Lecture Notes in Computer Science 9599

Commenced Publication in 1973
Founding and Former Series Editors:
Gerhard Goos, Juris Hartmanis, and Jan van Leeuwen

Editorial Board

More information about this series at http://www.springer.com/series/7409

Alessandro de Gloria · Remco Veltkamp (Eds.)

Games and Learning Alliance

4th International Conference, GALA 2015
Rome, Italy, December 9–11, 2015
Revised Selected Papers

 Springer

Editors
Alessandro de Gloria
Università di Genova
Genoa
Italy

Remco Veltkamp
Information and Computer Science
University of Utrecht
Utrecht
The Netherlands

ISSN 0302-9743   ISSN 1611-3349 (electronic)
Lecture Notes in Computer Science
ISBN 978-3-319-40215-4   ISBN 978-3-319-40216-1 (eBook)
DOI 10.1007/978-3-319-40216-1

Library of Congress Control Number: 2016941299

LNCS Sublibrary: SL3 – Information Systems and Applications, incl. Internet/Web, and HCI

Printed on acid-free paper

This Springer imprint is published by Springer Nature
The registered company is Springer International Publishing AG Switzerland

Preface

The Games and Learning (GALA) Conference reached its fourth edition in the beautiful setting of the cloister by Giuliano da Sangallo, at the Sapienza University in Rome. The conference took place during December 9–11, 2015, in Rome, Italy, and was organized by the Serious Games Society and The University of Genoa.

The conference provides the opportunity for meeting and discussing the main and emergent topics within a community of experts on serious games, which is growing year after year and involves academic, industrial developers, teachers, and corporate decision makers. Participants from four continents gave talks and organized workshops promoting knowledge share, technology transfer, and business development.

This year, the number of submissions has significantly grown along with the quality of the talks and the papers.

It was an honor to have Dr. Marco Marsella (EC) and Prof. Jung Hyun Han (University of Korea) as keynote speakers. Dr. Marsella, as representative of the European Commission, presented the new opportunities of research in the field of serious gaming and the new ICT calls in the framework of the H2020 program. Professor Jung Hyun Han opened the second day of the conference presenting the status of research on serious games in Asia and introducing a new frontier of collaboration.

The conference featured five different sessions of paper presentation and four workshops/tutorials.

The workshops/tutorials, held during the first day of the event, covered the following topics: games for health, games for mobility, pervasive gaming, and urban mobility. The Games for Health Workshop was organized by the University of Milan (Laura Anna Ripamonti and Dario Maggiorini) and built upon the increasing relevance of applied gaming approaches and gamification techniques for health and rehabilitation. The Games for Mobility Workshop, held by the University of Genoa (Francesco Bellotti and Riccardo Berta), analyzed and discussed the latest achievements and trends in the field of serious games and gamification for mobility and intelligent transportation systems. The Pergamon Workshop, held by professor Jacqueline Cawtson (DMLL-COVUNI), presented pervasive games as direct networking opportunities for creatives, academics, entrepreneurs, and game developers to expand into the serious games market. The Proto World Tutorial, held by Dr. Jannicke Baalsrud Hauge (BIBA), provided hands-on experience with a simulation game environment to model and plan urban mobility.

The paper sessions concerned such topics as: serious game design, tools, analytics and decisions making, pedagogy, and health. Beside these, the conference hosted two poster sessions collecting short papers related to serious games and their applications.

As in 2014, the selected best papers of the GALA Conference will be published in a dedicated special issue of the *International Journal of Serious Games*, the scientific journal managed by the Serious Games Society, which is a great reference point for academicians and practitioners to publish original research work on serious games and to be informed about the latest evolutions in the field.

The next GALA conference event will be held in Utrecht during December 5–7: http://www.galaconf.org/2016/.

December 2015   Alessandro De Gloria

Games and Learning Alliance
4th International Conference, GALA 2015
Rome, December 9–11, 2015
Revised Selected Papers

GALA 2015 was organized by the Serious Games Society and the University of Genoa.

General Chair

Alessandro De Gloria   University of Genoa, Italy

Program Chairs

J. Michael Spector   University of North Texas, USA
Remco C. Veltkamp   University of Utrecht, The Netherlands

Workshop and Tutorial Chairs

Games for Mobility

Francesco Bellotti   University of Genoa, Italy
Florian Häusler   Fraunhofer FOKUS, Germany

Games for Health

Laura A. Ripamonti   University of Milan, Italy
Dario Maggiorini   University of Milan, Italy

Program Committee

Anissa All	University of Gent, Belgium
Alessandra Antonaci	ITD-CNR, Italy
Sylvester Arnab	Coventry University, UK
Jon Arambarri	Virtualwaregroup, Spain
Aida Azadegan	The University of the West Scotland, UK
Jannicke Baalsrud Hauge	BIBA, Germany
Per Backlund	Högskolan i Skövde, Sweden
Norman Badler	University of Pennsylvania, USA
Sylvie Barma	Université Laval, Canada
Francesco Bellotti	University of Genoa, Italy
Riccardo Berta	University of Genoa, Italy
Rafael Bidarra	TU Delft, The Netherlands
Staffan Bjork	Chalmers, Sweden
Rosa Bottino	ITD-CNR, Italy

Maira Brandao Carvalho	University of Genoa, Italy/Technical University of Eindhoven, The Netherlands
Sylvie Daniel	University Laval, Canada
Kurt Debattista	University of Warwick, UK
Shujie Deng	University of Bournemouth, UK
Michael Derntl	RWTH Aachen, Germany
Frank Dignum	Università of Utrecht, The Netherlands
Miguel Encarnação	University of Louisville, USA
Ester Fuoco	University of Genoa, Italy
Christos Gatzidis	Bournemouth University, UK
Manuel Gentile	ITD-CNR, Italy
Marja Heuvel-Van den Panhuizen	Utrecht University, The Netherlands
Valerie Hill	Texas Woman's University, USA
Dirk Ifenthaler	University of Mannheim, Italy
Carolina Islas Sedano	University of Eastern Finland, Finland
Michael Kickmeier-Rust	University of Graz, Austria
Ralph Klamma	RWTH Aachen, Germany
Silvia Kober	University of Graz, Austria
Milos Kravcik	RWTH Aachen, Germany
Niki Lambropoulos	Global Operations Division, Greece
Elisa Lavagnino	University of Genoa, Italy
George Lepouras	University of the Peloponnese, Greece
Theo Lim	Heriot-Watt University, UK
Sandy Louchart	Glasgow School of Art Digital Design Studio, UK
Dario Maggiorini	University of Milan, Italy
Katerina Mania	Technical University of Crete, Greece
Fabrizia Mantovani	Università di Milano Bicocca, Italy
Michela Mortara	IMATI-CNR, Italy
Rob Nadolski	Open University, The Netherlands
Aniket Nagle	ETHZ, Switzerland
Manuel Ninaus	University of Graz, Austria
Carmen Padron	ATOS, Spain
Lucia Pannese	I-maginary, Italy
Magda Popescu	Carol I National Defence University, Romania
Rui Prada	INESC, Portugal
Marius Preda	Institut National des Télécommunications, France
Elena Putti	University of Genoa, Italy
Matthias Rauterberg	TU Eindhoven, The Netherlands
Laura Anna Ripamonti	University of Milan, Italy
Ion Roceanu	Carol I National Defence University, Romania
Margarida Romero	Université Laval, Canada
Esther Judith Schek	Università di Milano Bicocca, Italy
Nicola Secco	University of Genoa, Italy
Ioana Stanescu	Carol I National Defence University, Romania
Kam Star	Playgen, UK

Erik van der Spek   TU Eindhoven, The Netherlands
Herre van Oostendorp   Utrecht University, The Netherlands
Peter Van Rosmalen   Open University, The Netherlands
Remco Veltkamp   Utrecht University, The Netherlands
Wim Westera   Open University, The Netherlands
Antonie Wiedemann   University of Genoa, Italy
Peter Wolf   ETH Zurich, Switzerland

Local Arrangements Committee

Elisa Lavagnino   University of Genoa, Italy

Publications Chair

Riccardo Berta   University of Genoa, Italy

Communication Chair

Francesco Bellotti   University of Genoa, Italy

Administrative Chair

Elisa Lavagnino   University of Genoa, Italy
Antonie Wiedemann   University of Genoa, Italy

Contents

A Model-Driven Framework for Educational Game Design

Bill Roungas[1]([envelope]) and Fabiano Dalpiaz[2]

[1] Department of Multi-Actor Systems,
Delft University of Technology, Delft, The Netherlands
v.roungas@tudelft.nl
[2] Department of Information and Computing Sciences,
Utrecht University, Utrecht, The Netherlands

Abstract. Educational games are a class of serious games whose main purpose is to teach some subject to their players. Despite the many existing design frameworks, these games are too often created in an ad-hoc manner, and typically without the use of a game design document (GDD). We argue that a reason for this phenomenon is that current ways to structure, create and update GDDs do not increase the value of the artifact in the design and development process. As a solution, we propose a model-driven, web-based knowledge management environment that supports game designers in the creation of a GDD that accounts for and relates educational and entertainment game elements. The foundation of our approach is our devised conceptual model for educational games, which also defines the structure of the design environment. We present promising results from an evaluation of our environment with eight experts in serious games.

1 Introduction

According to Zyda [35], a serious game is "a mental contest, played with a computer in accordance with specific rules, that uses entertainment to further government or corporate training, education, health, public policy, and strategic communication objectives". Educational games are a class of serious games having an educational/learning purpose in the context of primary or secondary school, higher education, etc.

Despite the recent traction that serious and games gained, thanks to the increasing usage by parents and teachers [30], and despite all the available technologies, the design process of these games have not changed significantly, and still largely relies on tools such as simple text editors and prototyping software systems [18].

Moreover, the usefulness of game design documents (GDDs) as design artifacts is being questioned. A recent survey by Sundström [29] shows that less than 50 % of game professionals believe that GDDs are an effective way to communicate the design of a game, and only 5 % read GDDs to analyze a specific aspect of game design.

A. De Gloria and R. Veltkamp (Eds.): GALA 2015, LNCS 9599, pp. 1–11, 2016.
DOI: 10.1007/978-3-319-40216-1_1

In this paper, we propose an approach that aims to make GDDs a useful artifact. Our hypothesis, also supported by Sundström's [29] research, is that GDDs are either hardly or inefficiently used due to a variety of reasons:

- *Inconsistency* [6]: the same concepts are documented using different terminology in the GDD, and some design decisions are conflicting.
- *Infrequent updates* [6]: after the initial stages, the GDD is not updated regularly.
- *Multiple communication means*: Bethke [5] identified three different ways of communication in a gaming company, (a) through an explicit GDD, (b) through digital means (emails, Skype, wikis, etc.), and (c) oral. Using multiple ways to communicate can potentially lead to communication loss or overload.
- *Heterogeneous users*. GDDs are used by professionals with different educational and/or professional background, like artists and programmers. This leads to high chances of different interpretations of the same text.

The solution that we propose is based on the construction of a conceptual model [32] of educational games that describes its main constituents and their relationships. Such model defines the structure of the GDD and provides a common ground for communication among heterogeneous stakeholders. We also present a model-driven, web-based environment that enables the creation of GDDs that align with our conceptual model. Specifically, we make the following contributions:

1. Based on our study of the literature, we identify and relate the elements of educational games into a conceptual model for the design of educational games.
2. We describe the main features of our web-based, model-driven design environment that can be used for building GDDs for educational games.
3. We report on a qualitative evaluation of our environment with eight experts in serious games (design), which aims to assess the perceived usefulness of our solution.

The rest of the paper is structured as follows. After reviewing related work in Sect. 2, we introduce the conceptual model in Sect. 3, and we present the web environment in Sect. 4. We discuss the results from the evaluation in Sect. 5, and conclude in Sect. 6.

2   Related Work

The Design, Play and Experience (DPE) framework [33] extends the Mechanics, Dynamics, Aesthetics (MDA) framework [12] (for designing entertainment games) for the design of serious games. DPE has four layers of components, one of which is MDA. Each layer has one subcomponent for each of the three pillars of DPE, meaning the Design, the Play and the Experience. The contribution of DPE is the methodology it proposes in order to analyze and process the design of serious games, which when combined with an agile design environment, it provides a solution applicable to the whole spectrum of serious games.

The Serious Game Design Assessment (SGDA) framework [22] takes a similar standpoint, and defines six main aspects for the design of a serious game that shall be successfully combined to achieve the game's purpose: content, aesthetics/graphics, fiction/narrative, mechanics, framing, and interaction.

The LEGADEE online authoring environment [18] guides designers through multiple toolbars that support different design roles. The approach is model-driven, and is realized through an online environment. LEGADEE's intention is to offer a methodology and tools to guide the various actors that participate in the learning game conception, such as clients, teachers, game designers and developers. Our approach shares the same spirit with LEGADEE, but focuses on educational games.

Amory et al. [2] conducted an experiment on twenty students aiming at identifying which game type is more suitable depending on the learning environment and which are the game elements that students find interesting or useful. Results showed that the preferred genres are the 3D adventure and strategy games, whereas the game elements that students identified as the most useful were logic, memory, visualization and problem solving. Based on the results from the experiment, the authors presented a model that links pedagogical issues with game elements.

Aleven et al. [1] propose a design framework that requires the aligned definition of three main aspects, always keeping in mind that educational games need to be both educational and fun:

1. Learning Objectives: they are identified and defined by answering three questions: (a) What is the required prior knowledge?; (b) What is the knowledge that players will acquire from the game?; and (c) What potential knowledge players can learn that goes beyond the scope of the game?
2. MDA [12]: this is used for designers need to define the mechanics and to influence the dynamics and the aesthetics of the game.
3. Instructional Principles, that define how the learning process will be conducted.

Our research is motivated by the fact that the existing frameworks are rather high-level, as they include abstract elements as opposed to concrete ones that can serve as a basis for a design environment. For example, many of these approaches use the term "Learning" without going deeper into the core elements that define learning. The next section will address this limitation by proposing a detailed conceptual model.

3   Conceptual Model

We describe how we combine research from different domains into a conceptual model that defines the core elements of educational games. Our aim is to tackle the inconsistency problem of GDDs, for the conceptual model guides the design of

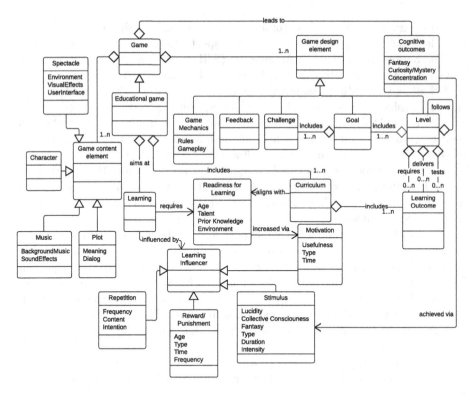

Fig. 1. Conceptual model of educational serious games

educational serious games by providing a common ground that should minimize misunderstandings by defining a standard terminology to be adopted.

The main challenge in this endeavor is how to combine the gaming aspects with the educational aspects. Our aim is to build a combined model as opposed to a simple merging of two independent models. To such extent, we started from a study of the literature from both fields, and we paid particular attention to the findings related with the interconnections between the two domains. The assembled conceptual model is shown in Fig. 1 using an UML class diagram.

A *game* consists of *game content elements* that represent its structural components; *game design elements* that explain the choices of the designers in terms of mechanics, goals, etc.; and desired *cognitive outcomes* that the game aims to trigger in the players. Among the cognitive outcomes that are to be evoked in the player, important ones are *fantasy* [17], *mystery and curiosity* [10], and *concentration* [8].

As far as game contents are concerned, we refer back to Aristotle's work [20], who defined the key dramatic elements to hold the attention of the audience as: well-defined, evolving *characters*; a *meaning* that stimulates intellect; *dialogs* that are memorable; *music* (or audio in videogames) that enhance the auditory experience; and *spectacle* to stimulate the visual experience.

Several game design elements are necessary to coordinate the dramatic elements into a genuine gaming experience: *goals* that the players shall strive for [4], *game mechanics* that determine the gameplay and constrain the possible behavior [27], increasingly hard *challenges* that keep the player engaged within a flow experience [8] (challenges are also part of the three dimensions of gameplay [9]), *levels* that split the game into multiple smaller episodes [4], and *feedback* that provides an immediate reaction on the players' actions [8].

An *educational game* is a type of game (see the is-a relationship) that aims at *learning* and does so by including a *curriculum* of knowledge to be transferred to the players. The curriculum is defined in terms of *learning outcomes* for the game [10] that define what knowledge the player is expected to achieve.

Our conceptual model details the main factors that affect the learning process. In the first place, learning requires that the learners/players have an adequate *readiness for learning* [31] in terms of age, talent, prior knowledge, and environmental factors: an excellent instructional method would not work when a misfit with the audience exists. Moreover, learning is affected by a number of influencing factors: the *motivation* [19] of the learner, the use of *repetition* to boost learning effectiveness [25], the provision of *stimuli* [13], and the inclusion of *rewards/punishments* [11] in response to positive and negative learning behavior.

A key chunk of the conceptual model is that relating *level* and *learning outcome*: every level requires the achievement of learning outcomes, delivers other outcomes, and tests outcomes as well. This structure enables defining an order relationship among levels in educational terms: a level that requires a certain learning outcome shall appear in the game only after a level that delivers such outcome has been successfully played.

4   Design Tool

The conceptual model is put in practice through the design and development of a web-based, model-driven environment for the design of educational games. In other words, the environment is aligned with the conceptual model in terms of the fields that are required to specify an educational game. Model-driven approaches have the advantage of being language independent [28]: the conceptual model can be used independently and contribute on building an environment with any programming language. As such, one could reuse the conceptual model to develop her own environment.

Web applications provide several advantages that help overcome some of the problems associated with GDDs: (i) they are accessible from everywhere and from multiple users; (ii) the look and feel can be easily customized; (iii) they can be accessed from a variety of devices; (iv) in comparison to desktop environments, they can achieve greater levels of interoperability.

In our environment[1], we made some implementation choices that are intended to facilitate the process of creation of high-quality, useful GDDs:

---

[1] Available at: http://seriousgamesdesign.com.

- *Semi-structured design environment.* Many game elements are common for all types of games, while some depend on the type of game and on the game studio. Thus, we designed a semi-structured environment which is more flexible than fully structured environments and at the same time more rigorous than free text.
- *Linkages of game objects.* Connecting the various objects in a GDD is crucial, as demonstrated by the many relationships between the classes that exist in our conceptual model of Fig. 1. Thus, we implemented these two features aiming at enabling game designers to "navigate" through the conceptual model:
  - *Hyperlinks.* Free text areas are enriched with the possibility for designers to link objects that they have already created, such as goals, challenges, character, audio files, etc. By doing so, the designer creates relationships between the current element and other ones. An example is shown in Fig. 2;
  - *Dropdown Menus.* The relationships between elements of Fig. 1 are implemented through dropdown menus, where the list includes objects that the designer has previously created and that can be accessed by navigating our conceptual model. An example is shown in Fig. 3. The usage of dropdown menus helps in two ways: (i) by only linking objects that already exist, this reduces the risk of inconsistency by referring to non-existing elements; (ii) changes in objects (e.g., renaming) are propagated automatically, without the necessity to apply the changes wherever the object is being referenced.
- *No predefined flow.* According to Meredith [21], decision makers on a design process face the dilemma: too much structure may stifle the creative process, while too little structure provides inadequate support. Therefore, given that we have opted for a relatively structured environment, we decided not to force designers to follow a specific sequence while designing their game (unlike the work by Marfisi-Schottman [18]). The prototype's layout resembles that of content management systems, where users can navigate freely to whichever page they want. This does not only gives more freedom to designers, but also offers a known, and thus more user-friendly, user interface.

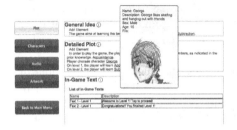

Fig. 2. Using hyperlinks in text areas to reference other GDD objects (here, a character)

Fig. 3. Dropdown menu: linking required, delivered, and tested knowledge to a level

Other important features of the prototype are the progress page and export options. The progress page is a dashboard for designers that shows the status of a GDD at a glance. We have partially implemented the customization of the exported document, depending on the stakeholder for whom is intended for.

Throughout our design process, we tried to adhere with the most important usability guidelines, especially those related with the key purpose of the environment: *Consistency* [23] and *Learnability* [16], by using standard terminology; *Clarity* [24], by introducing as few distractions as possible; and *Relevancy* [14], by keeping the concept of the environment aligned with the conceptual model.

5 Evaluation

We describe the process we followed to evaluate our environment and the outcomes of the analysis of the obtained results. The evaluation is intended not only to understand the strengths and weaknesses of our environment (so as to improve it), but also to collect feedback concerning the conceptual model which powers the environment in a model-driven engineering fashion.

The aim of the evaluation is to check the accuracy and comprehensiveness of the conceptual model, the usability of environment, and the benefits of features like hyperlinks and dropdown menus. More generally, our wish is to obtain insights concerning the extent to which our environment and Web 2.0 technologies can help game development teams to overcome the inconsistency and the lack of updates on GDDs and the problems associated with communication within educational game development teams.

We chose to conduct our evaluation through face-to-face interviews that are conducted after demonstrating the online environment. We have defined a plan for the evaluation and have taken several decisions with regard to the conducted interviews [34]:

- *Interview Type.* We decided for semi-structured interviews [26] through the use of a pre-defined set of questions to be rated on a Likert scale or through boolean values[2], followed by the possibility for the interviewees to comment on their response. This protocol combines the strengths of the structured, comparable results provided by scale-based questions with flexibility and richness of feedback from the oral comments.
- *Data Collection.* We decided to conduct face-to-face interviews at the subjects' working place (also known as first degree data collection techniques [15]). The reasons for this decision are (a) the possibility to demonstrate the environment in detail and also give the interviewees the opportunity to experiment with it, after the presentation, (b) the option to verbally explain aspects of the environment when the documentation is not sufficient, (c) the visual observation of the interviewees, which could provide additional feedback regarding their interaction with the environment, and (d) the informal comments of the

---

[2] Our questionnaire is available at: http://seriousgamesdesign.com/paper/ questionnaire/eval_form.php.

interviewees regarding aspects of the environment that would not be possible through an online questionnaire.

- *Selection of Subjects.* We decided to interview serious game experts from both the commercial gaming market and the academia. In total, we interviewed eight experts: three of them are working on serious game companies and five are working in academia. All of them work in the Netherlands.

The results from the individual interviews[3] are generally positive. All the interviewees found the idea very interesting, and the feedback we received gave us insights on how representatives from both the academic and the commercial communities of games perceive the present and the future of game design. The results to the closed questions are shown in Table 1. A comprehensive report is available in our online appendix.

The number of the interviewees does not allow us to make a statistically reliable generalization of the results. Nevertheless, due to the high expertise of the interviewees in serious games development, the results provide interesting information of how our environment can be adopted by academics and by professionals and can be potentially useful for the design of educational games and for further research.

Table 1. Summary of the responses to the questions to be answered via a 1-to-5 Likert scale or boolean values

ID	Question	Expert type	
		Market	Academic
1	Are all necessary elements present?	Y: 3, N: 0	Y: 4, N: 1
2.1	Is the non-predefined flow preferable to more structured flows?	Y: 2, N: 1	Y: 4, N: 1
2.2	How easy is the navigation in the website?	2.33 (sd: 0.6)	3.8 (sd: 0.8)
3.1	How important is linking game objects in a GDD?	5 (sd: 0)	4 (sd: 1)
3.2a	Are dropdown menus an efficient way to link game objects?	Y: 3, N: 0	Y: 5, N: 0
3.2b	Are dropdown menus faster than free text to link game objects?	Y: 3, N: 0	Y: 4, N: 1
3.3a	Are hyperlinks an efficient way to link game objects?	Y: 3, N: 0	Y: 5, N: 0
3.3b	Are hyperlinks faster than free text to link game objects?	Y: 3, N: 0	Y: 4, N: 1
3.3c	How useful is it to hover over a hyperlink to see an object's information?	4.67 (sd: 0.58)	4.8 (sd: 0.45)
4.1a	How effective is the environment to get a consistent GDD?	3.67 (sd: 0.58)	3.4 (sd: 0.89)
4.1b	How effective are Web 2.0 technologies to get a consistent GDD?	5 (sd: 0)	4.2 (sd: 0.84)
4.2a	How effective is the environment to keep GDDs up-to-date?	3 (sd: 1)	3.6 (sd: 1.14)
4.2b	How effective are Web 2.0 technologies to keep GDDs up-to-date?	3.67 (sd: 1.53)	4 (sd: 1.41)
4.3a	How effective is the environment to overcome communication problems?	3.67 (sd: 0.58)	3.8 (sd: 0.45)
4.3b	How effective are Web 2.0 technologies to overcome communication problems?	4.67 (sd: 0.58)	4 (sd: 0)

---

[3] Available at: http://seriousgamesdesign.com/paper/results/results.php.

Experts from both categories find that linking game objects (question 3.1) is an important feature to design serious games. Thus, an environment like ours can be of great help, by providing structure and facilitating the linkage of game objects. The interviewees reported the lack of game-specific tools that help game designers in documenting a game; this indicates a clear potential for an environment like ours.

Due to space limitations, we limit ourselves to outlining the most notable differences between the two expert categories in Table 1:

1. The question about the easiness of navigating through the environment (question 2.2) shows significant differences between the categories: 2.33 for the market experts and 3.8 for the academic experts. This can be explained by the fact that the academic experts have better understood the prototypical nature of the environment.
2. The average difference between the potential of our environment and of Web 2.0 technologies (question 4) is greater for the market experts than for the academic experts, especially in how they help overcome problems associated with game design documents: consistency (see questions 4.1a and 4.1b), updates (see questions 4.2a and 4.2b), and communication (see questions 4.3a and 4.3b).

Finally, we noticed that market experts perceived issues like user experience and user interface friendliness almost as important as the actual functionality of the environment, opening a whole new area for improving our prototypical environment.

6   Discussion

In this paper, we presented a conceptual model of educational games and an online environment based on that model. Our long-term objective is to study whether the usage of GDDs is limited due to the lack of effective tools or is rather due to the way educational games are developed. The preliminary evaluation that we conducted, which involved interviews with serious games experts, confirmed the absence of game-specific design tools, and has shown a positive attitude towards the potential benefit of a web, model-driven environment to mitigate the problems of GDD-based game design.

Our evaluation suffers from threats towards the validity affecting our evaluation. Internal validity is threatened by the use of a mixed approach that combines boolean questions with Likert scale questions: for homogeneity, we should have employed the same type of scale. Moreover, we have mostly demonstrated the tool, instead of letting the interviewees use it. Some of the questions are subject to confirmatory bias, i.e., the tendency of people of agreeing with the statements/questions. In terms of external validity, we have conducted a study with a small number of interviewees, all of which from the same geographic area. Moreover, there are threats concerning the credibility of the results, for we employed a custom questionnaire as opposed to validated questions.

This paper simply paves the way for future research in the field. The conceptual model can be further researched upon to identify any missing core element of educational games. These changes would obviously have to be mapped into the model-based design environment; maintaining this mapping could be facilitated by using a model-driven engineering development environment. Moreover, linking game mechanics with learning models, as depicted on the LM-GM model [3], will provide designers with a "dictionary" for adjusting the game mechanics to the learning objectives of the game. In the same spirit, the environment can be modified to produce all the necessary UML diagrams, as described in the ATMSG model [7], thus helping collaboration among the different stakeholders. The user interface and look-and-feel of the prototype can be greatly improved, especially in order to enable longitudinal studies on the effectiveness of our approach. Finally, case studies are necessary to fully validate our environment.

References

1. Aleven, V., Myers, E., Easterday, M., Ogan, A.: Toward a framework for the analysis and design of educational games. In: Proceedings of the IEEE International Conference on Digital Game and Intelligent Toy Enhanced Learning (DIGITEL), pp. 69–76. IEEE (2010)
2. Amory, A., Naicker, K., Vincent, J., Adams, C.: The use of computer games as an educational tool: identification of appropriate game types and game elements. Br. J. Educ. Technol. **30**(4), 311–321 (1999)
3. Arnab, S., Lim, T., Carvalho, M.B., Bellotti, F., Freitas, S., Louchart, S., Suttie, N., Berta, R., De Gloria, A.: Mapping learning and game mechanics for serious games analysis. Br. J. Educ. Technol. **46**(2), 391–411 (2015)
4. Baldwin, M.: Game design document outline (2005). http://ddijogos.xpg.uol.com.br/Baldwin_Game_Design_Document_Template.pdf
5. Bethke, E.: Game Development and Production. Wordware Publishing Inc., Plano (2003)
6. Brown, D.M.: Communicating Design: Developing Web Site Documentation for Design and Planning. New Riders, Berkeley (2010)
7. Carvalho, M.B., Bellotti, F., Berta, R., De Gloria, A., Sedano, C.I., Hauge, J.B., Hu, J., Rauterberg, M.: An activity theory-based model for serious games analysis and conceptual design. Comput. Educ. **87**, 166–181 (2015)
8. Csikszentmihalyi, M.: Flow: The Psychology of Optimal Experience, vol. 41. Harper Perennial, New York (1991)
9. Ermi, L., Mäyrä, F.: Fundamental components of the gameplay experience: analysing immersion. In: Worlds in Play: International Perspectives on Digital Games Research, p. 37 (2005)
10. Garris, R., Ahlers, R., Driskell, J.E.: Games, motivation, and learning: a research and practice model. Simul. Gaming **33**(4), 441–467 (2002)
11. Guthrie, E.R.: The Psychology of Learning. Harper, New York (1952)
12. Hunicke, R., LeBlanc, M., Zubek, R.: MDA: a formal approach to game design and game research. In: Proceedings of the AAAI Workshop on Challenges in Game AI, vol. 4 (2004)
13. Jung, C.G.: The archetypes and the collective unconscious. In: Handy, W.J., Westbrook, M. (eds.) Twentieth Century Criticism: The Major Statements. Light & Life Publishers, New Delhi, p. 205 (1974)

14. Koohang, A.: Expanding the concept of usability. Informing Sci. **7**, 129–141 (2004)
15. Lethbridge, T.C., Sim, S.E., Singer, J.: Studying software engineers: data collection techniques for software field studies. Empirical Softw. Eng. **10**(3), 311–341 (2005)
16. Lewis, J.R., Sauro, J.: The factor structure of the system usability scale. In: Kurosu, M. (ed.) HCD 2009. LNCS, vol. 5619, pp. 94–103. Springer, Heidelberg (2009)
17. Malone, T.W.: What makes things fun to learn? heuristics for designing instructional computer games. In: Proceedings of the 3rd ACM SIGSMALL Symposium and the First SIGPC Symposium on Small Systems, pp. 162–169. ACM (1980)
18. Marfisi-Schottman, I., George, S., Tarpin-Bernard, F.: Tools and methods for efficiently designing serious games. In: Proceedings of the 4th Europeen Conference on Games Based Learning ECGBL, pp. 226–234 (2010)
19. Maslow, A.H.: A theory of human motivation. Psychol. Rev. **50**(4), 370 (1943)
20. McKeon, R., Levinson, J.: Poetics: The Basic Works of Aristotle. Random House, New York (1941)
21. Meredith, R.: Creative freedom and decision support systems. In: Creativity and Innovation in Decision Making and Decision Support, pp. 30–46 (2006)
22. Mitgutsch, K., Alvarado, N.: Purposeful by design? a serious game design assessment framework. In: Proceedings of the International Conference on the Foundations of Digital Games, pp. 121–128. ACM (2012)
23. Nielsen, J.: Enhancing the explanatory power of usability heuristics. In: Proceedings of the SIGCHI Conference on Human Factors in Computing Systems, pp. 152–158. ACM (1994)
24. Palmer, J.W.: Web site usability, design and performance metrics. Inf. Syst. Res. **13**(2), 151–167 (2002)
25. Piaget, J.: Cognitive development in children: the piaget papers. In: Piaget Rediscovered: A Report of the Conference on Cognitive Studies and Curriculum Development, pp. 6–48. Ithaca School of Education, Cornell University (1964)
26. Robson, C.: Real World Research: A Resource for Social Scientists and Practitioner-Researchers, vol. 2. Blackwell Oxford, Oxford (2002)
27. Salen, K., Zimmerman, E.: Rules of Play: Game Design Fundamentals. MIT press, Cambridge (2004)
28. Schmidt, D.C.: Guest editor's introduction: model-driven engineering. Computer **39**(2), 0025–31 (2006)
29. Sundström, Y.: Game design and production: frequent problems in game development (2013)
30. Takahashi, D.: With a mobile boom, learning games are a $1.5B market headed toward $2.3B by 2017. GamesBeat (2013)
31. Vygotsky, L.S., Wollock, J.: The Collected Works of LS Vygotsky: Problems of the Theory and History of Psychology, vol. 3. Springer Science & Business Media, New York (1997)
32. Wand, Y., Storey, V.C., Weber, R.: An ontological analysis of the relationship construct in conceptual modeling. ACM Trans. Database Syst. **24**(4), 494–528 (1999)
33. Winn, B.: The design, play, and experience framework. In: Handbook of Research on Effective Electronic Gaming in Education, vol. 3, pp. 1010–1024 (2008)
34. Wohlin, C., Runeson, P., Höst, M., Ohlsson, M.C., Regnell, B., Wesslén, A.: Experimentation in Software Engineering. Springer Science & Business Media, New York (2012)
35. Zyda, M.: From visual simulation to virtual reality to games. Computer **38**(9), 25–32 (2005)

Steps to Design a Household Energy Game

Jan Dirk Fijnheer[1,2(✉)] and Herre van Oostendorp[1]

[1] Department of Information and Computing Sciences,
Utrecht University, Princetonplein 5, 3584 CC Utrecht, The Netherlands
{J.D.L.Fijnheer,H.vanoostendorp}@uu.nl
[2] Inholland University of Applied Science,
Wildenborch 6, 1112 XB Diemen, The Netherlands

Abstract. Research where gamification is used to influence household energy consumption is an emerging field. This paper reviews the design of games that aim to influence household energy consumption. The designs of ten games are analyzed. From this review, suggestions for the design of a new game have been identified, such as presence of a strong storyline, real live missions, customized game characters, monitoring the electricity meter, etc. Based on this comparative analysis, a new game focused on reducing energy consumption has been designed and its prototype is described and will be demonstrated at the conference. In the next stage of iterative design, end-users will be involved by means of focus groups. This considerate user-centered design process allows us to build a serious game that is effective in reducing household energy consumption.

1 Introduction

Gamification research has shown that the integration of serious games into real life could have positive effects on attitude and behavior [9]. Game design can be a valuable strategy for making non-game products, services, or applications, more enjoyable, motivating, and/or engaging the user [6]. The steps in designing a household energy game, which is presented in this paper, are part of a larger research project that will give insight into what the influence of playing in the real world is on sustainable behavior in the long term, and on attitudes towards sustainability. We focus specifically on energy consumption in households by means of electricity usage. The target is to contribute to the stimulation of individual sustainable behavior by studying how gamification can be a positive incentive for people to change their behavior regarding energy use at home. It aims to study whether this transfer from game play to real life behavior has a long-term character [9]. For this research project a game was designed that is to be used as a research instrument that will allow us to investigate different factors such as feedback, personal relevance and social interaction and that could strengthen the change in attitude and behavior. It is generally recommended that potential users of the game be involved in the development process [5]. This will be done in the next phase by means of focus groups. However, first the design of the game is established (step 1) by analyzing the designs of existing games that have a similar purpose. This is achieved by identifying a number of dimensions in the literature. Our assumption is that when the analysis (step 1) is done properly and potential users are

© Springer International Publishing Switzerland 2016
A. De Gloria and R. Veltkamp (Eds.): GALA 2015, LNCS 9599, pp. 12–22, 2016.
DOI: 10.1007/978-3-319-40216-1_2

involved in the design process (step 2), then this considerate user-centered game design will lead to a high quality game that is effective in reducing household energy consumption. We will first identify games that have similar, or at least partially similar, goals to the future game developed here (Sect. 2). The design of these games is analyzed with the dimensions/characteristics identified (Sect. 3). The optimum implementation of characteristics, and what might be lacking, will become clear from the considerate analysis. Based on this, suggestions are made (Sect. 4) for the final design of the game consistent with the research objectives. Finally, a description of our prototype will be presented.

2   Overview of Method to Analyze Energy Games

2.1   Goals

We have formulated six goals based on the requirements of the design of the game. The first goal is that the game makes players aware of sustainability issues concerning energy use at home. The game raises awareness. The second goal is the transfer of information about energy consumption so that players acquire more knowledge. The third goal is that players will be influenced by the game to change their behavior concerning energy consumption in real life. The fourth goal is that behavior in real life is integrated into the game by monitoring behavior in real life and using this information in the game progression. The fifth goal is that the game is played over a relatively long period of time and has several sessions. The sixth and final goal is that the game has a compelling and complex storyline that is able to engage players. A storyline in a game can be engaging because it stimulates our emotions [14]. A complex storyline includes a setting where game characters have to achieve goals and face multiple obstacles in reaching them [18].

2.2   Energy Games

Our game design is focused on energy use at home, specifically where personal behavior is involved. Games that also have this focus were chosen based on the above six goals. In February 2015, searches were performed in scientific databases and with the aid of public search engines. In these databases eight games were found that had been used as a research instrument with similarities to our research. These eight games are analyzed in this paper. The output of public search engines also suggested many games that are used for education and entertainment (but not for research) purposes. Unfortunately, only two additional games (*Joulebug* and *2020Energy*) are interesting to analyse because they have some similarities with our goals. Other games that came out of the search are not useful because they do not have a connection with real life energy consumption behavior and/or are too simple. The ten selected games are presented in the table of Appendix 1.

2.3   Characteristics of Game Design Analysis

Nineteen characteristics that are inspired by Prensky [14], Adams [1] and Schell [17] are distinguished to analyse the ten games. These characteristics are described in Table 1 in Appendix 1. The characteristics are clustered into five topics. The first topic is identification. A game is introduced by mentioning four general characteristics: (1) the year the game was released, (2) the research group/owner, (3) the purpose of the game (research, education or entertainment) and (4) the profile of the players. The second topic is Game Play. The game itself is described by mentioning (5) the description of the game type, (6) quality of the storyline, (7) the levels and progression (chronologic stages in difficulty) and (8) the representation of game characters. The third topic is Game Design. The presentation of the game and features are discussed by describing (9) the world (real life and/or in-game) where missions are accomplished, (10) the quantity of missions, (11) the possibility to customize, (12) feedback and rewards, (13) competition (high scores by oneself and/or competing against other players), (14) the quality of the graphic design, (15) real world effect (effect of behavior in the real world on progression in the game), (16) monitoring the electricity meter and (17) the duration of the game. The fourth topic is (18) the Technical Architecture that explains the technical design of the system. The fifth and final topic is Research Method. The research procedures of the eight games that are used as a research instrument are described, and (19) the kind of effects that are measured is mentioned.

3   Evaluation of the Implementation of Game Characteristics

The ten games that are selected have been analyzed and compared to each other by means of these nineteen characteristics. An overview of the results of this analysis is presented in Table 1 of Appendix 1. In the order of the five topics, the best implementations of characteristics and what is overall lacking are discussed. At the same time suggestions for the new design are made.

Topic 1. Identification. Characteristics Year (Char 1), Research group/Owner (Char 2) and Purpose (Char 3) are not discussed because they are only used to identify games. It is interesting to look closer at Player's profile (Char 4). In six games the game is played in family households, which include teenagers. There are good arguments to use family households as a study population. Family members all consume energy that can only be measured from an electricity meter, so it is reasonable and preferable that the whole family is involved in playing.

Topic 2. Game Play. Six different game types (Char 5) are mentioned. Two games are Simulation and Role-playing games, two games are Adventure and Role-playing games, two games are FarmVille like games and two games are Multiplayer games. *EnergyLife* is the only Eco-feedback game and *Joulebug* is the only Social mobile game. Implementing simulations can help players to prepare for real life missions. Role-playing can engage players more and adventure elements can be used for the storyline. Altogether, the games mainly focus on providing feedback on energy consumption. There are no games with a compelling and complex storyline (Char 6).

In general the games are not story-focused and miss the opportunity to enhance gameplay [17]. The games *Power Explorer* and *EnergyLife* have the best level and progression structure (Char 7). The strength of the game *Power Explorer* is the combination of normal gameplay and duels. *EnergyLife* has three levels with different activities. None of the games has levels that become more difficult during playing, and no game has the alignment of a compelling storyline and difficulty in playing. For our game it is preferable that a storyline will be implemented and missions become more complex when progression in the game is made. In seven games, game characters (Char 8) are used in the design. In the games *The Power House, EcoIsland* and *Powerhouse* the characters are family members that have some similarities with the characteristics of the players. Only in *EcoIsland* it is possible to "customize" the player's avatar. This feature should be implemented in the design of our game because it establishes a stronger connection between the game and reality [17].

Topic 3. Game Design. Eight games have real life (Char 9) energy saving missions. The game *Power House* has a strong combination by using both real life and in-game missions. It is preferable that in the design our game missions have to be carried out in real life. Using in-game missions to prepare players for real life missions is an option that should be considered. From six games we have no information about the quantity of missions (Char 10) available. The game *Power House* has, with ten missions, the most. In the games *EcoIsland* and *EnergyLife* customization (Char 11) is to some extent possible. In *EcoIsland* the avatars can be customized, and in *EnergyLife* a player can add two electrical devices to the five that are standard monitored. The customization of avatars and the addition of electrical appliances in the game is preferable, because it can have a positive influence on the involvement of the players. Seven of the ten games provide maximum feedback (Char 12) by means of points, badges/achievements and overviews of energy used or saved. All items should be implemented in our game design. In nine games players compete (Char 13) against themselves and others. Both should be implemented in our game. Only in the game *2020Energy* do players not compete against each other. Four games have high quality graphics (Char 14). The game *Power House* has the best graphics and can be used as an example for the development of the game for our research project. In seven games the player's behavior in the real world has a very strong effect on the game (Char 15). In our game it should be strong because real life missions will be implemented. In eight games the energy consumption is monitored (Char 16). This should be implemented in our game. Information that is obtained from continuously monitoring the energy consumption can be used to make progression in the gameplay. In the games *EnergyLife* and *Energy Chickens* electrical devices are monitored separately. This could be considered for implementation in our game if more specific feedback from individual appliances has to be provided. The duration of the games (Char 17) varies between a session to twenty-seven weeks. Four games are played for a month or more. Because we want to look at the long-term effects on behavior and attitude after playing the game it is plausible that the duration of our game should be extensive.

Topic 4. Technical Architecture. (Char 18) In six games the Technical Architecture is very advanced. The energy consumption is monitored and sometimes directly used in the game. For the game design of our project it is preferable that a real time connection between the electricity meter and game server is accomplished by using a datalogger with an Internet connection that is connected to the electricity meter in a household that has a WiFi network. The data of energy consumption will be sent to a database of a server. The option to cooperate with a network operator instead of using a datalogger is not recommended because the data transfer can be delayed. It is preferable that the game is basically an Internet page that is uploaded by a device (e.g. tablet) when the player logs in via an Internet browser.

Topic 5. Research Method. (Char 19) Knowledge, Attitude and Engagement are measured by means of questionnaires outside the game play. These questionnaires should be filled in before and after playing. Knowledge is also often measured with in-game quizzes and engagement can be measured by monitoring player's behavior during playing. These two options should be considered in our game design. Energy usage is measured by monitoring the energy meter. To set a good baseline for giving feedback about average energy consumption during playing, the energy consumption should be monitored before the game starts.

4   Conclusion

4.1   Meeting the Goals

First we will indicate to what extent the analysed games met the goals that are described in Sect. 2.1. The first goal is to make players aware of sustainability issues concerning energy use at home. To some degree almost all analysed games, except *Energy Chickens*, do this. The games *EcoIsland*, *Joulebug* and *2020Energy* also focus on energy use out of home. *Energy Chickens* is played in a work environment instead of a home but it is very likely that these players will also be more aware of energy use at home. The second goal is the transfer of information about energy consumption so that players acquire more knowledge. All analysed games do this. The games *Joulebug* and *2020Energy* also focus on other sustainability issues. The third goal is that players will be influenced by the game to change their behavior concerning energy consumption in real life. All analysed games do this more or less. This effect seems to be more likely when the electricity meter is part of the technical architecture. Because of this the games *The Power House* and *2020Energy* will only have indirect influence, as the energy usage is not measured. The games *The Power House* and *2020Energy* do not meet the fourth goal because the electricity meter is not connected to the game. Only the games *The Power House* and *2020Energy* do not meet the fifth goal that the game is played over a long period of time and has several sessions. The sixth goal is to have a compelling and complex storyline. Six games have a storyline, but unfortunately it is in all cases a very simple one. From this evaluation of goals that are met we conclude that the games *The Power House* and *2020Energy* do not meet many goals, other games do meet most of the goals and none of the games has strong storylines.

4.2 Required Design Features

From Sect. 3 and Appendix 1 we derive the following recommendations on design features to be implemented in the design of our game. Players should be all members of a household and play together. The game should have a compelling storyline and players have to accomplish real life missions that are provided by the game. Knowledge should be provided by questions in in-game quizzes. Missions should become more difficult over time and have a connection with the development of the storyline. The duration of a mission should depend on its intensiveness and will vary between one to three days. Depending on the quantity of missions the game should take at least more than a month to play. The game characters/avatars should have similarities with the players (customization). The world/setting of the game should have similarities with a household. Therefore specific devices of households should be present in the game world. Feedback should be provided by means of earned points, badges/achievements and overviews of energy used and saved. Players should be stimulated to achieve high scores and should be in competition with other households. The game should provide readings from the electricity meter and/or if technically possible readings from household appliances.

4.3 Final Design Prototype of the Game *The Power Saver*

In order of the five topics, we describe the final design of the prototype of our game 'The Power Saver'.

Topic 1. Identification. The game will be played in a household whereof in principle the whole family is involved (Char 4).

Topic 2. Game Play. It is an Eco-feedback, Multiplayer, Roleplaying and Point and Click Adventure game (Char 5). The game starts with an introduction of the story (Char 6). A family arrives at a dilapidated country house where something terrible has happened. The house used to be a peaceful place but that has changed dramatically caused by a failed experiment of a professor. The family enters the main hall of the house that contains several doors (Fig. 1a). Behind each door a room is situated where a game character in the form of a confused electrical device is placed. A ferret (former pet of the professor) called Kyoto guides the family in the game. Every week the family is asked to enter a preselected room. Before the door opens a quiz has to be played. A quiz contains questions that will prepare players for the missions that are occurring in that specific room. When the family enters the room a character in the form of a device that is in a confused state is shown (Fig. 1b). The family has to accomplish two missions to help the device character to get in a happy state (Fig. 1c). During the game the missions are getting more difficult (Char 7). Avatars of the family members are the central characters of the game (Char 8) (Fig. 1d).

Topic 3. Game Design. All missions (e.g. washing clothes on low temperatures) take place in the real world (Char 9). The game has fifteen missions, ten quizzes and an end-battle (Char 10). It will take two to three days to complete a mission. The missions are developed by the use of general energy saving measures. The family composition in

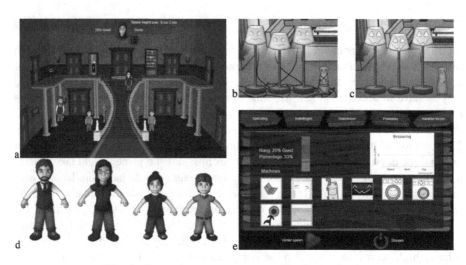

Fig. 1. Screenshots prototype game *The Power Saver*

the game is customised to the household (Char 11). In the prototype it is not possible to add specific devices from the household, though all general household devices are incorporated in the game. The player is getting feedback during playing (Char 12) (Fig. 1e). The energy use and savings are displayed in kWh and money. Also the savings per year is provided. A graph is used to give the player an overview of the energy use and a meter is developed to stimulate the energy saving behavior. The result of the quizzes is shown in a bar. The achievement of a completed mission is displayed with a badge of the happy device character corresponding with that mission. There is no competition (Char 13) with other households implemented in this prototype. In future versions this will be added. The quality of the graphic design (Char 14) is adequate (Fig. 1) and the navigation by the player is done by point and click on the screen. The player's behavior in the real world has a very strong effect on the game (Char 15), because real life behavior influences progress by means of completing missions and feedback of real life energy consumption that is monitored (Char 16) and presented continuously. The total period of playing the game is seven and a half weeks (Char 17).

Topic 4. Technical Architecture. An overview of the proposed technical architecture is shown in Fig. 2 (Char 18). A real time connection between the electricity meter and individual appliances and game server is accomplished by dataloggers with an Internet connection. The households have a WiFi network. The data of energy consumption will be sent to a database of a server at Utrecht University. The game is an Internet page that is uploaded by a device (e.g. tablet) when the player logs in via its Internet browser.

Topic 5. Research Method. Energy consumption is monitored a month before the game starts to set a good baseline of average energy consumption. All four effects of playing the game are measured (Char 19). Knowledge will be measured by using questionnaires before and after playing and the scores of quizzes in the game. Attitude will also be measured by using questionnaires before and after playing. Energy usage

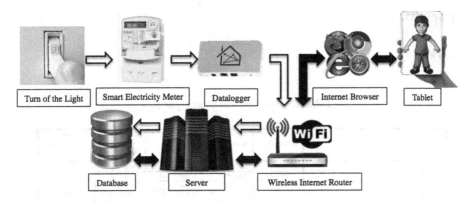

| Turn of the Light | Smart Electricity Meter | Datalogger | | Internet Browser | Tablet |

| Database | Server | Wireless Internet Router |

Fig. 2. Final design technical architecture of *The Power Saver*

will constantly be monitored from the energy meter. Engagement will be measured by using questionnaires before and after playing, by monitoring player's behavior during playing and monitoring how often the player logs in and what he/she is exactly doing for how long.

5 Discussion

In this review it is not yet taken into account what exactly the empirical effects are concerning behavior, knowledge and attitude, of design as a whole and/or of the individual characteristics. This can be equally important for making choices in the final design. A future paper will address this issue. We strive to develop a game based on user-centered design [5]. The presented prototype is not yet user-centered but just the outcome of the considerate part (step 1) of the game development process which consists of the analysis of the ten games, formulated goals and the skills of the developers. The next step is to involve the potential players in the design process. Eight families in the form of focus groups will evaluate this prototype. Four families evaluate the missions, quizzes, storyline and look and feel of the game. When adjustments in the game design have been made, the redesigned game is entirely played by the other four families. Based on this user study final adjustments are made and the game developed with this considerate user-centered design will be subsequently used in the research project. In our project we focus on a "value added" approach [12] where the effects of the features feedback, personal relevance (by means of customized avatars and addition of electrical appliances) and social interaction (by means of competition) on knowledge, attitude and behavior are examined. The technical developers have made it possible to add or remove these features in the prototype for future experiments. For example, feedback can be adjusted and competition between families can be added. However, we start our project with a "media comparison" approach [12] where the effect of the game is contrasted with another medium. During this experiment one group will play our game and a control group will receive the same information in the form of an intensive sustainability course that will take as long as the game and results will be compared.

Appendix 1

See Table 1.

Table 1. Overview ten energy games

Topic		Game / Characteristic	1 The Power House [2]	2 Power Agent [3][9]	3 EcoIsland [11]	4 Power Explorer [4][10]	5 Agents Against Power Waste [19]
Identi-ficatio		1 Year	2006	2007	2008	2008	2010
		2 Research group/ Owner	Bang et al.	Bang et al.	Kimura et al.	Bang et al.	Svahn, M.
		3 Purpose	Research	Research	Research	Research	Research
		4 Players profile	Teenagers	Teenagers in households	Households incl. teenagers	Teenagers in households	Households incl. teenagers
Game Play		5 Game type	Simulation & Role-playing	Adventure & Role-playing	FarmVille like	Multiplayer	Adventure & Role-playing
		6 Storyline*	+	+	--	+	+
		7 Levels & Progress*	+	+	--	++	?
		8 Game Characters *	+	+	+	+	--
Game Design		9 Mission world	In-game	Real life	Real life	Real life	Real life
		10 Mission quantity	?	7	?	2 duels	?
		11 Personification/ Customization	No	No	Yes	No	No
		12 Feedback and Rewards**	Combi.	Combi.	Combi.	Combi.	?
		13 Competition (Oneself/Other)	O/O	O/O	O/O	O/O	O/O
		14 Graphic Design*	-	+	-	++	-
		15 Real world effect*	--	++	++	++	++
		16 Monitoring elec. meter	No	Yes	Yes	Yes	Yes
		17 Duration	1 Session	1W	3W	1W	4W
		18 Technical Architecture*	-	++	+	++	++
Research Method		19 Measured Effect:					
		- Knowledge	?	Yes	No	Yes	Yes
		- Attitude	Yes	Yes	Yes	Yes	Yes
		- Energy usage	No	Yes	Yes	Yes	Yes
		- Engagement	Yes	Yes	No	Yes	Yes

Topic		Game / Characteristic	6 EnergyLife [7][8]	7 Joulebug	8 Power House [15][16]	9 2020 Energy	10 Energy Chickens [13]
Identi-fication		1 Year	2011	2011	2011	2012	2014
		2 Research group/ Owner	Gamberine et al.	Joulebug	Reeves et al.	ENERGY-BITS	Orlanda et al.
		3 Purpose	Research	Entertainment	Research	Education	Research
		4 Players profile	Adults in households	Trendy young adults	Adults in households	Teenagers	Office workers
Game Play		5 Game type	Eco-feedback	Social mobile	Multiplayer	Simulation & Role-playing	FarmVille like
		6 Storyline*	--	--	+	+	--
		7 Levels & Progress*	++	--	+	-	-
		8 Game Characters *	--	--	+	+	+
Game Design		9 Mission world	Real life	Real life	In-game & Real life	In-game	Real life
		10 Mission quantity	?	?	10 sessions	9	?
		11 Personification/ Customization	Yes	No	No	No	No
		12 Feedback and Rewards**	Combi.	Combi.	Combi.	Points & Ach.	Combi.
		13 Competition (Oneself/Other)	O/O	O/O	O/O	Oneself	O/O
		14 Graphic Design*	+	++	++	++	+
		15 Real world effect*	++	++	-	--	++
		16 Monitoring elec. meter	Yes	Yes	Yes	No	Yes
		17 Duration	16W	Infinite	2,5W	1 Session	27W
		18 Technical Architecture*	++	++	+	-	++
Research Method		19 Measured Effect:					
		- Knowledge	Yes	No	Yes	Yes	Yes
		- Attitude	Yes	No	?	Yes	Yes
		- Energy usage	Yes	Yes	Yes	Yes	Yes
		- Engagement	Yes	No	?	Yes	Yes

* --/-/+/++ ** Points, Badges/Achievements, Energy use/savings or a Combination (Combi.)

References

1. Adams, E.: Fundamentals of Game Design, 3rd edn. Peachpit, Pearson, Berkeley, London (2014)
2. Bang, M., Torstensson, C., Katzeff, C.: The PowerHouse: a persuasive computer game designed to raise awareness of domestic energy consumption. In: IJsselsteijn, W.A., Kort, Y. A., Midden, C., Eggen, B., Hoven, E. (eds.) PERSUASIVE 2006. LNCS, vol. 3962, pp. 123–132. Springer, Heidelberg (2006)
3. Bang, M., Gustafsson, A., Katzeff, C.: Promoting new patterns in household energy consumption with pervasive learning games. In: Kort, Y.A., IJsselsteijn, W.A., Midden, C., Eggen, B., Fogg, B.J. (eds.) PERSUASIVE 2007. LNCS, vol. 4744, pp. 55–63. Springer, Heidelberg (2007)
4. Bang, M., Svahn, M., Gustafsson, A.: Persuasive design of a mobile energy conservation game with direct feedback and social cues. In: Proceedings of the 2009 DiGRA International Conference: Breaking New Ground: Innovation in Games, Play, Practice and Theory. Digital Games Research Association (2009)
5. Benyon, D.: Designing Interactive Systems: A Comprehensive Guide to HCI and Interaction Design, 2nd edn. Pearson, Harlow (2010)
6. Deterding, S., Khaled, R., Nacke, L., Dixon, D.: Gamification: toward a definition. In: CHI 2011 Gamification Workshop Proceedings. ACM Press, Vancouver, BC (2011)
7. Gamberini, L., Jacucci, G., Spagnolli, A., Corradi, N., Zamboni, L., Perotti, M., Cadenazzi, C., Mandressi, S., Tusa, G., Björkskog, C., Salo, M., Aman, P.: Saving is fun: designing a persuasive game for power conservation. In: Proceedings of the 8th International Conference on Advances in Computer Entertainment Technology. ACM, NY (2011)
8. Gamberini, L., Spagnolli, A., Corradi, N., Jacucci, G., Tusa, G., Mikkola, T., Zamboni, L., Hoggan, E.: Tailoring feedback to users' actions in a persuasive game for household electricity conservation. In: Bang, M., Ragnemalm, E.L. (eds.) PERSUASIVE 2012. LNCS, vol. 7284, pp. 100–111. Springer, Heidelberg (2012)
9. Gustafsson, A., Katzeff, C., Bang, M.: Evaluation of a pervasive game for domestic energy engagement among teenagers. ACM Comput. Entertainment 7(4), 1–19 (2009)
10. Gustafsson, A., Bang, M., Svahn, M.: Power explorer – a casual game style for encouraging long term behaviour change among teenagers. In: Proceedings of the International Conference on Advances in Computer Entertainment Technology, pp. 182–189. ACM, NY (2009)
11. Kimura, H., Nakajima, T.: Designing persuasive applications to motivate sustainable behavior in collectivist cultures. PsychNology J. 9(1), 7–28 (2011)
12. Mayer, R.E.: Multimedia learning and games. In: Tobias, S., Fletcher, J.D. (eds.) Computer Games and Instruction, pp. 281–305. Information Age Publishing, Charlotte (2011)
13. Orlanda, B., Ramb, N., Langc, D., Houserd, K., Klinge, N., Coccia, M.: Saving energy in an office environment: a serious game intervention. Energ. Build. 74, 43–52 (2014)
14. Prensky, M.: Digital Game-Based Learning. Paragon House, Saint Paul (2001)
15. Reeves, B., Cummings, J.J., Scarborough, J.K., Yeykelis, L.: Increasing energy efficiency with entertainment media: an experimental and field test of the influence of a social game on performance of energy behaviors. Environ. Behav. 20(10), 1–14 (2013)
16. Reeves, B., Cummings, J.J., Anderson, D.: Leveraging the engagement of games to change energy behavior. In: CHI May 2011. ACM Press, Vancouver, BC (2011)
17. Schell, J.: The Art of Game Design: A Book of Lenses. Elsevier, Burlington (2008)

18. Stein, N., Glenn, C.: An analysis of story comprehension in elementary school children. In: Freedle, R.D. (ed.) Advances in Discourse Processes: New Directions in Discourse Processing, vol. 2, pp. 53–119. Ablex, Norwood, NJ (1979)
19. Svahn, M.: Persuasive pervasive games: the case of impacting energy consumption. Dissertation. Stockholm School of Economics, Stockholm, Sweden (2014)

D-CITE - A Serious Game to Analyze Complex Decision-Making in Air Traffic Management

Maria Freese[1]([✉]) and Sebastian Drees[2]

[1] German Aerospace Center (DLR), Institute of Flight Guidance,
Lilienthalplatz 7, 38108 Braunschweig, Germany
Maria.Freese@dlr.de
[2] HTW Berlin - University of Applied Science,
Treskowallee 8, 10318 Berlin, Germany
s0533094@htw-berlin.de

Abstract. Air Traffic is a complex system, where different stakeholders (e.g. Airlines, Airport, Air Traffic Controller, Ground-Handler) interact with each other. To optimize especially airport processes, cooperation between the above mentioned stakeholders is mandatory, but divergent goals and interests are supposed to have an influence on their decision-making process. Because of this, the way of collaborative decision-making seems to be a challenge. The aspects of human interactions during negotiations and human performance in planning activities are difficult to measure with conventional methods of real- and fast-time simulations. Serious Gaming is a new method in this research field to validate interaction processes in Air Traffic Management. The serious multiplayer game "D-CITE" (**D**ecisions based on **C**ollaborative **I**nteractions in **TE**ams) was developed to specifically analyze underlying factors that drive decision-making processes in an airport management environment. The aim of this paper is to illustrate the main ideas of D-CITE as well as to discuss the aspect of collaborative learning.

1 Introduction

Especially during critical events, the cooperation of various stakeholders at an airport is necessary. One such a critical event was the eruption of the Icelandic volcano *Eyjafjallajökull* in 2010. The results were massive restrictions in European and intercontinental air traffic due to the paralysis of large parts of European air traffic. Different stakeholder groups had to deal with challenges in this case, such that they had to cooperate in order to guarantee the most efficient air traffic. The process of this cooperative decision-making is very complex and different interests can affect the process of finding a solution. Out of these reasons the process of decision-making in the context of Air Traffic Management (ATM) must be analyzed. In this research field, there are some concepts which already focus on decision-making and its optimization. The concept of Total Airport Management (TAM) is one opportunity to increase the efficiency of service at airports. TAM is based on Airport-Collaborative Decision-Making (A-CDM; [1]).

© Springer International Publishing Switzerland 2016
A. De Gloria and R. Veltkamp (Eds.): GALA 2015, LNCS 9599, pp. 23–31, 2016.
DOI: 10.1007/978-3-319-40216-1_3

1.1   Airport Collaborative Decision-Making in Total Airport Management

The concept of A-CDM is based on the idea that different stakeholder (e.g. Air Traffic Control, airline companies, airport company, ground-handlers) have the possibility of using a common database [1, 2]. With the common database the exchange of information should be improved. The further development of A-CDM results in the concept of TAM. The assumptions are that decision-making processes and planning activities should happen in a cooperative way [3]. At this point, the distinction of cooperation and collaboration is relevant. Cooperation means that a group consists of different group members. Every group member is responsible for a different task. It is necessary to divide the general work to achieve a common goal. The handling of one subtask per person is useful for solving the task in general. The cooperation consists especially of the participation of each member. In contrast to cooperation there is no division of work during collaboration. All group members work together on certain tasks. The achievement of one common goal is in the foreground. Therefore every person has special skills, which are helpful to find a solution. All persons are equal. In the following the focus is on collaboration because every person is equal the whole team work together to achieve a common goal [4].

The concept of TAM consists of two main elements: the Airport Operation Center (APOC) and the Airport Operation Plan (AOP). An example for an APOC (Airport Control Center Simulator [ACCES] at the German Aerospace Center, Braunschweig) is depicted in Fig. 1. It is a virtual or physical control center, where relevant processes can be monitored, planned and controlled. An agent of each stakeholder group is sent to an APOC. They have to communicate as well as cooperate in order to analyze the current situation of an airport regarding certain critical events. Of course each agent has to represent the interests of the whole stakeholder group (especially in airport operating planning processes), but without cooperation, the workflow in an APOC functions inefficiently. This kind of a center consists of several key elements. In front of the room there is a video wall, on which information for all stakeholders is visible. Moreover each stakeholder has his or her own working station, where information only relevant to the particular stakeholder is visible. This is important because information may be different from stakeholder to stakeholder [1, 3]. To facilitate the collaborative decision-making process, this type of APOC is an important element. The second main element is the AOP. It is an operational plan for the next 24 h, which is collaboratively formulated. Information about flight processes and weather is visible.

Fig. 1. Airport Control Center Simulator (ACCES) at the Institute of Flight Guidance (DLR intern, 2015).

1.2   Air Traffic Management and Serious Gaming

Aspects of interaction during negotiations or decision-making processes and performance of humans in planning activities are difficult to measure with conventional methods of real- or fast-time simulations [5]. Gaming with a focus on serious pedagogical elements is a new method in this research field. The goal is to validate complex operational concepts in the ATM field and to optimize the decision-making process of different stakeholder agents. To simulate such processes, a digital multiplayer game, called D-CITE (**D**ecisions based on **C**ollaborative **I**nteraction in **TE**ams), was developed. There are several serious games with focus on training Air Traffic Controllers or Pilots as well as kinds of Management Simulation Games, but in contrast to most ATM-Games, D-CITE is solely designed to be played cooperatively. That's a special and relatively new focus in the context of ATM. In the following sections the main ideas of D-CITE are presented.

2   Serious Multiplayer Game "D-CITE"

D-CITE is a serious multiplayer game with a research focus on collaborative decision-making. In particular it is a research instrument to simulate and analyze decision-making in teams.

2.1   Requirements

D-CITE consists of several rounds. The number of rounds is set at the beginning of the game by the facilitator (APOC-Moderator). The difficulty of each game session can be adjusted by different planning scenarios for each session. In the actual scenario of D-CITE the number of complexity increases with the number of rounds. This means that the first round is very easy to understand (no critical event). In contrast to this, the players have to deal during the fourth round with a lot of critical events and a huge number of aircrafts.

The game is played cooperatively by a team of four to five players (see Table 1). The main goal of the team is to reach as many points as possible by collecting money and gaining customer-satisfaction points. It is necessary to share information because each player has only knowledge about the functionality of his or her own system. Therefore all players can only win or lose together. Moreover, the players have the secondary objective of attaining the highest possible economic success.

Teams can compete against each other by comparing the endpoints. The equation for computing the endpoints takes into account the amount of money collected or lost by each player and the passenger contentment. Passenger contentment is influenced by the outcome of the player's planning. The outcome corresponds to a simulation, which is calculated based on the player's planning. If the simulation is cancelled by a violation of rules, the player is informed by an error message. Other rules, which will not affect the simulation, may be added by the supervisor. The supervisor could for example set a time limit for each round.

Table 1. Roles of D-CITE [6].

Role	Description
Airline yellow	The Airline agent has the task of placing a certain number of airplane cards on the Standard Arrival Routes (STAR)
Airline salmon	The Airline agent has the task of placing a certain number of airplane cards on the Standard Arrival Routes (STAR)
(+ Airline lightblue)	(The Airline agent has the task of placing a certain number of airplane cards on the Standard Arrival Routes (STAR))
Ground-Handler	The Ground-Handler has the task of moving busses (for passengers) as well as pallet trucks (for cargo) from the depot to the stands, but also from and to any stand
Airport	The Airport is responsible for opening and closing the security checks

2.2   Game Boards

There are two phases of D-CITE: the planning phase and the simulation phase. Each phase includes a separate game board. During the seven steps of the planning phase it is necessary to change the already planned AOP because of critical events. Figure 2 shows the AOP, which is one of the main elements of the game. There are three main rows coloured blue, green and grey. The blue part symbolizes the four different Standard Arrival Routes, the green part stands for the landing time and the following parking position and the grey part informs the player about the take-off time of all airplanes. In summary the AOP visualizes the most relevant planning information of all airplanes. The plan is available to all players. In Addition to this AOP, each player has his or her own view (see Fig. 3).

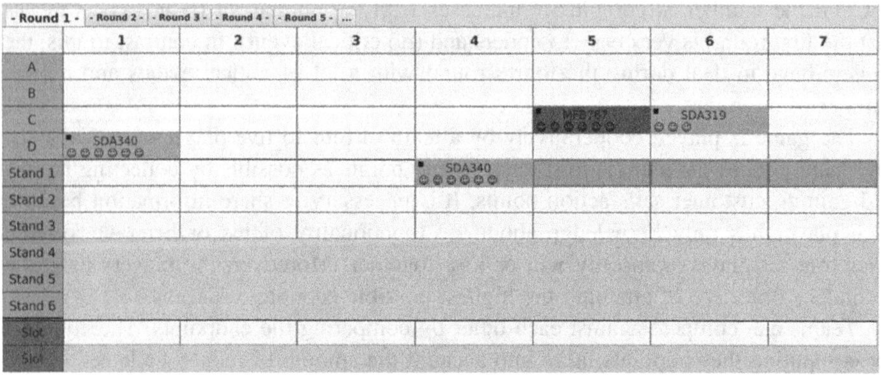

Fig. 2. Airport operation plan. (Color figure online)

The second phase is the simulation phase, which includes the game simulation board (see Fig. 4). The game board represents an airport with its main functions. As you can see, there are the Standard Arrival Routes, characterized by the letters A to D at

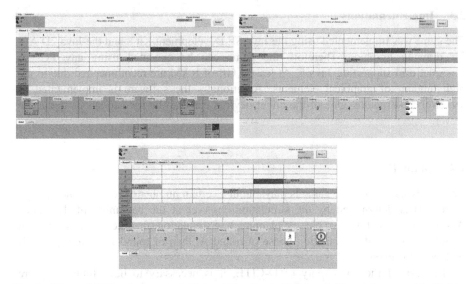

Fig. 3. View of Airline (upper area), Ground-Handler (middle) and Airport (lower area). (Color figure online)

the start of the flight routes. In addition, there is a critical zone (Terminal Maneuvering Area, [TMA]). Moreover, there are three stands, serving as the parking area of the airplanes, and one runway. Each role has its own area depicted. For the ground-handler there is an area for the busses and pallet trucks and for the Airport there are waiting halls for the outgoing passengers.

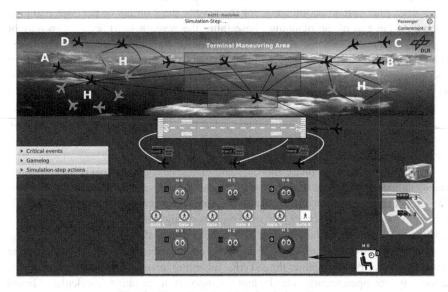

Fig. 4. Game board of the simulation phase.

2.3 Implementations

The game was implemented using the Java SE Development Kit 8 and the Java 2D API for drawing graphics. Therefore the game can be executed using any PC- or Mac-platform supporting Java 8. At least 4 GB of RAM are recommended due to the high amount of graphical elements. Additionally the software is implemented as server/client-structure. One of the client devices can also be used to start a dedicated server.

2.4 Game Play

As already mentioned the game is playable in a certain number of rounds. The number of rounds is determined by the simulation-observer at the beginning of the game. A round consists of the two phases: planning and simulation (first the planning phase of round A, second, the simulation phase of round A, then of round B). Every phase is divided into seven steps.

Because of the complexity of D-CITE, it is necessary to have training before playing the game. For this, an interactive tutorial was developed. An aircraft called "CITE" helps the user to understand not only the game surface but also how the game is played. After finishing the training, the game begins.

The focus during the game should be on collaboration and cooperation. As such, an already planned AOP for each round is presented at the start of the game. The players must reschedule the AOP because of incoming critical events during each round. Examples for these critical events can be: "Airport personnel strike: Passengers cannot enter Waiting Hall 1 for the next 3 steps" or "Weather: Storm - only 2 airplanes are allowed in the critical zone". The players must react to these events, change their planning, and communicate so as to come to a collaborative solution. To this end, each player must plan certain action cards for the sevens steps on his or her own planning tableau. At the end of the planning phase (after the seventh step), every step may or may not be planned with one action card. Because of communication and cooperation with each other, it can happen that the placement of cards results in (verbal) reactions of other players. Moreover it is for each role possible to get a simulation preview of his or her planning. This preview shows the planning results after each of the seven steps of a certain round. The players are able to optimize their planning and to give hints to other roles. The next phase, the simulation phase is starting, after all stakeholder agents have rescheduled the AOP. For each of the seven steps of a round the procedure is repeated. For this, the tokens are placed automatically.

During the simulation phase the outcome of the new planned AOP is being animated, including log messages showing details of each simulation step. At first the planned actions of each player-role are shown, namely placing airplanes on the STAR, opening, closing security checks or moving busses and pallet trucks. Afterwards the departure of an airplane is shown if it has been successfully dispatched. Then the boarding and movement of passengers between halls is animated as well as the movement of airplanes within the STAR, including planned landings. Further the airport pays for open security checks and a temporary team-rating is calculated based on the number of waiting passengers. There a various scenarios in which a simulation could be canceled. The team would then be required to correct the error, generate a new adjusted AOP and restart the simulation phase. After finishing the simulation phase, the next round starts. Therefore the players have to plan the next round regarding certain critical events. After rescheduling the AOP, the simulation phase is following. At the end of the game (set by the simulation observer) a screen with the results of all players is shown. The result-score is based on the one hand on the money collected by each player during the game, and on the other hand on the passenger satisfaction [6].

2.5 Playtest

Playtests to analyze the prototype were conducted with 32 participants (eight teams, one team consists of four players). After each playtest session the participants were to fill out a questionnaire. The general impression of the game concept, the comprehension of each player's role and the quality of the design of the play board were determined by the questionnaire. In Table 2 results are depicted.

Table 2. Selected results of first playtests ($N = 31$, one participant was excluded).

Category	No.	Description	Result
Game	1	Concept of the game	MW = 2 (Good)
	2	Fun during game play	71 %
	3	Factor of entertainment	60 %
	4	Degree of interaction	MW = 2,69 (High)
Role	1	Fast role immersion	87 %
	2	Easy role immersion	84 %
	3	Role comprehension	73 %
	4	Need for discussions	58 %
Design	1	Comprehensible game elements	77 %

The first question answered the question about the concept of collaborative decision-making. 29 participants liked the realization of the concept. 71 % of all players had fun during the D-CITE play session. That is important for the motivational aspect of playing a serious game. Additionally some participants named the collective planning tasks as main reason for having fun during their playtest session. The factor of entertainment is round about 60 %. To guarantee collaborative decision-making in a game, interactions are necessary. The degree of interactions in D-CITE is high. Almost all players (87 % and 84 %) could empathize with their role and many (73 %) were able to understand all their tasks. Most of the players (ca. 60 %) felt the need to take part in discussions. Participation in discussions is fundamentally for the collaborative decision making process. 77 % of the participants perceived the game elements were made intelligible. Consequently the design of D-CITE successfully supports the comprehension and the match flow of the game. During further playtests questions about the design of D-CITE were also asked, but the analyzation of the design of D-CITE is not focused in this paper.

3 Discussion

In summary, it could be illustrated that the cooperation of different stakeholder groups with divergent goals at an airport is very important because the whole system would fail, if only individual optimization is the base for decision-making. The main problem is that this results in complex processes. To simulate such kind of decision-making processes, a serious game seems to be the best method. For this, the serious multiplayer game D-CITE was developed and presented. It is a game for analyzing complex interaction and decision-making processes in ATM. But there is one main point which should be discussed. Traditionally serious games have their background in training or education. In this case neither the one nor the other background will be used. The aim of the game is on the one hand to demonstrate the complex interaction process, and on the other hand to show how cooperation works. But in D-CITE, a special kind of learning is implemented: collaborative learning [7]. The learning-by-doing approach is made possible by using a collaborative game-based learning situation. Various stakeholder groups of an airport collaborate and must decide which solution is the best one for the whole team. There are certain criteria, e.g. a common database and feedback, which should be considered [7]. The players should be able to communicate with each other and have access to information, not only about their own, but also about the performance of other groups. This point was also realized in D-CITE. One further aspect of collaborative learning is to get feedback. Feedback should have high priority especially within game-based-learning environments. During D-CITE, several hints and critical information may be shared among players. It is possible that each player can see the immediate effect of his or her actions on the AOP [8, 9].

Although D-CITE is a research method it could be also possible to use it as a learning game. In this context it would be possible to train the awareness of the relevance of information-sharing. [10] recommended a taxonomy of certain serious games components which consists of gaming and learning aspects. On the basis of these components, in Tables 3 and 4 one example of each category is depicted.

Table 3. Gaming components [10].

Category	No.	Element	Description	D-CITE
Gaming action	1	Movements	Move cards	Aircraft cards
Gaming tool	1	Feedback	Feedback about points	Team score
Gaming goal	1	Competition	Be the best team	Competition of different teams

Table 4. Learning components [10].

Category	No.	Element	Description	D-CITE
Learning action	1	Analyzing	Actual problem, compare	State of the art
Learning tool	1	Problem solving	Challenges	Critical events
Learning goal	1	Awareness	Perception of different learning aspects	Information-sharing

It is visible that already learning criteria exist. Because of these aspects it is possible to use D-CITE not only as a research instrument but also as a learning game. In this pedagogical context the training of the relevance of information-sharing is one application context.

4 Conclusion and Outlook

In the research field of ATM, serious gaming seems to be a relatively new method for the analysis of complex interaction processes. Because of the focus on human interaction, it is a suitable method to analyze interaction processes. In contrast to conventional methods of real- and fast-time simulations within D-CITE, it is possible to focus on the interaction of the players. The digital version of D-CITE is a simplified presentation of ATM-concepts, but it is more detailed than a paper-based game could be. One of the next steps is to answer how experts of ATM can realize the benefits of cooperation and collaboration by using serious gaming. Experiments are planned for the end of 2015.

References

1. Günther, Y., Inard, A., Werther, B., Bonnier, M., Spies, G., Marsden, A., Niederstrasser, H., et al.: Total Airport Management. Verfügbar unter (2006). http://www.bs.dlr.de/tam/Dokuments/TAM-OCD-public.pdf [27.03.2015]
2. EUROCONTROL. Airport CDM Operational Concept Document (2006). http://www.euro-cdm.org/library/cdm_ocd.pdf [27.03.2015]
3. Jipp, M., Depenbrock, F.S., Suikat, R., Schaper, M., Papenfuß, A., Kaltenhäuser, S., Weber, B.: Validation of multi-objective optimization for total airport management. In: Proceedings of the 8th Asian Control Conference (ASCC), Kaohsiung, Taiwan (2011)
4. Schmalz, J.S.: Zwischen Kooperation und Kollaboration, zwischen Hierarchie und Heterarchie. Organisationsprinzipien und -strukturen von Wikis. Verfügbar unter (2007). http://www.soz.uni-frankfurt.de/K.G/B5_2007_Schmalz.pdf [15.09.2015]
5. Meinecke, M., Suikat, R.: Evaluation of total airport management concepts via a game-based approach. In: 30th European Annual Conference on Human Decision-Making and Manual Control (EAM), Baunschweig, Germany (2012)
6. Freese, M., Drees, S., Meinecke, M.: Between game and reality: using serious games to analyze complex interaction processes in air traffic management. In: Proceedings of the 46th ISAGA Conference, Kyoto, Japan, June 2015
7. Romero, M., Usart, M., Ott, M., Earp, J., de Freitas, S.: Learning through playing for or against each other? Promoting collaborative learning in digital game based learning. In: Proceedings of the European Conference on Information Systems (ECIS) (2012). http://aisel.aisnet.org/ecis2012/93
8. Erev, I., Bornstein, G., Galili, R.: Constructive intergroup competition as a solution to the free rider problem: a field experiment. J. Exp. Soc. Psychol. **29**, 463–478 (1993)
9. Bornstein, G.: Intergroup conflict: individual, group and collective interests. Pers. Soc. Psychol. Rev. **7**(2), 129–145 (2003)
10. Carvalho, M.B., Bellotti, F., Berta, R., Rauterberg, M.: An activity theory-based model for serious games analysis and conceptual design. Comput. Educ. **87**, 166–181 (2015)

What Serious Game Studios Want from ICT Research: Identifying Developers' Needs

Grigorij Ljubin Saveski[1], Wim Westera[1(✉)], Li Yuan[2], Paul Hollins[2],
Baltasar Fernández Manjón[3], Pablo Moreno Ger[3], and Krassen Stefanov[4]

[1] Open University of the Netherlands, Heerlen, The Netherlands
{grigorij.saveski,wim.westera}@ou.nl
[2] University of Bolton, Bolton, UK
{l.yuan,p.a.hollins}@bolton.ac.uk
[3] Complutense University of Madrid, Madrid, Spain
{balta,Pablom}@fdi.ucm.es
[4] Sofia University "St. Kliment Ohridski", Sofia, Bulgaria
krassen@fmi.uni-sofia.bg

Abstract. Although many scholars recognise the great potential of games for teaching and learning, the EU-based industry for such "serious games" is highly fragmented and its growth figures remain well behind those of the leisure game market. Serious gaming has been designated as a priority area by the European Commission in its Horizon 2020 Framework Programme for Research and Innovation. The RAGE project, which is funded as part of the Horizon 2020 Programme, is a technology-driven research and innovation project that will make available a series of self-contained gaming software modules that support game studios in the development of serious games. As game studios are a critical factor in the uptake of serious games, the RAGE projects will base its work on their views and needs as to achieve maximum impact. This paper presents the results of a survey among European game studios about their development related needs and expectations. The survey is aimed at identifying a baseline reference for successfully supporting game studios with advanced ICTs for serious games.

Keywords: Serious game · Game industry · Technology · Game engine · Interoperability · Innovation · RAGE

1 Introduction

Serious games are games for non-leisure purposes [1]. Their potential for teaching and learning has been widely recognised. Thus far, however, seizing this potential has been problematic. While the leisure games industry is an established industry dominated by major non-European hardware vendors (e.g. Sony, Microsoft and Nintendo), major publishers, and a fine-grained network of development studios, distributors and retailers, the serious games industry displays many features of an emerging, immature branch of business: weak interconnectedness, limited knowledge exchange, absence of harmonising standards, limited specialisations, limited division of labour and insufficient evidence of the products' efficacies [2, 3]. The serious gaming industry is distributed

© Springer International Publishing Switzerland 2016
A. De Gloria and R. Veltkamp (Eds.): GALA 2015, LNCS 9599, pp. 32–41, 2016.
DOI: 10.1007/978-3-319-40216-1_4

over a large number of small independent players. There is no clearly functioning serious gaming sector with defined product and service qualities, competing suppliers and active users [2]. Growth figures for the wider domain of game-based learning are estimated to be in the region of 3–4 % per year until 2017 [4], which is well below the comparative estimated annual growth rate of 7 % of the leisure games market [5].

Still, conditions for a wider uptake of serious games are favourable. End-user connectivity as well as the market penetration of PCs and handheld devices do not present any barriers to the adoption of games. In recent years smartphones, tablets and social media have radically changed the media landscape outside school. Teachers, learners and parents urge schools to include these media in their school lessons and curriculum. The financial barriers for game development have receded as advanced tools for graphics design, media production and game creation have become accessible at low cost indeed some are available free of charge. There is increasing, empirical evidence of the effectiveness of serious games for learning and teaching [6], which is a critical factor in the acceptance of games as a learning tool.

The European Commission has designated serious games as a priority topic in its Horizon 2020 European Framework Programme for Research and Innovation. It envisions a flourishing serious games industry that both stimulates the creation of jobs in the creative industry sectors and helps to address a variety of societal challenges in education, health, social cohesion and citizenship. The RAGE project, which is funded as part of the Horizon 2020 Programme, is a technology-driven research and innovation project that will make available ICTs for supporting game studios at the development of serious games. In order to identify the needs and expectations of European game studios the RAGE project has carried out a series of in-depth stakeholder interviews with game development companies. This paper presents the main outcomes of this needs assessment grounded and interpreted within the context of game research and the game industry. Firstly this paper introduces the RAGE project and explains the motivation for this survey. Thereafter, the paper explains the conceptual underpinning of the survey and the method applied. It summarises the outcomes and concludes with a brief discussion.

2   The RAGE Project

The RAGE project (rageproject.eu) is a pan-European initiative to support the development of serious games. It is coordinated by the Open University of The Netherlands and includes 19 key partner participants from the game industry, the education sector and research centres from 10 European countries: Austria, Bulgaria, France, Germany, Italy, Portugal, Romania, Spain, United Kingdom and The Netherlands. RAGE will develop and validate a number of self-contained software modules that game developers can use for enhancing the pedagogical quality of their games. The software modules will facilitate the processing of data from logging and input devices to allow for learning analytics, emotional states capturing and stealth assessment of players, and enable strategic interventions and social representations that support personalised learning, game balancing, procedural animations, language analyses and syntheses, interactive storytelling, and other functions. One of the principal technical challenges of RAGE is to ensure interoperability of the software modules across the variety of game platforms that are used by game studios. While aiming for the widespread and sustained exploitation of the anticipated new technologies RAGE from the outset has deliberately engaged its main stakeholders in a co-design process. Importantly, we want to avoid the common mismatch between required and delivered ICT that can be observed everywhere, with costs of failure up to 2.5 % of the Gross National Product [7, 8]. The current survey is the first of the on-going stakeholder consultation required to identify developers' baseline needs and requirements.

3   Conceptual Framing

Game studios are a branch of creative industries, a term that emerged in the 1990s to connect the arts and other cultural activities with emerging digital technologies and the associated knowledge economy [9]. The creative industry product is innovative rather than routine, and can be characterised by originality, technical professional skill, uniqueness and quality [10]. Moreover the creative industries are expected to increasingly become the main driver of innovation and societal change, by the products and services they provide and as means of originating and sharing new ideas, knowledge and ways of working [11, 12]. While a variety of game market analyses and outlooks are available on a commercial basis - usually only available on a premium subscription basis - these tend to singularly cover the business perspective that is, they present macro-economic figures, e.g. market volumes, growth rates and segmentation and largely neglect other perspectives (cf. newzoo.com, superdataresearch.com, npd.com, forrester.com, idate.org). Additionally, most resources refer to the demand side of the overall game market, not the serious game market, but even less data about the supply side is available that would reveal how game studios view and deal with emerging technologies. When it comes to technology-driven innovation, however, a wider range of factors should be considered, including technology usage and the associated competences and knowledge management [13]. As RAGE aims to introduce a wide range of innovative technologies in the gaming sector the primary goal of our study is to understand the game studios' practices, strategies and expectations with regard to emerging technologies and to clarify how game studios - as part of technology-driven creative industries - balance production routines and innovative approaches. Figure 1 presents the conceptual model that was used for guiding this survey. Placing the game studios at the centre, it is important to collect details about (1) the games they deliver and (2) the customers and end-users that will use the games. Furthermore, (3) validation refers to the tools and mechanisms for establishing the effectiveness of the games for their purposes. Among the studios' means of production we distinguish (4) the pedagogical strategies that they apply, (5) the knowledge and information resources they rely on, and (6) the technological infrastructure and tools that they currently use for building the games. The latter is the main focus with in particular (6a) the platforms and programming languages the game studios use, the ways they deal with (6b) interoperability issues and how they view (6c) emerging technologies.

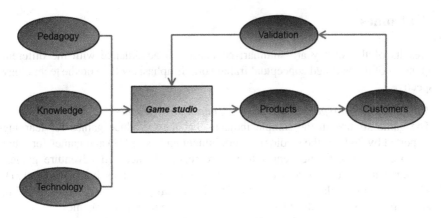

Fig. 1. Conceptual framework for the survey

4 Method

For this qualitative study we have opted for structured interviews rather than a questionnaire approach, as the latter does not match the in-depth detailed nature of the study and may have produced poor responses. A set of questions was elaborated for each of the framework components explained above. The final interview version contained 170 questions (61 yes-no questions, 73 open-ended questions and 36 Likert ratings). For practical reasons the interviews were arranged through online communications (Skype or phone) and the interviewers used an online questionnaire to guide the interview and to record the answers. This online questionnaire was not disclosed to the participants, however, in order to preserve the pursued interview setting. A priori, two test interviews were carried out to check for clarity and duration. Interview duration was typically less than one hour. Through the RAGE partner network we engaged with 21 game studios from 10 European countries. The average studio staff count was 32, which was strongly biased, however, by two large companies with around 200 employees. The other 19 studios have an average size of 14 employees (SD = 9). The respondents had senior positions in the studios (mean: 14 years of experience, SD = 9), either as CEO, creative director, owner, programmer, producer or as sales manager. With respect to the processing of the Likert scale data, which are ordinal, we follow Norman [14] in allowing parametric statistics for these. This results in despite the qualitative nature of the Likert labels, quantifiable scores that can be represented with the arithmetical mean, standard deviation, and estimated standard error of the mean, respectively, is it conditional to normality checks. The Likert scales (strongly disagree, disagree, neutral, agree, strongly agree) data were all converted into a linear metric at the interval $[-1, +1]$.

5   Outcomes

The results of the survey are summarized below, in accordance with the different components of the outlined conceptual framework. Emphasis will be on the technology perspective.

1. *The games: What type of games do the game studios produce?*
   The game studios in the sample indicate that they produce games for learning (reported by 76 % of the studios), entertainment games (57 %) and games for other purposes (67 %). Game genres that were reported, included adventure games, strategy games, quiz-based games, puzzle games, action games, both in 2D and 3D. The predominant player or learner mode was identified by most studios as being single player mode. Half of the studios also develop multiplayer games.

2. *The customers: Who are the studios' target customers and end-users?*
   The studios address diverse customer categories. They sell their games to companies (reported by 48 % of the studios), public organisations (43 %), education providers (38 %), individuals (38 %) and publishers (19 %).

3. *Validation: How do studios validate the effectiveness of their games for learning?*
   Most game studios claim to deliberately assess the effectiveness of their games for achieving pursued learning outcomes. They mostly rely on data that can be collected easily from game runs, e.g. logging and trace data, quizzes in the game, level achievement, internal ratings and performance scores. Some use (quick) questionnaires or rely on player community feedback. Three companies reported using randomised controlled trials collecting evidence. The validity of the approaches could not be established in this survey.

4. *Pedagogy: What pedagogical strategy do game studios use, if any?*
   When asked for their preferred approach toward pedagogy the game studios reported experiential learning pedagogy most often (76 %). Other approaches mentioned are guided instruction (62 %), quiz-based feedback (48 %) and problem solving (43 %). No detailed information was collected as to how game studios then further detail and implement these strategies in the games, and what level of expertise about instructional design they possess. In addition the studios were asked to rate the importance of diverse pedagogical strategies. Figure 2 presents the Likert rating results converted to the [−1, 1] interval. Horizontal bars reflect the standard error (not the standard deviation). Fundamentally all strategies receive some importance. The highest ranked strategies are natural feedback and debriefing after the game. Apparently, the game developers's priority is to avoid any interruptions of the game play, in order to preserve flow. Guidance and instruction during the game are rarely used, even though a vast body of evidence in instructional research demonstrates the inferiority of minimal guidance strategies [15].

5. *Knowledge: What are important information needs?*
   Participants were asked to rate the importance of diverse information and knowledge resources. The ratings are presented in Fig. 3.

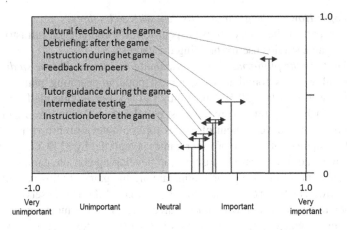

Fig. 2. The importance of pedagogical strategies

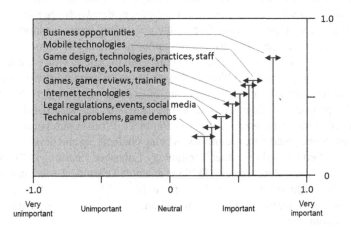

Fig. 3. The importance of various information and knowledge resources

Although the game studios appreciate a wide variety of knowledge resources, highest scores are assigned to resources about business opportunities, mobile technologies, game technologies, game design, best practices and potential new personnel. By answering the open-ended questions the game studios indicated the use of various external repositories (e.g. Unity Asset Store, Turbosquid, Three.js) for collecting game content (3D objects, textures, sound objects). Stock sites are regularly searched for reusable graphics and photographs. Software is retrieved from GitHub, Source-Forge, Bitbucket and Google play game services. Software troubleshooting is supported by consulting Stack Overflow as well as support sites and communities of game engine providers (Marmalade, Sony, Unreal). In addition game studios use online educational content and courses, for instance Moocs from Coursera and iVersity.

6. *Technology: How do the game studios deal with technology?*
   The larger part of the interview was spent to the technological infrastructure and tools that game studios use for building the games.

   (6a) *What are the platforms and programming languages that the studios use?*
   Windows was found to be the most popular operating platform (62 %), followed by Mac (38 %) and Linux (14 %). For mobile platforms Android (90 %) and iOS (86 %) are the most popular ones. A number of game studios reported the development of games for computer web browsers (62 %); the development of mobile browser games is reported by 33 %. Only 24 % of the game studios expressed an interest in developing console games. The significantly most popular game engine among the game studios is Unity (76 %), followed by Flash (38 %), and then Cocos2D (24 %). This observed dominance of Unity is consistent with other sources, e.g. [15]. The most popular programming language among the studios is C# (71 %), followed by C++ (67 %), JavaScript (48 %), objective C (33 %) and Java (33 %), which is quite similar to the latest Redmonk programming languages rankings [16].

   (6b) *Interoperability: What (learning technology) standards are used?*
   The studios reported a number of interoperability issues, or more specifically integration issues, such as linking games to existing systems (e.g. corporate systems, learning management systems), linking games with existing user data bases, compatibility problems with web browsers, portability to new hardware, and the integration and repurposing of existing game objects. SCORM was the predominant learning technology standard that was mentioned (43 %). Further interest was reported for xAPI (14 %). Whilst a number of the respondents highlighted interoperability as being challenging and of interest, very few identified or used any other Technology Enhanced Learning (TEL) standards such as those developed by IMS for example Learning Tools Interoperability (LTI) or Question and Test Interoperability (QTI) which would enable seamless data integration with learning management systems or virtual learning environments.

   (6c) *Emerging technologies: How do game studios judge emerging technologies?*
   Respondents were asked to rate importance of various emerging technologies for serious game development. The results are in Fig. 4. As can be observed from Fig. 4 all technologies receive some positive interest. Highest scores are assigned to learning analytics, the real time tracking of learning progress, adaptive gameplay and game evaluation, respectively, which all well exceed the level of importance. Other technologies seem to receive slightly more scepticism. Standard deviations are up to 0.7. This indicates that quite some studios dismiss these emerging technologies.

Through open-ended questions the participants were invited to expand on their scores. In many cases the answers were of tautological nature: we think technology X is important because we want our games to include it. In addition, positive scores were substantiated by the expectation that a particular technology would enhance the games' quality, either by allowing for better game play, increased credibility, supporting motivation or improve the learning. Commercial potential and practicability were also

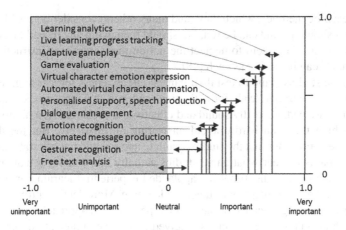

Fig. 4. Importance of various emerging technologies

mentioned as important factors. Negative scores were mainly motivated by doubts about the added value, and anxiety for complexity and cumbersome implementation. When it comes to emerging technologies game studios cautiously balance the pros and the cons in the context of their individual business.

5.1 Discussion and Conclusions

The objective of this survey was to provide a baseline reference for the alignment of ICT research and the serious game industry. Generally it is observed that the game studios expressed overall quite positive judgements about the importance of knowledge resources, pedagogical models, product validation and newly emerging technologies. Yet, the study allowed game studios to express a ranking of priorities, which could then inform the research ICT agenda. With respect to customers, the games, tools and infrastructure the game studios display the unrestricted diversity and fragmentation identified previously as a main characteristic of the serious game sector [2–4]. Major platforms are targeted, including mobile platforms. Many studios develop browser games. Exceptional is the predominance of the Unity game engine. Game consoles are avoided by most of the studios as platforms for serious games.

Serious game studios indicated the significant importance of pedagogy and the validation of the games' pedagogical effectiveness. Various pedagogical strategies were appreciated. Experiential learning was reported as the most popular approach used in the games. Natural feedback and debriefing (after the game) were ranked as the most important strategies, whereas guidance and instruction during the game are rarely used. Apparently, the game developers' priority is to avoid interruptions of the game play, in order to preserve flow. This seems to conflict, with a vast body of evidence in instructional research demonstrating the inferiority of minimal guidance strategies [17]. Further, serious game studios tend to present their games as the playful alternative for common teaching methods, which they (and many others) consider boring. They claim that learning should be and can be fun, but should then avoid any resemblance to traditional instruction. They seem to neglect the notion that sometimes instruction can be fun, and games can be boring as such [18].

Most game studios claim to test their games' effectiveness for learning. Some even use randomised controlled trials for collecting evidence. Asking serious game studios if their games are pedagogically sound and effective, is problematic, a highly coercive question, which they can hardly avoid answering affirmatively. But the depth and validity of the approaches that the studios claim to apply could not be established in this survey. It remains unclear what game studios actually know about pedagogical strategies. Puritans may comment that the applauded experiential learning approach is in fact not a pedagogical strategy, but a theory of learning. More detailed probing is needed into the operational significance of the studios' pedagogical approaches.

Although all knowledge resources received a positive appreciation, game studios assigned highest priority to information that enhances their business opportunities. Furthermore information about mobile technologies, game technologies, game design, best practices and potential new personnel received high ratings. A variety of external repositories are already accessed to support the work. Game studios designated interoperability as a major issue and many experienced practical difficulties when connecting their games to other systems. Despite these problems, only SCORM and to a lesser extent xAPI were mentioned as being used, and only a small number of studios referred to other Technology Enhanced Learning standards that might help to resolve the issues. It may suggest that the game studios have only limited awareness of these standards or that they do not consider (TEL) interoperability as an urgent topic. This may readily be associated with the fact that developers tend to perceive their applied games as "stand alone" creative solutions that offer learning activities independent of institutional learning management systems or virtual learning environments. With respect to the importance of emerging technologies highest rankings were given to learning analytics, real time tracking of learning progress, adaptive gameplay and game evaluation, respectively. Game studios are generally open and positive toward new technologies, but equally critical. They look for added value in terms of better games or commercial potential, and at the same time fear complex and cumbersome implementation.

Acknowledgements. The authors wish to thank the game studios that participated in the interviews. This work has been partially funded by the EC H2020 project RAGE (Realising and Serious Gaming Eco-System); http://www.rageproject.eu/; Grant agreement No. 644187.

References

1. Abt, C.: Serious Games. Viking Press, New York (1970)
2. Stewart, J., Bleumers, L., Van Looy, J., Mariën, I., All, A., Schurmans, D., Willaert, K., De Grove, F., Jacobs, A., Misuraca, G.: The Potential of Digital Games for Empowerment and Social Inclusion of Groups at Risk of Social and Economic Exclusion: Evidence and Opportunity for Policy. Joint Research Centre, European Commission (2013)

3. García Sánchez, R., Baalsrud Hauge, J., Fiucci, G., Rudnianski, M., Oliveira, M., Kyvsgaard Hansen, P., Riedel, J., Brown, D., Padrón-Nápoles, C.L., Arambarri Basanez, J.: Business Modelling and Implementation Report 2, GALA Network of Excellence (2013). www.galanoe.eu

4. Adkins, S.S.: The 2012–2017 worldwide game-based learning and simulation-based markets. In: Key Findings from Recent Ambient Insight Research, Serious Play Conference 2013. Ambient Insight, Monroe, WA (2013). www.ambientinsight.com/Resources/Documents/AmbientInsight_SeriousPlay2014_WW_2013_2018_GameBasedLearning_Market.pdf

5. PWC: Global Entertainment and Media-Outlook: 2012–2016. PriceWaterhouse-Coopers (2012)

6. Connolly, T.M., Boyle, E.A., MacArthur, E., Hainey, T., Boyle, J.M.: A systematic literature review of empirical evidence on computer games and serious games. Comput. Educ. **59**(2), 661–686 (2013). doi:10.1016/j.compedu.2012.03.004

7. Deursen, A., van Dijk, J.: Ctrl Alt Delete: productiviteitsverlies door ICT-problemen en ontoereikende digitale vaardigheden op het werk. Twente University, Enschede (2012)

8. Schönfeld, C.L.: Hoe IT projecten slagen en falen – Leren van pijnlijke ervaringen. Academic Service, Den Haag (2012)

9. O'Connor, J.: Creativity, Culture and Education. Arts Council England, Newcastle upon Tyne (2010). http://www.creativitycultureeducation.org/wp-content/uploads/CCE-lit-review-creative-cultural-industries-257.pdf

10. Caves, R.E.: Creative Industries: Contracts Between Art and Commerce. Harvard University Press, Boston (2000)

11. TSB: Creative industries Strategy 2013–2016. Technology Strategy Board, Swindon (2013). www.innovateuk.org

12. Potts, J., Cunningham, S.: Four models of the creative industries. Int. J. Cult. Policy **1201**(1), 163–180 (2008). doi:10.1080/10286630802281780

13. Nonaka, I.: The Knowledge-Creating Company. Harvard Bus. Rev. **69**(6), 96–104 (1991)

14. Norman, G.: Likert scales, levels of measurement and the "laws" of statistics. Adv. Health Sci. Educ. **15**(5), 625–632 (2010). doi:10.1007/s10459-010-9222-y

15. Global Game Jam (2015). http://globalgamejam.org/news/ggj-2015-official-stats

16. Redmonk programming languages rankings (2015). http://redmonk.com/sogrady/2015/01/14/language-rankings-1-15/

17. Kirschner, P.A., Sweller, J., Clark, R.E.: Why minimal guidance during instruction does not work: an analysis of the failure of constructivist, discovery, problem-based, experiential, and inquiry-based teaching. Edu. Psychol. **41**(2), 75–86 (2006)

18. Westera, W.: Games are motivating, aren't they? Disputing the arguments for digital game-based learning. Int. J. Serious Games (2015). http://journal.seriousgamessociety.org

The Double-Effect Approach to Serious Games in Higher Education: Students Designing and Developing Serious Games for Other Students

Peter Mayr[1(✉)], Harald Bendl[1], and Frauke Mörike[1,2]

[1] International Management for Business and Information Technology,
Duale Hochschule Baden-Württemberg Mannheim, Coblitzallee 1-9, 68163 Mannheim, Germany
Peter.Mayr@dhbw-mannheim.de
[2] Institute of Anthropology, Heidelberg University, Albert-Ueberle-Str. 3-5, 69120 Heidelberg, Germany

Abstract. This article introduces a student-centered, double-effect learning concept on the basis of Serious Games (SG), which has been developed and established at a higher education institution in Germany. The underlying principle of the concept is a two-tiered students-for-students-approach, which encompasses on the first level the design, development and implementation of a SG for project management by 3rd year students in Business Information Systems Engineering (BISE). The SG then gets incorporated into courses on the respective topic in other degree courses of the same institution. Given the promising potential of SGs in higher education in general and the multiple application options for Serious Games specifically in BISE, the authors argue that their concept can provide a solution for some of the limiting issues to enabling a broader application of SGs such as time-consuming and costly development or alignment of SGs to the curriculum of the target group.

1 Introduction

Current discourses on technology enhanced learning have widened the classic concepts on e-learning to the perspective of entire digital learning environments, which recur on familiar everyday life settings of the students to provide a more realistic framework for the learning contents [1]. Serious Games (SG) play an important role as an emerging paradigm in this context [2], as they enable for such a positioning of complex learning contents into a situation or setting familiar to the learners' experiential horizon.

1.1 The Double-Effect Approach to Serious Games in Higher Education

Taking that proposition into practical contexts of knowledge transfer in higher educa-tion, this article introduces a student-centered, double-effect learning concept on the basis of SGs, which has been developed and established at the Baden-Wuerttemberg Cooperative State University Mannheim (Germany). The underlying principle of the concept is a two-tiered students-for-students-approach which encompasses on the first level the design, development and implementation of a SG for project management by

A. De Gloria and R. Veltkamp (Eds.): GALA 2015, LNCS 9599, pp. 42–50, 2016.
DOI: 10.1007/978-3-319-40216-1_5

3rd year students in Business Information Systems Engineering (BISE), which then was incorporated on the second level into seminars on the topic for their peers in other degree courses of the same institution.

Given the findings of current studies on the promising potential of SGs in higher education in general (e.g. [3, 4]) and the multiple application options for SGs specifically in BISE [5, 6], the authors of this paper argue that their concept can provide a solution for some of the limiting issues to enable a broader application of SGs such as time-consuming and costly development [7], or alignment of SGs to the curriculum of the target group [8].

1.2   Serious Games in Business Systems Engineering Studies

The use of SGs in higher education can be regarded as an innovative method of activation for teaching, provided the availability of appropriate games that are tailored to both the educational objective and the target group. While such a utilization of SGs (namely students performing the user/player role) can be carried out in most if not all higher education subject areas, the interdisciplinary nature of BISE carries the potential for more extensive application opportunities of SGs and to approach some of the challenges encountered for the application of SGs in higher education.

As the students acquire knowledge on both business management and information technology in the course of their studies, they are not only able to play, but also able to implement or even develop SGs for other faculties [5, 9]. The combination of students' expertise in the commercial and technical arena enables the students in BISE to cover all skill profiles required for the design, development and implementation of a SG, as they are not only able to provide for the technical aspect of a SG but also for the relevant learning contents.

This approach has several advantages, as the students are familiar with issues of learning strategy and also well acquainted with the motivational potential of games, often from their own experience [10]. Therefore SGs can be used in BISE as a challenging interdisciplinary topic for study projects, which have as an outcome tailor-made target group oriented SGs with most current content ready for application, which can be offered at low cost for teaching of other faculties.

2   Case Study: The Serious Game brillianCRM – Designed and Developed from Students for Students

2.1   Setting the Grounds: The Baden-Württemberg Cooperative State University Mannheim

Baden-Wuerttemberg Cooperative State University (DHBW) in Mannheim offers an attractive and unique study method by combining theoretical studies at the university with practical experience at a partner company. The Bachelor degree programs at the DHBW Mannheim are recognized as intensive study programs (3 years), which have the interplay of theory and practical experience as leading principle: the dual degree program rotates on three month intervals, three months at the respective company and three months at the university. The regular change of location requires the students to be flexible and able to be highly engaged with individual study sections. Students from different companies, public and social institutes come together during their study periods at the DHBW Mannheim, work together in teams and implement joint projects, resulting in networks that benefit students even after they graduate.

The Bachelor degree program "International Management for Business and Information Technology" (IMBIT) garners an internationally orientated curriculum in the realms of BISE. The six study semesters cover an interdisciplinary spectrum of computer science, professional economics, and intercultural management, which are predominantly held in English, including a summer school one of the foreign partner universities. The lectures and seminars are complemented by six internship phases at accredited industry partners both on the supplier and user side of IT services such as Accenture, DB Schenker Logistics, Hewlett Packard, IBM, or Springer Publishing, in which the students can apply their acquired knowledge directly in the business environment in Germany and abroad.

2.2 Project Set-Up

Therefore, the double-effect concept to SGs firstly draws on the interdisciplinary nature of degree programs such as IMBIT and the strategic orientation of the DHBW Mannheim to align theoretical learning phases with a structured internship program in cooperation with industry partners, allowing for a set of students with an exceptional amount of practical experience in the later phase of their studies. Secondly, the DHBW facilitates a multidisciplinary network of professors, lecturers, and academic staff across faculties, departments, and degree courses through a practice of cross-lecturing, academic research groups and education projects. These prerequisites cater for a uniquely open environment in which cross-functional and innovative study projects can be realized, such as the one discussed here.

In the first phase of the project, 3rd year students of the graduate degree program IMBIT were given the task to design, develop and implement in twelve weeks a SG on Project Management. In general, the development of an IT solution in a joint IT project is part of the 3rd year curriculum, for which the students have by then acquired the necessary knowledge in both theory and industry internships to master a broad range of challenges. In a second phase, the serious game was incorporated into the didactic methodology of courses on project management in other Bachelor and Master degree courses of the same institution with a very positive response from the students on the method. Further feedback and suggestions of the students were gathered and used as key input for a third phase, a follow-up project a year later for the next 3rd year students to pick up, resulting a matured solution, which is now ready for university-wide application.

2.3   The brillianCRM Plot – A Brief Description

Upon starting the fully web-based SG brillianCRM (www.brillianCRM.com), the student enters into the role of the project manager for an international IT project. The employer of the project manager is a German consultant firm with headquarters in Hamburg, which specializes in the implementation of software for customer relationship management (CRM). The project is to be executed in Houston (Texas) at the headquarters of the fictitious client company Concrete Machinery Inc., a manufacturer of construction equipment.

Fig. 1. The graphical user interface of brillianCRM

The project task is to adapt the standard CRM software to the specific client/user requirements, for which the player in his role as project manager has not only to deal with the different stakeholders on the client side, but also with colleagues and a development team in India. The player goes through all major phases of a project from initiation, planning and implementation through to project completion. In each of the phases the player is required to apply the various methods of project management such as stakeholder and risk analysis, work breakdown structure, budgeting and scheduling. In the implementation phase, the player is confronted with various realistic crisis situations with characters from different cultural backgrounds to which they have to react with appropriate measure and communication (Fig. 2).

The users in their role as project manager have to correspond to both the requirements of the German boss, the stakeholders at the client's side (e.g. a very critical CFO, a sales manager, or the client's side project manager) and one's own team (e.g. project assistant and programmer). In order to successfully manage the project the user has to decide to go to different places and to use diverse forms of communication (email, phone, presentation). The users are given continually feedback on their project management performance on the three critical project dimensions time, cost and quality through a traffic light (see Fig. 1 - diamond in the top left). Overall, the students designed a SG based on both

Fig. 2. Acting characters in the game (finance director, Indian developer)

current project management standard and real-life scenarios from their own practical experience, which creates the atmosphere of a quasi-realistic project environment and can foster the students' immersion into the tasks and challenges to which they can apply learned concepts and methods.

2.4 The Student Serious Game Design and Development Project

The curriculum of the IMBIT Bachelor degree programme at the DHBW Mannheim envisages in the second and third year several courses on software development, such as an IT case study, an integration seminar, an IT project and a user experience (UX)/ design thinking workshop. Together with their practical experience from the internships in the industry the students have a broad range of skills at their disposal, ranging from project management, software design, programming up to UX. In summer 2014 then, a group of hardly thirty 3rd year students was given the task to design and implemented as part of their IT project a SG. The lecturers, who acted both as project sponsors as well as academic advisors, set the objective to deliver a running prototype of a SG featuring a number of technically correct and interesting learning tasks on management of a global IT project. Further requirements were that the SG should be web-based, support current devices with touch interfaces and can be used simultaneously by thirty to fifty players in the classroom. For the entire task from initial design up to implementation the semester schedule allowed for a maximum timeframe of eleven weeks.

The course had developed a mobile device enabled tourist information system for the city of Ladenburg (m-ladenburg.de) in the previous year as part of an IT case study and could thus build on the experience gained. The students organized themselves into four teams responsible for system design and programming, UX/Interface as well as the expert contents; the student project manager had an assistant.

To cater for the tight timeframe, the only viable approach reach the objective was agile development. The development of structure and content of the SG were kept separate from the software implementation, enabling the respective teams to work in parallel from the first moment onwards. The students chose a set up for the SG with a web browser as a front end, to deploy the game structure as XML tree and to store multimedia game contents in subdirectories of the server. The control program was written in Java and a Tomcat server set up to deliver the results pages created via JSP to the client. In addition to the Tomcat server on Ubuntu Linux several other open source components were used such as MySQL, JQuery, EasyUI and free TrueType typefaces and picto-grams.

Students described the UX requirements using personas, use cases and storytelling; consistent emotional appeal was a major aspect of the game. Students who want to play the SG can simply register with an email address and no other personal information except an (alias) name is required for user management. On the user account solely a hash of the salted password and the game score is saved. Lecturers using brillianCRM can create their own course groups, send out invites for the game, check the scores of the students and if required reset the game for their group.

The personal involvement of the students into this challenging project was remark-ably high and they over-delivered on the objective: On the day when their project presentation was due they did not only deliver the requested running prototype, but even a fully operational SG with a consistent look-and-feel, interesting learning tasks for the players and supporting marketing materials such as posters, slogan, jingle, video and Facebook page.

2.5   Application in the Project Management Lectures

The SG brillianCRM was then incorporated into the 2nd year lecturing sessions of two other undergraduate degree programs (International Business; Real Estate Manage-ment), as well as Master degree courses (Sales and Marketing and BISE) at the DHBW Mannheim. The SG was used as an activation method between theory-oriented lecturing phases: the students were not asked to play the entire game as a learning session on its own, but instead were asked to advance in the game only in correspondence to the topics they had just learned about. When the sequence was completed by all students, the lecture continued until the next sequence of the SG was played again to connect the learned content with a quasi-real situation. Other, more complex and reading-intense learning tasks of the game were then given as wrap-up or preparation for the next lecture.

The observed motivation of the students in the courses was extremely high and first unstructured feedback from the course participants very positive. The SG was assessed by the students as a useful supplement to traditional teaching methods, which helped to consolidate theoretical contents/methods and to experience their use "as in practice". The students furthermore felt motivated to start using project management tools such as MS project through their experience with MS Project plans in the SG's user challenges. The feedback gathered from the students using the game was then used as input for next year's group IMBIT students to further expand and optimize brillianCRM, bringing it to the solid maturity we have today.

3   Critical Review of the Approach

3.1   SG Design by Students for Students

The approach of SG design by students certainly featured direct benefits such as the inclusion of tailor-made teaching and learning contents as circumvented by the lecturers in their instructions to the student teams. This alignment to lecture plans was the first factor which enabled convenient integration of the SG into the teaching concept of other degree programs, while the marginal costs associated with its use both for students and lecturers clearly has to be regarded as the second factor. With regards to the application of the SG in other degree programs a crucial coefficient lays in the unique set-up of the DHBW which fosters a cross-linked teaching practice of its lecturers across different degree programs leading to a substantial flow of knowledge sharing about new initiatives and projects, such as the brillianCRM SG.

Another practical benefit of the students designing and developing the SG from scratch is its adaptability to new and/or enhanced SG contents: Apart from a planned extension of the SG brillianCRM to an application across the DHBW Mannheim, the latest IMBIT 3rd year students have just launched as their IT Project assignment a SG dealing with intercultural communication (www.brillianICM.com).

A critical aspect of this choice, however, lays in the limited scope which can be expected to be mastered by the students in the given timeframe. Consequently, the one or the other desirable game contents might not get implemented, the intellectual challenge is not completely harmonized across the tasks and the audio-visual configurations remain on a basic level.

3.2   Game Development-Based Learning as a Method for Software Development Teaching

Employing game development-based learning as a method to impart multi-dimensional skills and knowledge on software development suggests being a promising approach from various angles. The students exhibited a high level of dedication and engagement with the project due to the immediate results of their work and the direct application of it. The segmented structure of the SG design and development tasks allowed for attribution of individual performances, which is an often discussed topic on group work assignments. The costs to undertake such a project are very low, as the students utilized their own notebooks for development and collaborated via the network access of the DHBW. The budget of about fifty Euros per student was primarily allotted to the renting of a server share and usage rights/licenses for multi-media contents. Through these factors the project was independent from third party involvement and is a suitable foundation for cooperation projects with other faculties or universities, as neither royalty payments are incurred nor contractual agreements required.

The SG development required direct application of current practices in software development such as agile methods, UX/design thinking, project management, integration of multi-media contents and web-programming.

On a critical note stands the observation of the lecturers that students showed a tendency to focus on the areas they were already most familiar with and chose tasks within them rather than expanding their field of expertise to new fields. Through the subdivision into teams the organization of knowledge exchange between them beyond the direct SG design-related issues was barely possible (e.g. on new techniques discovered). Hence it is debatable, if homogeneous learning results could have been achieved.

4   Discussion

The implementation of such an ambitious task as a SG is certainly a challenge for the students as it requires the application and connection of acquired skills and expert knowledge from various multi-disciplinary fields such as project management, UX, software development, web programming as well as marketing/branding and requires a number of prerequisites on both BISE students' skill levels as well as institutional settings. The use of the concept to develop a SG by students and to use it in other courses is most primarily viable for topics which are required in the curriculum of a broad range of degree programs. For this reason "project management" had been selected as a first learning content for a SG development as it is an established subject at many German universities both in the technology and in the economic faculties. At the DHBW Mannheim the subject project management is taught in numerous degree programs as a compulsory module in a scope ranging from 2 to 4 credit points.

In summary, applying students' technical, expert and creative capabilities to develop SGs as an assignment gives them a sense of achievement with an immediate usable result and constitutes an effective solution to address some of the most common issues for SGs (Cost/Actuality/Curriculum Alignment). While a number of studies exist on the potential of game development-based learning [11], further insights into the hypotheses about SG design by students in conjunction with a more solid evaluation and measures will be needed to scale the "Serious Games from students for students"-approach with a direct application of the students' development in subsequent lectures for their peers.

Acknowledgments.   Special thanks goes out to our students of the WIMBIT11B and 12C courses and their inconceivable effort to bring the SG students-for-students development concept into practical existence. We also thank the students of the WIMBIT12A + B courses for their work on the new and latest SG from the IMBIT team: brillianICM.com.

References

1. Hugger, K., Walber, M.: Digitale Lernwelten: Annäherungen aus der Gegenwart. In: Hugger, K., Walber, M. (eds.) Digitale Lernwelten, pp. 9–20. VS Verlag, Wiesbaden (2010)
2. Bellotti, F., et al.: Designing a course for stimulating entrepreneurship in higher education through serious games. Procedia Comput. Sci. **15**, 174–186 (2012)
3. Abbott, D.: How to fail your research degree. In: Göbel, S., Ma, M., Baalsrud Hauge, J., Oliveira, M.F., Wiemeyer, J., Wendel, V. (eds.) JCSG 2015. LNCS, vol. 9090, pp. 179–185. Springer, Heidelberg (2015)
4. Bellotti, F., et al.: Serious games and the development of an entrepreneurial mindset in higher education engineering students. Entertainment Comput. **5**(4), 357–366 (2014)
5. Hakulinen, L.: Using serious games in computer science education. In: Proceedings of the 11th Koli Calling International Conference on Computing Education Research, pp. 83–88. ACM (2011)
6. Coelho, A., Kato, E., Xavier, J., Gonçalves, R.: Serious game for introductory programming. In: Ma, M., Fradinho Oliveira, M., Madeiras Pereira, J. (eds.) SGDA 2011. LNCS, vol. 6944, pp. 61–71. Springer, Heidelberg (2011)

7. Westera, W., Nadolski, R., Hummel, H., Wopereis, I.: Serious games for higher education: a framework for reducing design complexity. J. Comput. Assist. Learn. **24**(5), 420–432 (2008)
8. Lieberman, D.: Designing serious games for learning and health in informal and formal settings. In: Ritterfeld, U., Cody, M., Vorderer, P. (eds.) Serious Games: Mechanisms and Effects, pp. 117–130. Routledge, New York (2009)
9. Garneli, B., Giannakos, M.N., Chorianopoulos, K., Jaccheri, L.: Learning by playing and learning by making. In: Ma, M., Oliveira, M.F., Petersen, S., Hauge, J.B. (eds.) SGDA 2013. LNCS, vol. 8101, pp. 76–85. Springer, Heidelberg (2013)
10. Prensky, M.: Students as designers and creators of educational computer games: who else? Br. J. Educ. Technol. **39**(6), 1004–1019 (2008)
11. Wu, B., Wang, A.I.: A guideline for game development-based learning: a literature review. Int. J. Comput. Games Technol. **2012**, 1–20 (2012)

Instructions and Feedback in Connection with the Duration and the Level of Difficulty of a Serious Game

Alfredo Imbellone[✉], Giada Marinensi, and Carlo Maria Medaglia

Digital Administration and Social Innovation Center (DASIC),
Link Campus University, Via Nomentana, 335, 00162 Rome, Italy
{a.imbellone, g.marinensi, c.medaglia}@unilink.it

Abstract. The paper presents a study about the role of instructions and feedback within serious games in connection with the duration and with the level of difficulty of the game. Short and simple serious games can require to minimize instructions and feedback that otherwise risk to be perceived as obstructive for the game experience. Results obtained from a sample of 54 people show that both instructions and feedback are significantly linked to the expressed adequacy of the level of difficulty of the game. The expressed adequacy of the duration of the game has a significant role in mediating the relationship between the judgment on instructions and on the adequacy of the level of difficulty. The conclusion is that inadequate instructions and feedback are likely to be counterproductive, and they must be designed taking into account the duration and the level of difficulty of the game.

1 Introduction

A broad consensus is associated with the idea of learning through digital serious games, and game-based learning has reached an high popularity [1, 2]. Some authors, however, are skeptical about that, questioning if students are really motivated to learn, or they just want to play [3, 4]. According to this sort of criticism, edutainment is at risk of being limited to packaging and special effects, thus diminishing, instead of reinforcing, cognitive and metacognitive strategies [5, 6].

Research on game-base learning and serious games grew rapidly in the last years, but there are still few studies strongly based on causal relationships [7]. Instructions and feedback are widely studied in the field of educational serious games. The multifaceted nature of serious games, and their characteristic to be both serious and playful, reflect in most of the analyses about instructions and feedback.

Erhel and Jamet distinguish *learning instructions* and *entertainment instructions* within a serious game: the first ones are explicitly addressed to educational goals, the second ones encourage to play rather than to learn. According to their work, based on empirical evidence, while learning instructions can be considered more useful for the educational goals of the serious game, they are less appreciated by the players, who eventually prefer entertainment instructions that explain how to play, rather than prescriptions on what to achieve in terms of learning. Learning instructions are demonstrated to result in deeper learning, while entertainment instructions are more linked to

A. De Gloria and R. Veltkamp (Eds.): GALA 2015, LNCS 9599, pp. 51–60, 2016.
DOI: 10.1007/978-3-319-40216-1_6

accidental learning. However, entertainment instructions can result more effective if associated with feedback, which compensate the educational content [8].

Feedback, as well, is central to most pedagogic theories and was analyzed under different points of view [9–11]. A critical aspect of feedback within a serious game is its integration with game mechanics. Feedback must not distract the player while maintaining its positive effects, just like it must not interrupt the flow experience as stated by Csikszentmihalyi [12]. Feedback is one of the major facilitators of flow, but it must be properly designed to be as unobtrusive as possible not to delay or interrupt a flow experience. At the same time feedback must be harmonic with the Vygotsky's Zone of proximal development, otherwise excessive, or insufficient, challenge transmitted by feedback will induce anxiety, boredom, or apathy in the learner, especially when taking part to an educational serious game [13].

Dunwell et al. underlined the difficulty of inserting feedback within serious games. There is a strong relationship between the timing and content of feedback. Feedback must be provided autonomously and seamlessly alongside an engaging gameplay experience, and balancing these two factors is a substantial design challenge [14]. Bellotti et al. suggest to use feedback through the evolution of the serious game, observing the consequences of game actions, rather than being informed by an abstract and separated process [15].

The present paper wants to investigate the roles of instructions and feedback within a serious game, taking into consideration the duration of the game and the perceived level of difficulty as fundamental variables. The inspiration for the present paper originates from a case study on the impact of inadequate instructions and feedback in serious games. A previous study was, in fact, conducted on a set of 30 serious games for mobile devices, finding that both feedback and instructions were negatively linked to the willingness to play again [16]. This apparently anomalous finding can be interpreted as due to the perception of obstruction of feedback and instructions for the gameplay. A possible reason for this can be the extreme shortness and simplicity of the considered games. For this reason it seems of a certain interest to study a causal model formed by feedback and instructions together with the duration of the games and their perceived level of difficulty. Points of interest of the present study are those originating from its analysis of causal relationships in the field of serious games. In particular, this paper aims at showing which causal relationships are present among instructions, feedback, duration, and perceived level of difficulty for short and simple educational serious games.

2   The Serious Games

In 2012, at the end of a two-year European project, titled InTouch, a set of 30 serious games for mobile devices was developed. The set of 30 serious games was addressed to adult learners to be usable, to challenge players to confront them with work-related non-routine tasks.

Instructions within the games were extremely narrow. According to the classification given by Erhel and Jamet [8], learning instructions were given in the first frames of the games, together with the game scenario and the problem-based situation to be solved. For most games there were no entertainment instructions at all, since the game interactions were absolutely intuitive. Very short instructions were given, if necessary, indicating the number of correct answers/choices that were expected for each decision point. Feedback was given only in the last frame of the games, showing the final score and explaining why and how the given answers were, or were not, correct.

Figure 1 illustrates an example of instructions and feedback that were given within the games. The left part of the figure is a screenshot of a decision point within the games, where players were advised about the remaining time to answer and the number of correct answer for the proposed question. The right part of the figure is a screenshot of the last frame of a game, with the gained final score and an explanation of the outcome.

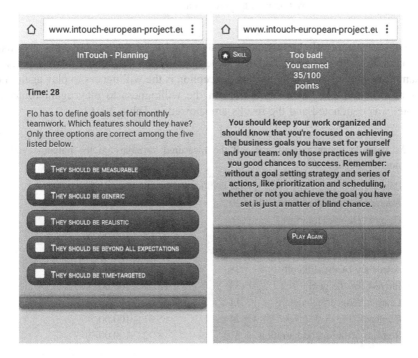

Fig. 1. Screenshots of a decision point and of a final frame of a serious game.

3 Scope and Hypotheses

A self-developed questionnaire was proposed to a group of 54 players after the completion of the games asking them to express on a 10 point Likert scale their opinion about the adequacy of the duration of the serious games, the design (graphic, interface), the fun of the gameplay, the instructions, the adequacy of the level of difficulty, the interest for the goal, the learning/educative content, the feedback, the realism of the game narration, the willingness to play again. Table 1 reports the average scores that were obtained for the measured variables.

Table 1. Average scores on a 10-point Likert scale (n = 54)

Variable	Score
Adequacy of the duration	6.6
Design (graphic, interface)	6.7
Fun of the gameplay	6.8
Instructions	8.1
Adequacy of the difficulty	6.7
Interest for the goal	6.1
Learning/educative content	6.4
Feedback	6.1
Realism of the game narration	6.8
Willingness to play again	5.7

Scores were generally high enough for all variables, or at least above the pass mark of 6 points. Roughly, it can be said that games were appreciated under many aspects by the sample of players. The only negative exception is the willingness to play again. For this reason a multiple linear regression on the willingness to play again (outcome variable) was conducted and the results are showed in Table 2 [16].

Table 2. Multiple linear regression of all the measured variables on the outcome variable "willingness to play again"

Predictor	Beta coefficient	t-value	Level of significance
Adequacy of the duration	.30	3.20	99.87 %
Design (graphic, interface)	−.16	−3.54	99.95 %
Fun of the gameplay	.70	7.62	100.00 %
Instructions	−.28	−4.07	99.99 %
Adequacy of the difficulty	.38	3.46	99.94 %
Interest for the goal	.33	13.22	100.00 %
Learning/educative content	−.11	−2.02	97.50 %
Feedback	−.24	−5.81	100.00 %
Realism of the game narration	.31	8.72	100.00 %

The regression coefficients for instructions and feedback are negative. At first sight it was quite surprising that instructions and feedback were perceived as contributing to discourage the willingness to play again. At the same time, the expressed adequacy of the duration and of the difficulty of the games resulted to be significant positive predictors of the willingness to play again. All these findings suggested to hypothesize that for short and simple games, like the ones that were considered, instructions and feedback could be perceived as obstructive for the gameplay. Players showed to desire to have fun while playing, and repeat their experience with the games, without stopping or interrupting the flow to receive instructions or feedback. This interpretation can be considered coherent with the fact that the games were not perceived as heavily educative, but rather a playful way to practice soft skills.

Starting from these results it was decided to deepen the analysis of the role of instructions and feedback within the serious games, investigating the influence of the perceived adequacy of the duration and of the difficulty. For the scope of the present study the four game variables of interest are thus the degrees of satisfaction expressed by the sample of users about: (a) the instructions, (b) the feedback, (c) the adequacy of the duration, and (d) the adequacy of the level of difficulty of the games.

The causal model to be tested reflects the order of appearance of the aforementioned variables within the serious games. Instructions are the first component that is given to the user at the very beginning of the game, while the perceived adequacy of the level of difficulty must be considered the final opinion of the user about the game. In between there are the opinions about the feedback and the adequacy of the duration of the games that can be considered as mediating variables. It is hypothesized that the quality of the instructions influences the opinion about the adequacy of the level of difficulty both directly and indirectly through the mediation of the feedback and of the adequacy of the duration of the games (Fig. 2). All causal relationships are hypothesized to be positive, since they represent the degree of satisfaction expressed by the users about the variables, as referred to the played games. It means that high values for the adequacy of the level of difficulty, for instance, are not necessarily equivalent to a very difficult game (in effect, the considered games were not difficult at all), but rather denote the appreciation for the challenge offered by the game that appears to be neither too difficult nor too easy.

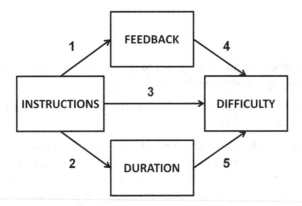

Fig. 2. Graphical scheme and numbers of the paths for the analyzed causal model.

4   Methods

This section contains an illustration of the methodology that was adopted in the present study: a description of the sample; the research procedure; the instruments and the statistical analyses that were adopted.

4.1 Participants

The target sample consisted of 54 workers of nine different Small and Medium-sized Enterprises (SMEs) operating in different business sectors (ICT, business support, education/training, etc.). The SMEs were selected on the basis of their willingness to participate in the study. Work positions were: 28 managers and 26 employees. 30 were males (56 %) and 24 were females (44 %). The mean age was 41.94 years (SD = 9.70).

4.2 Procedure

To test the developed kit of 30 mobile serious games the project partners held dedicated events (Learning Labs). During each Learning Lab a structured self-developed questionnaire was proposed to participants after the completion of the games.

Participation to Learning Labs and questionnaire compilation were obtained through an informed consent procedure asking for active consent from participants. Questionnaires took approximately 30 min to complete. Project staff members introduced the questionnaires, giving instructions about their compilation, explaining that they were voluntary and responses were anonymous and confidential. Project staff members were at the workers' disposal during the questionnaires' administration to answer questions and give explanations. All participants to different Learning Labs responded to the same questionnaire packet.

4.3 Measures

The self-developed questionnaire proposed to participants after the completion of the games was formed by the sections described below.

Demographics. An Identifying Information Form was used to collect demographic information: age, gender, working role.

Game variables. On a 10 point Likert scale it was asked to express one's appreciation about: (a) the instructions ("How adequate was the quality of the instructions?"), (b) the feedback ("How adequate was the quality of the feedback?"), (c) the duration ("How adequate was the duration of the games?"), and (d) the level of difficulty of the games ("How adequate was the level of difficulty of the games?").

4.4 Data Analysis

Preliminary Analysis. As a preliminary analysis, skewness and kurtosis of game variables were checked. Overall, all variables showed to conform to the normal distribution.

Correlation. As a first step the correlation matrix of all the variables was calculated.

Path Analysis. The path model involving the aforementioned four variables was analyzed with LISREL software package, using maximum likelihood estimation procedures [17]. The R-square percentage of variance of the adequacy of the level of difficulty explained by the model was reported, to estimate the completeness of the considered set of predictors for the outcome variable.

5   Results

Table 3 reports correlation coefficients of (a) the instructions, (b) the feedback, (c) the adequacy of the duration, and (d) the adequacy of the level of difficulty of the games. Level of significance of the correlation coefficients (p-values) is indicated in the table footnote.

Table 3. Correlation matrix of the variables involved in the analyzed causal model

Variable	Quality of instructions	Quality of feedback	Adequacy of duration	Adequacy of difficulty
Instructions	1.00	.40*	.79*	.79*
Feedback	.40*	1.00	.62*	.69*
Duration	.79*	.62*	1.00	.88*
Difficulty	.79*	.69*	.88*	1.00

* $p < 0.01$.

Table 4 reports the results of the path analysis with the levels of significance of the causal paths (p-values) indicated in the table footnote. Paths numeration is the same as indicated in Fig. 2.

Table 4. Path analysis coefficients estimates of the causal model

Path 1	Path 2	Path 3	Path 4	Path 5
.40*	.79*	.32*	.28**	.45*

$p < 0.01$; ** $p < 0.05$.

The R-squared value for the adequacy of the level of difficulty, considered as the final outcome variable, was found to be 0.85, which means that 85 % of the variance of the adequacy of the level of difficulty is explained by the considered model where the adequacy of the level of difficulty is predicted by the instructions, the feedback, and the adequacy of the duration.

The effect of the instructions (exogenous variable) on the adequacy of the level of difficulty (final outcome variable) is reported in Table 5, with the level of significance indicated in the table footnote. The direct effect is simply given by the coefficient of path 3. The indirect effect is composed by the sum of two parts: the one obtained by the meditation of the feedback (composition of paths 1 and 4) and the one obtained by the mediation of the adequacy of the duration (composition of paths 2 and 5).

Table 5. Effects of the quality of instructions on the adequacy of the level of difficulty

Variable	Total	Direct	Indirect (total)	Indirect through feedback	Indirect through adequacy of duration
Quality of instructions	.79*	.32*	.47*	.11	.36*

* $p < 0.01$; ** $p < 0.05$.

The instructions have a significant total effect on the adequacy of the level of difficulty, obtained as the sum of a direct effect (path 3 = 0.32) and an indirect effect. The indirect effect is given by the sum of a significant mediation of the adequacy of the duration (path 2 path 5 = 0.36), and a non-significant mediation of the feedback (path 1 path 4 = 0.11).

6 Conclusion

As a first conclusion, it must be said that the use of multivariate analysis allowed to understand much more deeply the learning and game mechanics rather than the merely descriptive results obtained by the satisfaction questionnaire. This is a useful indication for the evaluation of serious games to go beyond the simple measurement of a satisfaction questionnaire. In the considered case, what seemed to be a good level of satisfaction, when analyzed with multivariate technique, unveiled unexpected and non-trivial relationships among variables. The use of multilinear regression and of the path analysis, in fact, shed light on the effective role of game components and gave access to interesting interpretations and research perspectives herein illustrated.

The explanatory power of the considered model is quite significant, since 85 % of the variance of the adequacy of the level of difficulty is explained. This means that considering the instructions, the feedback, and the adequacy of duration as predictors of the adequacy of the level of difficulty was a right and enough exhaustive choice.

Results seem to confirm the hypotheses that there is a strong casual interrelationship among the instructions, the feedback, the adequacy of the duration, and the adequacy of the level of difficulty within a serious game.

Instructions showed to be strictly connected to the adequacy of the duration of the game (path 2), while the adequacy of the duration is strongly connected to the adequacy of the level of difficulty (path 5). Thus, instructions are significantly linked to the adequacy of the level of difficulty both directly (path 3) and indirectly through the adequacy of the duration of the game. It can be said that the adequacy of the duration of the games has a significant role of mediation in the relationship between instructions and the adequacy of the level of difficulty. It can be hypothesized that for short and simple games, like the ones that were analyzed, there should not be complex instructions, otherwise there is the risk that players perceive them as obstructive for the gameplay and inadequate in connection to the level of difficulty of the game.

On the contrary, the relationships between the instructions and the feedback (path 1) and between the feedback and the adequacy of the level of difficulty (path 4), even if significant, are not so strong to result in a significant indirect effect of the instructions on the adequacy of the level of difficulty through the feedback. This result is coherent with the findings by Erhel and Jamet who showed that the feedback enhances serious games' effectiveness, mostly if associated with entertainment instructions, while it acts separately from learning instructions like those that are present in the analyzed games [8].

It can be said that for the analyzed games, the instructions and the feedback contribute autonomously to the perception of the adequacy of the level of difficulty of the games. Attention must be paid both in the design of the instructions and of the feedback, so that both are coherent with the perception of the adequacy of the level of difficulty of the game, and none of them result to be obstructive for the gameplay.

The present study seems to confirm the suggestion to properly integrate feedback in the game, in order not to distract or bore the player [15]. This should be done especially for short and simple games, where players do not expect to find separate communication, but rather to test the consequences of their actions directly on the evolution of the game scenario.

The small sample size (n = 54) and the weak reliability of the instrument to measure the analyzed dimensions are the main limits of the present study. Instead of a generic self-developed satisfaction questionnaire, with one item for each variable, a validated instrument should be adopted, mapping multiple items to variables through factorization.

As a perspective for future work, what was found for short and simple serious games should be tested with other types of serious games (for instance more complex games with a longer duration) to check if the considered causal model is still valid. It should be tested if the role of the adequacy of the duration and of the level of difficulty is significant also when instructions and feedback, instead of being obstructive elements, positively contribute to enhance motivation and willingness to play again.

References

1. Hainey, T., Connolly, T.M., Stansfield, M., Boyle, L.: The use of computer games in education: a review of the literature. In: Felicia, P. (ed.) Handbook of Research on Improving Learning and Motivation Through Educational Games: Multidisciplinary Approaches, pp. 29–50. IGI Global, Hershey (2011)
2. Boyle, E., Connolly, T.M., Hainey, T.: The role of psychology in understanding the impact of computer games. Entertainment Comput. **2**, 69–74 (2001)
3. Okan, Z.: Edutainment: is learning at risk? Br. J. Educ. Technol. **34**, 255–264 (2003)
4. Healey, J.M.: The 'meme' that ate childhood. Educ. Week **18**(6), 37–56 (1998)
5. Olson, J.K., Clough, M.P.: Technology's tendency to undermine serious study: a cautionary note. Clearing House **75**(1), 8–13 (2001)
6. Schnotz, W.: Towards an integrated view of learning from text and visual displays. Educ. Psychol. Rev. **14**(1), 101–120 (2002)
7. Mayer, I., Bekebrede, G., Harteveld, C., Warmelink, H., Zhou, Q., Ruijven, T., Wenzler, I.: The research and evaluation of serious games: toward a comprehensive methodology. Br. J. Educ. Technol. **45**, 502–527 (2014)
8. Erhel, S., Jamet, E.: Digital game-based learning: impact of instructions and feedback on motivation and learning effectiveness. Comput. Educ. **67**, 156–167 (2013)

9. Kolb, D.A.: Learning styles and disciplinary differences. In: The Modern American College, pp. 232–255 (1981)
10. Mory, E.H.: Feedback research revisited. Handb. Res. Educ. Commun. Technol. **2**, 745–783 (2004)
11. Shute, V.J.: Focus on formative feedback. Rev. Educ. Res. **78**, 153–189 (2008)
12. Csikszentmihalyi, M.: Flow: The Psychology of Optimal Experience. Harper and Row, New York (1990)
13. Vygotsky, L.S.: Mind and Society: The Development of Higher Mental Processes. Harvard University Press, Cambridge (1978)
14. Dunwell, I., De Freitas, S., Jarvis, S.: Four-dimensional consideration of feedback in serious games. In: Digital Games and Learning, pp. 42–62 (2011)
15. Bellotti, F., Kapralos, B., Lee, K., Moreno-Ger, P.: User assessment in serious games and technology-enhanced learning. Adv. Hum.-Comput. Interact. **2013**, 2 (2013). ID 120791
16. Imbellone, A., Botte, B., Medaglia, C.M.: Serious games for mobile devices: the intouch project case study. Int. J. Serious Games **2**, 17–27 (2015)
17. Joreskog, K.G., Sorbom, D.: LISREL 8.8 for Windows [Computer software]. Scientific Software International Inc., Skokie, IL (2006)

Learning and Designing with Serious Games: Crowdsourcing for Procurement

Edward Oates[(✉)]

Centre for Defence Studies, Cranfield University, Defence Academy of the United Kingdom,
Shrivenham, SN6 8LA, UK
e.oates@cranfield.ac.uk

Abstract. This study takes a novel approach to defence procurement. Through the use of a Serious Game, developed using Open Source coding techniques and internally Crowdsourced, the design of defence equipment is developed through a wider than usual range of user perspectives. The aim is to reduce procurement cost by exposing defence equipment to a wide range of users ahead of the in-service phase, where re-work becomes more costly. Not previously reviewed the conjoining of a Serious Game, Open Source coding and Crowdsourcing has technical and cultural issues within UK defence. This is an interim report after the first year of work.

1 Introduction

The main themes of: defence procurement, serious games, open source coding and crowdsourcing, interlink in specific ways that require a short introduction. The paper then goes on to describe the study in further detail.

1.1 Defence Procurement Process

The UK Defence Procurement CADMID process (Concept, Assessment, Demonstration, Manufacture, In-Service, Disposal) (RUSI 2012; MODAF 2005) lends itself to simulations in the Demonstration and early Manufacture (D&M) stages (Fig. 1).

Typically, the simulation of a defence system in the manufacturer's test laboratory is supported by a small number of subject matter experts (SME) from the end-users' organisation. There is, however a weakness in this, as the small number of SMEs involved during D&M will inevitably view the emerging product from a relatively limited perspective. In contrast, 'The Wisdom of Crowds' (Surowiecki 2004, p. 10) identifies the need for high degrees of diversity and independent perspectives before choosing a solution. The issue to be addressed is: **How to get a large number of people to share their knowledge and experience within the D&M stages of defence procurement?** This paper offers the Crowdsourcing of Serious Games as a solution and presents a status report following one year of academic study.

© Springer International Publishing Switzerland 2016
A. De Gloria and R. Veltkamp (Eds.): GALA 2015, LNCS 9599, pp. 61–70, 2016.
DOI: 10.1007/978-3-319-40216-1_7

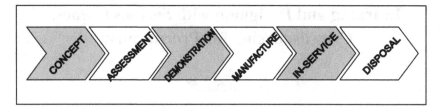

Fig. 1. CADMID Procurement Process described in JSP 886 (JSP 886 2015) is a linear procurement process designed to ensure defence systems are delivered to cost, time and quality.

1.2   Serious Games in Procurement

Serious Games for use at the Concept phase of defence procurement have been used within the Defense Advanced Research Projects Agency (DARPA 2015), where the game "ACTUV Tactics" was used to see what tactics might be developed for an un-manned submersible. Within UK, Niteworks (Niteworks 2015) acts as a focal point for government and industry partners to enhance future military capability where serious games might be used during the Concept phase.

Where the D&M stages begin to work with specific equipment capabilities the security requirements increase and this constrains the use of internet, allowing the use of defence intranet only. At this stage of the procurement process the capability has been defined and is passed to a project team for specific equipment implementation. It is at this stage of the procurement process that detailed human-machine interface design begins with a small number of subject matter experts (SME) working at the manufac-turer's site. Simulations are again used with agreed scenarios to pre-view the final equipment and whole system performance. With the mechanics and dynamics of the system and its synthetic environment already in place, it is the addition of 'gamification' that would take the next steps on to a Serious Game and the hosting on a web server to allow Crowdsourcing. This study takes those next steps.

If these D&M phases fail to find the optimal design, then expensive re-work is passed to the In-Service phase following feedback from the end user community. This drives the need for a Crowdsourcing construct to engage a diverse community early in the procurement process. Although simulation based acquisition is offered as a generally accepted process, as evidenced in the UK's Acquisition System Guidance (AOF 2015), the use of Crowdsourced Serious Games within a defence procurement project is novel and untested.

1.3   Crowdsourcing in a Procurement Process

Broadly speaking, development and procurement are processes undertaken by separate groups of people, with their finished product being used by another group of people. It is the author's experience that the loss of fidelity as requirements are passed in the text-based documentation process – within the User Requirement Document to System Requirement Document to Top Level Specification - from one group to another leads to costly in-service re-work and reduced user satisfaction. This closed, text-based process contrasts with a Crowdsourced game-based process that this paper proposes. The graphical interface provided by a Serious Game has the potential to convey the users' requirement in a more complete and meaningful way. When opened to defence users through Crowdsourcing a further benefit of agile design is offered.

Whether a project is run with 'big design up-front', or a more agile (DSDM 2015) 'enough design up-front' the user still needs to be engaged. With Crowdsourcing, that engagement is moved earlier in the procurement process. In the military context, user engagement can be impossible where the manufacturer is in a fixed location and the users are dispersed elsewhere in UK and on active service abroad. The crowd is geographically dispersed and groupings isolated. The medium for engaging the crowd, by default becomes the defence intranet.

1.4 Open Source in a Defence Network

As the game's functions and displays are developed incrementally through crowdsourcing, there has to be an in-house design and modification capacity to response to the users' feedback. In effect, the on-going design of the game becomes an Open Source project allowing users to propose coding changes and new function modules to the game.

It is possible for some commercial companies to have security clearances that allow access to the UK defence intranet. In such a case it is possible that the Serious Game development could be passed to a contractor. The down side of this is that the cost of the Serious Game would be added to the contract price. In view of this, an in-house Open Source approach is proposed.

A blog is used to allow feedback and discussions to take place. This also acts as a defence-wide media tool to advertise the game and encourage its use for fun, for game development, and for interface development.

In summary, the proposed concept is at the intersection of Serious Games, Crowdsourcing, and Open Source development.

2   Hypothesis

From the points raised above the hypothesis is that:

H1: Crowdsourcing with Serious Games for the design of defence equipment operator interface can be a more effective technique than current design methods.

The following will be used as measures of effectiveness.

H1a: The objective assessment of game score is taken as a Measure of Effectiveness when compared with the use of crowdsourced design features.

H1b: The objective assessment of time taken to achieve a game score is taken as a Measure of Effectiveness when compared with the use of crowdsourced design features.

H1c: The users' subjective expression of 'preferred' interface design is taken as a Measure of Effectiveness.

3   Methodology

The Serious Game is the central theme of the hypothesis, provides the vehicle for the Crowdsourcing, and by the nature of computer games provides a scoring value and duration from each game. The pre-developed game simulates an existing airborne maritime tactical display which has been in use un-altered for 20 years. The post-crowdsourced game will have all the features and displays suggested and added during the crowdsourcing process.

3.1   Game Overview

An example Serious Game was developed around an airborne maritime search task with a defined need to develop a new interface for an electronic warfare system. The specific case is an electronic support system where the users are given information on detected radars being operated against them. This is a surveillance task undertaken to develop situational awareness. Points are awarded for correct identification of ships and points deducted for incorrect identification. Time is limited by the fuel carried. The game has been in development through Crowdsourced feedback since September 2014. New functions and displays are being added throughout the Crowdsourcing period.

3.2   Objective Data Collection

Data Gathering.   At the end of the Crowdsourcing period a controlled trial will be used for data gathering. Running the game in a web browser from a standard file server does not allow data logging direct to the server. Instead, a log file records the functions used and the scoring achieved during the game. This file is then offered to the user to attach to an automated feedback email. It would be preferable to record data from a wide variety of users in uncontrolled conditions to increase the sample size. The fact that the players will have access to the log files brings in to question the validity of the data if uncontrolled trials are used.

Game Scoring.   The player scores points by the correct identification of ships in the game. At the start of the game there are 36 ships and as the sensors are used and detections made the ships' identification becomes known. This generates the score. In addition, the time-line is recorded with a more proficient operator, supported by improved displays, obtaining points faster.

Subject Matter Experts.   A sample of users will be gathered, and ranked according to years of experience in the use of relevant tactical displays. The group will be divided alternately by factor rank into two groups. One group will use the pre-developed game first and the other the post-crowdsourced game first to allow for learning during the trial. Data log files will be recorded. The groups will then swap games and the same game levels will be played again.

Trials Repetition. As the game uses random numbers to seed the game scenarios, it is planned to play the game a number of times. There will also be a degree of game learning by the Subject Matter Experts and this will be objectively assessed in the data analysis.

3.3 Data Analysis

The analysis will take game scores and durations as a measure of effectiveness. The data analysis will take a matrix of consecutive function selections, and an array of durations that the functions were in-use. These will be compared with final scores and game durations. The data will be inspected for correlations between pre-development functions (those existing before crowdsourcing) and the game scores and post-development functions (those developed through crowdsourcing) and their game scores. A similar analysis will be made against the game duration variable.

3.4 Game Play Questionnaire and Interviews

As there will be a subjective element to the measure of 'more effective', described as 'SME preferences', a questionnaire will ask for Likert Scale preference for the functions offered in the game. For each function, pre and post development, the answers from these questions will be used to rank their perceived usefulness.

There will also be a free text area for each question allowing the user to give further opinion on each function. These free text responses will be used in individual interviews to obtain further clarity on expressed preferences.

3.5 Literature Review Questionnaire

The literature review has identified several cultural factors that are associated with crowdsourcing (Luttgens et al. 2014, p. 357). Although not taken as a direct measure of effectiveness, these cultural aspects could impact the use of Crowdsourcing and Serious Games within MoD. These cultural factors will be used in a questionnaire sent to all users from the Crowdsourcing development period. These questions are:

Community Identity. To what extent do you identify with (feel a part of) this Serious Game community of players?
Consumer Producer. To what extent do you feel that you have control over the production of the tactical interface in the serious game?
Not Invented Here. To what extent do you resent the development of functions from outside the Procurement Stakeholder group?
Loss of Authority. To what extent do you feel that crowdsourcing subverts military authority and chain of command in the procurement process?
Social Media. To what extent do you think that social media web pages (Blogs, Ask A Question, Open Discussion) when hosted on defence servers are contrary to the military ethos.

Further cultural aspects may become apparent as the crowdsourcing activity continues and these will be added to the questionnaire.

4   Game Design in a Defence Environment

The mandated use of the UK defence intranet necessarily limits the code that may be used to create a Serious Game, as does the crowd from which an open source coding team may be formed. When selecting a language to work with it must be noted that Microsoft 'Notepad' will have to be the code editor, as no integrated development environment is available. The IE8 browser will have to be the interpreter and viewing window, but with the developer tools disabled. The crowd is likely to have been taught how to create a web page during schooling as part of the UK national curriculum and so will have been exposed to HTML and CSS. With these limitations in place the choice was made to initiate the Serious Game in JavaScript and jQuery. Various jQuery libraries could have been used to create the game, but given the expected rudimentary knowledge of web site coding within the crowd, a simple, universally applicable library (jQuery 2015) was chosen, with the benefit that any implementation of properties and methods would be explicit. With HTML5 and CSS3 not available, some Crowdsourced ideas required an alternative graphics package to 'Canvas'. The VML 'Raphael' library was chosen (Raphael 2015) as it is well documented on-line and in books. The basic routines of Timing Loops, Entity Control, and Z-Index manipulation are readily relevant and re-usable for anyone else wishing to build a game. A linked page is offered with advice on reference material and basic file structures for re-use. Attempts to connect with other people interested in writing Serious Games have not produced results.

Serious Games will often integrate with a server database to hold rankings and scorings. The UK defence intranet is tightly controlled and so this is not possible while retaining an agile Open Source coding theme. The game and all game files are held on a standard file server. Scorings are being held locally in a log file on the client and sent with other free-text feedback by email.

The subject of Game Design is well served by web sites and books. These were referred to and elements used to make the game attractive to many categories of user. Rigby and Ryan (2011, p. 139) identified: Competence (motivations to gain and display competence), Autonomy (motivations to control and direct one's own actions), and Relatedness (motivations to relate to others and achieve reciprocation) as reasons that people play games. The 'reward' scheme of on-screen medals was developed as a way of confirming 'competence'. The single-player game intrinsically supports 'autonomy', and the Defence Connect blog aims to support 'relatedness'. Other sources highlighted the need for a 'story'. Gibson (2015, p. 52), Iuppa and Borst (2012, p. 47), Thompson et al. (2007, p. 58) were referred to when writing the back-story and developing the story through the game levels. All of these aspects were developed from theoretical first-principles specifically for the UK defence environment.

5   Crowdsourcing the Serious Game

The benefit gained by seeking solutions outside of the traditional stakeholder community is summarised in Surowiecki's (2004, front cover) sub-title "why the many are smarter than the few", and by Page (2007, p. 158) as "diversity trumps ability". Page (2007, p. 162) describes the process by which a diverse group use their range of heuristics and perspectives to move from one local optimum solution to an interim solution to another interim solution, all the time improving until the group decides that no more improvements can be made. This situation leads to a winning solution. Page makes clear that it's the range of perspectives and heuristics that is important not the numbers of participants. Even taking a large number of people with high ability, if they have been through the same education process or the same set of experiences their restricted range of perspectives and heuristics will be smaller than the diverse group, and therefore less able to reach a winning solution. It's for this reason that a limited number of SMEs embedded with the manufacturer are unlikely to find an optimal user interface design during the defence procurement process.

5.1 Game Development

The game began development in June 2014 and went live on the UK defence intranet in September 2014. Accessible from a file server, the game consists of one HTML file that then references several JavaScript files and jQuery libraries. No file is greater than 100 Kb and loads within a few seconds when tested across the network.

The electronic warfare task was chosen as it is a task undertaken by all three armed forces, thereby making it more likely that a diverse user community could be developed. The UK defence procurement process would normally limit its engagement to those identified as the 'stakeholders' in accordance with the Acquisition System Guidance (AOF 2015). The stakeholders are those who will use, support or be affected directly by the new equipment. This is what makes the use of Crowdsourcing within the MoD procurement process so radical. Instead of limiting the engagement to the stakeholders only, the Crowdsourcing process seeks to include a wide range of people who will be outside the stakeholder group and outside the electronic warfare group of specialists.

Crowdsourcing, and indeed the whole concept of enterprise social media was new to UK defence until the arrival of the Defence Connect. The mix of security accreditations and connectivity across defence networks has limited the crowdsourcing initiative as the game has to be run on the higher security accredited defence intranet infrastructure. Those who only have access to Defence Connect can take part in the Blog, but are unable to experience the game itself.

5.2 Early Results

Data Log files returned with users' feedback emails are processed using R statistical analysis software using the 'qgraph' library (qgraph 2015). A network plot is produced (Fig. 3) which allows analysis of consecutive function selections and duration spent within the game functions. This will give frequency and duration per function data which will later be compared with game score and game duration data to address hypothesis H1a and H1b (Fig. 2).

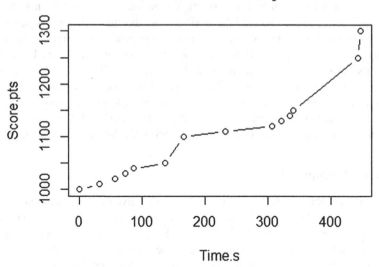

Fig. 2. The game score analysis plot from this one example game-play compares two measures of effectiveness: time, and game score. The increasing plot over time shows that all ship detections were correctly made. Incorrect identification of a ship gives a negative score.

6   Cultural Aspects of Gaming in Defence

From the description in the Game Design section there were significant technological issues. There are also cultural issues.

The Serious Game was developed as a 'grass-roots' activity without top-down direction. This contrasts with UK defence which is a strongly hierarchical organisation. While evidence has yet to be obtained through questionnaires, it may be that such a subversive action as playing a game without explicit direction from senior officers may be counter-cultural to the majority, and therefore unacceptable to be involved with.

Social media has been identified as being a security risk to defence personnel (UK Gov. 2011). While the younger people working in UK defence will have grown up with social media, the organisation tends to warn of the risks associated with it. This attitude is echoed in other western nations where press reports in relation to wiki-leaks is often seen as being 'bad for national security'. Future questionnaires will include specific questions to identify the effect of culture on the use of defence enterprise social media and the Serious Game in particular.

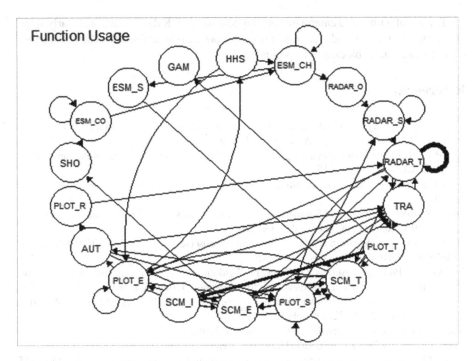

Fig. 3. Function usage provides a network of game functions used during a single game play. The functions are represented as nodes. The consecutive functions used are represented by edges. The width of the edges indicates the number of times consecutive functions have been used. For example, the thick line from and to the RADAR_T node shows repeated use of radar track while scan markers, and the PLOT_T to SCM_I line shows that track while scan markers are being passed to the inverse synthetic aperture radar mode for identification. A full legend and de-code has been omitted to save space in this short paper.

7   Conclusions

Simulations are regularly used within UK defence for training, but the use of a Serious Game to assist in the procurement 'Development and Manufacture' phases is a novel approach. A Serious Game developed to preview a user interface aims to reduce costly In-Service re-work and to increase user satisfaction.

To support an agile development process for the Serious Game, the UK defence intranet is able to support an Open Source coding team. With a blog on Defence Connect, a Serious Game is in use as a method of gaining a wide range of views and design ideas from inside and outside of the traditional procurement stakeholder group.

The use of Crowdsourcing for defence procurement has the potential to engage with a diverse range of people holding varying heuristics and perspectives. When filtered and aggregated by subject matter experts a Serious Game is proposed as a tool for learning and retaining corporate knowledge.

The use of games and enterprise social media within UK defence are at an early stage of acceptance. Culture and corporate norms of working practice will be subject to further study to understand blockages to progress.

References

AOF: Acquisition System Guidance (2015). www.aof.mod.uk. Accessed 20 July 2015

DSDM (2015). www.dsdm.org/. Accessed 20 July 2015

DARPA (2015). http://www.darpa.mil/program/anti-submarine-warfare-continuous-trail-unmanned-vessel. Accessed 20 July 2015

Gibson, J.: Introduction to Game Design, Prototyping and Development. Addison-Wesley, USA (2015)

Iuppa, N., Borst, T.: Story and Simulations for Serious Games. Focal Press, Waltham (2012)

jQuery (2015). jquery.com. Accessed 02 Oct 2015

JSP 886. www.gov.uk/government/uploads/system/uploads/attachment_data/file/405503/20150216-JSP886-Vol7Part8-05-TecDocs-v5_3-O.pdf

Luttgens, D., Pollok, P., Antons, D., Piller, F.: Wisdom of the crowd and capabilities of a few: internal success factors of crowdsourcing for innovation. J. Bus. Econ. **84**(3), 339–374 (2014)

MODAF (2005). http://www.modaf.com/files/MODAF%20Concepts%20and%20Doctrine%20Deskbook%20v0.1%2029%20Jul%2005.pdf

Niteworks (2015). www.niteworks.net. Accessed 20 July 2015

Page, S.E.: The Difference. Princeton University Press, Princeton (2007)

qgraph (2015). https://cran.r-project.org/web/packages/qgraph/qgraph.pdf. Accessed 01 Oct 2015

Raphael (2015). raphaeljs.com. Accesses 02 Oct 2015

Rigby, S., Ryan, R.M.: Glued to Games. Praeger, USA (2011)

RUSI: RUSI Defence Systems Spring 2012 – LPPV – Lessons for Defence Procurement article by Chis Maughan, p. 34 (2012). https://www.rusi.org/downloads/assets/201203_RDS_Maughan.pdf

Surowiecki, J.: The Wisdom of Crowds. Abacus, UK (2004)

Thompson, J., Berbank-Green, B., Cusworth, N.: The Computer Game Design Course. Thames and Hudson, London (2007)

UK Gov. (2011). https://www.gov.uk/government/news/defence-community-warned-of-risks-of-social-media. Accessed 20 July 2015

Development of Mobile Serious Game
for Self-assessment as Base
for a Game-Editor for Teachers

Andreas Herrler[1](✉), Simon Grubert[2], Marko Kajzer[2],
Sadie Behrens[3], and Ralf Klamma[2]

[1] Department of Anatomy and Embryology, FHML,
Maastricht University, Maastricht, The Netherlands
a.herrler@maastrichtuniversity.nl
[2] Chair of Information Systems and Databases, RWTH, Aachen, Germany
{grubert,klamma}@dbis.rwth-aachen.de,
marko.kajzer@rwth-aachen.de
[3] Department of Molecular and Cellular Anatomy,
Medical School, RWTH, Aachen, Germany
sbehrens@ukaachen.de

Abstract. Self-assessment is an important tool to improve student performance. A good serious game (SG) would be a very strong self-assessment tool because of the additional motivational aspects. However, self-assessment tools have to fit the learning matters of a course by 100 %, what general SG seldom do. The goal of this work is to build a simple SG editor each teacher can adjust to the learning goals of his course. Here we present the development of a game-editor for teachers for a puzzle-style game. By this editor teachers can edit their own course based game without sophisticated computer knowledge. The game mechanics meet the requirements of mobile- and micro-learning strategies. Furthermore, the game implements learning analytics for students as well as for teachers. The game engine and the editor are both based on standard Web technologies. The source code is maintained as an open source project to lower the barriers for further uptake.

1 Introduction

Serious Gaming combines relevant learning matter in an entertaining environment. Hereby serious games (SG) get an effective new element of studying [21]. Although self-assessment is known to be essential to self-directed life-long learning [2] it is frequently missing in offered educational material. As students regularly overestimate their knowledge and skills [1], they urgently need the possibility for self-assessment to check their real knowledge and to learn how to study [23]. Self-assessment should not be seen as a stressful experience but a chance for development. Therefore, we would like to offer SG for self-assessment to stimulate students to check their state of development more regularly. Improving techniques of self-assessment will improve the performance of students [19]. Students rate self-assessment only as relevant if it is perfectly fitting the course contents. Since SG are usually not developed by the teachers

© Springer International Publishing Switzerland 2016
A. De Gloria and R. Veltkamp (Eds.): GALA 2015, LNCS 9599, pp. 71–79, 2016.
DOI: 10.1007/978-3-319-40216-1_8

themselves, they rarely do so. Games, especially constructed for a course, have been shown to significantly improve the academic performance of medical students [13]. Therefore, teachers should get the chance to build SG by themselves. As teachers normally are not educated to develop SG, they have to ask companies to do so, which is very time- and cost-intensive [26].

The goal of this investigation was to develop a game editor for teachers with which teachers easily can build their own game, 100 % fitting the educational requirements of their course. In addition, the game should give students the chance to assess themselves and fill in missing learning matters.

2   Serious Game

At first we developed a SG and asked students for evaluation. The idea was to gain experience with the game design, the game mechanics and the game interactions before we started to design and implement the game editor for teachers. Our SG is a puzzle-style game. The game design is optimized for mobile devices. As we target mobile devices as tablets and smart phones for our SG editor we developed a SG that runs on the different mobile operating systems using the same developmental environment. After surveying different cross-development platforms [14], we opted for a combination of HTML5, JavaScript and CSS, the most popular now. This allowed us to deploy across different platforms with the same code base using available standard Web browsers on the devices. At the same time, we can access low-level libraries and system functionalities with the new HTML5 APIs. We chose the JavaScript libraries jQuery Mobile and jQuery UI to speed up the developmental process. For the game we implemented a client-server architecture. On the server we keep game and learner data in a central database. On top of the database we offer different Web services for the client-side games. To be prepared for mobile use, we added a HTML5 offline caching mechanism to support offline access to game data. Data cached on the client side are transferred to the server by AJAX with all data formatted in JSON.

The general setting of the game is as follows (Fig. 1): In the main menu the game can be chosen. We also implemented a small tutorial level to demonstrate the game mechanics and the possible game interactions to players. We arranged four galleries, one at each corner, containing the pieces the player is asked to arrange. The galleries are filled dynamically by a JavaScript function with content from the database or the cache. Pieces that are used multiple times in different sequences are shown only once. In the center four tiles are located with the same headers as the galleries. They represent 4 items related to each other in a logical manner. The player is asked to drag and drop the pieces in the appropriate tile. There is only one distinct logical matching solution for the user input. If the player is not able to finish the tiles he can press a *show me* button. Pieces placed incorrectly are highlighted in red, correctly placed ones in green. To learn more about the aspired learning goal an *e-learning* button can be chosen (Weblink). The player can choose between 4 levels of difficulty: easy – 3 given tiles, one to be filled in; medium – 2 given, 2 to be filled in; free – the user has to fill in all four tiles, but can choose which piece to start with; difficult – one tile given, the user has to fill in the rest.

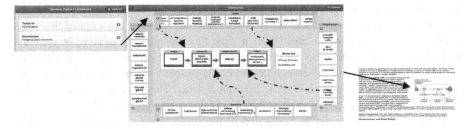

Fig. 1. Screenshots of the game showing a sequence rated as wrong. The 'Show me' would give the correct answer, pushing the 'E-Learning Link' button a webpage to study the topic. (Color figure online)

We evaluated, by questionnaire and focus group, the SG with a group of 10 medical students from Maastricht University and created a game instance with a content related to the learning matter students had to study at that time. Characteristics of the volunteers are: 90 % male, age 22.5 ± 2.1 yr (±SD), computer experience 13.1 ± 2.9 yr, use of computers 33.6 ± 18.5 h/w, game experiences 13.1 yr, playing games 3.8 ± 3.8 h/w. To test this game, they used PCs (Windows) 3 times, laptops 6×, Android tablets 1×, ipads 3×.

The students were asked to play the game several times, online as well as offline, if possible using different devices. After 5 days we asked them to fill in a questionnaire to assess the game in terms of its intention. The questionnaire contained 31 questions: on relevance, strengths and weaknesses ease of use, fulfillment of expectations, based on the ISONORM 9241/10 [22]. The answer are constructed as 5 point Likert scale.

All participants were invited to join a structured qualitative evaluation based on following questions: conceptual: What was good and what has to be improved?, process: What was good and what has to be improved?, What kind of games would you like to have in the future? Where do you see the benefit of such games? The discussion was recorded and typed. Thereafter, keywords were identified by two independent investigators. They were grouped as positive or negative statement and related to one of the four stimulating questions. Based on this we created a mind-map. Results of the questionnaire are: relevance as tool 4.4 ± 1.1, relevance of content 3.4 ± 1.3, learning by using the game 3.9 ± 0.4, feedback on performance 3.8 ± 0.9, ease of use 4.4 ± 1.1, self-explaining 4.1 ± 1.4, tutorial 4.6 ± 0.5, building up knowledge 3.9 ± 0.4, feedback on procedural mistakes 3.5 ± 0.9, period per game 4.5 ± 0.8, stability of gamer 3.5 ± 1.4, intermediate stop 3.3 ± 1.7, levels 2.6 ± 0.9, reaction time 4.5 ± 0.5), joy of playing 3.4 ± 0.9, meeting expectation 4.5 ± 0.5, future use of game 4.4 ± 0.5, recommend to other 4.0 ± 0.5.

The qualitative analysis revealed that students appreciated that the game could be played relaxing in between other learning activities, taking only 10–15 min, while one sequence took them between 10–30 s. Several students missed learning analytics and a way to compete with other students. Some students claimed more additional information and that the given links gave only basic information. In general, the e-links were rated as very useful. At that point only one level of difficulty was available and students asked for more difficult versions. They agreed that they knew the answers by heart after playing the game several times. Especially the feedback on whether an answer was wrong or correct was rated as very helpful. Students appreciated that they could play the game offline, making it a very flexible learning device. In general, students asked for a fancier layout of the game (under development by now). The user rated this game as a very valuable, nice and easily usable form of self-assessment and suggested more games related to other learning matters. The game was rated as useful to prepare for progress tests, course exams. Using this game motivated the user to study the topics asked in more depth. Sadly non of the students used the game in a mobile situation. They have to get more used to the game to implement this.

Based on feedback given by the students the game was adapted. Two bugs identified leading to instabilities have been solved, resulting in a stable running game. Talking about micro-learning, it is relevant that the game can be stopped any time after finishing one sequence. The state of the game is stored on the device and restored when re-opened. This information has been added to the tutorial, as well as further information on the different levels of the game, so that students know about this possibility. A second e-link is offered, one basic link for those still making mistakes and an advanced link containing more information in depth given to those solving a sequence correctly. Finally, students missed learning feedback and competition. We have implemented learning analytics given to students and teachers.

3 Game Editor for Teachers

After the optimization of the game, we developed the game-editor for teachers (Fig. 2).

The teacher's game-editor is set up to add new sequences to existing games or to create new games in a simple manner. To develop a new game the teacher can upload new pieces (PowerPoint templates; gif, png, jpg) and connections via a file uploading dialog. The files are used to create or edit a game. The uploaded pieces are grouped in sequences of four and can be selected in these groups when creating or editing a game. The game editor can choose a sequence of pieces and then drags and drops them on appropriate tiles. The designer chooses communication icons between tiles out of the standard symbol list. Finally, the e-learning links can be entered into additional input fields. All entered data are stored permanently in the game database and can be retrieved at any time by the game editor but also by the players at the time of game play. The data are stored according to a concept of game levels, so the game editor can design levels with different difficulties or different learning contents. In later versions also the design of levels with less than four pieces should be possible. Finally, the game editor/teacher will be able to select the players who have access to the game or offer it as open-source game, which is our main philosophy.

Six teachers from Maastricht University, The Netherlands as well as six teachers from the Medical School Aachen, RWTH, Germany have agreed to evaluate the game-editor by developing a game related to their educational activities (preclinical: anatomy, physiology, pharmacology; clinical: cardiology, orthopedics, anesthesiology). After having started building their games, they will be asked to fill in a questionnaire comparable to what students did, containing the same main topics: relevance,

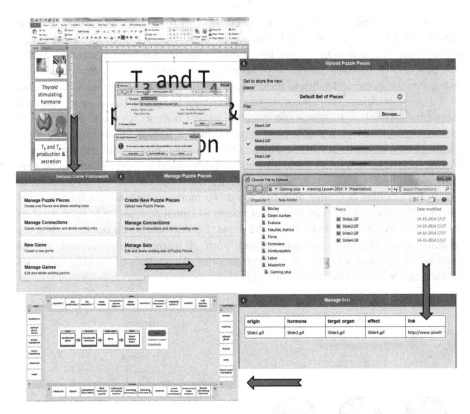

Fig. 2. Teacher's game-editor to edit a new game; different steps of editing are shown. (Color figure online)

usability, technical aspects, expectations and general questions (for results please contact the authors). Related to feedback, the game-editor for teachers got adapted.

4 Learning Analytics and Motivation Elements

Learning Analytics (LA) has recently become a major research area in technology enhanced learning. Research concentrates on predicting and steering the learning progress of individual learners with the goal of giving feedback to students and teachers as well as to stimulate students' activities. We used LA [15] to assess and analyze game traces from the database (https://www.mongodb.org/) through the GLEANER API (http://e-ucm.github.io/gleaner/) we concentrated on input traces, representing a learner interaction with the input device such as mouse clicks and logic traces representing events in the game logic. Through OpenID Connect of the provider Learning Layers (https://api.learning-layers.eu/o/oauth2/), users can authenticate and login to our application. For example, we modelled the game event "level_completion" storing information about the game (gameID) and the level (levelID). This trace has an additional result field that possible values "correct", "wrong" and "show me". For this game-based event, we have implemented an open badge (http://openbadges.org/) issued when the game logic cannot find a level after one has been completed. While this process is handled completely automatically without any interaction with instructors, the game editor has to think about game events and motivational elements for the game at design time. Another way of issuing badges is based upon statistics. Users earn themselves badges, experience points and high scores while being able to get learning feedback on a profile page, which is private to each player (Fig. 3). By the learning analytics students will see which of the sequences they missed most frequently to solve correctly to specify their learning activities on this topic. In the same way teachers can look up sequences most frequently solved incorrectly by all students to specify his teaching activities onto this topic. To motivate students the high score is shown with the two better and two lesser results to stimulate students to increase their performance by studying and redoing the game. Furthermore, open badges earned are collected over time and are summed up from all games, even different of this game-editor, to reach a higher level of performance. An analysis of learning outcomes by the game will be presented by an upcoming investigation.

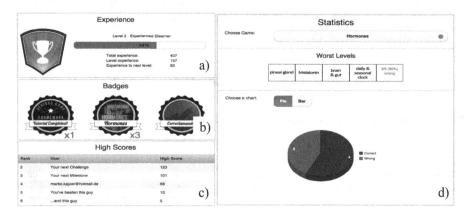

Fig. 3. Different parts of learning analytics and user motivation (a) general performance resulting from (b) badges over all games ever done and (c) high score; (d) learning analytics for students, teachers view is similar showing all students results per set. (Color figure online)

5   Discussion

The presented game-editor was developed on the educational purpose to give teachers the possibility to edit their own course-related SG in an easy and cheap way. To students it offers the possibility to assess their knowledge in a gamified surrounding and to improve it by using the given feedback and online learning facilities. We followed these goals as SG have been shown to enhance the traditional way of learning, increasing students' engagement to learning matter by feedback given and stimulating their learning activities [18].

Self-assessment has been shown to contribute to a deeper processing of learning, which stimulated us to set up the game as a self-assessment tool. Self-assessment is relevant especially to poor students because they tend to overestimate their own competencies [1]. Instant, task centred feedback, as given by the here presented game, is the most important part in self-assessment. It triggers learn-test cycles by repeating the game again and again to improve the gamers' results [4]. By choosing between different levels, as well as using e-learning links, students can adapt the game to their level of experience and personal educational needs [4]. As a form of formative assessment it is available to the students during their entire learning process adaptable to their pace of learning [27].

A game does not take more than 10–15 min, a sequence less than a minute. Fifteen minutes is about the time required for micro-learning [13]. Micro-learning has to offer a lot as supplementary element to the complex learning in the university, by working on small units with no overload on information. Students can use brief periods of time for studying, not used before [13], like traveling in a train or bus. Combining micro-learning with mobile learning is a further new dimension in higher education.

The game was developed with the educational intention of supporting self-assessment, micro- and mobile-learning, which are key elements of modern education [9]. Proof of concept by users is one of the milestones in game development [3]. Students' feedback showed that a good relation to the course is relevant for a high acceptance of the game [3]. On students' demand we added a second, advanced e-link, given when having solved a sequence correctly. To stimulate students to learn more in depth even when they solved a sequence correctly, the golden goal of a SG can be reached. By using basic or advanced e-links and choosing one of four difficulty levels students can adapt the game to their personal level of expertise, as asked for a SG [4].

There is the well-known paradox about the contradiction of playfulness and seriousness [10]. Because of the educational intention, we overlooked the quality of the game design and were asked to increase the elements of motivation and competition as relevant stimulating factors for a gamer to improve [16]. Although, knowing that scoring alone does not lead to better learning [7] we added motivation elements in the favor of edutainment. As suggested before [17] the user will see the neighboring results and not the high score after finishing the game, to induce competitive effects but not to disenchant him. Furthermore, he can collect batches and can reach different degrees of expertise (trainee, assistant, master, expert) to increase intrinsic motivation to play the games [7]. The batches earned are not only signs of mastering, there is also one batch named 'Please study'. Both kinds are intended to stimulate studying in a 'carrot and stick' approach.

Finally, teachers can analyze what, how long and often as well as with which success students play that game. Hereby, teachers can realize problems students face and adapt their teaching activities in that way that students will perform better in the nearby future [24]. The pedagogic most important aspect of SG is that it has been shown that SG work most effectively when they are offered in a blended approach [11], illustrating the relevance of a game 100 % fitting to the learning goals of the class. Developing games normally is a costly affair [12]. The here presented game-editor can be edited by each teacher requiring only standard computer skills. Although we know that such games can only achieve learning goals at the lower levels in Bloom's taxonomy [6] we expect a broad implementation into our curriculum. It will get even more relevant for student studies, as the game-editor is set up to export single sequences into electronic tests. As assessment drives students activities [25], such an implementation will stimulate the use of our SG for students' self-assessment and make it more viable.

References

1. Abadel, F.T., Hattab, A.S.: Patients' assessment of professionalism and communication skills of medical graduates. BMC Med. Educ. **14**, 28–34 (2014)
2. Antonelli, M.A.: Accuracy of second-year medical students' self-assessment of clinical skills. Acad. Med. **72**, 563–565 (1997)
3. Bartlett, E.: The publisher-developer relationship. In: Rabin, S. (ed.) Introduction to Game Development, pp. 857–879. Cengage Learning, Boston (2011)
4. Bellotti, F., Kapralos, B., Lee, K., Moreno-Ger, P., Berta, R.: Assessment in and of SG: an overview. Adv. Hum.-Comput. Interact. **2013**, 1–11 (2013)
5. Chen, S., Michael, D.: Proof of Learning: Assessment in SG. Gamasutra (2005). http://www.gamasutra.com/, (last visited 19 July 2015)
6. Connolly, T.M., Boyle, E.A., MacArthur, E., Hainey, T., Boyle, J.M.: A systematic literature review of the empirical evidence on computer games and SG. Comput. Educ. **59**, 661–686 (2012)
7. Delacruz, G.C.: Games as formative assessment environments: examining the impact of explanations of scoring and incentives on math learning, game performance, and help seeking. The National Center for Research on Evaluation, Standards, and Student Testing. Cresst report 796 (2011)
8. Eichler, S., Goertz, L., Kallenborn, M., Kraemer, W., Michel, P., Reiners, O.: Sieben gute Gründe für mobiles Lernen. Bitkom, Berlin (2014)
9. Eva, K.W., Regehr, G.: Self-assessment in the health professions: a reformulation and research agenda. Acad. Med. **80**(10 Suppl.), S46–54 (2005)
10. Gadamer, H.G.: Truth and Method. Seabury Press, New York (1975)
11. Graham, C.R.: Blended learning systems: definition, current trends, and future directions. In: Bonk, C.J. Graham, C.R. (eds.) Handbook of Blended Learning: Global Perspectives Local Designs, pp. 3–21. Pfeiffer, San Francisco, CA (2005)
12. Hendrix, M., Rolland, C.: Defining a metadata schema for SG as learning objects. IARIA, 14-19 (2012)
13. Hug, T.: Didactics of Microlearning: Concepts, Discoveries, Examples. Waxman, Berlin (2007)
14. Kapetanakis, M.: Cross-Platform Developer Tools 2012: Bridging the Worlds of Mobile Apps and the Web (2012). http://www.crossplatformtools.com, (last visited 17 July 2015)
15. Klamma, R.: Community learning analytics – challenges and opportunities. In: Wang, J.-F., Lau, R. (eds.) ICWL 2013. LNCS, vol. 8167, pp. 284–293. Springer, Heidelberg (2013)
16. Knight, J., Carly, S., Tregunna, B., Jarvis, S., Smithies, R., De Freitas, S., Mackway-Jones, K., Dunwell, I.: Serious gaming technology in major incident triage training: a pragmatic controlled trial. Resuscitation J. **81**, 1174–1179 (2010)
17. Moseley, A.: A case of integration: assessment and games. In: Connolly, T.M. (ed.) Psychology, Pedagogy, and Assessment in SG, pp. 342–357. IGI Global, Hershey (2014)
18. Norman, D.A., Spohrer, J.C.: Learner-centered education. Commun. ACM **39**, 24–27 (1996)

19. Pisklakov, S., Rimal, J., McGuirt, S.: Role of self evaluation and self assessment in medical student and resident education. Br. J. Educ. Soc. Behav. Sci. 4(1), 1–9 (2014)
20. Protopsaltis, A., Panzoli, D., Dunwell, I., De Freitas S.: Repurposing SG in health care education. In: 12th Mediterranean Conference on Medical and Biological Engineering and Computing (MEDICON 2010), Chalkidiki, Greece, 2010 (2010)
21. Prensky, M.: Listen to the Natives. Learn. Digit. Age 63(4), 8–13 (2006)
22. Prümper, J., Anft, M.: Fragebogen ISONORM 9241/10 (1993). http://www.ergo-online.de/, (last visited 17 July 2015)
23. Sandars, J.: The use of reflection in medical education. AMEE Guide No. 44. Med. Teach. 31(8), 685–6895 (2009)
24. Sliney, A., Murphy, D.: Using SG for assessment. In: Antonopolous, N., Ma, M., Oikonomou, A., Jai, L.C. (eds.) SG and Edutainment Applications, pp. 225–244. Springer Science & Business Media, Berlin (2011)
25. van der Vleuten, C.: The assessment of professional competence: developments, research and practical implications. Adv. Health Sci. Educ. 1, 41–67 (1996)
26. Westera, W., Hommes, M.A., Houtmans, M., Kurvers, H.: Computer-supported training of psycho-diagnostic skills. Interact. Learn. Environ. 11, 215–231 (2003)
27. Zimmerman, B.J.: Becoming a self-regulated learner: an overview. Theor. Into Pract. 41, 64–70 (2002)

Path of Trust: A Prosocial Co-op Game for Building up Trustworthiness and Teamwork

Konstantinos C. Apostolakis[1]([✉]), Kyriaki Kaza[1], Athanasios Psaltis[1],
Kiriakos Stefanidis[1], Spyridon Thermos[1], Kosmas Dimitropoulos[1],
Evaggelia Dimaraki[2], and Petros Daras[1]

[1] Information Technologies Institute, Centre for Research and Technology Hellas,
Thessaloniki, Greece
{kapostol,kikikaza,at.psaltis,kystefan,spthermo,dimitrop,daras}@iti.gr
[2] Ellinogermaniki Agogi, Pallini, Greece
dimaraki@ea.gr
http://www.iti.gr
http://ea.gr

Abstract. In this paper, a two-player digital game is presented, that attempts to balance the exciting game content and story-driven elements mostly associated with games in the entertainment industry with a serious game agenda. The latter focuses on teaching children aged 7–10 the importance of understanding the benefits of cooperation as well as expressing trustworthiness. Gamification of Prosocial Theory has led to several game mechanics being redefined, in order to turn traditional games' elements of competition into cooperation evaluation mechanisms. Using these mechanisms, children are called upon to adapt their gameplay behavior towards expressing prosociality and understanding each other's needs. Our experiments solidify this concept, by showcasing promising indications on the game's potential to help children understand when it is a good idea to adopt a prosocial behavior.

Keywords: Serious games · Prosocial behavior · Game design · Multiplayer games

1 Introduction

Current digital games targeting the education sector carry an unfortunate reputation among gamer communities in general. "Edutainment" is often mistakenly linked to low quality, as players feel such games fail to captivate their imagination. This fact leads to a significant blow to their effectiveness. Indeed, serious games can provide a very efficient means for skills acquisition, as they are usually defined in constrained environments that allow players to subliminally concentrate on the accomplishment of their task. In this respect, serious games categorized under the educational [9,16], recreational [4] or mind exercising character [5,17,18], strive to achieve their goals with the use of proper structures, all while presenting an attractive package. This however, often deliberately sacrifices the

A. De Gloria and R. Veltkamp (Eds.): GALA 2015, LNCS 9599, pp. 80–89, 2016.
DOI: 10.1007/978-3-319-40216-1_9

element of sheer enjoyment in favor of players achieving the desired progress [7]. In contrast to that, games developed purely for the entertainment industry tend to revolutionize society and culture, by offering engaging storylines, memorable characters and exciting game content. In many cases, such game titles have propelled the emergence of multi-billion dollar franchises, whose protagonists are unanimously regarded among our age's pop-culture icons. Such games however also receive criticism; often stemming from their depiction of violence and desensitization, elements around which most modern multi-million unit selling game plots revolve. In fact, studies that explore the impact of game violence on players' general behavior suggest the existence of certain relations between game content and attitudes related to aggression [2,3]. If we were to accept however that exposure to violent games breeds anti-social and aggressive behaviors in minors, we should not overlook the opposite: Positively affecting the formation of a child's personality through non-violent, "prosocial" games, in which helping and caring for others will assist children in comprehending that trusting and exhibiting prosocial behaviors have long-term and well-grounded beneficial results. In this respect, studies showing the relationship between violent and continuous gameplay habits and anti-social behaviors should be extended towards prosociality. Prosociality is in itself a complex concept and is comprised of many core domains, which include empathy, social competence, emotional intelligence, trust, fairness, compassion, generosity and cooperation [13,19]. Already, strong findings are exhibited in related studies [11]. Yet, only a few games exist wherein main characters model helpful and completely non-violent behaviors [1], while the scope of prosociality is usually not intended, it rather manifests itself by chance, in an attempt to gear the game towards certain groups of players, with intent on entertainment.

In this paper, we present a digital co-operative game that focuses on helping young children acquire prosocial skills necessary for developing positive relationships, understand the importance of teamwork and evaluate trustworthiness. Our goal is that children in danger of social exclusion will benefit from our game, which is tailored to teach prosocial skills that can help them appreciate and recognize the value of understanding other people's needs. More specifically we focus on the skills of identifying the benefits of cooperation and expressing trustworthiness, by fabricating these concepts into certified game mechanics that we show are capable of producing favorable gameplay experiences while subliminally promoting prosociality traits to children in need of developing a sense of accomplishment based upon self-control and school performance [15].

The remainder of this paper is organized as follows: Sect. 2 delivers a complete description of the game design and backstory, Sect. 3 outlines the technical details of the game architecture and user motion control configurations available, while Sect. 4 offers a look on small-scale experiments held in school environments for children aged 7–10. Finally, Sect. 5 concludes with a discussion on interesting findings and future work.

2   Gamification of Prosocial Theory

As mentioned before, we set out to build a game based on prosocial theory, and the definition of expressing trustworthiness and identifying the benefits of cooperation [19]. Our ultimate goal was to produce an engaging storyline and game content; elements primarily associated with the entertainment games industry, but fused with scientifically proven game mechanics in order to create a serious game for a non-leisure context (prosociality), in a way that delivers beneficial outcomes for players. We then set out to shape an imaginative game world around these game mechanics. We chose the endless running games genre as a basis for our prosocial game. Endless, or infinite running games, are platform games in which the player character is continuously running through a procedurally generated, seemingly endless game world in an attempt to go as far as possible or collect as many points as they can, before the character inevitably "dies". We chose this genre as it requires a limited set of game controls making it well-suited for our target audience of children aged 7–10. Furthermore, the genre is representative of the influential impact games in the entertainment industry bring to society and culture, being especially popular and enjoying particular success in mobile platforms [20].

2.1   Gameplay Example and Background

Path of Trust (PoT) is a cooperative game where the objective is to collect treasure while navigating through a maze inside an Egyptian tomb, avoiding mummies and traps. The player who assumes the role of wandering around (henceforth referred to as the Muscle) is attributed with Sensory Deprivation (see next paragraph) while their partner, unable to directly determine the course of movement, uses a top-down map view to navigate both of them safely through the maze, without being caught (henceforth referred to as the Guide). A sense of trust must be built between both players in order for the game to be completed; the Muscle player must trust their partner to provide guidance away from danger and the Guide must trust their partner to follow directions. We enrich this basic idea with a colorful backstory and cheerful, immersive 3D graphics to flesh out these characters' world. Screenshots of the final product are shown in Fig. 1.

2.2   Game Mechanics

As previously mentioned, PoT is a serious game intended to help children understand (a) the benefits of cooperation; and (b) when it is the right time to express trustworthiness. Prosocial theory dictates that people often make the mistake of believing there is a fixed pie of benefits and negotiation or that cooperation is an act of dividing the pie. However, the benefits of cooperation are rooted in the expansion of the pie and identifying how they might be increased, a core part of knowing when it is a good idea to cooperate [8]. This dictates that an element of competition must be apparent as the game progresses: players must not be

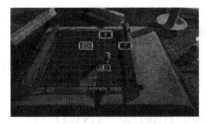

Fig. 1. Gameplay screenshot of the Guide top-down map view (left); player is briefly shown the contents of the three adjacent rooms. Gameplay instance of the Muscle 3D endless running platform view (right); direction input from the Guide displayed with an arrow on the top.

explicitly told to cooperate in order to win the game, lest the concept of adopting this behavior is diminished as a means to a reward. Instead, we intend to help children comprehend the notion of beneficial results tied to the decision of whether to cooperate or not. Our ultimate goal is for players to realize they can achieve far greater results when following a shared agenda, by agreeing to obey particular and specific rules of conduct. In our case, the benefits correspond to collecting pieces of treasure found in the Tomb. We also introduced the element of time, where players race against time trying to collect as much treasure as possible. **Unequal Pay** [6] is a game mechanic designed to introduce the element of competition and a desire to switch roles. It dictates that one player (e.g. the Muscle) is rewarded higher for accomplishing a task (i.e. collecting a treasure piece) than the other. Both players are meant to realize the benefits, as well as formulate a desire for re-routing resources. Hence, we introduce the mechanic of **Switching Places**, which allows players to pass through a 3D Magic Portal, after which the character roles, gameplay, graphics and benefits are switched. As the weaker party at the end of the bargain (e.g. the Guide) is aware of when the opportunity to switch places presents itself, it is up to the player to determine when to propose a bargain for the benefits to be exchanged. Likewise, it is up to the other player to evaluate the proposition and understand whether the offer was birthed out of a justified feeling of fairness or pure greed.

Having one another's trust is vital to cooperation [12]. It is important to have the skills necessary to communicate to others that one can be trusted and will make a good cooperation partner. We model the expression of trustworthiness through a second set of game mechanics. **Sensory Deprivation and Game World Navigation** [10] affect the ability to move from one place to another, when the correct way is not always obvious. Spatial immersion is achieved and heightened by having the player maneuver through the game world while aware of the latter size and depth. The game uses this heightened immersion to provide an exciting game-play experience, where the player navigating through the 3D world is constantly in the thrill of what lurks around the next corner. By removing the sensory element of a mechanic such as Game World Navigation in a cooperative game, we provide a platform for which trust between both players is essential to survive. We further enhance this platform with **Fog of War**, a lack of information about the game world until a specific area is observed or explored [14]. These elements can help build trust between both players; if the trust is broken, the Muscle is caught by one of the traps, which means both players do not succeed.

3   Game Setup and Natural User Interface (NUI)

PoT is a browser game, based on a server-client architecture. The game can be played either using a traditional approach (e.g. keyboard) or through a gesture-driven Natural User Interface (NUI). The game clients are responsible for rendering the game and deploying the NUI, while preserving synchronization with the server. The latter handles matchmaking, and actual game instance processes, updating the game state on both clients based on inputs received in the previous game cycle. A web browser is initialized at each client in order to execute game actions and display the two Muscle/Guide game worlds to the users. This setup makes PoT independent of input devices, thus allowing multiple player input configurations to be used for gameplay. A diagram of this server-client architecture and flow of game data is depicted in Fig. 2.

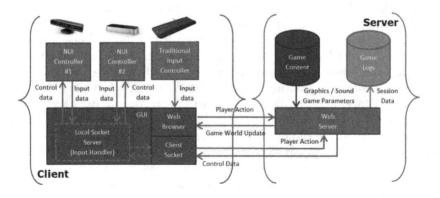

Fig. 2. PoT architecture diagram.

PoT offers three distinct configurations for receiving input from the players. Each player is free to choose his/her preferred configuration. Players are presented with a choice of using a traditional keyboard interface (controlling actions via the arrow keys), or gesture-driven NUI controllers built for the Microsoft Kinect and Leap Motion 3D controller. Simple gesture recognition using the Kinect sensor is done by tracking skeletal joints on the players' hands to determine whether a valid gesture (left/right arm extended, both arms extended forward) is performed. Gesture recognition with the Leap Motion controller on the other hand, is modelled as a subsequence-matching problem. Enabling and disabling sensor tracking is determined via control signals received from the server, which specifies the time frames in which input from the sensor is expected. If applicable, keyboard input on the other hand, is passed directly via the browser module.

4 User Study Results

We set out to test our game and proof of concept in small-scale studies held in a suburban private school located near Athens, Greece. The game sessions took place in two adjacent classrooms in order to assure that no physical communication between the participants was feasible. Therefore, the players' only means of communication was restricted to the commands given inside the game. PoT was played on mid-end laptops, connected via LAN. Each laptop was equipped with a different sensor configuration; one equipped with the Kinect sensor while the other with the Leap Motion controller. One laptop was arbitrarily selected to host the PoT server; both were synchronized using an NTP synchronization scheme. The study included 16 students at the age group of 8–9 years old (4 boys 12 girls). Approximately, 62 % of the participants had played some type of videogame before, while less than half had played games that involved any kind of interaction with other players. Each session consisted of anonymous pairing of players, i.e. participants were unaware of their teammate's identity. A brief description of the game background, as well as an explanation on the gestures for each respective sensor was given separately to each participant before the session. Each session had a predefined time limit set at 5 min. As an additional endgame condition, the game was declared victorious for the player who first accumulated 10 treasure points, leaving the possibility open for both players to reach that goal simultaneously. At the end of each session, the participants were asked to fill in a questionnaire about the game, as well as the conditions of the experiment.

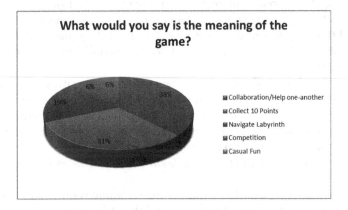

Fig. 3. Experimental results obtained from questionnaire studies, regarding players assessments towards the meaning of the game. (Color figure online)

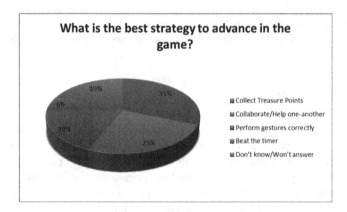

Fig. 4. Experimental results obtained from questionnaire studies, regarding players assessments towards the strategy required to win the game. (Color figure online)

Our results were derived from short, open-ended questionnaires, adjusted in language and presentation to the particular age group. A visual evaluation question for rating the game on two axes (easy-hard and boring-fun) along with a few open-ended, short-answer questions about the game experience were included in each questionnaire form. The questionnaires were distributed to students in groups of four after their game session. Questions were read out-loud and students were allowed time to fill in their answer. Answers were grouped and represented by key words in students' responses. Students generally rated their experience as rather enjoyable, and while assessments on the game challenge were varied, most students found the game to be relatively easy to play. Regarding the participants' grasp of the true meaning of the game, the most common open answers involved the general concept of collecting treasure, players' collaboration, helping one another, and navigating the labyrinth. Interestingly, as can be seen in Fig. 3, only one of the participants focused on the competitive element of collecting points to win. A similar trend in assessments was observed with regard to the question of what it takes to win in the game, as demonstrated in Fig. 4, where "collecting treasure" and "collaboration" were the most salient elements for students.

Players were also asked to evaluate their relationship with the other player, in which, approximately 19 % identified their partner as a pure adversary. Interestingly, 31 % of the players acknowledged an element of competition, but still admitted to recognizing their partner as team player, identifying the benefits they gained through cooperation. The remaining participants clearly identified the other player as a trustworthy cooperation partner. This assessment is shown in Fig. 5.

Finally, players were asked to evaluate the endgame result. In an interesting observation, ten out of sixteen players declared they felt that they had won or lost the game "as a team", despite some of the participants accumulating fewer points than their partner at the endgame. Players who made this statement noted their

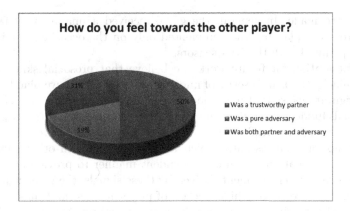

Fig. 5. Experimental results obtained from questionnaire studies, regarding players assessments towards the other participant. (Color figure online)

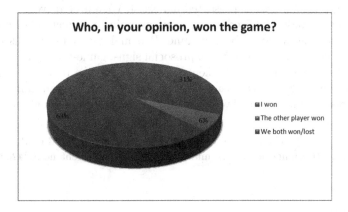

Fig. 6. Experimental results obtained from questionnaire studies, regarding players assessments towards the endgame result. (Color figure online)

partner had benefited from their willingness to cooperate and therefore, felt like they too shared in their partner's success. This trend is demonstrated in Fig. 6.

5   Conclusion

Our user study questionnaire results clearly demonstrate that PoT succeeded in conveying the importance of teamwork to children within the age group 7–10, as the majority of participants felt they had either won or lost the game together or had evaluated their cooperation as a lead towards beneficial outcomes. Also noteworthy is the fact that many players felt they could trust their partner to lead them safely around the labyrinth; even those players who admittedly realized a competitive spirit in their interactions were able to identify whether it was a good idea to trust their partner after propositions of following a certain direction were made. In general, the game received a unanimously favorable reaction from the players, who commented only on the occasional difficulty in getting acquainted with the NUI sensors.

As a foundation for future work, we believe that prosocial skills must be measured efficiently using a series of information cues. Hence, we plan to use our input configurations, so that multimodal signals related to gameplay behavior as well as signals hidden in our game mechanics will be linked to our target prosocial concepts. In our session trials described in Sect. 4, we have collected vision-based facial and motion analysis data, which we plan to fuse with other gamer profile data, and evaluate in a context-dependent manner to provide quantitative indicators related to engagement. Driven by these signals, the game will be personalized in order to achieve higher levels of player interest and thus, maximize the chances of achieving our prosocial learning objectives. Along these lines, we aim to present game content that differs for each child according to specific learning needs, social background, character, gender, etc. Input has been acquired in the form of questionnaires, as presented in Sect. 4. We aim to drive game content and mechanics to individualized patterns, maintaining a correct balance between skills and challenge imposed by the game. Personal gamer profiles listing data on gameplay behavior, the amount of prosocial signs, game-related achievements and signs of engagement must be kept. These should then be updated in order to develop adaptation mechanisms so that engagement is maintained at high levels, addressing particular play styles and needs at an individualized level.

Acknowledgments. The research leading to this work has received funding from the EU Horizon 2020 Framework Programme under grant agreement no. 644204 (ProsocialLearn project).

References

1. Anderson, C.A., Bushman, B.J.: Effects of violent video games on aggressive behavior, aggressive cognition, aggressive affect, physiological arousal, and prosocial behavior: a meta-analytic review of the scientific literature. Psychol. Sci. **12**(5), 353–359 (2001)
2. Anderson, C.A., Bushman, B.J.: Human aggression. Psychology **53**(1), 27 (2002)
3. Anderson, C.A., Gentile, D.A., Buckley, K.E.: Violent Video Game Effects on Children and Adolescents. Oxford University Press, New York (2007)
4. Anderson, C.A., Gentile, D.A., Dill, K.E.: Prosocial, antisocial, and other effects of recreational video games (2012)
5. Baniqued, P.L., Kranz, M.B., Voss, M.W., Lee, H., Cosman, J.D., Severson, J., Kramer, A.F.: Cognitive training with casual video games: points to consider. Front. Psychol. **4**, 1–19 (2013)
6. Brams, S.J., Jones, M.A., Klamler, C.: Proportional pie-cutting. Int. J. Game Theor. **36**(3–4), 353–367 (2008)
7. Buday, R., Baranowski, T., Thompson, D.: Fun and games and boredom. Games Health Res. Dev. Clin. Appl. **1**(4), 257–261 (2012)
8. Colman, A.M.: Cooperation, psychological game theory, and limitations of rationality in social interaction. Behav. Brain Sci. **26**(02), 139–153 (2003)

9. Dostál, J.: Educational software and computer games-tools of modern education. J. Technol. Inf. Educ. **1**(1), 24–28 (2009)

10. Finnegan, D.J., Velloso, E., Mitchell, R., Mueller, F., Byrne, R.: Reindeer & wolves: exploring sensory deprivation in multiplayer digital bodily play. In: Proceedings of the First ACM SIGCHI Annual Symposium on Computer-Human Interaction in Play, pp. 411–412. ACM (2014). ISO 690

11. Gentile, D.A., et al.: The effects of prosocial video games on prosocial behaviors: international evidence from correlational, longitudinal, and experimental studies. Personal. Soc. Psychol. Bull. **35**, 752–763 (2009)

12. Jones, G.R., George, J.M.: The experience and evolution of trust: implications for cooperation and teamwork. Acad. Manag. Rev. **23**(3), 531–546 (1998)

13. Keltner, D., Kogan, A., Piff, P.K., Saturn, S.R.: The sociocultural appraisals, values, and emotions (SAVE) framework of prosociality: core processes from gene to meme. Annu. Rev. Psychol. **65**, 425–460 (2014)

14. LeBlanc, M.: Tools for creating dramatic game dynamics. In: Salen, K., Zimmerman, E. (eds.) The Game Design Reader: A Rules of Play Anthology, pp. 438–459. MIT Press, Cambridge (2006)

15. Matysiak Szóstek, A., Soute, I.: Support of social skill development in children age 7–10 through technology aided games (2010)

16. McClarty, K.L., Orr, A., Frey, P.M., Dolan, R.P., Vassileva, V., McVay, A.: A literature review of gaming in education. In: Gaming in Education (2012)

17. Nouchi, R., Taki, Y., Takeuchi, H., Hashizume, H., Nozawa, T., Kambara, T., Kawashima, R.: Brain training game boosts executive functions, working memory and processing speed in the young adults: a randomized controlled trial. PloS One **8**(2), e55518 (2013)

18. Owen, A.M., Hampshire, A., Grahn, J.A., Stenton, R., Dajani, S., Burns, A.S., Ballard, C.G.: Putting brain training to the test. Nature **465**(7299), 775–778 (2010)

19. Penner, L.A., Dovidio, J.F., Piliavin, J.A., Schroeder, D.A.: Prosocial behavior: multilevel perspectives. Annu. Rev. Psychol. **56**, 365–392 (2005)

20. Purchese, R.: Temple Run 2 is the fastest-spreading mobile game ever. Eurogamer. http://www.eurogamer.net/articles/2013-02-01-temple-run-2-is-the-fastest-selling-mobile-game-ever

Digital Game Design as a Complex Learning Activity for Developing the 4Cs Skills: Communication, Collaboration, Creativity and Critical Thinking

Margarida Romero$^{(\boxtimes)}$

Université Laval, Québec, Canada
margarida.romero@fse.ulaval.ca

Abstract. In this study, digital game design is analyzed as a team-based knowledge modelling process. In the context of a graduate seminar, the students were organized in teams and were asked to design a serious game. In the early stages of the process, each team had the possibility to engage in a topic suggested by the professor or decide their topic of interest. Half of the teams choose a suggested topic (herd immunity, intergenerational communication, active ageing); the other half proposed a topic of their choice (inuits and micmacs, banker-customer relationship, French as a Foreign Language). In both cases, the students should engage in a participative design process which requires a learner-centered analysis. We analyze both the digital game design process and outcomes of the game design from the perspective of social participation and the 4C competencies deployed in the game design process: communication, collaboration, creativity and critical thinking.

1 Introduction

Digital game design is a knowledge modeling activity for learners of different ages. It engages the learners in a decision-making process of a complex system which includes the narrative, the characters' representation and their behaviors, and the mechanics allowing the user to reach the game objectives. The game creation process engages the learners into a meaningful constructivist activity [1, 2] requiring a high level of creativity and collaboration [3]. Our study aims to analyze a team-based serious game design process from the perspective of knowledge modeling, social participation and the 21st century competencies engaged in the game design process. Those outlined key competencies are communication, collaboration, creativity and critical thinking. In the next section, we introduce game design as a team-based knowledge modeling activity, before exploring the context of the course, the game design process and its outcomes.

2 Game Design as a Team-Based Knowledge Modelling Activity

Games are a structured forms of play [4] which aims at engaging one or more person in an interactive and enjoyable activity. Everyone can create games and define the rules of structured play in analogic contexts. During the 20th century, digital game creation

© Springer International Publishing Switzerland 2016
A. De Gloria and R. Veltkamp (Eds.): GALA 2015, LNCS 9599, pp. 90–99, 2016.
DOI: 10.1007/978-3-319-40216-1_10

required a certain level of computing literacy that prevented non-specialized computer professionals to create games. Nowadays, the evolution of the Internet and game engine platforms makes everyone capable of designing games and even creating playable indie-style games [5–7]. Our interest in the game design activity is not focused in the professional process of creating marketable games, but in the game design activity itself as a sociocultural and knowledge modeling activity [8]. Game creation is an activity that engages the user in the definition of a game universe and scenario based on a real or imaginary socio-historical context, where characters can introduce life narratives and interaction that display either known social realities or entirely new ones. Game creation is a knowledge modeling expression that allows the creation of different game universe and characters. As for knowledge modeling, it is a "cross-disciplinary area that deals with approaches to acquire, refine, analyse, capture, model and describe knowledge in a way so as to facilitate its preservation and to ensure that it can be aggregated, substituted, improved, shared and reapplied" [9, p. 1]. For Jonassen and Land [10], computers could be cognitive tools that support the knowledge modeling process both individually and collaboratively. In the field of computer sciences, knowledge modeling is considered a fundamental activity in the "design of computer-based systems for supporting human cognitive tasks in complex socio-technical systems" [11]. In our study, we engage the learners in the design of a serious game based on a topic related to a social challenge of their choice. By designing the game they should inquire, analyze and model the topic of their social challenge. They have to structure it as a game, including game and learning objectives, narrative mechanics [12, 13], game mechanics and learning mechanics [14].

3 Game Design as Social Participation

Based on the critical play, characterized by Flanagan as "a careful examination of social, cultural, political, or even personal themes that function as alternates to popular play spaces" [15, p. 6], participative critical game design aims to develop games which considers social inclusion from the design process and which are designed or developed by the end-users or who invites end-users to the design and development process in collaboration with other end-users or game professionals. Critical game design aims to develop an awareness of games as socio-cultural objects [16]. The critical game design process also values the knowledge experience of the community members interviewed during the game design process. The result of the digital game design is not the goal; instead, we focus on the critical game design process. The critical game design process is a participative learning experience [1, 17, 18] that is able to engage the game designers with society and the participants in a powerful knowledge modeling activity [19].

4 Participative Game Co-creation Process and Outcomes

4.1 Context

Hybrid Course Enrolled by Onsite and Online Students. The course "Game based learning, serious games and gamification of education" is an elective seminar for the postgraduate students of the master and doctorate program in educational technology of Université Laval (Québec, Canada). The course is enrolled by 24 students (12 onsite students and 12 online students). The majority of online students are located in Canada (n = 11; GMT-5 to GMT-8), excluding one student located in Tunisia (GMT+1).

The course accounts for 3 credits, organized as 3 h per week of synchronous class activity available to online students through the videoconference system Adobe Connect, 3 h of team-based autonomous activity and 3 h of individual activities.

Course Structure. The course is structured in two main periods in order to create two prototypes (Fig. 1).

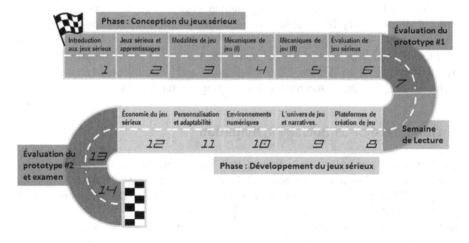

Fig. 1. Course structure and the two main periods and prototypes.

The first prototype should include the learning objectives, the game modalities, the game and learning mechanics, the evaluation strategy of the learning objectives and the evaluation of the gameplay. Based on the feedback received by the panel of experts composed by game development professionals, researchers, the course professor and other students not enrolled in the course, the team should improve the prototype and develop a second release defining the type of technologies they consider the best for their game design. The students are not required to engage in the development of the game. They are only required to produce a mock-up or a sketch of the look and feel and interface of their prototype that could help a third person to understand the game interface and interactivities.

Team Constitution Process. Teams were constituted the first day of the course after an introduction of each of the participants. They had to focus on their main competences in relation to game design. Teams were composed by two onsite students and two online students. A total of 6 teams were constituted during the first session of the course. Each team had the possibility to engage in a topic suggested by the professor or decide their topic of interest. Half of the teams decided to engage on the suggested topics (herd immunity, intergenerational communication, active ageing); the other half engaged in a topic of their choice (aboriginal inuits and micmacs, banker-customer relationship, and French as a Foreign Language). In both cases, the students had to identify the social challenges related to their topic and engage with the community during the serious game design process. The teams having decided to engage on topic suggested by the professor had the 'advantage' of having to their disposition a list of resources that were already selected to facilitate their analysis of their topic. They were also offered to contact specialist in their topic.

Participative Game Design Methodology. The students are introduced to digital game design through a 6 steps methodology aiming to facilitate the decision-making concerning the game modalities, game and learning mechanics and evaluation. The table below introduces the methodological procedure and reflective questions in each of the six steps of the proposed methodology (Table 1).

Table 1. Game design methodology.

Heading level	Font size and style
Learning objectives	Learning objectives are the key point in starting to design the digital game based learning (DGBL) activity. In this step, the students are invited to identify the formal or informal learning context, define which of the learning objectives will be part of the learning assessment and which type of feedback (or group awareness) will be offered as a display of progression to the learners during the game or gamification activity
Learner-centered need analysis	The learner-centered need analysis aims to analyze the learners' prior knowledge and competences (PKC) in order to organize the learning objectives in levels considering the Zone of Proximal Development [20] and the optimal difficulty to try to achieve a certain level of flow [21]. Based on the learners' diversity in terms of PKC, the team could decide to organize the learning modalities in order to adapt the game to the diversity or evaluate the cooperative game dynamics that could help overcome the learners' PKC diversity. The learner-centered need analysis should also analyze the learners' language and computer literacy, their preferences, context and technological resources in order to take decisions in the following steps

(Continued)

Table 1. (*Continued*)

Heading level	Font size and style
Game modalities	In order to decide the game modalities, the learners are invited to identify the existing serious games that could fit the learning objectives. In case an existing serious game matches the objectives, they should identify the pedagogical integration requirement. In case there is not an existing serious games fitting the requirements, the teams could decide to repurpose an existing game, such as using *Angry Birds* for learning mathematics. A third alternative is to design and create a game. Furthermore, the teams can opt for educational gamification and add the game components (e.g. public scoring and competitive team, reward system…) to an educational situation All the students enrolled in our course the students decided to create their game because no existing serious games fitted the learning objectives
Game rules, learning and game mechanics	The teams should decide the individual or collaborative context of the game and define the game rules. The game rules should be aligned with the learning objectives (first phase) and the learning assessment and feedback (fifth phase) in order to incentivize the learning progression in the game. The game mechanics structures the interaction and control processes allowing the player to advance in the game. The teams are introduced to the existence of primary and secondary game mechanics [22] and are invited to identify the learning mechanics and game mechanics (LM-GM) based on the LM-GM model proposed by Arnab and collaborators [14]
Learning assessment and feedback	In this phase of the game design methodology, the team should analyze the effective impact of the game on the learning objective achievements. The learning assessment and feedback should derivate from the learning objectives (first phase). According to the needs identified in the second phase (learner-centered need analysis), there are three main types of assessment that could be introduced in the game: diagnostic, formative and summative assessment. Individual and collective feedback could be displayed to the players through knowledge group awareness widgets [23, 24] in order to ensure the learner is aware of her/his progression
Gaming and learning experience	This last phase aims to evaluate the player gaming and (positive) learning experience. The teams are introduced to the works of Kiili in relation to the flow experience [25] and the criteria for improving it. Kiili focus on the importance of immediate feedback, clear goals and challenges that are matched with the current learners' knowledge and skills to place them in the flow activity state

5 Game Design Process

Each of the team has completed the game design successfully. The game design process has been evaluated according the six steps methodology and the assessment criteria associated to each step of the methodology. The game design outcomes have been evaluated by a panel of experts composed by professionals, researchers and other students not involved in the course. The learners 4C's "super skills" for the 21st century (communication, collaboration, creativity and critical thinking) [3] have been evaluated by the professor based on the game design process and team-based tutoring activities (Fig. 2).

Fig. 2. Screenshots of one the games designed by the intergenerational communication team [26].

Game Design Process. The figure below introduces the average results of the teams engaged in a suggested topic by the professor (having received more guidance in the initial steps of the process) and the average results of the teams engaged in a self-defined topic (Fig. 3).

We observe the teams designing a game based on a suggested topic have higher performances in the game design process documentation, the definition of the learning objectives of the game and the learning assessment strategy of the learning strategy. Self-defined topic teams outperform in the learner-centered context analysis, the game universe, game modalities, game mechanics and learning mechanics scores.

Evaluation of the 4Cs. The figure below introduces the average level of the 4Cs skills among the students in the suggested topic teams and self-defined teams (Fig. 4).

We observe that the learners composing the teams working on a self-defined topic clearly outperform their counterparts in the suggested topic teams in terms of communication and collaboration. The learners taking part in the suggested topic teams only show a slight advantage in the creativity skills.

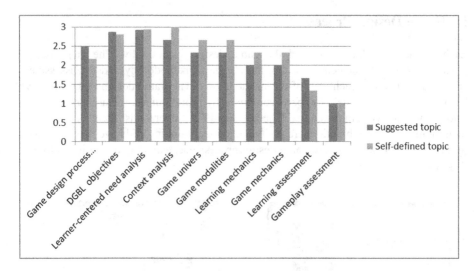

Fig. 3. Average results in the game design process of self-defined and suggested topic teams. (Color figure online)

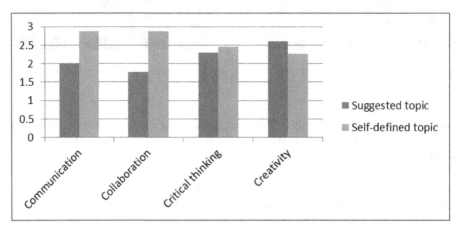

Fig. 4. Average results in 4Cs process of self-defined and suggested topic teams. (Color figure online)

6   Discussion

The graduate students enrolled in the "Game based learning, serious games and gamification of education" course reported a high level of engagement. The students' satisfaction with the course was high: onsite students' showed a 92.4 % of satisfaction in the questionnaire of satisfaction deployed at Université Laval for evaluation the quality of the teaching activities; within the same questionnaire, the online students reported a 88.6 % of satisfaction, which could be due to some of the quality difficulties in videoconference sessions. The students' reported feeling secure with a step-by-step methodology that allowed them to be creative in their design while having certain guidance in the process.

In terms of the design game process, the evaluation shows differences at the different stages. The 4Cs skills of students having chosen to work on a topic already suggested by the professor and those having preferred to engage in a game design topic of their choice were varying. We can observe that students having preferred a topic already prepared by the professor have better defined the serious games learning objectives and the game design documentation, but their performance is lower in all the other aspects of the game design process than the free-chosen topic teams. We can discuss this result as an initial advantage of having selected an already prepared topic, which helped the teams to focus directly on the learning objectives and documentation in the early stages of the game design process while their free-chosen topic counterparts were still defining what they would work on. However, despite the initial advantage, the teams working on predefined topics were less performant in the subsequent steps of the game design process. We should hypothesize about the possibility that learners having preferred to follow the professor suggestions could have a preference for higher guidance from the professor, which was less available in the subsequent steps of the game design process. We can also discuss this early advantage as a consequence of having more time in the first steps of the game design process than the teams working on defining their own topic.

In terms of the 4Cs skills, we observe that the free-chosen topic teams outperform in communication and collaboration. We can discuss this advantage under the lens of their small group development process [27] which engaged the team members to better know each others' preferences while deciding their serious game topic. At the opposite, the teams working on an already defined topic accelerated their "forming" stage of their group development process which does not developed the same degree of cohesion, communication and collaboration in the subsequent stages.

The differences observed in the teams according their engagement in an already defined topic could be also discussed under the lens of the individual traits of students that prefer to follow the professor suggestions, which shows less autonomy and initiative than their counterparts.

The objective of engaging the graduate students in a knowledge modeling process through a digital game design process has been achieved for all the students and teams. Digital game design is a powerful learning activity that has the capability to engage learners not only in K12 [28] but also in Higher Education [29].

Acknowledgments. The author aims to acknowledge the contribution to the revision of this manuscript by Hubert Ouellet, fellowship within the Ageing + Communication + Technology (ACT) project funded by the Social Sciences and Humanities Research Council of Canada (SSHRC).

References

1. Hassan, M.M., Moreno, A., Sutinen, E., Aziz, A.: On the participatory design of Jeliot mobile: towards a socio-constructivist mlearning tool. In: 2015 International Conference on Learning and Teaching in Computing and Engineering (LaTiCE), pp. 120–123 (2015)
2. Wingrave, C., Norton, J., Ross, C., Ochoa, N., Veazanchin, S., Charbonneau, E., LaViola, J.: Inspiring creative constructivist play. In: CHI 2012 Extended Abstracts on Human Factors in Computing Systems, pp. 2339–2344 (2012)
3. Romero, M., Usart, M., Ott, M.: Can serious games contribute to developing and sustaining 21st-century skills? Games Cult. J. Interact. Media 10(2), 148–177 (2015)
4. Prensky, M.: The motivation of gameplay: the real twenty-first century learning revolution. Horizon 10(1), 5–11 (2002)
5. Ke, F., Im, T.: A case study on collective cognition and operation in team-based computer game design by middle-school children. Int. J. Technol. Des. Educ. 24(2), 187–201 (2014)
6. Richard, G.T., Kafai, Y.B.: Responsive make and play: youth making physically and digitally interactive and wearable game controllers. In: Nijholt, A. (ed.) More Playful User Interfaces, pp. 71–93. Springer, Singapore (2015)
7. Woods, C.: The rise of interactive game development and multimedia project creation among school-aged children. In: Society for Information Technology and Teacher Education International Conference, vol. 2015, pp. 1971–1975 (2015)
8. Romero, M.: Critical game creation as intergenerational social participation. In: First Person Scholar, Different Games, 16 September 2015. Special Issue
9. Dutta, B., Madalli, D.P.: Trends in knowledge modelling and knowledge management: an editorial. J. Knowl. Manag. 19(1) (2015)
10. Jonassen, D., Land, S.: Theoretical Foundations of Learning Environments. Routledge, New York (2012)
11. Ham, D.-H.: Modelling work domain knowledge with the combined use of abstraction hierarchy and living systems theory. Cogn. Technol. Work 17, 575–591 (2015)
12. Jenkins, H.: Game design as narrative architecture. Computer 44, 53 (2004)
13. Lim, T., et al.: Narrative Serious Game Mechanics (NSGM) – insights into the narrative-pedagogical mechanism. In: Göbel, S., Wiemeyer, J. (eds.) GameDays 2014. LNCS, vol. 8395, pp. 23–34. Springer, Heidelberg (2014)
14. Arnab, S., Lim, T., Carvalho, M.B., Bellotti, F., de Freitas, S., Louchart, S., Suttie, N., Berta, R., De Gloria, A.: Mapping learning and game mechanics for serious games analysis. Br. J. Educ. Technol. 46, 391–411 (2014)
15. Flanagan, M.: Critical Play: Radical Game Design. MIT Press, Cambridge (2009)
16. Squire, K.: Cultural framing of computer/video games. Game Stud. 2(1), 1–13 (2002)
17. Kayali, F., et al.: Participatory game design for the INTERACCT serious game for health. In: Göbel, S., Ma, M., Baalsrud Hauge, J., Oliveira, M.F., Wiemeyer, J., Wendel, V. (eds.) JCSG 2015. LNCS, vol. 9090, pp. 13–25. Springer, Heidelberg (2015). doi:10.1007/978-3-319-19126-3
18. Khaled, R., Vanden Abeele, V., Van Mechelen, M., Vasalou, A.: Participatory design for serious game design: truth and lies. In: Proceedings of the First ACM SIGCHI Annual Symposium on Computer-Human Interaction in Play, pp. 457–460 (2014)
19. Romero, M., Lille, B., Kichkina, N., Bourgault, M., Proulx, J.-N., Patino, A.: Apprentissage intergénérationnel en Univers Social par le biais d'une création de récit de vie sur la migration. In: CICE-2015 Proceedings, University of Toronto, Mississauga, Canada (2015)
20. Vygotsky, L.S.: Mind and Society: The Development of Higher Mental Processes. Harvard University Press, Cambridge (1978)

21. Csikszentmihalyi, I.S.: Optimal Experience: Psychological Studies of Flow in Consciousness. Cambridge University Press, Cambridge (1992)
22. Fabricatore, C.: Gameplay and game mechanics design: a key to quality in videogames. In: Proceedings of OECD-CERI Expert Meeting on Videogames and Education (2007)
23. Chavez, J., Romero, M.: Group awareness, learning, and participation in Computer Supported Collaborative Learning (CSCL). Procedia-Soc. Behav. Sci. **46**, 3068–3073 (2012)
24. Pifarré, M., Cobos, R., Argelagós, E.: Incidence of group awareness information on students' collaborative learning processes. J. Comput. Assist. Learn. **30**, 300–317 (2014)
25. Kiili, K.: Digital game-based learning: towards an experiential gaming model. Internet High. Educ. **8**(1), 13–24 (2005)
26. Boutin, J., Corbeil, A., Dumont, L., Roy, S.: Designing a serious game for intergenerational learning in a camping scenario. In: Proceedings of the Silver Gaming Intergenerational Summer School, Québec, vol. 1 (2015)
27. Johnson, S.D., Suriya, C., Yoon, S.W., Berrett, J.V., La Fleur, J.: Team development and group processes of virtual learning teams. Comput. Educ. **39**(4), 379–393 (2002)
28. Bates, M., Brown, D., Cranton, W., Lewis, J.: Facilitating a games design project with children: a comparison of approaches. In: Proceedings of the European Conference on Games-Based Learning, pp. 429–437 (2010)
29. Ozoran, D., Cagiltay, N., Topalli, D.: Using scratch in introduction to programming course for engineering students. In: 2nd International Engineering Education Conference (IEEC 2012), pp. 125–132 (2012)

Social Practices for Social Driven Conversations in Serious Games

Agnese Augello[1], Manuel Gentile[2]($^{(\boxtimes)}$), and Frank Dignum[3]

[1] ICAR - National Research Council of Italy,
Viale delle Scienze - Edificio 11, 90128 Palermo, Italy
augello@pa.icar.cnr.it
[2] ITD - National Research Council of Italy,
Via Ugo La Malfa 153, 90146 Palermo, Italy
manuel.gentile@itd.cnr.it
[3] Utrecht University, Princetonplein 5, De Uithof, 3584 CC Utrecht, The Netherlands
F.P.M.Dignum@uu.nl

Abstract. This paper describes the model of social practice as a theoretical framework to manage conversation with the specific goal of training physicians in communicative skills. To this aim, the domain reasoner that manages the conversation in the Communicate! [1] serious game is taken as a basis. Because the choice of a specific Social Practice to follow in a situation is non-trivial we use a probabilistic model for the selection of social practices as a step toward the implementation of an agent architecture compliant with the social practice model.

Keywords: Social practice · Serious games · Physicians training · Communicative skills

1 Introduction

Effective communicative skills are important in different fields, and are the basis of every social relation. Serious games can be useful in this context, as a valid approach to train people to properly carry out conversations by means of simulation of dialogues with virtual characters. See e.g. [2–4].

The use of virtual agents for this purpose is particularly useful because it allows us to also bring social elements of interactions into the simulations [2]. They can be used to provide learners with a continuous feedback, showing the effects of their conversational choices on the emotions and behavioural changes of the interlocutors [1,5].

An area where conversations play an important role in everyday practice are the medical consultations. Training physicians to communicate better has several positive effects on patients' well-being. For example a good communication enhances patients' treatment adherence [6], leads to greater patient disclosure of sensitive psychosocial information and foster a reduction in patients' emotional distress [7]. It is generally agreed that better doctor-patient interaction leads to

A. De Gloria and R. Veltkamp (Eds.): GALA 2015, LNCS 9599, pp. 100–110, 2016.
DOI: 10.1007/978-3-319-40216-1_11

better diagnosises, which in turn can lead to huge (financial and human) cost savings in hospital tests and treatments.

Several Serious Games have been designed in this context. E.g. [1,8]. Communicate![1] is a serious game used by medical students to learn the best communication strategies to establish a valid and trusted relationship with the patient by means of consultations with virtual characters. SimSensei Kiosk [8], a dialogue system that conducts interviews related to psychological distress conditions, shows several benefits of using virtual agents from the perspective of the patient. In particular the patient, interacting with a virtual agent shows more openness to the conversation, not feeling judged by another human interlocutor.

Most agents that are used in these applications are based on scripts and reactive rules to respond to users. Unfortunately this leads to quite predictable and simple dialogs. Thus the challenge is to design agents that are more pro-active and are able to autonomously take their decisions according to their expectations and the evolution of the game. This would be more in line with Clark [9] who claims that a dialogue is a joint activity that must consider both individual and social processes.

The social context has a key role in the deliberative process of agents and is particularly important in a conversational context, where the deliberative process regards the choice of the most proper utterance. Conversation has a social effect because it contributes to changes in people (beliefs, attitudes, etc.), social relations, and the material world [10]. In the other hand the social structure, the social practice and the social agents involved in the social interaction determine the actual conversation utterances that are used [10]. As a matter of fact different communication strategies can be used according to the specific social context.

It is important therefore to formalize how the social context influences the deliberation process of agents. Existing techniques often do not fully model this type of situational deliberation of agents. The social context is often dealt with as a set of norms that add complexity to the cognitive model of the agent, complicate the deliberative process and that restrict agents application to the particular application domain for which they have been designed [11].

In order to address this issue we intend to use the concept of social practice as modeled in [11]. Social practices refer to everyday practices and the way these are typically and habitually performed in a society. In [11] social practice are used to create agents that are able to sense the physical and social aspects of the current situation, but act not in a simple reactive way, but pro-actively choosing a plan of actions suitable to reach their both social and functional goals.

In this paper, the model of social practice as a theoretical framework to manage conversation with the specific goal of training physicians in communicative skills is analyzed. To this aim, the domain reasoner that manages the conversation in the Communicate! [1] serious game is taken as a basis. We see how scenarios build with Communicate! can be replicated using Social Practices in order to subsequently show how the Social Practice model enhance the scenarios in a flexible and natural way. Because the choice of a specific Social Practice to follow in a situation is non-trivial we use a probabilistic model for the selection of social practices as a step toward the implementation of an agent architecture compliant with the social practice model [11].

2   Training Communication Skills for Medics

Let us consider the following scenario. A doctor is at the desk of his office in the hospital where he works. Someone knocks at the door. Because it is his consultation hour he expects a patient. Thus the doctor invites the person to come in. He habitually sees a lot of patients, following standard conversational protocols aimed to obtain useful information from the patient such as the existence of particular pathologies and the symptoms of the disease.

When the doctor receives a patient he activates a plan of actions related to the conversational protocol that should lead him to understand the patient's problems and to give the patient the right therapeutic treatment.

When the doctor does not know the patient who has just entered the room, he will first introduce himself properly and ask some general background questions to establish a trusted relationship with the patient.

Once he starts the conversation he will have some expectations about the type of responses the patient will give. If the expectations are not met he might change his ideas about the patient and reconsider his next moves in the conversation. E.g. if a patient seems not to acknowledge a symptom or fact, it might be the patient is worried or distracted and needs first to be put at rest. However, if an emergency occurs the doctor should interrupt the consultation and start a totally different practice (belonging to the emergency). If he did not handle this type of emergency very often he will have to deliberate to a greater extent (based on his medical knowledge and other cases) to determine the right plan of action.

The scenario described above shows the complexity of autonomous agents for this kind of games.

In order to have a concrete reference model for the medical context, we start from the work done in the Communicate! project. First the scenario model defined in the Communicate! serious game is briefly introduced. Then, the "anamnesis" scenario is analyzed in order to understand how scenarios build with Communicate! can be replicated using Social Practices in order to manage the conversation in a flexible and realistic way.

3   Communicate! Dialogue Management

The scenario model defined in the Communicate! project allows the designer to specify:

- a set of parameters, that represent the dialogue state;
- one or more conversation trees, in which the nodes are the player's statements and the computer's statements;
- a sequence of interleaves, that represent a sort of dialogue phase in which one or more conversation trees could take place.

The Communicate! serious game is based on the structural dialogue state app-roach, in which the interleaves, the trees and the statements represent the dia-logue grammar. The dialogue state is defined by the scenario parameters' scores, by the lasts computer's statements and by a set of emotions' scores. The basic set of emotions managed in Communicate! are: happiness, anger, surprise, con-tempt, disgust, fear and sadness.

According to the current dialogue state, a domain reasoner selects the pos-sible moves (the player statements) among which the player could choose the move to carry forward the dialogue. In fact, the player statements represent the dialogue moves that update the elements of the dialogue state (the parameters and the emotions of the virtual character).

3.1 The "Anamnesis" Scenario

The situation described in Sect. 2 is managed by a specific scenario defined in the framework of the Communicate! project [1], the "anamnesis" scenario. In this scenario, the user plays the doctor role and holds a consultation with a virtual patient.

The dialogue is "started" by the player who assumes the role of the doctor. The player has to choose among a number of possible expressions. Each of these expressions leads to the activation of a conversation tree.

Let us suppose the player, among the different possibilities, chooses the fol-lowing sentence to proceed the scenario: "I see you are a patient of Dr. Aarts" This player statement, produces a "surprise" effect in the agent that realizes that he will have an interview with an unknown doctor.

In terms of social practice, this element of "surprise" is the result of a viola-tion of an expectation of the social practices activated by the patient. Infact, as shown to the player at the beginning of the game, the patient expects to have an interview with his own doctor, that is the patient agent has activated the social practice *consulting my doctor*. This lead the patient agent to re-evaluate the situation and to select a new practice *consulting an unknown doctor*.

The scenario manages the case in which the doctor directly introduces him-self to the patient in the initial phase of the dialogue, as well as the case in which this greeting and presentation take place later. Of course, the two alternatives produce different effects on the virtual patient. In the former case, a positive effect on the "happiness" of the patient is achieved; instead in the latter case, an effect of "displeasure" of the patient is obtained. These two alternatives can be interpreted in the light of the social practices selected by the patient. The practice contains a norm which states that the doctor and patient should intro-duce themselves if not known yet in order to show respect. If the doctor does not make this introduction at the start this gets a social meaning of showing disrespect to the patient. So the "disappointment" of the patient could be seen as a consequence of the "violation" of the social norm.

The Communicate! scenario envisages that the doctor provides more informa-tion to the patient about himself and his role within the hospital. In particular, the doctor is still in training with the patient's doctor. Knowing that the one

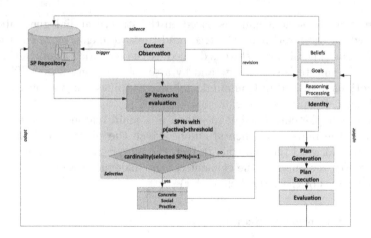

Fig. 1. Architecture for social reasoning [11]

who is in front of him is a doctor in training leads the patient agent to a state of "anger" if he is in an emotional state of "contempt". However, if the patient is in a state of "happiness", he goes to a state of "surprise".

The analysis of this portion of the dialogue shows that the effect of a communicative actions depends largely on the context in which they are uttered. Especially, the social meaning of the utterance depends on the social practice. Thus the ensuing emotional state of the patient also depends on this practice.

4   Social Practice Agent Architecture

The structural dialogue state approach used in Communicate! is a viable solution to manage scripted dialogues. Although this is a good starting point, from an educational point of view it is important to allow the player to experience more varying and realistic dialogues. In order to overcome the lack of flexibility of this approach, several approaches have been proposed in literature.

For example, structural dialogue state approach has often been contrasted with plan-based approaches [12,13]. Anyway, dialogue plan-based approaches require a great effort in the definition of commonsense knowledge and procedural processing, often leading to the creation of an opaque solution.

Moreover, to improve the educational effectiveness, the game should allow the user to play both the roles (doctor or patient), allowing the doctor to experience the patient point of view [14]. To this aim, a design of the game that models both the agents roles is required.

In this work, the model of social practice is introduced in order to overcome the limitations of both structural dialogue state and plan-based approaches, sharing the motivation with the work of Traum and Larsoon [15].

The proposed agent's architecture (Fig. 1) puts the identification of the social context at the basis of the deliberative process of the agents. The social context is modelled according to the theory of social practice (Sect. 4.1). The identification of the most appropriate social practice allows for a dynamic management of the dialogue within the serious game, allowing the conversation to follow a specific but not rigid flow, and restricting considerably the number of possible sentences that may be issued by the agent and at the same time facilitating the understanding of the utterances of the interlocutor. Starting from the observation of the context an agent updates his beliefs and goals, and activates a set of possible social practices. He then triggers an internal reasoning process in order to select the most appropriate social practice (Sect. 4.2). Finally, according to the selected social practice he starts a deliberation process in order to manage the conversation within the context of that practice. When the available information is not enough to activate a single social practice, the agent will interact with the user in order to obtain additional information that discriminates the context further and leads to one social practice being the most suitable.

In this paper the focus is on the social practice modeling and selection, as highlighted in the figure.

4.1   The Model of Social Practice

In this section the model of social practices described in [11] is analysed in the context of a doctor-patient dialogue. According to [11], the aim of the social practice model is to provide a representation scheme that allows the implementation of cognitive agents able to use the social practice as a first-class construct in the agent deliberation process. In the following, the components of the social practice model are described by referring to a specific social practice (*"Doctor Patient Dialogue"*) concerning the scenario of a doctor-patient interview. Table 1 summarizes the components of the social practice under investigation.

- *Physical Context* focuses on the identification of the environment elements, that are both the physical objects with a meaningful role in the practice (*Resources*), the agents (human beings or autonomous systems) involved in the practice (*Actors*) and the locations of objects and actors (*Places*).

   In the analyzed scenario at least two people are expected to take part in the practice, the interview takes place in a hospital, inside a room and at a specific time. Among the various resources available in this context, we can highlight the medical instruments visible in the room including the doctor's coat.
- *Social Context* describes the social interpretation of the elements sensed in the environment, in particular in [11] a distinction is made between the so called *Roles*, describing specific behaviours that can be expected from specific actors, and the interpretation of all the other elements, called *Social Interpretation*. Moreover the *Norms* identify the rules that are expected inside a social practice. As an example, in the analyzed scenario, we can identify a physician role and a patient role, and in some cases a relative of the patient. The doctor-patient dialogue generally takes place during consultation hours in a special room used for the purpose. Finally, the type of clothing, and in particular the colour of the coat worn by the doctor are usually indicative of the "role"

Table 1. The doctor-patient dialogue as a social practice

Abstract Social Practice	Doctor Patient Dialogue
Physical Context	
Resources	current time,medical instruments
Places	hospital,office
Actors	doctor1, patient1
Social Context	
Social interpretation	consulting room,consulting time,doctor has medical skills
Roles	doctor, patient, relative of the patient, nurse
Norms	patient is cooperative, doctor is polite
Activities	welcome, presentation, patient's data gathering, patient symptom description constative(answer,confirm,disagree,agree) directive(ask,instruct,request)
Plan patterns	
Meaning	support the patient, create trust, eliciting patient's problems and concerns, treatment and solution possible, empathic opportunity, empathic response
Competences	listening effectively, being supportive and empathic, use effective explanatory skills, adapt conversation to patient, discussing treatment options understandable

(doctor, assistant, nurse) that the professional has in the hospital. Different norms can be related to the roles of doctor and patient. As an example the doctor during the interview should totally reserve his attention to the patient; if suddenly there is an emergency, the norm is no more applicable. For what concerns the role of the patient it is important that he is cooperative.

- *Activities* are possible course of actions that agents can perform. In a fine-grained analysis, every communicative act of the agent can be considered as an activity. At this level we tie communicative acts to the speech act classification [16] and not to specific utterances. Listing all the possible language productions is not possible and certainly not efficient; moreover, this allows us to organize the individual communicative acts in communication protocols. Non communicative acts such as moves, gestures and so on can be also considered at this level. In a coarse-grain analysis, a set of simple actions can be considered as an activity; it is a sort of a scene in the plan of actions of the agent aimed to reach a specific sub-goal. As an example a scene can be a set of communicative and non communicative acts used by the doctor to welcome the patient into the room.
- *Plan Patterns.* A plan pattern is a pattern on the basis of which an agent can construct a plan to reach a goal. A plan pattern consists of an ordered set of scenes with a specific sub-goal that restrict the type of plans that can

be used. As an example, the doctor will start and follow a specific protocol for the patient consultation. The protocol can be structured in the following scenes: Welcome and Presentation, Personal Data acquisition (biographic data, pathologies, medical treatments, allergies, ...), Description of the symptoms. The goal of the protocol is to start a doctor/patient relation and to proceed to the consult, however the situation can evolve and lead to quit (dotted lines in the image) the social practice. For example if the doctor acquiring the information recognizes that another doctor could be more competent for the patient's issues (in this case the doctor has not the competences required by the practice), or if the patient shows an untrusted or disrespectful behavior (in this case a violation of a norm), the doctor can switch to another practice.

- *Meaning.* This part of the social practice model, is used to define social meanings for the agent's activities and plans. Considering communicative acts as activities, every act can assume a different meaning depending on the context of the dialogue, the cognitive status of the agents and so on. As an example, communicative acts could be classified from an empathic point of view according to the classification proposed by [17] (i.e. empathic opportunity, empathic response, etc.). At the same time, the meaning of communicative acts includes its intended effects [9]. Of course these examples are not exhaustive of all the other different types of meaning that could be associated to the communicative acts.
- *Competences* Competences are defined as the abilities an agent should have to perform the activities of the social practice. Amongst the medical skills required to interact with the patient there are several communication skills recommended to physicians [18,19]. For example, physicians should *listen effectively, being supportive and empathic, use effective explanatory skills, discuss treatment options in a simple way.* At the same time, patients should have health literacy skills in order to have an effective dialogue.

4.2   A Probabilistic Reasoner for Social Practice Selection

Starting from the observation of the context and according to his identity the agent activates a set of possible social practices. Based on his beliefs and goals it subsequently selects the most appropriate social practice. We propose a probabilistic reasoner for this selection process, because often not all information is available or certain. In those cases the agent will use its experience and derive as much information as possible to make a selection.

The elements of the physical environment and their social interpretation related to a social practice, are represented in a causal graph. An example for the practice *"Doctor Patient Dialogue"* is shown in Fig. 2. From the root node, representing the activation of the social practice, depart causal nodes representing its relevant elements (i.e. place, current time, ...). The states of these nodes are the possible social interpretations of such elements; for example the *consulting time* is the social interpretation of the physical resource *current time*. The causal links are expressed by means of conditional probability tables. The Bayesian networks allow the designer to adopt a top-down approach to formalize its initial knowledge about the social practice. In later versions learning algorithms will be implemented to allow the agent to learn the tables of conditional probabilities related to the social practices, but we leave that out for the moment. The algorithm of social practice selection is shown in Fig. 1, and explained below according to the scenario described in Sect. 2. First, the observation of the context and the identity of the agent produces an initial selection of practices. If the agent has the role of doctor and he is at the hospital, possible social practices are for example those related to consulting patients and the management of an emergency. According to the available information it is possible to set evidences in the causal graphs associated with the different social practices. In particular if the *current_time* is a *consulting_time* and the doctor is inside a consulting_room, the analysis of the activation probabilities of the possible practices shows that the practice related to a patient consultation (*doctor_ patient_dialogue*) has the highest probability, as shown in Fig. 2. In particular even if the agent does not yet know who is his interlucotor, according to the model of the activated social practice, he estimates that he should be a patient with a high probability.

When the situation evolves several things might happen. The person either can be indeed a patient, an hospital employee (is wearing some hospital stuff), or can be not alone. Depending on the actual situation the expectations of the social practice are confirmed and the practice is continued or the social practice is reevaluated with the new information. When a social practice is chosen the agent can start a further context analysis in order to discriminate among more concrete social practices that lead to more specific plan patterns, roles, norms etc.

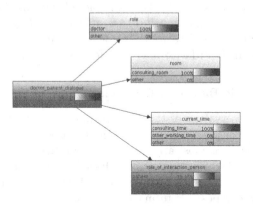

Fig. 2. The decision network activation for the *Doctor_Patient_Dialogue* social practice

5   Conclusion

In this paper we have given some initial steps showing the usability of social practices for managing dialogues in serious games. Mainly we have shown that social practice captures both the physical as well as the social context and thus forms an important source of information for the interpretation and generation of speech acts. Having this context available as source of information allows for a more accurate interpretation of the utterances as they can be compared to the expected type of utterances according to the practice. Because social practices do not enforce a fixed script but rather indicate usable plan patterns they allow for flexibility in the dialogue while still ensuring a (joint) goal to be achieved.

Of course, there are many open questions such as the connections between different social practices, the learning and adaptation of the agent and we have also not shown the actual dialogue manager that is used by the agent to generate the actual utterances. The first steps are to fully implement the agent architecture and using a simple dialogue planner as in Communicate! produce at least the same dialogues but on the fly. Moreover, the Information State approach [15] will be analyzed in order to verify if a dialogue manager defined according to this approach could be used as a valuable deliberation engine for an agent compliant with the social practice model.

Acknowledgements. We are grateful to Prof. J. Jeuring, for his useful explanation of the Communicate! project and for providing us the scenarios of the game.

References

1. Jeuring, J., et al.: Demo: Communicate! - a serious game for communication skills. In: Conole, G., Klobučar, T., Rensing, C., Konert, J., Lavoué, É. (eds.) Design for Teaching and Learning in a Networked World. Lecture Notes in Computer Science, vol. 9307, pp. 513–517. Springer, Heidelberg (2015). http://doi.org/10.1007/978-3-319-24258-3_49

2. Swartout, W., Artstein, R., Forbell, E., Foutz, S., Lane, H.C., Lange, B., Morie, J., Noren, D., Rizzo, S., Traum, D.: Virtual humans for learning. AI Mag. **34**(4), 13–30 (2013)

3. Babu, S.V., Suma, E., Hodges, L.F., Barnes, T.: Learning cultural conversational protocols with immersive interactive virtual humans. Int. J. Virtual Reality **10**(4), 25–35 (2011)

4. Dargis, M., Koncevics, R., Silamikelis, A., Kirikova, M.: Game-based Training of Communication Skills in Requirements Engineering. In: REFSQ Workshops 2014, pp. 147–148 (2014)

5. Traum, D.R., Swartout, W.R., Marsella, S.C., Gratch, J.: Fight, flight, or negotiate: believable strategies for conversing under crisis. In: Panayiotopoulos, T., Gratch, J., Aylett, R.S., Ballin, D., Olivier, P., Rist, T. (eds.) IVA 2005. LNCS (LNAI), vol. 3661, pp. 52–64. Springer, Heidelberg (2005)

6. Dimatteo, M.R.: Physician communication and patient adherence to treatment: a meta-analysis. Med. Care **47**(8), 826–834 (2009)

7. Roter, D.L., Hall, J.A., Kern, D.E., Barker, L.R., Cole, K.A., Roca, R.P.: Improving physicians interviewing skills and reducing patients' emotional distress: a randomized clinical trial. Arch. Intern. Med. **155**(17), 1877–1884 (1995). doi:10.1001/archinte.1995.00430170071009

8. Morency, L.P., Stratou, G., DeVault, D., Hartholt, A., Lhommet, M., Lucas, G., Morbini, F., Georgila, K., Scherer, S., Gratch, J., Marsella, S., Traum, D., Rizzo, A.: SimSensei demonstration: a perceptive virtual human interviewer for healthcare applications. In: AAAI Conference on Artificial Intelligence, North America, March 2015

9. Clark, H.H.: Using Language. Cambridge University Press, Cambridge (1996)

10. Fairclough, N.: Analysing Discourse: Textual Analysis for Social Research. Psychology Press, London (2003)

11. Dignum, V., Dignum, F.: Contextualized planning using social practices. In: Ghose, A., Oren, N., Telang, P., Thangarajah, J. (eds.) COIN 2014. LNCS, vol. 9372, pp. 36–52. Springer, Heidelberg (2015). doi:10.1007/978-3-319-25420-3_3

12. Cohen, P.R.: Dialogue modeling. In: Cole, R., Mariani, J., Uszkoreit, H., Batista-Varile, G., Zaenen, A., Zampolli, A., Zue, V. (eds.) Survey of the State of the Art in Human Language Technology, pp. 234–240. Cambridge University Press, Cambridge (1997)

13. Sadek, D., De Morim, R.: Dialogue systems. In: De Mori, R. (ed.) Spoken Dialogues with Computers. Academic Press, New York (1998)

14. McCurdy, N., Naismith, L., Lajoie, S.P.: . Using metacognitive tools to scaffold medical students developing clinical reasoning skills. Papers from the 2010 AAAI Fall Symposium on Cognitive and Metacognitive Educational Systems, Arlington, Virginia, USA, 11–13 November 2010, vol. FS-1001. AAAI (2010)

15. Traum, D., Larsson, S.: The information state approach to dialogue management. Curr. New Dir. Discourse Dialogue **15**, 325–353 (2003). doi:10.1007/978-94-010-0019-2

16. Searle, J.R.: Speech Acts: An Essay in the Philosophy of Language. Cambridge University Press, Cambridge (1969)

17. Suchman, A.L., Markakis, K., Beckman, H.B., Frankel, R.: A model of empathic communication in the medical interview. JAMA **277**(8), 678–682 (1997)

18. Maguire, P., Pitceathly, C.: Key communication skills and how to acquire them. BMJ (Clinical Research Ed.) **325**(7366), 697–700 (2002). doi:10.1136/bmj.325.7366.697

19. Travaline, J.M., Ruchinskas, R., D'Alonzo, G.E.J.: Patient-physician communication: why and how. J. Am. Osteopath. Assoc. **105**(1), 13–18 (2005)

A Comparison of Methodological Frameworks for Digital Learning Game Design

Alysson Diniz dos Santos[1](✉) and Piero Fraternali[2]

[1] Universidade Federal do Ceara, Instituto Universidade Virtual,
Av. Humberto Monte, s/n, bloco 901, Fortaleza 60440-554, Brazil
`alysson@virtual.ufc.br`
[2] DEIB, Politecnico di Milano, Via Ponzio 34/5, 20133 Milan, Italy
`piero.fraternali@polimi.it`

Abstract. Methodological frameworks guide the design of digital learning game based on well founded learning theories and instructional strategies. This study presents a comparison of five methodological frameworks for digital learning game design, highlighting their similarities and differences. The objective is to support the choice of an adequate framework, aiming to promote them as a way to foster principled digital learning games design. This paper concludes that: *(i)* interactivity, engagement and increasing complexity of challenges are fundamental factors to digital learning game design; *(ii)* the pedagogical base, the target, the possibility of doing game assessment and the presence of practical guidelines are the selection criteria that influence most the choice of a methodological framework, and *(iii)* the development of digital learning games - preferably by different research teams - is needed to provide empirical evidence of the utility of framework-based design.

Keywords: Digital learning · Educational · Games · Game-based learning · Methodological frameworks

1 Introduction

Although digital learning games (DLGs) are well established as a research field [1], strong scientific evidence of the claimed benefits - *e.g.* higher user motivation, better selective attention and improvements on analytical, spatial and psycho-motor skills, among others [2] - is still required to support DLGs design, development and usage [1]. The use of established learning theories and instructional strategies on the design of the DLGs is fundamental to enhance game-based learning [3]. With games grounded on learning theories and instructional strategies, researchers would be able to manipulate key variables and determine which factors have the greatest effect on learner motivation and achievement [3].

Recently, researchers proposed methodological frameworks to guide DLGs design coupling learning theories and instructional strategies with traditional game design aspects [4–8]. This paper presents a further look on these frameworks, analyzing their similarities, highlighting their differences, and investigating to which extent they were tested and used. Such a study may help the

© Springer International Publishing Switzerland 2016
A. De Gloria and R. Veltkamp (Eds.): GALA 2015, LNCS 9599, pp. 111–120, 2016.
DOI: 10.1007/978-3-319-40216-1_12

selection for a framework to base a DLG design, give insights on framework development and application to DLG design and, ultimately, contribute to improving DLGs effectiveness, through the use of adequate design methods. Specifically, the objectives of this work are:

- to identify and illustrate the most prominent frameworks for DLG design;
- to establish a comparison among them, highlighting their similarities and differences and,
- to expose open problems and research opportunities for both framework and DLGs designers.

Previous studies [3,9–11] examined the pedagogical foundations that grounded DLGs design. Nevertheless, none of these cite any methodological framework directly. Ibrahim and Jaafar (2009) [5] discuss four methodological frameworks that influenced the conception of their own model, the Educational Game Design Framework (described in Sect. 6). However, the authors did not establish any comparison among the presented frameworks, using them just to support the proposal of their own approach.

The following Sects. 2, 3, 4, 5 and 6 describe each analyzed methodological framework. Section 7 presents a comparison of the analyzed approaches, Sect. 8 discusses open problems and research directions, and Sect. 9 summarizes the findings of the paper.

2   RETAIN Model

The Relevance Embedding Transfer Adaptation Immersion & Naturalization (RETAIN) model is founded on instructional methods and learning theories that are closely aligned with modern game design principles [7]. The RETAIN model is based on six mains aspects: relevance, embedding, transfer, adaptation, immersion and naturalization.

Relevance addresses three different aspects: *(i)* the learning materials should be relevant to learners, their needs and learning style; *(ii)* the instructional units should be relevant to one another, *i.e.*, instructional units should be introduced and set in context with previously learned materials; and *(iii)* the game has to be relevant to reality, which includes insights on how to use the fantasy, *i.e.* the fiction supported by the narrative, commonly present in games. A related aspect refers to appropriately *embedding* content into the game fantasy. The intent is to integrate the educational content in such a way as to make it intrinsic to the fantasy context of the game. Learning and gameplay should function together seamlessly [7].

Knowledge *transfer* and *adaptation* are tightly related. The first aspect refers to the ability to teach player-learners how to transfer knowledge from one situation to another, and can be achieved through recall stimulation. The second refers to knowledge acquisition and can be achieved through *assimilation* - interpreting events in terms of previous known ones - and *accommodation* - alteration or creation of new knowledge, expanding the player understanding [7].

Immersion is the creation of a belief in the enveloping fantasy of the digital environment. It can be measured hierarchically from a simple interaction/reaction to being fully engaged to the context of the game. Adequate interactivity and a high level of engagement (provided by well-designed games) favor immersion [7].

Naturalization refers to automaticity or spontaneous knowledge, in which a learner uses the learned information habitually and consistently, monitors it, but does not have to devote significant mental resources to think about it. Games that are re-playable, *i.e.* the player enjoys to play repeated times, stimulate naturalization [7].

To simplify the framework use, the authors defined a table that classifies each of the five presented aspects in four levels (from 0 to 3). Each level has its set of requirements for the game to be considered at that level in a specific aspect. In a typical example, a game would be: level 1 in relevance, level 2 in embedding, level 2 in transfer, level 0 in adaptation, level 3 in immersion, and level 2 in naturalization. In addition, the authors classified the importance of each aspect, by the definition of a weighting scale. The table coupled with the weighting scale can be used to orient the development of a DLG and to evaluate the effectiveness of an already-developed one. No game so far declared to use RETAIN in its design.

3   The 'I's Framework

The 'I's framework [8] is based on a constructivist point of view, *i.e.* the players should learn by constructing new knowledge, connecting a new to a prior experience. The framework consists of a hierarchy of six elements, organized from low to high importance: *identity, immersion, interactivity, increasing complexity, informed teaching, instructional.*

Identity refers to the ability of capturing player's attention and tricking him into believing he is a unique individual within the environment - through a selectable avatar, for example. With a strong sense of identity and presence a player later can easily feel immersed and emotionally engaged with the game. *Immersion* is about having a heightened sense of presence in the environment, being engaged with the content and thus intrinsically motivated to succeed in the challenge of the game. The author argues that through high *interactivity*, adequate challenge level, appropriate feedback and user interface a game can harness immersion [8].

Adequate *increasing complexity* enhances the education provided by the game. Game challenges should fit the player increasing ability, aiming at a pleasurable frustration state - in which the player feels stimulated to try harder when facing a defeat. A DLG has to provide good level design and reward system to support adequate increasing complexity. Regarding feedback, *informed teaching* approaches embedded assessments within DLGs. A DLG can use in-game data (server-side data, ID, time, location, patterns of use and interaction, chat-logs and other tools) to run a posteriori analysis on players' proficiency [8].

Being *instructional* is the aim of any DLG. To achieve it, a DLG should present the previous elements - identity, immersion, interactivity, increasing complexity and informed teaching. Furthermore, other aspects can enhance the instructional power of the DLG. It should be adequately integrated to the curriculum, being re-playable and connected to traditional lab activities. The teacher should be responsible for creating scaffold-structuring interactions and developing instruction in small steps, based on tasks the learner is already capable of performing independently.

The author presents a game concept, which exemplify the DLG design process. However, no game so far reported to use the 'I's framework in its design.

4   Game Object Model II

The Game Object Model II (GOM-II) relates pedagogical dimensions of learning with game elements, based on the object oriented conceptual design paradigm [4]. The framework is focused on the development of adventure educational games and is organized around five core concepts: *definition, narrative, gender, social collaboration and challenges-puzzles-quests*:

The *definition* of a DLG refers to its learning potential. A well defined DLG should: *(i)* require the player to learn new strategies and skills and solve evermore complex challenges or puzzles; *(ii)* identify and exploit complex relationships between simulated and real characters, and *(iii)* solve ethical dilemmas [4].

The *narrative* defines the fantasy of the game. A good narrative should allow players to actively construct their own meaning/understanding through the use of plot devices (*e.g.* back story and cut scenes). The *gender* considers the different perspectives between male and female players. In order to be gender-inclusive, the DLG conflict design should include appropriate role models. The *social collaboration* concerns the social practice side of learning. An educational game should harness dialog, altruism, reciprocity, collective action and solidarity to support the development of a community of peers [4]. The *challenges-puzzles-quests* are the core of the learning activities. Well designed challenges generate tacit knowledge through knowledge exposition, conversations and reflection.

GOM-II is an evolution of the GOM framework, successfully used to design the academic adventure game Zadahr [12]. GOM-II was developed based on insights acquired on the design of the educational adventure game γKhozi [4,13]. However, no game so far is reported to use GOM-II in its design.

5   Three Layered Thinking Model

The Three Layered Thinking Model aims at supporting the design of web-based educational games, and stresses the importance of decreasing task complexity to adapt to limited budget environments. The model is structured in three levels, in which the *pedagogic level* (knowledge production) and the *achievement level* (knowledge outcomes) influence the core *design level* [6].

The *pedagogic level* relates to the knowledge production targeted by the DLG. On this level, the designer has to transform curriculum into game goals, considering the previous skills of the player and the desired knowledge enhancement. The *achievement level* relates to the knowledge outcomes of the DLG. A designer needs to conceive a DLG aiming to achieve a higher knowledge production [6].

The *design level* is the core level, aimed to guarantee the requirements of the pedagogic level and to achieve the motivators of the achievement level. It includes designing the style, task and interface of the DLG. The style design of the DLG, *i.e.* the definition of game genre, number of players, camera style, *etc*, should match the game goals (defined on the pedagogic level). The task design of the DLG, *i.e.* the design of levels, challenges and puzzles, should enhance players knowledge and skills through challenge provision. The tasks should consider the player previous skills and the desired knowledge enhancement (defined on pedagogic level) and also provide pleasure and challenge (motivators of achievement level) to the player. The game interface design should help the player keep concentrated in the game (another motivator of the achievement level) [6].

The authors carried out the design and development of three games to empirically test the Three Layered Thinking Model. The games were applied on a group of 120 undergraduate students of a web-based course on introduction to software applications. The authors tested different game styles, tasks and interfaces to achieve different curriculum goals. They conducted surveys to assess the motivation of the games, isolating and weighting the four motivators (skill, challenge, concentration and pleasure). They also used log data to assess the time spent on the game and how frequently the students played the game. Results indicated that the produced games do encourage learners engagement [6].

6   Educational Games Design Framework

The Educational Game Design Framework (EGDF) is focused on producing games for higher education, in which students need to self-learn specific subjects or materials, with integrated self-assessment modules. The model combines three main factors: game design, pedagogy and learning content modeling [5].

In *game design*, the focus is on usability and multi-modality. The DLG design should consider the usability test items of effectiveness, efficiency and satisfaction, based on ISO 9241 [15] and on the heuristics of Pinelle [16]. The multi-modality component uses the multimedia aspect of the game to provide fun and engage. In this aspect, the authors suggest the use of the heuristics of Malone [17] to generate challenge, fantasy, and curiosity in the game.

The *pedagogy* ensures that the DLG meets the learning outcomes. The authors suggest that the DLG subject selection should consider Bloom's taxonomy of learning outcomes [18] and motivation theory [19] to evaluate how the game affects students' motivation. The pedagogy should lead to appropriate *learning content modeling*, providing verifiable learning outcomes, in order to guarantee the achievement of learning goals. No game developed with this framework was found in the literature.

7   Comparison

The above mentioned frameworks aim at establishing patterns and guidelines for effective DLGs design. A comparison among them clarifies the underlying common characteristics and distinct aspects. Such a comparison has a twofold purpose: first it serves as a initial step for a DLG designer interested to adopt a methodological framework, and secondly unveils open problems and opportunities for further research and experimentation.

7.1   The Pedagogical Base

To some extent, all analyzed frameworks cite some learning theory that pedagogically justifies their development. Table 1 relates the frameworks with their pedagogical bases, which are briefly recalled in the rest of this Section.

Table 1. Learning theories used in the frameworks

Framework	Pedagogical base
Retain	Blooms taxonomy of educational objectives [18], Piaget's schemes [22] and Gagne's events of instruction [23]
'I's	Vygotsky zones of proximal development [20] and Piaget's schemes [22]
Game Objective Model - II	Vygotsky zones of proximal development [20]
Three Layered Thinking	Blooms taxonomy of educational objectives [18] and Siang and Rao hierarchical theories of learning [21]
EGDF	Blooms taxonomy of educational objectives [18]

Bloom's taxonomy of educational objectives states that targeted academic content needs to be introduced and reused in a hierarchical manner [18]. This is the most popular pedagogical base, being used in three of the analyzed frameworks (RETAIN, EGDF and Three Layered Thinking). This is due to the close alignment of Bloom's main argument with the digital gaming activity itself. In most games, to advance to the next level, the player is required to learn the rules of gameplay (and thus the associated learning objects) and how to apply them on the present level.

Piaget's schemes relate learning with adaptation, which is composed of assimilation and accommodation. Assimilation is the process of understanding world through existing schemes, whereas accommodation is the process of building new schemes [22]. RETAIN and 'I's frameworks state the importance of adapting the increasing complexity of challenges in a DLG to provide assimilation and accommodation to the player.

Vygotsky zones of proximal development (ZPD) focus on the difference between a child's actual and potential levels of development [20]. ZPD is the pedagogical base of two frameworks (GOM-II and 'I's). A well-designed DLG acts as a mentor, to move players from their actual to their potential development level [4].

The selection of a learning theory depends on what needs to be taught, how it is to be taught, and to whom it is being taught [7]. Therefore, the knowledge about the underlying pedagogical base is important for the designer to choose the methodological framework adequate to his case.

7.2   Interactivity, Engagement and Progression of Challenges

Two other elements are common to all analyzed frameworks - interactivity and engagement; and increasing complexity of challenges.

Interactivity and engagement are fundamental to immerse the player. A fully immersed player intellectually invests in the context of a game - which is ideal for the learning situation [7]. *Interactivity* and *engagement* are fundamental factors to immerse a player. Interactivity should be approached through appropriate feedback and user interface [8], possibly grounded on usability [16] and ergonomic design [5,15]. Engagement should be promoted by adequate narrative [4] and challenges design [6]. The heuristics of Malone [5,17] could be considered to provide higher engagement. Specifically about *immersion*, three frameworks (GOM-II, Three Layered Thinking and 'I's) cite the concept of flow, linking four factors - skill, challenge, concentration and pleasure - to the achievement of the state in which people are so involved in an activity that nothing else seems to matter [14].

Increasing complexity of challenges is fundamental to keep the player immersed. Increasing complexity of challenges is a common feature to all kinds of digital games. In DLGs it is specially important, considering that challenges should promote both pleasure and learning. Adequate challenges increasing complexity should consider player previous skills [6] and previous learned materials [7], aiming at a *pleasurable frustration* state, in which the player feels stimulated to try harder when facing a defeat [8].

7.3   Targets, DLG Design, Assessment and Experimental Validation

Table 2 compares the analyzed frameworks in terms of their target, the presence of practical game design guidelines, the availability of assessment data of DLGs and the frameworks experimental validation.

The analyzed frameworks can be classified according to the *target* as generalists or specialists. The generalist RETAIN and 'I's frameworks can be used to design any kind of DLG to any target audience. On the other hand, the specialist frameworks focus on a platform (web-based games in three layered thinking framework), a target audience (higher education students in Educational Game Design Framework) or a game genre (adventure games in GOM II). Specialist frameworks offer specific guidelines to their target (*i.e.* platform, target audience or game genre). Regarding *practical guidelines* to support the DLG design, EGDF suggests the utilization of heuristics [16,17] to provide usability and to

Table 2. Frameworks comparison table

Framework	Target	Practical guidelines to game design	DLG assessment	Experimental validation
RETAIN	Generalist	No	Yes	N/A
'I's	Generalist	No	No	N/A (game concept presented)
Game Objective Model - II	Specialist (adventure games)	No	Yes	N/A
Three Layered Thinking	Specialist (web-based games)	No	No	Empirically tested - 3 developed games
Educational Game Design Framework	Specialist (higher education students)	Yes	No	N/A

engage the player. The other four frameworks are limited to high-level methodological guidelines and do not provide procedural guidance to structure the development process of a DLG. It is also possible to use two frameworks, RETAIN and GOM-II, to *assess* already developed DLGs. The first uses a score from 0 to 63, in which the higher the score, the better the designed DLG, while the second proposes the use of a checklist to control the presence of all the necessary criteria established by the framework. Finally, about *experimental validation*, only the Three Layered Thinking framework was validated in a field study. The DLGs were developed for the same team that created the framework, and evaluated with a group of undergraduate students. The 'I's framework presents a game concept, developed according the framework guidelines. However, no study was found detailing the actual implementation. All the other frameworks consider the experimental validation as a future work [4,5,7,8].

8   Open Problems and Prominent Research Issues

The methodological frameworks are still lacking a thorough and independent assessment. Although based on previous research and strong instructional theories, few DLGs were designed and no updates for the frameworks were encountered in recent years - the most recent is the 'I's framework from 2010. Moreover, all the developed DLGs were published by the same research teams that developed the frameworks, what indicates the nonexistence of an active community of users. Although GOM-II and Three Layered Thinking are more mature in relation to the other frameworks, no game was actually designed with GOM-II and the empirical testing of Three Layered Thinking was carried out by the same research team that proposed the framework. To overcome this issue, further research should focus on **the design of framework-based DLGs**. Only through empiric use, the frameworks would be adequately assessed (and possibly updated) and a community of users can appear.

Another issue is the absence of information about *how the frameworks principles can be applied to game design in practice*. Framework-based designed DLGs would also help to solve this issue and would permit further investigations, for example: (i) how to map learning goals to game goals; and (ii) how to test the effectiveness of design practices suggested by the frameworks. In addition, with diverse framework-based designed DLGs, it would possible to establish comparisons among them, investigating, for example, how the guidelines on generalist frameworks correlate with different game mechanics. Finally, the DLGs should preferably be **designed by different research teams** from the ones that developed the framework. This would testify about the real applicability of the frameworks, meanwhile a bigger community of users is more likely to bring useful insights for frameworks updates.

9   Conclusions

The comparison *(i)* indicates that interactivity, engagement and increasing complexity of challenges are fundamental factors to DLGs design; and *(ii)* establishes pedagogical base, target, presence of practical guidelines and possibility of game assessment as selecting criteria to guide the choice for a framework. This paper detected two main research issues: *(i)* the lack of independent assessment, and *(ii)* the uncertainty about how the principles can be applied to game design in practice. Both issues should be approached through design and development - preferably by different research teams - of framework-based DLGs. This would provide important empirical data to the field, validating the frameworks, stimulating their popularization, and enabling further scientific investigation.

References

1. Connolly, T.M., Boyle, E.A., MacArthur, E., Hainey, T., Boyle, J.M.: A systematic literature review of empirical evidence on computer games and serious games. Comput. Educ. **59**(2), 661–686 (2012)
2. Susi, T., Johannesson, M., Backlund, P.: Serious games: an overview (2007)
3. Kebritchi, M.: Examining the pedagogical foundations of modern educational computer games. Comput. Educ. **51**(4), 1729–1743 (2008)
4. Amory, A.: Game object model version II: a theoretical framework for educational game development. Educ. Technol. Res. Dev. **55**(1), 51–77 (2007)
5. Ibrahim, R., Jaafar, A.: Educational Games (EG) design framework: combination of game design, pedagogy and content modeling. In: International Conference on Electrical Engineering and Informatics, 2009, ICEEI 2009, vol. 1, pp. 293–298. IEEE (2009)
6. Fu, F.-L., Yu, S.-C.: Three layered thinking model for designing web-based educational games. In: Li, F., Zhao, J., Shih, T.K., Lau, R., Li, Q., McLeod, D. (eds.) ICWL 2008. LNCS, vol. 5145, pp. 265–274. Springer, Heidelberg (2008)
7. Gunter, G.A., Kenny, R.F., Vick, E.H.: Taking educational games seriously: using the retain model to design endogenous fantasy into standalone educational games. Educ. Tech. Res.Dev. **56**(5–6), 511–537 (2008)
8. Annetta, L.A.: The "I's" have it: a framework for serious educational game design. Rev. Gen. Psychol. **14**(2), 105 (2010)
9. Catalano, C.E., Luccini, A.M., Mortara, M.: Guidelines for an effective design of serious games. Int. J. Serious Games **1**(1) (2014)
10. de Gloria, A., Bellotti, F., Berta, R.: Serious games for education and training. Int. J. Serious Games **1**(1) (2014)

11. Dondlinger, M.J.: Educational video game design: a review of the literature. J. Appl. Educ. Technol. **4**(1), 21–31 (2007)
12. Amory, A.: Building an educational adventure game: theory, design, and lessons. J. Interact. Learn. Res. **12**(2), 249–263 (2001)
13. Amory, A.: Learning to play games or playing games to learn? A health education case study with Soweto teenagers. Australas. J. Educ. Technol. **26**(6), 810–829 (2010)
14. Csikszentmihalyi, M., Csikzentmihaly, M.: Flow: The Psychology of Optimal Experience, vol. 41. Harperperennial, New York (1991)
15. Standard, I.: Ergonomic requirements for office work with visual display terminals (VDTs) part 11: Guidance on usability. ISO Standard 9241–11: 1998. International Organization for Standardization (1998)
16. Pinelle, D., Wong, N., Stach, T.: Heuristic evaluation for games: usability principles for video game design. In: Proceedings of the SIGCHI Conference on Human Factors in Computing Systems, pp. 1453–1462. ACM (2008)
17. Malone, T.W.: What makes things fun to learn? Heuristics for designing instructional computer games. In: Proceedings of the 3rd ACM SIGSMALL Symposium and the First SIGPC Symposium on Small Systems, pp. 162–169. ACM (1980)
18. Bloom, B.S.: Taxonomy of Educational Objectives: The Classification of Education Goals by a Committee of College and University Examiners. David McKay, New York (1956)
19. Kanfer, R.: Motivation theory and industrial and organizational psychology. In: Dunnette, M.D., Hough, L.M. (eds.) Handbook of Industrial and Organizational Psychology, vol. 1, 2nd edn, pp. 75–130. Consulting Psychologists Press, Palo Alto. CA (1990)
20. Vygotsky, L.S.: Mind in Society: The Development of Higher Mental Process. Harvard University Press, Cambridge (1978)
21. Siang, A.C., Rao, R.K.: Theories of learning: a computer game perspective. In: Proceedings of the Fifth International Symposium on Multimedia Software Engineering, 2003, pp. 239–245. IEEE (2003)
22. Piaget, J.: The Origins of Intelligence in Children, vol. 8, 5th edn. International Universities Press, New York (1952)
23. Gagne, R.M.: Instructional Technology: Foundations. Routledge, New York (2013)

Immersive Technologies and Natural Interaction to Improve Serious Games Engagement

Raffaello Brondi[1], Giovanni Avveduto[1(✉)], Marcello Carrozzino[1],
Franco Tecchia[1], Leila Alem[2], and Massimo Bergamasco[1]

[1] PERCRO Laboratory, Scuola Superiore Sant'Anna, Pisa, Italy
{r.brondi,g.avveduto}@sssup.it
[2] Games Studio, University of Technology, Sydney, Australia

Abstract. Newly available technologies and natural interaction in video games are reshaping the role of immersion and interaction on game enjoyment. The current work aims at assessing a highly immersive setup exploiting natural user interaction, combining Head Mounted Display and a depth camera, with the objective of evaluating its use as a platform for Serious Games through a series of experiments whose results are presented and discussed. Initial findings suggest that the introduced technological setup offers high level of engagement and facilitate the achievement of the flow state.

Keywords: Natural User Interfaces · Player engagement · Mixed reality · Flow · Serious Game · Virtual Reality

1 Introduction

Enjoyment is an important aspect of the game experience, as it is one of the factors mostly contributing in motivating users to play. Newly available technologies are reshaping the way we experience video games and in particular immersion and social interaction. Players can customize their experience, choosing the most familiar and effective forms of communication by using the new interaction technologies. The spreading of devices interfacing users with computers by using the innate human means of communication (e.g. voice and gestures), has empowered paradigms of natural interaction, namely Natural User Interfaces (NUIs), which relevantly impact both on communication and immersion. Moreover, the availability of cheap highly immersive visualization systems, such as low-cost head mounted displays (HMDs), is bridging the gap between video games and immersive Virtual Reality applications. Spatial presence and flow are considered key concepts [16] to explain how such immersive experiences commonly lead to better performance and enjoyment. The role of flow in gaming, and in particular in Serious Gaming (SG) [1], has been increasingly recognized as one of the most important factors contributing to a pleasant and effective user experience. Moreover, immersive VR is able to foster acquiring knowledge in a non-symbolic

© Springer International Publishing Switzerland 2016
A. De Gloria and R. Veltkamp (Eds.): GALA 2015, LNCS 9599, pp. 121–130, 2016.
DOI: 10.1007/978-3-319-40216-1_13

world very similar to the real one, thus increasing information retention [10] which is typically one of the most important learning goals of SGs [9].

This paper aims at assessing a shared immersive system, featuring natural interaction, with the objective of evaluating its use as a platform for SGs. After presenting the relevant literature related to the use of NUIs in Serious Games, the paper introduces the adopted technological setup and the experiments designed for its assessment. Results are finally presented and discussed.

2   Literature Review

The recent availability of low-cost devices able to acquire physical properties of users (body gestures, speech, etc.) has made possible the design and developments of NUIs, i.e. transparent interfaces allowing users to execute complex interactions. This is particularly true in games and in Virtual Reality, in which the operation to be performed are commonly simulations of corresponding real tasks. NUIs give users the opportunity of performing such tasks exactly the same way they would do in real life.

The use of NUIs in mainstream video games have been recently strongly fostered by the appearance of devices (such as the Nintendo WiiMote or the Microsoft Kinect) allowing tracking users' motion and, therefore, enabling intuitive interaction paradigms. The same has happened in the field of Serious Games, where the use of NUIs has been proven to increase the appeal and intuitiveness of SGs for rehabilitation [11] and for exercises in the elderly [4]. The real-time detection and analysis of body motion provides feedbacks able to engage users in achieving better results [12]. In training, NUIs make it possible to develop SGs that educate how to properly follow procedures and also how to physically behave to perform the required operations by accurately monitoring body position and posture [17]. The same applies in every sector of learning where physical actions are relevant.

Brondi et al. [3] have shown how setups combining immersive display with a NUI lead to a substantial increase in enjoyment with respect to standard desktop setups in Collaborative VEs. While performances seem not to fully benefit from such platforms, although a careful and dedicated interface design could overcome this issue. Sajjadi et al. [13] investigated whether the choice of interaction mode/controller has an impact on the game experience testing a collaborative game using an Oculus Rift. They observed that almost all participants using the HMD looked for alternative ways of communication trying to use gestures to interact with the partner even if not enabled by the technological setup. Lindley et al. [8] focus on the impact of the new interfaces involving body movements on player engagement and social behaviour claiming that the amount of social interaction is higher when using input devices which allow body movements.

3   Method

In the following, the technological setup and the interaction metaphors under evaluation are first introduced, then two experiments aimed at evaluating the system are presented. The first one has aimed at evaluating system usability, awareness and embodiment using a qualitative analysis through questionnaires. The last experiment has aimed at comparing the natural versus the classical (using Keyboard and Mouse) interactions in a playful context. In the latter experiment user engagement, social presence, performances, satisfaction and awareness have been compared using questionnaire results.

3.1   Technological Setup and Interaction Metaphors

In order to provide a high immersion to the user and to enable a natural interaction with the VE, a setup including HMD displays and depth cameras has been used [14,15].

The two experiments have been conducted using two different versions of the system. The first prototype uses an Oculus Rift DK1 and an Optitrack tracking setup made up of 8 cameras. Subsequently, the system has been upgraded using the Oculus DK2 and exploiting the included positional tracker.

The HMD connected to the workstation provides visual feedback. A depth camera mounted on top of the helmet, and integral to it, is used both for the real-time 3D capture of the user body and for fingers tracking. The reconstructed 3D mesh of the body is coherently co-located in the virtual environment. The user is able to naturally interact with the VE by grabbing and moving virtual objects in his/her peripersonal space.

In the first version, three reflective markers placed on the HMD enable Optitrack positional-rotational tracking. The orientation data coming from the inertial unit built-in the Oculus are fused with the data coming from the optical tracker. The Optitrack system allows to track a wider space than the DK2's positional tracking module used in the second version.

We will refer to this setup as "OU" from here on.

3.2   First Experiment

A pilot test has been performed in order to evaluate the first prototype and the implemented NUI, by observing how the users interacted with the system and how they felt while navigating the virtual environment and manipulating objects using their own bodies.

The experiment has consisted in a single-player immersive game, where participants have had to perform an assembly task as quickly as possible. Each user wearing the system has been free to walk in a 4 × 4 m virtual room partitioned by walls. Six objects acting as landmarks have been placed in the room: a table, a refrigerator, a sofa, a painting, a chair and a TV Set. Eighteen floating coloured toy boxes have been spread across the room. The painting depicting a specified layout of seventeen boxes has been placed on a wall. The aim of the task has been to recreate the layout by grabbing the floating boxes and placing them on the table.

Participants. A total of 14 volunteers took part to the study, 7 male and 7 female, aged between 24 and 57 years (32.71±9.12). Before the experiment they have filled the informed consent to participate in the experiment and an entry questionnaire to collect demographic and background informations. Previous experiences with 3D gameplay (1.86 ± 1.1) and HMD (2.28 ± 1.32) have been assessed on a 5-point Likert Scale from 1 to 5.

Procedure. First the users have played an entry session to get familiar with the system and the NUI. The average duration of this stage has been 158.3 ± 52.7 s. Players were free to decide when to stop. Once the familiarization session has ended, the assembly task has started.

The toy blocks have been spread across the room. They have been arranged in three groups close to the landmarks in order to force navigating the whole environment and making landmarks noticeable. The room and furniture arrangement has been designed to enforce obstacle avoidance in order to test navigation ability and spatial awareness.

Metrics. Upon completion of the assembly task, participants have been asked to complete a questionnaire aimed at collecting subjective measures about awareness, embodiment and ease of interaction. Measurements have been assessed on a 5-point Likert scale from 1 to 5. Furthermore they have been asked to produce a sketch map of the VE on which they had to locate the landmarks. Similarly to Huang and Alem [5], a quantitative assessment of the mental representation of the virtual space has been evaluated using a score ranging from 0 to 6. The two experimenters have assigned a score to the sketches based on the number of remembered landmarks. The map evaluation for each user has been given by averaging the independent estimations done by experimenters.

Task completion time and user's position over the time have been recorded.

3.3   Second Experiment

The experiment has aimed at comparing the OU system with a traditional Keyboard & Mouse gaming interface (referred as "KM") as interaction devices. The study has focused on the impact of the different technological setups and interaction metaphors on user engagement, social presence, awareness and performances.

The experiment has adopted a within-subjects design and has been based on a collaborative multi-player jigsaw puzzle game purposely developed. Players have had to work together in order to solve the puzzle before the time (7 min) expires. Two players physically located in different rooms have played the collaborative game sharing the same VE using two identical networked setups. The actions performed by each player have been immediately visible to the partner. During KM sessions the mouse pointer of the partner has been visible to the player. During OU sessions the RGBD captures of the two players bodies have been streamed between the two setups. A proxy for each player, made by a textured mesh reconstructed from the RGBD data and a virtual head replicating the user movements, has been shown in the VE. The participants have been able to communicate both verbally — through headsets — and using their bodies (e.g. using gestures).

Participants. A total of 24 subjects, 15 males and 9 females healthy subjects, aged between 23 and 50 (32.04 ± 6.84) took part to the experiment. Each of them filled an entry questionnaire, based on a 5 points Likert Scale from 1 to 5, to collect demographic and background information: experience with the use of computers (average 3.88 ± 0.85), videogames (average 3.12 ± 1.33), immersive virtual displays (average 2.54 ± 1.21), puzzle games (average 3.04 ± 1.2) and online puzzle games (average 1.83 ± 1.05).

Procedure. During the recruitment, participants have been asked to play a single player version of the puzzle game using the KM setup. The pre-experiment has aimed at assessing the skills of each participant in solving a puzzle in order to form twelve pairs with similar dexterities.

The players have been hence divided on the two identical networked setups. The subjects, spatially not co-located, were able to communicate by using only the communication channels provided by the setup. Before starting the experimental sessions, each user has performed a 5 min trial session to get familiar with the OU setup playing a simplified single player version of the puzzle game.

Each pair have therefore played two game sessions, one for each interaction metaphor. The order in which the two game sessions have been presented to different dyads has been randomized.

Metrics. At the end of each game session, players have answered a subset of the Game Engagement Questionnaire (GEQ) [2] (competence, flow, tension-annoyance, challenge, negative and positive affect), a subset of the Social Presence in Gaming Questionnaire (SPGQ) [7] (empathy and behavioural involvement), awareness and satisfaction questions. An exit questionnaire has been presented to both players in order to collect their preferences and motivations, friend relationship, general impressions and suggestions. Finally an informal debriefing session between the experimenters and both players has been conducted to further register impressions and anecdotes.

Objective measurements recorded have included: (1) completion time and score, (2) frame-rate and network latency, (3) outcome and tiles positions, (4) positions and headings of player head. Experimenters attended all the sessions taking notes of noteworthy events.

4   Results

The outcomes of the first experiment have been analysed in order to assess the liking of the OU system when navigating in a VE and accomplishing a simple task. The Mean and Standard Error of the Mean (SEM) are reported for the questionnaire's answers. Results of the second experiment have been used to compare the different technological setups and interaction metaphors. A Wilcoxon signed-rank test has been used to statistically compare questionnaires results and performances for the two conditions as the distribution of the data was not Gaussian.

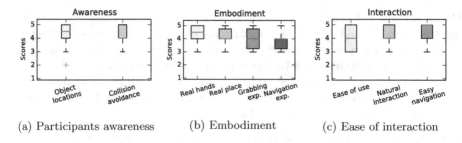

(a) Participants awareness   (b) Embodiment   (c) Ease of interaction

Fig. 1. Results of the first experiment

4.1   System and NUI Assessments

During the first experiment the developed interface has been tested in order to obtain a first indication of the levels of embodiment and awareness reachable. Furthermore the overall complexity of the interface using a basic interaction with the VE — pick and drag — has been also evaluated. The average time needed by the participants to accomplish the assembly session has been 455.35 ± 113.04 s.

Awareness. Figure 1a reports the level of spatial awareness (4.21 ± 0.26) and self awareness (4.28 ± 0.19) reached during the experiment. The 78.57 % of the participants have been able to correctly estimate the size of the VE. The subjects have been able to remember almost all the landmarks encountered (4.71 ± 0.91).

Embodiment. As shown in Fig. 1b, the subjects have had a strong feeling of embodiment. They have perceived the virtual proxy as a real representation of themselves (4.43 ± 0.17) and they have been convinced to be in a real physical place (4.14 ± 0.18). Furthermore the participants have strongly perceived both the interaction with the virtual objects (4.0 ± 0.21) and the navigation in the VE (3.86 ± 0.18) as a real physical tasks.

Interaction. As reported in Fig. 1c, participants have found the interaction with the virtual objects easy (4.0 ± 0.23) and natural (4.28 ± 0.19). They have also found easy to navigate the VE (4.57 ± 0.17).

4.2   Systems and Interactions Comparisons

During the second experiment, the classic KM system has been compared with the OU in order to evaluate their impact on performances, game engagement, social presence, awareness and satisfaction.

Performances. Figure 2a shows participants' performances during the first and the second half of the game for each session. Results report a significant increment $(W(23) = 45.0, p = 0.025)$ in the number of correctly positioned tiles in the KM session during the second half of the game.

Only 41.7 % of the pairs have won the OU game session while the 75 % have completed the puzzle in the KM session. As reported in Fig. 2b, players have

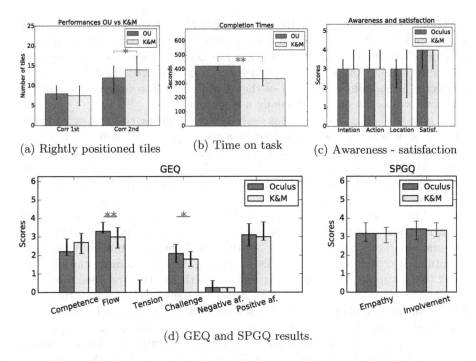

(a) Rightly positioned tiles   (b) Time on task   (c) Awareness - satisfaction

(d) GEQ and SPGQ results.

Fig. 2. Results of the second experiment (*$p \leq 0.05$; **$p \leq 0.01$). Bars reports 25th and 75th percentiles. (Color figure online)

completed the puzzle significantly faster ($W(23) = 21.0, p = 0.0002$) during KM sessions.

GEQ. The results of GEQ questionnaire indicate an overall positive evaluation of both setups (see Fig. 2d). Players have reported a higher level of flow ($W(23) = 35.0, p = 0.009$) as well as challenge ($W(23) = 22.5, p = 0.0105$) during OU sessions.

SPGQ. Participants have high-rated both social components, Empathy and Behavioural Involvement. No relevant differences have been found (see Fig. 2d).

Awareness and Satisfaction. As reported in Fig. 2c, players have had a good awareness of the other's actions, locations and intentions in both setups.

All the participants have rated both experiences as very satisfying. When asking *"Which kind of user interface do you prefer?"*, 16 players (66.7 %) have answered the natural one.

5   Discussion

Almost all the players have enjoyed the proposed immersive system. Participants have highly rated usability and immediacy of the NUI during the first experiment. The majority of the subjects (66.7 %) of the second experiment have found the NUI preferable to the classic KM interface even if it resulted to be more challenging. The OU experience has been perceived as more engaging and entertaining. Almost all the participants who preferred the KM metaphor appreciated the lower complexity of the interface, which resulted more familiar and comfortable for people who daily use computers.

A high level of embodiment has been registered during the first experiment. Players have believed to be involved in a real experience thanks to the high immersion and sense of presence induced by the system. Allowing users to manipulate virtual objects using their own hands and to navigate in the virtual system using their own body has greatly improved their embodiment. Participants during OU session have perceived their own proxy and the partner's one more as a physical presence rather than virtual. Experimenters have indeed observed that when navigating in the VE the subjects have tended to avoid collisions with physical objects — like walls — as they do in real life. Only three of them have intentionally crossed the virtual walls — breaking the embodiment illusion — in order to accomplish the task more quickly. Nonetheless the first time they have tried to cross the virtual wall they have been extremely careful because they have felt like hitting a real one. During the second experiment, several collisions have happened between the proxies of the participants. The absence of any physical feedbacks when passing through the partner's representation has been perceived by some players odd and sometimes a bit annoying, while cheerful by others.

Both games have been designed in order to stimulate participant's movement. In both experiments the subjects have reported high levels of awareness. During all the time they have been conscious of what was happening and how to reach their goal. During the second experiment high levels of awareness have been registered for both the modalities. The essential KM interface has resulted to be more functional to the task but, as observed by the experimenters and highlighted in the open questions, less fun and more impersonal.

Flow experience is one of the key factor to make a game engaging. The mental state reached in this condition makes the players completely engrossed in the game. During the second experiment, even if players have reported a high level of flow in both setups, the psychological absorption has been significantly greater in the OU session than in KM (see Fig. 2d). The subjects have felt completely disconnected from the real world. As a consequence of the deep absorption, the break between the virtual and the real world has been described by participants as considerably sharper during the OU sessions in both the experiments, as also reported in [6].

In the GEQ results of the second experiment, the OU system has been rated more challenging than the KM. However only one player has found the OU metaphor not enjoyable and too complex to be used. The majority of players (75 %) have considered the KM metaphor more immediate and faster. Nonetheless, most participants (71 %) during the final debriefing have asserted to appreciate more the OU metaphor (*"I felt like I was really playing with him a real puzzle!"*).

6   Conclusion

The developed system has proven to be an interesting alternative to the classic desktop interface. The NUI have beaten the classic keyboard & mouse setup in terms of flow reached during the game. The deep immersion provided by the system has led to a greater absorption in the game. A natural interaction with the environment allows users to act and communicate like they do in real-life. Games can be played without the mediation of any interface and interacting with the VE using the own body. This turns out to be extremely important to improve embodiment, engagement and awareness in the subject: *"It was like playing a real puzzle"*. The adoption of a photo-realistic representation of user's body in a coherently rendered virtual scenario has induced a strong feeling of embodiment without the need of a virtual avatar as a proxy. The user's ability to grasp and manipulate virtual objects using their own hands has not only provided an intuitive user interaction experience, but it has also improved user engagement.

Even if the natural interaction has been described as more intriguing and enjoying, it has resulted to be also more challenging; better performances have been achieved using the classic Keyboard & Mouse setup. Nonetheless, in the second experiment during KM sessions, experimenters have observed that many players have tried to use body language and gestures to interact with each other, even if these forms of communication were not enabled, as similarly reported in [13]. Hence providing a natural interaction seems to be important during social activities but further investigations have to be carried out to ease the NUI and filling the performance gap.

Given these results, allowing users to manipulate virtual objects with their own physical hands and to navigate the virtual space using their physical body has the potential to not only improve users interaction but also spatial understanding and self perception. Considering these characteristics, we believe that this system can be proficiently used for designing effective Serious Games.

References

1. Arnab, S.: Gala report on flow for serious games, August 2014. http:// seriousgamessociety.org/index.php/2014-07-11-14-15-51/explore/134-media/796- gala-report-on-flow-for-serious-games
2. Brockmyer, J.H., Fox, C.M., Curtiss, K.A., McBroom, E., Burkhart, K.M., Pidruzny, J.N.: The development of the game engagement questionnaire: a measure of engagement in video game-playing. J. Exp. Soc. Psychol. **45**(4), 624–634 (2009)
3. Brondi, R., Alem, L., Avveduto, G., Faita, C., Carrozzino, M., Tecchia, F., Bergamasco, M.: Evaluating the impact of highly immersive technologies and natural interaction on player engagement andow experience ingames. In: Chorianopoulos, K., Divitini, M., Hauge, J.B., Jaccheri, L., Malaka, R. (eds.) ICEC 2015. LNCS, vol. 9353, pp. 169–181. Springer, Cham (2015)
4. Cornejo, R., Hernández, D., Favela, J., Tentori, M., Ochoa, S.: Persuading older adults to socialize and exercise through ambient games. In: 2012 6th International Conference on Pervasive Computing Technologies for Healthcare (PervasiveHealth), pp. 215–218. IEEE (2012)

5. Huang, W., Alem, L.: A usability and spatial awareness study of near-eye displays. In: 2012 IEEE International Conference on Systems, Man, and Cybernetics (SMC), pp. 906–911. IEEE (2012)

6. Jennett, C., Cox, A.L., Cairns, P., Dhoparee, S., Epps, A., Tijs, T., Walton, A.: Measuring and defining the experience of immersion in games. Int. J. Hum. Comput. Stud. **66**(9), 641–661 (2008)

7. de Kort, Y.A., IJsselsteijn, W.A., Poels, K.: Digital games as social presence technology: development of the social presence in gaming questionnaire (SPGQ). In: Proceedings of PRESENCE, pp. 195–203 (2007)

8. Lindley, S.E., Le Couteur, J., Berthouze, N.L.: Stirring up experience through movement in game play: effects on engagement and social behaviour. In: Proceedings of the SIGCHI Conference on Human Factors in Computing Systems, pp. 511–514. ACM (2008)

9. Mitchell, A., Savill-Smith, C.: The use of computer and video games for learning: a review of the literature (2004)

10. Morrison, J.E., Fletcher, J.D.: Cognitive readiness. Technical report, DTIC Document (2002)

11. Rego, P.A., Moreira, P.M., Reis, L.P.: Natural user interfaces in serious games for rehabilitation. In: 2011 6th Iberian Conference on Information Systems and Technologies (CISTI), pp. 1–4. IEEE (2011)

12. Saini, S., Rambli, D.R.A., Sulaiman, S., Zakaria, M.N., Shukri, S.R.M.: A low-cost game framework for a home-based stroke rehabilitation system. In: 2012 International Conference on Computer and Information Science (ICCIS), vol. 1, pp. 55–60. IEEE (2012)

13. Sajjadi, P., Cebolledo Gutierrez, E.O., Trullemans, S., De Troyer, O.: Maze commander: a collaborative asynchronous game using the oculus rift & the sifteo cubes. In: Proceedings of the First ACM SIGCHI Annual Symposium on Computer-Human Interaction in Play, pp. 227–236. ACM (2014)

14. Tecchia, F., Avveduto, G., Brondi, R., Carrozzino, M., Bergamasco, M., Alem, L.: I'm in VR! using your own hands in a fully immersive MR system. In: Proceedings of the 20th ACM Symposium on Virtual Reality Software and Technology, pp. 73–76. ACM (2014)

15. Tecchia, F., Avveduto, G., Carrozzino, M., Brondi, R., Bergamasco, M., Alem, L.: [Poster] Interacting with your own hands in a fully immersive MR system. In: 2014 IEEE International Symposium on Mixed and Augmented Reality (ISMAR), pp. 313–314. IEEE (2014)

16. Weibel, D., Wissmath, B.: Immersion in computer games: the role of spatial presence and flow. Int. J. Comput. Games Technol. **2011**, 6 (2011)

17. Williams-Bell, F., Kapralos, B., Hogue, A., Murphy, B., Weckman, E.: Using serious games and virtual simulation for training in the fire service: a review. Fire Technol. **51**(3), 553–584 (2014)

Voluntary Play in Serious Games

Esther Kuindersma[1(✉)], Jelke van der Pal[1], Jaap van den Herik[2], and Aske Plaat[2]

[1] Netherlands Aerospace Centre (NLR), Amsterdam, The Netherlands
Esther.Kuindersma@NLR.nl
[2] Leiden Institute of Advanced Computer Science, Leiden University, Leiden, The Netherlands

Abstract. Voluntariness is an important feature of games. Serious game designers intend to generate engaging gameplay, which implies that voluntary play should be equally important for serious games as for entertainment games. This paper describes the outcome of a study on the impact of voluntariness on learning in a serious game. The results of 19 participants, randomly assigned to voluntary and mandatory gameplay, are analyzed to identify possible differences. The findings of this study suggest that, contrary to the opinion of many game designers, being required to play a serious game does not necessarily take the fun out of the game.

Keywords: Serious games · Effectiveness · Learning effect · Freedom of choice

1 Introduction

Serious games are "games that do not have entertainment, enjoyment or fun as their primary purpose" [1]. Over the last two decades they have become a substantial research topic in the educational field [2]. Especially the effectiveness of serious games has been much researched. These studies mainly focused on comparing the effects of serious gaming to those of traditional learning methods [3]. However, traditional learning methods are usually mandatory in nature, whereas serious gaming may have be expected to have a more voluntary character offering a student freedom of choice. Psychological studies have revealed positive effects of freedom of choice on motivation and participation [4, 5], making it plausible that it will also have a positive impact on the learning effect. Yet, to the best of our knowledge, no studies have taken into account the possible impact of freedom of choice within serious gaming (i.e., voluntary versus mandatory gameplay) on the effectiveness of the games.

The purpose of this study is to determine whether, and to what extent, gameplay (duration and score) and learning effect (test scores) of a serious game are affected by students' freedom of choice to play this game.

2 Background of the Study

Games have been used in training for centuries [6]. Although the term 'serious game' had been used in different contexts before [7], Abt [8] introduced the term in relation to instruction. In his view, the instructional aspect did not have to be incorporated into the

© Springer International Publishing Switzerland 2016
A. De Gloria and R. Veltkamp (Eds.): GALA 2015, LNCS 9599, pp. 131–140, 2016.
DOI: 10.1007/978-3-319-40216-1_14

game itself, but could also be part of the context. In 2002 the term moved toward digital games [9]. Nowadays, serious games are defined as (digital) games with a main purpose other than entertainment, enjoyment or fun [1]. When the main purpose is educational, serious games are also known as instructional games or game based learning.

At the basis of the definition of serious games lies the definition of games in general. Salen and Zimmerman [10] define games as "systems in which players engage in an artificial conflict, defined by rules that result in a quantifiable outcome", and McGonigal [11] defines them as "activities with a goal, rules, a feedback system, and voluntary participation". Other scholars on game and play also include "voluntary" or "free" in their definitions of games [1, 12–15]. While there is not a particular definition of games that is universally accepted, game designers have reached considerable consensus about the main principles of games, although a game does not necessarily need to satisfy all principles. Games often have rules, goals, a storyline, and outcomes; they offer inter-action, feedback, and competition. Furthermore, and critically important: they are played voluntarily and they are fun, or as they can be frustrating at times – at least they are 'immersive' or 'engaging'. A game should deeply absorb the player.

Most definitions of serious games originate directly from game definitions. Especially on account of the fun characteristic of games the term "serious games" appears to be an oxymoron. If games are fun by definition, they cannot be serious at the same time [16]. Also, games are non-productive and separate from the real world [12], whereas serious games have specific learning objectives related to life or work skills [14]. Callois [13] has even stated that it ceases to be play when this play of a game is forced. Thus, games should be played voluntarily. Yet serious games are meant to be instructional and instruction is typically non-voluntary [14]. This paradox may have an impact on player attitude and as such on the learning effect of the serious game. Players may have a more positive attitude when they are allowed the freedom to choose to play a serious game. In contrast, Huizinga [12] also stated that play is a serious activity, and that fun and serious do not necessarily exclude one another.

Offering learners a choice in their assignments empowers them to take control, which provides them ownership of the learning process and motivates them to be engaged. This increases interest and, with that, it increases time spent on the chosen assignment [17]. The freedom to choose what, when, and how to contribute in the learning process can motivate learners to actively participate and accomplish more [18]. These factors have also been identified as having a positive impact on the effectiveness of serious games.

In a study of forced play, Heeter et al. [4] found that non-gamers, with little or no experience with digital games, are likely to be at a disadvantage in serious gaming, as obtaining the intended effect of a serious game depends on how well the game is played. The negative affect that non-gamers experience in a game are expected to interfere with learning or with the cognitive benefits. Their study also showed that resistant players have less attention for the game they have to play and that they experience less positive and more negative feelings about that game. They would not play the game if they did not have to. Heeter et al. concluded that serious games are least effective for players who dislike a game and most effective for those who like it.

Closely related to freedom of choice is the topic of consent. Mollick and Rothbard [5] examined the role of consent as a psychological response to "mandatory fun" in gamification in the work environment. They found that games which employees consented to significantly increased their positive affect, while resistance resulted in a decrease in positive affect and a marginal decrease in performance. They also identified two sources of consent. Employees who play games outside of work were more likely to consent to them in other settings, and individuals who were allowed to choose which game to play showed higher levels of consent and perceived control. The latter may coincide with the freedom to choose to play a serious game or not, leading us to expect that playing a serious game voluntarily will increase positive affect and possibly performance.

Based on the motivating aspect of choice and the original definition of games we expect that voluntariness or freedom of choice will have a positive impact on the learning effect of serious games.

3   Experiment

The purpose of our experiment is to determine whether using the game voluntarily as a learning tool will result in improved player performance as opposed to mandatory gameplay. The experiment consists of a short training and a test of knowledge and application questions. The independent variables in this research are each participant's gender, age, and interest in gaming. The dependent variables are game score, test score, and time spent playing the game. In this section the recruitment of participants and the experimental design will be discussed, followed by the procedure and the materials.

3.1   Participants and Design

Participants have been recruited through various social media and by personal invitation. They were told the experiment related to aviation, but the focus on gaming was not disclosed. Only persons over the age of 18 were selected to participate. They were asked to give their informed consent before being registered. As an incentive participants were offered a chance to win a € 100 gift certificate. Chances of winning are related to completing all stages of the experiment, not to personal results.

A total of 64 persons registered for the experiment and completed an online survey with demographic information and levels of motivation and prior knowledge. They were randomly assigned to one of two groups, resulting in a voluntary gameplay group of 29 participants and a mandatory gameplay group of 35 participants. The participants will be referred to as 'voluntary players' and 'mandatory players' respectively. In the experiment voluntary players will be free to decide if and how long they want to play the game, while mandatory players will be required to play the game for at least ten minutes. Twenty participants completed the training and its test. Post-experiment surveys show that many participants did not finish their participation due to other priorities. There were 9 completes from mandatory players and 11 from voluntary players. One complete in the voluntary group was disqualified, because the participant indicated to accidentally have finished the test without playing the game. The experiment was completed in a valid way by 10 men and 9 women with a mean age of 39 (SD = 15). The groups did not differ significantly in terms of age, gender and interest in gaming.

The participants' prior knowledge on aviation and meteorology, as reported on the online survey with a possible score of ten, had a mean score of 4.16 (SD = 2.39) and did not differ significantly between test groups. However, mandatory players were more motivated to participate in the experiment than voluntary players (One-way ANOVA: $F(1,17) = 9.28, p < .05$).

3.2   Procedure and Materials

The experiment consisted of four stages, shown in Fig. 1. All materials were available online. Participants could complete all stages online at their own computer and at their own convenience. Registration took place by the participant providing an e-mail address and indicating their valid age and informed consent with a check mark. At the time of registration each participant was randomly assigned to a treatment group and gained access to a webpage with the experiment instructions and materials. After registration each participant provided demographic information, information concerning prior knowledge of aviation and meteorology, and their personal motivation for participating in the experiment in an online questionnaire.

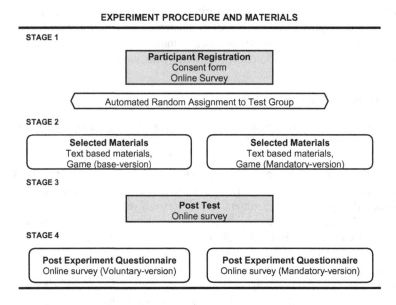

Fig. 1.   Schematic representation of the procedure stages and corresponding materials

The participants were then asked to study the text based materials and play the game. Voluntary players were free to decide if and how long they played, while mandatory players were told to spend a minimum of ten minutes playing. The text based instruction consisted of 13 webpages, offering information about cloud classification, characteristics of different cloud types, possible hazards, and the impact of clouds on aviation. It showed drawings and photographs of different types of clouds. Both test groups had unlimited access to the same set of text based materials.

The CloudAtlas Game. The game is identical for both test groups, but for the mandatory players the webpage enforced a ten minute minimum of active gameplay before allowing the player to take the test. The game is played in an internet browser using the keyboard as the input device. The objective is to fly an aircraft as far as possible (Fig. 2). During flight the player encounters the types of clouds that have been addressed in the text based instruction. Applying their knowledge about clouds and possible hazards, the players must decide to fly through a cloud, go over or under it, or land the aircraft to wait for the danger to pass. The impact of cloud hazards (i.e., icing, turbulence or lightning) on the aircraft is visualized on screen and results in increased fuel consumption. Consistent with reality, flying above a certain altitude requires oxygen. A limited supply of oxygen is available at the start of the game. During the game extra amounts of fuel and oxygen can be picked up to prolong the flight. The player may also encounter balloons and flocks of birds. Colliding with these must be avoided, because this will immediately end the game. In all other cases the game will end when the player runs out of fuel or oxygen. The distance traveled by the aircraft translates into a game score. Picking up score boosters during flight adds to the score, while making unnecessary landings leads to a deduction of points.

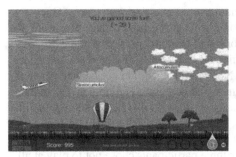

Fig. 2. Screenshot of the game

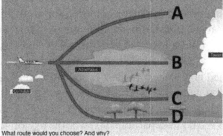

Fig. 3. Test item: application question

Tests. Participants studied the materials and played the game at their own pace and were free to proceed to the test when ready. Mandatory players had to play at least ten minutes for the test to become available. The test consisted of 11 knowledge questions and 7 application questions. In the knowledge questions participants were asked to reproduce cloud characteristics and recognize clouds from drawings and photographs. In the application questions players had to apply their knowledge to a certain situation. For example, a picture was presented of an aircraft and a certain type of cloud, with a number of possible routes drawn in the picture (Fig. 3). Participants were asked to choose the best route, taking into consideration safety, comfort and efficiency. They were also asked to explain their reasons for choosing this specific answer. Application questions were assigned higher weights than knowledge questions. Test scores were calculated as the percentage of points earned of a maximum of 49 points.

After the test participants were presented with the post experiment questionnaire. This questionnaire solicited more information on prior knowledge and gaming preferences. The voluntary players were asked about the extent of the freedom of choice they experienced in choosing to play or not to play the game. The mandatory players were asked whether they would have played the game when given a choice.

Upon completion of the test and the questionnaire, participants were informed about the follow-up and about their chance of winning the gift certificate.

The questionnaires used in the experiment have been constructed specifically for this study. No validated survey questions pertaining to voluntariness or game enjoyment were found in literature. Several questionnaire items use a ten point scale. Such a scale is easily understood [19] across age groups and education levels, and provides better data for analysis [20]. The use of an even scale avoids the neutral midpoint, forcing the participants to make a distinct choice for each item. Furthermore, the use of a ten point scale is common in both customer satisfaction surveys and game reviews.

4   Results

A total of 19 participants completed the experiment by taking the final test, 16 of them played the game. Game scores ranged from 721 to 4770, and test scores from 25 to 77. Table 1 shows the means and standard deviations on game and test scores. One-way analysis of variance controlled for motivation (ANCOVA) showed that there were no statistically significant differences in test scores and game scores between the groups.

T-tests revealed that there were no significant differences in test score and game score between male and female participants. Nor was there a difference between gamers and non-gamers for test score. However, gamers did achieve a higher game score than non-gamers ($F(1,17) = 8.35$, $p < .01$). Participants aged 40 and below scored significantly higher in the game ($F(1,17) = 15.58$, $p < .01$) and on the test ($F(1,17) = 4.90$, $p < .05$) than participants over the age of 40.

The length of gameplay varied widely, as three participants chose not to play at all, while two participants played for more than half an hour. The number of tries varied from zero to 22. Table 1 reveals that mandatory players played an average of 13.4 min longer than voluntary players (One-way ANOVA: $F(1,17) = 23.50$, $p < .001$). There was a significant effect of gameplay type on the amount of time played using prior motivation as covariate, $F(1, 16) = 10.98$, $p < 0.01$.

Table 1. Means and standard deviations for voluntary and mandatory gameplay groups

Measure	Test group			
	Mandatory (n = 9)		Voluntary (n = 10)	
	M	SD	M	SD
Gameplay (min)	16.8	8.2	3.4	2.9
Test score (%)	48.7	18.3	44.9	11.3
Game score	2723	1332	1092	1085

A t-test revealed that there was no significant difference in length of gameplay between male and female players. Nor was there a difference between gamers and non-gamers. Females did however have a lower average time per game attempt $(F(1,14) = 5.90, p < .05)$. Participants over the age of 40 also had a lower average time per attempt than younger participants $(F(1,14) = 4.64, p < .05)$.

We expected to see two subsets of players in both test groups: those who played only as long as required (up to 12 min) and those who continued playing (more than 12 min). Table 2 shows counts and percentages for these subsets. Within the voluntary group we also expected to find players who did not play at all and players that only played to get an idea of the game by playing three tries or less (Table 3).

Table 2. Subsets in mandatory and voluntary gameplay groups

		Gender		Gaming interest	
		Male (n = 10)	Female (n = 9)	Non-gamer (n = 11)	Gamer (n = 8)
Mandatory (n = 9)	Less than 12 min	1	2	2	1
	More than 12 min	5	1	2	4
Voluntary (n = 10)	Less than 12 min	4	6	7	3
	More than 12 min	0	0	0	0

Table 3. Subsets in voluntary gameplay group

		Gender		Gaming interest	
		Male (n = 10)	Female (n = 9)	Non-gamer (n = 11)	Gamer (n = 8)
Less than 12 min (n = 10)	No play	2	1	3	0
	3 tries or less	2	2	2	2

After the test, participants were asked how much they had enjoyed playing the game on a scale from 1 to 10 (M = 6.56, SD = 1.55). There was no significant difference between the test groups or between male and female participants. Younger participants however enjoyed the game more than older participants $(F(1,17) = 8.96, p < .01)$, and gamers enjoyed it more than non-gamers $(F(1,17) = 5.49, p < .05)$.

Mandatory players were asked how they felt about being obligated to play the game for a minimum amount of time. In general participants were neutral about this (M = 2.11, SD = .78). They were also asked if they would play the game if they were given a choice. Almost 78 % indicated they would. A correlation for the data revealed that the feeling about being obligated to play and the decision to play the game if not mandatory, were not significantly related, $r = .44, n = 9, p = .23$. A positive decision to play the game if it was not mandatory was not associated with a neutral or positive feeling about being obligated to play the game. Voluntary players were asked about the amount of freedom they experienced in choosing to play or not play the game on a scale from 1 to 10. The experienced levels of freedom ranged from 6 to 10, with a mean of 8.20 (SD = 1.69) and did not differ between gamers and non-gamers, male and female players or younger and older participants.

5   Discussion

Test Scores. This study sought to investigate the impact of freedom to choose to play or not play a serious game on the learning effect of this game. The learning effect of the serious game was measured by a test taken shortly after the training. We expected voluntary players to play the game longer and then perform better on the test than mandatory players. In effect, the data showed that mandatory players spent more time playing the game. The time spend on training does not appear to be a factor. Performance does not differ statistically between the two groups. There are several candidate causes for this. The group of voluntary players may have been able to extract knowledge from the game more efficiently than the mandatory players. It is also possible they were more successful in studying the written materials. Finally, there may be design issues with the game or the test. The game may not be as effective as expected or the test may not be valid.

Gameplay. The second aspect of interest was gameplay, measured in game score and duration. Contrary to our expectations voluntary players played for a shorter period of time than mandatory players and made less attempts. All voluntary players decided to quit playing the game within ten minutes. This raises the question why. Apparently voluntary players did not become fully engaged in the game, even though they rate the game about the same for enjoyment as the mandatory players do. Two thirds of the mandatory players play more than two minutes beyond the ten minute minimum, showing that the game in fact can be engaging. This outcome may indicate that a minimum time requirement is beneficiary for gameplay, as it forces the participant not to give up at the first setback.

Motivation. Players may have been extrinsically motivated to participate in the experiment by the chance of winning a € 100 gift card. This extra motivation can be expected to have been equal between the voluntary and mandatory players.
In line with the findings of Fulton et al. [17] we expected freedom of choice to motivate voluntary players and encourage them to accomplish better results. Additionally it would be understandable for a mandatory player to have a negative feeling about the obligation to play. However, voluntary players did not do better on the test, nor did they score higher on the level of enjoyment than mandatory players. Mandatory players reported a neutral feeling about having to play the game for a minimum amount of time, not a negative one. Possibly the fact that one participates voluntarily in the experiment changes the way one feels about an obligation to play the game. Alternatively these outcomes may possibly be caused by the limited number of participants or the game design. Further research is needed to clarify this.

Mandatory players even indicated that they would play the game if it was not mandatory. Although the following results were not significant with the number of participants in the current study, they do indicate an interesting trend. The percentage of mandatory players, who said they would play the game without the obligation, was higher than the percentage of voluntary players who actually did. The gameplay duration estimated by the mandatory players was also higher than the time played by the voluntary players.

Non-gamers. While the study focused on the differences between voluntary and mandatory players, some other results were found. Women and non-gamers played shorter and achieved lower scores than men and gamers respectively. This may be indicative of the general gaming skills of these groups. However, they did not perform worse on the test. These outcomes do not support the findings of Heeter et al. [4], who concluded that non-gamers are likely to be at a disadvantage in serious gaming. Also, the negative affect Heeter et al. found has not been established in the current study, despite the fact that non-gamers enjoyed the game less than gamers.

6 Limitations and Future Research

This study had a limited number of participants. By recruiting through social media we aimed to reach a large number of participants, but in fact the number of participants was limited. The group difference on prior motivation would probably not have occurred with a larger sample size or a different assignment strategy (pair matching). From the 64 initial registrations, only 19 persons completed the experiment. This dropout rate may also have influenced the results. Also mandatory participation to the study (as part of a regular course) would be of interest as this would provide a normal motivation setting for students in which the effects of voluntary gameplay can be observed without self-selection issues. It is intended to repeat the CloudAtlas experiment taking the above recommendations into account.

Another interesting angle for future research is the effect of different mandatory minimum amounts of gameplay on the total duration of gameplay to establish a recommended minimum.

7 Conclusion

This study aimed to determine whether and to what extent gameplay and learning effect of a serious game are affected by the freedom to choose to play or not to play the game. We expected that using the game voluntarily as a learning tool would result in improved player performance in a test, in comparison to the results after mandatory gameplay. This result was not found. However, it was found that mandatory gameplay in the CloudAtlas game does not ruin the enjoyment and engagement in the game, which contradicts the assumption of many game design theorists and practitioners that games need to be played voluntarily in order to be engaging, fun, and effective.

References

1. Michael, D., Chen, S.: Serious Games: Games That Educate, Train and Inform. Thomson, Boston (2006)
2. Wu, W., Hsiao, H., Wu, P., Lin, C., Huang, S.: Investigating the learning-theory foundations of game-based learning: a meta-analysis. J. Comput. Assist. Learn. **28**(3), 265–279 (2011)
3. Wouters, P., Van Nimwegen, C., Van Oostendorp, H., Van Der Spek, E.: Meta-analysis of the cognitive and motivational effects of serious games. J. Educ. Psychol. **105**(2), 249–265 (2013)
4. Heeter, C., Lee, Y., Magerko, B., Medler, B.: Impacts of forced serious game play on vulnerable subgroups. Int. J. Gaming Comput.-Mediated Simul. **3**(3), 34–53 (2011)
5. Mollick, E., Rothbard, N.: Mandatory fun: consent, gamification and the impact of games at work. The Wharton School Research Paper Series (2014)
6. Susi, T., Johanneson, M., Backlund, P.: Serious games - an overview. Technical paper, University of Skövde, Skövde (2007)
7. Djaouti, D., Alvarez, J., Jessel, J., Rampnoux, O.: Origins of serious games. In: Ma, M., Oikonomou, A., Jain, L. (eds.) Serious Games and Edutainment Applications, pp. 25–44. Springer, London (2011)
8. Abt, C.: Serious Games. Viking Press, New York (1970)
9. Sawyer, B., Rajeski, D.: Serious Games: Improving Public Policy Through Game-Based Learning and Simulation. Woodrow Wilson International Center for Scholars, Washington (2002)
10. Salen, K., Zimmerman, E.: Rules of Play: Game Design Fundamentals. MIT Press, Cambridge (2004)
11. McGonigal, J.: Reality Is Broken. Penguin Press, New York (2011)
12. Huizinga, J.: Homo Ludens: A Study of the Play Element in Culture. Beacon Press, Boston (1955)
13. Callois, R.: Man, Play and Games. University of Illinois Press, Champaign (1961)
14. Garris, R., Ahlers, R., Driskell, J.: Games, motivation, and learning: a research and practice model. Simul. Gaming **33**(4), 441–467 (2002)
15. Prensky, M.: Computer games and learning: digital game-based learning. In: Raessens, J., Goldstein, J. (eds.) Handbook of Computer Game Studies, pp. 97–122. MIT Press, Cambridge (2005)
16. Breuer, J., Bente, G.: Why so serious? On the relation of serious games and learning. Eludamos J. Comput. Game Cult. **4**(1), 7–24 (2010)
17. Fulton, S., Schweitzer, D.: Impact of giving students a choice of homework assignments in an introductory computer science class. Int. J. Sch. Teach. Learn. **5**(1), 20 (2011)
18. Becker, K.: How much choice is too much? INROADS **38**(4), 78–82 (2006)
19. Hernon, P., Whitman, J.R.: Delivering Satisfaction and Service Quality: A Customer-Based Approach for Libraries. American Library Association, Chicago (2001)
20. Coelho, P., Esteves, S.: The choice between a five-point and a ten-point scale in the framework of customer satisfaction measurement. Int. J. Market Res. **49**(3), 313–339 (2007)

Game and Learning Mechanics Under the Perspective of Self-determination Theory for Supporting Motivation in Digital Game Based Learning

Jean-Nicolas Proulx[✉] and Margarida Romero

Université Laval, Québec, Canada
jean-nicolas.proulx.1@ulaval.ca, Margarida.Romero@fse.ulaval.ca

Abstract. Using digital games in the classroom has been associated with higher levels of motivation among the students of different educational levels. However, the underlying psychological factors involved in the process have been rarely analyzed considering the self-determination theory (SDT) components and their relation to the optimal experience or flow [12]. In this paper, we aim to introduce a theoretical framework where the use of digital games in the classroom is analyzed through the game and learning mechanics of the LG-MG model [5] and the relation of the mechanics with the components of the SDT. The implications for the use of digital games in the classroom in order to promote the students' motivation is discussed in the last section of the paper.

1 Introduction

Understanding the effects of the use of digital game in an educational context is a complex task due to the complexity and diversity of educational ecosystems in terms of knowledge diversity, group dynamics, the evaluative context of the digital game use and the use of a certain digital game. The use of the digital games in educational contexts has been related to the development of the 21st century skills such the 4Cs (communication, collaboration, creativity and critical thinking) [30], the development of problem solving and literacy skills [16], the entrepreneurship attitudes and skills [8, 9], the contribution to cultural heritage [2], to intergenerational communication and learning [25, 29], and motivation [4, 10]. In the next section we analyze the link between the current use of digital game in the classroom and the effects on students' motivation based on an international literature review including different levels of education. After the current state of the analysis of games under the lens of their effects on motivation, we introduce the self-determination theory (SDT) [32] and analyze their links to the game and learning mechanics of the LG-MG model [5].

2 Digital Games in Education and Their Relation to Motivation

Educational psychologists have warned about a priori stereotype linking the use of new technologies in education, such as digital games, and the expected increase of motivation [1]. The research having analyzed the use of digital games in education has pointed to

© Springer International Publishing Switzerland 2016
A. De Gloria and R. Veltkamp (Eds.): GALA 2015, LNCS 9599, pp. 141–150, 2016.
DOI: 10.1007/978-3-319-40216-1_15

overall positive links between the use of digital games and their motivational effects among the learners [17, 18, 27]. Connolly, Boyle, MacArthur, Hainey and Boyle [10] mention that over a review of more than 70 empirical researches on the use of serious games in the classroom, the most observed positive impacts were "affectivity and motivation" (33) and "learning" (32). Also, the potential of serious games to foster intrinsic motivation is mentioned in many researches [41]. Since the activity is considered fun by gamers, they would be willing to spend more time and energy to complete it [41]. In addition, two key factors that are associated with computer games are autonomy (possibility to make relevant choices) and competence (the task represents a challenge while being achievable) which are elements of the self-determination theory that positively influence motivation [41].

Beside motivation, games also have the potential to inspire the interest, creativity and social interactions of those who use them [37]. Although he sees great potential in the use of games in education, Squire [36, p. 4] seems to think that there many contextual elements to take into account for motivation to emerge : "motivation for the gamers in my study was thus not simply a "property" or variable that they either had or did not have; motivation emerged through the intersection of students' goals and life histories, the game's affordances, and the institutional context". Even if he observed the emergence of motivation in the context of his study on the use of the game *Civilization 3* in the classroom, Squire [36] does not attribute the appearance of motivation only to the use of a game but to a coherence between different factors. Also, according to Filsecker and Hickey [14, p. 138] "kinds of cognitive strategies used might well be what distinguish motivated and unmotivated learners (Renkl 1997)." This brings the hypothesis that serious games have indeed the potential to foster motivation and learning, but this potential might not turn into a concrete form if certain conditions regarding the game and the learning context are not met.

The analysis of the use of digital games under the lens of the self-determination theory is explored in the next section as a theoretical framework that could help explore the underlying components in the relation between the use of digital games and the motivational effects.

3   Self-determination Theory (SDT) and Motivation

3.1   Introduction to Self-determination Theory (SDT)

The self-determination theory (SDT) is a theory of motivation developed by psychologists Edward Deci and Richard Ryan [32]. According to the SDT, people are directed towards growth and gain fulfillment through the integration of their experiences toward the development of a cohesive sense of self. In order to achieve growth, people should be able to develop three aspects:

- **Autonomy**: the need to feel in control of the own objectives and behaviors. According to Deci and Ryan [6, p. 63] "within SDT, autonomy for any given action is a matter of degree. Central to the theory is a continuum of motivational or regulatory styles that range heteronomy (controlled regulation) to autonomy or true self-regulation".

- **Connection or Relatedness**: the need of belonging and attachment to other people.
- **Competence**: the need to develop a certain level of knowledge and skills to develop tasks with a certain competence.

Applying the SDT perspective to education lead to consider that learners should be able to develop a certain level of competence, in connection with other people (peers, teacher/s, parent/s…) within a certain margin of autonomy that allows them to feel in control of the learning task and their activities within the task. According to the literature review of Reeve [26], the autonomy of the learners is related to their well-being in the classroom. According to Reeve, having a certain degree of autonomy motivates the learners and allows them to be more creative and choose optimal-level of difficulty challenges. The review of Reeve points to the key role of the teacher in allowing the learners' to have a certain level of autonomy in order to allow them to develop their orientation to grow, feeling more competent, more confident, more open-minded and creative.

A decade after proposing the SDT, Ryan and Deci [33, p. 179] highlight a positive link between the teacher who facilitates a certain degree of autonomy and the degree of engagement and motivation of the learners : « various studies of elementary and high school students (e.g., Hardre and Reeve 2003; Jang et al. 2007; Skinner and Belmont 1993) have shown that teachers' autonomy support is related to students' autonomous motivation and engagement ».

A literature review was performed by Taylor and colleagues [38] on 18 studies that "assessed the relation of motivation types according to SDT to school achievement" [38, p. 344] by using the Academic Motivation Scale (AMS) from Vallerand and Bissonnette [39]. Taylor and colleagues [38] found out that "intrinsic motivation and identified regulation have a moderately strong positive relation with school achievement" [38, p. 345] in the context of secondary education. Also, they observed that "introjected and external regulation had a weaker, but significant negative relation with school achievement" [38, p. 345] and that "amotivation had a strong, negative relation to school achievement" [38, p. 345]. In another study, Guay et al. [19] assessed the validity of some of the AMS constructs that were criticised, by using the exploratory structural equation modeling (ESEM) [7]. In that study, Guay and colleagues [19] found out that "ESEM results corroborate the factor validity of the AMS responses" [19, p. 72] among post-secondary students. That last study conclude to the validity of the AMS that was used in prior research analysed in the literature review of Taylor and colleagues [38]. Based on these prior studies on the SDT construct and its relevance on the study of motivation factors in the use of digital games in education, we introduce in the next section the continuum of autonomy and motivation within the SDT.

3.2   The Continuum of Autonomy and Motivation Within the SDT

Within the self-determination theory, different types of motivations are distinguished based on the different reasons or goals that will contribute to the birth of a new action

[33]. Their perspective on the concept of motivation led Deci and Ryan [13] to establish boundaries between different types of motivation according to goals and objectives that guide the action. According to this theory, "motivation concerns energy, direction, persistence and equifinality—all aspects of activation and intention" [32, p. 69]. Then, motivation is divided into three categories. Lack of motivation is referred to as "amotivation" [34]. Intrinsic motivation "refers to doing something because it is inherently interesting or enjoyable [33, p. 55]" and Extrinsic motivation "refers to doing something because it leads to a separable outcome. [33, p. 55]".

Amotivation	Extrinsic motivation				Intrinsic Motivation
Non Regulation	External Regulation	Introjected Regulation	Identified Regulation	Integrated regulation	Intrinsic Regulation
Lack of motivation	Controlled Motivation	Autonomous Motivation			
Lowest Relative Autonomy	← —————————————————————→				Highest Relative Autonomy

Fig. 1. Continuum in the self-determination according to the type of regulation and autonomy [34].

The primary difference between SDT and other motivations theories is discussed by Gagné and Deci [15, p. 340]: "the focus of SDT is on the relative strength of autonomous versus controlled motivation, rather than on the total amount of motivation. We maintain that it is important for a motivational theory to differentiate types of motivation and to use them in making predictions because research has shown that, whereas autonomous motivation facilitates effective performance and well-being, controlled motivation can detract from those outcomes, particularly if the task requires creativity, cognitive flexibility, or deep processing of information". Essentially, the self-determination theory evaluates the quality of motivation based on the degree to which it is "self-determined" or "autonomous".

3.3   The SDT and the Optimal Experience of Flow

Intrinsic motivation could be related to the optimal experience state or "flow experience". This concept was introduced by Csikszentmihalyi [11] and can be defined as a complete state of cognitive absorption or engagement into a task, in which the individual is not affected by thoughts or emotions unrelated to the task [12]. The theory of self-determination would be relevant to study a phenomenon such as optimal experience, since it takes into account different types and levels of motivation [23]. Kowal and Fortier [23] researches indicate that participants who had a self-determined motivation reached the highest states of flow experience. According to them, the self-determined or "autonomous" (see Fig. 3) forms of motivation can help to reach the flow state while controlled motivations seemed to have the opposite effect. Furthermore, a significant relationship was found between self-determined extrinsic motivation and the flow experience [23]. A similar link was established with Somuncuoglu and Yildirim [35] who suggested that students whose motivation was autonomous were more likely to be deeply engaged in their learning process. This notion of "deep engagement" concerning students in a task was also interpreted by Lee [24] as the presence of the flow experience. Also, Lee's study [24] suggests that students with autonomous motivation are less likely to procrastinate and more likely to reach the flow. Conversely, students who procrastinate showed a more controlled motivation and did not reach the flow [24]. Thus, fostering autonomous motivation among learners would increase the chances that they reach the optimal experience and be deeply engaged in their task. However, in a school context, tasks and lessons are not necessarily intrinsically motivating [24]. Therefore, it can be complex to reach the flow experience or intrinsic motivation in a school setting. Several current researches linked the flow, motivation and the use of serious games in class (e.g. [6, 21, 31]). Just like the flow experience, commercial games are deemed to "absorb" the player in such a manner, it can be difficult to stop playing [40]. Since the level of motivation generated by the school system for students is generally low, education world could benefit from the motivation and commitment that can arise games [40].

4 The Game and Learning Mechanics Under the Perspective of the Self-determination Theory (SDT)

4.1 Game and Learning Mechanics

Serious game mechanics (SGM) are the "game components that translate a pedagogical practice/pattern into concrete game mechanics directly perceivable by a player's actions" [6, p. 395]. According to Arnab and collaborators [6, p. 396], the game mechanics should support "intrinsic experiential learning (…). Knowledge acquisition and skill training should be obtained through game mechanics (e.g., Quests, cascading information, leader boards, goals, levels, badges, role play, tokens, etc.)". Basing themselves on Bloom's revised model made by Anderson and collaborators [3], Arnab and collaborators classified game mechanics according to the degree of thinking skill required. Figure 2 introduces the *Learning Mechanics - Game Mechanics* (LM-GM) model proposed by Arnab and collaborators [5]. According to Arnab and collaborators [6, p. 396] "Overall, the LM-GM model aims at providing a concise means to relate pedagogy intentions and ludic elements within a player's actions and gameplay, i.e., SGMs".

Game Mechanics		THINKING SKILL	Learning Mechanics	
○ Design/Editing ○ Infinite Game play ○ Ownership ○ Protégé Effect	○ Status ○ Strategy/Planning ○ Tiles/Grids	CREATING	○ Accountability ○ Ownership ○ Planning ○ Responsibility	
○ Action Points ○ Assessment ○ Collaboration ○ Communal Discovery ○ Game Turns	○ Pareto Optimal ○ Resource Management ○ Rewards/Penalties ○ Urgent Optimism	EVALUATING	○ Assessment ○ Reflect/Discuss ○ Collaboration ○ Hypothesis ○ Incentive ○ Motivation	
○ Feedback ○ Meta-game ○ Realism		ANALYSING	○ Analyse ○ Identify ○ Experimentation ○ Observation ○ Feedback ○ Shadowing	
○ Capture/Elimination ○ Competition ○ Cooperation ○ Movement	○ Progression ○ Selecting/Collecting ○ Simulate/Response ○ Time Pressure	APPLYING	○ Action/Task ○ Imitation ○ Competition ○ Simulation ○ Cooperation ○ Demonstration	
○ Appointment ○ Cascading Information ○ Questions And Answers	○ Role-play ○ Tutorial	UNDERSTANDING	○ Objectify ○ Tutorial ○ Participation ○ Question And Answers	
○ Behavioural Momentum ○ Cut scenes/Story ○ Goods/Information	○ Pavlovian Interactions ○ Tokens ○ Virality	RETENTION	○ Discover ○ Guidance ○ Explore ○ Instruction ○ Generalisation ○ Repetition	

LOTS to HOTS

Fig. 2. *Learning Mechanics - Game Mechanics* (LM-GM) [5].

4.2   Game and Learning Mechanics Under the Perspective of the SDT

Game mechanics involve a certain degree of interaction between the player and the game artifact or other persons involved in the game activity. Retroactivity is a key aspect of the game mechanics as a mechanism of interaction, allowing the learner to advance within the game [22]. Because of the existence of an interaction, digital games provide some degree of extrinsic motivation based on the retroactions of the game. This characteristic has been highlighted as a positive aspect of games [13]. Digital games can also promote the emergence of intrinsic motivation when the player-learners are engaged in a game, allowing them to develop a certain activity autonomy, an autonomous motivation and a certain degree of intrinsic regulation.

Figure 3 shows game mechanics (at left) and learning mechanics (at right, italic) according to their potential extrinsic and intrinsic motivation potential. None of the game, nor learning mechanics are considered in the amotivation zone of the SDT, because games always provide a certain level of interaction with the game artifact of the characters or other players [22]. Some of the game and learning mechanics of the LM-GM model have not yet been classified under the SDT perspective because of the neutral aspect or their potential that can be considered under the two perspectives. For instance, the meta-game and realism. LM-GM model was based on Bloom's learning theory in order to facilitate the learning process, because not all serious games are effective learning tools. This reality also apply for motivation, because not every serious games can be described as 'motivating' or 'fun' and using a motivational theory such as SDT to support LM-GM model might increase the fun factor. According to Katz and

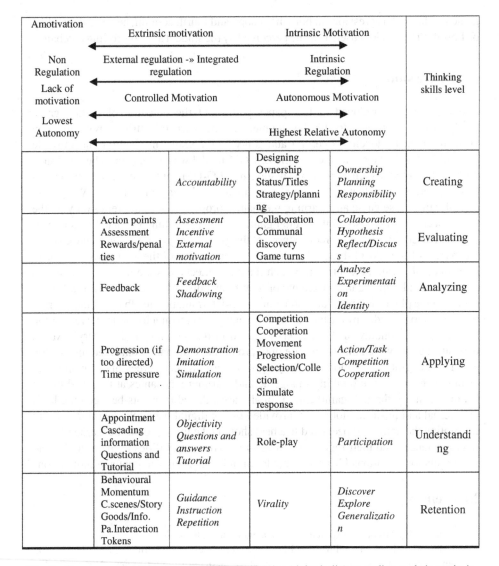

Amotivation					
Non Regulation / Lack of motivation / Lowest Autonomy					Thinking skills level
		Accountability	Designing Ownership Status/Titles Strategy/planning	*Ownership Planning Responsibility*	Creating
	Action points Assessment Rewards/penalties	*Assessment Incentive External motivation*	Collaboration Communal discovery Game turns	*Collaboration Hypothesis Reflect/Discuss*	Evaluating
	Feedback	*Feedback Shadowing*		*Analyze Experimentation Identity*	Analyzing
	Progression (if too directed) Time pressure	*Demonstration Imitation Simulation*	Competition Cooperation Movement Progression Selection/Collection Simulate response	*Action/Task Competition Cooperation*	Applying
	Appointment Cascading information Questions and Tutorial	*Objectivity Questions and answers Tutorial*	Role-play	*Participation*	Understanding
	Behavioural Momentum C.scenes/Story Goods/Info. Pa.Interaction Tokens	*Guidance Instruction Repetition*	Virality	*Discover Explore Generalization*	Retention

Fig. 3. Game mechanics (left) and learning mechanics (right, italic) according to their extrinsic and intrinsic motivation potential.

Assor [20, p. 11], "In order for choice to be motivating, it has to be based on a careful match between the various options and the students' needs, interests, goals, abilities, and cultural background. In addition, considerable attention should be paid to the context and manner in which the choice is provided." It would be interesting to investigate if this situation also affects motivation in SGM. Thus, the context in which digital games are pedagogically integrated would introduce additional factors which could affect the SDT continuum perception from the perspective of the learner. For instance, we put the game mechanic 'progression' in both the second and fourth column, because depending on how this mechanic is used it can be perceived by the student as a controlling mechanic.

5   Discussion

The framework introduced in this paper points out the potential of certain game mechanics to contribute to the development of the learners' intrinsic regulation by allowing them to develop a certain autonomy, autonomous motivation and intrinsic regulation. While we are aware that the LM-GM model was not meant to be combined with another theory such as SDT, we believe that LG-GM could use self-determination theory in order to evaluate the motivational impact of the game mechanics. We should consider that these game and learning mechanics properties does not relies only on the game mechanics but also on the digital game integration within a situated educational activity that could enhance or reduce those of the game. Analyzing the game and learning mechanics of the LM-GM model [5] from the perspective of the SDT shows the need to evaluate them in the context in which the game mechanics are used. In instance, a game designed with a game mechanic of 'communal discovery' could permit a certain degree of the player-learners' autonomy and self-determination feedback. If the instructional support provided by the teacher does not integrates too much of external regulation reducing the autonomy of the learners engaged in the 'communal discovery'. At the opposite a game which mechanics are only promoting externally controlled motivation could be integrated in a more challenging task with higher degrees of autonomy and team engagement by promoting this game and learning mechanics at the level of the learning activity through gamification. In all cases, the adjustments between the level of external and intrinsic motivation provided by the digital game, the learning activity integrating the game and peers and teachers should take into account the learners' level of competences and their regulation and co-regulation capabilities to avoid under and overregulation situations [28] which could diminish their engagement and motivation.

References

1. Amadieu, F., Tricot, A.: Apprendre avec le numérique. Retz (2014)
2. Anderson, E.F., McLoughlin, L., Liarokapis, F., Peters, C., Petridis, P., de Freitas, S.: Developing serious games for cultural heritage: a state-of-the-art review. Virtual Reality 14(4), 255–275 (2010)
3. Anderson, L.W., Krathwohl, D.R., Bloom, B.S.: A Taxonomy for Learning, Teaching, and Assessing: A Revision of Bloom's Taxonomy of Educational Objectives. Allyn & Bacon, Boston (2001)
4. Anyaegbu, R., Ting, W., Li, Y.: Serious game motivation in an EFL classroom in Chinese primary school. Turk. Online J. Educ. Technol. 11, 1 (2012)
5. Arnab, S., Lim, T., Carvalho, M.B., et al.: Mapping learning and game mechanics for serious games analysis. Br. J. Educ. Technol. 46, 391–411 (2014)
6. Arnab, S., Lim, T., Carvalho, M.B., et al.: Mapping learning and game mechanics for serious games analysis. BJET 46(2), 391–411 (2015)

7. Asparouhov, T., Muthén, B.: Exploratory structural equation modeling. Struct. Eqn. Model.: Multidiscip. J. **16**(3), 397–438 (2009)
8. Bellotti, F., Berta, R., De Gloria, A., et al.: Designing a course for stimulating entrepreneurship in higher education through serious games. Procedia Comput. Sci. **15**, 174–186 (2012)
9. Bellotti, F., Berta, R., De Gloria, A., et al.: Serious games and the development of an entrepreneurial mindset in higher education engineering students. Entertainment Comput. **5**(4), 357–366 (2014)
10. Chang, S., Lin, S.S.J.: Team knowledge with motivation in a successful MMORPG game team: a case study. Comput. Educ. **73**, 129–140 (2014)
11. Csikszentmihalyi, M.: Play and intrinsic rewards. J. Humanist. Psychol. **15**, 41–63 (1975)
12. Csikszentmihalyi, M.: Flow, the Psychology of Optimal Experience, Steps Towards Enhancing the Quality of Life. Harper & Row Publishers Inc., New York (1991)
13. Dunwell, I.: Four-dimensional consideration of feedback in serious games. In: de Freitas, S., Maharg, P. (eds.) Digital Games and Learning, pp. 42–62. Continuum Publishing, New York (2011)
14. Filsecker, M., Hickey, D.T.: A multilevel analysis of the effects of external rewards on elementary students' motivation, engagement and learning in an educational game. Comput. Educ. **75**, 136–148 (2014)
15. Gagné, M., Deci, E.L.: Self-determination theory and work motivation. J. Organ. Behav. **26**(4), 331–362 (2005)
16. Gee, J.P.: Why are video games good for learning. Unpublished Manuscript. **23** (2007)
17. Groff, J., Howells, C., Cranmer, S.: The Impact of Console Games in the Classroom: Evidence from Schools in Scotland. Futurelab, UK (2010)
18. Gros, B.: Digital games in education: the design of games-based learning environments. J. Res. Technol. Educ. **40**(1), 23–38 (2007)
19. Guay, F., Morin, A.J., Litalien, D., Valois, P., Vallerand, R.J.: Application of exploratory structural equation modeling to evaluate the academic motivation scale. J. Exp. Educ. **83**(1), 51–82 (2015)
20. Katz, I., Assor, A.: When choice motivates and when it does not. Educ. Psychol. Rev. **19**(4), 429–442 (2007)
21. Kiili, K., de Freitas, S., Arnab, S., Lainema, T.: The design principles for flow experience in educational games. Procedia CS **15**, 78–91 (2012)
22. Koster, R.: A Theory of Fun for Game Design. O'Reilly, Sebastopol (2013)
23. Kowal, J., Fortier, M.S.: Motivational determinants of flow: contributions from self-determination theory. J. Soc. Psychol. **139**, 3 (1999)
24. Lee, E.: The relationship of motivation and flow experience to academic procrastination in university students. J. Genet. Psychol. **166**(1), 5–15 (2005)
25. Newman, S., Hatton-Yeo, A.: Intergenerational learning and the contributions of older people. Ageing Horiz. **8**(10), 31–39 (2008)
26. Reeve, J.: Self-determination theory applied to educational settings (2002)
27. Ritzko, J.M., Robinson, S.: Using games to increase active learning. J. Col. Teach. Learn. (TLC) **3**(6), 45–50 (2011)
28. Romero, M., Lambropoulos, N.: Internal and external regulation to support knowledge construction and convergence in computer supported collaborative learning (CSCL). EJREP **9**(1), 309–330 (2011)
29. Romero, M., Loos, E.: Intergenerational game creation. Engaging elders and secondary level students in intergenerational learning about immigration through participative game design. In: EDEN, p. 167 (2015)

30. Romero, M., Usart, M., Ott, M.: Can serious games contribute to developing and sustaining 21st-century skills? Games Cult.: J. Interact. Media **10**(2), 148–177 (2015)
31. Romero, M., Usart, M., Ott, M., Earp, J., de Freitas, S., Arnab, S.: Learning through playing for or against each other? ECIS **5**, 1–15 (2012)
32. Ryan, R.M., Deci, E.L.: Self-determination theory and the facilitation of intrinsic motivation, social development, and well-being. AP **55**(1), 68 (2000)
33. Ryan, R.M., Deci, E.L.: Intrinsic and extrinsic motivations: classic definitions and new directions. Contemp. Educ. Psychol. **25**(1), 54–67 (2000)
34. Ryan, R.M., Deci, E.L.: Promoting self-determined school engagement. Handbook of Motivation at School, pp. 171–195 (2009)
35. Somuncuoglu, Y., Yildirim, A.: Relationship between achievement goal orientations and use of learning strategies. JER **92**(5), 267–277 (1999)
36. Squire, K.: Changing the game: what happens when video games enter the classroom. Innov.: J. Online Educ. **1**(6), 1–20 (2005)
37. Squire, K.: Video Games and Learning: Teaching and Participatory Culture in the Digital Age. Technology, Education–Connections (the TEC Series). ERIC (2011)
38. Taylor, G., Jungert, T., Mageau, G.A., et al.: A self-determination theory approach to predicting school achievement over time: the unique role of intrinsic motivation. Contemp. Educ. Psychol. **39**(4), 342–358 (2014)
39. Vallerand, R.J., Bissonnette, R.: Intrinsic, extrinsic, and amotivational styles as predictors of behavior. J. Pers. **60**(3), 599–620 (1992)
40. Westera, W.: Games are motivating, aren't they? Disputing the arguments for digital game-based learning. Int. J. Serious Games **2**, 2 (2015)
41. Wouters, P., Van Nimwegen, C., Van Oostendorp, H., Van Der Spek, E.D.: A meta-analysis of the cognitive and motivational effects of serious games. J. Educ. Psychol. **105**(2), 249 (2013)

Mobile Game Based Learning Based on Adaptive Curricula and Location Change

Erik Frank, Richard Lackes, and Markus Siepermann[✉]

Technische Universität Dortmund, Otto-Hahn-Str. 12, 44227 Dortmund, Germany
{erik.frank,richard.lackes,markus.siepermann}@tu-dortmund.de

Abstract. With the diffusion of mobile technologies, the classic learning process of class room learning as well as e-learning has changed. Mobile devices enable individuals to learn anywhere and anytime, even if only little time is available. Usually, m-learning is often seen as e-learning on mobile devices. This disregards the real potential of m-learning. Instead, the characteristics of mobility should be taken into account when designing m-learning, namely different places of learning and the process of location change. In this paper, we therefore introduce the concept of location-sequence-based learning (LSBL) that explicitly considers these characteristics. Then, we combine LSBL with the concept of game based learning (GBL) in order to even enhance the motivational aspect of both concepts.

Keywords: M-Learning · Sequence-based learning · Location-based learning · Education

1 Introduction

In a traditional manner, teaching is a location-bound communication process. In most cases, knowledge is transferred by word of mouth. But like other areas of communication, education has been extensively influenced by new information technologies. Starting from multimedia based systems, e-learning systems passed through tremendous developments, now providing sophisticated intelligent tutoring tools with automatic generation and marking of exercises, e.g. [18, 20, 22], or being game based learning systems based on commercial games, e.g. [2, 7, 9], or developed for special purposes, e.g. [1, 21]. With the emergence and increasing use of mobile technologies in the past years, mobile learning (m-learning) has gained much importance as an e-learning domain. Often, m-learning is just seen as e-learning but with mobile devices. However, from our perspective, the core of the matter is not entirely conceived yet. M-learning is not based on the mere extended spectrum of portability of existing e-learning concepts [23] but offers rich opportunities for new e-learning concepts. Indeed, mobile devices are the crucial technical innovation which led to the development of particular m-learning concepts, but the emphasis on mobility should not focus on the technology. It is just a means to an end. Substantial innovation lies with the learning process. Latter has changed radically due to the mobility and locomotion of the learning individual.

© Springer International Publishing Switzerland 2016
A. De Gloria and R. Veltkamp (Eds.): GALA 2015, LNCS 9599, pp. 151–160, 2016.
DOI: 10.1007/978-3-319-40216-1_16

In this paper, we want to deliberate location-based learning and introduce the concept of location-sequence-based learning (LSBL). Therefore, in the next section, we first have a look at the concepts of e-learning and m-learning. Then, we discuss location-based learning and introduce the idea of LSBL. In Sect. 4, we develop this idea and show how game based learning (GBL) can benefit from this concept. In Sect. 5, we formalize location-sequence-based game based learning and give an example of use in Sect. 6. The paper closes with a summary and some limitations in Sect. 7.

2   E-Learning and M-Learning

Diverse forms of learning can be differentiated that are not mutually exclusive i.e. tutored learning, collaborative or work group learning and ego-learning. Subject to the curriculum and educational objectives, the approaches may complement one another in a reasonable manner and therefore are with good cause. Both, tutored learning and collaborative learning are communicative forms of learning. Dialogue-oriented processes of this kind require chronological synchronism of individuals involved in the learning process. Spatial synchronism is often beneficial, but not in any case.

Knowledge transfer in tutored learning is unidirectional. As for collaborative learning, the distributed knowledge fragments of work group members are gathered and combined. In common use, it is referred to as socialization of knowledge. With regard to the transfer of knowledge, respective control and the measurement of learning success are unspecified. In case of ego-learning, documented knowledge is internalized by means of self-study [16]. Respective success depends on fitting knowledge documents, prior education, and intellectual constitution of the learning individual.

Any kind of synchronism, both chronological and spatial, requires to some degree coordination and a provision of resources. Linked transaction costs must be compensated with synchronization benefits. E-learning imparts curriculum to groups and individuals non dependent on time and location. It serves to present and distribute digital teaching materials [15].

Leidner and Jarvenpaa (1995) refer to virtual learning as to the use of diverse information technologies such as IP conferencing or distributed work spaces in order to transcend physical boundaries of the classroom and therefore annihilate spatial synchronism [11]. The independence of time and location implies that learning becomes a continuous process. At the same time, it can be suited to the individual learning requirements. Both, the temporal progress and the intensity of knowledge generation can be harmonized with regard to the learning individual and lead to an improved education [11].

At first, these independencies of e-learning and computer-based learning respectively have been considered as the crucial improvement to allow for separated study groups [19]. IT-based interpersonal communication as a characteristic aspect of e-learning is of course linked to it [8]. But the pure peripheral use of information technology within learning processes should be regarded just as the most rudimental form of e-learning. The actual task rather is to replace humans as tutors and study group participants with some sort of teaching machine i.e. an intelligent software solution.

In recent years, the propagation of mobile technologies advanced rigorously. Mobile devices and wireless data communication are almost ubiquitous. Hence, m-learning is in the focus of attention as an emergent e-learning domain [13]. The all out technical configuration of mobile devices caused e-learning to proceed on the go and thus use idle time in a reasonable manner. The high accessibility of mobile devices can significantly improve dialogue control and as a result preserve time synchronism to a certain degree. For example, the questions of the learning individual can be answered promptly by ever attainable and qualified tutors or members of a study group. This leads to expeditious learning achievements and avoids the threat of meanders.

E-learning in general is characterized as location independent, yet only m-learning as a special form enables people to acquire knowledge anywhere and at any time. However, it is subject to the precondition that the learning process can be halted and resumed regardless of the location without any problems.

Nevertheless, m-learning exceeds porting of existing e-learning solutions with regard to technical specifications of mobile devices. Suppose that a learning process is initiated at location A and continues at location B. In use of non-mobile technology, it is referred to as classic e-learning without consideration, though we often mistake such a succession as m-learning if mobile IT is deployed. Likewise, the distance between A and B is of no relevance. But for classification purposes, just a change of location seems appropriate. Hence, m-learning has to be considered literally as e-learning on the go.

Separate aspects of m-learning bear on returned ambient data of the mobile device. In this respect, dynamic context and positioning data has to be mentioned at first. But in addition, vital data may be returned as well e.g. in order to coach an athlete and point out running flaws. In principle, such data can be used to monitor the learning process and/or adjust the curriculum to the learning environment. The respective situational learning may in turn cause an initial effect to be observed at a much earlier stage. In this regard, sequence-based learning and location-based learning represent the genuine innovation of m-learning. We should refer to e-learning as m-learning but in this kind of appropriation.

3   Location-Based and Location-Sequence-Based Learning

M-learning may be classified as location-based learning and/or location-sequence-based learning (LSBL). Both forms are closely linked to a location or relocation and are characterized by a location-adaptive and/or situational learning process. With regard to location-based learning the curriculum adapts to the learning environment. The interactive museum guide is a popular example. Depending on the current position, relevant information about works of art is made available to the visitor on his museum tour [10].

Mobile position-fixing can be based on GPS, RFID or use of integrated image recognition [5]. In specific scenarios it is conceivable that not just the location, but also the sequence of location change may affect the curriculum and learning process. In case of mutual dependent curricula, e.g. knowledge which requires knowledge of a different kind, lessons can be learned subject to the specific location sequence. We refer to such use as sequence-based learning.

Intelligent solutions will direct users across concerted lessons and supervise the sequence-based learning process. Given such kind of sequence-sensitive m-learning within the context of the before mentioned example, the respective sequence can alter with regard to the greater educational objective. Thus, visitors can look at the works of art in a different order and learn about different aspects – either about distinct schools of art and techniques or about artists of a specific epoch. We call this sequence-sensitive m-learning location-sequence-based learning.

Mobile technologies are just a basic prerequisite to enable mobile learning. Classic e-learning applications on mobile devices are not the key innovation, albeit just as legitimate. The true potential of m-learning lies with the altered learning process.

Both, location-based learning and LSBL are pure forms of contextual learning. Under the terms of such paradigms, learning proceeds if the learning individual handles new information put in a contextual order which seems sensible [17]. The context exists in situ. Thus, people rather accept the depicted knowledge which for this reason will have a quasi everlasting effect. On this account, it is of major importance to delve into the aforementioned forms of m-learning.

4   Location-Sequence-Based Game Based Learning

Depending on the sequence of visited points of interests, e.g. sights of a city, objects of art in a museum or subsequently used vivariums in a zoological garden, the taught curricula differ, when using sequence-based learning. Therefore, the learning objectives are not, compared to location-based learning, bound statically to a place, but they are determined by the individually chosen "learning path" of the learning individual, i.e. the sequence of visited points of interest.

Sequence-based learning systems shall be flexible enough to generate and present meaningful information through a user-defined sequence of points of interest. Although an integrated recommender system can generate proposals how to continue the learning path in a most "reasonable" way, a strong paternalism with restrictive learning sequences is not intended. Such flexibility allows the learner to choose his learning path regarding to his individual curiosity so that certain locations may be visited with priority and others may be ignored. A learner's curiosity defines his effort to gain and learn specific information. Thus, open learning environments with places of self-determined acquisition of information foster the psychic energy of individuals to learn. With the accompanying engagement in an issue, learning can take place [4].

Sequence-based learning systems cannot cultivate the curiosity of a learner, but in such systems the curiosity can unfold freely and individually as it is not trimmed by a preset learning process. This fosters the intrinsic motivation of an individual to deal with certain issues and to learn about them [14]. If curricula are strictly preset because the learning path respectively the learning process is determined a priori, a learner's curiosity and with this his willingness to learn is verifiable inhibited [3]. This allows for the assumption that free, sequence-based learning can lead to an increased learning success because of the learner's pure intrinsic motivation contrary to an often enforced extrinsic motivation by institutionalized learning.

LSBL alone already offers great opportunities to stimulate the intrinsic learning motivation of individuals. This motivation can even be enhanced if we combine LSBL with GBL, another often used method for the motivation of learners. While the potential of GBL is its interactivity and its capability to demonstrate topics in a manageable and closed surrounding [6], LSBL offers a flexible basis of individual learning paths for such interactive surroundings. Because LSBL is more a concept than an instance of e-learning, it is not restricted to specific applications but can easily integrated in GBL settings. Then, the GBL part offers the setting of the game and the game play while LSBL offers the relations between the lessons to be learned.

A typical example for the combination of GBL and LSBL is an adventure game in which the learner takes the role of the hero who has to solve a quest (GBL setting). The adventure is composed of different places where the player can travel to (virtually as well as physically). At each place, information is hidden that comprises the lessons to be learned (LSBL part). The player can choose which information he acquires in order to solve his quest (LSBL part). Several solution paths are conceivable so that it is not necessary to gather all information provided (LSBL part). The player wins the game if he manages to solve his quest (GBL).

5   The Location-Sequence-Based Game Model

In general, the learning environment of a location-sequence-based game system consists of several points of interest (places) where the different lessons to be learned are located. The combination of places and lessons shall be called curriculum. Each lesson belongs to a superior field of teaching that is classified into different issues. Then, at each place, learners can choose which lesson of that specific place they want to learn. The available lessons at each place depend on the knowledge that a learner acquired beforehand. The formal model for the system can be described as follows: The learning system L is a hexatuple, consisting of a set P of N places, a set I of M issues, a set C, of curricula, the player's dynamic knowledge K, a similarity function sim and an access function $access$:

$$L_s = (P, I, C, K, sim, access) \tag{1}$$

The N places p_n, $n = 1, \ldots, N$, build the set P of points of interests:

$$P = \{p_n | n = 1, \ldots, N; N > 1\} \tag{2}$$

The field of teaching is classified into M different issues i_m:

$$I = \{i_m | m = 1 \ldots, M; M > 1\} \tag{3}$$

At each place, different issues can be taught. The combination of a place p_n and an issue i_m is called curriculum. A curriculum is the specific instance of an issue at a given place. The set of curricula is defined as:

$$C = \{c_{nm} | (p_n, i_m) \in P \times I\} \tag{4}$$

The curricula of each issue i_m at different places p_n can be compared among themselves in regard to their similarity:

$$sim:C \times C \times I \to [0, 1] \qquad (5)$$

The similarity function $sim()$ shall be 1 for $sim(c_{nm}, c_{nm})$ and symmetric so that $sim(c_{nm}, c_{km}) = sim(c_{km}, c_{nm})$. The learner starts the game at a random place $p_r \in P$ and passes through the learning process in a variable sequence of places. This first place is chosen by the learner as a starting point, driven by his individual curiosity and intrinsic motivation. At this point, the learner chooses the curricula c_{rm} of the place p_r that he is interested in. The set of those chosen curricula is his initial knowledge K_1 of the game:

$$K_1 = \{c_{rm} | c_{rm} \in C; learner\ is\ in\ p_r; 1 \leq r \leq N\} \qquad (6)$$

The learning process will be continued with this initial knowledge and expanded continuously at each place. Let

$$P_v \subseteq P \qquad (7)$$

be the set of points of interest that the learner has visited during the game, p_j the actual new place, and K_l the learner's gathered knowledge. Let $\sigma \in [0, 1]$ be a predefined system parameter acting as a threshold for the similarity of curricula. Then, the learner gets access to all curricula of place p_j that exceed the similarity threshold σ if compared to all curricula of his knowledge already gathered beforehand:

$$access(p_j, P_v, K_l) = \{c_{jm} | sim(c_{jm}, c_{nm}) \geq \sigma; c_{nm} \in K_l\} \qquad (8)$$

Out of this set of curricula, the learner can choose which curricula he wants to look at. After that, his complete knowledge is:

$$K_{l+1} = K_l \cup \{c_{jm} | c_{jm} \in access(p_j, P_v, K_l)\} \qquad (9)$$

6   Example

Subsequently, we illustrate the game design presented in the previous section with the example of a detective story in a zoological garden. Players are exposed to the following setting.

Mama Marmot has collected a basket of blueberries that she placed in front of her cave. But when she wanted to give the berries to her children, the basket was completely empty. Help Mama Marmot to find out who is the berry thief.

Players can visit four places where different animals live: The house of marmots (p_1), the house of elephants (p_2), the house of cougars (p_3), and the house of bears (p_4). The available issues shall be limited to the topics genus (i_1), habitat (i_2), diet (i_3), and behavior (i_4). The similarity of the species in regard to the issues $(i_1, \dots, i_4)$ is shown in

Fig. 1. At the outset, knowledgeable experts must explicitly determine the respective degree of similarity.

		Genus				Habitat				Diet				Behavior		
	p_1	p_2	p_3	p_4	p_1	p_2	p_3	p_4	p_1	p_2	p_3	p_4	p_1	p_2	p_3	p_4
marmot p_1	1.0	0.2	0.4	0.5	1.0	0.1	0.8	0.8	1.0	0.8	0.2	0.7	1.0	0.7	0.3	0.5
elephant p_2		1.0	0.1	0.2		1.0	0.2	0.5		1.0	0.3	0.5		1.0	0.4	0.6
cougar p_3			1.0	0.6			1.0	0.8			1.0	0.6			1.0	0.2
bear p_4				1.0				1.0				1.0				1.0

Fig. 1. Similarity of the species in terms of issue

Now, the player can choose which place he wants to visit first. As a starting point, the house of marmots may be suitable to find out more about the circumstances of the crime. There, the player can choose which curricula he wants to have a look at. The player does not possess any previous knowledge. Therefore, he reviews all available curricula so that his knowledge is initiated with $K_1 = \{c_{11}, c_{12}, c_{13}, c_{14}\}$. As the visitor opts for the marmot enclosure (p_1) as the starting point of the tour, he sets to a certain extent the issue-related focusing of the following learning process. He learns about the marmot living in America, Asia and Europe, being primarily an herbivore but also eating insects or snails, and living in small colonies.

The next place the player visits shall be the house of elephants (p_2). The curricula available to the player depend on the knowledge he gathered beforehand and the similarity threshold that we assume to $\sigma = 0.5$. That means that the curricula on the elephant's diet and behaviour are provided to the player (see Fig. 2).

	elephant p_2			
	i_1	i_2	i_3	i_4
marmot p_1	0.2	0.1	**0.8**	**0.7**

Fig. 2. Similarity of marmot and elephant concerning player's knowledge K_1

The player decides to learn about the elephant's diet and learns that elephants, like marmots, are herbivores. Thus, his knowledge is extended by curriculum c_{23} to $K_2 = \{c_{11}, c_{12}, c_{13}, c_{14}, c_{23}\}$. In addition, also the set of all visited places $P_v = \{p_1, p_2\}$ is

	bear p_4			
	i_1	i_2	i_3	i_4
marmot p_1	**0.5**	**0.8**	**0.7**	**0.5**
elephant p_2			0.5	

Fig. 3. Similarity of marmot and elephant with bear concerning player's knowledge K_2

extended by p_2. Thereafter, the player visits the bear (p_4) and again the similarity between the players knowledge and the curricula concerning the bear is considered (see Fig. 3).

Because of the similarities between the marmot and the bear, the player is provided with all curricula concerning the bear. The player decides to learn curricula c_{42} and c_{43} telling him that bears live in the northern hemisphere but once lived also in northern Africa, being omnivores. Extending his knowledge with curricula c_{42} and c_{43}, his new knowledge is $K_3 = \{c_{11}, c_{12}, c_{13}, c_{14}, c_{23}, c_{42}, c_{43}\}$ and the new set of visited places is $P_v = \{p_1, p_2, p_4\}$.

In the next step, the player visits p_3 being the only place where he has not been before. Due to the similarity with marmot and bear concerning habitat and with the bear concerning the diet (see Fig. 4), both curricula of the cougar are provided. The player decides to have a look at both curricula learning that the cougar is a pure carnivore living in North and South America. His knowledge is extended with both curricula c_{32} and c_{33}, to $K_4 = \{c_{11}, c_{12}, c_{13}, c_{14}, c_{23}, c_{32}, c_{33}, c_{42}, c_{43}\}$ and the set of visited places is $P_v = \{p_1, p_2, p_3, p_4\}$.

		cougar p_3			
		i_1	i_2	i_3	i_4
marmot	p_1	0.4	**0.8**	0.2	0.3
elephant	p_2			0.3	
bear	p_4		**0.8**	**0.6**	

Fig. 4. Similarity of marmot, elephant, and bear with cougar concerning player's knowledge K_3

Now, the player analyses his knowledge excluding the cougar from the list of thieves because of being a carnivore that does not eat berries. He discovers that still two suspects remain, both eating berries. One of them, the bear, lives in the same region as marmots do. Concerning the habitat of the elephant, the player did not gather any information. Therefore, he decides to go back to the elephant. Because his current knowledge K_4 is greater than the knowledge K_1 was when he first visited the elephant, more curricula about the elephant are now available to him (see Fig. 5). Therefore, the curriculum c_{22} concerning the elephant's habitat is now provided. The player extends his knowledge to $5 = \{c_{11}, c_{12}, c_{13}, c_{14}, c_{22}, c_{23}, c_{32}, c_{33}, c_{42}, c_{43}\}$ and learns that elephants live in the savanna

		elephant p_2			
		i_1	i_2	i_3	i_4
marmot	p_1	0.2	0.1	**0.8**	**0.7**
cougar	p_3			0.2	0.3
bear	p_4		**0.5**	**0.5**	

Fig. 5. Similarity of marmot, cougar, and bear with elephant concerning player's knowledge K_4

and the jungle of Africa and Asia, but not in the mountains or steppes like marmots do. Finally, the player can conclude that the bear has stolen Mama Marmot's berries.

7 Conclusion

Curricula can be imparted through location-based learning and LSBL in a new manner. Contextual and situational learning of this kind can add to faster acquisition of knowledge because of stimulating the intrinsic motivation of learners. In combination with GBL, the motivation of individuals to learn can even more be fostered. Thus, it is a future challenge to develop location-sequence-based game based learning environments which get essentially accepted and are forthright employed. Since recreation for many people is an expensive good, it is crucial to escape work life in time off. Concerning this matter, simulations, games, and role play seem most suitable for peripheral learning [12]. Such forms of learning are entertaining, reduce perceived idle time and stimulate the self-determined development of knowledge. In the end, the effect of learning seems most sustainable if people verily enjoy learning in recreational pauses.

In this paper, we presented the concept of such a learning system. Despite its great motivational advantages, there are still some limitations. First of all, the similarity function has to be designed very carefully for each application. If not, it may be possible that players cannot solve the game because they cannot gather all information that is needed for the quest. Then, this will discourage the player. Secondly, due to the quest to be solved, there are usually some information that players have to acquire in any case. This restricts the flexibility of the LSBL to some degrees.

References

1. Baker, A., Navarro, E.O., van der Hoek, A.: An experimental card game for teaching software engineering processes. J. Syst. Softw. **75**(1–2), 3–16 (2005)
2. Bittanti, M. (ed.): Civilization: Virtual History, Real Fantasies. Ludilogica Press, Milan (2005)
3. Bruner, J.S.: Towards a Theory of Instruction. Harvard University Press, Cambridge (1966)
4. Csikszentmihalyi, M., Hermanson, K.: Intrinsic motivation in museums: why does one want to learn? In: Hooper-Greenhill (ed.) The Educational Role of the Museum, Routledge, pp. 146–160 (1999)
5. Efrat, A., et al.: Using and determining location in a context-sensitive tour guide: the GUIDE experience. IEEE Comput. Spec. Issue Location-Based Comput. **34**(8), 35–41 (2001)
6. Gade, P.A.: The Influence of Trainee Gaming Experience and Computer Self-Efficacy on Learner Outcomes of Videogame-Based Learning Enviroments. U.S Army Research Institute for the Behavioral And Social Sciences, Arlington (2005)
7. Gee, J.P.: Good video games and good learning. Phi Kappa Phi Forum **85**(2), 33–37 (2005)
8. Kerres, M.: Multimediale und Telemediale Lernumgebungen: Konzeption und Entwicklung. Oldenbourg, München (2001)
9. Kolson, K.: The politics of SimCity. Polit. Sci. Polit. **29**(1), 43–46 (1996)
10. Kusunoki, F., Sugimoto, M.: Toward an interactive museum guide system with sensing and wireless network technologies. In: Proceedings of IEEE International Workshop on Wireless and Mobile Technologies in Education, Växjö, Sweden, pp. 99–102 (2002)

11. Leidner, D.E., Jarvenpaa, S.L.: The use of information technology to enhance management school education: a theoretical view. MIS Q. **19**(3), 265–291 (1995)
12. Leigh, E., Spindler, L.: Simulations and games as chaordic learning contexts. Simul. Gaming **34**(1), 53–69 (2004)
13. Looi, C.K., Sun, D., Wu, L., Seow, P., Chia, G., Wong, L.H., Soloway, E., Norris, C.: Implementing mobile learning curricula in a grade level: empirical study of learning effectiveness at scale. Comput. Educ. **77**, 101–115 (2014)
14. Malone, T.W., Lepper, M.R.: Making learning fun: a taxonomy of intrinsic motivations for learning. In: Snow, R.E., Farr, M.J. (eds.) Aptitute, Learning and Instruction: III. Conative and Affective Process Analyses. Erlbaum, Hilsdale, NJ, pp. 223–253 (1987)
15. Minass, E.: Dimensionen des E- Learning, p. 27. Smartbooks, Heidelberg (2002)
16. Nonaka, I., Takeuchi, H.: The Knowledge-Creating Company: How Japanese Companies Create the Dynamics of Innovation. Oxford University Press, New York (1995)
17. Nygaard, C., Andersen, I.: Contextual learning in higher education: curriculum development with focus on student learning. In: Milter, R.G., et al. (eds.) Educational Innovation in Economics and Business IX. Breaking Boundaries for Global Learning, pp. 277–294. Springer, Dordrecht (2004)
18. Patel, A., Kinshuk.: Intelligent tutoring tools – a problem solving framework for learning and assessment. In: Iskander, M.F., et al. (eds.) Proceedings of 1996 Frontiers in Education Conference – Technology-Based Re-Engineering Engineering Education, Salt Lake City, USA, pp. 140–144 (1996)
19. Pospisil, R., Millar, J.W.L.: Building the momentum for M-Learning via the ECU advantage project. In: Proceedings of ASCILITE: Balance, Fidelity, Mobility: Maintaining the Momentum? Brisbane, Australia (2005)
20. Siepermann, M.: Lecture accompanying E-Learning exercises with automatic marking. In: Richards, G. (ed.) Proceedings of World Conference on E-Learning, Chesapeake, USA, pp. 1750–1755 (2005)
21. Sindre, G., Natvig, L., Jahre, M.: Experimental validation of the learning effect for a pedagogical game on computer fundamentals. IEEE Trans. Educ. **52**(1), 10–18 (2009)
22. Thomas, P., Waugh, K., Smith, N.: Experiments in the automatic marking of ERDiagrams. In: 10th Annual Conference on Innovation and Technology in Computer Science Education, Monte de Caparica, Portugal, pp. 27–29 (2005)
23. Traxler, J.: Mobile learning: it's here but what is it? Interact. J. **9**(1), 1–12 (2005)

A Design Framework for Experiential History Games

Nicholas Lytle and Mark Floryan[✉]

Department of Computer Science, University of Virginia,
85 Engineers Way, Charlottesville, VA 22903, USA
{nal3gc,mfloryan}@virginia.edu

Abstract. This article presents empirical studies of a serious game focusing on various aspects of the American Civil War. We developed and deployed four distinct modules of our game for use within a fifth grade classroom in Virginia, USA. Of the first three modules deployed, only one lead to statistically significant results from pre-test to post-test. We used qualitative information from these first three trials to develop a design framework for experiential serious games of this form. We then developed and tested a fourth module by applying this framework and found significant learning improvements with this fourth module. This paper presents our game, results of empirical studies within a fifth grade classroom, and our proposed design framework identifying key aspects of the learning environment. Our results provide support for our hypothesis that application of this framework leads to increased learning gains. While we do not suggest that our framework is complete or exhaustive, we believe that designers of similar educational games can benefit by employing the principles of this framework directly.

Keywords: Serious games · Experiential learning · History education · Elementary education

1 Introduction

American students lack of knowledge in United States History is well documented. On the *National Assessment of Educational Progress* in 2014, 82 % of U.S. 8th grade students were not considered to be proficient in U.S. History knowledge.[1] In addition, there are well documented gender and racial gaps in history knowledge in elementary education, and the gap between public school students and those in private schools is significant. Comparatively, the number of 8th grade students that reported using computers for history/social studies education in school has increased significantly from 2010 to 2014 (18 % to 25 %), a promising indication that technology may be able to contribute to the solution to this problem.

---

[1] http://www.nationsreportcard.gov/hgc_2014/files/2014_history_appendix.pdf.

© Springer International Publishing Switzerland 2016
A. De Gloria and R. Veltkamp (Eds.): GALA 2015, LNCS 9599, pp. 161–170, 2016.
DOI: 10.1007/978-3-319-40216-1_17

While there have been many developments in educational and serious games that focus on STEM knowledge or topics, there have been relatively few developments for history-based games in the United States, especially American history. This is countered by the fact that U.S. History is the subject in which the smallest percentage of 8th and 12th grades students were tested as being proficient[2].

Agnor Hurt Elementary School, the school where the tests reported in this study were conducted, has a lower passing rate in history tests overall (70%) than both the corresponding district (85%) and state (84%). The school has also scored more poorly on the *fifth Grade Virginia studies test* (scoring 72% vs. 77% at Division and 85% at state).[3]

2   Related Work

While there exist relatively few serious games explicitly focusing on history in the scientific literature, many games are designed to be experiential in nature (including, but certainly not limited to [9–11]). These games allow the player to learn through direct experience within a simulated environment. Additionally, many frameworks exist for the design of educational games, but few relate specifically to experiential games. As one example, Akkerman et al. [9] describe a framework for developing a history game, Frequentie 1550, employing storification, but this framework is not entirely general in its utility to game designers. While some frameworks are very specific (and clearly useful when applied under the necessary constraints) many are quite general [2,4,5]. For example, Hunicke [3] describes the MDA framework for game design, but does not explicitly include educational purposes and does not provide specific meaningful heuristics for measuring a games application of the framework. Other frameworks [2,5,8], while very useful as general strategies for design, don't recommend explicit design principles, rendering their application somewhat difficult. Dondlinger [12] presents an overview of common strategies employed by successful educational games (goals, narrative, etc.), implying a useful concrete framework. In general, it seems most frameworks are either broadly constructed (useful in their ability to help us with general strategies for educational game design) or fitted to a particular problem (concrete and useful but only within a constrained problem space). One goal of this work is to attempt to provide a meaningful step towards bridging this gap, in which a fairly broad category of game (experiential games) might have a relatively concrete framework applied.

3   Our Game - A Nation Divided

A Nation Divided is a web-based game developed in Javascript using a rendering engine called *PIXI.JS*. The game is played from a top-down perspective as the player takes control of a nameless protagonist (see Fig. 1, left) navigating the

---

[2] http://www.nationsreportcard.gov/.

[3] https://p1pe.doe.virginia.gov/reportcard/report.do?division=2&schoolName=1797.

game world. The player interacts with other non-playable characters and entities and in many cases, the player is able to choose what response to give to these characters from a list of options.

The game currently contains four distinct modules (more detail below) focusing on distinct aspects of the American Civil War. In each module, the player is placed in a specific location and must complete a variety of tasks. This includes activities such as reading newspapers, communicating with townspeople, and engaging historical figures such as Harriet Tubman, Abraham Lincoln, etc. The quests for each module can be completed in any order, but all must be completed to progress to the ending segment. For many quests, the player must supply a non-playable character with the correct response to a question (or series of questions) to make progress. This helps ensure that the player understands a piece of information within the domain before continuing. If the player is unable to supply the correct answer to that character, there are characters within the vicinity that give hints or help.

Fig. 1. While playing, students walk around town interacting with historical figures and locals (left). Every module contains a unique end game scenario quizzing the students knowledge (right).

After all of the tasks are completed, the final section of a given module is available to the students. These ending scenarios are unique to each module and have their own interaction scheme and win condition. For example, Module 3 (Mid-war) features an end-game segment that tasks players to control a Union blockade and shoot down ships that have Confederate identifiers (Fig. 1, right). These ending segments usually tie back to the theme or plot that was developed in the previous section.

The game employs a cartoony aesthetic with colorful graphics and light, calming music. While there are certainly aspects of the time period that could have been explored or shown in a more detailed, mature light, the game was specifically designed for an elementary classroom setting and the design was catered around this intended young user. The dialogue, the primary vehicle for delivering information in the game, was not developed to be completely in-line with the speaking mannerisms of individuals in the 1800s. Instead, the primary goal was to make comprehensible and engaging dialogue that an average 5th grader could read and understand.

As stated earlier, the game contains four distinct modules, details of which follow:

1. **Underground Railroad:** Taking place on a southern cotton plantation in the 1850s, the player must aid Harriet Tubman in collecting supplies, information, and travelers to take on the Underground Railroad. Once ready, the player must complete a turn-based board game moving a group of runaway slaves from city to city navigating away from slavers trying to catch the party. The game is completed when either the slaves are caught (resulting in a game over) or the slaves are able to escape out of the country.
2. **Secession:** Set in an unspecified Virginian plantation in the year 1860, the player is tasked with delivering newspapers containing the news that Abraham Lincoln has been elected president. The player must present the correct newspaper to the non-playable characters (either a northern abolitionist newspaper or a southern newspaper) based off of the information and views that they relate to the player. On completion, the game shows each southern state seceding from the Union in order coupled with information about the beginning of the Civil War.
3. **Mid-war:** Set in 1862 on an unspecified Virginia plantation, the player must help General McClellan with a series of tasks for the Union. This includes relaying messages to Union naval officers, helping wounded soldiers remember which battles they took place in, and aiding Clara Barton and her nursing staff. Once completed, the player takes control of a Union blockade shooting down ships that have concepts associated with the Confederacy (e.g. Virginia, General Lee, Stars and Bars, etc.) and allowing ships that have concepts associated with the Union to pass.
4. **Gettysburg:** Set in Gettysburg, Pennsylvania during the Consecration of the National Cemetery at Gettysburg (1863), the player is tasked by Abraham Lincoln to collect information about what happened during the battle and how people are reacting. The player must piece a timeline of events from General Meade, ask for Frederick Douglass's opinion on the battle and war, and help reporters get the facts of the battle. Afterwards, the player aides Lincoln in constructing the Gettysburg Address by select the correct missing word in a segment of the address given its synonym.

Although similar to one another, each module is unique in exactly how material is presented and game mechanics are designed. The following section attempts to taxonomize the framework of our game.

4   Our Design Framework

Chronologically, we developed a framework for designing modules within our system after the deployment of modules 1–3 (Underground Railroad, Secession,

Mid-war) in the classroom, and before the design and development of module 4 (Gettysburg). The reasoning for this is two fold. Firstly, we observed large variation in the efficacy of the first three modules in the classroom (see methodology and results below) and wished to develop a theoretically understanding of how our various designs affected learning in the classroom. Additionally, we hoped to design the final module (Gettysburg) by applying our framework directly as a more robust test to validate the framework. Thus, one can observe that this framework is somewhat retrospective with regards to our first three modules (designed via qualitative and quantitative results of those interventions), but was applied and validated directly through the final Gettysburg module.

We identified nine design variables and posit that these affect the quality of an educational game, especially those similar in structure to our game.

1. **Spatial Clustering:** Spatial Clustering involves the degree to which related entities in the game are visually (spatially) located near one another. For example, a module that places a Union general (e.g., General Grant) near union soldiers is advantageous. This qualitative measure implies that designers can take advantage of the visual nature of the medium by spatially categorizing related elements for the player, assisting the player in forming a taxonomy of the information. This can also be done with certain groups in highlighting roles and viewpoints. Having all of the slave characters in the cotton fields while the white plantation masters and workers were outside of the fields (Module 1) serves to highlight differences between groups and form relationships between groups and roles.

2. **Temporal Clustering:** High temporal clustering occurs when all of the events chronologically fit into a small time-period. The higher range in time leads to low temporal clustering. For example, a module covering the entire American Civil War will have lower temporal clustering than a module focusing on one year within the war.

3. **Clearly Defined Goals:** Well documented in educational gaming [1,6,12], a module with clearly defined goals makes clear to the student what task is at hand and what must be achieved. Additionally, these goals should be concrete and actionable. Quests in the game that are easily identifiable to the player (e.g., talking to 10 clearly visible wounded soldiers) are easier for a student to accomplish than quests that are not (e.g., finding a canteen hidden on the map but occluded).

4. **Thematically Defined Ending:** This principle states that ending sequences (whether cinematic or interactive) should be closely tied to the activities the player was performing in the main mission to avoid a feeling of separation or exclusion. For example, Module 1's ending in which the player takes control of a runaway party of slaves on the Underground Railroad was a direct extension of the narrative developed from the previous segment in which the player had to collect supplies to get ready for the journey.

5. **Interactive Ending:** This principle states that modules should have a separate game as the ending sequence rather than a passive activity. We observed that modules with this feature tended to be better at engaging the students,

encouraging them to continually play after completion. For example, many students continually played the ending game for Module 3 (the Union blockade game) as it was the most developed and most interactive game of the 4 modules. Conversely, no students went through the slideshow of information about the beginnings of the Civil War found in Module 2 more than once.

6. **Difficulty of Gaming the System:** Gaming the system [13,14] occurs when students attempt to maneuver through an educational (or any) system in an unintended way (usually by leveraging the feedback given). An activity scoring well on this dimension might be a task forcing students to put ten events in history in proper order. Because this task has many combinations (too many to reasonably guess each), it is difficult for a student to game the system (i.e., try every combo until the player can move on without considering the content and/or purpose of the activity). This is best exemplified in our system in Module 4 (Gettysburg) in the segment where the player must aide General Meade in piecing together a timeline of events. Because each required input has 5 different options, most students elected to not attempt a guess and check approach to the quest.

7. **First-Hand Interaction:** This principle involves the degree to which a student can directly interact with any artifacts of interest. For example, a module that discusses a famous historical figure would have less first-hand interaction than a module that allows the player to directly speak with that figure. In examining questions related to identifying people, it was found that the questions that had the subject present in the game performed better. In general, we posit that increased first-hand interaction is likely preferable.

8. **Breadth of Quests:** This refers to the number of unique quests any given module has. For example, Module 1 (The Underground Railroad) had 7 small quests while Module 2 (Secession) had 2 larger quests. While Module 1 was the most successful, we believed that there is most likely a hard limit on how many individual quests a module can contain before a player can become overwhelmed. This limit could also be more related to the number of actions in a module than the number of quests.

9. **Depth of Quests:** In addition to breadth of quests, depth of quests refers to the amount of actions necessary for the completion of a single quest. For example, a quest that requires a student to deliver 10 newspaper is said to be deeper than a quest that only requires the player to speak to 4 naval officers. We posited that there was a hard limit on how deep a quest could be before the task becomes overwhelming or frustrating to the player.

Table 1 below presents the degree to which each of our four modules address the nine principles in our design framework. The lead game designer was asked to identify each module as having low (red in table below), medium (yellow in table below), or high (green in table below) application of the principle in question. A rating of low approximately means that less than 25 % of the module correctly applies the principle. Yellow was given if between 25 and 75 % of the module content addresses the principle in question, while green indicates that most (more than 75 %) of the content is a direct application of the principle in question.

Table 1. A visual representation of how well each of our four modules applies the various aspects of our design framework. Green implies a strong application, yellow a medium application, and red a weak application of that particular principle.

	Spatial Clustering	Temporal Clustering	Clear Defined Goal	Thematically Defined Ending	Interactive Ending	Hard to Game	First-hand Interaction	Breadth of Quests	Depth of Quests
Underground Railroad									
Secession									
Mid-war									
Gettysburg									

5   Methodology

For each module, students from a small elementary school in Virginia were taken out of the classroom for an hour long period of time. Each student was a 5th grader who was learning the material discussed in the game that year in their classroom. Each student was given a school laptop computer to access the game as well as pencils and pens to answer the pre and post test questions. Some students participated in multiple test sessions while others did not. The number of students that participated in each test session varied from module to module. This information is provided in the Results section under Table 2.

The test sessions were divided into three main sections: the pre-test, the game playing session, and the post test. Between each of these sections the students were given instructions on what he or she would be doing by the researchers and the teacher. During each section, the teachers and researchers would provide clarification to any student asking questions or provide help to the student when asked if it did not directly influence their ability to complete the task (e.g. getting paper). Each student was given a unique identifying number that was held constant between all three sections. The teacher was able to know which student was tied to each number, but the researchers did not.

During the pre and post-test sessions, each student was given a test that included a number of multiple choice questions related to the material discussed in the game. These questions were all modeled after Virginia Standard of Learning (SOL) style questions for the 5th grade Virginia Studies SOL and some were direct questions from previous SOL exams. The students were able to answer the questions in any order they chose and were given 15 min to complete the assessment. In some sessions, some questions appeared on both the pre and post test for that session and some questions appeared on multiple test sessions.

Between the pre and post test sessions, the students had up to 30 min to play the game. Students were allowed to ask the teachers and researchers clarifying questions but were not given information on exactly where to go or how to complete a task. Any technical difficulties that happened during this period were handled by the researchers. The students were not strictly discouraged from collaborating with other students playing the game unless a student was explicitly telling other students how to complete certain tasks. If a student completed the entirety of the game, he or she was encouraged to continue exploring within the game until the time limit for gameplay was up.

6   Results

Table 2 below summarizes the pre test to post test score changes over all four modules. Three modules led to improvements in scores (modules 1, 3, and 4). Modules 1 and 4 were the only two that show statistically significant results ($p < 0.05$). Both of these modules also contain medium to high effect sizes.

Table 2. Overall results comparing pre test to post test scores across all four test sessions (one test per module)

Module	n	x_1	σ_1^2	x_2	σ_2^2	p	Cohen's D
Underground Railroad	17	0.614	0.176	0.739	0.147	**0.012***	**0.766**
Secession	20	0.611	0.224	0.572	0.208	0.384	0.180
Mid-war	15	0.550	0.210	0.633	0.208	0.191	**0.398**
Gettysburg	18	0.346	0.225	0.438	0.234	**0.008****	**0.398**

We also performed an analysis of learning gains across various question types, in order to obtain some sense of student learning across categories. Table 3 below summarizes these results. Modules 1 and 4 performed well on questions regarding *people* (important players during various times of the war). Additionally, module 1 displayed improvements on *analysis* questions. Two modules (3 and 4) show significant improvements in questions regarding *events*. There were no significant improvements on questions regarding viewpoints or facts & terms.

Table 3. P-Values of T-Tests from pre to post test broken down by question type. Red highlights indicate that the mean decreased. Bold indicates statistically significant changes.

Module	n	People	Geography	Viewpoints	Facts	Events	Analysis
U. Railroad	17	**0.007****	N/A	0.999	0.168	N/A	**0.013***
Secession	20	0.090	0.517	0.209	N/A	0.825	N/A
Mid-war	15	0.178	N/A	0.334	N/A	**0.006****	N/A
Gettysburg	18	**0.003****	0.668	0.104	0.999	**0.049***	0.496

7   Conclusions and Future Work

We were pleased to find that overall, the Underground Railroad module and the Gettysburg module displayed the highest learning gains, as they tended to fit our model more closely than the other two modules. We thus believe that our data provides some support for the hypothesis that our framework is a useful tool for designing educational games of this form. We are, however, hesitant to claim that our framework provides sufficient or necessary conditions for effective educational game design. Our intention with this work was to make progress towards useful design principles for game designers constructing experiential games geared towards younger students (elementary in our case). To this effect, we feel that although our framework is not authoritative or complete, it provides useful insight and progress towards a robust set of design principles for educational games. To this end, we note that our most promising result from this work is the increase in learning gains observed with module 1 (Underground Railroad) and module 4 (Gettysburg), the two modules which most closely apply the principles from our framework. Some meaningful insight might be gleaned by re-examining our framework and the degree to which these two modules fit various features (see Table 2 above). In particular, features that were closely applied in our successful modules and not in unsuccessful modules may prove to be more important for design. These features include spatial clustering, providing a clearly defined goal, and providing a thematically defined ending. Thus, these design considerations may very well be the subjects of immediate further inquiry as they have shown promise as a potential indicator of success in the classroom.

Likewise, framework features that are ignored by our two unsuccessful modules might indicate a lowest-common denominator for ineffective design. Features fitting this category include providing a thematically defined ending, having it be difficult to game the system [13], and providing a clearly defined goal. These features, in fact, could prove to be necessary features of any successful design, a conclusion supported by related literature [6,7,12].

Additionally, our analysis breakdown by question might provide some indication of design elements that help reinforce various types of knowledge. For example, identifying important people within the war was most successful in modules with high spatial clustering, a result that may indicate that clustering helps students categorize the major players more accurately. Questions regarding events showed most improvement in modules 3 and 4, potentially indicating that features unique to those modules (first hand interaction, interactive endings) improve learning in this area. Both of these claims require further investigation, but may generalize to other related situations.

In conclusion, the purpose of this work was to investigate the use of educational games for history education. We developed an initial framework based on results of three modules used within a 5th grade classroom, and applied this framework to a fourth module for validity. Our results show that the best pre to post-test learning gains occurred in modules that most closely applied our design framework. While we don't claim that this fully validates our framework, it does provide evidence that the ideas therein are worthy of further exploration as we attempt to make progress towards a robust set of design principles for educational game design. We thus hope that educational game designers can find utility in thinking about the aspects of our design framework and how these features might affect the efficacy of a resulting game implementation.

Acknowledgements. We would like to thank Andy Barron, David Amin, Zane Laughlin, Adrian Lee Gloria, and the rest of the development team (http://people. virginia.edu/~nal3gc/civilwarcredits). We would also like to thank Mia Shand, along with all of the faculty, staff, and students of Agnor Hurt Elementary School for their participation in the study.

References

1. Charsky, D.: From edutainment to serious games: a change in the use of game characteristics. Games Cult. **5**, 177–198 (2010)
2. Westera, W., et al.: Serious games for higher education: a framework for reducing design complexity. J. Comput. Assist. Learn. **24**(5), 420–432 (2008)
3. Hunicke, R., LeBlanc, M., Zubek, R.: MDA: a formal approach to game design and game research. In: Proceedings of the AAAI Workshop on Challenges in Game AI, vol. 4 (2004)
4. Salen, K., Zimmerman, E.: Rules of Play: Game Design Fundamentals. MIT Press, Cambridge (2004)
5. Burgos, D., Tattersall, C., Koper, R.: Re-purposing existing generic games and simulations for e-learning. Comput. Hum. Behav. **23**(6), 2656–2667 (2007)
6. Prensky, M.: Computer games and learning: digital game-based learning. In: Raessens, J., Goldstein, J. (eds.) Handbook of Computer Game Studies, vol. 18, pp. 97–122. MIT Press, Cambridge (2005)
7. Gee, J.P.: Good Video Games+ Good Learning: Collected Essays on Video Games, Learning, and Literacy. P. Lang, New York (2007)
8. Kelly, H., et al.: How to build serious games. Commun. ACM **50**(7), 44–49 (2011)
9. Akkerman, S., Admiraal, W., Huizenga, J.: Storification in History education: a mobile game in and about medieval Amsterdam. Comput. Educ. **52**(2), 449–459 (2009)
10. Floryan, M., Woolf, B.: Rashi game: towards an effective educational 3D gaming experience. In: Proceedings of the IEEE International Conference on Advanced Learning Technologies, Athens, GA (2011)
11. Froschauer, J., et al.: Design and evaluation of a serious game for immersive cultural training. In: 2010 16th International Conference on Virtual Systems and Multimedia (VSMM). IEEE (2010)
12. Dondlinger, M.J.: Educational video game design: a review of the literature. J. Appl. Educ. Technol. **4**(1), 21–31 (2007)
13. Baker, R., et al.: Why students engage in gaming the system behavior in interactive learning environments. J. Interact. Learn. Res **19**(2), 185–224 (2008)
14. Cocea, M., Hershkovitz, A., Baker, R.S.: The impact of off-task and gaming behaviors on learning: immediate or aggregate? In: Proceedings of the 2009 Conference on Artificial Intelligence in Education, pp. 507–514 (2009)

Teaching Statistics and Risk Management with Card Games

Markus Siepermann[✉]

Technische Universität Dortmund, Otto-Hahn-Str. 12, 44227 Dortmund, Germany
markus.siepermann@tu-dortmund.de

Abstract. Very often, students lack of understanding and motivation for formal concepts like programming, modelling, mathematics, or statistics although these are key skills and very important for disciplines like risk management. In this paper, we present a learning system based on the simple card game High or Low that helps to teach fundamental principles of statistics and risk management. In addition, we provide a computer prognosis to the players. Results show that if students are forced to calculate the likelihood and make the decision which option to choose on their own, the outcome is acceptable. But if a computer generated prognosis is given, a high percentage of students rely on the prognosis even if it is obviously not correct.

Keywords: Card games · Game based learning · Statistics · Risk management

1 Introduction

Many business sciences disciplines like accounting, information systems, operations management, production management etc. require good skills in mathematics, statistics, or other formal concepts like algorithmic problem solving and modelling. But unfortunately, students often lack of these skills. Aggravating, they even dislike mathematics. In a non-representative short-survey, we asked students at the beginning of their studies why they have chosen to study business sciences. The response was alarming: More than one half of the students answered that they do not like mathematics and do not want to do that anymore so that they have chosen to study business sciences. Obviously, this is a dangerous misjudgement.

In addition, as regularly conducted course evaluations show, formal concepts like data or business process modelling as well as algorithmic problem solving are usually new to more than half of the students (see Table 1). This problem keeps active during all semesters of bachelor studies. Although the course evaluations also indicate that students are satisfied with the lectures (both lectures of Table 1 consecutively achieved 1st or 2nd place in lecture ranking during the past two years) and say that they have learned a lot, they still have problems with formal concepts after these courses as exam results show. Thus, there is a huge gap between the knowledge and the interests of students on the one side, and the skills that are needed in business sciences and job requirements on the other side. This gap has to be closed during studies. But unfortunately, students often show an aversion against these skills and lack of motivation to learn them.

© Springer International Publishing Switzerland 2016
A. De Gloria and R. Veltkamp (Eds.): GALA 2015, LNCS 9599, pp. 171–180, 2016.
DOI: 10.1007/978-3-319-40216-1_18

Table 1. Previous knowledge of students concerning formal concepts

	Semester	New topic	High learning effect
Algorithmic problem solving	2013	56.3 %	57.9 %
	2014	61.4 %	51.3 %
	2015	40.7 %	71.4 %
Modelling	2012/2013	74.4 %	76.7 %
	2013/2014	84.6 %	84.6 %
	2014/2015	80.0 %	89.2 %

Thus, a major challenge for teaching is to motivate students to learn such skills as they are key job qualifications. If the intrinsic motivation for learning is missing, games can be an appropriate measure to extrinsicly motivate students to learn [7, 16, 20, 29]. In addition, playing games is one of the most effective [1, 5, 6] and natural ways to learn [11]. In the case of online games, additional advantages like student tracking, online assessment, user feedback, or community features can be realised [18].

For business sciences, an important topic in statistics is the concept of likelihood and conditional probability that is used in many disciplines like risk management or supply chain management. For this topic, we developed a learning system based on the simple card game *High or Low* to teach these basic principles of statistics. There, the player has to decide if a masked card is higher or lower than an uncovered card. If the situation is too risky, the player has the choice to fold.

The remainder of this paper is organised as follows. In the next section, we give a short overview of existing games used for teaching. In Sect. 3 we introduce the cards game based learning system that we developed to teach and practice the concept of likelihood and evaluation of risk situations. Section 4 presents some initial analyses of the game. The paper closes with a discussion of the results and future prospects.

2   Literature Review

Game based learning (GBL) is often seen as the simple combination of videogames and education [18]. Although already the interaction with computers can improve the motivation [28], this bears the danger of reducing games to the motivational aspect [12]. If GBL is only used as a vehicle to motivate students extrinsicly, its real potential is misconceived [24]. Therefore, we use the definition of Salen & Zimmerman (2004) that "a game is a system in which players engage in an artificial conflict, defined by rules, that results in a quantifiable outcome" [23]. This definition clearly distinguishes games and therefore GBL from the concept of gamification. Gamification comprises any attempt to use game concepts for teaching and learning such as the use of leader boards in class rooms or game time as a reward for good learning [17]. In these cases, the learning process is separated from the game so that students can easily get bored [10]. The same holds for badly designed games that are either too simple [12] or where the learning content is put into the game as an interruption so that the content has to be learned in order to proceed in the game. As a result, it is difficult to keep the learners' engagement high [9] as they are not motivated to learn skills because they are convinced to need them. On the contrary, learning the content runs the risk of getting cumbersome. Then, students tend to become good gamers and guessers instead of good learners [10] so that the learning output reduces and a deeper understanding of the underlying content cannot be achieved [17]. Therefore, it is crucial to find a balance between game fun and educational value [22].

One approach to provide game fun is to use existing commercial video games like SimCity [13] and derivates [27], Civilisation [3, 26], or World of Warcraft [8]. But it is not possible to use existing games for any conceivable learning situation [19]. Therefore, many authors developed special games for specific purposes to use the full potential of games.

A popular field of application for GBL is learning languages. Lin et al. (2008) for example developed a crossword game to learn English vocabulary [14]. Chen et al. (2010) as well as Liu & Liu (2005) focused on learning Chinese [4, 15]. Another field of application is computer sciences as many authors come from this discipline. Sindre et al. (2009) for example have built a kind of adventure game where the player is the hero who has to solve different quests in order to proceed in the game [25] while Baker et al. (2005) developed a card game that simulates the management of a software development project [2]. Pfotenhauer et al. (2009) use a Matlab simulation to teach cryogenic principles [21].

While the above mentioned games are especially designed to teach a certain topic, we use the underlying principles of the popular card game *High or Low* to teach fundamental principles of statistics. With the help of this game, we show how knowledge on statistics helps to achieve better results in the game and therefore how helpful statistics can be. Knowledge about statistics is needed in risk management where risk situations have to be quantified and evaluated. Then, on the basis of that evaluation, the decision on action alternatives has to be made. However, players also learn that, although statistics help us to judge a situation better, it is still possible that because of the uncertainty of the game and of life the less likely situation may occur so that invested money is lost.

3   The Game Concept

3.1   High or Low

The *High or Low* card game (see Fig. 1) is one of the simplest card games played with either 32 or 52 cards. For calculation simplicity, we restrict the game to 32 cards. The order of the cards colours shall be (from high to low) spades, hearts, diamonds, clubs, the order of the cards shall be ace, king, queen, jack, 10, 9, 8, and 7. Then, the gameplay is as follows: Initially, the player has a sum of 100 coins that he can use to play the game. In the first step, the dealer (here: the computer player) takes the first two cards from the pile of cards and shows one card to the player. The other card is hidden. If the first card is spades ace or clubs 7, it is immediately put to the pile of used cards and the next card is drawn. Otherwise, the player has three options:

- He can fold and do nothing.
- He can say that the next card will be higher and bet an amount of his coins.

– He can say that the next card will be lower and bet an amount of his coins.

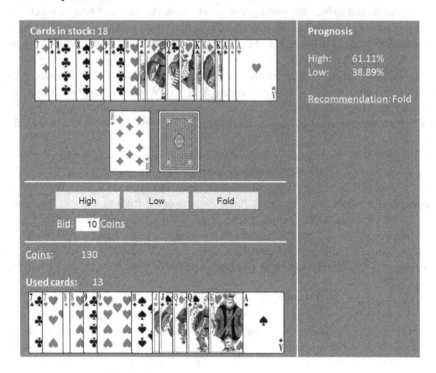

Fig. 1. User interface of the *High or Low* game

If the player folded, the first card is put on the pile with the played cards. The hidden card is not shown and placed in the pile of unused cards. If the player is wrong, his bid is lost. If he is right, he won the doubled bid. The game continues until there are only two cards left. Then, the cards are shuffled again. If the player has lost all of his coins, he lost the game.

3.2   Calculating the Likelihood

When playing this game, a common mistake is to assume that the likelihood to guess high or low correctly is 50 % because the player has two options for guessing. But obviously, this is not correct. The likelihood that the hidden card is higher or lower than the revealed card depends on the value of the revealed card and the cards that are still in stock. Let us assume a complete new stock and the first card being spades 10. Then, the likelihood that the hidden card is higher than spades 10 is $16/31 = 51.61$ %. That means that good players should calculate the likelihood at each step depending on the current shown card and the cards that are still in stock or respectively that are already played. Then, if the player orientates to the likelihood, he will be successful in the long-run. But he has to keep in mind that although he orientates to the likelihood, it is still possible to lose a round. For example, if the first revealed card is hearts ace, the likelihood that the hidden card is lower is $30/31 = 96.77\%$. But it is still possible that the next card is spades ace (with a likelihood of 3.22 %).

3.3 Game Modes

Now, the system provides different modes to the player. In the *basic mode*, the player gets all information about the stock and the pile of used cards. He cannot only see the revealed card but also the list of cards that are still in stock and the number of cards already played. This helps to correctly calculate the likelihood in each round. In the *advanced mode*, information about the stock and played cards is hidden.

To be successful in the game, it is not only important to calculate the likelihood correctly, but also to apply this knowledge to the game and to judge the situation. For example, this is a useful skill for risk management where different situations have to be measured and evaluated. Then, on the basis of this evaluation, a decision has to be made. Let us have a look at our initial example with the first card revealed being spades 10. The likelihood that the hidden card is higher than spades 10 is 51.61 %. A risk neutral decision maker would therefore choose the option high card. The reason is that the expected revenue is greater than zero. If we assume a bid of 100, the expected revenue is 3.22. Thus, placing a bid on high leads to a positive revenue in the long-run. However, it is not advisable to place all coins because it is still possible and quite likely to lose the bet. At first sight, most people would therefore choose the option to fold because the situation between high and low is nearly balanced which contradicts the concept of neutral decision making.

For teaching purposes, a so-called *prognosis mode* can be applied to the basic and advanced mode. In this mode, the system calculates the likelihood and gives a recommendation to the player which option to choose. There, the system acts like a risk neutral decision maker. That means that only if the likelihood of choosing high or respectively low is exactly 50 %, the recommendation is to fold. Two sub-modes are implemented: The *teaching mode* calculates the likelihood and gives a recommendation while the *practice mode* gives only a recommendation.

The *teaching mode* has the purpose to explain the fundamentals of the game, the underlying statistics and risk concepts. The player can reproduce in each step how the likelihood is calculated. Then, on the basis of the likelihood, the correct option has to be chosen. If the expected outcome of an option is positive, this option should be chosen. In the practice mode, the player has to calculate the likelihood on his own. The recommendation for an option then only indicates if the likelihood was calculated correctly.

In addition, an *assessment mode* can also be applied to the basic and advanced mode that also provides several sub-modes. In the first mode, the player has to calculate the likelihood of one of the options high or low and write the percentage rounded to the second decimal place into the answer box but without choosing high or low. This mode tests if the player calculates the likelihood correctly. In the second sub-mode, the player again has to calculate the likelihood of one option. Then, after giving the answer, he has to choose the option of a risk neutral decision maker. This mode tests if the calculation of the likelihood is correct and if the player has understood the concept of risk neutral decision making. In the third mode, the player gets the recommendation of the system which option to choose. But this recommendation is not necessarily correct. In addition, the player has to place a bid if he chooses the high or low option. This mode tests if the player only relies on the prognosis or calculates the likelihood on his own. As the player has to place bids, we can judge if the player just guessed or calculated correctly: If he calculated the likelihood correctly, his bids should correspond to that likelihood. The higher the correct likelihood is, the higher his bid should be. That means that the grading depends on how the player plays the game and not on the number of coins that he won.

4 Analysis

We used the above presented game during summer term 2015 in a preliminary study to observe how students use the system. 42 students participated in the study and played the game several times. 63 % of the participants were male and 37 % were female.

Because of its early stage, the system was not used for assessment and grading in exams. In the basic assessment mode 1, the likelihood was usually calculated correctly. In assessment mode 2, in general the decisions were correct. But however, we observed deviations from the optimal decision strategy: Usually, only when the likelihood exceeded 60 %, students tended to choose high or low instead of fold. A conceivable reason can be that the risk adjustment of students is not necessarily risk neutral but risk-averse. Therefore, only a likelihood significantly higher than 50 % can lead to a decision high or low instead of fold. However, this behaviour should be examined further in future studies.

Table 2. Interpretation of Cramér's V

Value	Interpretation
0.00 – 0.10	No intercorrelation
0.10 – 0.30	Weak intercorrelation
0.30 – 0.60	Average intercorrelation
0.60 – 1.00	Strong intercorrelation

Assessment mode 3 was not tested as described in Sect. 3. Instead, we observed how students rely on the prognosis and the given recommendation without placing bids. This is very interesting in the field of risk management. There, it is important not to completely rely on prognoses and given key indicators but to critically analyse them and come to an own well-founded decision. Now, in this mode, the player's only information is the revealed card and the recommendation which option to choose. If desired, the player has to track the sequence of played cards on his own in order to know which cards are played and which are still in the stock. The recommendation was manipulated as follows: The fold recommendation was given for a likelihood between 50 % and 55 %. If the likelihood was between 85 % and 100 % no manipulation was done to avoid a fast detection of the manipulation. Between 55 % and 85 %, the recommendation was inverted from high to low and vice versa. In the first two rounds of each game, no manipulation was done to avoid a fast detection of the manipulation. We used Cramér's V to measure the association between the players' decisions and the recommendations of the system. The common interpretation of Cramér's V is given in Table 2.

Without manipulation, 79 % of the players have a strong intercorrelation between their decision and the recommendation and 21 % have an average intercorrelation. Because Cramér's V is a measure that expresses only the strength of a relation and that does not reveal its direction, i.e. if it is positive or negative, we have to check separately if the players followed the recommendation. Figure 2 shows the relation between the given recommendations and the players' decisions if manipulations are possible. As we can see, all players followed the correct recommendations. Concerning the manipulated recommendations, 70 % did not follow and chose another option in more than 75 % of all wrong recommendations, but 22 % of all players still followed the wrong recommendations leading to bad decisions on which option to choose.

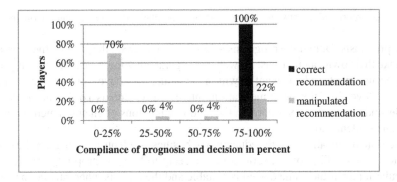

Fig. 2. Match between recommendation and player decision

If we have a look on those players, who strongly rely on the recommendations, we get an interesting result. Then, there is a difference in gender when using the recommendation. If there is no manipulation during the game throughout, 92 % of the male players have a strong intercorrelation between their decision and the recommendation in comparison to 71 % of the female players. But when the prognosis is manipulated and the recommendations can be wrong, the picture inverts. Then, 83 % of the male and 86 % of the female players still rely on the correct recommendation. But 64 % of the female players keep on relying on the wrong recommendations while only 50 % of the male players do so (see Fig. 3).

5   Discussion

Results show that in general students are able to calculate the statistical measures correctly if they are forced to do so. But concerning the risk adjustment, there is a deviation from risk neutral decision making, be it because of the students' general risk adjustment that is not necessarily neutral but may be risk taking or risk-averse, be it because of a misunderstanding in risk neutral decision making. Moreover, when additional tools like a prognosis are provided, a significant number of students tends to rely

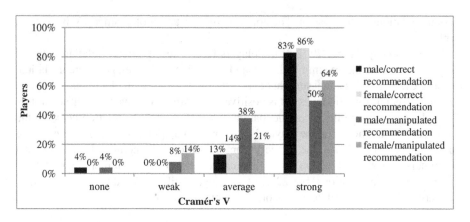

Fig. 3. Intercorrelation between recommendation and player decision depending on gender

on this prognosis. Only if the prognosis is obviously incorrect, they ignore the prognosis and make their own calculations. However, the game play improves the learning situation. Because most students want to win in the game, they have a critical look at prognoses and "override" the recommendation. Interestingly, there is a difference in gender. Female students tend to rely more on the recommendations of an automated prognosis than male students do.

There are implications for the education of business students as well as for the design of serious games. First of all, serious games seem to be an appropriate way to teach unpopular topics if the game design is suitable and the topic is inherently connected to the game itself. Then, students engage in the problem and learn to apply the basic theory. Secondly, business education should consider the differences in gender when teaching statistics and using prognoses. Because female students tend to rely more faithfully on tools even if the outcome is wrong, a special focus should be set on a critical reflection of supporting tools when teaching females in order to make them aware of possible errors in prognosis systems.

For game designers, the first implication is that the topic to be learned should inherently be connected with the game. If the underlying theory is a prerequisite to solve the game task, students are willing to learn and to apply the theory. Secondly, the results of manipulated prognoses show that games should not provide too much help and too many supporting tools. If so, students may rely on these tools and "just play" the game. A suitable solution could be to include obviously false results so that players are forced to verify the results of the supporting tools and therefore to apply their knowledge.

As always, some limitations are present. First of all, the number of participants was quite small. Future studies should collect more data and analyse that data more deeply. By now, the bids were not analysed at all but they could provide useful information about the strategies of the players, in particular when and why they followed and deviated from recommendations. Possible reasons could be a risk-averse instead of a risk neutral risk adjustment or a misunderstanding of risk neutral decision making. However, the present study cannot answer this question. Secondly, because of the small sample, the differences in gender may not be representative. But it would be interesting to analyse if and why female students tend to rely more on prognosis tools than male students do. Thirdly, we did not analyse until now if the use of the system really leads to a better understanding of statistics, decision making under risk and the use of prognosis tools. A future step will be to analyse the impact of the game on assessment and grading.

The system itself can also be expanded. In the current form, it is a single player game against a computer system. The introduction of a leader board would foster the competition. This could lead to a deeper engagement of students and could lower the belief of some students in the quality of the prognosis.

References

1. Asan, A.: School experience course with multimedia in teacher education. J. Comput. Assist. Learn. **19**, 21–34 (2003)
2. Baker, A., Navarro, E.O., van der Hoek, A.: An experimental card game for teaching software engineering processes. J. Syst. Softw. **75**(1–2), 3–16 (2005)
3. Bittanti, M. (ed.): Civilization: Virtual History, Real Fantasies. Ludilogica Press, Milan (2005)
4. Chen, Z.H., Liao, C.C., Chan, T.W.: Learning by pet-training competition: alleviating negative influences of direction competition by training pets to compete in game-based environments. In: 2010 IEEE 10th International Conference on Advanced Learning Technologies (ICALT), pp. 411–413 (2010)
5. Cole, J.M., Hilliard, V.R.: The effects of web-based reading curriculum on children's reading performance and motivation. J. Educ. Comput. Res. **34**, 353–380 (2006)
6. deLeon, L., Killian, J.: Comparing modes of delivery: classroom and on-line (and other) learning. J. Public Aff. Educ. **6**, 5–18 (2000)
7. Ebner, M., Holzinger, A.: Successful implementation of user-centered game based learning in higher education: an example from civil engineering. Comput. Educ. **49**(3), 873–890 (2007)
8. Gee, J.P.: Good video games and good learning. Phi Kappa Phi Forum **85**(2), 33–37 (2005)
9. Jackson, G.T., McNamara, D.S.: Motivational impacts of a game-based intelligent tutoring system. In: FLAIRS Conference, pp. 1–6 (2011)
10. Ke, F.: A case study of computer gaming for math: engaged learning from gameplay? Comput. Educ. **51**(4), 1609–1620 (2008)
11. Kickmeier-Rust, M.D., Albert, D.: Micro-adaptivity: protecting immersion in didactically adaptive digital educational games. J. Comput. Assist. Learn. **26**, 95–105 (2010)
12. Kirriemuir, J., McFarlane, A.: Literature review in games and learning. A NESTA Futurelab Research report - report 8 (2004)
13. Kolson, K.: The politics of SimCity. Polit. Sci. Polit. **29**(1), 43–46 (1996)
14. Lin, C.P., Young, S.S.C., Hung, H.C.: The game-based constructive learning environment to increase english vocabulary acquisition: Implementing a Wireless Crossword Fan-Tan Game (WiCFG) as an example. In: Fifth IEEE International Conference on Wireless, Mobile and Ubiquitous Technology in Education, WMUTE 2008, pp. 205–207 (2008)
15. Liu, Z., Liu, Z.: Building an intelligent pedagogical agent with competition mechanism to improve the effectiveness of an educational game. In: Workshop on Educational Games as Intelligent Learning Environments (2005)
16. Maloy, R.W., Edwards, S.A., Anderson, G.: Teaching math problem solving using a web-based tutoring system, learning games, and students' writing. J. STEM Educ. **11**(1&2), 82–90 (2010)

17. McClarty, K.L., Orr, A., Frey, P.M., Dolan, R.P., Vassileva, V., McVay, A.: A literature review of gaming in education. Gaming in education (2012)

18. Moreno-Ger, P., Burgos, D., Martínez-Ortiz, I., Sierra, J.L., Fernández-Manjón, B.: Educational game design for online education. Comput. Hum. Behav. **24**, 2530–2540 (2008)

19. Nagle, R. (2001). Enrichment games and instructional design: Can game-based learning transfer to other domains. http://www.imaginaryplanet.net/essays/literary/games/games6.php

20. Papastergiou, M.: Digital game-based learning in high school computer science education: impact on educational effectiveness and student motivation. Comput. Educ. **52**(1), 1–12 (2009)

21. Pfotenhauer, J.M., Gagnon, D.J., Litzkow, M.J., Blakesley, C.C.: Designing and using an online game to teach engineering. In: Frontiers in Education Conference, W2C, pp. 1–5 (2009)

22. Prensky, M.: Digital Game Based Learning. McGraw-Hill, New York (2001)

23. Salen, K., Zimmerman, E.: Rules of Play: Game Design Fundamentals. MIT Press, Cambridge (2004)

24. Siepermann, M., Lackes, R., Börgermann, C.: Generic question-and-answer based business games. JADLET J. Adv. Distrib. Learn. Technol. **1**(2), 34–43 (2013)

25. Sindre, G., Natvig, L., Jahre, M.: Experimental validation of the learning effect for a pedagogical game on computer fundamentals. IEEE Trans. Educ. **52**(1), 10–18 (2009)

26. Squire, K., Barab, S.: Replaying history: engaging urban underserved students in learning world history through computer simulation games. In: Sixth International Conference of the Learning Sciences. Lawrence Erlbaum Associates, Santa Monica, United States (2004)

27. Starr, P.: Seductions of sim: policy as a simulation game. Am. Prospect **5**(17), 19–29 (1994). Spring

28. Vogel, J.J., Greenwood-Ericksen, A., Cannon-Bower, J., Bowers, C.A.: Using virtual reality with and without gaming attributes for academic achievement. J. Res. Technol. Educ. **39**, 105–118 (2006)

29. Wang, L.C., Chen, M.P.: The effects of game strategy and preference-matching on flow experience and programming performance in game-based learning. Innovations Educ. Teach. Int. **47**(1), 39–52 (2010)

Simulation-Based Serious Games for Science Education in Elementary and Middle Schools

Seungho Baek, Ji-Young Park, and JungHyun Han$^{(\boxtimes)}$

Korea University, Seoul, Korea
{bshsqa,lemie,jhan}@korea.ac.kr
http://media.korea.ac.kr

Abstract. This paper presents serious games developed for the science subject in elementary and middle schools, specifically for the chapters of "Force and Motion" and "State Change of Water." The components of each chapter were thoroughly analyzed, and then a game-based curriculum was developed for the components classified as having high- or mid-level difficulties in both teaching and learning. Based on the curriculum, the PC-based game "Force and Motion" implemented frictional/gravitational/magnetic force simulations, and the mobile game "State Change of Water" implemented particle-based fluid simulations. The games were evaluated by elementary and middle school teachers, and the evaluation results showed that simulation-based serious games are promising tools for improving the learning effects in science subject.

Keywords: Serious games · Simulation · Science education

1 Introduction

The usefulness of serious games has been proved in many fields including education, training, and healthcare. In fact, serious games are currently being used in the real-world education fields, and it is agreed upon that they are especially well suited to motivate learners. In the subjects of mathematics and foreign languages, for example, many commercial games are available. However, the educational potential of serious games is not yet proven in the science subject. There would be many reasons for this, but an important one is that games in the science subject require *physics-based simulation*, which is hard to implement at real time especially for non-rigid objects.

This paper presents serious games developed for the science subject in elementary and middle schools. Unlike the previous games that largely focused on visual effects rather than physically correct simulations and consequently would often lead students to fatal misconceptions, the serious games presented in this paper are intended to be faithful to the physics laws: the PC-based game "Force and Motion" implemented frictional/gravitational/magnetic force simulations, and the mobile game "State Change of Water" implemented particle-based fluid

© Springer International Publishing Switzerland 2016
A. De Gloria and R. Veltkamp (Eds.): GALA 2015, LNCS 9599, pp. 181–188, 2016.
DOI: 10.1007/978-3-319-40216-1_19

simulation. The games were evaluated by elementary and middle school teachers, and the evaluation results show that simulation-based serious games are promising tools for improving the learning effects in science subject.

This paper is organized as follows. Section 2 reviews the related studies. Section 3 overviews how the games have been designed and developed. Sections 4 and 5 detail "Force and Motion" and "State Change of Water," respectively. Section 6 presents the evaluation results, and Sect. 7 concludes the paper.

2   Related Work

The status of serious games in the history of game development has been studied in Zyda [1]. With the advent of Nintendo Wii and Wii Fit, the integration of home video games and fitness or healthcare is now taken as granted [2]. Research on the potential of serious games in rehabilitation training [3,4] confirms their effectiveness, and Sánchez and Olivares [5] and Mouaheb et al. [6] discussed serious games as an education tool.

Various research works reported that computer or video games are actually effective in boosting learning effects. Connolly et al. [7] have proved that serious games can lead to positive functional development, and De and Jarvis [8] have shown improvement of education/training effects with the use of serious games. Wrzesien and Raya [9] applied interactive game content to science education and investigated its effectiveness. Yusoff et al. [10] studied the design trend of serious games.

3   Game Design and Development

The research and development efforts presented in this paper were conducted on two chapters of the science subject in elementary and middle schools: "Force and Motion" and "State Change of Water." To develop serious games for scientific learning, analyzing the components of the chapters is essential. Given the standards for learning achievement, we estimated the *teaching-learning difficulty* of each component. The teaching-learning difficulty is classified as either high, mid, or low. Table 1 shows the analysis results for "Force and Motion."

When the teaching-learning difficulty was estimated, many factors were considered: if the component contains abstract concepts which are far from everyday life, if it requires the students to comprehend the time-spatial relationships, if it requires to conduct experiments which are actually hard to implement, etc. A team of elementary and middle school teachers and professors of educational institutes participated in the process, making the estimated difficulties highly acceptable in the community.

For the components classified as having high- or mid-level difficulties, the team of teachers and professors worked with the game designers to develop the game-based curriculum. For this purpose, the game's goal was first defined and then the game scenario was designed. The focus was not only on the learning motivation and effect but also on enhancing the visual realism.

Table 1. Analysis of the components in "Force and Motion" chapter.

Goals for education curriculum	Achievement standard	Achievement standard details	Teaching-learning difficulty			Game development method
			high	mid	low	
Understanding that, between magnets, there are attractive and repulsive forces. Activity: find magnetic poles	Can find magnetic poles and explain the attractive and repulsive forces	Can classify objects into those attracted to a magnet and those not			O	Actual experiment is more appropriate. Not fit for game
		Can find magnetic poles		O		Using a magnet's attractive and repulsive forces, obtain a game item or evade a monster
		Can explain the forces that exist between opposite poles and same poles		O		
Understanding the magnetic feature of pointing towards a certain direction. Activity: make a compass	Can explain a magnet has the property of pointing towards a certain direction	Can find a magnet's direction	O			Find directions using a magnet
		Can make a compass with a magnetized nail		O		Make a compass using magnetizable objects
Making a tool or toy using magnetic properties. Activity: make a toy using magnets	Can make a tool or toy using magnets	Can design and develop a toy that uses magnet	O			Using magnets, land from high altitude
Finding examples for the usage of magnets in daily environment	Can give examples for the usage of magnets in daily environment	Can find examples for the usage of magnets in daily environment		O		using a magnet, find objects.

4   Force and Motion

"Force and Motion" is a 3D PC game, where students can learn the principles about gravity, friction, and magnetic forces, which are taught in the corresponding chapter in the science subject. Figure 1-(a) and -(b) show the screen shots for game lobby and stage selection, respectively. The game consists of three roller-coaster stages. The user can move to the next stage only when the current stage's mission is completed. In the first stage, "The Rift of Dwarves" shown in Fig. 1-(c), the train can advance forward by solving a series of quizzes about force and motion. In this stage, the users should apply their prior knowledge to solve the quizzes. When they fail to solve a quiz, a couple of hints are provided.

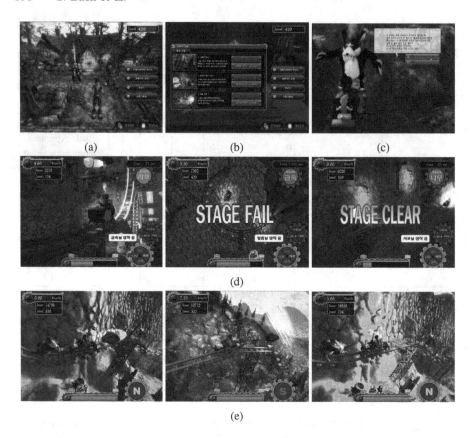

Fig. 1. Screen shots of "Force and Motion." (a) The game lobby. (b) Stage selection. (c) The fist stage for quiz. (d) The second stage for learning the frictional and gravitational forces. (e) The third stage for learning the magnetic forces.

The second stage is named "The Gold Mine of the Owl King," where a user navigates a sleigh on the rail. The rail has a complex structure: some parts of the rail are straight but others are curved, even including 360° circular path. While navigating through a series of milestones, the user's mission is to pass through a milestone at a certain period of time. The rail's material dynamically changes and can be either ice, metal, or wood. On the other hand, the user can select the material of the sleigh runners out of ice, metal, wood, and sand paper so as to adjust the frictional force, control the sleigh speed, and complete the missions on milestones. In addition, the width of the sleigh runners can be adjusted by the user. The wider, the more frictional force! See Fig. 1-(d) for the screen shots of the second stage.

The user may go through a trial-and-error loop. For example, the combination of ice rail and ice runners would make the sleigh overly fast, precluding the user's completing the mission. In contrast, the combination of wood rail and sand-paper runners would make the sleigh overly slow, even making the sleigh fall off the rail for the case of 360° circular path. While completing the stage, the user can gradually overcome misconceptions and eventually embrace the correct concepts. The user will be able to learn the frictional properties of materials easily observed in everyday life and how the frictional forces change depending on the contact areas.

In the third stage, "The Orange Mountain Range," the user will learn the magnetic forces. Many obstacles are on the rail. They are all magnetic rocks. The north and south poles of an obstacle are visualized using the red and blue colors, respectively, which are quite familiar to students. In addition, the magnetic field induced by each obstacle can be inferred from compasses, which are scattered around the obstacle. The obstacles can be thrown away by using the huge bar magnet attached in front of the sleigh. It can be rotated by the user. If the north pole of the obstacle faces the sleigh, for example, the use should rotate the bar magnet such that its north pole faces the obstacle. Then, the repulsive force between them throws the obstacle away. Otherwise, the sleigh will crash into the obstacle. Figure 1-(e) shows the screen shots of the third stage.

"Force and Motion" is developed using Unity, a game development tool. In Unity, users can write a *script* describing the behaviour of an object. For example, a magnet's behaviour [11] caused by other magnets is described in a script, which computes the force and torque acting on the magnet. Then, Unity's internal rigid-body simulation module moves the magnets as described by the script.

5   State Change of Water

"State Change of Water" is a 2D game on smart mobile devices such as smart phones and tablets. The goal of the game is to control the water flow so as to preserve as much water as possible till the final destination. It provides an easy and simple interface and so, for example, the water flow can be controlled by tilting the device, as shown in Fig. 2-(a).

In addition, the game is intended to effectively relay the learning content about the properties of water, such as the state changes between ice, water, and vapor. If the water follows a path with many holes or flows over a porous object, for example, the use can decrease the temperature below zero and freeze the water, as illustrated in Fig. 2-(b), so as to be able to avoid the holes or the porous object. In contrast, when a volcano region is chosen at a branch point, for example, the water would be evaporated, as shown in Fig. 2-(c). It would them make it hard to successfully complete the mission.

This game was developed using a particle-based fluid simulation method [12], which was implemented also in Unity scripts. Both water and vapor are simulated as particles whereas ice is simulated as a rigid body. Fluid simulation requires a lot of computation time and it is currently impossible to implement real-time 3D fluid simulation at mobile devices. That is why we adopted 2D fluid simulation.

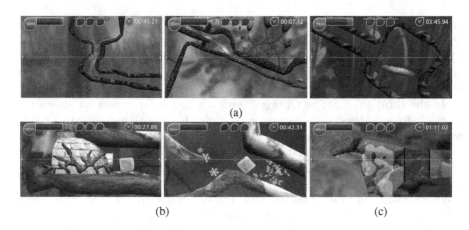

Fig. 2. Screen shots of "State Change of Water." (a) Water. (b) Ice. (c) Vapor.

6   Evaluation

"Force and Motion" and "State Change of Water" were evaluated using the tool proposed by Jung et al. [13] The evaluation elements are listed in Table 2. In each of "State Change of Water" and three stages of "Force and Motion," a group of science class teachers was involved: 7 teachers in "The Rift of Dwarves," 6 in "The Gold Mine of the Owl King," 8 in "The Orange Mountain Range," and 4 in "State Change of Water." After playing the games, the subjects were asked to rate from one to four on each evaluation element. The evaluation results are shown in Table 3. The teachers also provided comments on the strengths and weaknesses of the games and how to improve the games.

The evaluation results indicate that the *teaching-learning content* requires improvement in general. "The Gold Mine of the Owl King" and "The Orange Mountain Range" scored the lowest whereas "The Rift of Dwarves" and "State

Table 2. The elements to be evaluated for serious games.

Evaluation elements	
Teaching-learning contents	Validity of purpose, validity of contents, practicality of contents, reliability of contents, systemicity of contents, appropriacy of quantity
Teaching-learning strategy	Motivation, learner control, feedback, consideration of learner level, system to help learning
Screen organization	Appropriacy of design, freshness of design, convenience of design
Technology	Systemicity of management, security
Economics morality	Copyright protection, human rights protection, personal information protection, economics

Table 3. Evaluation results.

Games		Average scores					Average
		Teaching-learning contents	Teaching-learning strategy	Screen organiza-tion	Technology	Economic-morality	
Force and Motion	The Rift of Dwarves	2.31	3.00	2.33	3.00	2.65	2.89
	The Gold Mine of the Owl King	1.62	2.60	2.33	3.50	2.26	2.44
	The Orange Mountain Range	1.62	2.40	2.00	3.00	2.15	2.44
Earth and Moon		2.78	1.85	2.60	2.33	3.25	2.41
State Change of Water		2.56	2.15	2.40	3.00	3.00	2.47
Average		2.18	2.40	2.33	2.97	2.66	

Change of Water" scored above 2. The teachers commented that the curriculum
is well organized and adheres well to the content to be learned. However, they
advised that, in "The Orange Mountain Range," the directions given to the
users be made clearer and the sleigh speed control in "The Gold Mine of the
Owl King" be made both more realistic and more intuitive.

Regarding the *teaching-learning strategy*, "The Rift of Dwarves," "The Gold
Mine of the Owl King," and "The Orange Mountain Range" scored relatively
high, but "State Change of Water" scored low. The scenarios of all games were
highly evaluated, but the teachers advised that some game features such as
monotonous background music, the overall difficulty, and low rewarding system
be improved.

The *screen organization* scored below 2.5. The reasons for such low scores
have been analyzed to be the low quality of the graphics and inconvenient user
interfaces compared to those of commercial games. These would be the inherent
weakness of the prototype games, but the evaluation results imply that serious
game developers should put more efforts into the graphics and user interfaces.

The average score of the *technology* element is 2.97, which is the highest among the evaluation elements. It was not unexpected because fric-
tional/magnetic forces and particle-based fluid simulations are novel techniques,
which are hard to find even in commercial games.

The *economics-morality* element also scored high. It was because the games
were made free and available to all users who can access and download the games
through Internet. However, the elementary school teachers advised that the game
character's animation and costumes be made more appropriate for elementary
school students.

7   Conclusion

This paper presented serious games developed for the science subject in elementary and middle schools: "Force and Motion" and "State Change of Water."
The games were evaluated by teachers. The evaluation results showed the potential of serious games in science subject and also their limitations. For example,
the teachers' comments that the game-based curriculum is well organized and

adheres well to the content to be learned imply the potential of serious games as a complementary tool for science education. On the other hand, low-rated evaluation on the game organization, user interfaces, and the graphics implies that serious game developers should put more efforts into those aspects in order to motivate the learners in elementary and middle schools.

Acknowledgments. This work was supported by Institute for Information & communications Technology Promotion(IITP) grant funded by the Korea government(MSIP)(No.R0115-15-1011, Physics-based solutions for science experiments in e-Book).

References

1. Zyda, M.: From visual simulation to virtual reality to games. Computer **38**(9), 25–32 (2005)
2. Göbel, S., Hardy, S., Wendel, V., Mehm, F., Steinmetz, R.: Serious games for health: personalized exergames. In: Proceedings of the International Conference on Multimedia, MM 2010, pp. 1663–1666. ACM, New York (2010)
3. Kim, Y.S., Kim, N.Y., Cho, S.H.: A study on the positive impact of a persuasive game and its potential for social change literacy. J. Korea Game Soc. **14**, 39–48 (2014)
4. Kim, K., Lee, Y., Oh, S.: Development and analysis of a walking game 'paldokangsan3' using kinect. J. Korea Game Soc. **14**, 49–58 (2014)
5. Sánchez, J., Olivares, R.: Problem solving and collaboration using mobile serious games. Comput. Educ. **57**(3), 1943–1952 (2011)
6. Mouaheb, H., Fahli, A., Moussetad, M., Eljamali, S.: The serious game: what educational benefits? Procedia-social and behavioral sciences. In: 4th World Conference on Educational Sciences (WCES-2012), Barcelona, Spain, 02–05 February 2012, vol. 46, pp. 5502–5508 (2012)
7. Connolly, T.M., Boyle, E.A., MacArthur, E., Hainey, T., Boyle, J.M.: A systematic literature review of empirical evidence on computer games and serious games. Comput. Educ. **59**(2), 661–686 (2012)
8. De Freitas, S., Jarvis, S.: Serious games-engaging training solutions: a research and development project for supporting training needs. Br. J. Educ. Technol. **38**(3), 523 (2007)
9. Wrzesien, M., Raya, M.A.: Learning in serious virtual worlds: evaluation of learning effectiveness and appeal to students in the e-junior project. Comput. Educ. **55**(1), 178–187 (2010)
10. Yusoff, A., Crowder, R., Gilbert, L.: Validation of serious games attributes using the technology acceptance model. In: 2010 Second International Conference on Games and Virtual Worlds for Serious Applications (VS-GAMES), pp. 45–51. IEEE (2010)
11. Thomaszewski, B., Gumann, A., Pabst, S., Straßer, W.: Magnets in motion. ACM Trans. Graph. (TOG) **27**(5), 162 (2008)
12. Müller, M., Charypar, D., Gross, M.: Particle-based fluid simulation for interactive applications. In: Proceedings of the 2003 ACM SIGGRAPH/Eurographics Symposium on Computer Animation, SCA 2003. Eurographics Association, Aire-la-Ville, Switzerland, pp. 154–159 (2003)
13. Jung, H., Lee, C., Jhun, Y.: Development and application of an evaluation tool for serious games. J. Korean Assoc. Inf. Educ. **18**(3), 401–412 (2014)

English Vocabulary Learning System Based on Repetitive Learning and Rate-Matching Rule

Jinsuk Yang, Kyoungsu Oh[✉], and Kiho Youm

Department of Media, Soongsil University, Sangdo 1-dong,
Dongjak-gu, Seoul, Republic of Korea
{ispio,oks,youmkh}@ssu.ac.kr

Abstract. In this paper, we propose an efficient English vocabulary learning system using repetitive learning and the rate-matching rule. The proposed system provides a learning method based on the user's learning skill. By using the proposed system, users can solve exam-style questions wherever and whenever they choose. Efficient repetition learning is provided by using repetition periods based on the forgetting curve for long-term memory. The answered questions are then evaluated to update the user's learning skill and the question difficulty. Due to this adaptive difficulty adjustment, users almost always receive questions that are appropriate for their skill level. If users answer questions correctly or learn more than the defined amount, then the proposed system provides them with encouraging feedback imagery. This is very similar to being rewarded for an achievable challenge in a game, and it can encourage users to study consistently.

1 Introduction

Many approaches to using computer programs to increase study efficiency have been researched, and experiments have shown that computer games are very effective at improving learning performance [5–7]. We propose an efficient English vocabulary learning system that includes beneficial features of computer games, providing an efficient review method and a learning method based on the user's skill level. [2] reviewed 10 learning methods and verified that two of them, practice testing and distributed practice, have much higher utility. These useful learning methods are applied to our memorization system. In order to retain information in the long-term memory, appropriately timed review is necessary. We have users review at a time based on the forgetting curve [1], which is used for many study systems. Maintaining the user's study flow by giving them appropriate questions is also important. Therefore, we adaptively adjust the user's learning skill and question difficulty according to an evaluation of the answered questions. In our system, the "Glicko-2 rating system" [4] is employed to determine the user's skill level and question difficulty. Additionally, we give users immediate feedback when they answer a question correctly and the amount of learning surpasses predefined levels. This type of feedback is similar to that found in computer games. Gamification in serious games has been attempted in various ways. However, the approaches focused more on either game style or content in many cases. We apply game design theories, balancing, and rewards to motivate users to study with our efficient learning system.

© Springer International Publishing Switzerland 2016
A. De Gloria and R. Veltkamp (Eds.): GALA 2015, LNCS 9599, pp. 189–195, 2016.
DOI: 10.1007/978-3-319-40216-1_20

The proposed system consists of the User, Client (mobile devices), and Server (Amazon Web Services). Figure 1 shows an overview of the proposed system. Each user has skill points, a score, and a level. The skill points indicate the user's actual learning level. This value is not shown to the user, and it is modified according to an evaluation of the user's answers to questions. The score is a numerical value that represents the amount of study. It is always shown to the user, and it increases when the user solves a question correctly. The level is very similar to that found in computer games. It increases depending on predefined score levels. Since we use mobile devices as our client, portable learning is possible. This allows users to study wherever and whenever they want. The client sends questions that have several blanks in a word, and the user must select letters to fill in the blanks. The answer to the question is evaluated, and the client sends the result to the server. The server receives the evaluation from the client to adjust the user's level and the question difficulty. If the user's answer is correct, then our system increases the user's skill points and score. Otherwise, our system decreases the skill points. At the same time, the question difficulty is adjusted based on the user's skill adjustment. According to our adaptive difficulty adjustment, the user's skill level and question difficulty are always determined correctly, and users receive questions that are appropriately difficult. After modification, the server sends a new question to the client. The proposed system employs a review method based on the forgetting curve in order to facilitate efficient memorization. When our system sends a new question, it attempts to find one that the user has to review immediately and sends it. If there can be no review questions due to insufficient time, then our system selects a question that has never been solved and is appropriate for the user.

Fig. 1. System overview

2   Exam-Style Practice Questions and Appropriate Feedback

Figure 2 shows an example question in our client. Users only see it while they are studying and do not need to care about others, such as review. At the top of Fig. 2, the current question (word), meaning of the word, answer choices, and pass button are shown. The difficulty of the question is shown on the left side of the meaning panel, and the number of times the user has studied this word is indicated on the right side by several star images. For example, the word "apple," which has one star on the upper-right-hand side, was sent to the user at least one day ago, and the user answered it correctly.

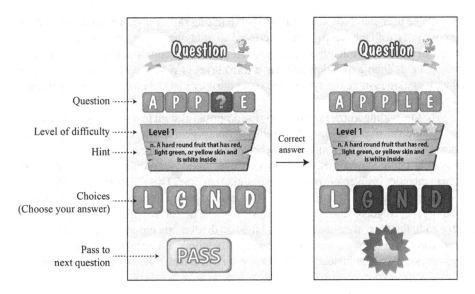

Fig. 2. Example of exam-style practice question

Users select answers that correspond to the blanks in the word after reading the meaning of the word. If the answer is wrong, the word is shown after the user answers the other 14 questions. Otherwise, our system increases the user's score and shows an image that encourages the user (right side of Fig. 2). When the score reaches the predefined score, our system shows another image that celebrates the fact that the user has leveled up.

3 Adaptive Difficulty Adjustment and Repetition Management

Our system evaluates the user's answers in order to adaptively adjust their learning skill and the question difficulty. After the adjustment, a new question is selected based on the review period or the user's learning skill. The Glicko-2 rating system is one of the most popular rating systems used to measure and manage the player's skill level in games, such as chess. The Glicko-2 rating system uses a rating and the ratings deviation (RD) for each player. For instance, the gaming skill of a player who has a rating of 1500 and an RD of 50 is between 1400 and 1600 with a 95 % chance. Therefore, a lower RD is associated with a more accurate rating. By playing the game many times, the RD decreases steadily, but it can increase if the player goes a long time without playing the game.

We use the Glicko-2 rating system to determine the user's skill points and question difficulty. The user and question ratings determine the skill points and difficulty, respectively. Question solving in our learning system is the same as game matching in chess. If a user answers a question correctly, then the user's rating will increase and the question rating will decrease. Otherwise, the user's rating will decrease and the question rating will increase. When our system selects a new question, it refers to the user's rating. As a result, the user can study according to their learning skill. Providing questions that are appropriately difficult keeps users interested in studying. After many users solve the same question, the difficulty of the question changes to appropriate difficulty, so it is more suitable than a question that has a fixed level of difficulty. As with the original Glicko-2 rating system, our system decreases the user's RD when the user does not study for a long time.

When providing a question to a user, the proposed system first searches for questions that require the user's review. According to the forgetting curve (Fig. 3) proposed by Ebbinghaus [3], our system checks whether the question needs to be reviewed. The forgetting curve shows memory reduction over time. According to the curve shape, human memory is inversely proportional to elapsed time. This theory suggests that users should review after an appropriate period in order to retain information in the long-term memory. [1] contends that the first review should be performed after 10 min, the second after 24 h, the third after one week, and the fourth after one month. After four reviews, users can retain memories for approximately six months. We employ [1] 's suggestion in our system, except instead of 10 min, we set one hour as the first review period.

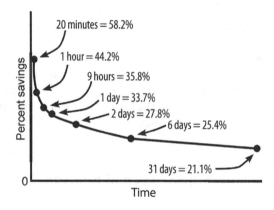

Fig. 3. Forgetting curve proposed by Ebbinghaus

Figure 4 shows the process of answering a question. After a user answers a question, the client evaluates the answer and sends the result (correct or incorrect) with question information (repetition count and study time) to the server. The server updates the user's rating, RD, and question rating according to the evaluation. If the answer is correct, the system increases the number of repetitions of the question in order to select the question in the next review period automatically. Otherwise, the question appears after the user studies the other 14 questions.

Figure 5 shows the process of selecting a question that will be sent to a user. First, our system searches for questions that need to be reviewed by referring to the current repetition count of questions and the time in which a user studied them. Questions with an elapsed time greater than the corresponding review period are selected as candidates. For each candidate, we compute review importance by using (1).

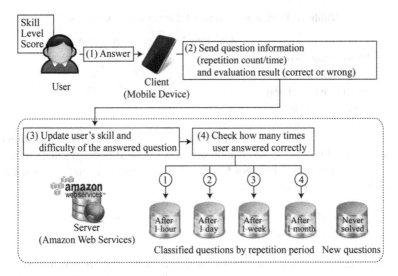

Fig. 4. Answering process

$$\text{Review importance} = (\text{elapsed time} - \text{review period})/\text{review period} \qquad (1)$$

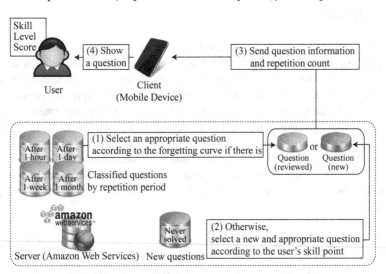

Fig. 5. Question-selection process

The review importance is always positive, and O means that it is time to review immediately. The questions in Table 1 (A, B, and C) have repetition counts of 1, 2, and 3, respectively, and each has an elapsed time of more than one day. The proposed system selects Question A, which has the greatest review importance, as the next question, since Question A might be removed from a user's memory stochastically.

Table 1. Review importance of three example questions

	Question A	Question B	Question C
Elapsed time (day)	2	8	31
Repetition	1	2	3
Repetition period (day)	1	7	30
Review importance	1	1/7	1/30

If there are no appropriate review candidates, then our system finds a new question from the question pool. At this time, the system searches for questions that satisfy the conditions in Eq. (2) to select suitable ones for users. An arbitrary question is selected as the next one among those found.

$$(\text{User's rating} - (2 * \text{User's RD})) < \text{Question rating} <$$
$$(\text{User's rating} + (2 * \text{User's RD})) \tag{2}$$

Finally, the selected question is sent to the client and shown to the user in the exam style. As a result, users can review at the appropriate time or solve a new question that is appropriately difficult.

4   Conclusion

In this paper, we proposed an efficient English vocabulary learning system providing an efficient review method, an approach for ensuring appropriate difficulty levels, and effective learning strategies. It is possible for users to enhance memorization by simply solving the exam-style practice questions provided by the proposed system at their convenience. The proposed system performs adaptive difficulty adjustments to ensure appropriate difficulty levels and gives users immediate feedback in order to encourage them. These features are very similar to those found in computer games. This is why our approach is considered a kind of gamification of education. The proposed system prevents users from losing interest in memorization learning, so it can improve learning performance. Moreover, our system can easily be extended to other areas of study, such as mathematics and science.

Acknowledgments.   This work was supported by the Korea Science and Engineering Foundation(KOSEF) grant funded by the Korea government (MEST) (No. 2011-0012214).

This work was supported by Institute for Information & communications Technology Promotion(IITP) grant funded by the Korea government(MSIP) (No.10047039, Development of the realtime inspection SW and reverse engineering SW based on multiple 2D x-ray images and CT images).

References

1. Buzan, T.: Use Your Head. Rajpal & Sons, Delhi (1982)
2. Dunlosky, J., Rawson, K.A., Marsh, E.J., Nathan, M.J., Willingham, D.T.: Improving students' learning with effective learning techniques promising directions from cognitive and educational psychology. Psychol. Sci. Public Interest **14**(1), 4–58 (2013)
3. Ebbinghaus, H.: Über das gedächtnis: untersuchungen zur experimentellen psychologie. Duncker & Humblot (1885)
4. Glickman, M.E.: The Glicko-2 system for Rating Players in Head-to-Head Competition. Accessed Oct. 2003
5. Ke, F., Grabowski, B.: Gameplaying for maths learning: cooperative or not? Br. J. Educ. Technol. **38**(2), 249–259 (2007)
6. Virvou, M., Katsionis, G., Manos, K.: Combining software games with education: Evaluation of its educational effectiveness. J. Educ. Technol. Soc. **8**(2), 54–65 (2005)
7. Wong, W.L., Shen, C., Nocera, L., Carriazo, E., Tang, F., Bugga, S., Ritterfeld, U.: Serious video game effectiveness. In: Proceedings of the International Conference on Advances in Computer Entertainment Technology, pp. 49–55 (2007)

An Information Theoretic Approach for Measuring Data Discovery and Utilization During Analytical and Decision-Making Processes

Matthew Daggett[✉], Kyle O'Brien, and Michael Hurley

Massachusetts Institute of Technology Lincoln Laboratory, 244 Wood Street,
Lexington, MA 02420, USA
{daggett,kyle.obrien,hurley}@ll.mit.edu

Abstract. Across many commercial, government, and military environments, multi-level decision-making processes rely on complex sociotechnical systems. Human dynamics are a significant driver of the overall effectiveness of these processes, yet the characterization of both the intra- and inter-individual performance contribution is limited by sparse, qualitative, and often subjective observations. Recent advances in quantitative human-machine instrumentation have made possible greater objective study of users interacting with data; however, performance metrics leveraging these measurements are often narrow and ad hoc. When assessing the analytical and decision-making performance of teams, it is critical to know the information that members have observed, synthesized, and acted upon, and ad hoc approaches can be insufficient. In this paper we present a novel assessment framework based on the principles of Shannon information theory. We detail how this framework can holistically characterize decision information flows and describe its application to assess teams' abilities to effectively discover data during serious games.

1 Introduction

Today, from commercial operations control centers to expeditionary military detachments, complex sociotechnical enterprises exist that are composed of sensors, systems, networks, and people, all of which interoperate to synthesize and disseminate information for various echelons of decision-makers. Within these enterprises, the most scarce and critical component is the human, whose contribution can be the biggest performance driver of the overall enterprise, yet is often the least understood. Few methods exist that effectively characterize the analytical performance of humans in these contexts and traditional techniques

This work was sponsored by the Assistant Secretary of Defense for Research and Engineering under Air Force Contract FA8721-05-C-0002. Opinions, interpretations, conclusions, and recommendations are those of the authors and are not necessarily endorsed by the United States Government.

A. De Gloria and R. Veltkamp (Eds.): GALA 2015, LNCS 9599, pp. 196–207, 2016.
DOI: 10.1007/978-3-319-40216-1_21

such as systems analysis or modeling and simulation are insufficient in accounting for human dynamics (both intra- and inter-individual). Advanced training and experimentation platforms, such as serious games, provide new paradigms for the deeper study of human performance; however, assessment techniques remain largely qualitative, subjective, and anecdotal. These limitations hinder our ability to draw objective conclusions and optimize parameters influencing success.

Since 2007 we have been working to address these challenges through the development of Humatics; a novel research methodology used to quantitatively measure human behavior, rigorously assess human analytical performance, and provide data-driven ways to improve the effectiveness of individuals and teams. Humatics incorporates three major areas of research including system-level, physiological, and cognitive instrumentation; assessment methodology and metrics development; and performance feedback and behavioral recommendation. In this paper, we describe how two components of this methodology, system instrumentation and information theoretic metrics, can be employed to characterize the performance of teams' abilities to discover and utilize data during a serious game.

2 Information Theoretic Metrics

Many analysis- and decision-oriented tasks require humans to synthesize and assess information from multiple sources with varying degrees of data volume, velocity, variety, and veracity. For these tasks, performance is defined by how well humans can separate relevant pieces of information from a background of irrelevant information, akin to a farming combine that separates wheat from chaff. Measuring and tracking these different information quantities through multiple steps of a team analytical or decision process can be challenging, and traditional approaches requiring multiple ad hoc assessment techniques often fail to combine in a way that represents holistic team performance. To overcome this we have repurposed techniques from the field of communications, specifically Shannon information theory, as the mathematical foundation for making these measures of relevant and irrelevant information. Thus, we can then draw an analogy to the classical problem of receiving information over a noisy channel, where the relevant information (the "signal") is mixed with the irrelevant information (the "noise"), which "corrupts" the comprehension of the relevant information in the decision-making process. For the purposes of this paper, we will focus on applying this assessment methodology to characterize the performance of teams in a serious game; however this technique can be applied to many other datasets used during training or real-world operations.

To instantiate this information theoretic assessment process, we start with a discrete-valued information dataset, hereafter known as the "scenario," and completely label it to denote which pieces of information are relevant or irrelevant to the task being studied. We then expose users to the scenario dataset during a serious game and record their analytic behaviors that denote when information is being observed. Next, an evaluation algorithm determines which type of information was observed during each measurement and several information measures can be computed and combined to assess user performance. This section will describe the key components of the evaluation process and then introduce the formal terminology and theoretical results that can be applied generally to any system.

2.1   Data Curation, Instrumentation, and Accumulation

The first step in the evaluation process involves labeling scenario data to obtain "ground truth." In this process, we discretize the scenario data into individual pieces of information and then classify each piece as relevant or irrelevant, depending on the applicability of the information to the analytic or decision task at each time-step in the scenario. Relevant data are that which the user should focus their effort on, as the discovery and understanding of this information will lead to success in solving the scenario. Conversely users should avoid the irrelevant information, as it will only consume resources and corrupt the understanding of the scenario. Labeling is a one-time process and the results are used for evaluation purposes only, and are not shared with the users.

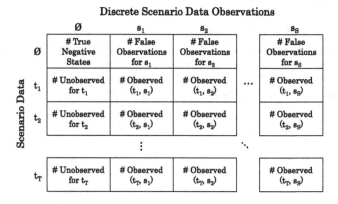

Fig. 1. The accumulation matrix associates instrumentation observations to scenario ground truth

The second step involves collecting measurements of user interactions with the scenario data during a task and is usually achieved through instrumentation of the software tools being used to explore the scenario data. Where possible, instrumentation should directly measure the data being inspected by an analytic behavior, but there are instances where proxy measurements or heuristics are needed to properly match a user behavior to the scenario data.

Once the scenario data are labeled and instrumentation data are collected, we have the necessary inputs for a formal information theoretic evaluation. The next step is to compute a joint probability density function between the scenario

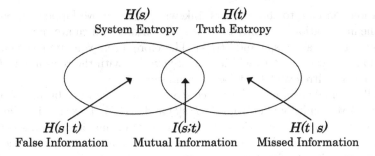

Fig. 2. Venn diagram representing the system and truth entropies and their relationships to the subsequent conditional entropies

ground truth and the system instrumentation data. To represent the joint distribution, we utilize a two-dimensional matrix whose rows correspond to each scenario-related data element and whose columns correspond to the amount of information accumulated with respect to that element. We refer to this as an *accumulation matrix* and it is shown in Fig. 1.

To populate the accumulation matrix, row ϕ for the scenario truth data contains the counts for all the irrelevant elements and each relevant element has its own row. For the observed data columns, each observed element has its own column, and column ϕ has the counts of unobserved elements. The amount of information is found by recursively analyzing system observations for each scenario-related data element and summing the number of instances when the user inspected those elements. The final step is filling in the (ϕ, ϕ) cell, which is a count of true negatives, or the number of irrelevant elements that the users did not access or observe. With a complete accumulation matrix, information measures can now be defined and calculated.

2.2   Information Measure Definitions

In this section, we describe the general evaluation algorithm and introduce the information measures. This paper concerns itself with "relevant" and "irrelevant" information, while much of our underlying work in information theory involved multi-target trackers and classifiers where measures of "true" and "false" information were evaluated [1,2]. To maintain a degree of continuity with previous publications, the pairs of terms are used interchangeably.

The first information measure that we compute is *entropy*. Conceptually, entropy is a measure of uncertainty about the types of items contained in a particular data set and it increases as more data types are present or are more equally likely to appear in the data set. As shown in Fig. 2, the entropies of the scenario ground truth data, t, and system instrumentation data, s, are represented by the regions $H(t)$ and $H(s)$, respectively. The third entropy, $H(s,t)$, is the entropy of the combined data sets. The region where the two information sets overlap represents the *mutual information*, $I(s;t)$, which quantifies the information common to the two sets. Likewise, the non-overlapped regions represent the information that only one data set contains, which are the *conditional entropies*, written as $H(s|t)$ and $H(t|s)$. Therefore, users who are more effective at triaging the scenario data will have more overlap with the relevant (or truth) dataset and less irrelevant (or false) information.

Finally, a single overall performance score for users can be obtained from the sum of the two conditional entropies, $H(s|t)$ and $H(t|s)$. This sum is called *total conditional entropy* or *variation of information* [3], and lower sums correlate to better performance. This measure satisfies the mathematical definition of a metric, making it effective for comparing the relative performance of different users.

To effectively understand the data triage performance of users, we compute two additional, derived performance measures; the *Information Completeness*, $I(s;t)/H(t)$, which is the relative fraction of relevant (true) information discovered, and the *False Information Ratio*, $H(s|t)/H(t)$, which is the ratio between the amount of irrelevant (false) information generated and the amount of relevant (true) information available for discovery. Information Completeness provides a measure of how much of the relevant information has been discovered by users, whereas the False Information Ratio provides a measure of how much effort has been spent on observing irrelevant information, thus potentially degrading scenario comprehension. These measures can be visualized in the form of an Information Coverage (IC) plot as shown in Fig. 3.

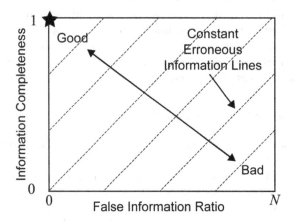

Fig. 3. This figure depicts an example IC plot where the Information Completeness and the False Information Ratio are visualized on the y-axis and x-axis, respectively. This plot shares some of the same characteristics as the Receiver Operation Characteristic (ROC) plot from signal detection theory. Ideal performance of $(0,1)$ denoted by the star is where all the relevant information has been discovered and no irrelevant information was observed. The lines of constant erroneous information show where the total conditional entropy is constant and overall performance is equal.

2.3 Calculating Information Measures

The information theoretic measures are estimated from the counts of occurrences of different actions during an analytic task. Given a filled accumulation matrix, probabilities of occurrence are estimated by normalizing each bin by the total number of counts in the matrix $p(t, s) = n_{t,s}/N$.

The standard functions from information theory generate the entropies for the full matrix $H(t, s)$, the truth $H(t)$, and the observations $H(s)$:

$$H(t, s) = -p(t, s) \log p(t, s), \tag{1}$$
$$H(t) = -p(t) \log p(t), \tag{2}$$
$$H(s) = -p(s) \log p(s), \tag{3}$$

where we estimate the marginal probabilities as $p(t) = \sum_s n_{t,s}/N$ and $p(s) = \sum_t n_{t,s}/N$.

The mutual information and conditional entropies are obtained from

$$I(t, s) = H(t) + H(s) - H(t, s), \tag{4}$$
$$H(t|s) = H(t, s) - H(s), \tag{5}$$
$$H(s|t) = H(t, s) - H(t). \tag{6}$$

Finally, the total conditional entropy score is computed by the following equation:

$$S = H(t|s) + H(s|t) = 2H(t, s) - H(t) - H(s). \tag{7}$$

Over time, we have moved from estimating information theoretic measures with naive methods to more advanced methods that account for limited statistics on the count sizes and that also provide covariance estimates on the information theoretic measures so that the significance of the analyses can be reported [4–7]. A software package has been developed that provides estimates using both techniques and is available for public download [8]. For the purpose of clarity, the naive approach has been described here.

3 Applications

The generality of this approach yields many assessment applications, from training and serious gameplay to real-world daily operations. In this section we detail how this approach was used to assess the effectiveness of users performing geospatial analysis tasks during a serious game. However, we have also applied it in other contexts such as understanding how users extract and synthesize information from text documents in order to develop their situational understanding.

3.1 Network Discovery Serious Game

In 2009, researchers at MIT Lincoln Laboratory developed a serious game [9,10] to better understand how analysts use multisource textual and geospatial data

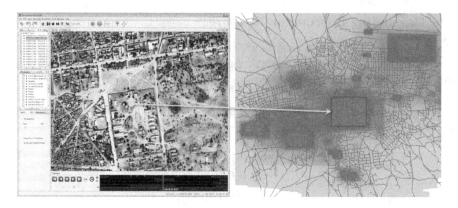

Fig. 4. Game client screen capture depicting viewport instrumentation (Color figure online)

to make risk-informed decisions. The goal was to establish an analytical baseline and conduct research regarding what new tools and techniques might improve human analytical performance over that baseline.

In the game, competitive teams of varying size and composition self organize their roles and responsibilities to analyze the scenario data effectively and make the expected decision outcomes. The scenario is based around a scripted storyboard where an organized crime network is operating in a city to incite violence (kidnappings, riots) and then quickly disperse into the background populace of the city. Teams are given relevant and irrelevant news and police reports to cue them to observable events in a collection of airborne video. Teams then analyze the video to follow suspect vehicles from overt events to their sources and destinations in order to unravel the network of facilities used by the crime organization. Teams are given 90 min to analyze the video and reports to accrue evidence before codifying what they know by identifying which facilities (sites) should be interdicted by law enforcement to disrupt the network.

The scenario storyboard was used to develop a probabilistic vehicle traffic model in order to produce vehicle movements, or tracks, for the scenario vehicles we want the teams to find. We then embed those tracks into realistic background traffic movements that simulate the normative movements of the city population. Using this combined track dataset as input, video modeling and simulation tools were used to produce a video dataset rendered at every point in the city's geospatial extent over all time-steps in the scenario. The video and report data are displayed and manipulated in a software client that was purpose-built for this research and is instrumented for post-game analysis.

3.2   System Instrumentation

Software instrumentation built into the game client records various user actions at specific intervals, such as where the player is looking in data-space, known

Fig. 5. Scenario and background data representations for sites and tracks (Color figure online)

as the viewport. The viewport data are recorded each second and includes the current time during gameplay, the time in the scenario being displayed, and the geospatial bounding-box of the video data currently being viewed in the map tool. Figure 4 shows a screen capture of a client display where the video displayed in the client on the left corresponds to the blue viewport outline on the heat-map on the right, as indicated by the yellow arrow.

After the viewport data are logged, they are correlated with the scenario ground truth to determine which relevant (scenario crime network) and irrelevant (background population) tracks or sites are in the field of view at each scenario time-step. A graphical representation of the scenario and background information is shown in Fig. 5. On the left plot, we want the players to discover the scenario sites annotated with the red icons and not the background sites denoted with a yellow dot. Similarly for the right plot showing the vehicle track extents, we want the players to focus on the red scenario vehicle tracks and not on the yellow background population tracks.

3.3   Building the Game Accumulation Matrix

For the accumulation matrix for this game, rows correspond with each scenario-related vehicle track and columns correspond to the amount of information accumulated about that track through time. The amount of track information is found by recursively analyzing viewports for each scenario-related track and summing the number of instances when the user inspected the track, however multiple observations of the same vehicle at the same time were only counted as a single observation. To score performance on discovering scenario sites, we can compute another accumulation matrix by a similar process, where the rows are treated as stationary "tracks" that are valid for the entire duration of the game.

3.4   Data Discovery Performance Assessment

In this section we will demonstrate the utility of the information theoretic metric approach using the aforementioned serious game. During the development of
this game, a key research question was how to determine the number of players required for sufficient team performance given the difficulty and complexity
of the scenario. We hypothesized that there are diminishing returns to adding
more and more players on a team, and that there may be an optimal team size
for this game. Generally this design process can be ad-hoc and anecdotal, but
we explored a more systematic approach by varying team size over a series of
experiments and assessed performance across several dimensions. For simplicity
we focus the following examples on assessing player performance while inspecting
vehicle tracks, however the process is the same for site inspection performance.

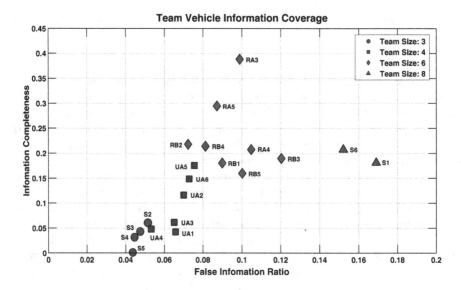

Fig. 6. Information Coverage performance as a function of team size

In Fig. 6 an Information Coverage plot is shown depicting the performance
of 20 teams of size N players, where N was chosen to be 3, 4, 6, and 8.
The Information Coverage plot was introduced in Fig. 3. For this exercise, the
3- and 4-person teams have $N-1$ game clients; players at the computers perform
analysis and the player without a computer coordinates the efforts of the other
players and performs data synthesis. For the 6- and 8-person teams there are
$N-2$ game clients per team, with the two non-computer players sharing the
leadership and synthesis roles.

There are a number of insights that we can obtain from this plot. For this
game, there is much more information than can be effectively discovered by a

team of 3. Their performance indicates that some relevant scenario information is discovered along with some irrelevant information, but performance is bounded by limited manpower. The 4-person teams start to show a divergence in performance where most of those teams observed similar amounts of irrelevant information, but half the teams (UA2, UA5, UA6) achieved much higher Information Completeness. In the case of the 6-person teams, we see a much bigger divergence where some teams (RA3 and RA5) are able to make effective use of their additional manpower to discover more relevant information while minimizing additional irrelevant information, whereas the rest of the 6-person teams only increase their irrelevant information with the additional manpower. The teams of 8 continue this trend and during in-person game observations these teams failed to have effective teaming strategies leading to poorer integration of collective information and worse overall decision performance.

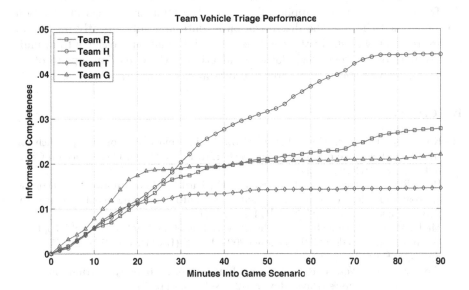

Fig. 7. Convergence of information completeness as a function of scenario time

While Fig. 6 illustrates the ability to compute holistic performance throughout the entire game, diagnostic metrics are also desired. Figure 7 shows an example where the information theoretic metrics were computed every two minutes of a 90-min exercise, for four teams of five players with $N-1$ game clients. In this example we present Information Completeness plotted as a function of time during the game as a way to measure how well teams are converging onto the relevant information. As seen in Fig. 7, Team G has better discovery performance than the rest of the teams early on, but at ~25 min into the scenario their performance flat-lines. Team H continuously observes relevant information up to the 75 min mark where they move from a discovery workflow to a decision workflow in order to submit their game answers, and subsequently had a more complete answer set than the other teams.

After several years of experimentation with over 80 teams of different configurations and sizes we have found that smaller amounts of observed irrelevant information are correlated with a higher probability of correct site discovery. Additionally, observing greater amounts of irrelevant information is correlated with higher false alarm probabilities during the game decision making process.

4   Conclusion

In this paper we have shown that information theoretic metrics can be used to improve the quantitative study and objective assessment of human analytic and decision-oriented processes, and we demonstrated its application to measuring information discovery during a serious game. While we describe one specific use, the framework has broad applicability given the number of ways information can be defined through the discretization of data and subsequently measured. Future research will study the combination of information measures from multiple sources of heterogeneous data and identifying their relationships to other aspects of performance, such as perceived awareness, uncertainty, or risk.

References

1. Kao, E.K., Daggett, M.P., Hurley, M.B.: An information theoretic approach for tracker performance evaluation. In: IEEE 12th International Conference on Computer Vision (ICCV) (2009)
2. Holt, R.S., Mastromarino, P.A., Kao, E.K., Hurley, M.B.: Information theoretic approach for the performance evaluation of multi-class assignment systems. In: Proceedings of SPIE 7697:76970R/1-12 (2010)
3. Meilă, M.: Comparing clusterings by the variation of information. In: Schölkopf, B., Warmuth, M.K. (eds.) COLT/Kernel 2003. LNCS (LNAI), vol. 2777, pp. 173–187. Springer, Heidelberg (2003)
4. Wolpert, D.H., Wolf, D.R.: Estimating functions of probability distributions from a finite set of samples. Phys. Rev. E **52**, 6841–6854 (1995)
5. Wolpert, D.H., Wolf, D.R.: Erratum: estimating functions of probability distributions from a finite set of samples. Phys. Rev. E **54**, 6973 (1996)
6. Wolf, D.R., Wolpert, D.H.: Los Alamos National Laboratory Report No. LA-UR-93-833 (1993) (unpublished). Send email to comp-gas@xyz.lanl.gov with subject "get 9403002" to get an encoded postscript version. "9403001" might also be helpful to the reader
7. Kao, E.K., Hurley, M.B.: Numerical estimation of information theoretic measures for large data sets. MIT Lincoln Laboratory Technical Report 1169, Lexington, MA (2013)
8. Kao, E.K., Hurley, M.B.: Estimation of information theoretic measures from associated data samples. http://www.ll.mit.edu/mission/isr/InfoTheoreticMetrics/InfoTheoreticMetrics.html
9. Won, J.C.: Influence of resource allocation on teamwork and performance in an Intelligence, Surveillance, and Reconnaissance (ISR) "Red/Blue" exercise within self-organizing teams. Ph.D. thesis, Tufts University (2012)

10. Won, J.C., Condon, G.R., Landon, B.R., Wang, A.R., Hannon, D.J.: Assessing team workload and situational awareness in an Intelligence, Surveillance, and Reconnaissance (ISR) simulation exercise. In: IEEE First International Multi-Disciplinary Conference on Cognitive Methods in Situation Awareness and Decision Support (CogSIMA) (2011)

Collecting Human Habit Datasets
for Smart Spaces Through Gamification
and Crowdsourcing

Giovanni Cucari, Francesco Leotta$^{(\boxtimes)}$, Massimo Mecella, and Stavros Vassos

Dipartimento di Ingegneria Informatica, Automatica e Gestionale,
Sapienza Università di Roma, Rome, Italy
`cucari.1192481@studenti.uniroma1.it`,
`{leotta,mecella,vassos}@dis.uniroma1.it`

Abstract. A lot of research in the last years has focused on smart spaces, covering aspects related to ambient intelligence, activity monitoring and mining, etc. All these efforts require datasets to be used for experimental purposes and as benchmarks for novel techniques. Such datasets are today difficult to obtain as, on the one hand, building smart facilities is expensive, requiring considerable costs for maintenance and extension, and, on the other hand, freely available datasets are scarce, not continuously updated and contain a limited set of sensors, thus not allowing the evaluation of algorithms that require the availability of specific categories of sensors. To this aim, we have built a prototype smart virtual environment producing sensor logs on the basis of activities performed by users as if they were really acting in a physical smart space.

1 Introduction

A smart space is "an environment centered on its human users in which a set of embedded networked artefacts, both hardware and software, collectively realize the paradigm of *ambient intelligence (AmI)*" [9]. In AmI, the *knowledge* of environment dynamics and of users behaviors and preferences is employed to interpret sensors output in order to perform appropriate actions on the environment. *Sensor data* is first analyzed to extract the current *context*, which is a convenient abstraction of the state of the environment. This context is analyzed to make decisions that modify the environment by means of *actuators*.

AmI lays at the intersection between many different research areas including artificial intelligence (AI) and human-computer interaction (HCI). The validation of proposed techniques requires the availability of specific facilities (e.g., smart houses) containing a multitude of sensors and actuators. Unfortunately, this aspect represents a bottleneck for the development of new techniques in AmI. On the one hand, building such facilities is expensive, requiring considerable costs for maintenance and extension. In the vast majority of cases, datasets are not freely available to the community; freely available ones (e.g., CASAS[1]

---

[1] https://wsucasas.wordpress.com.

A. De Gloria and R. Veltkamp (Eds.): GALA 2015, LNCS 9599, pp. 208–217, 2016.
DOI: 10.1007/978-3-319-40216-1_22

and Tracebase [8] projects) are not continuously updated and contain a limited set of sensors, which do not allow the evaluation of algorithms that require the availability of specific categories of sensors. Additionally, the specification of the sensors, in terms of accuracy, performance and layout, is usually unknown.

A viable approach to deal with the lack of datasets is to employ crowd-sourcing and gamification [10] to gather them from users. This paper presents a prototype 3D virtual environment available as a Facebook application, allowing users to replicate their own lifestyle and habits. The environment additionally contains a set of virtual sensors, which the final user is completely unaware of, whose measurements are anonymously stored and aggregated into datasets. The design of such a software facility raises interesting challenges like *(i)* ensuring the truthfulness of reported behaviors, and *(ii)* fostering user engagement.

The paper is organized as follows: Sect. 2 presents the virtual environment and the architecture of the overall system. Section 3 provides details about the two usability rounds of evaluation that led the development of the final prototype, which include the technique for assessing the truthfulness of the users presented in Sect. 4. Section 5 presents the result of the evaluation of the final prototype. Section 6 discusses related work and Sect. 7 concludes the paper.

2   The Virtual Environment: Design Principles

The virtual environment consists of a house with six rooms (kitchen, bath-room, utility room, living room, bedroom and study-room with gym), which can be explored and manipulated by the user through a character. Figure 1(a) shows a bird's-eye view of the house. The creation of such an environment is nowadays noticeably simplified by the availability of rapid development envi-ronments, which allow to deploy the very same application on various plat-forms (e.g., Android, iOS, Windows Phone, common browsers) without major changes. In particular, we decided to develop our environment using Unity[2], and to integrate the game in the Facebook platform as an external application avail-able at https://apps.facebook.com/1544863072467612/. This integration allows to obtain useful information about the user's preferences that can be used to make the environment more attractive; it is possible, for example, to have a male or female character according to the gender of the user.

The point of view of the game consists of a third person camera placed behind the character. In order to simplify the comprehension of the gaming dynamics the game screen is divided in two sections, as shown in Fig. 1(b). The left side is devoted to show the current state of the character (e.g., the name, the current score and the mission state) together with currently owned and usable objects. The right side is devoted to the interaction with objects in the house. All the interaction menus with the objects of the house (not currently owned by the character) appear on the right side of the screen.

It is possible for the character to interact with all the objects of the house. Objects are classified into categories; for example some of the objects (e.g., the

---

[2] https://unity3d.com/.

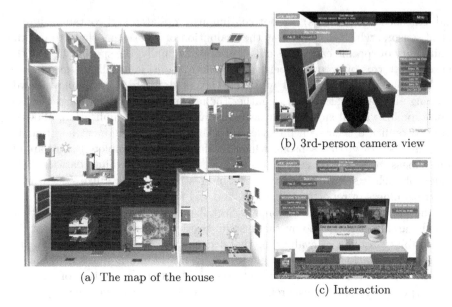

(a) The map of the house

(b) 3rd-person camera view

(c) Interaction

Fig. 1. The virtual environment

cabinet, the oven) may contain other objects and are called *container objects*. The user can navigate the environment by using either the mouse or the keyboard. As soon as the character enters the range of action of an interactive object, it will receive a visual feedback indicating the available operations. These latter are object-specific or category-specific; for example, the oven (i.e., a container object) can be filled with all the objects that can be cooked (another example of object category). Some of the objects are carried by the character; this way, we can obtain natural ways of interaction, like having a coffee while comfortably seated on the couch watching TV, as shown in Fig. 1(c).

Time is a fundamental component of the environment; the interaction with some objects can be, in the real world, time consuming but the user could not be incline to wait a "real" amount of time while playing a game. This is the reason why the virtual environment supports a neat distinction between *physical* and *virtual* time. Physical time represents a notion of time as perceived by people in the real world, i.e., it reflects the time actions would take if really executed. Virtual time instead marks the passing of time within the virtual environment, i.e., the time the user spends in front of the game. Keeping track of physical time is important for two reasons; on the one hand, showing physical time to user helps in providing the required degree of realism; on the other hand, datasets produced by the virtual environment will contain real timestamps that are indeed required by vast majority of ambient intelligence techniques. As an example, objects that perform a transformation of other objects (for example the preparation of a toast by the toaster) have an associated timer that lasts few seconds of virtual time, while increasing of few minutes the physical time.

The sensor logs produced during the interaction with the virtual environment take the form of a sequence of events of the type $\langle ts, s, v \rangle$, where ts is a physical timestamp, s is a string identifying the source sensor, and v is the value measured by the sensor. Here we want to remark the difference between actions performed inside the environment (that are not present in the log) and events represented in the log that come instead from a set of installed, invisible to the user, sensors.

In the current release two types of sensors (usually available in real smart space facilities) are present in the environment, namely switch sensors triggering when a door is opened/closed, and presence sensors deployed within all the rooms. The latter are installed on the ceiling facing downwards following a grid layout covering the entire room. The virtual environment has been designed in order to make it simple to add new sensor classes; however, certain sensors can be difficult to be emulated inside a virtual environment especially when physical processes are involved (e.g., accelerometers, temperature sensors).

From an architectural point of view, the virtual environment acts as client-side of a back-end, in which data (i.e., users, generated sensor logs, missions completed) are stored and managed. Additionally, the server-side hosts a service implementing the truthfulness scoring task (see Sect. 4); all the auxiliary data needed for this task is stored in the database in the form of serialized software objects together with scores obtained by users and user rankings.

3   Usability Evaluation

The first stage of evaluation (conducted at the beginning of March 2015) involved five experts with experience in gaming, thus enabling us to get trustworthy advices and opinions about the visual environment. In this case, the experts were required to conduct an evaluation whose main purpose is to identify usability problems in a design; user-relevant feedback because the experts had gaming knowledge. The experts first attended an interactive seminar where the application was introduced and demonstrated. They were then individually asked to conduct the usability evaluation of the application.

The critical usability problems found by the experts were: *(i)* not clear interaction modality, whether based on keyboard or on point&click; *(ii)* lack of a proper visual feedback when interacting with objects, and having the possibility to interact with all objects, not only some of them; *(iii)* slower movement of the character, more precise, and capability to locate where the character is in the house; *(iv)* messages and instructions should be not too formal, but more natural and immediate, based on common language. The second version of the virtual environment was developed, following the received feedback, during March 2015, and a second evaluation was conducted in the period between 1 April and 9 April 2015, through a private invitation message on Facebook. This larger evaluation involved 20 persons who were asked to perform three missions:

1. **Exploratory mission:** In order to acquire a certain confidence with the environment, the user is free to explore the house and to use all the objects.

2. **Truthful morning routine:** The user is asked to carry out the actions done during an usual morning in a truthful way (as he/she would do in real life).
3. **Untruthful morning routine:** The user asked to carry out the actions of the mission in a untruthful or uncommon way.

The users were 12 males and 8 females, with an average age of 26, 5 years. The 60 % of users are students, 30 % workers and the last 10 %, in the period of the test, were looking for a job. A result of the experiment was also to obtain a reliable dataset, being generated in an unrestricted way by users, who also had the task of labeling their missions as truthful or untruthful.

The content of the feedback covered several topics, and ranged from the detection of bugs to the request of new features. The requests were interesting, in fact the 70 % of users asked to add the action "wash the hands" in the bathroom, and the 20 % reported the lack of the action "make the bed". The high number of requests for the same action showed that there was an obvious lack in the design phase because we had not inserted fundamental actions in a morning routine.

4   Ensuring Truthfulness

Let us consider the environment E where a single user character (i.e., a virtual character moved by the user) interacts with a set of objects $O = \{o_1, o_2, \ldots, o_{n_O}\}$. Given a set of object categories $C = \{c_1, c_2, \ldots, c_{n_C}\}$ and the set O, the function $f_M : O \mapsto 2^C$ associates to each object in O a set of categories in C. The interaction with the environment happens through a set of actions $A = \{a_1, a_2, \ldots, a_{n_A}\}$. A single action $a_i \in A$ takes as input a list of objects, each belonging to a specific category in C, thus a signature like $a_i\left(c_{i_1}, c_{i_2}, \ldots, c_{i_{n_{a_i}}}\right)$.

For the sake of brevity, let us suppose the availability of an alphabet $\Sigma = \{\sigma_1, \sigma_2, \ldots, \sigma_{n_\Sigma}\}$. If n_O and $max_i\{n_{a_i}\}$ are finite, it is always possible to associate to any valid instantiation of each action a unique symbol in Σ using a two-way function. Symbols in Σ can be represented, for example, using two lowercase letters from the English alphabet (for simplicity) (e.g., $\sigma_j =$ *Take an apple by the fridge* $\mapsto$ "aa", $\sigma_k =$ *Take an orange by the fridge* $\mapsto$ "ab"). This representation of symbols can be easily extended in case a bigger Σ set is needed.

Let us denote the set of human habits with $H = \{h_1, h_2, \ldots, h_{n_H}\}$. A user performing a specific habit $h_i \in H$ executes an ordered sequence of actions belonging to Σ^+. If we denote with $\mathcal{H}_i = \left\{s_{i_1}, s_{i_2}, \ldots, s_{i_{n_{H_i}}}\right\}$ the set of executions of the habit h_i, we want to define a function $f_{h_i} : \mathcal{H}_i \mapsto \mathbb{R}$, specific to the habit h_i, that assign to a single string in $\mathcal{H}_i$ a score representing its truthfulness. We will also denote with $\mathcal{S} = \bigcup_{k=1}^{n_H} \mathcal{H}_k$ the set of all the strings. During the heuristic evaluation, for example, we had $n_H = 3$, thus we had three different sets $\mathcal{H}_1$, $\mathcal{H}_2$ and $\mathcal{H}_3$ containing the different executions of the requested habits.

The task of ensuring truthfulness has been already addressed using manual consensus-based techniques [6]. It falls into the broad category of player classification techniques [1]. In this paper, we consider a reported behavior s_{i_j} to be truthful only if there exists a subset of similar reported behaviors in $\mathcal{H}_i$. If we suppose the cardinality $|\mathcal{H}_i|$ big for any given i, one possible way to design the truthfulness function f_{h_i} is to cluster the strings in $\mathcal{H}_i$ according to a specifically designed distance measure, and to assign scores according to the result.

Given two strings s_1 and s_2, a string similarity metric measures the similarity between two strings. Following the heuristic evaluation, we developed a distance measure d_n inspired by the seminal Jaro-Winkler distance function [11]. Given the Jaro distance d_j, we define our distance function as:

$$d_n\left(s_1, s_2\right) = d_j\left(s_1, s_2\right) + \left(\left(\left(a \cdot p_1\right) + \left(l_{max} \cdot p_2\right)\right)\left(1 - d_j\left(s_1, s_2\right)\right)\right) \qquad (1)$$

where (i) $a = \frac{[\# \text{ common sequences}]}{|s_1| + |s_2|}$ is the number of common patterns with respect to the overall length of strings, (ii) $l_{max} = \frac{max(\text{length of common sequences})}{|s1| + |s2|}$ is the length of the longest common pattern with respect the cumulative length of strings s_1 and s_2, (iii) p_1 and p_2 are scaling factors (in our implementation we fixed both to 0.1), and (iv) $|s_1|$ and $|s_2|$ are the lengths of strings s_1 and s_2.

In order to aggregate similar sequences of actions into groups according to the defined distance measure, we employed the DBSCAN clustering algorithm [4]. DBSCAN requires two parameters (ϵ and $MinPts$) that have been experimentally selected by manually evaluating the results of the first stage of evaluation. As soon as a new mission for the habit h_i is completed by a user, a new string s is generated and added to the set $\mathcal{H}_i$. Running DBSCAN on $\mathcal{H}_i$ (now including s) produces a set of clusters $\mathcal{C}_i = \left(C_{i_1}, C_{i_2}, \ldots, C_{i_{n_{C_i}}}\right)$. For the sake of brevity we will denote with C_s the cluster assigned to the new string s.

We employed the size of the clusters in $\mathcal{C}_i$ in order to compute the score to assign to the new string s. In particular, we can assign to any cluster $C_j \in \mathcal{C}_i$ a weight $p_i = \frac{|C_j|}{|\mathcal{H}_i|}$ that represents the percentage of samples in $\mathcal{H}_i$ covered by C_j. If we denote with p_s the weight associated to the cluster C_s a simple strategy could be to use this weight as a score correction factor, thus assigning higher scores to strings belonging to the biggest clusters. This kind of approach would acknowledge high truthfulness to a reported behavior if there are many other users reporting a similar behavior for the specific habit.

This approach has a main drawback: it fosters user to perform habit in a standardized manner, thus encouraging them not reveal their real habits. In order to cope with this issue, we can define a set of coefficients $W = \{w_1, \ldots, w_z\}$ where the w_k coefficients is assigned to the k-th biggest cluster. The m-th biggest cluster, for any $m > z$, will have a coefficient w_m equal to 1 (no corrections to the weight of the cluster). If we denote with w_s the coefficient assigned to the cluster C_s, the correction weight assigned to the string s will be $\widetilde{p}_s = p_s \cdot w_s$. This way it is possible, by tuning the set W, to slightly penalize behaviors belonging the biggest cluster in order to foster slightly unusual behaviors.

The system calculates the final score by taking into account not only $\widetilde{p}_s$ but also the number of actions carried out during the mission with respect to the average length of the strings belonging to $\mathcal{H}_i$. This way, reported behaviors containing many repetitions of patterns are penalized.

5 Final Evaluation

The evaluation of the final prototype started on June 26th with private messages on Facebook and public posts, shared between friends, on Facebook wall. Overall, the final experimentation was conducted on 32 end-users (20 male and 12 female), with an average age of 26. The evaluation consisted of completing four missions together with a questionnaire: morning routine (in a working day), morning routine (in ah holiday), evening routine and relax routine. The questionnaires were structured as follows:

- the first questionnaire collected information about the user background; it was filled only once;
- the second questionnaire collected information about ease of access to the game functionalities, evaluation of game experience and ease to understand the logic of the game; it was requested to be filled at the end of each mission;
- the third questionnaire collected users' suggestions.

From the first questionnaire, the 31,3 % of users declared not to be an usual gamer whereas only the 9,4 % consider themselves as expert gamers. On a scale of 1 to 5, the average declared gaming experience is 2.59. The 75 % of the user tried or knew life simulation games like "The Sims", therefore they did not have difficulty in understanding the logic of the game. 69 % of the users did not know smart spaces before the experiment and 75 % of them never experienced a smart space, but 83,3 % of these latter expressed interest in this type of environment.

The second questionnaire provided the following information. Figure 2(a) shows how even though in the vast majority of cases users did not find any difficulties in controlling the character, there is room for improvements in this area. From Fig. 2(b) and (c) we deduce that instead the comprehension of the logic of the game was always very high, and most of the users were able to easily replicate the desired behavior. Figure 2(d) shows the results on the overall experience within the game: in the Morning Routine (in a working day) mission most of the user (35 %) had a good experience in the game (grade 4), the 25 % assigned a grade 5 and another 25 % gave a grade 3. Taking into account the 4 missions, about 70 % of users evaluate good (grade $\geq$ 4) his experience.

The third questionnaire concerned technical problems/bugs or suggestions for improvements. We can group received feedback in 3 macro-categories: *technical suggestion* (46,2 %), *bugs* (23 %) and *request of new features* (30,8 %). Most of the suggestions concerned the addition of actions, e.g., "dry your hair after showering", "other actions with the phone". Other suggestions had a technical nature, e.g., the preference for another game view, improvements of the environment surrounding the house and a better character control. Technical problems due to bugs in the system were experienced by the 11 % of users, the 47 % did not find any problems of this type, whereas the remaining 42 % did not answer.

5.1 Correctness of the Truthfulness Algorithm

Data gathered during the final evaluation allowed us to estimate the performance of the clustering algorithm in terms of accuracy. In particular, accuracy has been

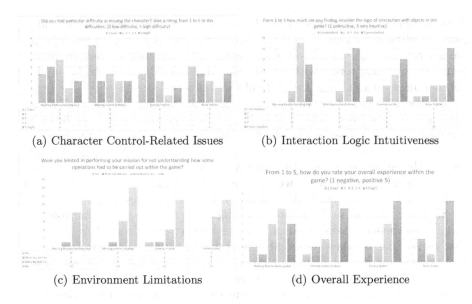

(a) Character Control-Related Issues   (b) Interaction Logic Intuitiveness

(c) Environment Limitations   (d) Overall Experience

Fig. 2. Analysis of the final evaluation questionnaires (Color figure online)

evaluated by comparing the cluster in which a specific mission was assigned with the "ground truth" declared by the user at the end of the mission when users were requested to evaluate their behavior as either "usual", "particular" or "unusual". We measured *accuracy* as "the proportion of true results (both true positives and true negatives) among the total number of cases examined" [12]. In our case we expect that actions declared as "usual" by the user will be grouped in clusters of size greater than 1. Similarly, we expect that actions declared "unusual" or "particular" by the user will be classified as "noise" and assigned to clusters of size 1. We recall the reader that our truthfulness assessment algorithm does not provide a boolean outcome of truthfulness, providing instead a score. Nonetheless, given the limited size of the dataset (with respect to the expected runtime size), the assumption can be considered fair.

If we consider a *true positive* as an action declared "usual" and assigned to a cluster of size ≥ 2, and a *true negative* as an action declared "unusual" or "particular" and assigned to a cluster of size 1 (correctly), the measured accuracy value is 70,5 %. Even though the validity of this result is limited by the size of the dataset, we believe this result witnesses the quality of the proposed approach.

6   Related Work

To the best of our knowledge, this work represents the first attempt to gather smart space datasets by employing crowdsourcing and gamification. The reader may notice a certain analogy with famous simulation games like "The Sims".

A major difference here lies in the fact that "The Sims" does not intend to model realistic situations. "The Sims" game implements a series of rewards that are not related to the likelihood of characters behavior; instead they are related to (short and long term) wishes and goals that provide points to be used to obtain objects or to change the state of the character.

Generic tools for generating datasets of agents moving into pervasive environments are presented in [5,7]. The former tool generates a dataset based on a transition matrix representing the probability-causal relations between all the sensors; as a consequence, the generated sensor log is tightly coupled to the model. The latter tool aims at the massive generation of big datasets and applies a more sophisticated strategy where actions are simulated into a virtual environment and a layered strategy is employed to produce sensor logs.

Similarly, authors in [2] propose a configurable dataset generation tool able to generate realistic logs based on a virtual smart space consisting of agents that behave "as if" they were real inhabitants of the actual smart space. The tool takes as input a set of hand-made models of human habits expressed using a declarative process modeling language. Such a virtual environment can be configured to contain a certain set of sensors and actuators, hence allowing to evaluate technique for AmI over a set of different smart space configurations.

Both [2,7], similarly to our approach, decouple actions performed in the environment from sensor measurements. Their main limitation is the employment of hand made models that necessarily limit the realism of the produced dataset.

Finally, the CASAS project has recently launched the "Smart Home in a Box" program [3][3], which is intended to gather a huge amount of sensor data from worldwide deployed installations obtained by freely shipping sensor kits abroad. This approach, even though promising, does not solve the issue related to the limited variety of sensors as these latter cannot be freely chosen.

7   Conclusions

In this work, we presented a 3D environment able to generate truthful smart space datasets through gamification and crowdsourcing. As such approach has been successfully applied to other areas, its employment in the smart space area is promising. The environment contains sensors invisible to the final user, thus allowing the generation of datasets tailored on the final application.

Even tough at the current stage the proposed approach is able to generate realistic datasets, improvements are needed in order to maximize system effectiveness. As a first point, user engagement represents an important aspect of gamification. Rewards represent a usual way to engage users. Being the system designed to be integrated in a massive social network like Facebook, it allows the game to access important information to this aim, including user preferences. This information can be used to turn scores into rewards that can be valuable to the final user. These rewards can either be in-app extensions or may consists

---

[3] http://smarthome.ailab.wsu.edu/.

of external products and services (i.e., prizes). In order to increase their scores, users could also be asked to participate in the evaluation of played-back (user generated) routines as truthful or not as part of the game.

As a second point, our approach is used to generate sensing data related to a single character that moves and acts in the smart space. Real smart spaces, however, may contain multiple persons at the same time each performing his own habits. This introduces an additional complication to systems that analyze sensing data, as most of the widely used sensors generate measurements that are not assigned to a specific person. As a consequence, an extension to the environment could be the support to multiple users in the same environment. Again, the on-line nature of our environment noticeably simplifies this aspect.

Acknowledgements. This work has been partly supported by the EU project VOICE (621137), the Italian cluster SM&ST - Social Museum and Smart Tourism, and the Italian project NEPTIS.

References

1. Bauckhage, C., Drachen, A., Sifa, R.: Clustering game behavior data. IEEE Trans. on Comput. Intell. AI Game **7**(3), 266–278 (2015)
2. Caruso, M., Ilban, C., Leotta, F., Mecella, M., Vassos, S.: Synthesizing daily life logs through gaming and simulation. In: Proceedings of 2013 ACM Conference on Pervasive and Ubiquitous Computing Adjunct Publication, UbiComp 2013 Adjunct, pp. 451–460. ACM, New York (2013)
3. Cook, D., Crandall, A., Thomas, B., Krishnan, N.: Casas: a smart home in a box. Computer **46**(7), 62–69 (2013)
4. Ester, M., Kriegel, H.-P., Sander, J., Xu, X.: A density-based algorithm for discovering clusters in large spatial databases with noise. In: KDD, vol. 96, no. 34, pp. 226–231 (1996)
5. Helal, A., Mendez-Vazquez, A., Hossain, S.: Specification and synthesis of sensory datasets in pervasive spaces. In: IEEE Symposium on Computers and Communications, pp. 920–925 (2009)
6. Kamar, E., Horvitz, E.: Incentives for truthful reporting in crowdsourcing. In: Proceedings of the 11th International Conference on Autonomous Agents and Multiagent Systems, vol. 3, pp. 1329–1330. International Foundation for Autonomous Agents and Multiagent Systems (2012)
7. Merico, D., Bisiani, R.: An agent-based data-generation tool for situation-aware systems. In: 7th International Conference on Intelligent Environments (2011)
8. Reinhardt, A., Baumann, P., Burgstahler, D., Hollick, M., Chonov, H., Werner, M., Steinmetz, R.: On the accuracy of appliance identification based on distributed load metering data. In: Proceedings of the 2nd IFIP Conference on Sustainable Internet and ICT for Sustainability (SustainIT), pp. 1–9 (2012)
9. Tazari, M.-R., Furfari, F., Fides-Valero, Á., Hanke, S., Höftberger, O., Kehagias, D., Mosmondor, M., Wichert, R., Wolf, P.: The universAAL reference model for AAL. In: Handbook of Ambient Assisted Living, vol. 11, pp. 610–625 (2012)
10. Von Ahn, L.: Games with a purpose. Computer **39**(6), 92–94 (2006)
11. Winkler, W.E.: Overview of Record Linkage, Current Research Directions. Statistical Research Division, US Census Bureau, Washington, D.C. (2006)
12. Metz, C.E.: Basic principles of ROC analysis. In: Seminars in Nuclear Medicine, vol. 8, pp. 283–298. Elsevier (1978)

Comparing Game Input Modalities: A Study for the Evaluation of Player Experience by Measuring Self Reported Emotional States and Learning Outcomes

Stavroula Bampatzia[✉], Angeliki Antoniou, and George Lepouras

Human-Computer Interaction and Virtual Reality Lab, Department of Informatics and Telecommunications, University of Peloponnese, Terma Karaiskaki, 22100 Tripolis, Greece
{s.babatzia,angelant,gl}@uop.gr

Abstract. As new game controllers such as the Microsoft Kinect for Xbox are introduced into the market, new forms of game interaction are introduced such as gestures, voice and eye tracking, which raise some questions regarding the user experience. Is it possible that different input methods provide a more usable game setting and affect the player's emotions and learning process? In this paper, a 2D game about the history of photography was designed and implemented to test these hypotheses. Two prototypes of this game were created, with the first requiring input only via mouse, while the second requiring input via voice and gestures (Kinect). Two different groups tested these two prototypes. The findings from previous pilot experiments indicated that using Kinect as an input method caused higher valence and dominance levels than the use of mouse and were further validated here. Additionally, the learning outcomes of players were not affected by the input method.

1 Introduction

Games have been used over the last years in numerous domains and fields, assisting different goals and purposes. In particular, serious games, games with a purpose that it is not pure entertainment, have been used in education [1] and training [2], in medicine [3], in rehabilitation [4], in cultural heritage [5] and in many more domains.

Especially in regards to education, games have been exploited over the last years with remarkable results [6] and they are recognized as significant learning tools increasing learning motivation [7]. The field of game-based learning is now well established to provide the theoretical framework and the tools for further practice [8]. Games can increase critical thinking, support analysis and synthesis of information, reuse of knowledge in new situations [9] and add significant value to the instructional effectiveness of different domains [10]. Other cognitive elements benefited by games are memory skills, motor abilities, spatial perception and others [11]. Cognitive benefits have been also found in different types of games, like exergames [12]. Games can also be an excellent framework for situated learning (learning that is not disconnected from the real world) [13]. Even populations with special needs and learning difficulties can be benefited from well-designed educational games [14].

© Springer International Publishing Switzerland 2016
A. De Gloria and R. Veltkamp (Eds.): GALA 2015, LNCS 9599, pp. 218–227, 2016.
DOI: 10.1007/978-3-319-40216-1_23

In addition and in regards to emotions, it seems that games can increase the arousal levels of the players [15]. For example, games have been associated with an increase in arousal benefiting different cognitive tasks such as memory tasks [16]. The different emotions players experience during game play are recorded by different studies [17] and the role of these emotions in learning is evaluated. Furthermore, games can be now designed to also evoke specific emotions [18].

Finally, it seems that game input modalities are particularly important [19]. It also seems that emotions experienced during the game can be affected by game input modalities, since for example complex input methods were found to increase gamers' arousal levels [20]. From the literature review, there seems to be a lack of studies investigating the effect of game input modalities in relation to emotions experience by the player. There are also studies showing indications that game input modalities might affect game learning outcomes [21]. Thus, this study investigates the gaming experience of the participants in terms of self-reported emotions (e.g. valence, arousal, dominance and tiredness), usability issues of games with different input modalities and learning outcomes in regards to game input modalities.

2   Related Work

There are indications that input modalities are very important. For example, it was found that gestural user interfaces (both Nintendo Wii and Microsoft Kinect) can increase immersion and improve user experience [19]. In particular, using Kinect as an input modality can improve interaction efficiency and enhance immersion in 3D virtual systems [22]. Kinect-assisted instruction was also studied in educational settings and significant educational benefits were found [23]. Furthermore, primary school students seemed to prefer Kinect over mouse input in educational applications, despite the usability problems they experienced with the former [24].

Many studies attempt to measure user arousal levels, emotions and overall user experience. Tan et al. developed a system to understand users' emotions by observing their body postures [25]. McDuff developed an emotional prosthetic to allow users to reflect on their own emotions and to predict valence, arousal and engagement [26].

Especially, concerning games, input modalities are also important. In a recent study, full body gestures were easier to use than mouse and keyboard when a game book was used for interactive storytelling [27]. Another study, compared mouse and keyboard over gamepad controls in first person shooter games. Players had usability problems with gamepad controls but self-reported equal overall experience for both [28]. Game input methods have been also studied in medicine with chronic pain rehabilitation patients [29] and in psychology where motion-based touchless games were found to be better for autistic children [30]. More complex input methods were found to increase arousal levels, despite of increases in complexity [20].

Emotions, arousal levels and overall experience are also measured in games [31]. For example, user facial expressions have been studied to assess user experience [25]. Another study, evaluated affective usability experiences of an exergame for older users [32]. Different methods have been tried, like attempting to evaluate player experience in games by including self-characteristics (personality traits) assessment in the evaluation process [33]. Games not only try to assess the experience and measure different arousal aspects, but sometimes they also use this information as user feedback. For example, a video game used biofeedback to help psychiatric patients to learn relaxation skills and develop new emotional regulation strategies [34]. Finally, Nacke et al. provide an overview of affective input mechanisms for games, like gaze interaction and eye tracking, electromyography, galvanic skin response, electrocardiography, heart rate measurement, strain sensors, temperature sensors, and electroencephalography [35].

Especially, regarding game input modalities and learning outcomes there are indications that input modalities affect the quality of learning and the establishment of associations between concepts [21]. Game input modalities also seem to play a role in group educational gaming activities [36]. According to [37] new input modalities such Kinect, can boost student motivation and promote learning. Using gestures and other body movements can enhance the comprehension of learning material by students [38]. However, the field of Kinesthetic learning is relatively new and requires further investigation.

Therefore, this study investigates the gaming experience of the participants in terms of self-reported arousal levels and emotions as well as usability issues of games with different input modalities. It also studies the effect of game input modalities in regards to learning outcomes.

3   Method

Hypotheses: There were four main research hypotheses, all directional based on previous research findings, as described above and our previous pilot study [32]: 1. The self reported emotions of the players of the Kinect prototype will be more positive than the self reported emotions of the players of the mouse prototype. 2. There will be a difference in the perceived usability between the two groups (one using mouse and the other using Kinect input) and mouse users will have higher usability scores. 3. The game will enhance the learning process. 4. The game input modality will affect the learning outcomes and Kinect users will have higher learning scores. In our study the independent variables are: input modalities (i.e. Kinect & Voice, Mouse) and the dependent variables are: self reported emotions (i.e. Valence, Arousal, Dominance, Tiredness), self reported usability and learning outcomes.

In order to study the first hypothesis, that the emotional state and more particularly the arousal, the valence, the dominance and the tiredness levels of the participants will be affected by the game input method, we used a between subjects analysis. To study the usability differences of the two game input methods, we also followed a between subjects design. To study the third hypothesis, about the learning efficiency of the game itself, a within subject design experiment was performed. Finally to explore if the game input modality affects the learning outcomes of this game, we selected a between subject design comparing the total scores between the two groups (one group using mouse input and the other using Kinect input) after the game.

Game Type: The game designed for the purposes of this research aimed to inform the player about the history of photography. The specific topic was chosen for two main reasons: 1. To the designers' knowledge, this is a unique game dealing with the history and techniques of artistic photography, 2. Certain types of games and games of certain topics seem to be associated with increased stress levels and depression levels [39] which need to be avoided here, since the game theme should not interfere with the stress levels to be measured. Therefore, a neutral topic was chosen in order to expand players' knowledge on artistic photography.

Game: The game is called "Watch through the glass" and is implemented as a desktop application where the player can use the mouse or the Microsoft Kinect Sensor as an input device. A demo of the mouse version of the game can be found at: https://www.youtube.com/watch?v=VP-KqPaT7yE. The game consists of three different levels. In the first level, players have to listen to a recording about the life and works of three famous photographers by pressing the play button (first prototype) or by parsing it with their hand (second prototype) and then they have to sort the artist's photographs by chronological order. They have the opportunity to listen to the recording unlimited times. In the first prototype (mouse input) they can place the photographs by drag and drop. In the second prototype (Kinect input) they first have to put their hand over the image, they can select it by saying "Hi" and then move their hand to the desired position and place it by saying "Ok". In the second and in the third levels of the game, players have to read some information about the work of some photographers and then to recall this information in order to answer to six questions. Players, who use the mouse, can select the answer by placing an orange check mark on the desired answer. Players who use Kinect, can select an answer by just parsing the answer with their hand. In order to keep playing the game, players have to press the yellow dart (first prototype) or they have to parse it (second prototype) in every screen of the game.
The objective of the player is to collect as many credits as possible. During the whole game, players can see their current score in the bottom left corner of the screen. For each correct answer, they earn one credit. At the end of the game they can see their total score. Moreover, between the three levels of the game, players receive feedback about the correct answers of the level they have just finished. In the course of the game, information is provided about the technological advancements of the camera over the last two centuries. Participants can sort the photographs or select an answer only once. This requires them to be certain before providing their responses and it also prevents them from randomly selecting, placing pictures and answering questions.

This game was designed for two different input modalities (mouse, Kinect). It was developed in Processing which is an open source programming language. The game was projected on a wall in a large scale and each user participated alone and only in one of the two prototypes of the game.

Subjects: There were 36 adults (18 males, 18 females) who completed the pilot experiment. Their ages ranged from 18 to 35 years of age (M = 24.56, SD = 4.01). All the participants were fluent in English as the simple instructions and the game environment were in English. The majority of the participants had no previous knowledge on the topic of the game.

Procedure: In particular, there were 2 groups of 18 people in a between subjects design. The first group played the game only with the mouse (first prototype) and the second group played the game only with the Kinect (second prototype). Each session lasted a maximum of 30 min, in order to avoid experiment fatigue.

Before each session, all the participants were asked to complete one short questionnaire with demographic questions regarding their age and their previous experience with gaming and various input modalities. They also had to evaluate their alertness and emotional state (e.g. tiredness, arousal, dominance and valence). Next, the researchers provided instructions and explained to the player the goal of the game and what she was going to deal with. In the second group, participants had to play a short demo of the game, which lasted a maximum of 3 min in order to learn how to use the Kinect. After each session, participants were asked again to complete a second questionnaire about their physical and emotional state and to evaluate the system and the game.

The questionnaires to evaluate the emotions of players and the usability of each input method were built by the researchers based on standardized questionnaires, the 5-step Self-Assessment Manikin (SAM) scales [40], the System Usability Scale (SUS) [41] and the Post-Study Usability Questionnaire (PSSUQ) [42]. As far as the learning outcome questionnaires, there were 8 multiple choice questions asking people to recollect information they learned in the game (Q1: What is illustrated by the image?, Q2: What did the photographer Henri Cartier Bresson talk about?, Q3: Who took this picture?, Q4: Who is this photographer?, Q5: On what subject did Bruce Davidson focus on his work ?, Q6: Who was taking pictures of Che Guevara?, Q7: Who took this picture?, Q8: Which photographer is famous for fashion photography?). Their responses were imported to the SPSS 20 to be analyzed statistically. The same questionnaire had to be answered before and after the game.

4   Results

In order to validate our first hypothesis, that the arousal, the valence, tiredness and the dominance of participants will be different after the experiment in the two groups, we run the non parametric Mann-Whitney U test. This analysis showed us that the valence of players with Kinect *(M = 4.39, SD = 0.60)* was greater than the valence of players with mouse *(M = 3.67, SD = 0.68)* after the game *(U = 77.0, p = 0.003, r = 0.49)*. Moreover, the dominance in the second group (Kinect input) *(M = 4.06, SD = 0.63)* was greater than the dominance in the first group (mouse input) *(M = 3.22, SD = 0.80)* *(U = 77.00, p = 0.003, r = 0.49)*. However, we did not elicit any significant difference in arousal *(U = 133.00, p = 0.312, r = 0.168)* and in tiredness *(U = 158.00, p = 0.905, r = 0.019)* between the groups after the game. Thus, Hypothesis 1 is partially confirmed findings inline with pilot study results.

Checking the usability of the two input modalities, players in the mouse condition *(M = 4.61, SD = 0.85)* found their input modality easier than players in the Kinect version *(M = 3.89, SD = 1.02)* *(U = 91.00, p = 0.013, r = 0.414)*. We also discovered that people who played in the mouse condition *(M = 4.33, SD = 1.23)* were more satisfied by the use of that input method than those who played with the Kinect *(M = 3.78, SD = 1.00)* *(U = 102.50, p = 0.042, r = 0.338)*. However, players using the Kinect *(M = 4.22, SD = 1.21)* reported that they would like to play this game again with the Kinect compared to players using the mouse *(M = 3.11, SD = 1.36)* *(U = 87.00, p = 0.013, r = 0.413)*. Finally, the players using the mouse *(M = 4.50, SD = 0.70)* reported that it was easier to identify the actions they were expected to perform during the game than those using the Kinect *(M = 3.78, SD = 1.16)* *(U = 102.50, p = 0.043, r = 0.337)*. Hypothesis 2 was also confirmed.

By the statistical analysis of data related with the learning outcomes of the game, we discovered through the Wilcoxon Signed-ranks Test that in both groups the total scores after playing the game were higher than before playing the game. In detail, the total score after the game of players with mouse *(M = 5.78, SD = 1.80)* was significantly different than their total score before playing the game *(M = 3.83, SD = 1.61)* *(Z = −3.24, p = 0.001)*. Also, the total score after the game of layers with Kinect *(M = 5.44, SD = 1.33)* was significantly different than their total score before playing the game *(M = 3.77, SD = 1.55)* *(Z = −3.138, p = 0.002)*. Apart from the total score of the players, significant difference was presented in some questions (see Table 1). Hypothesis 3 was confirmed, too.

Table 1. Within subject design - Learning outcomes from pre and post questionnaires

Input Modality (Groups)	Questions	Results
Mouse	Q4	$Z = -3.31, p = 0.001$
	Q6	$Z = -3.16, p = 0.002$
Kinect	Q1	$Z = -2.00, p = 0.046$
	Q4	$Z = -2.12, p = 0.034$
	Q7	$Z = -1.89, p = 0.058$
	Q8	$Z = -2.33, p = 0.020$

Lastly, we run a between subject design experiment to identify whether significant differences exist in the prior knowledge of the subjects of the two groups. We found that the subjects of both groups had similar knowledge of this field *(U = 160.000, p = 0.949, r = 0.01)*, indicating a balanced split between the two experimental groups. Then, the results from the Mann-Whitney U test indicated that the total scores of both groups after playing the game were not significantly different *(U = 137.000, p = 0.419, r = 0.134)*. However, for only one post question (Q6) the score of players with mouse *(M = 0.94, SD = 0.23)* was significantly higher than the score of players with Kinect *(M = 0.61, SD = 0.50)* *(U = 108.000, p = 0.018, r = 0.110)*. Therefore, hypothesis 4 was not confirmed.

5 Discussion

The results of the analysis indicate that there are significant differences between the groups that tried the different game input methods. In particular, Kinect users reported being happier and more dominant (higher self esteem) after playing the game, compared to the mouse users. Different input methods were found to affect the participants' emotional state and in particular, reported attractiveness to an event (valence) and self esteem (dominance). This finding might be due to the unfamiliarity of the users with such an input method. Most participants were experienced mouse users but they did not have previous experience with the Kinect. Therefore the novelty of the device might be responsible for the significant findings. However, the fact that the users were involved in full body interaction might have also played a role, since users are forced to behave like extraverts (i.e. moving vividly and speaking loudly). From psychology research [43], it is known that extraverts report more positive emotions. Since the Kinect forced people to behave like extraverts, what might affect out results could be also the phenomenon explained by Bem (self perception theory) showing that when an individual is forced to behave in a certain manner, the individual perceives her own behavior and starts feeling in the same way [44]. At this stage, it seems difficult to separate the two effects and future works can focus on participants that are experienced in full body interaction, in order to eliminate the novelty effect.

Concerning usability, overall participants did not face any difficulties in any of the two conditions. However, the mouse was considered more usable compared to the Kinect, since it scored significantly higher. It is important to note here, that despite this usability differences between the two input methods, Kinect users reported higher satisfaction and dominance levels. It seems that in a game the usability of an input method is not by itself sufficient to predict the users' game satisfaction. Nonetheless, novel input methods, such as the Kinect, seem to be more engaging for the players and increase the willingness of players to use them more in the future. On the other hand, the players found the interaction with traditional input methods, such as the mouse, more familiar and predictable.

Regarding the knowledge outcomes of the game, users in both groups showed a significantly better understanding of the field of the history of photography after playing the game, showing that the game did affect the learning outcomes. Nevertheless, there was no significant difference between the performance and therefore the knowledge outcomes of the users in the mouse condition compared to the Kinect condition, implying that the game input modality did not affect learning.

6   Conclusions

The significance of the present findings implies that game input methods can affect the emotional state of players. This can be further studied in order to better map game input methods with different emotional states of users. There might be a connection between game input modalities and user engagement which could be also explored further. The present work provided useful insights into different game modalities, which have not been compared by previous works. Our future work will collect further data, including both self-reports and physiological measurements, from a larger and more diverse sample of users. For example, people more experienced with the Kinect should be used as subjects of future experiments to avoid possible novelty effects, as the ones possibly expressed here. Additionally, since the nature of the game could sensibly affect the results, a range of different games could be designed and tested as a next step. An interesting aspect that could be explored in future works is the application of the same experimental setup as part of game therapy, involving subjects suffering from addiction (addiction patients often have underlying depression and have low arousal levels [45]). Game input methods seem to affect the overall gaming experience and affect users in different ways. Being a relatively new research field, game input modalities need to be further studied since they could have a major impact at the HCI community.

Acknowledgments. We would like to thank all the participants who agreed to take part in the experiments. Secondly, we are mostly grateful to E. Roumelioti, V. Bravou and A. Vasilakos for their help in developing the game, graphic design and sound editing.

References

1. Ma, M., Bale, K., Rea, P.: Constructionist learning in anatomy education. In: Ma, M., Oliveira, M.F., Hauge, J.B., Duin, H., Thoben, K.-D. (eds.) SGDA 2012. LNCS, vol. 7528, pp. 43–58. Springer, Heidelberg (2012)
2. Azadegan, A., Riedel, J.C., Baalsrud Hauge, J.: Serious games adoption in corporate training. In: Ma, M., Oliveira, M.F., Hauge, J.B., Duin, H., Thoben, K.-D. (eds.) SGDA 2012. LNCS, vol. 7528, pp. 74–85. Springer, Heidelberg (2012)
3. Bouchard, B., Imbeault, F., Bouzouane, A., Menelas, B.-A.J.: Developing serious games specifically adapted to people suffering from alzheimer. In: Ma, M., Oliveira, M.F., Hauge, J.B., Duin, H., Thoben, K.-D. (eds.) SGDA 2012. LNCS, vol. 7528, pp. 243–254. Springer, Heidelberg (2012)
4. Dores, A.R., Carvalho, I.P., Barbosa, F., Almeida, I., Guerreiro, S., Leitão, M., de Sousa, L., Castro-Caldas, A.: Serious games: are they part of the solution in the domain of cognitive rehabilitation? In: Ma, M., Fradinho Oliveira, M., Madeiras Pereira, J. (eds.) SGDA 2011. LNCS, vol. 6944, pp. 95–105. Springer, Heidelberg (2011)
5. Antoniou, A., Lepouras, G., Bampatzia, S., Almpanoudi, H.: An approach for serious game development for cultural heritage. J. Comput. Cult. Herit. **6**, 1–19 (2013)
6. Kebritchi, M., Hirumi, A.: Examining the pedagogical foundations of modern educational computer games. Comput. Educ. **51**, 1729–1743 (2008)
7. Cordova, D., Lepper, M.: Intrinsic motivation and the process of learning: beneficial effects of contextualization, personalization, and choice. J. Educ. Psychol. **88**, 715–730 (1996)
8. Prensky, M.: Digital game-based learning. Comput. Entertain **1**, 21 (2003)
9. Ferreira Franco, J., de Deus Lopes, R.: Three-dimensional digital environments and computer graphics influencing K-12 individuals' digital literacy development and interdisciplinary lifelong learning. In: ACM SIGGRAPH Asia 2009 Educators Program, p. 15 (2009)
10. Šisler, V., Brom, C., Cuhra, J., Činátl, K., Gemrot, J.: Stories from the history of Czechoslovakia, a serious game for teaching history of the Czech lands in the 20th century – notes on design concepts and design process. In: Herrlich, M., Malaka, R., Masuch, M. (eds.) ICEC 2012. LNCS, vol. 7522, pp. 67–74. Springer, Heidelberg (2012)
11. Verhaegh, J., Fontijn, W., Hoonhout, J.: TagTiles: optimal challenge in educational electronics. In: 1st International Conference on Tangible and Embedded Interaction, pp. 187–190 (2007)
12. Gao, Y., Mandryk, R.: The acute cognitive benefits of casual exergame play. In: SIGCHI Conference on Human Factors in Computing Systems, pp. 1863–1872. ACM (2012)

13. de Aguilera, M., Mendiz, A.: Video games and education: (Education in the Face of a "Parallel School"). Comput. Entertain **1**, 10 (2003)
14. Paniagua Martín, F., Colomo Palacios, R., García-Crespo, Á.: MAS: learning support software platform for people with disabilities. In: 1st ACM SIGMM International Workshop on Media Studies and Implementations that Help Improving Access To Disabled Users, pp. 47–52 (2009)
15. Reuderink, B., Mühl, C., Poel, M.: Valence, arousal and dominance in the EEG during game play. IJAACS **6**, 45 (2013)
16. Jeong, E., Biocca, F.: Are there optimal levels of arousal to memory? effects of arousal, centrality, and familiarity on brand memory in video games. Comput. Hum. Behav. **28**, 285–291 (2012)
17. Gutica, M., Conati, C.: Student emotions with an edu-game: a detailed analysis. In: 2013 Humaine Association Conference on Affective Computing and Intelligent Interaction, pp. 534–539. IEEE Computer Society, Washington, D.C. (2013)
18. Wang, N., Marsella, S.C.: Introducing EVG: an emotion evoking game. In: Gratch, J., Young, M., Aylett, R.S., Ballin, D., Olivier, P. (eds.) IVA 2006. LNCS (LNAI), vol. 4133, pp. 282–291. Springer, Heidelberg (2006)
19. Francese, R., Passero, I., Tortora, G.: Wiimote and Kinect: gestural user interfaces add a natural third dimension to HCI. In: International Working Conference on Advanced Visual Interfaces, pp. 116–123. ACM (2012)
20. Lankes, M., Hochleitner, W., Hochleitner, C., Lehner, N.: Control vs. complexity in games: comparing arousal in 2D game prototypes. In: 4th International Conference on Fun and Games, pp. 101–104. ACM (2012)
21. Zarraonandia, T., Bellucci, A., Aedo, I., Díaz, P.: Exploring interaction possibilities in educational games: a working proposal. In: 14th IEEE International Conference on Advanced Learning Technologies. pp. 640–641. IEEE (2014)
22. Liao, H., Long, X.: Study on virtual assembly system based on Kinect somatosensory interaction. In: 2013 International Conference on Information Science and Cloud Computing, pp. 55–60. IEEE (2013)
23. Villaroman, N., Rowe, D., Swan, B.: Teaching natural user interaction using OpenNI and the Microsoft Kinect sensor. In: 2011 Information Technology Education Conference, pp. 227–232. ACM, New York (2011)
24. Vrellis, I., Moutsioulis, A., Mikropoulos, T.: Primary school students' attitude towards gesture based interaction: a comparison between Microsoft Kinect and Mouse. In: 14th IEEE International Conference on Advanced Learning Technologies, pp. 678–682. IEEE (2014)
25. Tan, C.S.S., Schöning, J., Luyten, K., Coninx, K.: Informing intelligent user interfaces by inferring affective states from body postures in ubiquitous computing environments. In: 2013 International Conference on Intelligent User Interfaces, pp. 235–246. ACM (2013)
26. McDuff, D., Karlson, A., Kapoor, A., Roseway, A., Czerwinski, M.: AffectAura: an intelligent system for emotional memory. In: SIGCHI Conference on Human Factors in Computing Systems, pp. 849–858. ACM, Chicago (2012)
27. Kistler, F., Sollfrank, D., Bee, N., André, E.: Full body gestures enhancing a game book for interactive story telling. In: Si, M., Thue, D., André, E., Lester, J., Tanenbaum, J., Zammitto, V. (eds.) ICIDS 2011. LNCS, vol. 7069, pp. 207–218. Springer, Heidelberg (2011)
28. Gerling, K.M., Klauser, M., Niesenhaus, J.: Measuring the impact of game controllers on player experience in FPS games. In: 15th International Academic MindTrek Conference: Envisioning Future Media Environments, pp. 83–86. ACM (2011)

29. Schönauer, C., Pintaric, T., Kaufmann, H.: Full body interaction for serious games in motor rehabilitation. In: 2nd Augmented Human International Conference, p. 4. ACM, New York (2011)

30. Bartoli, L., Garzotto, F., Gelsomini, M., Oliveto, L., Valoriani, M.: Designing and evaluating touchless playful interaction for ASD children. In: 2014 Conference on Interaction Design and Children, pp. 17–26. ACM (2014)

31. Bampatzia, S., Roumelioti, E., Antoniou, A., Lepouras, G., Bravou, V.: Comparing game input modalities: a study for the evaluation of player experience by measuring emotional state and game usability. In: 9th International Conference on Research Challenges in Information Science, pp.13–15. IEEE, Athens (2015)

32. Billis, A.S., Konstantinidis, E., Ladas, A., Tsolaki, M.N., Pappas, C., Bamidis, P.D.: Evaluating affective usability experiences of an exergaming platform for seniors. In: 10th International Workshop Biomedical Engineering, pp. 1–4. IEEE, Kos (2011)

33. Birk, M., Mandryk, R.L.: Control your game-self: effects of controller type on enjoyment, motivation, and personality in game. In: SIGCHI Conference on Human Factors in Computing Systems, pp. 685–694. ACM (2013)

34. Fernández-Aranda, F., Jiménez-Murcia, S., Santamaría, J., Gunnard, K., Soto, A., Kalapanidas, E., Bults, R., Davarakis, C., Ganchev, T., Granero, R., Konstantas, D., Kostoulas, T., Lam, T., Lucas, M., Masuet-Aumatell, C., Moussa, M., Nielsen, J., Penelo, E.: Video games as a complementary therapy tool in mental disorders: PlayMancer, a European multicentre study. J. Ment. Health **21**, 364–374 (2012)

35. Nacke, L.E., Mandryk, R.L.: Designing affective games with physiological input. In: Workshop on Multiuser and Social Biosignal Adaptive Games and Playful Applications in Fun and Games Conference (2010)

36. Valadez, J., Ferguson, C.: Just a game after all: violent video game exposure and time spent playing effects on hostile feelings, depression, and visuospatial cognition. Comput. Hum. Behav. **28**, 608–616 (2012)

37. Hsu, H.: The potential of Kinect in education. IJIET **1**(5), 365–370 (2011)

38. Chao, K., Huang, H., Fang, W., Chen, N.: Embodied play to learn: exploring Kinect-facilitated memory performance. Br. J. Educ Technol. **44**, E151–E155 (2013)

39. Morgan, B., Burkett, C., Bagley, E., Graesser, A.: Typed versus spoken conversations in a multi-party epistemic game. In: Biswas, G., Bull, S., Kay, J., Mitrovic, A. (eds.) AIED 2011. LNCS, vol. 6738, pp. 513–515. Springer, Heidelberg (2011)

40. Morris, J.: SAM: the self-assessment manikin; an efficient cross-cultural measurement of emotional response. J. Advertising Res. **35**, 63–68 (1995)

41. Brooke, J.: SUS-A quick and dirty usability scale. Usability Eval. Ind. **189**(194), 4–7 (1996)

42. Lewis, J.R.: Psychometric evaluation of the post-study system usability questionnaire: the PSSUQ. In: Human Factors and Ergonomics Society Annual Meeting, vol. 36, pp. 1259–1260. SAGE Publications (1992)

43. Watson, D., Clark, L.A.: Extraversion and its positive emotional core (1997)

44. Bem, D.: Self-perception: an alternative interpretation of cognitive dissonance phenomena. Psychol. Rev. **74**, 183–200 (1967)

45. Koob, G.F., Le Moal, M.: Neurobiology of drug addiction. In: Stages and Pathways of Drug Involvement: Examining the Gateway Hypothesis, pp. 337–361. Cambridge University Press, New York (2002)

Supporting Collaborative Serious Game Studies Online

Francesco Bellotti[1(✉)], Riccardo Berta[1], Alessandro De Gloria[1], Michela Ott[2],
Maria Magdalena Popescu[3], and Jannicke Baalsrud-Hauge[4]

[1] DITEN - University of Genova, Via Opera Pia 11/A, 16145 Genoa, Italy
{franz,berta}@elios.unige.it, alessandro.degloria@unige.it
[2] Institute for Educational Technology - National Council of Research (CNR-ITD), Genoa, Italy
ott@itd.cnr.it
[3] Carol I National Defense University, 68-72 Panduri St., Bucharest, Romania
mpopescu03@gmail.com
[4] BIBA, University of Bremen, Bremen, Germany
baa@biba.uni-bremen.de

Abstract. While a lot of papers have argued for the educational potential of serious games, the field is still young and methods and tools are needed in order to support effective and efficient design. The SG Studies Database is an instrument devised to allow sharing structured information about SGs. This information can be used by scholars and practitioners also to perform comparative analysis and identify components and modules that could be used in different games. The SG Studies database, which is freely available online on the site of the Serious Games Society, relies on a SG description model, that has been defined in order to allow a structured description of SGs, considering the perspectives of different stakeholders and contexts of use, and spurring the identification of SG components and their relationship with pedagogical theories and expected outcomes. The SG Studies database has already been used as a tool to support identification of reusable patterns and components in SGs, in order to identify best practices and favor module re-use. Other meta studies are possible in the future on the database by any parties.

1 Introduction

Serious Games (SGs) are now spread and used in a variety of environments (formal and informal education, training, advertising, fitness, etc.) and for a variety of topics, ranging from curricular activities (biology, history, languages, etc.) to management (finance, logistics, value chain, etc.) and personnel training (healthcare, salesmen, waiters, etc.).

Several classifications and ontologies have been proposed in literature and databases are being maintained, in order to allow a description and/or support the use of SGs in different contexts. For instance, a non-exhaustive list of resources includes the following:

- Classifications, providing dimensions for SG classification. Examples include: [1–6].

A. De Gloria and R. Veltkamp (Eds.): GALA 2015, LNCS 9599, pp. 228–237, 2016.
DOI: 10.1007/978-3-319-40216-1_24

- Repositories, featuring databases of SGs. Examples include Engage Learning[1] and Serious.gameclassification.com[2]
- Blogs, focusing on news from the SG market and applications. Significant examples include the Serious Games Society (SGS) Blog[3] and The Serious Games Market[4].
- Analysis and ontologies, going more in detail with the analysis of the game goals and components. The SGS' SG Knowledge Management System[5] and, with much more examples but with less detail, Serious.gameclassification.com (see footnote 2).

SG studies provide focused analysis of one or more SG along the above mentioned dimensions. Studies may be monographic (on a single game or topic) or comparative (comparing different SGs). In any case, they should critically present and analyze state of the art SGs.

Game studies are not a novelty. "Games studies"[6] is a well-known journal available online since 2001. Some studies, as another example, have shown amazing properties of legend games such as Tetris (e.g., [7, 8]).

However, the field needs to be refined and extended, particularly in the specific direction of SGs. As the number of developed SGs and related articles increases (e.g., [9, 10]), we think it is necessary to develop and support an "engineering" approach, systemizing the studies, allowing comparative analysis and homogeneous data collection. How can SG studies be characterized? We believe that a cornerstone will be the study of SG mechanics, that are game components able to achieve pedagogical goals through enjoyable features (e.g., [11, 12]). The SG Studies Database is intended as a tool through which scholars and practitioners can systematically describe and analyze SGs, supporting sharing and development of knowledge.

SGs should be critically analyzed and presented in order to allow different types of stakeholders to achieve different goals, such as grasping the main features of a game, compare different games on homogeneous dimensions, assess the impact and educational and entertainment value and the advancement over the state of the art. This is expected to be beneficial for scientist ad technology researchers, as they can get inspiration from the market and think of solutions to overcome the present limits. SG studies may present the perspective of different stakeholders involved in the process (e.g., end-users, teachers, families, designers, content developers).

This paper presents the concept of the SG Studies Database tool, developed by the Games and Learning (GaLA) project [13] and now publicly available in the Serious Games Society's (SGS) website (see footnote 5). Through this tool, structured and semi-structured information is being collected for several games. The system is freely accessible and new analysis can be added on demand. The goal is to develop knowledge, based on empirical evidence, on SG mechanics, their deployment in different contexts and their effectiveness.

---

[1] http://www.engagelearning.eu.

[2] http://serious.gameclassification.com.

[3] http://seriousgamessociety.org.

[4] http://www.seriousgamesmarket.com.

[5] http://studies.seriousgamessociety.org.

[6] http://gamestudies.org/.

2 SG Classification and Taxonomies

A lot of work has been done about SG categorization, and literature has some important papers on this topic. Taxonomies have been proposed classifying SG according to different criteria, such as application domains [2], markets [3], skills [14, 15], learning outcomes [4]. These categorizations show the educational (some put it also more simply, speaking of concreteness or closeness to the real-world) added value of SGs with respect to games, for which a meaningful categorization can still be considered the one by [16], that involves the following categories: action games, adventure games, fighting games, puzzle games, role-playing games, simulations, sport games, strategy games. A more recent taxonomy is slightly more simple: action games, strategy games, adventure games, simulation games, puzzle game educational games.

A very comprehensive and transversal approach to SG classification has been proposed by [1], which rapidly became a reference, proposing a matrix of two major criteria: market (the application domain) and purpose (initial purpose of the designer). Items in the first dimension include: government, defense, marketing, education, corporate, etc. Items in the second include: advergames, games for health, games at work, etc.

[5] introduces the following categories based on the psycho-pedagogical and technical level of games:

- Mini Games for Young Children. Often the game genre is based on trivia, puzzle, memory, or drill and practice (in a positive sense) styles.
- Simulation Games, that basically pursue a drill and practice approach to certain procedural, strategic, or tactic skills.
- Off-the-Shelf Games/Moddings. This approach uses commercial off-the-shelf games for educational purposes.
- Game-like Enhancements for Learning Material. Such approach incorporates small games as training for a specific limited set of skills.
- Competitive Educational Games. This term indicates games with a primarily educational purpose that – at the same time – can compete with commercial entertainment games as well as with conventional learning environments. These may be considered the real SGs.

An original hypercube taxonomy has been presented in [17], which involves 4 dimensions:

- Purpose – ranging from fun/enjoyment to training/learning.
- Reality – ranging from imitation of real and fictitious contexts to proving abstract visualizations such as in games like Tetris.
- Social Involvement – ranging from single player games to massively multiplayer games.
- Activity - ranging from active game types (e.g., action games or – even with a physical dimension – the Nintendo Wii game play) to passive game types (where at the end of this continuum the passive perception of a movie is situated).

Along the years, an ever huger number of SGs have been developed, and now some repositories are available online, with related taxonomies for cataloguation and search.

Djaouti, Alvarez and Jessel have created serious.gameclassification.com (3168 featured games, as of July 2015), a collaborative classification of SGs, which is a reference at world level [6]. The selected classification dimensions (that are a clear extension of the [1] model) are:

- Gameplay (game-based vs. play-based – games have fixed goals to achieve; core rules represented by bricks constituting a game)
- Purpose (Education, information, marketing, subjective message broadcast, training, goods trading, storytelling)
- Market (Entertainment, State & Government, Military & Defence, Healthcare, Education, Corporate, Religion, Culture & Art, Ecology, Politics, Humanitarian & Caritative, Media, Advert, Scientific Research)
- Audience (Type: General Public, Professionals, Students; age groups)

Additional user-contributed keywords are also possible.

This description of games is simple, but has allowed a good, and ever growing and improving classification of a variety of SGs.

In a subsequent academic paper [18], the same authors have refined their approach defining the "Gameplay/Purpose/Sector" (GPS) taxonomy, which involves:

- Gameplay: rules, objectives, conflicts, etc.
- Purpose: create awareness, teach, train, broadcast a message, etc.
- Sector: health care, military, government, business, etc.

In the specific field of rehabilitation, [19] have presented a survey and classification towards a taxonomy.

Imagine[7] is a Lifelong Learning Programme EU project which includes a game directory, where game descriptions can be searched by such categories as:

- Genre: action, puzzle, trivia, etc.
- Subject categories: agriculture, medicine, science, sports, etc.
- Target audience: primary, secondary, tertiary, vocational, lifelong learning
- Learning objective: memory, dexterity/precision, applying concepts and rules, decision making, social interaction, ability to learn

Engage learning[8] is a EU LifeLong Learning Programme (LLP) project that has built a portal for game-based learning. This includes a catalogue of descriptions of games used for learning (even if also non-educational games are listed, like BioShock). The catalogue of games for learning includes localization and cultural issues as well as information about quality and rating. The reviews contain case studies of how these games may be used in a classroom environment and suggested implementation of the game. The experience of the reviewer is tabled and a walkthrough to reduce the learning curve is detailed. The search categories of the Engage database include:

- Game platform: PC, Nintendo Wii, Sony PSP, Nintendo DS, etc.

---

[7] www.imaginegames.eu.
[8] www.engagelearning.eu.

- Genre/Type of game: action, racing, puzzle, etc. and a list of specific SG types: SG-business, SG-exergaming, SG-healthcare, SG-military, etc.
- Learning objectives: memory, dexterity/repetition, applying concepts/rules, decision making, social interaction, ability to learn
- Schooling level: primary, secondary, adult
- Learning purpose: motivational, cognitive skills, spatial awareness, motor skills, social interactions, and a set of curricular topics: history, maths, physics, sports, etc.
- Rating descriptors: bad language, discrimination, drugs, sex, violence, etc.
- Learning curve: less than 5 min, 5–30 min, 30–60 min, more than 60 min

[20] have reviewed 28 studies with empirical data from a learning outcome perspective to outline the effectiveness of SGs. They conclude that serious games potentially improve the acquisition of knowledge and cognitive skills. Moreover, they seem to be promising for the acquisition of fine-grid motor skills and to accomplish attitudinal change. However, not all game features increase the effectiveness of the game. The work gives recommendations including the alignment of learning outcome(s) and game type, the alignment of the game complexity and human cognitive processes, attention for cognitive and motivational processes, research on specific mitigating factors like sex on game effectiveness and, finally, developing new ways of assessing game effectiveness. Such conclusions are inline with the concerns expressed in [21], that highlight the need for scientific and engineering methods for building games as means that provide effective learning experiences.

3   A Knowledge Management System for Serious Games

In the above sketched context, we identified in particular a lack of automatic tools to support knowledge acquisition and management in the SG domain. Thus, the GaLA project committed to the development of a Knowledge Management System (KMS) for SG description and study. Conceptually, we have built the system mainly on the basis of the above mentioned taxonomies and the definition of metrics that keep into account both the entertainment (e.g., [22, 23]) and, overall, pedagogical value of SGs (e.g., [24–26]). Definition of suited metrics for learning is key since "serious games will only grow as an industry if the learning experience is definable, quantifiable and measurable" [27], which calls in particular for in-game seamless (or stealth) assessment [28, 29].

The KMS has been designed to allow experts to create a hierarchical network of entities (units of knowledge that we call SG descriptors), that describe a SG according to a predefined ontology (see below). Descriptors involve texts, keywords and other multimedia assets for representing a SG. Descriptors concern game elements and mechanics, game design and implementation aspects, modalities of use of SGs, pedagogical principles. Some entities can be linked among each other. Definition of links (e.g., among game mechanics, pedagogical principles or goals, development tools) is important to connect various facets of a complex multidisciplinary field. This approach, in fact, intends offering a global overview and supporting a connected exploration of the SG field. The objective is to offer a service able to manage knowledge for:

- allowing an in-depth understanding of SGs through a detailed description of their mechanisms. The Game Ontology (GOP) project[9] does this only for games, without pedagogical concerns, that are key for SGs.
- better applying games into learning and training contexts, considering pedagogies. A more detailed (pedagogical) classification and analysis would enhance the service provided by the Engage project[10]. Engage provides good information on the use of games, but is finalized to make a search inside the game database (i.e., find the description of a game satisfying certain key-words). Our approach, instead, aims at supporting advanced multidimensional searches considering all the fields touched by SG research.
- designing new games. This can be achieved through an in depth analysis of game mechanisms, pedagogical aspects, modalities of use, development tools, etc.

The KMS consists of a relational database where tables store data about descriptors and links among them. Data for each covered SG can be inserted through an online user interface. The KMS' structure relies on the SG Description Model (SGDM) which involves the following sections:

- General description: free description, keywords, technologies and technical data, target market and users, application domain, estimated learning curve and learning time.
- SG as a learning environment: user assessment, feedback, sociality, graduality of learning/scaffolding, personalization.
- SG components: the game main mechanics are described in general and with the specific SG case. Each mechanics can be linked with one or more pedagogical approach (described later) and learning goals, and the link must be explained and evaluated. Typical components include: rules, goals, entity manipulation, support for assessment, Other, more technical, components include: algorithms, game engine, interoperability and standards, psychological aspects.
- Context of use. Possible contexts of use of the game are described in terms of environment, learner and teacher role, learning topics, pedagogical approaches (e.g., situated learning, problem-based learning) and learning goals (cognitive, psycho-motoric, affective, soft-skills, etc.). The educational value of a game is due not only to intrinsic features, but also to the ways in which it is deployed (e.g., in class, in a museum, in the leisure time, in corporate training) and used (to motivate, to verify knowledge acquisition; with a specific role by a teacher, parent etc.) (Game-based learning).
- Analysis/assessment. This section provides metrics for the SG along various dimensions, such as effectiveness, efficiency, pleasantness of use, diffusion of the game, feedback and assessment support, exploitability in one or more learning contexts, capability of motivating and engaging the user.

Concerning pedagogy, a SG is described along two main dimensions: theoretical frameworks and learning outcomes. Several different frameworks are listed, and can be

---

[9] https://www.gameontology.com.
[10] http://www.engagelearning.eu.

used for describing a SG: personalism [30], situated learning, experiential learning, constructivism, etc.

The outcomes are divided into: cognitive, psycho-motorial, affective and soft-skills.

- Cognitive (related to mental skills; this point refers to knowledge building and to the development of intellectual skills)
  - Remembering, understanding, applying, analysing, evaluating, creating [24]
- Psycho-motorial (i.e., skills related to physical movement, coordination, and use of the motor-skill areas)
  - Perception, set, guided response, mechanism, complex overt response, adaptation, origination [25]
- Affective (related to attitudes; this point includes the manner in which we deal with things emotionally, such as feelings, values, appreciation, enthusiasms, motivations, and other attitudes)
  - Receiving phenomena, responding to phenomena, valuing, organization, internalizing values [26]
- Soft-skills (personal attributes not easy to quantify, and sometimes described as intangible, that enhance an individual's interactions, job performance and career prospects)
  - Intra-personal: self-reflection, self-control, self-motivation, self-discipline, ability to learn, strategic thinking, creativity
  - Inter-Personal: empathy, team working, conflict management, communication, negotiation, collaboration, decision making; cultural empathy

4   Current Status of the System

The structure of the database has been implemented and over 60 SG descriptions (the SG studies) have been prepared by GaLA partners following the SGDM. Given the nature of the system, a proper validation cannot avoid extensive user testing and analysis of a huge quantity of data. However, in order to have prompt feedback on the methodology, we have performed two kinds of analysis: an expert evaluation exploiting a questionnaire on usability of the system (effectiveness, efficiency and pleasantness of use) and an early analysis of the first available data. The questionnaire confirms the validity of the approach, even if describing each SG required a significant amount of time (around 20 h). Preliminary SG data analysis revealed emergence of some recurrent mechanics (e.g., score computation, informative feedback, simple user interaction, extensive use of texts and question-based dialogues and interactions) and their relationship with pedagogical goals.

Exploiting information in the database, [11] have developed a model for SG analysis and conceptual design based on activity theory, namely the Activity Theoretical Model for SGs (ATMSG). The ATMSG provides a systematic and more detailed representation of educational serious games, depicting the ways that game elements are connected to each other throughout the game, and how these elements contribute to achieving the desired pedagogical goals. The ATMSG has also been applied to classify the elements of a SG and identify how it could have been refactored and expanded following the

Service Oriented Architecture (SOA) paradigm [31, 32]. This is an important step towards enhancing design and development of SGs.

5   Conclusions and Future Work

While a lot of papers have argued for the educational potential of SGs, the field is still very young and methods and tools are needed in order to support effective and efficient design. The SG Studies Database is an instrument devised to allow sharing structured information about SGs. This information can be used by scholars and practitioners also to perform comparative analysis and identify components and modules that could be used in different games.

The SG Studies database relies on a SG description model, that has been defined in order to allow a structured description of SGs, considering the perspectives of different stakeholders and contexts of use, and spurring the identification of components and their relationship with pedagogical theories and expected outcomes. This is a major difference with respect to the previous approaches to SG classification and description.

Thanks to these features, the SG Studies Database has already been used as a tool to support identification of reusable patterns and components in SGs, in order to identify best practices and favor re-use (e.g., [11, 12]). Other meta studies are possible in the future by any parties, as the tool is freely available online.

There are a number of challenges in the future of SG research, mostly related to a necessary increase in the educational effectiveness through a pleasant gaming experience (e.g., by improving human-computer interaction, student and teacher analytics and modeling). The SG Studies database is intended as a tool where issues and solutions for SG design and deployment can be presented and evaluated by a variety of stakeholders.

The next development steps will include the development of tools for simplified interaction, advanced visualization, querying and data-mining, with the goal of allowing scholars and practitioners to answer research questions and identify emerging trends in SG design and deployment, exploiting machine-learning facilities enabled by the database structure. This is a major innovation that we are targeting for the next future.

A final point may concern a specialization for supporting users with special needs (e.g., [33, 34]).

References

1. Sawyer, B., Smith, P.: Serious game taxonomy. Paper presented at the Meeting Serious Game Summit 2008, Game Developer Conference
2. Zyda, M.: From visual simulation to virtual reality to games. Computer **38**(9), 25–32 (2005)
3. Michael, D., Chen, S.: Serious Games: Games that Educate, Train, and Inform. Thomson Course Technology, Boston (2006)
4. Egenfeldt-Nielsen, S.: Overview of research on the educational use of videogames. Digital Kompetanse **3**(1), 184–213 (2006)
5. Kickmeier-Rust, M.D.: Talking digital educational games. In: Kickmeier-Rust, M.D. (ed.) Proceedings of the 1st International Open Workshop on Intelligent Personalization and Adaptation in Digital Educational Games, Graz, Austria, pp. 55–66 (2009)

6. Djaouti, D., Alvarez, J., Jessel, J.P., Methel, G., Molinier, P.: A gameplay definition through videogame classification. Int. J. Comput. Game Technol. (2008). Quarter 1, Hindawi Publishing Corporation

7. Hoogeboom, H.J., Kosters, W.A.: The theory of tetris. Nieuwsbrief van de Nederlandse Vereniging voor Theoretische Informatica 9, 14–21 (2005)

8. Tsuruda, K.M.: A closer look at tetris: analysis of a variant game. Atlantic Electron. J. Math. 4(1), 23–34 (2010)

9. Pannese, L., Morosini, D.: Serious games to support reflection in the healthcare sector. Int. J. Serious Games 1(3), 5–14 (2014). http://dx.doi.org/10.17083/ijsg.v1i3.30

10. Barbieri, A., Tesei, A., Bruzzone, A., Roceanu, I., Beligan, D.: Learning impact evaluation of the serious game "Cultural Awareness – Afghanistan Pre-deployment". Int. J. Serious Games 1(3), 15–33 (2014). http://dx.doi.org/10.17083/ijsg.v1i3.27

11. Carvalho, M.B., Bellotti, F., Berta, R., De Gloria, A., Islas Sedano, C., Baalsrud Hauge, J., Hu, J., Rauterberg, M.: An activity theory-based model for serious games analysis and conceptual design. Comput. Educ. 87, 166–181 (2015). ISSN: 0360-1315, http://dx.doi.org/10.1016/j.compedu.2015.03.023

12. Arnab, S., Lim, T., Carvalho, M.B., Bellotti, F., de Freitas, S., Louchart, S., Suttie, N., Berta, R., De Gloria, A.: Mapping learning and game mechanics for serious games analysis. Br. J. Educ. Technol. (2014). doi:10.1111/bjet.12113

13. Bellotti, F., Berta, R., De Gloria, A.: Games and Learning Alliance (GaLA) supporting education and training through hi-tech gaming. In: IEEE International Conference on Advanced Learning Technologies (ICALT), Rome, Italy, 4–6 July 2012, pp. 740–741 (2012). Art. no. 6268245, doi:10.1109/ICALT.2012.146

14. Kirriemuir, J., McFarlane, A.: Literature Review in Games and Learning Report 8: Futurelab Series (2004). http://hal.archives-ouvertes.fr/docs/00/19/04/53/PDF/kirriemuir-j-2004-r8.pdf

15. Riedel, J, Baalsrud Hauge, J.: State of the art of serious gaming for business and industry. In: 17th International Conference on Concurrent Enterprising: Collaborative Environments for Sustainable Innovation, Aachen, Germany. Centre for Operations Management, RWTH Aachen, Aachen (2011)

16. Herz, J.C.: Joystick Nation. Little Brown & Company, Boston (1997)

17. Kickmeier-Rust, M.D., Peirce, N., Conlan, O., Schwarz, D., Verpoorten, D., Albert, D.: Immersive digital games: the interfaces for next-generation e-learning? In: Stephanidis, C. (ed.) HCI 2007. LNCS, vol. 4556, pp. 647–656. Springer, Heidelberg (2007)

18. Djaouti, D., Alvarez, J., Jessel, J.P., Rampnoux, O.: Origins of serious games. In: Ma, M., Oikonomou, A., Lakhmi, C., Jain, L.K. (eds.) Serious Games and Edutainment Applications, pp. 25–43. Springer, London (2011)

19. Rego, P., Moreira, P.M., Reis, L.P.: Serious games for rehabilitation: a survey and a classification towards a taxonomy. In: 5th Iberian Conference on Information Systems and Technologies (CISTI) (2010)

20. Wouters, P., van der Spek, E.D., van Oostendorp, H.: Current practices in serious game research: a review from a learning outcomes perspective. In: Connolly, T., Stansfield, M., Boyle, L. (eds.) Games-Based Learning Advancements for Multi-sensory Human Computer Interfaces: Techniques and Effective Practices, pp. 232–250 (2009)

21. Greitzer, F.L., Kuchar, O.A., Huston, K.: Cognitive science implications for enhancing training effectiveness in a serious gaming context. J. Educ. Resour. Comput. 7(3), 2–16 (2007)

22. Cowley, B., Charles, D., Black, M., Hickey, R.: Toward an understanding of flow in video games. Comput. Entertainment 6(2), 1–27 (2008)

23. Cziksentmihalyi, M.: Flow: The Psychology of Optimal Experience. Harper & Row, New York (1990)

24. Anderson, L.W., Krathwohl, D.A.: A Taxonomy for Learning, Teaching, and Assessing: A Revision of Bloom's Taxonomy of Educational Objectives. Longman, New York (2001)
25. Harrow, A.J.: A Taxonomy of the Psychomotor Domain: A Guide for Developing Behavioral Objectives. McKay, New York (1972)
26. Krathwohl, D.R., Bloom, B.S., Masia, B.B.: Taxonomy of educational objectives: the classification of educational goals. In: Handbook II: The Affective Domain. David McKay Company (1964)
27. Ritterfeld, U., Cody, M., Vorderer, P. (Hrsg.): Serious Games: Mechanisms and Effects. Routledge, Taylor and Francis, Mahwah (2009)
28. Shute, V.J., Ke, F.: Games, learning, and assessment. In: Ifenthaler, D., Eseryel, D., Ge, X. (eds.) Assessment in Game-Based Learning: Foundations, Innovations, and Perspectives, pp. 43–58. Springer, New York (2012)
29. Bellotti, F., Kapralos, B., Lee, K., Moreno-Ger, P., Berta, R.: Assessment in and of serious games: an overview. In: Advances in Human-Computer Interaction (2013). Article ID 136864, doi:10.1155/2013/136864
30. Maritain, J.: La personne et le bien commun, The Person and the Common Good, by John J. Fitzgerald. University of Notre Dame Press, Notre Dame (1985)
31. Carvalho, M.B., Bellotti, F., Hu, J., Baalsrud Hauge, J., Berta, R., De Gloria, A., Rauterberg, M.: Towards a service oriented architecture framework for educational serious games. In: 15th IEEE International Conference on Advanced Learning Technologies (ICALT 2015), Hualien, Taiwan, pp. 147–151 (2015). doi:10.1109/ICALT.2015.145
32. Carvalho, M.B., Bellotti, F., Berta, R., De Gloria, A., Gazzarata, G., Hu, J., Kickmeier-Rust, M.: A case study on service-oriented architecture for serious games. Entertainment Comput. 6, 1–10 (2015). doi:10.1016/j.entcom.2014.11.001
33. Curatelli, F., Bellotti, F., Berta, R., Martinengo, C.: Paths for cognitive rehabilitation: from reality to educational software, to serious games, to reality again. In: Gloria, A. (ed.) GALA 2013. LNCS, vol. 8605, pp. 172–186. Springer, Heidelberg (2014). doi: 10.1007/978-3-319-12157-4_14
34. Curatelli, F., Martinengo, C.: Design criteria for educational tools to overcome mathematics learning difficulties. In: Proceedings of Virtual Worlds for Serious Applications Conference, VS-GAMES 2012, Genova, 29–31 October 2012. Procedia Computer Science, vol. 15C, 2012, pp. 92–102. Elsevier B.V. Publ., The Netherlands

Interesting, but not Necessarily Effective: Testing a Serious Game with Socially Disadvantaged Children

Christoph Klimmt[1(✉)] and Semhar Ogbazion[2]

[1] Department of Journalism and Communication Research, Hanover University of Music, Drama, and Media, Expo Plaza 12, 30539 Hanover, Germany
christoph.klimmt@ijk.hmtm-hannover.de
[2] Department of Communication, University of Münster, Bispinghof 9-14, 48143 Münster, Germany
semhar.ogbazion@uni-muenster.de

Abstract. Serious games are often hoped to outperform conventional instruction techniques particularly in educationally challenging contexts. The present study tested a German serious game designed to teach fundamentals of civic engagement with a class of elementary school children (N = 26, mean age 10 years) from a socially disadvantaged urban population. Findings suggest that the young players liked the new mode of learning, but effects of playing on domain knowledge were not observed. We discuss the results with regard to the preconditions that serious games have to meet just as conventional instruction techniques when players/learners are facing specific challenges such as social disadvantages.

1 Introduction

Among the many purposes for which serious games are being developed, knowledge dissemination and instruction certainly belong to the most prominent [1, 2]. The strategic intention in educational serious games is to utilize both their features that can enable or support desired cognitive processing (e.g., visualization, interactive exploration, feedback) and features that increase learner motivation (e.g., competitive setup, reward delivery through entertaining elements) [3]. With these potentially powerful attributes, serious games may achieve educational success in contexts where conventional instruction techniques reach their limits. For instance, if learners are facing difficulties due to the abstractness of a knowledge domain, the mentioned features of serious games could lead to comprehension levels that would be difficult to achieve with classic classroom instruction [4].

One of the populations that often face specific educational challenges are socially disadvantaged learners [5]. Poverty and related problematic life circumstances can have negative effects on learners' abilities and motivations to participate effectively in formal education [6]. For instance, socially disadvantaged children are at greater risk to face attention problems [7] and to develop problem behavior in class contexts [8], both mechanisms through which effective learning is often undermined. Against this background, techniques of gamification or even entire serious games could help to overcome problems of educational effectiveness with socially disadvantaged children, as they may

© Springer International Publishing Switzerland 2016
A. De Gloria and R. Veltkamp (Eds.): GALA 2015, LNCS 9599, pp. 238–244, 2016.
DOI: 10.1007/978-3-319-40216-1_25

achieve a better fit between learners' specific motivations and (processing) abilities than conventional instruction methods.

The present research tested the responses of socially disadvantaged elementary school students to a serious game. Standardized and qualitative data were collected to find out whether disadvantaged children exhibit learning success and how they react to the playful instruction in terms of interest, motivation, and intention to continue the experience. With our experiment, we intend to expand the state of research on serious games beyond media-centered perspectives of educational impact towards an understanding of the complex interactions between game attributes and preconditions resting in the personality and social circumstances of the learner.

2 The (Assumed) Educational Power of Serious Games in Instructing Disadvantaged Learners

The remarkable chances that video game technology and design have to offer to educators have been conceptualized and demonstrated in various contexts [2, 3, 9, 10]. While beneficial design elements and associated desirable player responses are manifold (including perceptual, cognitive, and motivational dimensions), the perspective on socially disadvantaged learners renders a few selected elements of serious games particularly relevant.

First, an instructional serious game can possibly overcome motivational barriers that formalized, classic instruction is often facing when confronted with disadvantaged students. Due to various problems and experiences, disadvantaged students have a greater probability to feel uncomfortable in school settings and in performance situations in particular [11]. Attending and participating in formalized educations implies more stress for disadvantaged learners, so a rather informal, playful, non-serious setting such as a video game should have greater chances for instructional success because learners should approach them with less anxiety, reluctance, and (expected) frustration.

Second, research on poverty consistently shows that the cognitive abilities of many disadvantaged children fall behind the average abilities of middle-class learners [12]. Understanding complex, abstract information, processing instructional messages, and making sense of a continuous flow of educational material is thus a much greater challenge for disadvantaged children than for learners without poverty burden. Therefore, the characteristics of serious games that are bound to interactivity and individualization of learning experiences should be of particular usefulness for disadvantaged learners. These design features should allow them or their instructor to set the pacing, the number of repetitions of content presentation, and, depending on specific design elements, also the quality of content presentation such as abstractness or redundancy across modalities (e.g., text, pictures, audio) to levels that correspond optimally to their cognitive abilities [13]. A specific aspect of cognitive challenges that serious games can respond to more effectively than most conventional instruction techniques is reading skills. Disadvantaged children often face particular difficulties when learning activities involve reading and working with long texts, and such literacy problems spill over to more general academic performance [14]. Serious games offer rich alternatives to text-based content delivery, including interactive self-experiences of knowledge domains that could otherwise only have been described by text [15]. Hence, game-based education could function as a workaround for text and reading-associated challenges that disadvantaged children have to struggle with.

Third, disadvantaged children frequently display problems to focus their attention on organized learning activities (attention regulation) [16]. Attention problems in turn undermine effective take-up, processing, comprehension, and memorization of educational materials and are thus an important factor in understanding the inferior average learning outcomes of disadvantaged children. The unique combination of interactivity and motivational appeal that (well-designed) serious games have to offer may counteract such attention regulation problems most effectively. Gaming has been shown to result in flow experiences [17], a state of sustained focused attention on an ongoing activity that includes intense activation of cognitive resources and continued problem solving. Games seem to establish flow experiences by capturing users' attention through interactive involvement – players need to make decisions and observe the outcomes of their actions, which triggers new challenges to process [18]. Because games attract user attention continuously, this effect could compensate for the attention regulation problems that many disadvantaged children are bringing into a learning situation. As a result, serious games should have greater chances to overcome attention-based learning problems than conventional instruction of socially disadvantaged children.

In sum, among the many attributes of serious games, the three aspects listed here – informal and playful setting, customization to cognitive abilities, and continuous support for attention regulation – seem to represent key capacities of games as instructional medium that could be of particular value in educating disadvantaged learners. On top of these capacities, the general characteristics that apply to all learners/players (e.g., enjoyment, interactive storytelling) should not be forgotten; however, with regard to specifically targeting disadvantaged learners, they are assumed to play rather an auxiliary role.

Given the optimistic arguments for the potential capacity of serious games to match well with the specific learning requirements of disadvantaged children, the present research tested the response of such children to an instructional serious game that was developed outside of academic projects. With regard to the relevant outcome variables, we established the following research questions:

RQ1. How effective is an instructional serious game for knowledge construction in socially disadvantaged children?

RQ2. How do socially disadvantaged children respond in terms of motivation and interest to an instructional serious game?

3   Method

A sample of 26 children (13 girls) aged 9 to 12 years (M = 10.2 years) from a socially disadvantaged district of a major German city (500,000 + inhabitants) participated in an experiment. Following written parental consent and in collaboration with their local school, the children were invited to play a serious game about civic engagement and democratic principles for 30 min. Gaming took place in a special classroom equipped with computers. After the playing time, the children filled in a brief questionnaire, and 14 of them were asked to stay afterwards for an additional semi-structured interview about their gaming and learning experience. Hence, a mixed-method approach was taken to investigate the disadvantaged children's responses to the serious game.

The game that was used for the study was "Eugens Welt" ("Eugen's world"), a browser-based point-and-click adventure. The mission of the game is to connect to various non-player characters (NPCs) who are neighbors in a multistory apartment building. By resolving mini-quests and mini-games, players learn about living in a local community, democratic decision making, civic engagement, and conflict resolution. The more tasks the players resolve, the more progress towards the game goal (reaching the rooftop apartment) is achieved. In order to access the rooftop, 80 percent of the in-game quests must be completed successfully. "Eugens Welt" was created by public institutions in Southern Germany (including a public broadcast station) and is part of a larger cross-media project on civic school education. The game has won several national prizes for excellent serious game design (impressions from actual gameplay can be found at https://www.youtube.com/watch?v=oAtPPuC1IAo).

To assess the outcomes of playing, several measures were employed. A simple knowledge test on issues that the game addressed (e.g., on how people should behave respectfully in a community) was constructed; in a pre-post-test design, participants gave answers to this 5-item test with a maximum of 8 correct answers before and right after playing the serious game. Moreover, the post-play questionnaire addressed game enjoyment, liking of the protagonist (Eugen), and the level of attention during gaming, each measured by a single item. Those children who also participated in the qualitative interview were asked, among other game-related issues, what they had liked about the game (and what not) and whether they had learned something they had not known before.

4   Results

The comparison of knowledge test scores before and after playing the serious game revealed no increase in domain knowledge; however, the test turned out to be relatively easy, as children achieved almost 75 % correct responses before playing. The post-play average score was exactly the same value (Table 1).

Table 1. Average scores (and standard deviations) of the pre- and post-play knowledge test (5 questions with a maximum of 8 correct answers overall) (N = 26)

Knowledge score prior to playing	5.81 (1.27)
Knowledge score after playing	5.81 (1.63)

The participants rated their game experience very positively, liked the protagonist, reported to have tried hard to complete the game and to have been very attentive during gameplay (Table 2). However, they had severe difficulties in completing the game; only four participants managed to reach the game goal (the rooftop apartment) by fulfilling 80 percent of the in-game tasks.

Table 2. Average scores (and standard deviations) of the participants to questions about their responses to the game. Each concept was measured by a single item scaled from 1 (minimum/not at all) to 5 (maximum/to full extent) (N = 26).

Enjoyment	4.08 (1.13)
Liking of protagonist	3.96 (1.00)
Investment of effort ("tried hard")	4.46 (0.99)
Attention during game play	4.12 (1.11)

The analysis of the qualitative interviews that were conducted with 14 of the participants revealed interesting additional insights. First, several interviewees found the game extremely difficult, for instance, because they failed to understand quest descriptions, had problems in understanding text-based instructions, or were lost with in-game navigation. A few players even misunderstood the role of the protagonist (Eugen) and took him for a competing NPC. Second, participants' responses to a question about whether players had recognized relationships between game content and their personal social life circumstances were rather shallow; the children reported perceived similarities between game objects (buildings, interior) and their own living environment, but mostly failed to recognize more abstract matches that would have resonated with the game's educational goal such as 'I know conflicts similar to those in the game from my family'. Third, the interviewed players agreed in not having learned something new from the game – nobody mentioned incidents of insight or notable knowledge growth during gameplay. And fourth, various children welcomed the informal, playful setting and answered that they would like to play again or to use the game as tool in school instruction.

5   Discussion

With the current sample size and focus on one single game, the generalizability of the present study findings is of course limited. However, the obtained pattern of results is worthwhile of discussion with regard to the complexities and preconditions that game-based instruction seems to face in disadvantaged learners just as other instructional media do. The findings suggest that the children from a school district with above-average social disadvantage (a) were very focused on the game, (b) liked playing very much, (c) found the game extremely difficult, and (d) did not acquire any new knowledge from 30 min of game usage in spite the fact that the entire content of the game is 'purely' educational.

Our interpretation of this pattern is that serious games do not necessarily work better for disadvantaged learners just because they are games. The participants reported comprehension problems with regard to text information provided in the game, to rules and game mechanics, and even the role of the protagonist. Hence, similar deficits emerged that had been studied in the context of conventional instruction, including literacy problems and specific cognitive limitations [12, 14]. The serious game used in the present study was obviously not yet sufficiently customized to these requirements of disadvantaged learners.

In addition, the cognitive load that the game seems to have imposed due to perceived high levels of difficulty is probably the reason for why players did not generate new knowledge and made only peripheral inferences from the game content to their personal live conditions [19]. The fact that they mentioned only superficial connections such as buildings and people indicates heuristic processing – the players had not enough cognitive resources to both play the game and derive higher-order learnings from its content simultaneously. Hence, the interactivity, which contributes to the motivational appeal of serious games – and did so in the present study as well – is also a cognitive *challenge* that is of particular relevance to socially disadvantaged learners. These learners seem to need a higher level of 'gaming literacy' [20] before they are ready to benefit from (customized) serious games. Alternatively, designers of serious games for disadvantaged learners will need to find ways to reduce cognitive complexity, for instance through simpler modes of interaction or substantially expanded tutorials that help players to automatize interaction so that cognitive capacity is saved for processing and comprehension of educational content.

Overall, the present experiment suggests that the great opportunities that serious games have to offer for instruction will not necessarily become manifest 'automatically'. For disadvantaged learners, careful tailoring of the game and its content (e.g., the amount of text to read; the accessibility and usability) is just as important as it is for conventional instruction methods. The current players had fun and liked the game, and this is certainly an advantage that other instruction methods cannot bring about as reliably as a digital game. But in order to function as effective medium of instruction, the complex preconditions of learners need to be well-considered in game design and the educational context of serious game applications.

References

1. Gee, J.P.: What Video Games Have to Teach Us About Learning and Literacy. Palgrave McMillan, New York (2003)
2. Wouters, P., van Nimwegen, C., van Oostendorp, H., van der Spek, E.D.: A meta-analysis of the cognitive and motivational effects of serious games. J. Educ. Psychol. **105**, 249 (2013)
3. Ritterfeld, U., Cody, M., Vorderer, P. (eds.): Serious Games: Mechanisms and Effects. Routledge, New York (2009)
4. Westera, W., Nadolski, R., Hummel, H., Wopereis, I.: Serious games for higher education: a framework for reducing design complexity. J. Comput.-Assist. Learn. **24**, 420–432 (2008)
5. Engle, P.L., Black, M.M.: The effect of poverty on child development and educational outcomes. Ann. N. Y. Acad. Sci. **1136**, 243–256 (2008)
6. Brooks-Gunn, J., Duncan, G.J.: The Effects of poverty on children. Future Child. **7**, 55–71 (1997)
7. Noble, K., McCandliss, B., Farah, M.: Socioeconomic gradients predict individual differences in neurocognitive abilities. Dev. Sci. **10**, 464–480 (2007)
8. Qi, C.H., Kaiser, A.P.: Behavior problems of preschool children from low-income families. review of the literature. Top. Early Child. Spec. Educ. **23**, 188–216 (2003)
9. Clark, D.B., Tanner-Smith, E.E., Killingsworth, S.S.: Digital games, design, and learning. A systematic review and meta-analysis. Rev. Educ. Res. **86**, 79–122 (2016)

10. Connolly, T.M., Boyle, E.A., MacArthur, E., Hainey, T., Boyle, J.M.: A systematic literature review of empirical evidence on computer games and serious games. Comput. Educ. **59**, 661–686 (2012)
11. Hamre, B.K., Pianta, R.C.: Can instructional and emotional support in the first-grade classroom make a difference for children at risk of school failure? Child Dev. **76**, 949–967 (2005)
12. Stipek, D.J., Ryan, R.H.: Economically disadvantaged preschoolers: ready to learn but further to go. Dev. Psychol. **33**, 711 (1997)
13. Pinelle, D., Wong, N., Stach, T.: Heuristic evaluation for games: usability principles for video game design. In: Proceedings of the SIGCHI Conference on Human Factors in Computing Systems. ACM, New York, pp. 1453–1462, April 2008
14. Miles, S.B., Stipek, D.: Contemporaneous and longitudinal associations between social behavior and literacy achievement in a sample of low-income elementary school children. Child Dev. **77**, 103–117 (2006)
15. Peng, W., Lee, M., Heeter, C.: The effects of a serious game on role-taking and willingness to help. J. Commun. **60**, 723–742 (2010)
16. Howse, R.B., Lange, G., Farran, D.C., Boyles, C.D.: Motivation and self-regulation as predictors of achievement in economically disadvantaged young children. J. Exp. Educ. **71**, 151–174 (2003)
17. Sherry, J.L.: Flow and media enjoyment. Commun. Theor. **14**, 328–347 (2004)
18. Klimmt, C., Hartmann, T., Frey, A.: Effectance and control as determinants of video game enjoyment. CyberPsychol. Behav. **10**, 845–847 (2007)
19. Sweller, J.: Cognitive load during problem solving: effects on learning. Cogn. Sci. **12**, 257–285 (1988)
20. Klimmt, C.: Key dimensions of contemporary video game literacy: towards a normative model of the competent digital gamer. Eludamos – J. Comput. Game Cult. **3**, 23–31 (2009)

Involving Cognitively Disabled Young People in Focused Mini SGs Design: A Case Study

Francesco Curatelli[1(✉)], Chiara Martinengo[2],
Elisa Lavagnino[1], and Antonie Wiedemann[1]

[1] DITEN, University of Genova, Via Opera Pia 11/A, 16145 Genoa, Italy
curatelli@unige.it, {lavagnino,wiedemann}@elios.unige.it
[2] DIMA, University of Genova, Via Dodecaneso 35, 16146 Genoa, Italy
martinen@dima.unige.it

Abstract. In this paper, we propose the design of a mini SG *Il Negozio di Viola* having as its objective the acquisition by disabled young people of the concepts of cost, revenue and gain in the context of a selling transaction, which are concepts very difficult to internalize by people with cognitive problems. This mini SG makes it possible to have a real experience, even if in a simulated environment, on the concept of gain. Moreover, we will show that the direct involvement in the design of the mini SG by M., a young with neuro-motor disabilities, has made it possible to identify and solve the semantic problems that disabled users may encounter in the use of the game, which is the greatest difficulty in the design of this kind of mini SGs. This involvement has also contributed to improve her cognitive abilities and awareness to have an active role in the development of software tools that can be useful for other people.

1 Introduction

During the last years there it has become apparent that the suitable use of Information and Communication Technologies (ICT) can foster the participation in the information society, better social relations, improved job possibilities and, in general, the active participation in the life of society and to its cultural heritage [1]. In particular, one of the major challenges concerns the transition from integration to inclusion of people with cognitive disabilities either caused by neuromotor or other types of problems. In this context, an important sector for the inclusion of a disabled person (for it concerns the management of important activities of daily life) is the *basic economic field*. With this term we mean what involves the basic activities of the use of money and the management of the logical-mathematical meanings that are the basis of all activities in this area. In fact, people with neuromotor and/or cognitive disabilities have typically significant difficulties in this field; therefore, a major challenge is the identification of strategies and the design/implementation of software tools that make able people with cognitive abilities to manage this important field as early as their schooling age.

Concerning the use of software tools, a role of major importance is played by learning tools that also emphasize the game aspects, such as Games-Based Learning and Serious Games (*SGs*). They refer to games whose purpose is not limited to pure entertainment

© Springer International Publishing Switzerland 2016
A. De Gloria and R. Veltkamp (Eds.): GALA 2015, LNCS 9599, pp. 245–254, 2016.
DOI: 10.1007/978-3-319-40216-1_26

[2, 3] (although having fun during game playing is a major feature [4]), and for which suitable assessment methodologies have been proposed [5, 6].

In fact, during the last years many studies on SGs for disability has been done [7–9], and many research projects have been developed [10–12]. However, the SGs for disabled people often have very limited cognitive objectives, while conversely the SGs for non-disabled people have the opposite problem: the required cognitive level is simply too high for the target students. To solve this problem, we have proposed the use of simple focused SGs (*mini SGs*) with more complex and articulated cognitive goals, in order to allow disabled people to perform more complex gaming, also describing some mini SGs implemented [13, 14]. In particular, the cognitive goals are not simply limited to the mechanical use of the money, but concern the much more important acquisition of the mathematical meanings involved and the ability to properly manage problematic situations.

In this paper, we propose the design of a mini SGs having as its objective the acquisition of the concepts of cost, revenue and gain in the context of a selling transaction. Promoting this acquisition by disabled young people, at least in cases where their cognitive situation permits it, is very useful in their adult life. In fact, it is possible that people with disabilities could be in their adult life in the position of sellers, for example if they want to earn money through the sale of products built by themselves. Section 2 describes the difficulties that arise in this area for young people with cognitive difficulties, which are especially due to the impossibility to make real experiences about, because the usual experience is to be buyers and not sellers. In Sect. 3 we propose the design of the mini SG *Il Negozio di Viola* (*The Viola's shop*) as a virtual environment to make real experiences in this field and to manage the mental representation with the related mathematical concepts. Finally, Sect. 4 present as a key idea of this work, the direct involvement in the design of the mini SG by M., a young with neuro-motor disabilities, who has given a fundamental contribution to overcome the greatest difficulty in the design of mini SGs for disabled people: to identify and solve the semantic problems that a disabled user may encounter in the use of the game, and to ensure that the UI helps to solve the problems of this situation. Moreover, the involvement by M. has also been a significant improvement of her cognitive abilities, self-esteem, and awareness to have an active role in the development of software tools that can be useful for other people.

2   The Problematic Situation: Gain in a Sale

An area of major importance in the daily life of people is surely the economic field, which comprises basic and more complex operations such as to recognize the different coins and banknotes, make payments, make changes of coins or banknotes with others of equal value, make purchases with rest or with discount, calculate the cost of the produced goods, up to more and more complex situations. Acting in this field makes it possible to acquire useful mathematical skills; this is because there is a dialectical and mutually reinforcing interaction between the operational capabilities in using money and the different meanings of the mathematical operations that underlie the real activities.

In previous papers [13, 14] we have proposed the use of paths of cognitive rehabilitation within the economic field. In particular, we have highlighted the synergistic action between experiences made in the concrete reality and the use of focused mini SGs, which make it possible to acquire the different mathematical meanings by activities taking place in virtual environments that recall the related real environments, although in a simple and schematic way. We have also noted that, in cases where learning difficulties are mild, a greater cognitive progress is obtained by preceding the activities with SGs by some real experiences. But on the contrary, in presence of more severe cognitive difficulties, the use of software programs makes it possible a more relaxed approach than experiencing the same situations in the reality [15]. Moreover, in case of severe motor disabilities the use of mini SGs makes up for the objective difficulty to frequently make real experiences.

In addition, for some situations in the economic field it is very difficult to have a direct real experience also by non-impaired people, and even more for people with cognitive difficulties. One of these is the trade from the point of view of the seller; in fact, the typical real experience is to be on the side of the purchaser, not on the side of the seller. In this situation, the problems involve assessing costs, revenues and earnings. Although these concepts only require operations of addition or subtraction, they needs some mental operations which are very critical for people with cognitive difficulties. The first is the acquisition of a mental representation of the situation, and then the use of a significant capacity of imagination and abstraction. Another ones are the ability to control several sequential steps, the use of the correct linguistic expressions and the control of their meanings, and the use of non-immediate meanings of addition and subtraction.

In this section we will describe some theoretical and practical lab activities on this issue, during which several learning difficulties have been detected. Teamwork has been used because is much more effective for cognitive improvement. In fact, it allows the participants to make comparison of the adopted strategies, so leading to the control of their mental operations and to a significant improvement of their meta-cognitive abilities [16, 17]. The work has been carried out gradually, starting from a linguistic approach, and has been attended by three young people: M., 19, with spastic tetraparesis, D., 14 and Mi, 11, both with aspecific learning difficulties.

The first phase has been focused on a reflection on the term *gain*, which is used, in everyday language, with multiple meanings either real or figurative. Common experience of all the young people was that parents *gain* with their work. In the second phase of the work, reflections have been carried out on the fact that every object that is needed for daily life must be first produced and has a cost. Here the young people have proposed concrete examples about, some ones industrially produced (such as clothes, shoes and appliances), other ones home produced (such as cakes, pizzas and toasts).

In the third phase, to better understand the concept of cost, the attention has been focused on the design of the preparation of a number of toasts, which are a very simple food of whom the young people were familiar with both the ingredients and the method of preparation. This has required the definition of the amount of raw food needed and of the related costs with the calculation of the cost for each toast.

All these activities have been very tiring for the young people and have had to be carefully followed by the tutors. However, the fact of facing a situation within the context of a real field experience [18–21]) and which recalls concrete experiences of real life did motivate the young people to look for a solution, without being discouraged by early failures. Moreover, the laboratory approach [22] has got the young people used to explain and motivate their solving strategies, right or wrong they were, and has allowed them to understand the reasons of their errors, by comparison of the different solutions proposed. Therefore, a meta-cognitive process has been triggered which has often put them able to correct by themselves the solving process, better understanding the meaning of the operations used. In the fourth phase, we have considered the sale of toasts in a snack bar which involves the concepts of revenue and gain. During this last phase several difficulties have been detected:

- Linguistic problems in finding the most suitable expressions to describe the various situations.
- Difficulties in the management of the mental representation of the different phases and in their time schedule.
- Linguistic-semantic difficulties in the use of the expression *"more money than at the beginning"*, by which trying to identify the gain. Initially, all the young people have perceived as *"new"* the entire amount of money given by the buyer to the seller to pay the toast. Moreover, D. also showed a confusion with the situation of the rest of the money. Instead, at a certain point M. found most congenial the expression *"money that has been added"*, which was perceived more evocative of the fact that the money available was increased over time.
- Difficulties in the management of the mathematical meanings.
- To obtain lasting acquisitions.

All these difficulties are due to the total lack of a real experience by the young people, which makes it very difficult to build a mental representation of the situations.

3   The Design of the Mini SG: Il Negozio di Viola

The three young people who have participated to the lab works described in Sect. 2 had already had a significant experience in the use of some mini SGs. In fact, they have used the software programs *CoLT2* (*COin Learning Tool*), *Il Cambiamonete* (*The Coin Exchanger*), *Attenti al Cambio!* (*Watch the Exchange!*), *Attenti al Resto!* (*Watch the Change!*), *Attenti alla Spesa!* (*Watch your Shopping!*) [23]. With the aid of these programs, the young people have attended to several lab works, either individualized or in group, in the latter case with mini SGs which provide two-player games. The use of these software programs has allowed the young people to acquire a conscious (and not just functional) use of the money in purchasing situations, has enabled the acquisition of mathematical meanings, also increasing their cognitive and metacognitive skills [14].

To make possible a real experience, even if in a simulated environment, on the concept of gain it has been designed the mini SG *Il negozio di Viola* (*The Viola's shop*). The game aims to simulate trading in a shoe store; we have chosed this industrially produced article because the shoe stores are the stores where M. happens to go more often. The software program has a simple and schematic graphical, with limited movements, but recalls effectively the significant aspects of the real environments. Moreover the learning objectives are integrated very effectively with those of the game. It is provided an overall map of the environments, where the trading situations may occur (the Viola's shop and the Shoe factory); within this map the Viola's van and the customers' cars are represented and moved (Fig. 1).

Fig. 1. The overall map

The game begins with the scene of the empty shop and Viola who notes that she must go to the factory to buy some shoes. Then, in the map it is represented the movement of Viola's van from the shop to the Factory where it is allocated the following scene. In the Factory, Viola can buy only a pair of shoes and with limited money; the prices are without cents and, if for example her wallet contains 30 €, on the shelf there are several kinds of shoes with a cost greater than or equal to 30 € (at least one equal). This means that the portfolio resets after the purchase. After the return to the shop (also displayed on the map), the program automatically sets for the shoes a selling price greater than the factory cost. The selling situation proceeds in a similar way but with the customer moving from his house to the shop and trading to sell a pair of shoes. After the sale, it takes place (with the aid of carton bubbles) a dialogue between Viola and the player who must select one among several predefined answer. This dialogue, which is based on the comparison of wallet content during the different phases of the sale, leads the player to the awareness that there has been a gain and to the ability to quantify it, by separating, in the revenue, the part of the money that covers the cost and the *"new"* money.

As already mentioned, the main difficulty in designing a mini SGs in the basic economic field is to identify and manage the possible semantic difficulties that may occur during the game to young people with cognitive problems. This is the reason why our program software have always been designed on the basis of the results of the theoretical and practical lab works done with the young people. Moreover, during the implementation phase, they have been tested repeatedly, not only to detect any programming errors, but also to receive the feedback comments by the young people with cognitive difficulties, and have modifying them accordingly. In the design of Il Negozio di Viola the situation was even more delicate, given the lack of real experiences by the participants and the less successful results obtained in this field with the theoretical and practical lab works.

For all these reasons we decided to involve M., not only in the use of the mini SG, but also in its design; this is in order to find the best solutions right together with her. We have considered M. ready to give her effective contribution, not only for the cognitive progresses she made in several years of lab works and use of mini, but also for her acquired expertise in the use of COTS games (such as *The Sims*, *Kinectimals unleashed*, *My Little Baby*) that also involve situations in the basic economic field. The intervention of M. in the design, which will be described in detail in the next Section, has produced two results; on the one hand it has provided information far more precise and targeted to implement the program. In fact, just because she herself has cognitive difficulties on this topic, her intervention in the design of the UI has determined solutions which are effective in dealing the previously analyzed difficulties, so leading to good management of the mental representations and related mathematical concepts. On the other hand it has been an important formative opportunity for M., as it has made it possible to develop and use different cognitive and metacognitive abilities.

4   The Intervention of M. in the Design and Implementation

The intervention of M. in the design of the mini SG *Il negozio di Viola* has taken place in different directions. First of all, the work involved monitoring the effectiveness and functionality of the graphical aspects that are represented in the different scenes (the overall map, the shop of Viola, the factory) and the visibility of the writings in the cartoon bubbles. For example, M. pointed out that it was not immediately clear to her that the image of the shoes represented a pair and suggested to put a written warning that the image actually depicts the box with the pair of shoes.

Subsequently, it has been verified if the various steps required by the program were clearly understandable and easily feasible. For example, when Viola goes to the factory to buy shoes there is the problem of calculating the amount of money contained in the wallet to decide which pair to buy among the pairs of shoes on the shelf. As M. was able to easily do mental computation in some cases, but not in others, initially we proposed the solution to add a money counter in the wallet area. But instead M. argued that: (1) she preferred to proceed by trial and error in the purchase, as just happened when she had played COTS games, and (2) this was a very useful training to become faster in the calculation. Following this suggestion, it has been added the possibility to change the choice of the shoes to buy. In another situation, M. had not noticed that, after returning from the factory to the store after buying there, the price of shoes had been increased by the program by adding the Viola's gain. So, when she read the cartoon bubble who explained this, she argued that it would be useful to return to the shop and check this fact. Therefore, we have included this possibility, which was not present before.

The main and most significant contribution of the intervention of M. has been in improving the semantic clarity of the contents in the dialogues with Viola concerning the control of the wallet and cash register in the different steps, and the calculation of the gain. Actually, in the first version tested by M. the control and the calculation of the gain occurred in two dialog windows like Fig. 2:

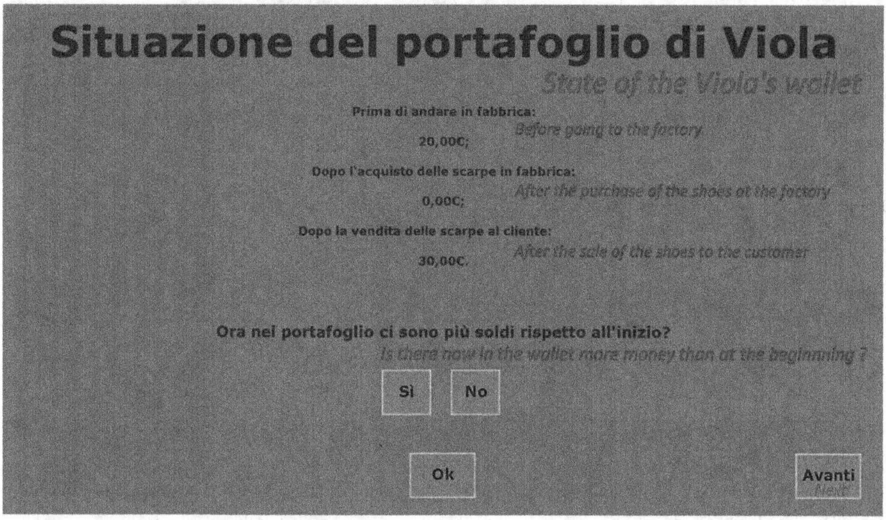

Situazione del portafoglio di Viola
State of the Viola's wallet

Prima di andare in fabbrica:
20,00€;
Before going to the factory

Dopo l'acquisto delle scarpe in fabbrica:
0,00€;
After the purchase of the shoes at the factory

Dopo la vendita delle scarpe al cliente:
30,00€.
After the sale of the shoes to the customer

Ora nel portafoglio ci sono più soldi rispetto all'inizio?
Is there now in the wallet more money than at the beginning ?

Sì   No

Ok   Avanti
Next

Fig. 2. 1st dialog window (initial)

The caption *"now in the wallet there is more money than in the beginning"* was not clear to M, because it did not immediately redirect her to the state of the wallet before going to the factory. In addition, M. found that the mere use of numbers for the calculation of the gain was largely inadequate because it would have required to her higher abstraction abilities than she had at that moment. M. found a way to make this fundamental step more accessible both from the semantic and the operational points of view; in fact, she suggesting that the money in the wallet could be shown at any step. The program has been modified accordingly, and the first dialog box of Fig. 2 has become as shown in Fig. 3 and these changes are essential to ensure that the UI solves the difficulties that have been discussed in Sect. 2. The figures remember in a synoptic way the different contents of the wallet and the corresponding state of the shelf of the store, and the captions, whose content has been suggested by M., refer in much clearer way to the time sequence of the transactions. This makes it possible to realize more easily that, after the sale, the money is actually increased with respect to the initial situation.

In the next window (Fig. 4) it is possible to drag the extra money into a specific box. If this operation is done properly the program outlines that this is actually the gain collected after the sale, so obtaining the conceptual connection goal of the mini SG.

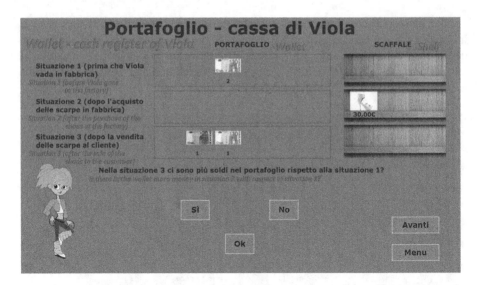

Fig. 3. 1st dialog window (final)

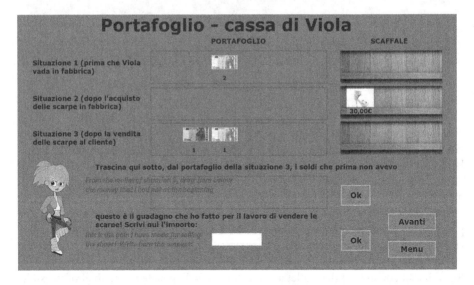

Fig. 4. 2nd dialog window (final)

Instead, in the following window the player is asked to drag the money into a specific box so that at the end the wallet contains only the money gained in the transaction. This makes it possible for the player to internalize the fact that the revenue (the sum paid by the customer) is actually the sum of the money given to the factory (the cost) and the sum gained, and that the gain is the difference between revenue and cost.

5   Conclusions

In this paper, we propose the design of a mini SG *Il Negozio di Viola* having as its objective the acquisition of the concepts of cost, revenue and gain in the context of a selling transaction by disabled young people. After a first experimental version, it was decided to structure the game in different levels, to grade the difficulty of the activity and the cognitive skills required. At present it has been implemented a complete version of the first level, the most important and critical, whose goal is the acquisition of the concept of gain and of a concrete methodology for its assessment. The full implementation of the higher levels will be the subject of further research.

The involvement by M., a young with neuro-motor disabilities, in the design on the mini SG *Il Negozio di Viola* has made it possible to directly verify the semantics difficulties in using the game and to find the more suitable design solutions. Moreover it has also been a significant contribution to the improvement of her cognitive abilities, self-esteem, and awareness to have an active role in the development of software tools that can be useful for other people. So, we argue that the experimentation that has been done in this field is also a contribution not only to the validation of the effectiveness of SGs as educational tools for people with cognitive difficulties [24] but also to the recognition of the importance of their active participation in the design of the educational tools. In other words, we think that the active role by the final users in the design of SGs targeted to the cognitive improvement of disabled young people should be, when possible, included in the design and implementation phase of the program tools itself.

Acknowledgments. We are highly indebted to all the young people we have followed, and in particular to M., who has been deeply involved in the improvement of the mini SG. They are the only important subjects of our researches.

References

1. European Union: Ministerial declaration. In: Conference on ICT for an Inclusive Society (2006). http://ec.europa.eu/informationsociety/events/ictriga2006/doc/declarationriga.pdf
2. Bellotti, F., Berta, R., De Gloria, A.: Games and learning alliance (GaLA) supporting education and training through hi-tech gaming. In: Proceedings of the ICALT 2012, pp. 740–741 (2012)
3. Bellotti, F., Berta, R., De Gloria, A., D'Ursi, A., Fiore, V.: A serious game model for cultural heritage. ACM J. Comput. Cult. Heritage 5, 17:1–17:27 (2012)
4. Connolly, T.M., Boyle, E.A., MacArthur, E., Hainey, T., Boyle, J.M.: A systematic literature review of empirical evidence on computer games and serious games. Comput. Educ. 59, 661–686 (2012)
5. Bellotti, F., Kapralos, B., Lee, K., Moreno-Ger, P., Berta, R.: Assessment in and of serious games: an overview. Adv. Hum. Comput. Interact. 2013, 1:1–1:11 (2013). Article ID 136864
6. Carvalho, M.B., Bellotti, F., Berta, R., De Gloria, A., Sedano, C.I., Hauge, J.B., Hu, J., Rauterberg, M.: An activity theory-based model for serious games analysis and conceptual design. Comput. Educ. 87, 166–181 (2015)
7. Grammenos, D., Savidis, A., Stephanidis, C.: Designing universally accessible games. Comput. Entertain. 7(8), 1–29 (2009)

8. Yuan, B., Folmer, E., Harris, F.C.: Game accessibility: a survey. Univers. Access Inf. Soc. **10**, 81–100 (2011)

9. Evett, L., Ridley, A., Keating, L., Merritt, P., Shopland, N., Brown, D.J.: Designing serious games for people with disabilities game, set and match to the Wii. Int. J. Game-Based Learn. **1**, 11–19 (2011)

10. Lanyi, C.S., Brown, D.J., Standen, P., Lewis, J., Butkute, V., Drozdik, D.: GOET European project of serious games for students with intellectual disability. In: Proceedings of the CogInfoCom, pp. 1–6 (2011)

11. Hussaan, A.M., Sehaba, K., Mille, A.: Helping children with cognitive disabilities through serious games. In: Proceedings of the ASSETS 2011, pp. 251–252 (2011)

12. Lanyi, C.S.S., Brown, D.J.: Design of serious games for students with intellectual disability. In: Proceedings of the India HCI, pp. 151–160 (2010)

13. Martinengo, C., Curatelli, F.: Percorsi e Software Didattici per il Recupero di Difficoltà Cognitive in Ambito Logico-Matematico. In: Difficoltà di Apprendimento e Didattica Inclusiva, vol. 1, pp. 195–209. Erickson (2013)

14. Curatelli, F., Bellotti, F., Berta, R., Martinengo, C.: Paths for cognitive rehabilitation: from reality to educational software, to serious games, to reality again. In: De Gloria, A. (ed.) GALA 2013. LNCS, vol. 8605, pp. 172–186. Springer, Heidelberg (2014)

15. Curatelli, F., Martinengo, C.: Mondi Reali e Virtuali per lo Sviluppo Cognitivo di Ragazzi Disabili. In: Proceedings of the DIDAMATICA, Genoa (2015)

16. Martinengo, C., Curatelli, F.: Laboratori e Tutorati: Proposte per Affrontare le Difficoltà in Matematica dalla Scuola Primaria all'Università. In: Proceedings of the GRIMED, Lucca (2015)

17. Pesci A.: Cooperative learning and peer tutoring to promote students' mathematics education. In: 10th International Conference Models in Developing Mathematics Education, Dresden, pp. 486–490 (2009)

18. Boero, P.: The crucial role of semantic fields in the development of problem solving skills. In: Ponte, J.P., Matos, J.F., Matos, J.M., Fernandes, D. (eds.) Mathematical Problem Solving and New Information Technologies, pp. 77–91. Springer, Heidelberg (1992)

19. Boero, P.: Experience fields as a tool to plan mathematics teaching from 6 to 11. In: Proceedings of the II It-De Symposium on Didactics of Mathematics, vol. 39, pp. 45–62 (1994)

20. Kolb, D.A., Boyatzis, R.E., Mainemelis, C.: Experiential learning theory: previous research and new directions. In: Sternberg, R.J., et al. (eds.) Perspectives on Thinking, Learning, and Cognitive Styles. The Educational Psychology Series, pp. 227–247. Erlbaum, Mahwah (2001)

21. Conway, P.F., Sloane, F.C.: International Trends in Post-Primary Mathematics Education: Perspectives on Learning, Teaching and Assessment. National Council for Curriculum and Assessment, Dublin (2006)

22. Piochi, B.: Una certa idea di Matematica. In: Atti Matematica & Difficoltà, Bologna, vol. 17, pp. 79–90 (2011)

23. Curatelli, F., Martinengo, C.: Design criteria for educational tools to overcome mathematics learning difficulties. Procedia Comput. Sci. **15**, 92–102 (2012)

24. Girard, C., Ecalle, J., Magnan, A.: Serious games as new educational tools: how effective are they? A meta-analysis of recent studies. J. Comput. Assist. Learn. **29**, 207–219 (2013)

Read, Play and Learn: An Interactive E-book for Children with Autism

Vedad Hulusic[1(✉)] and Nirvana Pistoljevic[2]

[1] University Sarajevo School of Science and Technology,
Hrasnicka cesta 3a, 71000 Sarajevo, Bosnia and Herzegovina
vhulusic@gmail.com
[2] Teachers College, Columbia University,
525 West 120th St., New York, NY 10027, USA

Abstract. Serious games can easily engage students, captivate and maintain their attention allowing them both learning with an adult, or on their own. But, teaching children with developmental disabilities like ASD, requires special set of tools and methods, due to decreased level of attention towards stimuli presented and lessened capability to learn in ways typical children do. Interactive multisensory computer based instruction seems to be a good match for these diverse learners because it offers multisensory learning experience, interactive practice with constant feedback, increased learning opportunities, and customization to each child's needs. In this paper we present a web-based interactive educational e-book designed to engage a learner with additional auditory-visual stimulation related to the text being read in two languages, and by providing multi layered questions about the story read, for comprehension. Our educational goals were to teach children novel vocabulary, counting, identifying numbers and colors, and responding to inference questions.

Keywords: Children · Autism · Interactive e-book · Learn unit · Education

1 Introduction

Autism Spectrum Disorder (ASD) is a neurodevelopmental disorder that is detectable or apparent early in development, before age 2 [20], and its characterized by the lack of language development, socialization and development of patterns of rigid, repetitive, auto-stimulating behaviors that interfere with over-all functioning of a person [3]. Children with ASD often have difficulty processing sensory information, by under- or over-processing different inputs, which in turn affects their learning. Studies have shown that children with autism may master more educational objectives using a computer compared to traditional teaching strategies, and are more interested and motivated to learn through computer-assisted instruction [7,34]. Price compared comprehension and information acquisition across two conditions: reading interactive e-books (on iPads)

A. De Gloria and R. Veltkamp (Eds.): GALA 2015, LNCS 9599, pp. 255–265, 2016.
DOI: 10.1007/978-3-319-40216-1_27

vs. printed books with 30 students diagnosed with ASD, and found positive outcomes for each participant using e-books [23]. In addition, teachers' survey reveled that the students found iPads motivating, which made them reinforcers, and in turn decreased their inappropriate behaviors in the classroom.

For over 50 years, research showed that the basic teaching unit, upon which all learning and teaching are based on is a three-term-contingency (i.e. a learn unit) [15,16,27]. A learn unit is an observable and measurable interaction between a teacher and a learner, and it consists of two or more antecedent-behavior-consequence contingencies. A-antecedent is a stimulus/stimuli presented by a teacher or a computer/teaching device (i.e. visual stimuli - picture of a bird and an auditory stimuli - find a bird); B-behavior is a response to an antecedent (i.e. student touching a bird on the screen); and a C-consequence is delivered in a way of reinforcement for correct responses and correction for an incorrect responses. Corrections for incorrect response guide the student to emit a correct? Response, in order not to demotivate a learner and to provide him/her with a learning opportunity. Skinner's tree-term-contingency has been proven effective not only as a teacher-student interaction, but as one between a learner and a teaching device, famous Skinner's teaching machine [27,28] or Emurian et al. 's computerized instruction [10]. Therefore, a serious game we have designed and developed, is entirely based on the learn unit, an interlocking three-term con-tingency between a computer that presents visual and auditory antecedents and delivers feedback, and a student who emits the responses to the computer's antecedents [18].

Serious games have become an effective tool in treatment of various physical and psychological limitations, as well as education of diverse populations. Using this medium users are exposed to deeply engaging, visually dynamic, rapidly paced, and highly satisfying experiences, in comparison to conventional teaching methods and therapies [13]. In addition, serious gaming has contributed to several fields, such as education [9], simulation [25], health [2], cultural heritage [1] and others.

Serious games have been used for medical applications, including treatment of ASD [33], and can be divided into educational and treatment games. Each of these categories can be further divided into subcategories [22]. Existing games, focusing on treatment of social interaction with children with ASD, are used to reinforce emotion recognition [26], facial recognition [30], and foster collaboration through computer gaming [4,5]. Noor et al. reviewed articles from 2011 and 2012, putting the focus on technology and serious games classification, as well as on the developed serious games for treating children with ASD and/or for education [22]. Another review by Zakari et al., considering articles from 2004 to 2014, divided them across several criteria: technology platform, 2D/3D, learning objectives and type of interaction [35]. According to these classifications, our game could be defined as a tablet/desktop/laptop, 2D, touch-screen for learning counting 1–10, identifying letters, colors and objects, and understanding the semantics of the scene and narration.

2   The Life of "The Wolf in Love"

"The Wolf in Love" e-book has two ancestors: an inclusive theatre play and an interactive tactile (hard copy) children's book.

2.1   The Theatre Play

The theatre play was initiated by *EDUS-Education for All*, a non-for-profit organization that advances education for children with and without disabilities in Bosnia and Herzegovina in order to create an opportunity for children with ASD to engage in creative activity with typically developing peers. Marija Fekete-Sullivan wrote a screen play and the children's book storyline [12]. The play was then created in co-operation with the *Aparat Thetre* and *SARTR* (Sarajevo War Theatre), and has been performed several times by children actors with and without developmental disorders, Fig. 1.

2.2   The Hard Copy

Following the success of the play and children's enjoyment, which was mainly a result of the idea of respecting the differences and ignoring false boundaries between children, a children book with tactile stimulations and interactive elements (pulling, flipping, texture changes, and similar) was designed and printed with the support of UNICEF-BH, Fig. 1. The book was aimed to stimulate and reinforce comprehensive development and school readiness skills as the main precondition for realizing the full individual potential of a child. It was designed to provide stimulation for 3 to 12 year-old children with and without disabilities, especially focusing on the multisensory learning needs of children with ASD. The book was also bilingual (Bosnian-Croatian-Serbian and English languages), and each page had options for discovery learning and tactile sensations in order to draw and keep children's attention. For younger learners or children with disabilities, each page provided learning not only through auditory stimulation of

Fig. 1. A scene from the theatre play (left) and the children interaction with the printed book (right).

someone reading to them, but through full sensory exploration learning per each page as well (i.e. texture changes, manipulative parts of a page, strong colors and salient target characters, letters, numbers, etc.). Older learners were able to read the story but also to learn words in a second language since on each page, text was printed in both BHS and English languages as direct translations. These objectives were all aligned with the BH educational curriculum.

2.3   The E-book

According to the UNICEF-BH MICS Survey, only 56 % of children in Bosnia and Herzegovina, ages birth through 5 years-old, have at least 3 children's books in the house [31]. However, we are aware of the trends in the world today where media dominate children's lives through watching TV, playing video games, reading stories through e-readers, tablets, and smartphones. In the USA, the percent of children with access to some type of smart mobile device at home (e.g. smartphone, tablet) has jumped from 52 % to 75 % from 2011 to 2013 [17]. Seventy-two percent of children ages 0–8 use a mobile device for some type of media activity such as playing games (63 % of the time), watching videos, using apps, or reading books (only 30 % of the time) [17]. Video games in particular provide an ideal multimedia tool that presents concepts in a way that are engaging, informal, and fun for children [24]. Therefore, a potential benefit of educational video game is the value of generating engagement and motivation to learn for a student [6]. New multimedia and interactive features of the animated electronic storybooks were found superior when it comes to vocabulary acquisition in kindergartens compared to static e-book version of the same text in Netherlands [29]. Also, eye-tracking studies have demonstrated that children fixate longer on details in illustrations that are highlighted in the text [32]. Glenburg and Langston demonstrated that comprehension is better when the text is followed by illustration as pictures help to build mental models [14].

Guided by all these findings, we have designed our interactive e-book to attract attention of a learner, to engage him/her by features additional to the text being read in two languages (i.e. auditory stimulation when clicked on a certain object in the scene: naming the object or making a related sound) and by providing a multi layered question about the scene or story read. The questions on each page increase in difficulty to accommodate different levels of learners (young or a child with a disability vs. older typically developing child), Table 1.

One of the goals of both the entertainment and serious games is adaptivity and dynamic content generation [8,19], in order to efficiently balance the game flow and thus avoid frustration and/or boredom. In our game this is achieved by allowing the user to skip to the next page without being forced to answer the higher-level questions. In addition, the order of predefined answers is randomized and multiple target stimuli for "point to" type of questions are provided.

In addition, the cartoon-like, low-fidelity graphics in our game is used for several reasons. The first one is that the same graphics has been used in the printed book. As this is an extension we wanted to preserve the same visual appearance. Secondly, the targeted population for our game is used to this graphics style from

Table 1. The educational goals were to teach children to identify target objects (i.e. learn the vocabulary), 1:1 correspondence or learning to count objects from 1 to 10, to identify numbers 1–5, identify colors, and respond to inference questions.

Question	Educational goal
1	Selection-based question always with varied antecedents (i.e. "point to", "find", "where is", "touch")
2	1:1 correspondence question, teaching children to count objects
3	Production responding, an inference question, where the child reads a short text and makes conclusions based on the comprehension of the story

various children books and cartoons. Finally, we wanted to avoid the "Uncanny valley" phenomenon [21], in which a high-fidelity human-like computer-generated character is less preferred than its cartoon-like counterpart.

Our overall goal was to enrich the book reading experience for different levels of readers and to provide an engaging learning environment for children with disabilities, especially multisensory needs of children with ASD. The game can be accessed at http://edusbih.org/book/.

3   E-book Development

The e-book was developed using several web technologies: HTML5, CSS3, JavaScript, jQuery and AJAX. These technologies allow for easy-to-use, real-time interaction through the web-based front end.

Fig. 2. Three scenes from the e-book: scene 2 (left), scene 5 (middle) and scene 10 (right).

In the web implementation of the e-book, the pages were called scenes. There are 13 scenes in total, named *scene1.html* through *scene13.html*, Fig. 2. By default, when the e-book is started, *scene1.html* is loaded. All scenes are displayed through a single file, *index.html*. This is achieved through a navigation controller that loads a requested scene by switching the current html content with the content of the corresponding scene through AJAX, Fig. 3. At the same

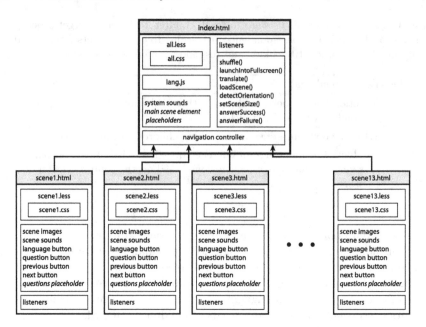

Fig. 3. A schematic view of the game structure.

time, JavaScript method *loadScene*, defined within *index.html*, resets the global variables *was_corrected* - used to indicate the correction; and *questions_active* - indicating if the questions were triggered. At this point the event listeners take over and wait for the user to interact with the game.

All html files have event listeners which are responsible for the page interaction. *index.html* controls the logic for the questions and answers, the language selection and for scene traversal, Fig. 4. Individual scene files are responsible for the events at each particular scene, e.g. playing the sounds, hiding and showing the elements, selecting the questions, and initiating the corrections.

All the styling, including visual appearance, sizes, positions and effects, is done using *Less elements* preprocessor [11]. Namely, each scene has its own *.less* file which defines the above-mentioned features for that page. On top of that, there is an *all.less* file which defines the general page appearance including the language and question bar (Fig. 4), responsiveness, correction and animations.

Everything in the application that can be translated has its key in the *lang.js* file. By clicking on the language selection button, the method *translate()* is called. The method translates all the system and local strings that are defined for the corresponding scene. The language can be selected at the opening scene, and also toggled throughout the game. This is an important feature that fosters learning a foreign language.

Each scene contains three question, two of which have three provided answers. For each such question only one of them, within its html element of the class *answer*, has class *correct* assigned. Questions that require interaction with

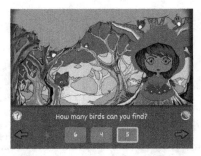

Fig. 4. A correction indicating the correct answer. Bottom box: the question button (top left), the language button (top right), the question and answers (middle), navigational buttons (bottom left and right) (Color figure online).

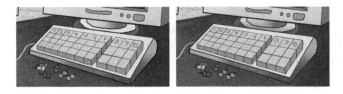

Fig. 5. Correction invoked after an element other than the keyboard had been touched (Color figure online).

the active scene elements, i.e. that use the "where is", "point to" or similar antecedent, have their own logic implemented within their belonging scene. This logic is based on an additional listener that checks if the touched element has a class *correct* assigned to it. If so, the answer is considered as correct. For each correct answer the "applause" sound is played and one of the text responses ("Great job!", "Excellent!", "That's correct!") is randomly provided. In case of the incorrect answer the correction is invoked. All the provided answers are shuffled using the method *shuffle()* in the *index.html* file.

The correction for the incorrect answers is provided by either adding the blinking yellow frame to the correct answer (Fig. 4) for the questions with the provided answers, or by adding a red halo around the correct object (Fig. 5) for the questions with the "pointing to" antecedent.

In each scene there are a number of interactive elements. These elements, when touched, either make corresponding sound, such as tweeting for bird or howling for wolf, or are being named in the selected language. At the same time, they are either smoothly scaled up and down, so they gently pop up, or animated so they move across the scene. This is achieved by assigning the *scale-animation* class to the corresponding element, and defining the animation code in the corresponding *.less* file.

Finally, each scene has a bilingual narration, which is part of the storyline that introduces the child to the current scene. It is triggered by either clicking on the narrating character if in the scene (Fig. 6), or on any non-interactive element

Fig. 6. The visual appearance of the narration once triggered.

in the scene if the narrator is not present. Once triggered, it is both displayed visually on a predefined spot and played audibly. All the voice overs and the object naming audio files have been narrated by children.

4   Conclusions and Future Work

Our interactive e-book provides a multisensory experience to relate basic learning concepts to children through game-like experience. Children can hear the text being narrated in one of the two languages of their choice, they can read along and practice reading skills or just relay on visual stimuli and textually respond to it. They can engage in a game to explore each page of the book or for younger users, just the interactivity and animations on each page are something to retain their attention. It is a multiuse, multilevel educational interactive application of the latest research in education, interactive e-books and serious games.

Since this is a pilot project, the e-book has only been preliminary tested with several children with and without developmental delays, in order to eliminate any potential technical malfunctioning. Nonetheless, it showed an indication of a great potential, as all children seemed to enjoy using it and expressed high interest in reusing it. The next step is to test the e-book and its interactive features on the acquisition of the novel vocabulary, foreign language vocabulary, 1:1 correspondence (i.e. counting), colors, and comprehension of the story. We would like to compare the effect and the experiences of children with disabilities with typically developing children.

On the other side, there were many considerations and limitations on the technical side of the game development, which could be overcome in the future and allow for further technical enhancement of the game. One such consideration was the scene transition. A simple transition, where the internet connection is over 1Mbps, has been straightforward to implement and it is rendered smoothly without any delays. However, for lower bandwidths, which are not uncommon in this region, and also for mobile connections (3G and similar), we implemented the background scene loading that allows the user to interact with the current scene while the next one is being loaded. Once the requested scene is loaded, the transition is made.

One of the main limitations in the development was the input graphics that we had from the designing team of the printed book. Namely, all the graphics were raster, and only partially layered, which made it impossible to extract many scene objects from the background without major interventions on the drawings. Furthermore, it restricted the game resolution and object animations. In the future versions of the e-book we will make more scene object interactive and potentially improve the object animations. In addition, we will make the game more responsive so that it fits all the screen size factors and ratios more naturally.

Acknowledgments. The authors would like to thank employees of the non-for-profit organization EDUS-Education for All. We would also like to thank Bakir Husovic and Namik Mesic for helping with the game development. Finally, we would like to thank everyone who was involved and supported the development of the theatre play, printed book and the e-book. The pilot project was funded by the UNICEF-BH.

References

1. Anderson, E.F., McLoughlin, L., Liarokapis, F., Peters, C., Petridis, P., de Freitas, S.: Developing serious games for cultural heritage: a state-of-the-art review. Virtual Reality **14**(4), 255–275 (2010)
2. Arnab, S., Dunwell, I., Debattista, K.: Serious games for healthcare: applications and implications, pp. 1–370 (2013)
3. American Psychiatric Association: Diagnostic and Statistical Manual of Mental Disorders (DSM-5®). American Psychiatric Pub. (2013)
4. Battocchi, A., Gal, E., Sasson, A.B., Pianesi, F., Venuti, P., Zancanaro, M., Weiss, P.: Collaborative puzzle game-an interface for studying collaboration and social interaction for children who are typically developed or who have autistic spectrum disorder. In: Proceedings of 7th ICDVRAT with Art Abilitation, pp. 127–134 (2008)
5. Battocchi, A., Pianesi, F., Venuti, P., Ben-Sasson, A., Gal, E., Weiss, P.: Collaborative puzzle game: fostering collaboration in children with autistic spectrum disorder (ASD) and with typical development. In: 2009 Virtual Rehabilitation International Conference (2009)
6. Bourgonjon, J., Valcke, M., Soetaert, R., Schellens, T.: Students perceptions about the use of video games in the classroom. Comput. Educ. **54**(4), 1145–1156 (2010)
7. Chen, S.H., Bernard-Opitz, V.: Comparison of personal and computer-assisted instruction for children with autism. Ment. Retard. **31**(6), 368–376 (1993)
8. Correa, O., Cuervo, C., Perez, P., Arias, A.: A new approach for self adaptive video game for rehabilitation-experiences in the amblyopia treatment. In: 2014 IEEE 3rd International Conference on Serious Games and Applications for Health (SeGAH), pp. 1–5. IEEE (2014)
9. De Freitas, S.I.: Using games and simulations for supporting learning. Learn. Media Technol. **31**(4), 343–358 (2006)
10. Emurian, H., Hu, X., Wang, J., Durham, A.: Learning java: a programmed instruction approach using applets. Comput. Hum. Behav. **16**(4), 395–422 (2000)

11. Fadeyev, D.: Less elements. http://lesselements.com/
12. Fekete-Sullivan, M.: Zaljubljeni vuk/The Wolf in Love. EDUS (2015)
13. Foreman, J.: Next-generation educational technology versus the lecture. EDU-CAUSE Rev. Mag. **38**(4), 12–22 (2003)
14. Glenberg, A.M., Langston, W.E.: Comprehension of illustrated text: pictures help to build mental models. J. Mem. Lang. **31**(2), 129–151 (1992)
15. Greer, R.D.: The teacher as a strategic scientist: a solution to our education crisis? Behav. Soc. Issues **1**(2), 25–41 (1991)
16. Greer, R.D.: Designing Teaching Strategies: An Applied Behavior Analysis System Approach. Academic Press, New York (2002)
17. Holloway, D., Green, L., Livingstone, S.: Zero to Eight: Young Children and Their Internet Use. LSE, London (2013)
18. Hulusic, V., Pistoljevic, N.: "LeFCA": learning framework for children with autism. Procedia Comput. Sci. **15**, 4–16 (2012)
19. Lopes, R., Bidarra, R.: Adaptivity challenges in games and simulations: a survey. IEEE Trans. Comput. Intell. AI Games **3**(2), 85–99 (2011)
20. Luyster, R., Richler, J., Risi, S., Hsu, W.L., Dawson, G., Bernier, R., Dunn, M., Hepburn, S., Hyman, S.L., McMahon, W.M., et al.: Early regression in social communication in autism spectrum disorders: a CPEA study. Dev. Neuropsychol. **27**(3), 311–336 (2005)
21. Mori, M., MacDorman, K.F., Kageki, N.: The uncanny valley [from the field]. IEEE Robot. Autom. Mag. **19**(2), 98–100 (2012)
22. Noor, M., Shahbodin, F., Pee, C., et al.: Serious game for autism children: review of literature (2012)
23. Price, A.: Making a difference with smart tablets. Teacher Librarian **39**(1), 31–34 (2011)
24. Rieber, L.P., Noah, D.: Games, simulations, and visual metaphors in education: antagonism between enjoyment and learning. Educ. Media Int. **45**(2), 77–92 (2008)
25. Shelton, B.E., Hedley, N.R.: Using augmented reality for teaching Earth-Sun relationships to undergraduate geography students. In: The First IEEE International Workshop on Augmented Reality Toolkit, p. 8. IEEE (2002)
26. Silver, M., Oakes, P.: Evaluation of a new computer intervention to teach people with autism or asperger syndrome to recognize and predict emotions in others. Autism **5**(3), 299–316 (2001)
27. Skinner, B.F.: Teaching machines. Science **128**(3330), 969–977 (1958)
28. Skinner, B.F.: The Technology of Teaching. Appleton-Century-Crofts, New York (1968)
29. Smeets, D., Bus, A.: The interactive animated e-book as a word learning device for kindergartners. Appl. Psycholinguistics **22**(1), 1–22 (2014)
30. Tanaka, J.W., Wolf, J.M., Klaiman, C., Koenig, K., Cockburn, J., Herlihy, L., Brown, C., Stahl, S., Kaiser, M.D., Schultz, R.T.: Using computerized games to teach face recognition skills to children with autism spectrum disorder: the lets face it! Program. J. Child Psychol. Psychiatry **51**(8), 944–952 (2010)
31. UNICEF-BH: Bosnia and Herzegovina Multiple Indicator Cluster Survey (MICS) 2011–2012. UNICEF-BH (2013)
32. Verhallen, M.J., Bus, A.G.: Young second language learners visual attention to illustrations in storybooks. J. Early Childhood Literacy **11**(4), 480–500 (2011)
33. Wang, Q., Sourina, O., Nguyen, M.K.: Eeg-based "serious" games design for medical applications. In: 2010 International Conference on Cyberworlds (CW), pp. 270–276. IEEE (2010)

34. Whalen, C., Massaro, D.W., Franke, L.: Generalization in computer-assisted intervention for children with autism spectrum disorders. In: Real Life, Real Progress for Children with Autism Spectrum Disorders, pp. 223–233. Brookes Publishing Co. (2009)
35. Zakari, H.M., Ma, M., Simmons, D.: A review of serious games for children with Autism Spectrum Disorders (ASD). In: Ma, M., Oliveira, M.F., Baalsrud Hauge, J. (eds.) SGDA 2014. LNCS, vol. 8778, pp. 93–106. Springer, Heidelberg (2014). http://dx.doi.org/10.1007/978-3-319-11623-5-9

MindSpace: Treating Anxiety Disorders in Children with a CBT Game

Barbara Göbl[1], Helmut Hlavacs[1(✉)], Jessica Hofer[2], Isabelle Müller[2], Hélen Müllner[2], Claudia Schubert[2], Halina Spallek[2], Charlotte Rybka[2], and Manuel Sprung[2]

[1] Research Group Entertainment Computing, University of Vienna, Vienna, Austria
helmut.hlavacs@univie.ac.at
[2] Faculty of Psychology, University of Vienna, Vienna, Austria

Abstract. We describe the design process and implementation of the serious game MindSpace. MindSpace provides a playful setting for treating children with a variety of social and specific anxiety disorders. A modular approach is explained, taking a closer look on cognitive-behavioral techniques such as exposure tasks, psycho-education or coping techniques and how they are implemented within a game setting. Also, special focus is paid to the needs of our target group by putting a strong emphasis on usability and motivational factors and hence, therapy adherence.

1 Introduction

Anxiety disorders are among the leading psychological conditions in children and adolescents. Research undertaken in western countries reports prevalence figures of 10 % and higher, with anxiety disorders accounting for half of the diagnosed psychological conditions. Additionally, these disorders often show high co-morbidity with affective disorders such as depression. They can potentially lead to anxiety disorders and depression in adult age, substance abuse or even suicide attempts [11,22].

Cognitive Behavioural Therapy (CBT) is an established treatment form to tackle these psychological conditions. Meta-studies show that CBT is a highly effective treatment method and leads to reduced symptoms for both anxiety and depression [17].

However, several issues remain. Low availability of trained CBT therapists often leads to long waiting lists. Given the high prevalence of anxiety disorders, this lead to exploration of different alternatives to face-to-face treatment, such as group treatment, self-help delivered via telephone or computer supported treatment [18,19]. Also, financial or time related problems create the need for easier access to psychological treatment [15].

These problems have certainly supplemented the research undertaken in the field of computerized CBT (CCBT). Many approaches to CCBT have been taken so far and found to be effective when used as part of a therapeutical intervention, as well as when used on their own [15]. The method of computerization can be

© Springer International Publishing Switzerland 2016
A. De Gloria and R. Veltkamp (Eds.): GALA 2015, LNCS 9599, pp. 266–275, 2016.
DOI: 10.1007/978-3-319-40216-1_28

tailored to the group of targeted clients and the specific anxiety disorder. Video games have become a popular approach when dealing with children and adolescents. Surveys show that children are very familiar with video games and a large percentage has access to the necessary hardware. In 2014, 99 % of households in Germany were in possession of a computer or laptop, 94 % had smart phones. 81 % of children reported to use the internet on a daily basis and nearly half said they played video games at least several times a week [7].

By developing the serious game *MindSpace*, we aim to address the above mentioned issues concerning childhood and adolescent anxiety and support therapists and children during treatment.

2 Related Work

A variety of CCBT programs have been developed during recent years, specializing on different psychological conditions and their treatment. The choice of how to computerize therapy is heavily dependant on resources, disorder and target group. For example, virtual reality programs are used for treating and exploring social phobias for adults [8,13], while video games are found to cater well to the needs of children and adolescents [4].

Regarding our young audience, projects such as *BRAVE-ONLINE* [20,21] and *Camp Cope-a-lot* [12] come into focus. *BRAVE-ONLINE* mimicks sessions as they take place in face-to-face therapy and is accompanied by a therapist who is introduced via telephone and keeps up contact via mail. It aims to attract children with cartoon images and appropriate multimedia content. The *Camp Cope-A-Lot* CD (CCCD) targets children aged 7–12. Various media are used to provide affective education, teach relaxation techniques, give homework and go through exposure situations. To motivate the child, computer games are introduced as rewards. Instructions are included to allow non-trained supervisors to support the child. Applied in clinical trials, both CCCD and BRAVE-ONLINE have successfully improved anxiety symptoms. *gNats* [6] provides a video game approach to CBT, targeting 10–15 year old adolescents. It is intended to be used alongside face-to-face therapy and showcases the positive responses of both clinicians and adolescents to CCBT. Another example is *Treasure Hunt*, also fully implemented within a game setting and designed to support face-to-face therapy. The player is taken upon a ship and sent on a treasure hunt. Several tasks and mini-games include the principles of CBT. It is important to mention, that evaluation of programs who are exclusive to face-to-face treatment showed improvement in anxiety and depression, even without the help of trained therapists [19].

3 Psychological Background

CBT is used to treat many different psychological conditions, such as post-traumatic stress disorder, anxiety disorders, depression, or even eating disorders [3]. It combines cognitive and behavioral aspects and is based on the idea of emotion, thoughts and behavior deeply affecting our well-being [14]. One of the main goals is to identify, control and adjust irrational behaviour and damaging thoughts. Typically, cognitive-behavioral therapy is very structured, problem oriented and follows a specific manual [10]. Some of the main aspects included in child CBT treatments were paid special attention in our work: assessment, psycho-education, coping techniques, exposure procedures and contingency management [9].

Assessment refers to both a first diagnosis as well as monitoring of the changes over time. Tools such as report inventories and behavioral observation are used to gather information for treatment. During *Psycho-Education*, children are taught about anxiety, its physiological symptoms and its behavioral and psychological basics. Inaccurate views on anxiety and treatment are addressed to positively influence cognition and expectations. *Coping Techniques* include methods to help the child relax such as breathing techniques and muscle relaxation. Also, anxious children tend to misinterpret ambiguous situation, leaning towards maladaptive thoughts or *self-talk* to trigger anxiety. An important task of CBT is to make children aware of their *self-talk* and help them analyze and adapt their thoughts. *Exposure* refers to a gradual confrontation with the client's fears. Counterconditioning combines exposure with incompatible reactions such as relaxation. Extinction, on the other hand, confronts a client with anxiety triggering stimuli while using cognitive and behavioral techniques to control the situation and lower anxiety to a lower, manageable level. Finally, *Contingency Management* stresses the consequences of a client's behavior, setting behaviour modification as a major goal. A traditional approach within cognitive-behavioral therapy is to work with rewards.

4   MindSpace

To address the problem of child anxiety disorders, *MindSpace*[1] was developed by an interdisciplinary team of computer scientists and psychologists. MindSpace is a 2D jump 'n' run game including concepts and therapy modules loosely based on the "Modular Approach to Therapy for Children with Anxiety, Depression, Trauma, or Conduct Problems" [5] (MATCH-ADTC, henceforth MATCH). MATCH is an evidence-based, specialized CBT manual giving instructions on how to proceed throughout child CBT. MATCH modules are independent and allow for a flexible order do help individualize therapy and work on the child's main condition as well as any accompanying problems. This child-tailored approach was transferred to MindSpace. Different modules were implemented, starting with the "Fear Ladder", "Fear Thermometer" and "Maintenance" representing the assessment, as described above. Psycho-education and coping techniques are conveyed by "Learning About Anxiety", "Quick Calming" and "Cognitive STOP". Exposure tasks are included in the "Practicing" module and finally, "Rewards" refer to contingency management.

---

[1] http://barbarella.cs.univie.ac.at/mindspace/MindSpace.html.

4.1 Game Design and Use of the Game

MindSpace targets children aged 7–12 diagnosed with anxiety disorder. It has no prerequisites and was designed to be easily accessible, both regarding the skill level of the player as well as the hardware it runs on.

To accommodate the skill of our young players several precautions were taken. All stages of the game provide an optional tutorial, both as text as well as audio to accommodate young children's reading capabilities. Furthermore, menus and buttons are mostly represented by graphics only, using simple, recognizable symbols throughout the game. Game graphics and player characters are designed in comic style, tailored to our young players.

There are a number of aspects that characterize MindSpace's unique approach to CBT. Firstly, while many programs are based on linked multimedia content, we provide an extensive game environment. Hence, it holds special appeal for children, leading towards higher engagement and better motivation to finish training. Secondly, MindSpace is very flexible in adapting to the specific fears of children as it provides a large set of different anxieties and situations for exposure tasks. Lastly, MindSpace was designed to be self-explanatory, hence, while possible to use it as addition to face-to-face therapy, it is also intended to work with little to no assistance from care givers or psychotherapists (Fig. 1).

Fig. 1. Fear Ladder and Fear Thermometer (Color figure online)

4.2 Let's Play MindSpace

After creating an account and choosing a player figure, the player will go through an introductory phase, introducing the game and its context as well as gathering data about his or her anxieties. The chosen figure will be represented in all exposure videos later on.

The Fear Ladder. This screen provides a list of pre-selected anxieties, represented with an icon and text, that can be sorted within the steps of the ladder. The steps are arranged bottom-up from 1 to 10 and colored from green to red, to emphasize the severity of the anxiety. The player can drag up to 10 anxieties in the steps of the ladder but must at least place 1 item in the top-most spot. This step can optionally be taken with the help of a therapist or the parents to discuss the order. The game will henceforth focus on the top-most anxiety.

The Fear Thermometer. The next screen, the *Fear Thermometer*, prompts the child to select an order of situations regarding the chosen anxiety. 11 different situations need to be placed to fill ten slots of the thermometer, thus creating a list of gradual exposure steps the player will be confronted with during the game. One situation will be left unsorted, meant to represent a situation the player decides that they are already somewhat comfortable with. The intention is to start the player off with a good feeling, as they leave the first situation behind them right at the start. After completing the introductory steps, the player will be taken to the cockpit of his space craft.

The Cockpit. The cockpit is a fully graphical representation of the game's main menu and hence the central point for accessing all further modules. A pop up explains the controls to the player, inviting him to explore the cockpit with his mouse pointer, as every graphic linked to a menu item is also linked to an audio file. Hovering over a button starts a track explaining its function. Before venturing further into space though, the player has to take astronaut training. This training is necessary to enter the later stages of the game, as it represents learning about coping techniques and psycho-education. Altogether, five menu options are provided, each linking to another module of the game, within the cockpit:

The Education Button. This button starts the astronaut's training. Clicking these items will create a pop-up window offering play buttons for 3 different videos that teach the astronaut about anxiety and coping techniques.

Open Space and the Solar System. This menu option leads to the solar system where ten planets represent a level each, whereas a level represents a situation that has been sorted into the fear thermometer in earlier steps. Flags mark the planets a player has managed to conquer wholly, giving them a sense of accomplishment and providing sub-goals to boost morale. Clicking on a planet starts a jump 'n' run level that lands the space craft on the planet's surface where the player will have to go through exposure situations but can also collect up to 100 stars to trade in for playroom items. Exposure situations are depicted as comets that collide with the surface. While the player can optionally pause to delay the exposure, there is no way to continue exploring the planet without finishing the exposure. Level menus include a button to exit the level and go

Fig. 2. Jump 'n' run levels display many different worlds

back to the solar system as well as playing short videos to rehearse coping and relaxation techniques (Fig. 2).

The Playroom. The playroom represents a major part of the motivational system of the game, hence the module "Rewards". While players have to collect stars during the jump 'n' run levels, this is where they can use the stars to exchange them for toys and items for their playroom. The more stars they collect, the more items are available and can be placed via a simple drag & drop mechanism to furnish their room.

The Statistics Display. This screen provides an overview over the child's progress throughout the game. Anxiety ratings for each individual level are gathered. To accommodate our young players, these statistics are displayed using fear thermometer graphics which indicate, both by colour as well as number, the ratings taken during the game.

4.3   In-Game Exposure and Monitoring

The exposure situations are one of the core modules within the game, representing the "Practicing" module. Each planet/level represents one of the situations sorted by the child using the fear thermometer. Exposure videos depict 15 different anxieties divided into 11 situations, each of them in different versions for both male and female players. This results in a total of 330 videos integrated in MindSpace, adding up to about 165 min of exposure material. Videos are composed using an age appropriate comic style. They depict situations in third person perspective, starring the character chosen by the player. Common anxieties such as darkness, public speaking, school, strangers or traffic accidents are covered.

Choice of anxieties was based on statistical data about pre-valence of specific anxieties in children [2]. Before and after exposure, measurements are taken on

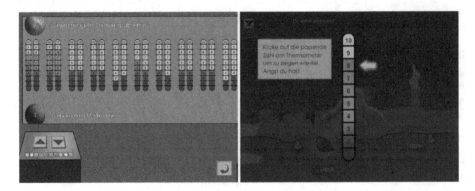

Fig. 3. The fear thermometer is a recurring motive used to display statistics and measure in-game anxiety (Color figure online)

a scale from 1–10 indicating how much fear the child feels at this moment. This serves two purposes. Firstly, ratings throughout the game's levels can be viewed by the child itself or e.g. a therapist to monitor progress. Secondly, if a high value of 9 or above is given, a pop-up appears optionally providing a rehearsal of coping and relaxation techniques to support anxious children. As soon as a level is finished, measurements for this level are displayed and the player is praised for his achievement. As described above, progress can be monitored within the game by navigating to the statistics display from the cockpit. This functionality represents the "Maintenance" module. Children can see their progress and how treatment is helping them (Fig. 3).

4.4 In-Game Psycho-Education and Coping Techniques

Psycho-education and coping techniques are included using instructional videos. Astronaut training consists of 3 implemented MATCH [5] modules. An instructor takes you through the training units. In *Learning About Anxiety*, the goal is to introduce the workings of anxiety. This video shows that anxiety occurs naturally, happens to everyone and how it manifests within our bodies. Understanding is an important motivational factor for later practice and treatment. The second video, *Cognitive STOP* introduces the STOP method. The children are taught to replace worried thoughts with better, helpful thoughts to handle anxious situations. Lastly, the *Quick Calming* video introduces relaxation techniques, helping the child to handle anxiety and relax when being fearful. As anxiety triggering situations often come up in public, it's important for the child to have a way to deal with it quickly.

4.5 Game Development

MindSpace is based on Flash and ActionScript 3. It has low hardware requirements and can be run in any browser, independent of platform, using the free

Fig. 4. Images from "Learning About Anxiety" and "Cognitive STOP"

Flash Player. The game has been taken through an iterative process of development and testing. Each module has gone through several repeated phases of programming and game testing, as well as a final check whether psycho-therapeutic aspects have been fully implemented (Fig. 4).

4.6 Experiences and Evaluation

Preliminary evaluation has been performed. Studies show that learning disabilities show high morbidity with anxiety disorders, affecting nearly a third of children with learning disabilities [16]. Hence, participating children were all pupils at schools for children with special education needs to put the focus on assessing MindSpace as preemptive method to avoid anxiety and lower anxiety-symptoms in children. 22 children, ages 7–11, were recruited and tested using a wait list control design. Interventions targeting young, anxious children have successfully improved quality of life [1] and as mentioned above, childhood anxiety is a problem best tackled early on. Thus we believe that preventive measures are an important task.

While current results on effectiveness are inconclusive, feedback on MindSpace has been quite positive. Children readily engaged in the game over the course of several sessions. Both our reward system and game play received praise and provided motivation to further complete levels and exposure tasks.

5 Conclusion

This paper provides a closer look on the CCBT game MindSpace and how psychological principles are implemented within a game setting. For one, we try to give insight into design considerations regarding our special target group. Both usability and game play need to be tailored to age and abilities. Also, therapy adherence is a important factor in psychological treatment that we tackle by including a reward system and additional motivational factors. Many of these motivational aspects are inherent to game settings e.g. specific goals and sub-goals, such as finishing a level.

If the need should arise, MindSpace can be expanded on many levels. While an extensive set of specific and social phobias is already included, the modular nature of the game makes it easy to extend these lists even further. To simplify fear ratings and exposure analysis, physiological measurements might be included, e.g. by using computer mice measuring galvanic skin response.

Finally, further experimental evaluation of MindSpace poses an important future task. While separate modules can be singled out for testing, such as efficacy of exposure tasks or the reward system, testing the overall effect of the game within clinical test groups is a long-term goal.

References

1. Aures, S., Bradtke, N., Schmidtchen, S.:Prävention von Angststörungen im Grund-schulalter (2006). http://www.gwg-ev.org/sites/default/files/aures.pdf. Accessed 13 Apr 2015
2. Beesdo, K., Knappe, S., Pine, D.S.: Anxiety and anxiety disorders in children and adolescents: developmental issues and implications for DSM-V. Psychiatr. Clin. North Am. **32**(3), 483–524 (2009)
3. Butler, A.C., et al.: The empirical status of cognitive-behavioral therapy: a review of meta-analyses. Clin. Psychol. Rev. **26**(1), 17–31 (2006)
4. Ceranoglu, T.A.: Video games in psychotherapy. Rev. Gen. Psychol. **14**(2), 141–146 (2010)
5. Chorpita, B.F., Weisz, J.R.: MATCH-ADTC: Modular Approach to Therapy for Children with Anxiety, Depression, Trauma, or Conduct Problems. PracticeWise, LLC, Satellite Beach (2009)
6. Coyle, D., et al.: Exploratory evaluations of a computer game supporting cognitive behavioural therapy for adolescents. In: Proceedings of the SIGCHI Conference on Human Factors in Computing Systems, CHI 2011, pp. 2937–2946. ACM, Vancouver (2011)
7. Feierabend, S., Plankenhorn, T., Rathgeb, T.: JIM 2014 Jugend, Information, (Multi-) media. Basisstudie zumMedienumgang 12- bis 19-Jähriger in Deutsch-land. Medienpädagogischer Forschungsverbund Südwest. http://www.mpfs.de/fileadmin/JIM-pdf14/JIM-Studie%5C_2014.pdf. Accessed 1 Feb 2015
8. Felnhofer, A., et al.: Afraid to be there? Evaluating the relation between presence, self-reported anxiety and heart rate in a virtual public speaking task. Cyberpsychol. Beh. Soc. Netw. **17**(5), 310–316 (2014)
9. Gosch, E.A., et al.: Principles of cognitive-behavioral therapy for anxiety disorders in children. J. Cogn. Psychother. Int. Q. **20**(3), 247–262 (2006)
10. Kendall, P.C. (ed.): Child and Adolescent Therapy: Cognitive-Behavioral Proce-dures, 4th edn. The Guildford Press, New York (2011)
11. Kendall, P.C., et al.: Clinical characteristics of anxiety disordered youth. J. Anxiety Disord. **24**(3), 360–365 (2010)
12. Khanna, M.S., Kendall, P.C.: Computer-assisted CBT for child anxiety: the coping cat CD-ROM. Cogn. Behav. Pract. **15**(2), 159–165 (2008)
13. Klinger, E., et al.: Virtual reality therapy versus cognitive behavior therapy for social phobia: a preliminary controlled study. Cyberpsychology Behav. **8**(1), 76–88 (2005)

14. Kognitive Verhaltenstherapie. http://www.gesundheitsinformation.de/kognitive-verhaltenstherapie.2136.de.html. Accessed 5 Mar 2015

15. March, S., Spence, S.H., Donovan, C.L.: The efficacy of an internet-based cognitive-behavioral therapy intervention for child anxiety disorders. J. Pediatr. Psychol. **34**(5), 474–487 (2009)

16. Margari, L., et al.: Neuropsychopathological comorbidities in learning disorders. BMC Neurol. **13**, 198 (2013)

17. Mitte, K.: Meta-analysis of cognitive-behavioral treatments for generalized anxiety disorder: a comparison with pharmacotherapy. Psychol. Bull. **131**(5), 785–795 (2005)

18. Proudfoot, J., et al.: Clinical efficacy of computerised cognitive-behavioural therapy for anxiety and depression in primary care: randomised controlled trial. Br. J. Psychiatry **185**(1), 46–54 (2004)

19. Proudfoot, J., et al.: Computerized, interactive, multimedia cognitive- behavioural program for anxiety and depression in general practice. Psychol. Med. **33**, 217–227 (2003)

20. Spence, S.H., et al.: A randomized controlled trial of online versus clinic-based CBT for adolescent anxiety. J. Consult. Clin. Psychol. **79**(5), 629–642 (2011)

21. Spence, S.H., et al.: Online CBT in the treatment of child and adolescent anxiety disorders: issues in the development of BRAVE-ONLINE and two case illustrations. Behav. Cogn. Psychother. **36**, 411–430 (2008). (Special Issue 04 July 2008)

22. Steinhausen, H.-C., et al.: Prevalence of child and adolescent psychiatric disorders: the Zürich epidemiological study. Acta Psychiatr. Scand. **98**(4), 262–271 (1998)

Development and Testing of a Serious Game for the Elderly (Title: 'Paldokangsan3')

KyungSik Kim[1(✉)], YoonJung Lee[2], and DooNam Oh[3]

[1] Department of Game Development, Hoseo University,
Hoseo-ro 79 Beon-gil 20, Baebang-eup, Asan-si, Chungnam, South Korea
kskim@hoseo.edu
[2] Department of Social Welfare for the Elderly, Hoseo University,
Hoseodae-kil 12, Dongnam-ku, Cheonan-si, Chungnam, South Korea
yoon2525@hoseo.edu
[3] Department of Nursing, Hoseo University, Hoseo-ro 79 Beon-gil 20,
Baebang-eup, Asan-si, Chungnam, South Korea
doonoh@hoseo.edu

Abstract. Old people are prone to get weak in their physical bodies as well as their memorizations. We have developed a serious game for the elderly named 'Paldokangsan3' which is a walking game strengthening legs as well as the ability of memorization with the interface of motion capture using Kinect. Also we have evaluated the usability test of 'Paldokangsan3'. This game machine has been installed in a senior house for one month that the elderly could play the game as they like in the house. Most participants played 2–3 times a day for a month even though most of them are suffering mild cognition impairment. They showed good subjective satisfactions in their interviews that we could go on the project further to expand its applications.

1 Introduction

Computer games are useful bidirectional media which have features of repeating something with fun [1]. Among them, there are serious games with a special purpose such as education and training, not just for amusement [2].

The societies of the whole globe have increasing numbers of old people living longer with medical and scientific achievements. However old people are prone to get weaker in their muscle and power with their bodies receding, hence easy to get sick with little activities. Also the ability of memorization is decaying with the ages. Therefore they need repetitive performance and trials to maintain their vitalities on their physical bodies as well as their mental activities [3].

This research is to utilize serious games to improve the life of the old people. We have developed a serious game 'Paldokangsan3' recently which is a walking game to strengthen their bodies with memorizing to help their memorization abilities for that purpose [4–6].

The aim of this paper is to describe the latest development of 'Paldokangsan3' about its design and its effect analysis as well as the usability test with two experiments. 'Paldokangsan3' has features focusing on walking a shopping street with full attention

© Springer International Publishing Switzerland 2016
A. De Gloria and R. Veltkamp (Eds.): GALA 2015, LNCS 9599, pp. 276–285, 2016.
DOI: 10.1007/978-3-319-40216-1_29

of memorization to buy some designated items. It has the concept of mall walking which permits the player with visional fun as well as physical exercise. It is dealing with five common diseases of the elderly (Dementia, Depressions, Osteoporosis, Diabetes Mellitus, and Hypertensions). The mission of the game is to buy some good items walking the shopping street which are good for the selected disease. 'Paldokangsan3' is using Kinect as its interface of motion capturing of the player with intuitive gestures. The expected effect is improvement of memorization, concentration to find out something in the vision and mental health through entertainment.

The first experiment was done with 25 volunteers of more than 65 years old in Cheonan senior center in Korea in Nov in 2013. They tried the game in whole three levels once a day for ten days. They were all focused on the game to remember the mission and to make correct decision with the gestures walking inside a small area to be captured by Kinect.

The data had been analyzed to show that the number of times of playing the game was positively correlated with the score with 99 % of confidence, negatively correlated with the number of steps and duration time to finish it with 99 % of confidence. Also we got the good results of adaptation and vicariousness, and self-esteem.

We have done the second experiment for the usability test [7] of 'Paldokangsan3' in Dec in 2014 for one month in Asan senior house in Korea. We have installed the game machine there for the elderly to play the game in their convenient time without any intervention. Most participants played 2–3 times a day for a month even though some of them were suffering mild cognition impairment. We have collected their data through inspection, questionnaire and interviews by the researchers as well as in-game measurement for the play. The results showed good adaptation of the game for the period.

2 Related Works

Games for the elderly has been developed and utilized in Japan first where the ratio of old population of more than 65 years old is one of the biggest countries in the world. Their games are 'Taiko Drum Master' to move both arms following the music [8], 'Hebi Hebi' to strengthen the muscles of the leg for the elderly not to be fallen down [9], and recently 'Sit-up' by Kyushu rehabilitation center [10].

There have been several researches on games related to the old person's physical and mental problems: applications for entertainment and information retrieval could compensate for age-related physiological and cognitive shortcomings [11]. Serious games are not only useful for healthy behavior, but generally for cognitive learning (knowledge and skills), motor skills, affective learning (attitude change, motivation) and communicative learning [12].

Recently domestic researches for the elderly are active for the improvement of physical movement and rehabilitation [13]. Some of them are the personal training system for exercise and rehabilitative training [14], game with Wii-mote to improve cognition with activities [15], and game by motion capturing with 3D depth camera to help exercise and rehabilitation [16].

Hoseo University has been supporting for the research of serious games for the elderly since 2009. We had analyzed the needs of middle and elder generation about serious games for the elderly, and got the result (1) elder generations prefer leisure activities such as mountain climbing, walking, yoga, golf and travel for health, interest, the development for oneself and relieving stress; (2) they don't prefer game activity for leisure, but prefer to use serious game for health, simulation, medical treatment and sports than middle generation [17]. We focused on the walking game that the original version 'Paldokangsan1' was first developed in 2011 with wire connected interfaces and announced abroad [18, 19], and 'Paldokangsan2' in 2012 with Bluetooth connected interfaces [5].

3   Development of 'Paldokangsan3'

3.1   Design Concept of the Game

In human vision, the useful field of view (or UFOV) is the visual area over which information can be extracted at a brief glance without eye or head movements [20]. Generally UFOV size decreases with age most likely due to decreases in visual processing speed, reduced attentional resources, and less ability to ignore distracting information [21]. UFOV performance is correlated with a number of important real-world functions including risk of an automobile crash. Performance can be improved by computer based training [22].

In the beginning of this research in 2008, we had collected the survey of the old people about their leisure activities and analyzed that (1) elder generation prefers leisure activities such as mountain climbing, yoga, golf, walking and travel, etc., for health, interest, the development for oneself and relieving stress; (2) they don't prefer game activity for leisure, but prefer to use serious game for health, simulation, medical treatment and sports than middle generation [17]. We started to make a walking game for the elderly in 2010 [18].

We focused on UFOV to make our new serious game for the elderly. By the repeated reaction on UFOV, we thought their bodies and mental abilities could be improved much better. We have decided to develop a walking game with vision giving the scene on the screen just as seen by the walker. So the movement of the scene should be adjusted with the steps of the player. Also to control the scene and the steps, we needed a useful and comfortable interface for the elderly.

'Paldokangsan3' has the game concept of 'mall walking' to give walking action with visional pleasure as well as memorization. Walking to buy something in the mall or shopping area could help the player to concentrate on the game with little exhaust and longer play time. Its intention is to raise memorization, concentration, vitality by strengthening the UFOV. According to the player there should be several levels of difficulties. Also the game should give feedbacks to the player if the choice was right or wrong. We put different sound effect with color on every selection of the item in the game. And the final score with daily ranking and weekly ranking would show the accomplishment of the player [6].

3.2 Game Play

Figure 1 shows 4 screens of the game interface of 'Paldokangsan3'. The game starts with selecting a disease to get a mission that is to buy some items in the market, and walking the shopping street selecting those items following the remembering. The average time to finish the mission would be 2–3 min for one level. The player may forget what to buy: then a chance coin can be used to reshow the mission for five seconds in the screen.

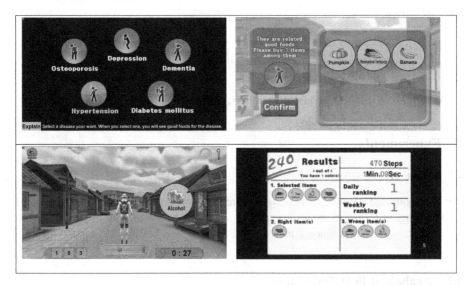

Fig. 1. Game Interface of 'Paldokangsan3': (1) first screen of selecting a desease(up-left), (2) mission screen for target items to buy in the market street(up-right), (3) play screen showing the avatar and the item of the store in the market street with no.steps, and duration time (down-left), (4) final score screen of the player at the end of each level (down-right)

The game has three levels. The first level is to remember three items with half round, and the second level is to remember four items with another half round. And the final level is to remember six items with another full round of the market place.

3.3 Game Interface – Kinect

Using Kinect, it becomes so easy to control the game with just a gesture. We have asked the old to walk in a small circle to count the steps, to use right hand to traverse in the menu, and to use left hand for selection and confirmation. Also we have added a gesture of remembering the mission and gesture of discarding a wrong item for the usage of the coin in the game.

One of the biggest benefits of using the Kinect interface is the business model. If the player has the Kinect and PC with big monitor or TV which can be connected to PC, he or she can download the software online to use them in the own environment.

3.4 Score of the Game

The score is an important factor for the player to get feedback from the game. When the player has finished each level of the game, the score would be given at the end for at least 10 s (Fig. 1(4)):

$$Score = (no.\ of\ correct\ items) * K_1 - (no.\ of\ wrong\ items) * K_2 + (no.\ of\ coins) * K_3$$
$$+ (standard\ time - duration\ time) * K_4.$$

Where K_1, K_2, K_3, K_4: constant numbers, time unit: s.

4 Experiments

4.1 First Test (2013)

We have collected 25 volunteers of ages more than 65 year old (20 women and 5 men) for the game in Cheonan senior community center in Korea to play the game once a day for total of 10 days since 8th Nov. 2013.

4.2 Analysis of First Test (2013)

The data was collected in the game machine accumulating automatically when the game played. And they were analyzed statistically to find correlation between several factors using SPSS with T-test.

The number of times of playing the game is found to be deeply correlated to most factors with the confidence of 95 % as in the Table 1 (by **). The score was increased while the duration time was decreased with the number of times of the play. That meant the most player could memorize better, and finish the mission faster as the number of play increased.

That means that the more repetition, the more correct and faster accomplishment.

In the previous work [6], the adaptation of the game and vicariousness for the avatar improved correspondingly through the game with the confidence of 99 % and 95 % respectively. And memorization of good foods for some diseases increased with confidence of 95 % but for the general memorization of the player was not proved to have the confidential relationship. The analysis showed also the self-esteem has been increased after the game with the confidence of 99 %.

Table 1. Correlations of factors of 25 players (number of times of the game, average score of each level, average duration time of each level, average number of steps of each level and average number of steps per second)

		No. times	Score			Avg. score	Avg. duration time	Avg. no. step/sec
			Level 1	Level 2	Level 3			
No. times		1						
Score	Level 1	0.461**	1					
	Level 2	0.439**	0.519**	1				
	Level 3	0.309**	0.276**	0.494**	1			
Average score		0.623**	0.721**	0.793**	0.787**	1		
Duration time	Level 1	−0.664**	−0.626**	−0.524**	−0.313**	−0.692**		
	Level 2	−0.244**	−0.214**	−0.167**	−0.101	−0.270**		
	Level 3	−0.207**	−0.188	−0.013	0.005	−0.060		
Avg. dur. time		−0.531**	−0.537**	−0.431**	−0.186*	−0.552**	1	
No. steps/s	Level 1	0.511**	0.577**	0.433**	0.240**	0.576**	−0.756**	
	Level 2	0.504**	0.411**	0.439**	0.263**	0.504**	−0.720**	
	Level 3	0.387**	0.260**	0.048	0.306**	0.268**	−0.737**	
Avg. no. steps/s		0.554**	0.546**	0.434**	0.311**	0.590**	−0.818**	1

**Confidence of 0.95

4.3   Usability Test (2014)

Usability elements has been classified in 8 areas: if control is easy (easiness), if it's not hard to learn how to control it (learnability), etc. as in Table 2.

This game machine was installed in a senior house in Asan for one month that the old could play the game as they like in the house. It was because it was secured from visitors outside that they have plenty of time to check and investigate the machine on their own.

However the habitants were small that just 8 persons were collected as volunteers among 20 persons of total habitants. We decided to continue our tests with the research of Nielsen [23] that the results of at least 5 participants were found similar to big participants, and the research of Todd and Benbasat [24] that the evaluation of human satisfaction was possible with 2–20 small samples because the amount of information collected through the analysis of language protocol were so abundant.

The participants of our second experiment were in ages from 60 to 88. Most of them were men with little education background and were suffering mild cognition impairments without any personal families.

Table 2. Questionnaire for usability evaluation (2014)

Area	No	Contents
Easiness of game control	Q1	Has the walk recognized well?
	Q2	Has the arm motion recognized well?
	Q3	Was the game good to control as you want?
	Q4	Could you see if your choice was correct or not?
Learnability of game play	Q5	Was it easy to understand how to control the game?
	Q6	Could you remember easily to the method to control the game?
Memorability	Q7	Was the game helpful to remember good foods for a specified disease?
	Q8	Was the game helpful for your normal memorization ability?
Challenge	Q9	Did you think you would like to the game do better next time?
	Q10	Did you feel to continue to play the game for the next level?
Efficiency	Q11	Has it got easier to play the game as you repeat the game?
Tension	Q12	Could you be concentrated on the game in the process of it?
Familiarity	Q13	Was the background of the game familiar to you?
	Q14	Did you feel the avatar just like you in the game?
Satisfaction	Q15	Was the game good to play continuously?
	Q16	Was tie game interesting to play?

4.4   Analysis of Usability Test (2014)

Most participants played 2–3 times a day for a month even though most of them were suffering mild cognition impairment. They showed good subjective satisfactions in their interviews also.

The result of questionnaire in Table 2 is shown in Table 3. They were checked after 1st week and 2nd weeks. Table 3 describes: as time goes on, learnability, memorability, challenge, tension and satisfaction gets lower while easiness, efficiency and familiarity gets up. To analyze the result in average value, the scores of tension and satisfaction were very high. That means there were no difficulties in concentration and immersion in the game play with higher satisfaction with new stimulus of computer game.

Figures 2, 3 and 4 shows daily average scores for each level of the game, daily average duration time of the play, and total number of players in a day for each. X-axis is for date and Y-axis for values (LV: level of the game in the figures). They have been collected for 1 month without naming the players. They shows steady increase of scores with small variations, and decrease of duration time also.

Table 3. Result of usability test (We tried twice: 1st week later and 2nd week later)

Area	1 week later	2 weeks later	Change	Average
Easiness	3.47	3.88	Up	3.68
Learnability	3.94	3.38	Down	3.66
Memorability	3.88	3.63	Down	3.76
Challenge	4.00	3.75	Down	3.88
Efficiency	3.75	4.00	Up	3.88
Tension	4.13	4.00	Down	4.07
Familiarity	3.50	3.50	No	3.50
Satisfaction	4.44	4.13	Down	4.29

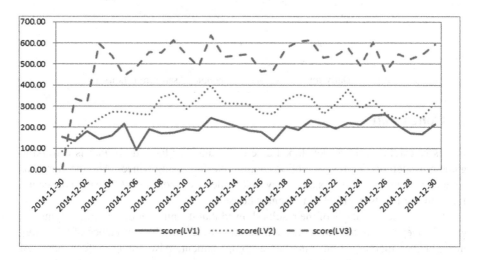

Fig. 2. Daily average scores for each level (Asan senior house)

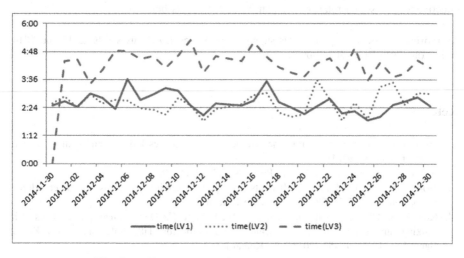

Fig. 3. Daily average duration times (Asan senior house)

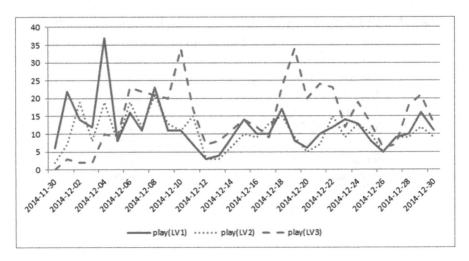

Fig. 4. Daily total no. of plays (8 people, Asan senior house)

5   Conclusion

In this research, we have developed a serious game for the elderly that is a walking game plus memorization with motion capture interface using Kinect. And the game has been tested twice: first for its efficiency to 25 elderly of more than 65 years old, second for usability test to 8 elderly in a senior house.

The statistical analysis of the results showed that the number of times of playing the game is deeply correlated to scores and duration time with the confidence of 99 % that means better memorization with fast accomplishment. Also for the effectiveness of concentration and vitality of the participants, we had good confidence of 95 %.

We found also the game was good enough to collect people as galleries that another effectiveness of social relationship can be added for its benefits.

Acknowledgments. This project was supported by Hoseo University's FRC 2013 and 2014 project (no: 2013-0125, 2014-0092).

References

1. 2014 White Paper on Korean Games Guide to Koran Games Industry and Culture. Korea Content Agency (2014)
2. Abt, C.C.: Serious Games. Viking Press, New York (1970)
3. Jeon, H.K., Kim, M.Y.: The benefits of aquatic exercise programs for older adults. J. Coaching Dev. **5**(2), 69–76 (2003). (In Korean)
4. Kim, K.-S., Oh, S.-S., Ahn, J.-H., Lee, S.-H., Lim, K.-C.: Development and analysis of a walking game using controllers of armrests and footboards (Title: Paldokangsan). J. Korea Game Soc. **11**(6), 43–52 (2011). (In Korean)

5. Kim, K.-S., Oh, S.-S., Ahn, J.-H., Lee, S.-H., Lim, K.-C.: Development and analysis of walking game using controllers of hand buttons and footboards (Title: Paldokangsan2). J. Korea Game Soc. **13**(3), 95–104 (2011). (In Korean)
6. Kim, K.-S., Lee, Y.-J., Oh, S.-S.: Development and analysis of walking game 'Paldokangsan3' using kinect. J. Korea Game Soc. **14**(1), 49–57 (2014). (in Korean)
7. Nielsen, J.: Designing Web Usability: The Practice of Simplicity, Indianapolis. New Riders Publishing, Indiana USA (2000)
8. http://taikopsp3.namco-ch.net/
9. http://www.namcobandaigames.com/
10. Tach, D.: Video Game Uses Kinect to Help Stroke Patients Walk, Kyushu University, Asahi Shinbun, 27 November 2012
11. Gerling, K.M., Masuch, M.: Exploring the potential of gamification among frail elderly persons. In: CHI 2011 Workshop on Gamification, Vancouver, BC, Canada
12. Wouters, P., Van der Spek, E., Van Oostendorp, H.: Current practices in serious game research: a review from a learning outcomes perspective. In: Connolly, T. (ed.) Games-Based Learning Advancements for Multi-sensory Human Computer Interfaces: Techniques and Effective Practices, pp. 232–250. IGI Global, Hershey (2009)
13. Seo, J.-M.: A design consideration element and serious game for disabled person. Korea Soc. Comput. Inf. **16**(1), 81–87 (2011). (In Korean)
14. Ryu, W., Kang, H., Kim, H.: Development of personal training system using serious game for rehabilitation training. J. Korea Game Soc. **9**(3), 121–128 (2009). (In Korean)
15. Ok, S., Kim, D.: Serious game design for rehabilitation training with infrared ray pen. J. Korea Game Soc. **9**(6), 151–161 (2009). (In Korean)
16. He, G.F., Woong, J., Kang, S., Jung, S.: Development of gesture recognition-based 3D serious games. J. Korea Game Soc. **11**(6), 103–113 (2011). (In Korean)
17. Lee, Y.-J., Ahn, J.-H., Lim, K.-C.: Analysis of the needs of middle and elder generation on serious game for the elderly. J. Korea Contents Assoc. **9**(10), 1–27 (2009)
18. Kim, K-S., Oh, S-S., Ahn, J-H., Lee, S-H.: Development of a walking game for the elderly using controllers of hand buttons and foot boards. In: Proceedings of the 17th International Computer Games Conference (CGAMES), Louisville, pp. 158–161 (2012)
19. Lee, S.-B., Baik, Y.-J., Nam, K.-C., Ahn, J.-H., Lee, Y.-J., Oh, S.-S., Kim, K.-S.: Developing a cognitive evaluation method for serious game engineers. Cluster Comput. **17**(3), 757–766 (2014). The Journal of Networks, Software Tools and Application. Print ISSN 1386-7857. Springer US
20. Ball, K., Wadley, V.G., Edwards, J.D.: Advances in technology used to assess and retrain older drivers. Gerontechnology **1**(4), 251–261 (2002)
21. Sekuler, A.B., Bennett, P.J., Mamelak, M.: Effects of aging on the useful field of view. Exp. Aging Res. **26**(2), 103–120 (2000)
22. Wikipedia (2014). http://en.wikipedia.org/wiki/Useful_field_of_view
23. Nielsen, J.: Why you only need to test with 5 users. Alertbox, Nielsen Norman Group (2000)
24. Todd, P., Benbasat, I.: An experimental investigation of the impact of computer based decision aids on decision making strategies. Inf. Syst. Res. **2**, 87–115 (1991)

Assistance for Older Adults in Serious Game Using an Interactive System

Minh Khue Phan Tran[1,2,3(✉)], François Bremond[1], and Philippe Robert[2]

[1] Stars, Inria, Sophia Antipolis, France
Francois.Bremond@inria.fr
[2] CoBTek Cognition Behaviour Technology EA 7276, Research Center Edmond and Lily Safra, University of Nice Sophia Antipolis, Nice, France
probert@unice.fr
[3] Genious Interactive, 3ter rue des Pins, Montpellier, France
m.phantran@genious.com

Abstract. Serious Games offer a new way to older adults to improve various abilities such as the vision, the balance or the memory. However, cognitive impairment causes a lot of difficulties to them when actively practicing these games. Their engagement and motivation are reduced rapidly when encountering successive problems without any help. In this paper, we present an approach to assist older adults in Serious Game using an interactive system. Three groups of players with different cognitive impairments (Mnesic Plaint, MCI and Alzheimer) have been tested with the system in a concentration-based game. As the experimental results, the players performed a high performance when playing with the assistance of the system, especially among Alzheimer group. The future work aims to perform this approach with a larger population and explore other factors which can influence on the players' motivation.

1 Introduction

In recent years, many researches proved that the video game, renamed under a special term «serious game», can boost mental skills for older adults [1, 2]. Moreover, many projects offer games in some specific problematics of them [3, 4].

This new technology can maintain motivation and improve engagement's player. However, there is a paradox among the older players: they could quickly discourage because of many difficulties due to lack of game culture or their fragile memory. Consequently, they cannot play alone and could abandon the game after a short use. The big challenge here is actively keeping them in game as long as possible by maintaining permanently their motivation and their engagement. For that, detecting their motivation level is necessary for determining the moment to help them.

The paper is organized as follows. In Sect. 2, we make an overview of many approaches related to player's engagement and motivation. Section 3 describes in details our approach. In Sect. 4, we present an experimental application of the system with 30 persons presenting the cognitive impairment (Mnesic, MCI and Alzheimer) through a concentration-based game. In the last section, we discuss a conclusion and future works to be presented later.

© Springer International Publishing Switzerland 2016
A. De Gloria and R. Veltkamp (Eds.): GALA 2015, LNCS 9599, pp. 286–291, 2016.
DOI: 10.1007/978-3-319-40216-1_30

2   Related Work

In the case of the use of gamification into the non-gaming context [5], intrinsic motivation and extrinsic motivation [6] exist together. But when the player is an older adult, intrinsic motivation is more important than extrinsic motivation.

Some works have been conducted to adjust the game design [7, 8] and the gameplay [9] as well as introduce new devices [10, 11] in the games. Also, a new source of motivation through the robot is slowly exploited. In Japan, animal therapy has been replaced by robot therapy in assisted activities [12] as well as improvement and prevention dementia for older adults. In the case of cognitive training, a socially assistive robot in [13] has been tested with patients with dementia in a specific music cognitive-base game. Some systems in Human-Machine Interaction estimate the attention's level of the user based on various factors such as face's orientation [14] or several backchannels' behaviours [15].

However, these approaches do not handle the difficulties generated by cognitive impairment such as lack of memory or distraction during the game. They cannot recognize the moment that the older players are distracted when they realize many wrong handlings or forgets the rules and do not know how to continue to play.

3   Interactive System

We have proposed an interactive system in order to provide several assistances to older adults. In [16], the proposed system interacts with the user in terms of his movements and his position in the related zones. In this paper, the system will focus on the gestures performed by older adults when they are playing the game in order to determine the situation for giving him help.

Figure 1 describes the structure of the interactive system, which is a combination of two modules: Recognition Module and Interaction Module. Thanks to the Kinect camera of Microsoft and the supplied Kinect SDK, the Recognition Module tracks and recognizes the player's gestures then sends them to the Interaction Module. The last one collects these information and combines with game states provided by the game in order to determine the type of interaction with the player through a 3D animated avatar. Here, the avatar can move, realize many expressions and give the verbal communications to player. The interest of a virtual avatar is demonstrated in the literature. Indeed, he can bring to players a feeling of companion [17], increase his attention and his sympathy [18] and more importantly, improve his interaction with the system [19].

4   Experiment

The aim of this experiment is to evaluate the efficiency of the proposed system for keeping actively the players in the game. Three groups of ten older adults, categorized by their cognitive state (Mnesic plaint, MCI, Alzheimer), are solicited, by the doctor, to perform a cognitive training session through a game during their memory consultation.

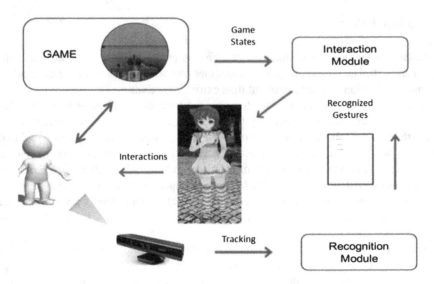

Fig. 1. Structure of the interactive system

Our hypothesis is that the proposed system can improve their performance as well as possible during the game.

4.1 Protocol

The session takes place in a private room, equipped with a screen, a game with Camera Kinect (Fig. 2) and the presence of a therapist. Each session lasts approximately 20 min. In short, there are three phases of the game:

- *Phase 1:* the player learns rapidly how to play the game with the therapist.
- *Phase 2:* the player plays the game alone without any helps.
- *Phase 3:* the player plays the game with the avatar's assistances.

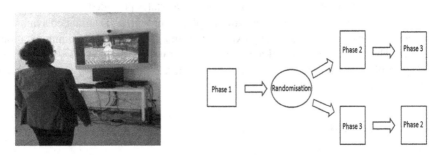

Fig. 2. Player interacts with the avatar   **Fig. 3.** Order of the phases for each player

The order of phases for one session is as follows: all the players begin with phase 1. Then, a randomization is made to determine between phase 2 and 3 in which one if the players continue as described in Fig. 3.

Players' performance is collected only in phase 2 and 3. It's presented by:

- Playing time of a phase: the duration when the players start the phase until the end of the phase.
- Score for the current phase.

4.2 Adaptation of System

In this experimentation, we designed the game in the simple manner so that the players can browse the menu, choose the level, follow the tutorial and play the game by only raising hands (left/right). Moreover, we elaborated all of communication texts with a psychologist in order to create a positive ambiance and encourage the players. In addition, we provide 3 types of assistance to the players:

- *Assistance against inactivity*: when the players do not interact with the game or the avatar for a while, the avatar recalls the players' attention and gives some expected guidelines according to the current game state.
- *Assistance against errors*: during the game, if the players make a lot of errors, the avatar supposes that they can forget the rules then recall them.
- *Assistance for tutorial*: when the players desire to realize a tutorial before playing the game, the avatar guides them basing on their gestures.

4.3 Experimental Results

Obviously, the players always finish the game and have a play time which is shorter in phase 3 than in phase 2 (Figs. 4 and 5). More importantly, two players in Alzheimer group abandon the game in phase 2. Indeed, without any help, the players spend much time to recall the rules of game, while in phase 3, thanks to the assistance against inactivity the players can continue and finish the game. The case of two abandoned players emphasizes the interest of assistance against inactivity. Their motivation tumbles down quickly when they cannot remember the rules of game.

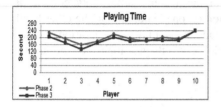 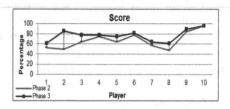

Fig. 4. The results of MCI group in phase 2 and phase 3

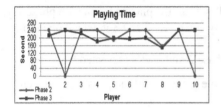 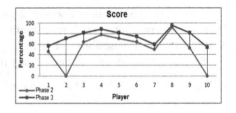

Fig. 5. The results of Alzheimer group in phase 2 and phase 3

The score of the players benefits also the assistance of system (Figs. 4 and 5). Thanks to the assistance against errors, the players can reduce the number of errors. Especially, Alzheimer group had a score more important than other groups.

In order to understand how the players appreciate the assistance of the system, we asked a short questionnaire at the end of each training session, concerning various characteristics of the avatar (voice, communication's text, appearance, animation and intervention). All of the players agree that avatar's voice is clear and the communication is understandable. 27 players think that the appearance is pleasant and the other three find it normal. Moreover, avatar's animation is judged natural by 26 players, normal by 2 players and still factice by the last two. Globally, the players appreciate positively the avatar as well as its interactions during the game.

5   Discussion and Conclusion

In this paper, we proposed an assistive system for older adults with the Serious Game. Because of the decline of their cognitive functionalities, they have a lot of difficulties to perform a successful session. They need real-time assistance. The more they are helped, the longer their motivation is maintained. An experiment was conducted with 30 older players categorized by their diagnostic (Mnesic Plaint, MCI and Alzheimer) during the memory consultation. The proposed system aims to maintain their motivation by keeping them actively and improving their performance during a cognitive training game. Therefore, the system uses a 3D animated avatar to give assistances (recalls, guidelines) according to the inactivity and the number of errors. As the experimental results, the players realized a high performance and use effectively the rules and guidelines of the game thanks to the assistances of the avatar. Future work consists in confirming these results with a larger population on one hand, and on the other hand, analysing more precisely the reason of errors made by the players. In addition, it could be also interesting to explore more factors which can influence their motivation (e.g. gameplay, music, new kind of assistance).

References

1. Belchior, P.D.C.: Cognitive training with video games to improve driving skills and driving safety among older adults. Dissertation Abs. Int. **68**(9-B) (2007)

2. Anguera, J.A., Boccanfuso, J., Rintoul, J.L., Al-Hashimi, O., Faraji, F., Janowich, J., Gazzaley, A.: Video game training enhances cognitive control in older adults. Nature **501**(7465), 97–101 (2013)
3. VERVE project. http://verveconsortium.eu/
4. Az@Game project. http://www.azagame.fr/
5. Sebastian, D., Miguel, S., Lennart, N., Kenton, O., Dan, D.: Gamification: using game-design elements in non-gaming contexts. In: CHI 2011 Extended Abstracts on Human Factors in Computing Systems, Canada (2011)
6. Deci, E.L., Ryan, M.R.: Intrinsic Motivation and Self-determination in Human Behavior. Springer, New York (1985)
7. Bouchard, B., Imbeault, F., Bouzouane, A., Menelas, B.-A.J.: Developing serious games specifically adapted to people suffering from alzheimer. In: Ma, M., Oliveira, M.F., Hauge, J.B., Duin, H., Thoben, K.-D. (eds.) SGDA 2012. LNCS, vol. 7528, pp. 243–254. Springer, Heidelberg (2012)
8. Ji-won, L., Seong-jun, P.: A study on interface design of serious game for the elderly. Adv. Sci. Technol. Lett. **39**, 159–163 (2013)
9. Tong, T., Chignell, M., Lam, P., Tierney, M.C., Lee, J.: Designing serious games for cognitive assessment of the elderly. In: Proceedings of the International Symposium of Human Factors and Ergonomics in Healthcare, vol. 3, pp. 28–35. SAGE Publications (2014)
10. Kretschmann, R., Dittus, I., Lutz, I., Meier, C.: Nintendo Wii sports: simple gadget or serious measure for health promotion? – A pilot study according to the energy expenditure, movement extent, and student perceptions. In: Proceedings of the GameDays 2010 – Serious Games for Sports and Health, Darmstadt, pp. 147–159 (2010)
11. Webster, D., Celik, O.: Systematic review of kinect applications in elderly care and stroke rehabilitation. J. Neuroeng. Rehabil. **11**(1), 108 (2014)
12. Wada, K., Shibata, T., Saito, T., Tanie, K.: Effects of robot assisted activity for elderly people and nurses at a day service center. Proc. IEEE **92**(11), 1780–1788 (2004)
13. Tapus, A., Matari, M.J.: The use of socially assistive robots in the design of intelligent cognitive therapies for people with dementia. In: IEEE International Conference on Rehabilitation Robotics, pp. 924–929 (2009)
14. Ishii, R., Nakano, Y.I., Nishida, T.: Gaze awareness in conversational agents: estimating auser's conversational engagement from eye gaze. ACM Trans. Interact. Intell. Syst. (TiiS) **3**(2), 11 (2013)
15. Vinciarelli, A., Pantic, M., Heylen, D., Pelachaud, C., Poggi, I., D'Errico, F., Schroeder, M.: Bridging the gap between social animal and unsocial machine: a survey of social signal processing. IEEE Trans. Affect. Comput. **3**, 69–87 (2012)
16. Minh Khue, P.T., François, B., Philippe, R.: Comment intéresser les personnes âgées aux Serious Game? In: JA-SFTAG 2014, France (2014)
17. Morandell, M.M., Hochgatterer, A., Fagel, S., Wassertheurer, S.: Avatars in assistive homes for the elderly. In: Holzinger, A. (ed.) USAB 2008. LNCS, vol. 5298, pp. 391–402. Springer, Heidelberg (2008)
18. Vardoulakis, L.P., Ring, L., Barry, B., Sidner, C.L., Bickmore, T.: Designing relational agents as long term social companions for older adults. In: Nakano, Y., Neff, M., Paiva, A., Walker, M. (eds.) IVA 2012. LNCS, vol. 7502, pp. 289–302. Springer, Heidelberg (2012)
19. Ortiz, A., del Puy Carretero, M., Oyarzun, D., Yanguas, J.J., Buiza, C., Gonzalez, M., Etxeberria, I.: Elderly users in ambient intelligence: does an avatar improve the interaction? In: Stephanidis, C., Pieper, M. (eds.) ERCIM Ws UI4ALL 2006. LNCS, vol. 4397, pp. 99–114. Springer, Heidelberg (2007)

Padua Rehabilitation Tool: A Pilot Study on Patients with Dementia

Stefano Cardullo[1,2(✉)], Pes Maria Valeria[3], Tognon Ilaria[3],
Pesenti Ambra[1,2], Luciano Gamberini[1,2], and Daniela Mapelli[1,2]

[1] Department of Psychology, University of Padova, Padua, Italy
stefano.cardullo@gmail.com
[2] Human Inspired Technology Research Centre (HIT),
University of Padova, Padua, Italy
[3] Centro Residenziale per Anziani, Cittadella, PD, Italy

Abstract. Over the past 20 years, research led to the development of new technologies to improve the quality of life of brain damaged patients. One of these technologies used for cognitive rehabilitation is the tablet devices. Here we present the results of the first iPad application for cognitive rehabilitation specifically designed and developed for Italian patients with acquired brain deficits, comparing three different treatment conditions. The results obtained reveal good level of appreciation and efficacy both in cognitive and in neuropsychiatric domain for the patients that used the Padua Rehabilitation Tool.

Keywords: iPad-based rehabilitation · Cognitive rehabilitation · Serious games · Dementia

1 Introduction

In the last decade we are witnessing a non-stop process in the development of new technologies. Rapidly new tools such as tablet devices are widely diffused among population and allow us to think about new generation of solutions in different domains of interest. One of these domains is the field of cognitive rehabilitation as part of neuropsychological rehabilitation.

At the most fundamental level, people undergoing cognitive rehabilitation require help to remediate, reduce or alleviate their cognitive deficits [1]. Sohlberg and Mateer (1989) [2] say that "Cognitive rehabilitation ... refers to the therapeutic process of increasing or improving an individual's capacity to process and use incoming information so as to allow increased functioning in everyday life" (p. 3). Cognitive rehabilitation can have the goal of intervening on: (1) disability, seeking to stimulate and improve altered functions by direct action on these functions (restoration), (2) promoting the use of alternative mechanisms or of preserved skills (compensation), or (3) using different strategies to help minimize problems resulting from the dysfunction (replacement) [3]. Moreover, considering that people with brain injury are likely to have a number of associated problems such as anxiety, depression, and difficulties with communication and social interaction, we need to address all these additional problems in the rehabilitation program.

© Springer International Publishing Switzerland 2016
A. De Gloria and R. Veltkamp (Eds.): GALA 2015, LNCS 9599, pp. 292–301, 2016.
DOI: 10.1007/978-3-319-40216-1_31

The background concept of neuropsychological rehabilitation is the neural plasticity. Years of research have demonstrated the capacity of the Central Nervous System (CNS) to functionally and structurally adapt in response to experience. Despite the assumption that changes in brain network can occur only in specific and critical periods, now we adopt the idea of a permanently plastic brain [4, 5]. Plasticity is not an occasional state of the nervous system; instead, it is the normal ongoing state of the nervous system throughout the life span [6]. Starting from this assumption the field of cognitive rehabilitation has begun to use this body of evidence to develop therapies that harness the key behavioral and neural signals that drive neural plasticity [7]. Literature has shown how technology could be a useful tool to achieve this aim and how the rapidly development of new technologies had an important impact on cognitive rehabilitation.

One of the most used technologies for rehabilitation is the Virtual Reality (VR). VR typically refers to the use of interactive simulations created with computer hardware and software to present users with opportunities to engage in environments that appear and feel similar to real world objects and events [8, 9]. Users interact with displayed images, move and manipulate virtual objects and perform other actions in a way that attempts to "immerse" them within the simulated environment thereby engendering a feeling of "presence" in the virtual world [10].

In the last few decades the VR field is transitioning into work influenced by video games. Because much of the research and development being conducted in the games community parallels the VR community's efforts, it has the potential to affect a greater audience. Given these trends, VR researchers who want their work to remain relevant must realign to focus on game research and development [11]. These changes led to the development of Serious Games.

While the rationale for the majority of games developed for consoles or PCs is purely entertainment, recreation or winning a stake, we can define serious games as: "a mental contest, played with a computer in accordance with specific rules, that uses entertainment to further government or corporate training, education, health, public policy, and strategic communication objectives." [11]. Clearly health care is one of the major application domain for introduce the concept of games designed for a serious purpose other than pure entertainment [12]. Computerized training programs could offer a more flexible, personalized approach to traditional cognitive training programs; they provide real-time performance feedback and can adjust to the user's ability level, keeping the activity engaging and fun. Computer and video games are designed to be fun and exciting and may provide motivation for the patients of all ages to adhere to the training program [13, 14]. This is possible thanks to a gamification process that transforms the normal rehabilitation exercises in more exciting and fun tasks. As result people get more chances to maintain higher interest on rehabilitation over time, even if we deal with elderly [15, 16]. Different applications of serious games have shown their benefits in cognitive rehabilitation for a various kind of patients [17–25]. Virtual environments can provide safe and customizable training, which can be tailored to the specific needs of each different patient. Moreover is possible to constantly monitor and analyze the user performance. Despite these important benefits the majority of VR system requires high cost technologies, they are large and difficult to move and require a specialist expertise to set up and operate. These factors prohibit such systems from being usable in some clinical environment and for home rehabilitation. Thanks to the advent of new technologies, such as the tablet devices, it is possible to go beyond these limits developing new kind of serious game and application for cognitive rehabilitation. Recently the efforts of researchers and clinician led to the development of new programs that use the tablet devices proving good results in rehabilitation [26–32]. Due to the lack of specific tablet application for cognitive rehabilitation in Italian language we designed and developed the first software for patients with acquired brain injury independently from their etiology: the "Padua Rehabilitation Tool (PRT)".

Here we present a pilot study to evaluate the possible effects of the use of PRT in patients with dementia comparing three treatment conditions: traditional, iPad based, and no treatment.

2 Methods

2.1 Participants

Fifteen patients with diagnosis of dementia (Mean age: 81; SD age: 8,6; 5 males) were recruited in an Italian residential center for elderly. Inclusion criteria were: age greater than 65, Clinical Dementia Rating Scale [33] score equal to 1 or 2, Mini Mental State Examination (MMSE) [34] score between 19 and 25 and the ability to use at least one upper limb. The patients were randomly assigned to the three treatment conditions: (1) no treatment, (2) traditional paper and pencil, (3) iPad based. The groups were not significantly different for age ($F_{2,12} = .099$, $p = .906$), education ($F_{2,12} = .035$, $p = .965$) and MMSE score ($F_{2,12} = .811$, $p = .468$). Refer to Table 1 for group and total sample descriptive statistics of age, education and MMSE score.

Table 1. Descriptive statistics of age, education and MMSE (t0)

| | | N | Mean | Std. Deviation | Std. Error | 95% Confidence Interval for Mean | | Min | Max |
						Lower Bound	Upper Bound		
AGE	iPad	5	81,80	10,83	4,84	68,36	95,24	66,0	92,0
	Traditional	5	82,80	8,23	3,68	72,58	93,02	70,0	91,0
	no treatment	5	80,20	8,64	3,87	69,47	90,93	68,0	91,0
	Total	15	81,60	8,68	2,24	76,79	86,41	66,0	92,0
EDUCATION	iPad	5	6,20	3,90	1,74	1,36	11,04	3,0	13,0
	Traditional	5	6,40	3,13	1,40	2,51	10,29	5,0	12,0
	no treatment	5	6,80	3,83	1,71	2,04	11,56	4,0	13,0
	Total	15	6,47	3,38	0,87	4,60	8,34	3,0	13,0
MMSE	iPad	5	22,24	1,90	0,85	19,88	24,60	20,4	24,0
	Traditional	5	22,66	2,09	0,93	20,07	25,25	19,3	24,0
	no treatment	5	21,22	1,48	0,66	19,38	23,06	19,4	22,7
	Total	15	22,04	1,81	0,47	21,04	23,04	19,3	24,0

2.2   Treatment Conditions

The patients were divided into three different treatment conditions: (1) no treatment, (2) traditional paper and pencil, (3) iPad based.

Patients in the no treatment conditions during five weeks followed the normal activity planned by the institution such as reading newspapers, watching TV, playing cards and more.

Patients in the traditional treatment conditions four times a week for five weeks (20 sessions) used classic paper and pencil materials for rehabilitation. They were engaged in exercises for different cognitive domains. This type of materials proved to be effective for cognitive rehabilitation [35]. The sessions were individual and each one lasted about one hour.

In the iPad based treatment condition patients used the "Padua Rehabilitation Tool" (PRT) for rehabilitation four times a week for five weeks (20 sessions). Each session lasted about one hour. The PRT consists of 35 exercises of cognitive stimulation grouped into the various functions involved: attention, memory, language, logic reasoning, recognition, orientation and motor control (Figs. 1 and 2).

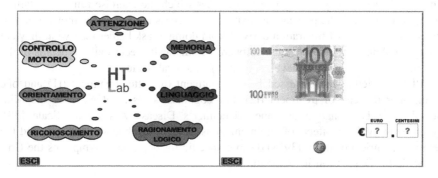

Fig. 1. Screenshots of "Padua Rehabilitation Tool".

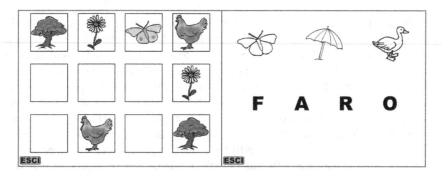

Fig. 2. Screenshots of "Padua Rehabilitation Tool".

The software runs on Apple© iPad® and it is built using Adobe® Flash Professional CC© with ActionScript 3.0 code (air for iOS). Thanks to the different cognitive domains involved in the exercises is possible to develop specific treatment programs tailored to the cognitive impairments of each user. Thus the PRT can be administered to patients independently from the acquired pathology (brain vascular disease, traumatic brain injury, neurodegenerative deficits, etc.). Given the importance of the link between learning mechanics and game mechanics [36], specific attention was paid during the developing phase of this tool. The PRT was designed with a simple interface and the stimuli used are not complex in order to allow an easy interaction to all the users. All the tasks utilize the same method of response ("tap gesture") after which a visual and auditory feedback is given to the participant both in case of correct or incorrect response. Accordingly to the errorless learning approach [37], is very important to avoid the implicit learning of errors during the performance. Because of that a feedback (positive or negative) must always given to the patient. The exercises consist of levels of increasingly difficulty. The main variables that vary are the number of stimuli, time of presentation, complexity of stimuli or scene, colors or shape of stimuli. Only one variable at time is modified to increase the difficulty of the exercise. In case of correct response the exercise automatically goes to the next level. In case of error the patients can retry the same level up to three times, after which the exercise runs out. Starting with a very easy task the patients can experience success increasing the motivation and decreasing the sense of frustration derived from doing a task harder than what they are able to do. After each response the software automatically record all the details of the performance (time response, level, score, ...) in a local database.

All the patients were assessed before treatment (t0) after treatment (t1) and one month after the end of treatment (t2). For cognitive assessment we used the Mini Mental State Examination and the Alzheimer's Disease Assessment Scale [38]. Moreover to evaluate effects of treatment in associated psychopathology we used the Neuropsychiatric Inventory [39] and more specific for depression symptoms the Cornell Scale for Depression in Dementia [40].

3   Results

Given the structure of the observed data, we used a mixed-effects model approach. The most important advantage of mixed-effects models is that they allow the researcher to simultaneously consider all factors that potentially contribute to the understanding of the structure of the data [41]. These factors comprise not only the standard fixed-effects factors controlled by the experimenter (in our case, time and group) but also the random-effects factors, in other words, factors whose levels are drawn at random from a population (in our case, patients). We used R (R Core Team, 2014) and package *lme4* [42] to perform a linear mixed effect analysis of the relationship between our dependent variables (MMSE, ADAS, NPI, CORNELL), times and groups. For each measure we used three models: a null one (m0) with only the random effect (intercept for patients), another one (m1) with the random effect and as fixed effects the time and group variables, and the last one (m2) with the random effect and as fixed effect the interaction between time and group. P-values were obtained by likelihood ratio tests of the full model with the effect in question (m2) against the other two models. We report here only the cases where the full model was significantly better to explain the observed data.

As can be seen in Table 2 for Mini Mental State Examination the full model revealed a significantly effect of the interaction between time and group $\chi^2(4) = 20.85$, $p < .001$.

Table 2. Results of comparison between different linear mixed effect models for MMSE

	AIC	BIC	χ^2	Df	p value
m0	240,66	246,09			
m1	235,25	247,9	13,41	4	0,009
m2	222,39	242,27	20,85	4	< 0,001

How can be seen in Fig. 3 the no treatment group had a significantly different performance during time compared with the other two groups. No differences were observed between the traditional treatment and the iPad group.

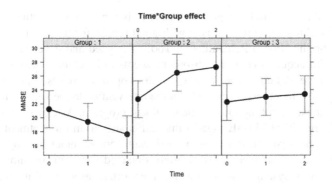

Fig. 3. Plot of the full model effects (MMSE)

Similar results were obtained for Neuropsychiatric Inventory (Frequency × Severity) (Table 3) where the full model revealed a significantly effect of the interaction between time and group $\chi^2(4) = 11.09$, p = .025. Even in this case the no treatment group had an opposite trend of results compared with the other two groups.

Table 3. Results of comparison between different linear mixed effect models for NPI (Frequency × Severity)

	AIC	BIC	χ^2	Df	p value
m0	344,59	350,01			
m1	342,97	355,62	9,62	4	0,047
m2	339,88	359,75	11,09	4	0,025

Moreover the traditional treatment group maintained the results one month after the end of treatment while the iPad group did not (Fig. 4).

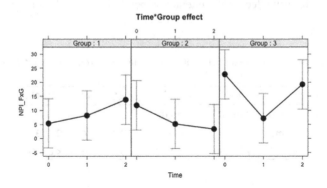

Fig. 4. Plot of the full model effects (NPI)

4   Discussion

The results of this pilot study suggest that, as already reported in literature [26, 27], the tablet device technology could be used with good results for the cognitive rehabilitation. In specific the "Padua Rehabilitation Tool", designed and developed specifically for patients with acquired cognitive disorders, seems to be efficacy with patients with neurodegenerative deficits. The variety of developed exercises and the different involved cognitive functions permit to tailor the intervention to the specific needs of the patients and adjust from time to time the treatment program. As expected by previous study [35] the results at MMSE suggest that, differently from no treatment group, the traditional treatment condition lead to a significantly improvement in cognitive functioning of patients. Moreover the iPad group obtained same results showing us the potentiality of this system. One of the most important aspects of treatment is the generalization to other aspect of daily life and not only in the specific cognitive functioning. People with cognitive impairment may have additional problems that should also be addressed in rehabilitation programs. The results at Neuropsychiatric Inventory suggest that the iPad treatment could have important results also in associate psychopathology. The demise of these results one month after the end of treatment could be explained by the small size of our sample: even changes in only one patient could counterbalance the small effect of the other patients. Actually one patient of the iPad group had an important worsening in medical conditions after the end of treatment. This led to an increase of symptoms of apathy and depression. The small size could also explain why in the other scales were not observed significantly results. For this reason one of the first purposes for the future is to enlarge the sample in order to get stronger conclusion by our results.

Furthermore the patients have shown interest and curiosity about the proposed treatment with PRT. They found it easy to use and engaging; they also asked to use this tool again in the future if needed. This is an important aspect that can explain why could be more useful a technological solution for treatment, like a tablet device, compared with more traditional tools.

References

1. Wilson, B.A.: Towards a comprehensive model of cognitive rehabilitation. Neuropsychol. Rehabil. **12**(2), 97–110 (2002)
2. Sohlberg, M.M., Mateer, C.A.: Cognitive Rehabilitation: Introduction to Theory and Practice. Guilford Press, New York (1989)
3. Bracy, O.L.: Cognitive rehabilitation: a process approach. Cogn. Rehabil. **4**, 10–17 (1986)
4. Draganski, B., May, A.: Training-induced structural changes in the adult human brain. Behav. Brain Res. **192**(1), 137–142 (2008)
5. Johansson, B.B.: Brain plasticity in health and disease. Keio J. Med. **53**(4), 231–246 (2004)
6. Pascual-Leone, A., Amedi, A., Fregni, F., Merabet, L.B.: The plastic human brain cortex. Annu. Rev. Neurosci. **28**, 377–401 (2005)
7. Warraich, Z., Kleim, J.A.: Neural plasticity: the biological substrate for neurorehabilitation. PM&R **2**(12), 208–219 (2010)
8. Sheridan, T.B.: Musings on telepresence and virtual presence. Presence Teleop. Virtual Environ. **1**(1), 120–126 (1992)
9. Weiss, P.L., Jessel, A.S.: Virtual reality applications to work. Work **11**(3), 277–293 (1998)
10. Weiss, P.L., Kizony, R., Feintuch, U., Katz, N.: Virtual reality in neurorehabilitation. In: Selzer, M.E., Cohen, L., Gage, F.H., Clarke, S., Duncan, P.W. (eds.) Textbook of Neural Repair and Neurorehabilitation, vol. 2, pp. 182–197. Cambridge University Press, Cambridge (2006)
11. Zyda, M.: From visual simulation to virtual reality to games. Computer **38**(9), 25–32 (2005)
12. Ma, M., Zheng, H.: Virtual reality and serious games in healthcare. In: Brahnam, S., Jain, L. C. (eds.) Advanced Computational Intelligence Paradigms in Healthcare 6. SCI, vol. 337, pp. 169–192. Springer, Heidelberg (2011)
13. Bozoki, A., Radovanovic, M., Winn, B., Heeter, C., Anthony, J.C.: Effects of a computer-based cognitive exercise program on age-related cognitive decline. Arch. Gerontol. Geriatr. **57**(1), 1–7 (2013)
14. Kueider, A.M., Parisi, J.M., Gross, A.L., Rebok, G.W.: Computerized cognitive training with older adults: a systematic review. PLoS One **7**(7), e40588 (2012)
15. Gamberini, L., Raya, M.A., Barresi, G., Fabregat, M., Ibanez, F., Prontu, L.: Cognition, technology and games for the elderly: an introduction to ELDERGAMES Project. PsychNology J. **4**(3), 285–308 (2006)
16. Gamberini, L., Barresi, G., Maier, A., Scarpetta, F.: A game a day keeps the doctor away: a short review of computer games in mental healthcare. J. CyberTherapy Rehabil. **1**(2), 127–145 (2008)
17. Burke, J.W., McNeill, M.D.J., Charles, D.K., Morrow, P.J., Crosbie, J.H., McDonough, S. M.: Optimising engagement for stroke rehabilitation using serious games. Vis. Comput. **25** (12), 1085–1099 (2009)
18. Conconi, A., Ganchev, T., Kocsis, O., Papadopoulos, G., Fernández-Aranda, F., Jiménez-Murcia, S.: Playmancer: a serious gaming 3D environment. In: International Conference on Automated solutions for Cross Media Content and Multi-channel Distribution, 2008, AXMEDIS 2008, pp. 111–117. IEEE, November 2008

19. Caglio, M., Latini-Corazzini, L., D'agata, F., Cauda, F., Sacco, K., Monteverdi, S., Zettin, M., Duca, S., Geminiani, G.: Video game play changes spatial and verbal memory: rehabilitation of a single case with traumatic brain injury. Cogn. Process. **10**, 195–197 (2009)

20. Cameirão, M.S., Bermúdez, I.B.S., Duarte Oller, E., Verschure, P.F.: The rehabilitation gaming system: a review. Stud. Health Technol. Inform. **145**(6), 65–83 (2009)

21. Lundqvist, A., Grundström, K., Samuelsson, K., Rönnberg, J.: Computerized training of working memory in a group of patients suffering from acquired brain injury. Brain Inj. **24** (10), 1173–1183 (2010)

22. Flavia, M., Stampatori, C., Zanotti, D., Parrinello, G., Capra, R.: Efficacy and specificity of intensive cognitive rehabilitation of attention and executive functions in multiple sclerosis. J. Neurol. Sci. **288**(1), 101–105 (2010)

23. Hilton, D., Cobb, S., Pridmore, T., Gladman, J., Edmans, J.: Development and evaluation of a mixed reality system for stroke rehabilitation. In: Brahnam, S., Jain, L.C. (eds.) Advanced Computational Intelligence Paradigms in Healthcare 6. SCI, vol. 337, pp. 193–228. Springer, Heidelberg (2011)

24. Gamberini, L., Cardullo, S., Seraglia, B., Bordin, A.: Neuropsychological testing through a Nintendo Wii console. Stud. Health Technol. Inform. **154**, 29–33 (2009)

25. Cardullo, S., Seraglia, B., Bordin, A., Gamberini, L.: Cognitive training with Nintendo Wii® for the elderly: an evaluation. J. CyberTherapy Rehabil. **4**(2), 159–161 (2011)

26. Kiran, S., Des, R.C., Balachandran, I., Ascenso, E.: Development of an impairment-based individualized treatment workflow using an iPad-based software platform. Semin. Speech Lang. **35**, 38–50 (2014)

27. Onoda, K., Hamano, T., Nabika, Y., Aoyama, A., Takayoshi, H., Nakagawa, T., Ishihara, M., Mitaki, S., Yamaguchi, S.: Validation of a new mass screening tool for cognitive impairment: cognitive assessment for Dementia, iPad version. Clin. Interv. Aging **8**, 353 (2013)

28. Dang, J., Zhang, J., Guo, Z., Lu, W., Cai, J., Shi, Z., Zhang, C.: A pilot study of iPad-assisted cognitive training for schizophrenia. Arch. Psychiatr. Nurs. **28**(3), 197–199 (2014)

29. Chan, M.Y., Haber, S., Drew, L.M., Park, D.C.: Training older adults to use tablet computers: does it enhance cognitive function? The Gerontologist **56**(3), 475–484 (2016)

30. Des Roches, C.A., Balachandran, I., Ascenso, E.M., Tripodis, Y., Kiran, S.: Effectiveness of an impairment-based individualized rehabilitation program using an iPad-based software platform. Front. Hum. Neurosci. **8** (2014)

31. Rand, D., Zeilig, G., Kizony, R.: Rehab-let: touchscreen tablet for self-training impaired dexterity post stroke: study protocol for a pilot randomized controlled trial. Trials **16**(1), 277 (2015)

32. White, J., Janssen, H., Jordan, L., Pollack, M.: Tablet technology during stroke recovery: a survivor's perspective. Disabil. Rehabil. **37**(13), 1186–1192 (2015)

33. Morris, J.C.: The Clinical Dementia Rating (CDR): current version and scoring rules. Neurology **43**, 2412–2414 (1993)

34. Folstein, M.F., Folstein, S.E., McHugh, P.R.: "Mini-mental state": a practical method for grading the cognitive state of patients for the clinician. J. Psychiatr. Res. **12**(3), 189–198 (1975)

35. Bergamaschi, S., Arcara, G., Calza, A., Villani, D., Orgeta, V., Mondini, S.: One-year repeated cycles of cognitive training (CT) for Alzheimer's disease. Aging Clin. Exp. Res. **25** (4), 421–426 (2013)

36. Arnab, S., Lim, T., Carvalho, M.B., Bellotti, F., Freitas, S., Louchart, S., Suttie, N., Berta, R., De Gloria, A.: Mapping learning and game mechanics for serious games analysis. Br. J. Educ. Technol. **46**(2), 391–411 (2015)
37. Baddeley, A., Wilson, B.A.: When implicit learning fails: Amnesia and the problem of error elimination. Neuropsychologia **32**(1), 53–68 (1994)
38. Mohs, R.C., Rosen, W.G., Davis, K.L.: The Alzheimer's disease assessment scale: an instrument for assessing treatment efficacy. Psychopharmacol. Bull. **19**(3), 448 (1983)
39. Cummings, J.L., Mega, M., Gray, K., Rosenberg-Thompson, S., Carusi, D.A., Gornbein, J.: The Neuropsychiatric Inventory comprehensive assessment of psychopathology in dementia. Neurology **44**(12), 2308–2314 (1994)
40. Alexopoulos, G.S., Abrams, R.C., Young, R.C., Shamoian, C.A.: Cornell scale for depression in Dementia. Biol. Psychiatry **23**(3), 271–284 (1988)
41. Baayen, R.H., Davidson, D.J., Bates, D.M.: Mixed-effects modeling with crossed random effects for subjects and items. J. Mem. Lang. **59**(4), 390–412 (2008)
42. Bates, D., Maechler, M., Bolker, B., Walker, S.: lme4: linear mixed-effects models using Eigen and S4. R Package Version **1**(4) (2013)

Biomechanical Analysis of Rehabilitation Exercises Performed During Serious Games Exercises

Bruno Bonnechère[1,2,3(✉)], Bart Jansen[2,3], Lubos Omelina[2,3], Victor Sholukha[1,4], and Serge Van Sint Jan[1]

[1] Laboratory of Anatomy, Biomechanics and Organogenesis, Université Libre de Bruxelles, Brussels, Belgium
bbonnech@ulb.ac.be
[2] Department of Electronics and Informatics (ETRO), Vrije Universiteit Brussel, Brussels, Belgium
[3] Department of Medical Information Technologies (MIT), iMinds, Ghent, Belgium
[4] Department of Applied Mathematics, Peter the Great St. Petersburg Polytechnic University, St. Petersburg, Russia

Abstract. The use of video games in physical rehabilitation is becoming more and more popular. A lot of studies are focusing on the clinical efficacy of such kind on new interventions. However there is still, currently, a lack of information about the importance of learning effect of the task (e.g. motions required to play the game). Therefore the aim of this study was to evaluate the importance of motor learning during rehabilitation exercises performed with specially developed Serious Games. Ten healthy adults played 9 sessions of games over a 3 weeks period. Different parameters were extracted from the games to performed functional and biomechanical evaluation. ANOVA and ICC were processed to evaluate reproducibility of measurement. The majority of the learning effect occurred during the very first session. Therefore, in order to allow regular monitoring the results of this first session should not be included in the follow-up of the patient.

1 Introduction

Commercial video games have significantly evolved over the last decade. Today computer performance and play experience allow new perspectives for rehabilitation. Thanks to new gaming controllers (Nintendo Wii Fit™, Microsoft Xbox Kinect™, etc.) video game playing has changed from a passive (i.e., the player is seated on a sofa) to an active experience: players have to move in order to interact with games.

Clinicians are now prospecting the new potential use of these games in rehabilitation mainly through testing available commercial games with patients suffering from various pathologies, mainly in the neurological field (e.g. cerebral palsy [1], stroke [2], Parkinson disease [3], elderly [4] ...). The term serious gaming is used to describe the use of commercial games in rehabilitation. Physical rehabilitation must be based on active exercises, and these new gaming strategies allow for this. Currently there are two

A. De Gloria and R. Veltkamp (Eds.): GALA 2015, LNCS 9599, pp. 302–311, 2016.
DOI: 10.1007/978-3-319-40216-1_32

main limitations with the use of commercial video games in rehabilitation. First of all these games are not adapted for rehabilitation (e.g. not based on physical rehabilitation exercises, based on speed, too complex visual background) since they are developed for fun and entertainment purposes. Therefore results of the clinical studies exploring the possibilities of the integration of such kind of exercises in physical rehabilitation did not, currently, present a high level of evidence [1–4].

Secondly, player motion accuracy requested by the player during the games is low while most therapists will aim to improve patient joint control and coordination. Furthermore there is currently no possibility to record the motion performed by the patients during exercises. However, collecting this information could be important to: (i) allow to provide direct feedback to patient and eventually correct the motion if they are not performed in the right way and (ii) to provide information to therapists in case of telerehabilitation exercises when the patient is performing exercises at home without the clinicians' supervision.

In order to tackle the above mentioned limitations, specific games must be developed for rehabilitation purposes. Such kind of games, called serious games (SG) (i.e. games designed with a primary purpose other than pure entertainment), must be designed taking into account real clinical needs and constraints (e.g. simple visual background, based on relevant clinical schemes, range of motion and speed required to perform the exercises must be adaptable …) and allow to record motions performed by the patients [5].

Since the release of the Nintendo Wii Balance Board™ (WBB) and the Microsoft Xbox Kinect™ (Kinect) in 2007 and 2010 respectively a lot of studies have been done in order to evaluate if these devices can be used to perform simple biomechanical evaluation (Kinect) and balance or posture assessment (WBB).

Concerning the Kinect there are studies exploring the possibilities of this device for posture assessment [6], gait analysis [7], functional evaluation [8] … The Kinect is a markerless motion capture system that provides a simple skeleton model allowing full body analysis [9]. Such kind of system seems to be accurate enough to track and monitor patients body movements during simple rehabilitation exercises. However, while results about repeatability of measurement performed with the Kinect are excellent [10], it appears that the skeleton model provided is not always stable and does not allow three-dimensional (3D) motion analysis (due to the small numbers of point) [8]. A model-based approach (MBA) has been developed in order to tackle these problems and allows 3D motion analysis with the Kinect [11].

It appears thus that specially developed SG coupled to the WBB and the Kinect sensor could be used to follow patients' evolution during rehabilitation exercises. However before being used in clinics to assess patients, the data collected during the games and parameters extracted from it must be repeatable from session to session or at least the progress made between the first and the last session due to a learning effect must be known. These data are important in order to quantify the part of the evolution of the patients due to clinical improvement and the part due to learning effect (if any).

Such kind of evaluation, done during the rehabilitation, has many advantages; (i) done in the natural environment of the patient (it is known that patients are not exhibiting the same performance when there are wearing underwear in a gait laboratory), (ii) when patients are immerged in the games they are less focused on the motion and on pain and can reach larger amplitudes than when there are asked to perform one particular motion, (iii) time saving and (iv) financially beneficial (the devices are affordable and since the evaluation is done within the therapy session there is no dual pricing).

Therefore, the aim of this study was to evaluate the repeatability of the measurements collected during rehabilitation exercises performed by healthy subjects with the Kinect sensor and to quantify the learning effect (the part of progress that are due to the familiarization of the games) in order to determine whether or not those parameters could be used to assess patient's status and follow up during the rehabilitation process.

2 Material and Method

2.1 Games

Two specific SG have been developed (snapshots of the games are presented in Figs. 1 and 2, movies of the games can be seen from http://www.youtube.com/ict4rehab) [5]. During the Wipe Out game, patients have to clean a screen covered by mud using a cloth, different configuration are possible (e.g. the screen can be divided in case of asymmetric disease) (Fig. 1). During the Pirates games subjects have to conduct a pirate to a treasure following a predefined path, different configurations are possible (from simple linear and symmetrical trajectories to asymmetric curves) (Fig. 2).

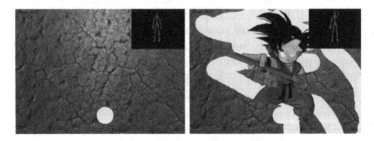

Fig. 1. The Wipe Out games (the skeleton provided by the Kinect is shown in the right corner)

The Kinect was connected to a laptop (Intel Core I5, Windows 7, 6 GB RAM) via USB connection and data were retrieved using custom-written software based on the Kinect SDK[1].

All the data collected were stored in C3D file format.

---

[1] http://www.microsoft.com/en-us/kinectforwindows/develop/downloads-docs.aspx.

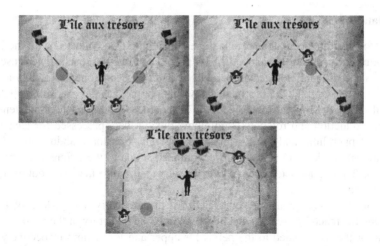

Fig. 2. The three different configurations of the Pirate game used in this study

2.2   Participants

Ten young healthy adults (age = 26 (4) years, height = 175 (12) cm, weight = 65 (12) kg, 3 females) participated in this study. No participant presented any neurological or orthopedic disorder and none of the subjects was taking medication at the time of the study that may have influenced balance, posture or limbs motions.

2.3   Procedures

The Kinect sensor was placed on a tripod at 1.5 m above the floor. Subjects stood at 2.5 m from the camera and the screen of the computer. Subjects were then invited to play the games. Each session comprised the following games:

For the Wipe Out games three different configurations were used to control the cloth: with the upper limb, the lower limb and with the trunk. When the game is controlled with upper or lower limbs the screen is virtually divided into two parts. For each of the configurations 3 repetitions were performed.

For the Pirate games two configurations were tested: with the upper limbs and with the lower limbs. As shown in Fig. 2 three different conditions were used: straight line from bottom to top (Configuration 1), straight line from top to bottom (Configuration 2) and curved path (Configuration 3). All of these configurations were symmetric.

Both the order of the games and the order of the configuration within the game were randomized. The duration of a session was approximately 15 min (depending on the ability of the subject).

In total 9 sessions were played (3 sessions per week) using the same protocol.

2.4   Data Processing

In order to get more accurate and reliable results all the data collected with the Kinect were optimized using the developed MBA [11]. Then two approaches were used: the first one is a traditional biomechanical analysis and the second one is a quality analysis of the motions. For the biomechanical evaluation the Ranges of Motion (RoM = Maximal angle – Minimal angle) for 3D shoulder motions (flexion/extension – abduction/adduction and rotations) and elbow flexion were processed for games controlled by upper limb and 3D hip motions (flexion/extension – abduction/adduction and rotations) and knee flexion for lower limb. Then due to the different nature of the task, two different parameters were processed to get more information about the quality of the motions.

For the Wipe Out game the total length of the trajectory, the surface of the trajectory and the reaching area (i.e. the 3D envelop of the trajectory of the wrist related to the trunk or the foot related to the pelvis for upper and lower limb respectively).

For the Pirate game a new variable was computed to assess the quality and accuracy of the motion. For the upper limb motion of the wrist related to trunk along Z axis (up and down displacement) and X axis (medio-lateral displacement) were plotted and a polynomial fitting was applied (1st degree for straight trajectories and 2nd degree for curved one) to finally obtain the error estimate (prediction).

Ratios between right and left side were processed for all those parameters because many pathologies are asymmetric or affects only one side [12].

2.5   Statistical Analysis

Normality of the data was checked using the Shapiro-Wilk test. Mean values and standard deviations were calculated. ANOVA tests for repeated measures were processed to compare the 9 sessions. In order to be more close to the clinical situation were testing is done before (pre-test) and after (post-test) the intervention, ANOVA tests were computed to compare results of the first and of the last session.

The test-retest reliability was investigated using Intra-class Coefficient Correlation (ICC) (two-way random average measures). All statistics and data processing were performed in Matlab (MathWorks, Natick, Massachusetts, U.S.A.).

3   Results

The Table 1 presents the results of the RoM reached during the different games. For clarity and in order to avoid overloading the tables, only results of the first and the last sessions are presented. ANOVA and ICC have been processed on the ratio between left and right side for the nine sessions.

Results about the quality of the motion performed during the games are presented in Tables 2 and 3 for the Pirate and the Wipe Out games respectively.

Table 1. Mean (std) results and statistics for range of motion, results are expressed in degrees. The difference is the difference between session 1 and 9 expressed in percentage

UPPER LIMB												
		Left side			Right side			Ratio				
		Session 1	Session 9	T-test	Session 1	Session 9	T-test	ANOVA	ICC	Pre-Post	Diff.	
Pirate	Flex.	106 (18)	101 (14)	0.40	91 (17)	88 (14)	0.52	0.78	0.55	0.54	+1%	
	Abd.	102 (33)	104 (34)	0.94	90 (26)	102 (25)	0.24	0.79	0.64	0.42	-10%	
	Rot.	57 (12)	64 (11)	0.31	59 (32)	61 (13)	0.81	0.86	0.75	0.51	-8%	
	Elbow	80 (23)	83 (18)	0.77	83 (16)	81 (24)	0.73	0.86	0.38	0.78	-6%	
Wipe	Flex.	142 (33)	138 (29)	0.78	136 (25)	127 (25)	0.39	0.09	0.44	0.35	-4%	
	Abd.	84 (17)	88 (29)	0.71	55 (13)	62 (14)	0.47	0.55	0.61	0.51	5%	
	Rot.	57 (18)	60 (19)	0.69	79 (31)	90 (32)	0.40	0.62	0.56	0.65	11%	
	Elbow	88 (28)	99 (13)	0.13	96 (27)	97 (16)	0.73	0.63	0.31	0.33	-11%	

LOWER LIMB												
		Left side			Right side			Ratio				
		Session 1	Session 9	T-test	Session 1	Session 9	T-test	ANOVA	ICC	Pre-Post	Diff.	
Pirate	Flex.	95 (14)	106 (16)	0.22	98 (30)	96 (21)	0.88	0.69	0.55	0.21	-12%	
	Abd.	91 (44)	95 (22)	0.84	103 (41)	100 (50)	0.93	0.31	0.44	0.77	-8%	
	Rot.	42 (14)	50 (15)	0.15	42 (12)	48 (14)	0.43	0.08	0.42	0.33	-4%	
	Knee	58 (16)	61 (15)	0.16	65 (24)	64 (20)	0.94	0.07	0.61	0.75	-7%	
Wipe	Flex.	60 (15)	56 (13)	0.61	61 (14)	57 (13)	0.63	0.67	0.12	0.78	0%	
	Abd.	86 (10)	81 (27)	0.59	84 (17)	72 (21)	0.31	0.28	0.27	0.64	-8%	
	Rot.	37 (8)	32 (13)	0.40	45 (13)	34 (15)	0.16	0.48	0.10	0.21	-15%	
	Knee	84 (29)	75 (30)	0.56	74 (18)	66 (25)	0.46	0.31	0.31	0.75	0%.	

Flexion, abduction and rotation are used for shoulder motions and for hip motions for upper limb and lower limb respectively.

Table 2. Mean (std) results and statistics for the quality score of the Pirate game, ratios between right and left side are presented. The difference is the difference between session 1 and 9 expressed in percentage

Pirate							
	Configuration	Session 1	Session 9	ANOVA	ICC	Pre-Post	Difference
Hands	1	117 (23)	116 (31)	0.96	0.20	0.98	0 %
	2	115 (22)	97 (12)	*0.008*	0.56	0.14	−15 %
	3	95 (17)	118 (24)	0.66	0.48	*0.04**	*+24 %**
Legs	1	114 (59)	57 (17)	*0.0003*	0.08	0.07	−50 %
	2	81 (47)	60 (44)	0.58	0.07	0.41	−26 %
	3	88 (33)	91 (12)	0.67	0.54	0.86	+2 %

* significant difference (0.05 level) ANOVA test

Table 3. Mean (std) results and statistics for the quality score of the Wipe Out game. The difference is the difference between session 1 and 9 expressed in percentage

Wipe Out							
	Parameters	Session 1	Session 9	ANOVA	ICC	Pre-Post	Difference
Hands	Length, cm	4779 (3102)	6195 (1732)	0.11	0.60	0.26	+30 %
	Surface, cm^2	2215 (1531)	2589 (993)	0.82	0.35	0.57	+17 %
	Volume, cm^3	24368 (14332)	24933 (10399)	0.69	0.59	0.93	+2 %
Legs	Length, cm	3800 (2384)	4632 (3285)	0.81	0.80	0.48	+22 %
	Surface, cm^2	2352 (1322)	2139 (1068)	0.11	0.42	0.61	−9 %
	Volume, cm^3	77710 (8808)	55540 (5225)	0.89	0.83	0.18	−28 %

4   Discussion

Two different approaches were tested to evaluate players' performance in this study; biomechanical analysis and quality analysis.

Concerning biomechanical analysis, the different RoM reached during the game was analyzed. The first important points to note is that for all games and all configurations no statistical significant differences were found between all sessions (ANOVA) or between the fist and the last session. Looking at the reproducibility of measurement two different patterns can be seen based on the different games. In the Pirate game the motion to perform is induced by the path and the player has to follow this trajectory, there is no flexibility. Higher ICC values were obtained for the Pirate games compared to the Wipe Out (mean ICC values = 0.58 against 0.48 for the upper limb and mean ICC = 0.50 against 0.20 for the lower limb). Although no difference was found in terms of RoM, results of the ICC seems to indicate that measuring only the RoM to define what has been done by a patient doing 30 s of exercises is too simplistic. Therefore, more complex analysis must be performed in order to summarize and synthetize what the patient has been performing during the rehabilitation exercises.

Two different kinds of scores were thus computed, one for each game, in order to get information about the quality of the motion performed during the games.

The configuration used in the Pirate games was developed in order to assess symmetry between both sides and to quantify the severity of the disease compared to the healthy, or less severely affected side. From a therapeutic point of view there is still a debate about the use of symmetric or asymmetric exercises for the limbs [13], or to train only the affected side [14]. Contrariwise from the assessment point of view, due to high inter subjects variability, it is common to compare affected and healthy side. Results of the evolution of the ratio between right and left side are presented in Table 2 for the 3 different configurations tested. While only one statistical significant difference was found (hands, configuration 3) between session 1 and 9, both ANOVA and ICC results are low. Instead of computing the ratio, statistics on the learning effect were computed on each side separately.

The Wipe Out game is less restrictive than the Pirate game since players are free to clean the screen without constraints. Therefore, scores relate to the trajectory path (length, surface and volume). No significant difference was found between the sessions, and good agreements were found for trajectory lengths and volume for both upper (ICC = 0.60) and lower limbs (ICC = 0.80). As for the time more reproducible results have been found for the lower limbs compared to upper limb.

In order to estimate the learning effect for every parameter the difference between results obtained during the second and the last sessions were computed since it appears that there is an important decrease between the first and the second session. The results are presented in the Table 4. ANOVA tests were used to determine if the observed difference was statistically significant or not.

Table 4. Learning effect for the different studied parameters (computed between session 2 and 9)

Parameters		Learning effect
Angles, Upper Limb	Pirate – Shoulder Flexion	+1 %
	Pirate – Shoulder Abduction	−7 %
	Pirate – Shoulder Rotation	−6 %
	Pirate – Elbow Flexion	−7 %
	Wipe Out – Shoulder Flexion	−3 %
	Wipe Out – Shoulder Abduction	3 %
	Wipe Out – Shoulder Rotation	8 %
	Wipe Out – Elbow Flexion	−9 %
Angles, Lower Limb	Pirate – Hip Flexion	−10 %
	Pirate – Hip Abduction	−6 %
	Pirate – Hip Rotation	−4 %
	Pirate – Knee Flexion	+2 %
	Wipe Out – Hip Flexion	+1 %
	Wipe Out – Hip Abduction	−6 %
	Wipe Out – Hip Rotation	−11 %
	Wipe Out – Knee Flexion	+2 %
Quality, Pirate	Upper Limb – 1	0 %
	Upper Limb – 2	−11 %
	Upper Limb – 3	−1 %
	Lower Limb – 1	***−40 %***
	Lower Limb – 2	−23 %
	Lower Limb – 3	+2 %
Quality, Wipe Out	Upper Limb – Length	+28 %
	Upper Limb – Surface	+3 %
	Upper Limb – Volume	−6 %
	Lower Limb – Length	−9 %
	Lower Limb – Surface	+21 %
	Lower Limb – Volume	−19 %

From the 28 parameters studied only one of them presented significant differences between session 2 and 9 (the error estimation of the Pirate [configuration 1] controlled with the legs). Concerning the RoM no clear trend clearly appears, some joints presented increased amplitudes while other decreased. It is important to note here that, while for the time a decrease is expected as an indicator of progress in the games, for the RoM a better control of the motion does not necessarily imply an increase of amplitude. Actually, from a neurological rehabilitation point of view, by working on the quality of the motion, the coordination between both limbs increases, decreasing coupled motions, decreasing adiodochokinesia … the quantity of the motion (i.e. RoM) required is going to decrease and therefore the energy needed to perform this exercises will also decrease [15]. The different scores related to the quality have been developed for this purpose.

This study focused only on a healthy population and would allow the creation of a database of healthy subjects for latter comparison with patients suffering from various pathologies. Therefore further studies will focus on establishing a larger database with children and elderly to analyze whether or not the age has any influence.

Patients will also be included to analyze if the different scores computed are representative of the severity of the disease.

5   Conclusion

The aim of this study was to determine whether or not some parameters obtained during specific serious gaming rehabilitation exercises with the Kinect are reproducible enough to monitor patients' evolution. Concerning the biomechanical analysis restricting this analysis to RoM is too simplistic and did not provide enough information. Therefore specific score must be processed according to the nature of the exercises to be performed and monitored. In conclusion we observed that the majority of the learning effect occurred during the very first session. Thus in order to allow regular monitoring the results of this first session must be considered as a familiarization and learning session and should therefore not be included in the monitoring.

References

1. Bonnechère, B., Jansen, B., Omelina, L., Degelaen, M., Wermenbol, V., Rooze, M., Van Sint Jan, S.: Can serious games be incorporated with conventional treatment of children with cerebral palsy? A review. Res. Dev. Disabil. **35**(8), 1899–1913 (2014). http://www.ncbi.nlm. nih.gov/pubmed/24794289
2. Putrino, D.: Telerehabilitation and emerging virtual reality approaches to stroke rehabilitation. Curr. Opin. Neurol. **27**(6), 631–636 (2014). http://www.ncbi.nlm.nih.gov/ pubmed/25333603
3. Arias, P., Robles-García, V., Sanmartín, G., Flores, J., Cudeiro, J.: Virtual reality as a tool for evaluation of repetitive rhythmic movements in the elderly and Parkinson's disease patients. PLoS One **7**(1), e30021 (2012). http://www.ncbi.nlm.nih.gov/pubmed/22279559
4. Webster, D., Celik, O.: Systematic review of Kinect applications in elderly care and stroke rehabilitation. J Neuroeng. Rehabil. **11**, 108–132 (2014). http://www.ncbi.nlm.nih.gov/ pubmed/24996956

5. Omelina, L., Jansen, B., Bonnechère, B., Van Sint Jan, S., Cornelis, J.: Serious games for physical rehabilitation: designing highly configurable and adaptable games. In: Proceedings of the 9th International Conference on Disability, Virtual Reality and Associated Technologies, Laval, France, pp. 195–201 (2012)
6. Clark, R.A., Pua, Y.H., Fortin, K., Ritchie, C., Webster, K.E., Denehy, L., Bryant, A.L.: Validity of the Microsoft Kinect for assessment of postural control. Gait Posture. **36**(3), 372–377 (2012). http://www.ncbi.nlm.nih.gov/pubmed/22633015
7. Pfister, A., West, A.M., Bronner, S., Noah, J.A.: Comparative abilities of Microsoft Kinect and Vicon 3D motion capture for gait analysis. J. Med. Eng. Technol. **38**(5), 274–280 (2014). http://www.ncbi.nlm.nih.gov/pubmed/24878252
8. Bonnechère, B., Jansen, B., Salvia, P., Bouzahouene, H., Omelina, L., Moiseev, F., Sholukha, V., Cornelis, J., Rooze, M., Van Sint Jan, S.: Validity and reliability of the Kinect within functional assessment activities: comparison with standard stereophotogrammetry. Gait Posture. **39**(1), 593–598 (2014). http://www.ncbi.nlm.nih.gov/pubmed/24269523
9. González, A., Hayashibe, M., Bonnet, V., Fraisse, P.: Whole body center of mass estimation with portable sensors: using the statically equivalent serial chain and a Kinect. Sensors (Basel) **14**(9), 16955–16971 (2014). http://www.ncbi.nlm.nih.gov/pubmed/25215943
10. Bonnechère, B., Sholukha, V., Jansen, B., Omelina, L., Rooze, M., Van Sint Jan, S.: Determination of repeatability of kinect sensor. Telemed. J. E Health **20**(5), 451–453 (2014). http://www.ncbi.nlm.nih.gov/pubmed/24617290
11. Sholukha, V., Bonnechère, B., Salvia, P., Moiseev, F., Rooze, M., Van Sint Jan, S.: Model-based approach for human kinematics reconstruction from markerless and marker-based motion analysis systems. J. Biomech. **46**(14), 2363–2371 (2013). http://www.ncbi.nlm.nih.gov/pubmed/23972432
12. Kagerer, F.A.: Control of discrete bimanual movements: How each hand benefits from the other. Neurosci. Lett. **584**, 33–38 (2015). http://www.ncbi.nlm.nih.gov/pubmed/25307124
13. Lee, D., Lee, M., Lee, K., Song, C.: Asymmetric training using virtual reality reflection equipment and the enhancement of upper limb function in stroke patients: a randomized controlled trial. J. Stroke Cerebrovasc. Dis. **23**(6), 1319–1326 (2014). http://www.ncbi.nlm.nih.gov/pubmed/24468068
14. van Delden, A.L., Beek, P.J., Roerdink, M., Kwakkel, G., Peper, C.L.: Unilateral and bilateral upper-limb training interventions after stroke have similar effects on bimanual coupling strength. Neurorehabil Neural Repair **29**(3), 255–267 (2015). http://www.ncbi.nlm.nih.gov/pubmed/25055838
15. Law, M.C., Darrah, J., Pollock, N., Wilson, B., Russell, D.J., Walter, S.D., Rosenbaum, P., Galuppi, B.: Focus on function: a cluster, randomized controlled trial comparing child-versus context-focused intervention for young children with cerebral palsy. Dev. Med. Child Neurol. **53**(7), 621–629 (2011). http://www.ncbi.nlm.nih.gov/pubmed/21569012

Gamification of a Truck-Driving Simulator for the Care of People Suffering from Post-Traumatic Stress Disorder

Corentin Haidon[1], Adrien Ecrepont[1], Benoit Girard[2],
and Bob-Antoine J. Menelas[1(✉)]

[1] Department of Mathematics and Computer Science,
University of Quebec at Chicoutimi (UQAC), Chicoutimi, QC, Canada
{corentin.haidon1,adrien.ecrepont1,bamenela}@uqac.ca
[2] GRAP, Occupational Psychology Clinic, Saguenay, QC, Canada
ben.girard@videotron.ca

Abstract. Victims of fatal injured accidents involving large trucks are mainly non-occupants of the trucks (more than 80 %). Therefore, it appears that truck drivers who had accidents are likely to suffer from *Post Traumatic Stress Disorder* while no research does address this need. This paper tackles this point by the mean of an exposition therapy through the use of Virtual Reality technologies. Our main contribution concerns the fact that we do not only exploit Virtual Reality to expose the user. We do create an environment that offers to the patient the possibility to act in order to recover his ability to face the traumatic situation. For this, we rely on the game mechanics and the personalization of the virtual environment to bring the trucker to be active while being exposed to the cues that are related to its fear. Doing so, he should reactivate his capacities and thus be able to act differently in such a traumatic situation.

1 Introduction

It is known that trucker do face multiples issues that may impact their psychological health. The ignorance of the route, the traffic, bad weather conditions as well as the dangerousness of the cargo constitute indeed professional conditions that may affect the psychological health of a trucker. In the same way, several personal conditions (remoteness of the family, physical health, fatigue and loneliness) may also have negative consequences on a trucker. All this seems to create an environment conducive to accidents that may have major impacts for the trucker and the company.

In fact, the last update (June 2015) regarding the highway traffic reports that in 2013 large trucks represented 4 % of all motor vehicles in the US [1]. Nevertheless, trucks were involved in 9 % of fatal crashes and 3 % otherwise (crashes having injuries and/or property damages). Moreover, in fatal crashes only 17 % of the victims were occupants of large trucks. This means that a

© Springer International Publishing Switzerland 2016
A. De Gloria and R. Veltkamp (Eds.): GALA 2015, LNCS 9599, pp. 312–322, 2016.
DOI: 10.1007/978-3-319-40216-1_33

majority of truck drivers who had an accident are likely to face post-traumatic problems. However, to the best of our knowledge, there is no research that targets the treatment of truckers suffering from **Post-Traumatic Stress Desorder (PTSD)**. Our research intends to answer this need. In general, the research for the treatment of PTSD among victims of road accidents is very recent, the few studies done on this domain show nevertheless encouraging results [2]. Our work is part of this niche. It concerns particularly accidents involving large trucks.

Use of Virtual Reality (VR) technologies in the fields of education, rehabilitation and neuroscience is increasingly recognized [3,4]. In particular, it was shown that for a majority of cases, the exploitation of VR tends to provide better results than traditional approaches because of their ecological validity [5,6] (an action is said ecological if it is similar to what happens in the daily life [7]). However the high cost in terms of development, usage and maintenance tends to limit the use of VR. **Serious Games** (**SG**: "games that do not have entertainment, enjoyment or fun as their primary purpose" [8,9]) turning on workstations appear to represent an alternative that may require a lower cost when compared to a VR system, although not being less effective than expensive and complex technologies [6,10]. In this view, we have designed a SG that simulates the driving of a truck for the care of people suffering from PTSD, using the work of Arnab et al. [11] for the game mechanics perspective.

The paper is organized as follows: related works are presented at Sect. 2, the theoretical approach is detailed in Sect. 3. Section 4 describes the proposed simulator before the conclusion in Sect. 5.

2   Related Work

Undergo an event where its physical or psychological integrity is threatened (war, terrorist attack, earthquake, traffic accident, etc.) may have major psychological impacts on a person. Beyond normal reactions (having hard time to sleep well and/or going over the details of the situation in its mind) that decrease with time, PTSD is a mental illness that can result from this particular event. PTSD appears to affect 6.8 % of the US [12], whether adults or children. Considering these statistics, the treatment of this mental disorder represents a major public health issue [13]. Besides the use of some medications (antidepressants), **Cue Exposure Therapy (CET)** offers an increasingly considered treatment. This approach amounts to gradually bring a person to face the stimuli that he fears.

This relies on the fact that fear is due to exaggerated physiological and behavioral responses to stimuli that are perceived as being more threatening than they actually are. The idea behind the Cue Exposure Therapy is thus to decrease the fear sensation throughout a gradual exposition to the stimuli while letting the person being able to control his emotional reactions [14]. Although, *in-vivo* (real-life) exposition remain an effective solution, the exposure can also be assumed through pictures, films, or mental imagery deducted from descriptions of the fear inducing stimuli (imaginary exposure) [15]. Nevertheless, *in-virtuo* exposure is another way to expose user by the use of Virtual Reality, what has been defined by North [16] as **Virtual Reality Therapy (VRT)**. VRT has proven especially useful when *in-vivo* exposition may not be exploited (e.g. patient may not be able to support a real-life exposition or the situation may be difficult to reproduce live) or when imaginary exposure is inefficient (e.g. because the person is not able to properly represent the source of anxiety in its mind) [2] by ensuring the ability to create a suitable and safe environment for the patient.

Several research areas as diverse as arachnophobia, agoraphobia and obsessive compulsive disorders have shown the benefit of using an in-virtuo exposition therapy [12,17–19].

In addition, it should be noted that VR technologies allow to set up situations: (a) that are interactive (the user may act on the environment) [20], (b) that are dynamic (they can be paced by an external party, such as a therapist) [12] and (c) that meet the needs of each patient (the situation is close to what frightens the patient). Therefore, we consider that it would be appropriate to use VR in order to not only expose the user to the frightening situation but also to let him recover the power to act inside this environment (on the truck in the present case). Doing so, the patient would be able to react differently in the traumatic situation. This approach is known as **Action-Cue Exposure Therapy (ACET)** [5].

The following describes our theoretical approach in exploiting a virtual world in order to design an Action-Cue Exposure Therapy for truck drivers suffering from post-traumatic stress disorders.

3   Theoretical Approach for the Design of an Environment Driving by ACET

Our analysis of different works on VR technologies to cure PTSD revealed that the full potential of VR is rarely reached. Considering an application such as Virtual Iraq [21]; a simulator where soldiers could revive a series of war events; it is clear that this work has paved the way to a very innovative approach. However, the exploited simulator does not allow the patient to be fully active in the environment, it only delivers visual and auditory stimuli to the patient.

Our goal is rather on an active treatment of the user where he could try to correct his reactions, what will assess the success of controlling his anxiety. As a therapeutic oriented solution and allow the user to be an actor, we designed a truck-driving simulator that is considered as a SG. This SG will be designed to teach [22,23] the user new associations to the stimuli that activate the fear sensation as identified by Powers et al. [24] as a way to overcome a trauma. For this, we rely on two axes to design a SG as efficient as possible: (a) the game elements that will support learning mechanisms, and (b) the personalization of the virtual environment. Next subsection details the gamification and the personalization inside the simulator.

3.1   Game Elements of the Simulator

To ensure a systematic approach over the game mechanics and their associated learning mechanisms, we analysed the simulator using Arnab et al.'s *Learning Mechanics-Game Mechanics (LM-GM) model* [11]. The LM-GM model is a tool created as an answer to the lack of methodology in the creation of SGs and their assessment, thus it features a methodology to map learning and game mechanics in this particular case.

Through the observation of the game loop (see Fig. 1), six main groups of game mechanics (GMs) have been identified based on those provided by the LM-GM model:

Movement, Simulate/Response and Realism[1]**:** As a driving-oriented simulation, the core of the gameplay consists in driving, what relates to the *Movement* of the player inside the virtual world. The *Response* of the vehicle, as an immediate feedback must remind the player the sensations experienced while driving in the real world, what lead to some *Realism* in the feedback.

Levels, Cascading Information and Behavioural Momentum[2]**:** The player experiences multiple sessions called *Levels*. Each level feature a final objective (destination, driving goal e.g. do not overturn, etc.). The organisation of levels ensure *Cascading Information* i.e. that the conditions evolve gradually to a situation more complex and closer to the traumatic situation. *Behavioural Momentum* is generated through the looping over levels.

Story and Information[3]**:** The *Story* takes place in the job assignation during the game. *Information*s are created around the mission such as the type of load of the truck, the client to deliver, etc.

Tokens[4]**:** *Tokens* are random elements (from the user perspective) that can affect the game state. In our case, tokens are controlled either by a random sequence, or by the supervisor. Weather conditions, time of the day and car crashes present on the road are an example of what can happen randomly during the play session. They are elements that will serve for the personalization of the game.

Feedback, Rewards and Status[5]**:** The main *Feedback* is given to the player at the end of a level so that he can assess his success or failure. Upon mission completion, the *Status* of the player is updated and his experience will eventually increase. *Reward* mechanisms can then be mapped to the experience of the player. The simulation provides also immediate feedback described previously as Response.

Design/Editing[6]**:** Although not being the main gameplay feature, we consider *Designing* the truck as an important factor to enhance the immersion and realism of the game. As explained earlier, our goal is to provide realistic and familiar surroundings to the player. By being able to customize the look of his truck, the player can identify the truck, hopefully leading to some positive reinforcement.

The GMs previously described have then been mapped to their associated learning mechanics (LMs):

Fig. 1. Game loop explicited with the LM-GM model

Exploration, Simulation and Action/Task: The user will learn through its *Exploration* of the world as well as the realistic *Simulation* of the truck that will respond to its *Actions*.

Repetition: *Repetition* will play an important part of the learning process as it will activate the "over-learning" [22] ability of the patient.

Guidance and Instructional: Through mission aspects, the player will be *Guided* and receive *Instructions* on how to deal with his objectives.

Feedback and Motivation: *Feedback* will be provided as indicators of the user progress, leading to potential *Motivation* to improve.

Ownership: The sense of *Ownership* of the truck is designed to improve the player involvement in his mission.

All of those associations, as well as their implementation that will be discussed later, are summarized in Table 1.

3.2   Personalization of the Game

We consider personalization, i.e. adapt the game to the user, as another important feature of the game. Aside of the game mechanics previously explained, personalization will act as a way to provide stimuli that may let the patient perceive the traumatic situation. To do so, we rely on the supervisor to adapt the game to the current mental state of the patient through tools that are provided (scenario/map editor, etc.). This customization is materialized through two main aspects that are customizing: (a) the environment (visual) and (b) the missions. Doing so, we offer the trucker an opportunity to reactivate his capacities for driving a truck and thus be able to act differently in the traumatic situation.

Such customization will also allow the supervisor to control the difficulty of the game through a combination of road type (e.g. linear highway surrounded by

Table 1. Game and learning mechanics of the simulator, based on the *LM-GM* model

Game mechanic	Learning mechanic	Implementation
Movement, Simulate/Response and Realism[1]	Explore, Simulation and Action/Task	Immersion through a HMD and a *racing wheel*
Levels, Cascading Information and Behavioural Momentum[2]	Repetition	Levels
Story and Information[3]	Guidance and Instructional	Radio messages & Level conditions (job given)
Tokens[4]		World events: Weather, Day Time, Car Crashes
Feedback, Rewards and Status[5]	Feedback and Motivation	Level change, Pop-up and Truck customization
Design/Editing (6)	Ownership	Customization of the truck

forest, urban road, forest path) and the conditions that affect the levels: weather, time of the day (affecting visibility and visual fatigue), car crash aside the road; the goal being to enable the patient to gradually approach and ultimately relive the situation that led to his trauma. The adaptation of the difficulty to the player has been recognized as a powerful learning component [23,25,26] and most games use formulas to calculate difficulty whereas our approach is on a fully human-controlled shaping of the game experience.

4 The Proposed Game

Previously mentioned elements (Table 1) led us to a design specially focused on the core game elements and the customization of an interactive photo-realistic environment created using the game editor *Unreal Engine 4*. The single-player game recreates the environment of the province of Quebec (Canada) in different weather conditions (sunny, snowy, rainy and icy) and at any time of the day (sunrise, noon, afternoon) and night.

4.1 Setup Overview

Different devices are available to the user to support the immersive nature of the system. One counts in particular: a "Head Mounted Display" for the visual modality and a *racing wheel*, a gearbox and pedals equipped with haptic feedbacks to control the vehicle (see Fig. 2).

A Head Mounted Display (HMD): Thanks to the HMD and the head-tracking system provided, the user has the ability to turn his head in order to fully appreciate the interior of its truck. This is particularly interesting, since it may reveal meaningful details about the dashboard meters and buttons. It also allows looking out the window and in the mirrors, providing a freedom of movement and a feeling of realism.

(a) Scene rendered through the HMD.   (b) A user experimenting the game, the HMD on his head and the wheel in hands.

Fig. 2. Current setup of the system.

A Set Having a Racing Wheel, a Gearbox and Pedals: Through the *Logitech G27 Racing Wheel*, the user is able to maneuver the truck (see Fig. 2). The steering wheel has a force feedback system, so it reacts to turns, shocks and speed in the same way as power steering. The shift lever can be chosen in automatic, sequential or manual mode. Different buttons, placed on the steering wheel and the gear lever, allow controlling the based functionality of the truck (headlights, turn signals, horn, radio etc.). All these elements cause both a change in the vehicle behavior and are also highlighted by a faithful visual representation via the orientation of the steering wheel and indicators on the dashboard.

4.2 Gameplay Through the Therapy Protocol

The therapy protocol that will be exploited with this interactive tool is a multi-sessions therapy (from 8 to 10). Although the second and later sessions being mostly identical, the first session is not made as a driving session but more as a discovery one.

The First Session. During the first session, the patient ends up in a parking lot where several types of trucks are stationed at reasonable distances. The patient can move at its own speed in that environment, allowing its progressive exposure and skills recovering. At this time the patient is asked to choose its preferred model of truck from a selection of well known trucks. His choices are then associated with its profile. This session will therefore be a first contact with the tool. It will allow to assess patient trauma level. Indeed, it is expected that patients with a high level of trauma may experience some difficulties in completing that session.

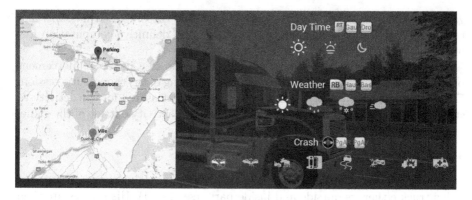

Fig. 3. A typical, well-known path to be followed by the driver. It should be noted that several environments (urban, forest, agglomeration) are located on this route.

Subsequent Sessions. During each other session, the player operates the game by driving a preselected truck from one point to another as stated in his mission (see Fig. 3), previously set up by the supervisor. At any time in the mission, the doctor will be able to change the course of events through different shortcuts (e.g. reset the weather to clean) if he decides so.

At the start of a mission, a Non-Player Character (NPC) will talk to the player through the radio of the truck. The narrative presentation used to transmit the job requirements and the conditions of the road aim to imitate a real job environment and support the immersion. While achieving special conditions (e.g. first 10 Km traveled), the NPC will also transmit praises, completing the feeling of positive reinforcement [26].

By completing a mission, the player gets rewarded through new options to customize his truck, as well as badges. A first reward appears after a certain amount of completed missions, unblocking the customization option inside the

(a) Different outside pattern are selectable for the customization of the truck.

(b) Different inside patterns are selectable.

Fig. 4. Customization of the truck (a) outside & (b) inside.

game. Later rewards are associated to the number of completed missions and traveled kilometers. At the time of this writing, no definitive computation formula has been decided as it is still a work in progress.

Assessing the player through the game is a first step in the reinforcement process, the second step being done during a debriefing of the therapeutic session. Either having succeeded of failed, or after the patient asking for the activity to stop, the patient is then invited to debrief about the activity outside of the game.

4.3   Customization of the Truck

Once the customization option unlocked, the user is able to change the design of his truck either its outside and inside parts (see Fig. 4). His choices are then associated to his profile. Giving the ability to edit the truck is used to bring the patient to express his attachment to his truck.

5   Conclusion and Future Work

This paper described the design of a simulator for truckers suffering from PTSD. For this, we used VR technologies in order to not only expose the user to the frightening situation, but also to let him recover his power to act in this environment. The proposed design relies on a theoretical approach centered on two elements that are detailed: the core game elements of the simulator and the personalization of the game.

As reaching the final version of the simulator is planned for the end of November 2015, we will run some user tests to assess the effectiveness of the proposed simulator.

References

1. NHTSA: Traffic safety facts (dot hs 812 150). U.S. Dept. of Transportation (2015)
2. Wiederhold, B.K., Bouchard, S.: Advances in Virtual Reality and Anxiety Disorders. Springer, New York (2014)
3. Bohil, C.J., Alicea, B., Biocca, F.A.: Virtual reality in neuroscience research and therapy. Nat. Rev. Neurosci. **12**(12), 752–762 (2011)
4. Botella, C., Breton-López, J., Quero, S., Baños, R.M., Garcia-Palacios, A., Zaragoza, I., Alcaniz, M.: Treating cockroach phobia using a serious game on a mobile phone and augmented reality exposure: a single case study. Comput. Hum. Behav. **27**(1), 217–227 (2011)
5. Girard, B., Turcotte, V., Bouchard, S., Girard, B.: Crushing virtual cigarettes reduces tobacco addiction and treatment discontinuation. CyberPsychol. Behav. **12**(5), 477–483 (2009)
6. Bourgault, N., Bouchard, B., Menelas, B.-A.J.: Effect of ecological gestures on the immersion of the player in a serious game. In: Ma, M., Oliveira, M.F., Baalsrud Hauge, J. (eds.) SGDA 2014. LNCS, vol. 8778, pp. 21–33. Springer, Heidelberg (2014)

7. Plantevin, V., Menelas, B.A.J.: Use of ecological gestures in soccer games running on mobile devices. Int. J. Serious Games **1**(4) (2014)

8. Michael, D.R., Chen, S.L.: Serious games: Games that educate, train, and inform. Muska & Lipman/Premier-Trade (2005)

9. Menelas, B.A.J., Otis, M.J.D.: Design of a serious game for learning vibrotactile messages. In: 2012 IEEE International Workshop on Haptic Audio Visual Environments and Games (HAVE), pp. 124–129. IEEE (2012)

10. Bouchard, B., Imbeault, F., Bouzouane, A., Menelas, B.-A.J.: Developing serious games specifically adapted to people suffering from alzheimer. In: Ma, M., Oliveira, M.F., Hauge, J.B., Duin, H., Thoben, K.-D. (eds.) SGDA 2012. LNCS, vol. 7528, pp. 243–254. Springer, Heidelberg (2012)

11. Arnab, S., Lim, T., Carvalho, M.B., Bellotti, F., Freitas, S., Louchart, S., Suttie, N., Berta, R., De Gloria, A.: Mapping learning and game mechanics for serious games analysis. Br. J. Educ. Technol. **46**(2), 391–411 (2015)

12. Garcia-Palacios, A., Hoffman, H., Carlin, A., Furness, T.U., Botella, C.: Virtual reality in the treatment of spider phobia: a controlled study. Behav. Res. Ther. **40**(9), 983–993 (2002)

13. Kessler, R.C., Berglund, P., Demler, O., Jin, R., Merikangas, K.R., Walters, E.E.: Lifetime prevalence and age-of-onset distributions of DSM-IV disorders in the national comorbidity survey replication. Arch. Gen. Psychiatry **62**(6), 593–602 (2005)

14. Foa, E.B., Kozak, M.J.: Emotional processing of fear: exposure to corrective information. Psychol. Bull. **99**(1), 20 (1986)

15. Scozzari, S., Gamberini, L.: Virtual reality as a tool for cognitive behavioral therapy: a review. In: Brahnam, S., Jain, L.C. (eds.) Advanced Computational Intelligence Paradigms in Healthcare 6. SCI, vol. 337, pp. 63–108. Springer, Heidelberg (2011)

16. North, M.M., North, S.M., Coble, J.: Virtual Reality Therapy. IPI, Colorado Springs (1996)

17. Carlin, A.S., Hoffman, H.G., Weghorst, S.: Virtual reality and tactile augmentation in the treatment of spider phobia: a case report. Behav. Res. Ther. **35**(2), 153–158 (1997)

18. Côté, S., Bouchard, S.: Cognitive mechanisms underlying virtual reality exposure. CyberPsychol. Behav. **12**(2), 121–129 (2009)

19. Meyerbröker, K., Emmelkamp, P.M.: Virtual reality exposure therapy in anxiety disorders: a systematic review of process-and-outcome studies. Depression Anxiety **27**(10), 933–944 (2010)

20. Menelas, B.A.J., Picinali, L., Bourdot, P., Katz, B.F.: Non-visual identification, localization, and selection of entities of interest in a 3d environment. J. Multimodal User Interfaces **8**(3), 243–256 (2014)

21. Cukor, J., Spitalnick, J., Difede, J., Rizzo, A., Rothbaum, B.O.: Emerging treatments for ptsd. Clin. Psychol. Rev. **29**(8), 715–726 (2009)

22. Marks, I.: Behavioral psychotherapy of adult neurosis. In: Garfield, S.L., Bergin, A.E. (eds.) Handbook of Psychotherapy and Behavior Change (1978)

23. Bíró, G.I.: Didactics 2.0: a pedagogical analysis of gamification theory from a comparative perspective with a special view to the components of learning. Procedia Soc. Behav. Sci. **141**, 148–151 (2014)

24. Powers, M.B., Smits, J.A., Leyro, T.M., Otto, M.W.: Translational research perspectives on maximizing the effectiveness of exposure therapy. In: Handbook of the Exposure Therapies, pp. 109–126 (2007)

25. Hanus, M.D., Fox, J.: Assessing the effects of gamification in the classroom: a longitudinal study on intrinsic motivation, social comparison, satisfaction, effort, and academic performance. Comput. Educ. **80**, 152–161 (2015)
26. Morris, B.J., Croker, S., Zimmerman, C., Gill, D., Romig, C.: Gaming science: the gamification of scientific thinking. Front. Psychol. **4**, 607 (2013)

Challenges for Serious Game Design

Designing the Game-Based Neurocognitive Research Software "Hotel Plastisse"

Ulrich Götz[1], Mela Kocher[1(✉)], René Bauer[1], Cornelius Müller[2],
and Bruno Meilick[3]

[1] Zurich University of the Arts ZHdK, Zurich, Switzerland
{ulrich.goetz,mela.kocher,rene.bauer}@zhdk.ch
[2] Human Interface Design, Hamburg, Germany
cornelius.mueller@me.com
[3] Erding, Germany
brunomeilick@googlemail.com

Abstract. In this paper we address the challenges in designing game-based training software for use in a neurocognitive context. The project "Hotel Plastisse" is a cooperative software development, designed by researchers of the Specialization in Game Design at the Zurich University of the Arts (ZHdK) and of the International Normal Aging and Plasticity Imaging Center (INAPIC) at the University of Zurich. The aim of the project was to create a game-based software tool for a training study, which allows the comparison of single-domain and multi-domain cognitive training of elderly people. As the demand for game-based training software in scientific or therapeutic contexts is expected to grow in the future, we would like to share our insights into the development of a game that follows game design principles while at the same time generating scientifically valuable data.

Keywords: Serious game · Applied games · Cognitive training software · iPad

1 Introduction

Bavelier et al. have previously reported their findings on neuroscientific research with commercial video games and highlighted promising research opportunities for collaboration between game designers and neuroscientists [1]. Our project is characterized by such a collaboration. "Hotel Plastisse" [2] is a game-based cognitive training software designed by the Specialization in Game Design of the Zurich University of the Arts (ZHdK) [3], based on scientific cognitive training principles outlined by the International Normal Aging and Plasticity Imaging Center (INAPIC) at the University of Zurich [4]. The software was used in a cognitive training study to investigate training-induced cognitive change in healthy people aged 65 to 75 years. This paper presents insights into the project's design decisions, which had to take into account both game design principles and the aim of generating scientifically reliable data.

© Springer International Publishing Switzerland 2016
A. De Gloria and R. Veltkamp (Eds.): GALA 2015, LNCS 9599, pp. 323–328, 2016.
DOI: 10.1007/978-3-319-40216-1_34

2   The INAPIC Study

2.1   Context

The INAPIC study focuses on describing effective training interventions against the attenuation of normal cognitive decline in healthy aging [5]. While both single-domain (i.e., focusing on one domain of training only) and multi-domain cognitive trainings (i.e., simultaneously focusing on several domains of training) have been researched separately [6], the main focus of this study is a comparison between single-domain and multi-domain cognitive training. Crucial to the study is the employment of a highly motivating setting that surpasses the usual standard of cognitive training tasks [7]. Rather than conducting a training study with commercial video games [8], the study team commissioned a custom-tailored game-based training software that fulfilled the dual functions of both motivating study participants and generating analyzable data.

2.2   Scientific Requirements

The study design and the specific nature of the target group created a number of set requirements for the game, which were established jointly by INAPIC and ZHdK. Pre-tests showed that the target group had limited game experience. Further, the study required that participants attend daily training for 50 days with individualized game difficulty that adapted to the participants' performance. The participants were to be split in four separate groups, three of which were established as different single-domain training groups, and one as a multi-domain training group, the latter simultaneously combining the tasks of all single-domain training groups. The domains to be trained by performing tasks in the game-based environment of "Hotel Plastisse" were spatial navigation, visuo-motor coordination, and inhibition. Significant requirements related to the scientific quality of the data to be obtained from the four groups. In order to set performance results of single-domain and multi-domain trainings in relation to each other, numerous parameters of the training software had to be comparable to each other, including e.g. a common visual framework, duration of tasks, breaks in between training units, frequency and speed of in-game events.

3   Hotel Plastisse – Design Strategy

3.1   User-Centered Design Meets Scientific Requirements

Previous experience in serious game design [9] led the ZHdK researchers and designers to follow a distinct user-centered approach, attending to the needs of both participants and monitoring scientists. A Master of Arts in Design project was additionally integrated into the design process of "Hotel Plastisse", specifically to identify the optimal usability and playability solutions for the target group [10].

The study design required 50 daily training sessions for a user group that – due to their age – required an especially user-friendly training setup, regarding both the software and hardware usability, as well as the training environment. These circumstances resulted in the choice of iPad 1, and once it became available, iPad 2, as training devices. The iPads were handed out with the pre-installed "Hotel Plastisse" software, providing comfortable access and making it possible for participants to train at home in their domestic surroundings, thus increasing acceptance and endurance during the training period. The hardware could easily be handled by the target group [11]. Since the iPads were set up to transmit the data of daily training sessions to a university server via wireless internet, there would be no need for participants to commute to the research lab during the study, but INAPIC researchers would still be able to closely manage the study and conduct individualized monitoring.

3.2 Creating a Narrative Frame

The ZHdK design team developed the setting of a hotel as an overall narrative frame for "Hotel Plastisse". This general setting allowed for the creation of a variety of story and task elements, which on the one hand could meet the requirements for the four training groups, and on the other, could be designed as sequential mini-games under a common theme. The metaphor of a hotel also helped structure the game: in a manner similar to returning to a software menu, the hotel receptionist introduces the participant/ player to tasks, which are to be performed in the respective hotel rooms. The player is given the virtual role of the hotel owner's nephew, who carries out the tasks assigned. The various mini-games all relate to the central metaphor, and create a plausible narrative string. At the same time, the setting guarantees a game environment to which the participants can relate from their own personal experiences.

3.3 Designing for Cognitive Training and Data Generation

In order to generate a diversity of game situations during training sessions, each of the three single-domain training categories of spatial navigation, visuo-motor coordination and inhibition, as well as the multi-domain training category, feature 5 separate mini-games. In total, "Hotel Plastisse" features 20 mini-games (Fig. 1).

The scientific requirements stipulate that effective cognitive training has to be supported by automatically adjusted levels of difficulty of the training software with respect to the mini-games. Therefore, a training score of 80 % or more in a given mini-game task completion leads to a more difficult iteration of the same mini-game on the following training day, which will allow for achieving an even higher score. A score between 80 % and 60 % of task completion will maintain the same level of difficulty, whereas a score below 60 % will lower the level of difficulty. As the level of difficulty can theoretically be raised every training day over the course of 50 days, each of the mini-games provides 50 levels of difficulty. After the completion of a mini-game course, a calculation of the score is transparently communicated to the participant/player, also displaying his/her performance record over the past training days. In addition to receiving complimentary or encouraging comments, the participant/player is notified of whether or not they receive a reward in the form of admission to a higher level of difficulty on the following training day. This information serves as motivation for the participants/players to give their best during each training session. A detailed

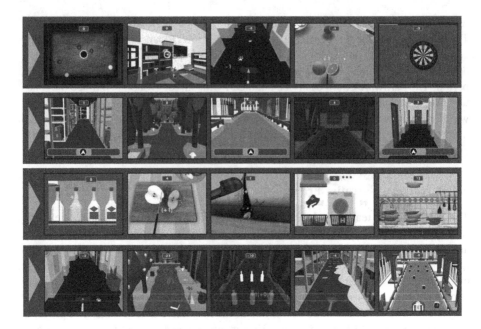

Fig. 1. Overview of the 20 mini-games in "Hotel Plastisse"

performance protocol of the participants' performance is transmitted to an INAPIC data server.

Once the participants agree to take part in the study, the training takes the following course: First, each participant is assigned to one of the four training categories of single- or multi-domain training. The participant agrees to train the same five mini-games of one training category every day, for 50 days. To do so, each day the participant starts the iPad application, logging-in with an assigned code name to begin the training session. The hotel owner Thomas welcomes the participant, and hands out an assignment for the first mini-game. A cutscene leads the participant from the lobby to a hotel room, where a specific mini-game task is to be performed. The cutscenes serve as time buffers, since all participants have to spend the same amount of time gaming every day. After the completion of the mini-game the participant receives motivational feedback, which consists of an encouraging text, the training score, and the training record accomplished so far. A cutscene leads back to the hotel lobby where Thomas sends the participant to the next mini-game. This procedure is repeated until all five training games have been completed, and Thomas bids the participant farewell for the day. This procedure takes place every day for the entire training period (Fig. 2).

4   Game Development Post-mortem

To optimize the gaming experience, video games tend to offer the player a maximum interactive control within their limitations. Conversely, the scientific requirements set for the development of "Hotel Plastisse" only permitted the strict parameters of testing

Fig. 2. Flowchart for the single-domain "Hotel Plastisse" training in spatial navigation

software, and not elaborated game mechanics (e.g. strategic player decisions, individual choice of narrative experiences or alternative routes, etc.). From a scientific point of view, "Hotel Plastisse" can be considered a valuable tool, as the software reliably creates comparable data from a high number of participants, thus laying the foundation for further research [5]. From the perspective of game design, the question remains whether participants experience "Hotel Plastisse" as a game with meaningful gameplay [12], or as a test. During the design process, possible in-game interactions had to be iteratively reduced to strengthen the comparability of the participants' performances within a limited set of measurable parameters. However, the design strategies discussed in 3 give rise to the participants' expectation that "Hotel Plastisse" is a game comparable to commercial video games. Therefore, user feedback will primarily deal with the software's game design components and not target its core nature of a test. The immanent nature of "Hotel Plastisse" produces a hybrid genre, a test in the guise of a game.

5 Conclusion

The call for future cooperation between neuroscience and game design, as made by Bavelier et al., implies complex teamwork: Specific scientific requirements must interconnect with game design requirements, resulting in a new, hybrid game genre, mixing game criteria with data generating tests. For optimal results, such hybrid games will have to be developed with close attention to both science and game design, taking their requirements, and public perceptions of their utility into account.

Acknowledgements. The authors would like to thank the following members of the core INAPIC team at the University of Zurich who developed the original research idea and initiated the collaboration with the ZHdK Zurich University of the Arts: Anne Eschen, Lutz Jäncke, Mike Martin, Susan Mérillat, Christina Röcke, Jacqueline Zöllig. Furthermore, Julia Binder and Ladina Costa-Bezzola were involved in the project.

References

1. Bavelier, D., Green, C.S., et al.: Brain plasticity through the life span: learning to learn and action video games. Ann. Rev. Neurosci. **35**, 391–416 (2012)
2. Cf. Project website. http://hotelplastisse.zhdk.ch. Accessed 16 Sep 2015
3. Website of ZHdK Specialization in Game Design. http://gamedesign.zhdk.ch. Accessed 16 Sep 2015
4. INAPIC. http://www.inapic.uzh.ch/index.html. Accessed 16 Sep 2015
5. Binder, J.C., Zöllig, J., Eschen, A., Mérillat, S., Röcke, C., Schoch, S.F., Jäncke, L., Martin, M.: Multi-domain training in healthy old age: Hotel Plastisse as an iPad-based serious game to systematically compare multi-domain and single-domain training. Front. Aging Neurosci. **7**, 137 (2015)
6. Buitenweg, J., Murre, J., Ridderinkhof, K.R.: Brain training in progress: a review of trainability in healthy seniors. Front. Hum. Neurosci. **6**, 183 (2012)
7. Jaeggi, S.M., Buschkuehl, M., Jonides, J., Perrig, W.J.: Improving fluid intelligence with training on working memory. Proc. Natl. Acad. Sci. (PNAS) (2008). www.pnas.org_cgi_doi_10.1073_pnas.0801268105. Accessed 16 Apr 2014
8. Basak, C., Boot, W.R., et al.: Can training in a real-time strategy video game attenuate cognitive decline in older adults? Psychol. Aging **23**(4), 765–777 (2008)
9. Applied Games at ZHdK. http://gamedesign.zhdk.ch/de/content/forschung/projekte. Accessed 16 Sep 2015
10. Master of Arts in Design project by Konradin Kuhn: Anforderungen an die Gestaltung von Spielwelten für Senioren am Beispiel des Serious Games "Hotel Plastisse", ZHdK Zurich University of the Arts, Master Thesis 2012. For download see http://hotelplastisse.zhdk.ch/publications/. Accessed 23 Oct 2015
11. Ijsselsteijn, W., Nap, H.H., de Kort, Y., Poels, K.: Digital game design for elderly users. In: Proceedings of the 2007 Conference on Future Play, pp. 17–22 (2007)
12. Salen, K., Zimmerman, E.: Rules of Play: Game Design Fundamentals. The MIT Press, Cambridge (2004)

Virtual Patients for Knowledge Sharing and Clinical Practice Training: A Gamified Approach

Federico Cabitza[1(✉)], Daniela Fogli[2], and Angela Locoro[1]

[1] Dipartimento di Informatica, Università di Milano Bicocca,
Viale Sarca, 336, 20126 Milano, Italy
{cabitza,angela.locoro}@disco.unimib.it
[2] Dipartimento di Ingegneria dell'Informazione,
Università degli Studi di Brescia, Via Branze 38, 25123 Brescia, Italy
daniela.fogli@unibs.it

Abstract. In this paper, we report the experimentation of QUESt, a Web-based tool designed to disseminate case-based knowledge in communities of experts, in the domain of medical training. To this aim, QUESt allowed the teachers of a specialization medical school to create virtual patients in the form of interactive online questionnaires and have students interact with these in a clinical contest. We discuss the results to argue that virtual patients and similar tools can foster the discussion and dissemination of case-oriented medical knowledge if used in lightly gamified initiatives, where participation is more important than winning.

1 Introduction

In this contribution, we advocate an approach to the sharing of medical knowledge that calls for technologies that effectively foster the participation of domain experts, in our case medical doctors. This participation is aimed at the discussion of circumscribed knowledge 'nuggets' and, possibly, at the emergence of practice-related knowledge from the usually silent front-line users [8], so as to build a sort of *collective knowledge* body.

The lack of ad-hoc tools that could specifically meet this high-level requirement motivated us in designing and deploying a lightweight technology, named QUESt [1], that allows doctors to create Virtual Patients in the form of adaptive online questionnaires that present short case reports, different diagnostic and treatment options, and collect preferred ways to 'solve' those cases.

Virtual Patients (VPs) "are clinical scenarios that play out on the computer screen" [3], where the computer plays the role of the patient and the learners interrogate it by typing or selecting questions and requesting information on laboratory or physical examinations; then, on the basis of the computer responses, the learners should be able to make a diagnosis and provide a management plan.

The study described in [4] revealed that VPs engaged medical students in higher critical thinking than students using paper cases. This ability is usually

© Springer International Publishing Switzerland 2016
A. De Gloria and R. Veltkamp (Eds.): GALA 2015, LNCS 9599, pp. 329–335, 2016.
DOI: 10.1007/978-3-319-40216-1_35

acquired through experience with a large number and broad range of case studies [5] and VPs appear as the aptest means to accomplish this task, since they also allow to sequence cases in an ideal mix in order to support different types of reasoning [3]: considering alternative hypotheses, reflecting on the key features of a case, or comparing it with other cases, by pattern recognition [2]. Last but not least, VPs put emphasis not only on arriving at a correct diagnosis, but also on the steps that lead to that diagnosis.

On the other hand, motivating learners and engaging them actively in training activity is becoming more and more important to reach an efficient and effective learning outcome. To this end, there is a growing interest in serious games [6] or in adopting gamification techniques [7] and introducing game design elements in non-game contexts, like the VP ambit.

For this reason, the VPs created with the QUESt system were experimented in a purposely gamified experience: a contest in which post-graduate doctors competed for the right interpretation of the case summary, the choice of the right diagnosis, the identification of the most appropriate treatment, while also employing the lower amount of resources. In case of an equal resource consumption, the winners would be selected for having limited the patient discomfort and risk, which were also assessed during the VP interaction.

This was made possible because each diagnostic and therapeutic option that our system made available to the respondents during the interaction with the VP was previously associated by the teachers with scores associated with the costs, time, risk and discomfort for the patient necessary to undertake the specific test or the treatment.

The QUESt system was specifically designed to facilitate the creation of VP-based contests also by non-programmers, as doctors are. This was in line with the need, discussed by [3], for better authoring tools for case development, as well as for new ways to assess the appropriateness of the clinical reasoning process. Accordingly, the main requirement of the QUESt system was to allow end users to create multi-page, dynamic online web questionnaires autonomously, as well as to extract the multiple paths of the choices and decisions made by the respondents, so as to assess their appropriateness and rank the performance within a gamified context.

The End-User Development (EUD) approach to the design of QUESt were aimed at: (i) making the VP development as much easy as describing it in (structured) natural language, by means of a configuration file written in YAML[1]; (ii) transforming the VP expressed by means of this structured description into an interactive online questionnaire to be presented to the medical students according to their interaction with the VP options.

---

[1] YAML is a simple machine-parsable data-serialization format designed for human readability and interaction with scripting languages such as Perl and Python, whose specifics are available at http://yaml.org/.

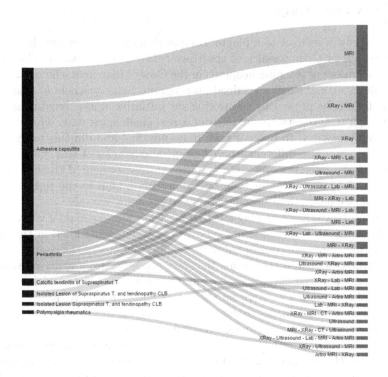

Fig. 1. The exam-diagnosis pathways for all the diagnoses given in the case at hand. (Color figure online)

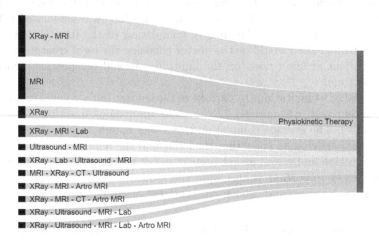

Fig. 2. The exam-therapy pathways for the most correct therapy for the case at hand. (Color figure online)

2   The Case Study

Our case study is relative to a playful competition initiative within the Special-ization School in Orthopaedics of the University of Milan (Italy). This school includes a number of teaching hospitals in the Great Milan area where post grad-uate students attend their specialization program. Some teachers of this school collaborated in the project by sponsoring the initiative among its students, and by drafting a case report on the basis of a real challenging case. This case was appropriately tweaked to make it even more puzzling and difficult to interpret, so as to become quite different from the typical examples of textbooks, as well as from routine interventions. Shortly put, the case presented to the students regarded a 55-year old woman, who was reporting a pain to the right shoulder that in the last month had become progressively more severe[2].

In our study, the game at play was that of "what would you do if you were the doctor in charge?". This game unfolded as the respondents filled in the online questionnaire: they were confronted with a short summary of the case; then they were supposed to choose the exams they felt necessary from a list of available options (the fewer, the better); each examination was associated with a concise report displayed after a random number of seconds (from 5 to 15). This delay was purposely added in order to deter the respondents from asking for all of the examinations in order to get more knowledge about the case. Moreover, each examination was associated with a cost and other contextual attributes (see above). After the presentation of the reports, the respondents were to select a diagnosis among a list of more or less plausible ones[3]; and then to choose both a therapy and a follow-up strategy according to the selected diagnosis.

The winners of the game were said to be obviously those who could select the right diagnosis and the appropriate therapy for that diagnosis; however, also the list of examinations that had been requested to find the right diagnosis was taken into consideration (i.e., the related decision path, which was associated with an aggregate score); as well as the time of completion of the questionnaire. The "one best" winner then would be the doctor choosing the right treatment for the (virtual) patient at lower cost (on the multidimensional perspective mentioned above) and time.

On a total of 94 invitations to partake in the contest (on a voluntary basis and with no incentives), we received 77 complete anonymous questionnaires (82 % response rate). The average completion times was 10 min.

All of the participants knew that the game and the related contest was just a gamified occasion and a well-meant pretext to get involved in a learning process where the most important things were the students' committed participation in solving the VP case and, above all, the later discussion of the case and the

---

[2] Reporting other medical details of this case would be out of the scope of this con-tribution.

[3] In our case study the correct diagnoses were more than one: "Adhesive capsulitis" was the most plausible and probable, followed by "Isolated Lesion of Supraspinatus T. and tendinopathy" and then "Calcific tendinitis of Supraspinatus T."

collected paths by the teachers. In particular, each practitioner was involved in the discussion of the case, as he/she was invited to compare his/her decisions with the ones of the teachers (and the winners), as well as of the colleagues (at least at a certain level of aggregation).

To this aim, the QUESt system had been also conceived to present a number of elements to be discussed after the students' interaction with the VP questionnaire: to this aim, it allowed for the extraction of many pieces of information from the response set and give them to the attention of the school teachers. For instance, by looking at the responses for the case at hand, Fig. 1 shows in form of infographic[4], the number of unique paths that had been undertaken by the practitioners involved[5].

Teachers deemed the "Adhesive capsulitis" as the most "correct" diagnosis for the case at hand. Forty-nine students out of 77 chose this diagnosis, while other six respondents chose a plausible alternative: all together 69% of the students got it right. The distribution of the decision paths is depicted in Fig. 1: this can also give an idea of which tests, and sequences of tests (i.e., paths), helped the respondents to identify the correct diagnosis, as well as which ones did not support the right reasoning toward the right answer. For instance, the diagram shows that the two paths "RMI" and "XRay - RMI" brought to the right diagnosis with a greater proportion than the other paths: these two examinations were then very useful to identify the correct diagnosis, but the best students chose only the RMI (the fewer tests, the better, as the lower the costs).

Figure 2 shows the numbers of paths for the right diagnosis that led to the most appropriate therapy (i.e., the physiokinetic therapy). The number of total respondents that had been able to associate the correct diagnosis with the correct therapy was much lower than in the case of diagnosis selection, i.e., 25 out of 77 (32%), exactly half of the good diagnosticians. Then, the task to build the right path of clinical decisions resulted to be a very challenging game, irrespective of the fake competition among colleagues, akin to the most difficult cases in real medical practice.

Table 1. The median, variance, interval for each costly dimension.

Item	Median	Variance	Min-Max value	Item	Median	Variance	Min-Max value
Money	190	65	20-540	Time	5	3	1-10
- Right	190	74	20-540	- Right	5	3	1-10
- Wrong	190	61	20-272	- Wrong	4	3	2-7
Risk	3	3	1-9	Discomfort	4	2	1-10
- Right	3	2	1-9	- Right	4	2	1-10
- Wrong	2	3	1-5	- Wrong	4	2	1-6

---

[4] All the infographics were created with the online tools available at http://raw. densitydesign.org.

[5] The order of the exams was relevant, e.g. the paths "XRay - MRI" and "MRI - XRay" were considered as two different diagnostic paths.

Table 1 reports the median, the variance and the min-max values interval of the aggregate scores (by sum of weights) associated with the paths built by the respondents (for each dimension: time, cost, discomfort, risk); both for the set of correct diagnoses, i.e., for the 53 respondents who "won the diagnosis game", and for the other 24 respondents who lost. The higher variance of the money-related item for the right diagnostic dimension (74 vs. 65) reflects the very different paths chosen by the doctors during the game before taking the correct decision.

3   Conclusions

The experience that we reported in this paper regards the use of QUESt, a system that was developed by following an EUD approach to allow doctors to create VPs autonomously and have them interact with trainees in terms of dynamic and multi-page online questionnaires. While the EUD part of this project was reported and validated in [1], here we focused on the learning experience that this system enabled. The medical teachers involved in this project applied QUESt to a learning initiative where their students had to be involved in a gamified contest and compete for the development of the best clinical path, in the shortest lapse of time and, most notably, with the lowest use of resources and risk: this latter element is at the core of the continuous quest of doctors for appropriateness of intervention and sustainability of healthcare. Winning this game was much less important than participation; moreover, the game gave both to students and teachers elements to discuss about a very difficult case, to understand why certain paths were more likely than others, and how the right choices could be made in the most efficient manner.

Our study then contributes in investigating how VPs and online questionnaires could be made suitable tools for medical training and for the continuous assessment of novices and trainees if used in a lightweight gamified context, where the competition does not regard being a good doctor, but rather making the best use of the resources available.

References

1. Cabitza, F.: On a QUESt for a web-based tool promoting knowledge-sharing in medical communities. Behav. Inf. Technol. **34**(6), 598–612 (2015)
2. Cendan, J., Lok, B.: The use of virtual patients in medical school curricula. Adv. Psysiol. Educ. **36**, 48–53 (2012)
3. Cook, D.A., Triola, M.M.: Virtual patients: a critical literature review and proposed next steps. Med. Educ. **43**, 303–311 (2009)
4. Kamin, C., OSullivan, P., Deterding, R., Younger, M.: A comparison of critical thinking in groups of third-year medical students in text, video, and virtual PBL case modalities. Acad. Med. **78**, 204–211 (2003)
5. Norman, G., Dore, K., Krebs, J., Neville, A.J.: The power of the plural: effect of conceptual analoies on successful transfer. Acad. Med. **82**(10 Suppl.), S16–S18 (2007)

6. Ricciardi, F., De Paolis, L.T.: A comprehensive review of serious games in health professions. IJCGT **2014**, 1–11 (2014)
7. Silva, F., Analide, C., Felgueiras, G., Pimenta, C.: Gamification, social networks and sustainable environments. IJIMAI **2**(4), 52–59 (2013)
8. Tucker, A.L.: An empirical study of system improvement by frontline employees in hospital units. M&SOM **9**(4), 492–505 (2007)

Gamified Platform for Physical and Cognitive Rehabilitation

Carina S. González[1(✉)], Pedro Toledo[1], Alberto Mora[2],
and Yeray Barrios[1]

[1] Department of Computer Engineering and Systems,
University of La Laguna, Santa Cruz de Tenerife, Spain
{carina,pedro,yeray}@isaatc.ull.es
[2] Department of Multimedia, Open University of Catalonia, Barcelona, Spain
amoraca@uoc.edu

Abstract. In this paper is described the design and development of a KINECT based interactive platform application aimed to physical rehabilitation and cognitive training of the minors in situations of illness. This platform, called TANGO:H, is highly configurable and customizable, thanks to exercises editor: TANGO:H Designer. So, the platform allows the adaptation of exercises and activities according to the specific characteristics of each user and user group.

Keywords: Physical rehabilitation · Cognitive training · Kinect · Exercises · Exergames

1 Introduction

The hospital classrooms (AH) provide educational services to students hospitalized during the period of compulsory education. The types of disease affecting these students are varied, but stand out the oncological, orthopedic, respiratory, diabetes and surgery. The time of admission to hospital may be of short duration (up to 5 days), medium duration (6–20 days) and long duration (over 21 days) and may affect the process of socialization and formation of the child. An average of 210 children a year is treated in the seven Canary hospital classrooms. Collaboration and discussion with clinicians (Pediatrics, Nursing and Physiotherapy) on the needs of this hospitalized population concluded that it was feasible to develop playful tools based on ICT and a scenario to boost and strengthen the physical and motor activity of hospitalized children and adolescents [1]. Note that this is a facet of their development so far unattended, but there are several researches tools for the rehabilitation purposes [2, 3]. These reasons have motivated the creation of the platform TANGO:H (Tangible Goals: Health), an open platform accessible and highly configurable to enable the creation, customization and adaptation of exercises and activities according to the specific characteristics of each user and user group.

Below we will analyze the requirements that we have followed in the design and development of the platform.

© Springer International Publishing Switzerland 2016
A. De Gloria and R. Veltkamp (Eds.): GALA 2015, LNCS 9599, pp. 336–341, 2016.
DOI: 10.1007/978-3-319-40216-1_36

2 Tango:H

TANGO:H is an application aimed to physical rehabilitation and cognitive training of the minors in situations of illness. It is also a tool for health promotion, where through social games and physical education patients can learn, exercise and interact with others. It is also a tool for professionals (therapists, educators, and psychologists) can create exercises adapted to the particular needs of each patient or user groups and monitor their evolution.

The power of TANGO:H lies in its capacity to generate exercises, i.e. it is not a static platform in which exercises or games are fully defined and integrated, but also allows the implementation of these through an editor that makes this task simple. The program is capable of interpret and execute the exercises previously created by the professional in the editor TANGO:H Designer (Tangible Goals: Health Designer). The interface for the end-user is an active video game, where the patient performs the exercises previously created as a game, interacting with the system through body movements and gestures. The combination between editor and game modules allows the creation of a variety of exercises, personalized and adapted to the characteristic of the patients.

To understand the composition and elements of the exercises you need to know a number of concepts that define the interaction with the application, as described in Table 1.

In order to consider a target as reached, the user will need to interact with it with any or all of the associated contact points whether it is a target with OR logic or AND logic respectively. Additionally, a special type of target can be assigned, the Dummy that should not be reached by the user.

The exercises will be displayed on screen step-by step, all targets belonging to a step will be shown on the game screen simultaneously. Once all step phases have been successfully completed, all targets will be replaced by the targets of the following step.

Using the established logic, the system classifies exercises in three different types: *(a) physical, (b) cognitive and (c) free*. Each exercise class is considered and evaluated differently at execution time.

In the *physical exercises*, the professional desires the user to perform a series of specific movements, making him to reach certain targets with one or more contact points. A large number of visual hints are required in order to communicate to the user the next movement to perform as intuitively as possible. The chosen method to indicate the user the next movement was to match the target and the points of contact highlighting them with the same colour. Furthermore, this exercise class requires a sequential structure that will allow the therapist to orchestrate the exercise at editing.

Moreover, with *cognitive exercises*, the educator is interested in avoiding visual hints that can give away the next target to be reached. Thus, for this exercise class, a set of targets will be presented making the user to engage in a cognitive task such as relate the sound of a cat with its visual representation (matching). Through the use of sound hints, the user will know the next target without making it too obvious. Cognitive tasks do not required a pre-establish order to reach the targets.

Table 1. Concepts and interaction elements in TANGO:H

Element	Description
Contact point	Represents a point of human body which allows user interaction with a target. The system currently has a total of 13 contact points enabled
Objective	This is the element that the user must meet one or more contact points. A Target consists of an image, or a region of the screen, to which accompanies a set of properties: - *Contact Point.* Can have one or many *Sound.* Plays when a contact point reaches the target - *Colour.* In TANGO:H represents the point of contact with which must be reached the Target
	A Target has associated one or more contact points, the interaction between them responds according to one of the three following behaviours: - *All at once.* All contact points should simultaneously reach the Target - *One.* At least one of the selected contact points must reach the Target - *Dummy.* This is a target that, although being reached, does not change the dynamics of the exercise, so it is not necessary define it Contact Points
Stage	A Stage is a group of targets. To overcome a stage, you must achieve all the objectives that comprise as: - *Synchronous.* The user must reach all the targets of the stage simultaneously - *Asynchronous.* The user must reach all the targets of the stage regardless of the order or the time instant in which it occurs
Step	A Step is a grouping of stages. To overcome a step, the user must complete the stages that compose it as: - *Sequential.* The user must overcome Stages in the order in which they were created - *Randomized.* The user must overcome Stages regardless of the order On the other hand, a step can be repeated as often as deemed necessary. The property that controls this is called iteration. Also you can assign a sound, so that, at the beginning the step plays itself
Exercise	An Exercise is a set of steps that are executed sequentially in the order in which they are defined. For the user to achieve an exercise, it must satisfy: - All sequentially steps or all phases grouped in each of the steps (sequentially or randomly) - All the targets that are grouped in each of the stages (synchronously or asynchronously) The visualization of the exercises in screen is done by Steps. That is, the targets that make a step will be presented simultaneously on the screen. Once achieved all targets of each of the phases that contains a step, they will be deleted from the screen, visualizing the next Step

In addition, the "free configuration" exercise type was added. This class allows the professional to create exercises on the editor ignoring any type of consideration established by the two previous types.

3   Games Modes

TANGO-H offers two game modes: (a) single or (b) multiplayer. In single mode the exercise will be conducted by one player in the categories described above (physical cognitive or free). Besides the traditional way of playing with a single user, in the multiplayer game mode two people can play sequentially or simultaneously, both competitively or collaboratively. This last mode has been possible by the functional detection of two human bodies concurrently.

In the sequential multiplayer mode, after selecting the game, the two players performing the same exercise of equal complexity, one after the other. However, in the simultaneous multiplayer mode, players will face the selected exercise simultaneously, working either in resolution as competing to reach as many points as possible. So, the competitive type shows the score for each player for the exercise performed, while in the collaborative multiplayer mode, users must work together to achieve the objectives, and the two users have the same score, time and stars.

4   Levels and Personalization

TANGO:H Designer includes the functionality to assign an action range to the objectives of an exercise. This action range shall be equal for all targets that make up the exercise, and requires the timing described in the previous section to detect whether or not the user is willing to play or is a step movement. The action range parameter defined from the TANGO:H Designer is included in the XML definition of exercise. It may also particularize this range with a factor that is assigned to the user.

All these settings for action range, both in the performance and in the user's profile, are evident in TANGO:H to the user executing the exercise, because when the user touches within the range (not necessarily in order) start counting the timing clock. This functionality can also create difficulty levels for exercises and users, and enables the designer to create groups of exercises that require different skills from simple to more complex. The level can be adjusted depending on the user's progress in treatment within the possibilities and needs of each patient [4].

5   Implementation and Validation

The Operating System (O.S.) employed as development platform has been Microsoft Windows 7©. When choosing the development platform, a study involving different alternatives was undertaken (drivers are available for all O.S. such as Linux).

One of the main factors considered when choosing Microsoft Windows© was its compatibility with Microsoft Kinect©. Another important factor in the decision is the large user base that this Operating System has, taking into account the objective to distribute the application to the largest number of users as possible.

The developed software has been implemented in C# on the .NET platform. The use of this platform guarantees the correct functioning of the application on Microsoft Windows© and eases the portability to future versions of this Operating System. In order to interact with Microsoft Kinect© the drivers developed by PrimeSense™ and the OpenNI™ libraries. OpenNI™ is an Open Source Framework that allows to develop applications for the Microsoft Kinect© device. OpenNI™ allows abstracting the data obtained from the device and using them to interpret the user position and pose through the generation of a virtual skeleton. This representation consists in thirteen contact points represented by different limbs and joints of which their position and orientation can be obtained in real time. The system development has focused in maintaining as much flexibility in exercise creation without affecting the usability of both product components. Additionally, the application has to adapt itself to the needs of the user. Therefore, it was crucial that the application was highly configurable and able to cover the cognitive needs or physical rehabilitation requirements. So, the adaptation is achieved through the logic introduced in application background responsible of executing the exercises defined in the XML.

We have followed in the design a User Centred Design (UCD) methodology [5], and validate the TANGO-H playability, usability and functionality with experts and children [6]. Note that 13 educational playability heuristics were evaluated, obtaining as educational playability average a value of 2.9, among values from 1 to 5 (Fig. 1).

Fig. 1. Validation of TANGO:H conducted with children

6 Conclusions

In this paper is described the design and development of a KINECT-based interactive platform, called TANGO:H. This platform is adaptable to the characteristics of the population it is intended: hospitalized children and in home care. Also, it is highly configurable and customizable, thanks to exercises editor: TANGO:H Designer. This feature allows health professionals and educators to create game-like exercises, adapted to the specific needs of end users and to the context in which the intervention will take place. Moreover, due to the diversity of users it targets, TANGO-H is an accessible platform that allows interaction with information systems without physical contact with the traditional control systems using KINECT sensor. Therefore, this tool allows compensation for physical inactivity of children in situations of illness and aims to help young hospitalized people in their recovery and, at the same time, support health professionals and educators. Also, this tool will help to normalize children providing them quality of life and wellbeing.

Acknowledgments. This work is funded by the research project SALUD-in: *"Interactive Virtual Rehabilitation Platform based on Social Games for Health, Physical Education and Natural Interaction Techniques"* PI2010/218 of Canarian Agency for Research, Innovation and Information Society.

References

1. Gonzalez, C., Toledo, P., Alayon, S., Munoz, V., Meneses, D.: Using information and communication technologies in hospital classrooms: SAVEH project. Knowl. Manag. E-Learn. Int. J. (KM&EL) **3**(1), 72–83 (2011)
2. Alankus, G., Lazar, A., May, M., Kelleher, C.: Towards customizable games for stroke rehabilitation. In: Proceedings of the 28th International Conference on Human Factors in Computing Systems, pp. 2113–2122. ACM (2010)
3. Cameirao, M., Bermudez, I., Duarte, O., Verschure, P.: The rehabilitation gaming system: a review. Stud. Health Technol. Inform. **145**, 65 (2009)
4. Hutzler, Y., Sherril, C.: Defining adapted physical activity: international perspectives. Adap. Phys. Act. Q. **24**(1), 1–20 (2007)
5. Nicholson, S.: A user-centered theoretical framework for meaningful gamification. In: Proceedings GLS 8.0 (2012)
6. González, C.: Student Usability in Educational Software and Games: Improving Experiences. Advances in Game-Based Learning (AGBL) Book Series. IGI Global, Pennsylvania (2012)

No Man Is a Monkey Island: Individual Characteristics Associated with Gamers' Preferences for Single or Multiplayer Games

Stefano Triberti[1]([⊠]), Daniela Villani[1], and Giuseppe Riva[1,2]

[1] Department of Psychology, Università Cattolica del Sacro Cuore,
Largo Gemelli 1, 20123 Milan, Italy
{stefano.triberti, daniela.villani,
giuseppe.riva}@unicatt.it
[2] Applied Technology for NeuroPsychology Lab,
IRCCS Istituto Auxologico Italiano, Via Magnasco 2, 20149 Milan, Italy

Abstract. Recent literature suggests that video games and serious games may be used to promote prosocial behavior and social abilities. Among several important open issues, a critical question regards what features of video games may be more suitable to address social skills promotion and morality education, for example single and multiplayer gaming. Since the research states that individual characteristics may drive media preferences/acceptance, here we analyzed individual differences (personality traits and social tendencies) among players who prefer single/multiplayer gaming. The results show that players who prefer multiplayer gaming were more agreeable, more empathic and less aggressive than the ones who prefer single player. Discussion deals with the importance of considering individual characteristics of the target population while designing video games or serious games for health interventions.

1 Introduction

Recent literature suggests that video games and serious games may be used to promote prosocial behavior [1, 2], social abilities [3, 4], and even morality education [5–7]. Indeed, since video games are interactive and can feature complex narratives, they can be used to place gamers inside moral dilemmas with the unique opportunity to reflect on the consequences of their own moral choices, possibly re-perform them again, this way engaging themselves into moral reasoning processes in a secure context. This opens to new opportunities for video games/serious games use in the field of education and life skills promotion. Indeed, life skills as effective communication, decision making, critical thinking, and empathy can be exercised in the context of social situations, which can be partially simulated by narratively-salient virtual environments [5]. However, applications in this field are still rare [8], and the research on this proposal is still in its infancy [6].

Among several important open issues, a critical question regards what features of video games may be more suitable to address social skills promotion and morality education. To address this question we have to consider that gamers' individual characteristics may orient their attitudes towards video games with different features.

A. De Gloria and R. Veltkamp (Eds.): GALA 2015, LNCS 9599, pp. 342–347, 2016.
DOI: 10.1007/978-3-319-40216-1_37

Indeed, the scientific literature states that personality can guide media preferences [9], which suggests that people may seek out entertainment that reflects aspects of their individual characteristics [10]. Therefore, it is possible that personality-related preferences have an influence on serious games and video games acceptance, which can be a key factor influencing games' effectiveness in the context of interventions for learning/education [11, 12]. Moreover, differences in personality traits and social abilities have shown to be associated with gamers' in-game behaviors and attitudes, which would be the key aspect in the context of intervention for social skills empowerment and/or morality education. Indeed, Joeckel and colleagues [13] argue that morality salience of media content serves as a guiding force in audience reactions, but this phenomenon is possibly influenced by individual attitudes. For example, gamers who preferred to play as evil characters and to perform evil actions inside video games resulted less agreeable, less empathic and more aggressive than gamers who preferred good characters/choices [5]. Moreover, gamers with anti-social motivations to play have been found less prone to feel emotional attachment towards fictional characters [14].

Concerning features of video games suitable to address social skills promotion and morality education, we consider that single and multi player games can offer different opportunities. For example, on the one hand, single player video games, which are certainly more widespread in the serious gaming scenario [15], are more useful to make the gamer focus on narrative contents and/or complex relationships and dialogues with fictional characters. On the other hand, multiplayer games may allow educators to generate and sustain real relationships and community building among real players. Indeed, multiplayer games are interesting for learning/education objectives, in that networking and team working are becoming the foundations of human performance in educational, organizational and recreational settings [16]. The experience of multiplayer video games is quite different from playing alone, in that it comprises the reward of being socialized into a virtual group/community of players and acquiring a reputation within it [17, 18]. Moreover, multiplayer online games experience may promote knowledge gain [19] and social influence among players [20, 21].

Teng [22] reported personality differences between multiplayer gamers and non-gamers: the first ones obtained higher scores in openess, conscientiousness and extraversion. Diversely, Collins and colleagues [23] compared problematic multiplayer gamers with non-gamers and they found that the first ones were higher in physical aggression and verbal aggression and lower in impulsivity and agreeableness.

Staring from these statements, we argue that it is worthy to explore the suitability of single player or multiplayer game designs for different attitudes, personality and abilities of video game players. The present contribution aims at addressing this issue, in order to identify possible individual dispositions towards game features which can be crucial for the development of effective games influencing the development of social skills.

2 Methods

205 video game players including 40 females ranging in age from 12 to 47 years (M = 24.85, SD = 4.98) participated in the research. In the context of a more broad research on game preferences [5], they were asked to write the name of a video game

character, representing their preferences in the video games world. Then, we categorized these characters as coming from single player games, or games with at least a multiplayer feature. This way, the total sample has been split between players with a preference for single player (120) or multiplayer games (85). Differently from other studies on the topic [23], the gamers constituting our sample were not problematic gamers, in that they were equally distributed among different amounts of gaming activity. Precisely, 59 players (28.8 %) used to play video games two times a week, 67 (32.7 %) used to play four-five times a week and 79 (38.5 %) used to play everyday.

We assessed personality based on the taxonomic structure derived from factor analytics consisting of five bi-polar dimensions that categorize the fundamental facets (traits) of human personality, that is, the Five Factor Model (McCrae & Costa, 2008) composed by *Openness*, such as curious, imaginative, and artistic people; *Conscientiousness*, such as efficient, organized, and thorough people; *Extraversion* such as sociable, energetic, and enthusiastic people; *Agreeableness*, such as forgiving, warm and sympathetic people; and *Neuroticism*, such as tense, irritable, and moody people. The Italian version [25] of the Big Five Inventory (BFI) [26] was used to measure each personality trait in the present study.

We then assessed social abilities of players by focusing on empathic abilities and aggression tendencies. Empathic abilities were evaluated using the Italian version [27] of the Interpersonal Reactivity Index [28], consisting of four dimensions: *Empathic Consideration* (feeling emotional concern for others), *Perspective Taking* (cognitively taking another's perspective), *Fantasy* (emotional identification with fictional characters), and *Personal Distress* (negative feelings in response to the distress of others).

Aggression tendencies were evaluated using the Italian version [29] of the Aggression Questionnaire [30] which is based on a multifaceted conception of aggression entailing four sub-traits: *Physical* and *Verbal Aggression* that represent the instrumental or motor components; *Anger* or *Rage* that constitutes the emotional or affective component, that is, the physiological arousal as preparation for aggression; and *Hostility*, which represents the cognitive component. Finally, *Aggression Total* was computed by the sum of scores on the four subscales.

3   Results

We performed analyses of variance with the preference for single or multiplayer gaming as the independent variable, and the personality traits and social abilities/tendencies as the dependent variables. No significant results emerged for Extraversion, Neuroticism, Openess, Conscientiousness, Hostility, IRI Personal Distress, IRI Perspective Taking and IRI Fantasy. Diversely, significant results emerged for the remaining variables. As Table 1 shows, gamers with a preference for multiplayer games were found to be more agreeable [$F(1,204) = 8.116$, $p = .005$, $\eta^2 = .038$], less verbally [$F(1,204) = 5.495$, $p = .020$, $\eta^2 = .026$] and physically aggressive [$F(1,204) = 3.887$, $p = .050$, $\eta^2 = .019$], less prone to emotional [$F(1,204) = 4.515$, $p = .035$, $\eta^2 = .020$] and total aggressive tendencies [$F(1,204) = 7.287$, $p = .008$, $\eta^2 = .035$] and more able to feel emotional concern for others [Empathic consideration: $F(1,204) = 5.087$, $p = .025$, $\eta^2 = .024$].

Table 1. Means and standard deviations from the performed analyses of variance for single and multiplayer games.

Questionnaires	Subscales	Single Player	Multiplayer
Interpersonal	Fantasy	24.15, DS = 4.72	23.65, DS = 5.06
Reactivity	Empathic Consideration*	23.05, DS = 4.3	24.41, DS = 4.12
Index	Perspective Taking	23.64, DS = 4.59	23.31, DS = 4.29
	Personal Distress	18.6, DS = 4.82	18.77, DS = 4.32
Aggression	Physical Aggression*	18.92, DS = 6.46	17.15, DS = 6.16
Questionnaire	Verbal Aggression*	15.47, DS = 4.16	14.14, DS = 3.78
	Anger*	16.89, DS = 5.59	15.35, DS = 4.31
	Hostility	21.19, DS = 6.88	19.6, DS = 5.64
	Aggression (Total)*	72.48, DS = 16.92	66.24, DS = 15.36
Big Five Inventory	Conscientiousness	3.27, DS = 0.72	3.46, DS = 0.72
	Openness	3.71, DS = 0.63	3.73, DS = 0.62
	Neuroticism	2.88, DS = 0.83	2.93, DS = 0.77
	Extraversion	2.81, DS = 0.84	2.94, DS = 74
	Agreeableness**	3.35, DS = 0.61	3.60, DS = 0.64

4   Discussion and Conclusions

Previous research has investigated the relationship between video game playing and gamers' personality traits quite often. To our knowledge, this is the first attempt to identify personality correlates of preferences for single/multiplayer gaming. The results of the present research suggest that, to an extent, personality traits and pre-existing social abilities may drive gamers' attitudes towards product features such as single/multiplayer gaming. While designing games for educational interventions to promote prosocial behavior and/or social skills, designers should take into account not only the best game features according to the intervention objectives but, where possible, the individual characteristics of a target population too. Personality differences can be important for game design, in that as Koster [31] says, different games appeal to different personality types and individual differences constitute an important element for long-term success of a product. Indeed, game design already considers individual differences in gaming style and personality, such as the well known gamers taxonomy provided by Bartle [32] which divides video game players among achievers, explorers, killers and socialisers. Focusing on personality differences related to game features, our results suggest that players less agreeable, less empathetic and more aggressive may feel more comfortable while engaging themselves into single player virtual experiences. On the contrary, players who are characterized by stronger social skills and a more positive attitude towards others may be more well disposed towards the opportunity of playing with other people. From a game design perspective, this results suggest that video games for health may include quick personality assessment tools (e.g. brief questionnaires) to assess players' characteristics, in order to provide advices about possible game features/modes to be chosen. Otherwise, taking into account information about players' personality the games could adapt themselves, for example giving more or less emphasis to some of the game contents (say: the presence and activity of other players) during the game instances. Further research should explore whether individual differences may also influence serious games' final effectiveness in the context of game-based interventions for health.

References

1. Koo, G., Seider, S.: Video games for prosocial learning. In: Schrier, K., Gibson, D. (eds.) Ethics and Game Design: Teaching Values Through Play. IGI Global, Hersey (2010)
2. Gentile, D.A., Anderson, C.A., Yukawa, S., Ihori, N., Saleem, M., Ming, L.K., Shibuya, A., Liau, A.K., Khoo, A., Bushman, B.J., Rowell Huesmann, L., Sakamoto, A.: The effects of prosocial video games on prosocial behaviors international evidence from correlational, longitudinal, and experimental studies. Pers. Soc. Psychol. Bull. **35**, 752–763 (2009)
3. Greitemeyer, T., Osswald, S., Brauer, M.: Playing prosocial video games increases empathy and decreases schadenfreude. Emotion **10**, 796–802 (2010)
4. Anderson, C.A., Shibuya, A., Ihori, N., Swing, E.L., Bushman, B.J., Sakamoto, A., Rothstein, H.R., Saleem, M.: Violent video game effects on aggression, empathy, and prosocial behavior in eastern and western countries: a meta-analytic review. Psychol. Bull. **136**, 151–173 (2010)
5. Triberti, S., Villani, D., Riva, G.: Moral positioning in video games and its relation with dispositional traits: the emergence of a social dimension. Comput. Hum. Behav. **50**, 1–8 (2015)
6. Weaver, A.J., Lewis, N.: Mirrored morality: an exploration of moral choice in video games. Cyberpsychol. Behav. Soc. Netw. **15**(11), 610–614 (2012)
7. Happ, C., Melzer, A., Steffgen, G.: Superman vs. BAD man? the effects of empathy and game character in violent video games. Cyberpsychol. Behav. Soc. Netw. **16**, 774–778 (2013)
8. Krebs, J.: Moral dilemmas in serious games. In: Proceedings of the 2013 International Conference on Advanced ICT, pp. 232–236. Atlantis Press, Paris (2013)
9. Kraaykamp, G., van Eijck, K.: Personality, media preferences, and cultural participation. Pers. Indiv. Differ. **38**, 1675–1688 (2005)
10. Rentfrow, P.J., Goldberg, L.R., Zilca, R.: Listening, watching, and reading: the structure and correlates of entertainment preferences. J. Pers. **79**, 223–258 (2011)
11. Lavender, T.: Homeless: it's no game-measuring the effectiveness of a persuasive videogame. In: 2nd European Conference on Games Based Learning, p. 261 (2008)
12. Yusoff, A., Crowder, R., Gilbert, L.: Validation of serious games attributes using the technology acceptance model. In: 2nd Internationl Conference on Games and Virtual Worlds for Serious Application, VS-GAMES 2010, pp. 45–51 (2010)
13. Joeckel, S., Bowman, N.D., Dogruel, L.: Gut or game? the influence of moral intuitions on decisions in video games. Media Psychol. **15**, 460–485 (2012)
14. Bowman, N.D., Schultheiss, D., Schumann, C.: "I'm attached, and I'm a Good Guy/Gal!": how character attachment influences pro- and anti-social motivations to play massively multiplayer online role-playing games. Cyberpsychol. Behav. Soc. Netw. **15**, 169–174 (2012)
15. Wendel, V., Gutjahr, M., Göbel, S., Steinmetz, R.: Designing collaborative multiplayer serious games. Educ. Inf. Technol. **2**, 287–308 (2013)

16. Argenton, L., Muzio, M., Shek, E.J., Mantovani, F.: Multiplayer serious games and user experience: a comparison between paper-based and digital gaming experience. In: De Gloria, A. (ed.) GALA 2014. LNCS, vol. 9221, pp. 54–62. Springer, Heidelberg (2015)
17. Yee, N.: Motivations for play in online games. Cyberpsychol. Behav. **9**, 772–775 (2006)
18. Ducheneaut, N., Yee, N., Nickell, E., Moore, R.J.: "Alone Together?" exploring the social dynamics of massively multiplayer online games. In: CHI 2006, pp. 407–416 (2006)
19. Hopp, T., Barker, V., Schmitz Weiss, A.: Interdependent self-construal, self-efficacy, and community involvement as predictors of perceived knowledge gain among MMORPG players. Cyberpsychol. Behav Soc. Netw. **18**, 468–473 (2015)
20. Trepte, S., Reinecke, L., Juechems, K.: The social side of gaming: how playing online computer games creates online and offline social support. Comput. Hum. Behav. **28**, 832–839 (2012)
21. Zhong, Z.J.: The effects of collective MMORPG (Massively Multiplayer Online Role-Playing Games) play on gamers' online and offline social capital. Comput. Hum. Behav. **27**, 2352–2363 (2011)
22. Teng, C.-I.: Personality differences between online game players and nonplayers in a student sample. Cyberpsychol. Behav. **11**, 232–234 (2008)
23. Collins, E., Freeman, J., Chamarro-Premuzic, T.: Personality traits associated with problematic and non-problematic massively multiplayer online role playing game use. Pers. Indiv. Differ. **52**, 133–138 (2012)
24. McCrae, R.R., Costa Jr., P.T.: The five-factor theory of personality. In: John, O.P., Robins, R.W., Pervin, L.A (Eds.) Handbook of Personality: Theory and Research, 3rd edn., pp. 159–181 (2008)
25. Ubbiali, A., Chiorri, C., Hampton, P., Donati, D.: Italian big five inventory. Psychometric properties of the italian adaptation of the big five inventory (BFI). Boll. di Psicol. Applicata. **59**(266), 37 (2013)
26. John, O.P., Donohue, E.M., Kentle, R.L.: The Big Five Inventory: Versions 4a and 54 (1991)
27. Albiero, P., Ingoglia, S., Lo Coco, A.: Contributo all'adattamento italiano dell'Interpersonal Reactivity Index. Testing-Psicometria-Metodologia **13**, 107–125 (2006)
28. Davis, M.H.: Measuring individual differences in empathy: evidence for a multidimensional approach. J. Pers. Soc. Psychol. **44**, 113–126 (1983)
29. Fossati, A., Maffei, C., Acquarini, E., Di Ceglie, A.: Multigroup confirmatory component and factor analyses of the italian version of the aggression questionnaire. Eur. J. Psychol. Assess. (2003)
30. Buss, A.H., Perry, M.: The aggression questionnaire. J. Pers. Soc. Psychol. **63**, 452–459 (1992)
31. Koster, R.: A Theory of Fun. O'Reilly Media, Sebastopol (2004)
32. Bartle, R.: Hearts, clubs, diamonds, spades: players who suit MUDs. J. MUD Res. **1**, 19 (1996)

N.O.T.E.: Note Over The Edge

Alessandro Riccadonna, Davide Gadia$^{(\boxtimes)}$, Dario Maggiorini,
and Laura Anna Ripamonti

Università degli Studi di Milano, Via Comelico 39, 20135 Milano, Italy
`alessandro.riccadonna@studenti.unimi.it`,
`{gadia,dario,ripamonti}@di.unimi.it`

Abstract. A cochlear implant is an electronic device surgically implanted to improve auditory perception in people suffering of severe hearing loss. While a cochlear implant supports a sufficient spoken communication, it is limited in the reception of more complex sounds. Long training sessions are needed in order to enhance the auditory abilities of the patients and, as a consequence, maintain a high level of interest and concentration during the training tasks is mandatory.

In this paper, we present N.O.T.E. (Note Over The Edge): a video game designed for auditory training of prelingually deaf children with cochlear implant. N.O.T.E. has been designed as an integrated and flexible system, using a game-based approach to present to the children a set of tests with different complexity, and allowing to the therapist a complete monitoring of the progresses of the training.

Keywords: Auditory training · Cochlear implant · Children · Video game

1 Introduction

The World Health Organization states [1] that over the 5 % of the world population (around 360 million people) suffers of hearing loss. In very severe cases [2], a cochlear implant is needed to provide a sufficient auditory perception. As of December 2012, approximately 324,000 people worldwide are using a cochlear implant [3]. This kind of device brings an actual improvement in the quality of life of people suffering hearing loss, but, however, the technical limitations of current cochlear implants do not allow to recover the complete functionalities of a normal hearing. Even if the limited number of frequencies elaborated by the device is usually sufficient to allow a satisfactory spoken communication with a single interlocutor, there are noticeable limits in the discrimination of speech intonation (questions or statements), and in the perception of more complex sounds, like e.g., melodic patterns. This situation is particularly critical in prelingually deaf children, because they cannot use their precedent experience regarding sounds and speech during the adaptation stage to the sounds processed by the cochlear implant.

A. De Gloria and R. Veltkamp (Eds.): GALA 2015, LNCS 9599, pp. 348–353, 2016.
DOI: 10.1007/978-3-319-40216-1_38

A long and accurate auditory training is considered a necessary stage in the adaptation to the new hearing condition and in the development of a finer recognition of sounds and speech [4–8]. Applications for auditory training developed for devices like smartphones and tablets can represent important tools to be integrated in a habilitation therapy due to their diffusion and portability. However, few studies in literature on auditory training have addressed the specific case of prelingually deaf children [6], and almost no tools exist which are explicitly developed for the training of these subjects.

In 2012, Zhou et al. [9] proposed the MOGAT system: a mobile application presenting a set of exercises designed for music training of prelingually deaf children. The presented validation proved how it is necessary to specifically design the auditory training for prelingually deaf children, including activities perceived as interesting and entertaining.

In this paper, we present N.O.T.E. (Note Over The Edge): a video game designed for the auditory training of prelingually deaf children. We embed training activities inside a video game rather than develop a set of different interactive exercises, because our purpose is to investigate if the characteristics of a video game (like e.g., interactivity, gameplay, sense of achievement [10]) can contribute in a positive way to the reception and interest of the children to the training plan proposed by the therapists [11–13].

In the next sections, after describing N.O.T.E., preliminary results obtained from a field experimentation are presented.

2 N.O.T.E.: Note Over The Edge

N.O.T.E. has been designed for 6–8 years old children with cochlear implants. Considering this target, a video game is the most appropriate choice as training environment, since it allows the schematic integration [10] of several different auditory and visual stimuli in an interactive application; a combination that optimizes the cognitive elaboration of informations [14].

After a preliminary analysis, it has been decided to develop N.O.T.E. as an "endless running game" for a tablet device, because the characteristics of this kind of game are easily adaptable to the nature of the planned tasks: the interaction is usually limited to a small number of predefined simple movements or actions, the game world and levels are generated procedurally and theoretically unlimited, and, if accurately designed and tuned, it is possible to keep high levels of attention and motivation [15].

In N.O.T.E., the player controls a swimmer who, surprised by a storm, must reach the seashore. The player swims from left to right, and she can move up and down on 5 different lanes. While swimming, the player finds some boxes floating in the water: as soon as she approaches a box, a notes sequence (monotonic, ascending, or descending) is played. On the basis of the evaluation of the amplitude of the notes sequence, the player must choose if she has to stay on the same lane, or move in a upper or lower lane. This choice will avoid obstacles (sharks or similar creatures), and select the only safe lane, where a lifebelt is waiting for the swimmer. If the swimmer reaches the lifebelt, her score is updated, and the velocity of the game is increased, otherwise the game is slowed down. Figure 1 shows some screenshots of the main stages of a N.O.T.E. level. The performance of the player is based on the overall number of correct evaluations, on the number of consecutive correct answers, and on the correlation between the time used before each decision and the complexity of the stimuli used in the level. This design allows a great flexibility in the characteristics and complexity of each single test and the overall levels, while keeping the player motivated and interested for long gaming sessions, therefore improving the efficacy of the auditory training.

An administration panel has been developed as a web application to allow the therapists to monitor the performances of the children, and to design new levels, by creating procedurally new notes sequences or uploading external music files. Therefore, the auditory training is controlled and based on a remote communication: the game uploads to a web server all the results from the gaming sessions, which will be available to the therapists in the administration panel while, if a network connection is available, the download of updated levels and exercises are performed at the beginning of each gaming session.

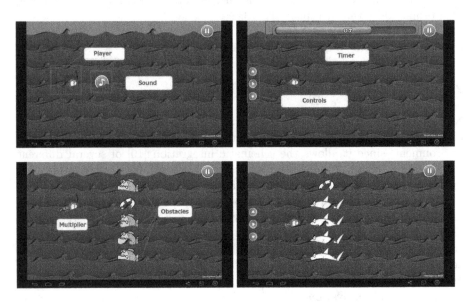

Fig. 1. Four screenshots of a N.O.T.E. level: the player meets a new sound box (top left); after hearing the notes sequence, the player must choose if move or not (top right); if the choice is correct, the multiplier (the lifebelt) will update the number of correct answers and it will speed up the game (bottom left); if the choice is wrong, the obstacle will update the number of wrong answers and it will speed down the game (bottom right)

3   Preliminary Validation

We have performed a preliminary testing session with a set of 5 children between 6 and 8 years old, all with cochlear implants since a period ranging from 11 to 26 months. Under the supervision of a parent, they have played with a version of the game developed to run in a web browser, to avoid possible differences between mobile devices. This version of N.O.T.E. consisted in 7 different levels with increasing complexity, each repeated 5 times.

In Fig. 2 we show the average percentage of correct answers and the average reaction times. We have divided the children in subsets on the basis of their age. It can be noticed how the average reaction times increase with the complexity of the levels, with the exception of the only 8 years old child, who however is the subject with a longer experience with a cochlear implant. Regarding the percentage of correct answers, it can be noticed how the percentage is always under 80 %, and that the preliminary results seem to suggest a different behaviour of the subsets of children regarding specific complexity levels: this trend requires a more accurate investigation, in order to check possible correlations between age, age of installation of the cochlear implant, and different thresholds in the notes variations.

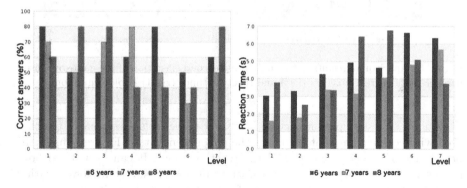

Fig. 2. Results of the preliminary tests: percentage of correct answers (left) and reaction times (right) (Color figure online)

We have also asked 3 normal hearing children to play with the same version used in the experiment, in order to have a benchmark. In Fig. 3 we show the average percentage of correct answers and the average reaction times of the children with cochlear implants (i.e., we present an average of the data presented in Fig. 2) compared with the averaged data from the normal hearing children. It can be noticed that the differences between the two sets of players are relevant: if the normal hearing children show an average reaction time almost constant through the different levels, the reaction times of the children with cochlear implants increase almost linearly with the level of complexity.

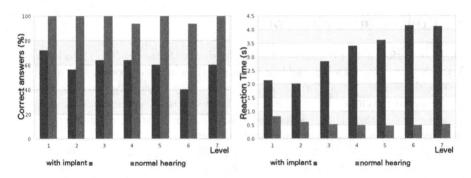

Fig. 3. Comparison of results between children with cochlear implants and normal hearing subjects: percentage of correct answers (left) and reaction times (right) (Color figure online)

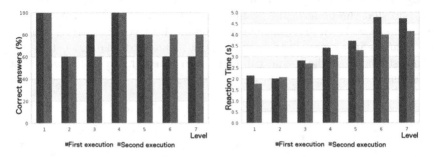

Fig. 4. Comparison of results between first and second execution of the game by a user: percentage of correct answers (left) and reaction times (right) (Color figure online)

Finally, as a very preliminary additional test, we have asked one of the children with cochlear implant to repeat the experimental test. Figure 4 shows the percentage of correct answers and the reaction times. It can be noticed how, in this second repetition, the reaction times in the last levels are lower, with a correspondent increase in the number of correct answers. Even if it is not possible to deduce final conclusions from a test with a single user, we interpret these results as a preliminary suggestion about the validity of the proposed approach.

4   Conclusion and Future Work

We have proposed N.O.T.E.: a game designed to be an effective tool for the auditory training of children with cochlear implants. The preliminary tests seem to validate the initial design choices: the game has been well received by the children involved in the first trials, and the results suggest that the approach proposed with N.O.T.E. can represent a valid tool to enhance the auditory perception.

A full validation with a larger number of subjects will be performed under the supervision of expert therapists as soon as all the protocols required in case of scientific tests involving children will be approved.

Future extensions will include the development of additional tools in the administration panel, in order to allow the therapists to create different and more accurate notes sequences, and the introduction of an achievement system in the game (trophies), in order to keep a high level of interest and motivation in the children.

Acknowledgements. The authors thank Dr. Antonio Mancuso and Dr. Massimo Grassi for their contribution in the design of N.O.T.E..

References

1. World Health Organization: Deafness, hearing loss (2015). http://www.who.int/mediacentre/factsheets/fs300/en/
2. Cochlear: Degrees of hearing loss (2015). http://www.cochlear.com/wps/wcm/connect/intl/home/understand/hearing-and-hl/what-is-hearing-loss-/degrees-of-hl
3. NIH Publication No. 11-4798: Cochlear Implants (2015). https://www.nidcd.nih.gov/health/hearing/pages/coch.aspx
4. Gfeller, K., Witt, S., Adamek, M., Mehr, M.R., Rogers, J., Stordahl, J., Ringgenberg, S.: Effects of training on timbre recognition and appraisal by postlingually deafened cochlear implant recipients. J. Am. Acad. Audiol. **13**(3), 132–145 (2002)
5. Galvin III, J.J., Fu, Q.J., Nogaki, G.: Melodic contour identification by cochlear implant listeners. Ear Hear. **28**(3), 302–319 (2007)
6. Galvin, J.J., Fu, Q.J., Shannon, R.V.: Melodic contour identification and music perception by cochlear implant users. Ann. N. Y. Acad. Sci. **1169**(1), 518–533 (2009)
7. Chen, J.K.C., Chuang, A.Y.C., McMahon, C., Hsieh, J.C., Tung, T.H., Li, L.P.H.: Music training improves pitch perception in prelingually deafened children with cochlear implants. Pediatrics **125**(4), e793–e800 (2010)
8. Petersen, B., Mortensen, M.V., Hansen, M., Vuust, P.: Singing in the key of life: a study on effects of musical ear training after cochlear implantation. Psychomusicol. Music Mind Brain **22**(2), 134–151 (2010)
9. Zhou, Y., Sim, K.C., Tan, P., Wang, Y.: MOGAT: mobile games with auditory training for children with cochlear implants. In: Proceedings of the 20th ACM International Conference on Multimedia, pp. 429–438. ACM (2012)
10. Koster, R.: Theory of Fun for Game Design, 2nd edn. O'Reilly Media, Sebastopol (2013)
11. Gaggi, O., Palazzi, C.E., Ciman, M., Galiazzo, G., Franceschini, S., Ruffino, M., Gori, S., Facoetti, A.: Serious games for early identification of developmental dyslexia. ACM Comput. Entertain. (2014, in press)
12. Maggiorini, D., Ripamonti, L.A.: LTC for seniors: an intelligent gaming solution. Int. J. Digit. Hum. (2014, in press)
13. Knutas, A., Ikonen, J., Maggiorini, D., Ripamonti, L.A., Porrasi, J.: Creating software engineering student interaction profiles for discovering gamification approaches to improve collaboration. In: Proceedings of 15th International Conference on Computer Systems and Technologies (CompSysTech 2014) (2014)
14. Paivio, A.: Dual coding theory: retrospect and current status. Can. J. Psychol. **45**(3), 255–287 (1991)
15. Csikszentmihalyi, M.: Flow: The Psychology of Optimal Experience. Harper and Row, New York (1990)

Smash! Sport Participation and Commitment by Game Design

Harald Warmelink$^{(\boxtimes)}$, Sean Vink, and Richard van Tol

HKU Innovation Studio, HKU University of the Arts Utrecht,
Lange Viestraat 2b, 3511 BK Utrecht, The Netherlands
{harald.warmelink,richard.vantol}@hku.nl,
seankvink@gmail.com

Abstract. The authors present *Smash!*, a game concept aimed at increasing participation in and commitment to tennis. A game design team was confronted with a theory of tennis student dropout based on a distinction between four tennis kid types: the Tryer, Buyer, Flyer and High Flyer. An initial problem articulation and goal definition phase led to a concept that should encourage the transitions from Tryer to Buyer to Flyer. The concept consists of three parts: (1) an online platform revolving around a personal avatar with which skill development is tracked and encouraged; (2) a smartphone app of mini-games to train tennis tactics; (3) a QR-coded personal club card for tennis students to find each other and play a virtual tennis match with. Contributions of and further research opportunities for the *Smash!* concept are reflected upon.

1 Introduction

The Dutch tennis federation (in Dutch, the Koninklijke Nederlandse Lawn Tennis Bond; KNLTB) is alarmed by the sport attrition they observe, i.e., sports club dropout. This kind of sport attrition is perceived as a problem, because sports clubs have traditionally played an important part in a community's physical activity. By providing sport facilities and opportunities, sports clubs at least increase the chance of children and adolescents becoming physically active [1, 2]. KNLTB approached the School of Games and Interaction of HKU University of the Arts Utrecht (or HKU for short), asking whether some kind of game-based design could attract Dutch youngsters to and retain them in tennis sports clubs once again.

With this question KNLTB presented a novel game design research challenge. Research into sport participation and commitment through game design is scarce. Related research has focused on enticing physical activity and exercise at home or a medical institution through game or gamification design, often as (part of) a prevention or treatment program for certain diseases, disabilities or trauma [3–8]. Although related, sport participation or commitment is not explicitly pursued in such research.

Given this lack of research as well as calls for further sports redesign [2, 9], we took the opportunity presented by KNLTB to explore whether or how game design could stimulate sport participation and commitment, fully realizing that what we would be doing is effectively a redesign of sports education one way or another, in this case tennis education.

© Springer International Publishing Switzerland 2016
A. De Gloria and R. Veltkamp (Eds.): GALA 2015, LNCS 9599, pp. 354–360, 2016.
DOI: 10.1007/978-3-319-40216-1_39

In this article we explain and discuss *Smash!*, a concept that was designed over a six-month period by a group of HKU students, supervised by a teacher and a researcher. We discuss the concept by juxtaposing it onto sport-/social-scientific theories of sport participation and commitment. By doing so we aim to prove the content and face validity of the concept [10].

2   Problem Articulation and Goal Definition

2.1   Tryers, Buyers, Flyers and High Flyers

At the start of the project KNLTB distinguished four kinds of young tennis learners, or 'tennis kids' in their own words, following four different levels of proficiency and involvement [11]:

- Tryers are children with little to no proficiency or understanding of game rules. Learning how to play the game of tennis is the most important factor in motivation. They often find 'the game' daunting.
- Buyers are the ones who actually say 'I play tennis'. They really want to play 'the game'. Having fun is their most important motivational factor for playing tennis. Tennis is often one of their many weekly activities.
- Flyers have made a commitment to tennis and identify themselves as 'a tennis player' rather than someone who 'plays tennis'. They love the game and have developed a strong sense of intrinsic motivation for tennis. Additionally, they want to be part of the tennis playing community, i.e., they want to have friends who are also tennis players. They have clear and simple expectations and a realistic view of their progress.
- High flyers are very competent and focused on a future in which tennis plays an important role. In the game they focus mainly on developing their movement and placement skills, as well as tactical play.

Continuing problem articulation, the design team attended the KNLTB 'Tennis Kids' teaching course. In this course the team learned the current approach to tennis training. Based on the course and the above basic distinction in tennis kids, the team further articulated the problem of tennis club dropouts.

The team envisioned that when young tennis players join the club as a Tryer, only some of them become a Buyer after their first few lesson cycles. Only few become a Flyer, and the amount of time it takes to become one is relatively long – a matter of years. Only very few become High Flyers, taking much more time to get there. The latter step is not a problem, however. The problem lies in the progression from Tryer to Buyer, and from Buyer to Flyer. That takes too long, resulting in only few actually making that transition.

2.2   Explaining Tennis Dropout

The team conceived that a potential cause for tennis dropout is the traditional method of teaching tennis, typified by countless repetitions on a long, gradual learning curve.

Through this method, tennis students must attain a basic level of skill proficiency before being ready to actually play the game. The method does not fit well with typical learning design in games. Deficiencies surface quickly and are even emphasised, which is closely followed by frustration. In the designers' view, this does not help sport participation and commitment. Opportunities needed to be sought to allow students to 'play the game' more quickly, though in different ways. This would create a more attractive and steeper learning curve.

Further problem articulation with the KNLTB led to the additional conclusion that tennis was often too marginalised and isolated in a tennis kid's life. Tennis participation suffers because it is then positioned as merely a weekly activity, nothing more. The design team wanted to evoke more enthusiasm for tennis and thus motivate tennis kids to become more involved with the sport by creating some sort of a meeting point where all forms of influence on a child's life come together (e.g. parents, friends, competencies, achievements). In any case, tennis needed to take on a more important and steady role in the child's life. It needed to become more ubiquitous.

2.3   A Focus on Learning Tennis Techniques and Tactics in a New Way

Information provided on child psychology, tennis and the KNLTB practice of teaching tennis to kids inspired the foundation of a new concept. The design team found that the KNLTB already makes use of a number of game mechanics in their youth curriculum, in order to make the learning curve less daunting. The most striking example is a game using a larger ball and a modified racket on a half-court. The tennis kid can earn a sticker for a job well done. This amounts to an 'easy mode' with a reward feedback loop (an extrinsic motivational factor). The easy mode seems to work well for Tryers, yet less for Buyers, as they already master the basic techniques.

Buyers and Flyers seem to develop intrinsic motivation mainly through playing the actual game of tennis. However, Buyers (need to) spend too much time refining techniques during training, i.e., the actual act of swinging a racket to hit the ball, in different ways. This leaves very little time to work on the tactics that are required for a truly representative and simply good game of tennis. Think of the need to really place the ball in a specific corner of the field. The two are of course interrelated. It is hard to apply a tactic if one has not yet mastered a technique. Moreover, sometimes it is hard to make the distinction between the two to begin with. Topspin is arguably both a technique and a tactic. The design team still chose to focus the concept for the applied game mainly on the transition from Buyer to Flyer by helping tennis kids learn the required tactics, rather than the basic techniques.

Following the entire problem articulation process, the design team concluded that this project would not entail a redesign of the tennis game itself. It was also agreed that it would not entail a change of tactics and techniques involved in playing tennis. Instead the design team chose to redesign how tactics and techniques are learned.

3   The *Smash!* Concept

3.1   A Personalized Web Application

The design team turned the grand and ambitious goal of tennis ubiquity and tactics training into an equally grand and ambitious platform that incorporated and supported different kinds of games, and offered a game-like experience itself as well (Fig. 1). This online platform was essentially a personalised web application. The platform revolves around an avatar created by the tennis kid. The avatar is actually a virtual representation of the tennis kid. Through skill points and achievements, skills can be improved and avatar personalization options become available.

Fig. 1. The online platform's design, with its skill points and achievements system.

The tennis kid can earn skill points and achievements by playing a smartphone application of mini-games (explained further on), or by playing virtual matches on the online platform itself against a computer-generated opponent, or another tennis kids' avatar. The tennis kid's own coach can also award skill points and achievements for applying knowledge gained during an actual tennis lesson. The tennis kid's parents can also award skill points, based on their observations of their child doing tennis-related activities, such as watching a tennis match, practicing a technique or doing tennis club chores.

In essence the skill points and achievement system are extrinsic motivational factors for tennis learning, visualised in the form of a changing avatar. The skill points and achievements are also part of a levelling system. Through skill points and achievements, the tennis kid advances in level, which in turn influences the outcomes of virtual matches played on the online platform.

3.2   A Smartphone Application of Mini-Games

The design team also designed a smartphone application of mini-games focused on tactics training (Fig. 2). This smartphone application is a continuation of the mini-games done during a tennis lesson, only now purely focused on tactics. A long-list of tactics was developed and ordered to create a tactics levelling system. The list included aiming, hitting modes (forehand and backhand, or volley, or smash), effect balls (topspin and slice), racket grip and higher-order strategy (aggressive, passive, or alternating). The online platform keeps track of the tactics trained in the mini-games.

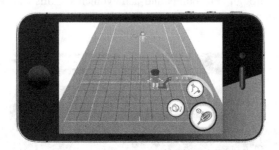

Fig. 2. The smartphone mini-game app's design.

3.3   Augmented Reality Game Through a QR-Coded Personal Club Card

A final component of the platform is an Augmented Reality (AR) game, by means of a QR-coded personal club membership card (Fig. 3). Put simply, a tennis kid uses the card to bring his/her avatar to life, provided he/she has a smartphone at hand. He/she can point a smartphone's camera on two membership cards: his/her own, and someone else's. The AR application picks up the two membership cards' QR codes, connects to the online platform to obtain both players' avatars, and then virtually projects the avatars on their respective membership cards to start an automated tennis match between the two. The winner is determined by each avatar's skill points and achievements as logged in the online platform. This result is then fed back into the online platform as well.

Fig. 3. The AR game's design, initiated by pointing a smartphone's camera on a QR-coded personal club card.

3.4   The Complete Concept

The entire concept is meant to support the involvement of the tennis kid's entire social surroundings in his/her development as a tennis player. In summary, the HKU designers expect that this entire concept will accomplish the following:

- The tennis kids will socialise more, finding each other to play virtual matches, discuss (game) tactics and compare avatars;
- The coach can test and build on theoretical knowledge (i.e., tennis tactics), the foundation of which can be laid by the mini-games. The tennis kid must also show the coach what he/she has learned to gain points and progress in the online platform;
- Parents of the tennis kid become involved with the experience of tennis by discussing and rewarding how their child practices skills outside of the tennis club.

The concept is expected to accomplish the above, because it emphasises both intrinsic and extrinsic motivational factors [12], thereby tapping into a factor known for being influential when it comes to sport participation and commitment: social support [1, 13, 14]. With this concept the tennis kid is provided with a wealth of motivation to become a true tennis player. The concept will give tennis kids the sensation of competence and autonomy, i.e., that they can learn and play tennis more quickly and more often than before, and that their social environment supports their tennis progression. That way the concept taps into the motivation a tennis kid has and needs to keep to successfully transition from Tryer to Buyer, and from Buyer to Flyer.

4   Conclusion

The design process led the HKU team to a multifaceted concept: a personalised web application for avatar administration and development by obtaining skill points and achievements, a smartphone application of mini-games for tactics training, and an automated, AR tennis game initiated by focusing a smartphone's camera on two QR-coded personal membership cards. The concept will give tennis kids the sensation that they can play tennis more often (though in different ways) than before, and it will activate the tennis kids' social circles.

Despite difficulties inherent to setting up play-tests with children (finding candidates, acquiring permission and supervision, and interpreting results), the design team was able to test a high-fidelity prototype with the target audience. Due to the small test group size and time constraints, only general feedback could be obtained, being overall positive and demonstrating the concept's potential nonetheless.

We argue that this article contributes to the fields of sport redesign for sport participation and commitment as well as applied game design in the domain of health. In fact, this article brings the two fields together in a novel way. The question remains whether the design expectations would actually be reached. An in-depth evaluation of a full-fledged working prototype of *Smash!* is a logical though daunting next step, indeed. In any case, we believe that there is huge potential for increasing sport participation and commitment by redesigning sports education through game design.

References

1. Biddle, S.J.H., Atkin, A.J., Cavill, N., Foster, C.: Correlates of physical activity in youth: a review of quantitative systematic reviews. Int. Rev. Sport Exerc. Psychol. **4**, 25–49 (2011)
2. Balish, S.M., McLaren, C., Rainham, D., Blanchard, C.: Correlates of youth sport attrition: a review and future directions. Psychol. Sport Exerc. **15**, 429–439 (2014)
3. Barry, G., Galna, B., Rochester, L.: The role of exergaming in Parkinson's disease rehabilitation: a systematic review of the evidence. J. NeuroEngineering Rehabil. **11**, 33 (2014)
4. Goble, D.J., Cone, B.L., Fling, B.W.: Using the Wii Fit as a tool for balance assessment and neurorehabilitation: the first half decade of "Wii-search". J. NeuroEngineering Rehabil. **11**, 12 (2014)
5. Joo, L.Y., Yin, T.S., Xu, D., Thia, E., Chia, P.F., Kuah, C.W.K., He, K.K.: A feasibility study using interactive commercial off-the-shelf computer gaming in upper limb rehabilitation in patients after stroke. J. Rehabil. Med. **42**, 437–441 (2010)
6. Hamari, J., Koivisto, J.: Social motivations to use gamification: an empirical study of gamifying exercise. In: Proceedings of the 21st European Conference on Information Systems SOCIAL, pp. 1–12 (2013)
7. Guy, S., Ratzki-Leewing, A., Gwadry-Sridhar, F.: Moving beyond the stigma: systematic review of video games and their potential to combat obesity. Int. J. Hypertens. **2011**, 179124 (2011)
8. Mellecker, R.R., McManus, A.M.: Active video games and physical activity recommendations: a comparison of the Gamercize Stepper, XBOX Kinect and XaviX J-Mat. J. Sci. Med. Sport **17**, 288–292 (2014)
9. Fraser-Thomas, J.L., Côté, J., Deakin, J.: Youth sport programs: an avenue to foster positive youth development. Phys. Educ. Sport Pedagogy **10**, 19–40 (2005)
10. Graafland, M., Dankbaar, M., Mert, A., Lagro, J., De Wit-Zuurendonk, L., Schuit, S., Schaafstal, A., Schijven, M.: How to systematically assess serious games applied to health care. JMIR Serious Games **2**, e11 (2014)
11. Pothuizen, R.: We hebben teveel buyers en te weinig flyers (2012). http://tenniskidsnl. blogspot.nl/2012/07/teveel-buyers-te-weinig-flyers.html
12. Ryan, R., Deci, E.: Intrinsic and extrinsic motivations: classic definitions and new directions. Contemp. Educ. Psychol. **25**, 54–67 (2000)
13. Kanters, M.A., Bocarro, J.N., Greenwood, P.B., Casper, J.M., Suau, L., McKenzie, T.L.: Determinants of middle school sport participation: a comparison of different models for school sport delivery. Int. J. Sport Manag. Mark. **12**, 159–179 (2012)
14. Santi, G., Bruton, A., Pietrantoni, L., Mellalieu, S.D., Saccinto, E.: Sport commitment and participation in masters swimmers: the influence of coach and teammates. Eur. J. Sport Sci. **14**, 852–860 (2014)

Engagement Mechanisms for Social Machines

Flávio S. Correa da Silva[1], Luiz Carlos Vieira[1(✉)], and Stefania Bandini[2,3]

[1] LIDET, University of São Paulo, São Paulo, Brazil
{fcs,lvieira}@ime.usp.br
[2] CSAI, University of Milano-Bicocca, Milan, Italy
bandini@disco.unimib.it
[3] RCAST, University of Tokyo, Tokyo, Japan

Abstract. Social machines are systems in which humans and computational agents work together. In order to create an effective social machine, one needs to design interaction protocols for agents to collaborate, program the computational agents and build mechanisms to engage humans into activities that are supportive to the goals of the machine. One approach to build engagement is to create opportunities for the experience of fun. The present work contains a discussion about how to design engaging and productive activities for social machines based on fun.

Keywords: Interaction models · Social machines · Engagement mechanisms · Fun

1 Introduction and Motivation

Social machines are socio-technical systems that combine the computational power of machines and the intelligence, creativity and common sense of humans. They are the convergence of interactive content systems - blogs, social networks, video sharing websites (*Social Software*), people who perform tasks which are trivial for humans but difficult for computers - e.g. solve CAPTCHAS or perform micro-tasks in crowd-based services (*People as Computational Unities*) and computer agents that are built to socialize with humans, create relationships, interpret or mimic human emotions (*Software as Social Entities*) [3].

Social machines are well fit to solve problems whose complexity is due to physical or functional distribution of data [18]. They can be particularly useful to solve complex problems of social and economic relevance [10]. Due to the inherent heterogeneity of agents in social machines, the analysis and design of these systems require novel methodological practices, blending existing techniques and experiences from applied social sciences and computational sciences to enable the participatory definition of goals, elicitation of resources and coordination of actions [4].

Even though the goals of a social machine can be beneficial for the human participants, they are not necessarily perceived by them as such. For example, economic policies and strategies proposed by the government, which aim

---

The authors thank FAPESP, CAPES and CNPq for financial support.

A. De Gloria and R. Veltkamp (Eds.): GALA 2015, LNCS 9599, pp. 361–367, 2016.
DOI: 10.1007/978-3-319-40216-1_40

at improving the overall quality of life, may be perceived as authoritarian by citizens. Hence, in many cases people involved in social machines do not feel motivated to act as suggested by the system, even if there are clear benefits for them in doing so. For example, interactive systems to monitor and suggest activities for patients undergoing therapeutic treatment, such as physiotherapy or care of senior citizens, may not be used just because they are perceived as dull.

Computational agents can be designed and implemented using standard techniques from agent based and distributed programming. Human agents, however, cannot be programmed in the conventional sense. At best, they can be convinced to behave according to prescribed rules, based on social norms to reward or punish behaviour depending on whether agents help or hinder the actions proposed by the machine to reach its goals.

The present work explores how human agents can be motivated to behave in such way that the goals of a social machine can be reached, discussing how activities can be designed to be simultaneously productive and a source of fun. As pointed out by scholars in behavioural economics and behavioural game theory [1,9], the motivations for individuals to engage into specific activities can be hard to explain using simplified models of pure rationality. Humans have individual preferences and memories that shape their attitudes through the evocation of emotions. This makes their motivations difficult to establish and to manage. Even when the global goals of a social machine are collectively accepted by the human agents that take part in it, additional incentive may be required for individuals to behave in such way that the machine as a whole works towards these goals [16]. Novelty, fantasy, meaningful goals, sense of control and constant feedback are fundamental to evoke *enjoyment* in the activities performed by each individual [6,14], which can be an important incentive for action.

2   Fun as a Reason for Engagement in Activities

People play with games and toys or do sports with no requirement for any external reward because such activities bring *pleasure*, *enjoyment* or *fun*. These three feelings are distinct, as can be illustrated by any individual working to appease hunger (pleasure), relaxing while listening to music (enjoyment), or anticipating the drop of a roller-coaster cart (fun). Games and toys are natural artefacts to evoke these feelings, but they can also be experienced in other contexts sometimes considered as "serious", with the common ground that there is always a sense of *intrinsic motivation* related to these feelings [14].

By interacting with objects and other agents, humans learn about the world in which they live and learn to cope with uncertainties [8]. As an *exploratory behaviour*, interactions build relational values that indicate the proper way to manipulate objects (based on physical affordances and socio-cultural constraints) [15] and to further relate with other agents, fostering complex group behaviour that involves competition, cooperation and coordination [8]. Interaction makes use of the senses, and sensed information is filtered into consciousness by *attention* according to individual *intentions*. Intentions are derived from previous experiences and steer future interactions by guiding the senses towards information considered relevant for each individual. The permanent construction of an image of oneself - called *self* and containing not only intentions but also memories, actions, desires, pleasures and pains - is directly related to the process of learning and to the experience of enjoyment in life [6].

Self motivation stems from curiosity, fantasy and challenge [6,14]. *Curiosity* relates to sensemaking of observable patterns that are unknown yet sufficiently understandable in order to capture one's interest. As a pattern is unfolded, its information gets "chunked" into the autonomous nervous system and the pattern becomes no longer interesting. *Fantasy* relates to mental images that are not necessarily captured by the senses, which help in the identification of new concepts using previously built conceptual models, this way aiding in the understanding of an external reality. Mental images also "rewind-and-replay" past experiences to achieve emotional mastery, and maintain optimal levels of mental arousal. *Challenges* are opportunities for action contained in any activity, physical or otherwise, that require skills to be exercised and contain goals that deliberate demand wilful focus of attention. Interactive systems such as video games can have other relevant attributes that derive from these three, such as sensation (sensory pleasure, derived from curiosity), narrative (empathy with characters and their stories, derived from fantasy) and fellowship (relationships that help creating or overcoming difficulties by competition or cooperation, derived from challenge) [12].

The Flow Theory [6] provides a conceptual foundation for self motivation, as it elucidates the distinctions between pleasure, enjoyment and fun. According to this theory, the state of flow occurs when an individual willingly focuses attention on a task because it offers meaningful challenges and difficult but achievable goals according to individual skills. Both levels of challenge and required skills must be above a personal threshold in order for enjoyment to emerge. If the challenge is too high, the task causes anxiety; if the required skills are too low, the task causes boredom. If both challenge and required skills are too low, the task is not interesting and causes apathy. Enjoyment can only happen when there is a constant "flow" between the levels of challenge and required skills (i.e. the task is slightly challenging until the individual is able to acquire the required skills to perform it, and then a new task is proposed which is again challenging and the cycle is repeated). To give a concrete example, the satisfaction of basic needs such as eating is merely pleasurable, but when it is featured together with well balanced challenges (e.g. when a gourmet is challenged to discover novel flavours) it generates a higher level of satisfaction that goes beyond pleasure.

Challenge is one of many facets of self motivation. Other aspects are also important, as enjoyable activities relate to freedom of choice and the provision of opportunities to use imagination and social skills. Fun is intuitively known to be more fleeting and intense than enjoyment or pleasure, and this is because there are different levels of engagement with activities [2]. When an object or a task is appealing to the senses (e.g. because it generates curiosity or is aesthetically appealing) an individual is primarily engaged in interacting with it. In this level goals and fantasy are not so important, awareness is not yet totally captured and an individual is only trying to satisfy early curiosity. As interactions occur, the individual can move to a second level of engagement in which she is engrossed by the interaction. Here, meaningful and achievable goals become important and attention gets so focused on the task that the individual may lose track of time. If the interaction proceeds satisfactorily, the individual may reach a level in which she is totally immersed in the interaction. In this level, the senses can be completely absorbed by the interaction and the individual may feel as being somewhere else. Fantasy becomes relevant as the individual may feel that she can make the difference in another world, feeling empathetic with the results of actions with respect to elements of the fantasy. Hence, pleasure and enjoyment are initial levels of satisfaction which, given appropriate conditions, can turn into fun as a more fleeting and intense emotion.

Other psychological aspects are also relevant to the exploration of fun. Emotions, either positive or negative, are particularly important, because they have a significant role in reasoning (by placing *markers* into choices, making them more or less relevant based on past experiences). This topic has been already discussed in detail elsewhere [17].

3   Fun by Design – Concepts and Examples

Designing for fun is challenging, as feelings depend upon preferences, memories and context, and vary with the presence of other agents and their relationships. As a consequence, the design of fun activities must be permanently assessed and adjusted based on feedback by the people involved in the interactions [11,13]. Good design guidelines include not only the provision of novel and surprising elements and meaningful goals, but also constant feedback about the progress in tasks and opportunities for action, and the provision of information in the form of stories and events about virtual characters and other participants. These guidelines usually help enticing curiosity and supporting fantasy, but they help specially evoking the sense of control, which is important for the state of flow.

Noteworthy examples of social machines in which at least some of these design practices have been employed to motivate actions through fun can be found in the literature. The Volkswagen company has maintained the *Think Blue* initiative to foster innovation in sustainability, with a natural focus on eco-friendly transportation. One branch of the *Think Blue* initiative is the *Fun Theory* campaign[1], which promotes projects in which everyday activities are redesigned to become engaging through fun. In one project, motion sensors and loudspeakers have been added to trash bins in public spaces, to create the illusion of extremely deep bins. This makes disposing of rubbish in the bin intriguing, leisurely and compelling. A second project added weight sensors and loudspeakers in the steps of staircases in a subway station. The steps are decorated as piano keys, and different notes are played as people climb up and down the stairs. This makes using

---

[1] http://thinkblue.volkswagen.com/com/en/blue-projects/thinkblue-fun-theory.html.

the stairs more fun than using escalators, motivating people towards a healthier behaviour and reducing energy consumption. Both projects mainly rely on curiosity and sensory feedback to produce fun.

Two other projects have been developed at the Brazilian IoT (Internet of Things) forum[2]. In the *On the Go* project[3] the goal is to balance the load of passengers, improve trip planning and reduce costs with underused vehicles in public transportation. Mobile devices are employed to track users, who play a game in which they have to catch specified vehicles at given time intervals in order to reach their desired locations. They are rewarded with points and badges as they succeed. Users generate data which can be used to optimise the management of the public transportation system. In the *Crowd for Care* project[4] there is also a game played using mobile devices. The system involves individuals as well as food manufactures, sport centres and parks. Institutions offer *health credits* that are earned by individuals as they consume available services. As users accumulate different levels of health credits, they are awarded with special benefits that are also health-related (such as free medical exams or Tai Chi Chuan classes). Both projects rely on challenges to motivate people, but fall short on the exploration of other aspects that are also relevant for fun, particularly fantasy. They still need to be field tested with real users to observe their reactions, preferences and if their initial interest persists along time.

A final, witty *counter*-example is presented by the design company *Superflux* in the video *Uninvited Guests*[5], in which it is clarified that a well engineered and evidently efficient socio-technical system may crash if the system is not explicitly supportive to self-motivation [7].

4   Conclusion and Future Work

This article has discussed potential scenarios for the use of social machines, and focused on how to motivate humans to act on behalf of global goals, based on notions of fun and enjoyment.

Specialised languages are required to build specifications, and corresponding computational platforms are required to support, manage and provide a computational realisation of social machines. An essential aspect to be represented in such languages is interaction between components, so that their internal behaviour can be abstracted and the resulting systems can be analysed as a whole. Additionally, since these languages should be used to communicate specifications as well as processing results to participants in social machines (i.e. humans who behave as components in social machines), they should be concise and simple to understand. Finally, in order to build social machines whose behaviour can be verified with respect to desired requirements and attributes, these languages should have a formal underpinning and the corresponding specifications

---

[2] http://www.iotbrasil.com.br/new/en/.

[3] http://onthegoproject.strikingly.com/.

[4] http://crowdforcare.strikingly.com/.

[5] http://www.superflux.in/work/uninvited-guests.

and processing results should be formally verifiable. A recent language for social machines is the *Lightweight, Situated, Stateful Social Calculus* (LS^{3}C). A detailed formal account of the LS^{3}C language can be found elsewhere [5]. We plan to use the LS^{3}C language to design and implement social machines, based on which we will be able to collect experimental data about the effectiveness of different strategies to motivate human components to behave in such way as to contribute to the functioning of social machines.

The plans for future work include building experiments to field test the ideas presented here, particularly focusing on scenarios related to the development of multi-player games to help in the monitoring and/or treatment of individuals requiring temporary or permanent special care.

References

1. Ariely, D.: Predictably irrational: the hidden forces that shape our decisions. Harper, New York (2010)
2. Brown, E., Cairns, P.: A Grounded investigation of game immersion. In: Extended Abstracts on Human Factors in Computing Systems, CHI 2004, NY, USA (2004)
3. Buregio, V., Meira, S., Rosa, N.: Social machines: a unified paradigm to describe social web-oriented systems. In: 22nd International Conference on World Wide Web (2013)
4. Correa da Silva, F.S., Robertson, D., Vasconcelos, W.: Experimental interaction science. In: Artificial Intelligence, Simulation of Behaviour - Annual Convention.2013: Workshop on Social Coordination - Principles, Artifacts and Theories (2013)
5. Correa da Silva, F.S., Robertson, D.S., Vasconcelos, W.W., Chung, P.W.H., Murray-Rust, D., Papapanagiotou, P.: LS^{3}C - the lightweight, situated, stateful social calculus. Technical report RT-MAC-IME-2015-02, Brazil (2015)
6. Csikszentmihalyi, M.: Flow: The Psychology of Optimal Experience. Harper, New York (1991)
7. Deci, E., Flaste, R.: Why We Do What We Do: Understanding Self-Motivation. Penguin, UK (1996)
8. Dubberly, H., Pangaro, P., Haque, U.: What is interaction? are there different types? Interactions **16**(1) (2009)
9. Gintis, H.: The bounds of reason : game theory and the unification of behavioral sciences. Princeton University Press, Princeton (2009)
10. Giunchiglia, F., Robertson, D.S.: The social computer - combining machine and human computation. University of Trento Technical report, DISI-10-036 (2010)
11. Hassenzahl, M.: We cannot design them. Emotions can be quite ephemeral. Interactions **11**(5), 46–48 (2004)
12. Hunicke, R., LeBlanc, M., Zubek, R.: MDA : a formal approach to game design and game research. In: 19th AAAI Challenges in Games AI Workshop (2004)
13. Isbister, K.: Enabling social play: a framework for design and evaluation. In: Bernhaupt, R. (ed.) Evaluating User Experience in Games: Concepts and Methods. Human-Computer Interaction Series, pp. 11–22. Springer, London (2010)
14. Malone, T.W.: What Makes Things Fun to Learn. A Study of Intrinsically Motivating Computer Games. Phd thesis, Stanford University (1980)
15. Norman, D.A.: The Design of Everyday Things, 2nd edn. Basic Books, USA (2002)

16. Schneier, B.: Liars and Outliers: enabling the trust that society needs to thrive. Wiley, Hoboken (2012)
17. Vieira, L.C., Correa da Silva, F.S.: Understanding fun. In: Videojogos 2014, Portugal (2014)
18. Weiss, G.: Multiagent Systems: A Modern Approach to Distributed Artificial Intelligence. The MIT Press, USA (2000)

Transportation Services Game: A Practical Tool to Teach Outsourcing Concepts on Logistics

Alvaro Gehlen de Leao[✉]

Pontifical Catholic University of Rio Grande do Sul, Av. Ipiranga, 6681,
Porto Alegre 90619-900, Brazil
gehleao@pucrs.br

Abstract. This paper will discuss the use of a simulation game that was conceived to teach concepts on logistics outsourcing of freight services. It will be presented a brief theoretical basis to support the design of simulation games based on game theory and operations research approaches. During the previous years, this kind of games was successfully applied on undergraduate and graduate courses in the Faculty of Engineering at Pontifical Catholic University of Rio Grande do Sul. Emerging results from this experience will be depicted in this paper, evaluating educational aspects of simulation games as a learning instrument, particularly the use of the Transportation Services Game.

1 Introduction

Increasing competition within their areas of influence has changed the characteristics of companies and educational institutions, which obligates them to adopt a choice of innovative approaches to improve performance of learning processes. According to Carvalho et al. [1], the serious games approach have increased its application in the educational environment, making the learning process through games more delightful and attractive than the traditional ones. Also, more attention is being given to the insertion of games in the academic curriculum [1, 2], providing a formal support for game-based educational initiatives. In this context, serious games have successfully amplified their use as an effective instrument to provide an enjoyable environment for learning in business and production engineering courses and in service-oriented or industrial enterprises [3].

1.1 Serious Games for Learning and Education

Serious games are expanding its use as a learning tool, including business and management games, which normally involves economics and production aspects. In this way, a serious game [4], to be an effective instrument for learning, must include several related actions to provide a concrete experience, allowing observations and reflections to conduct towards abstract concepts and generalizations and to formulate hypotheses to be tested which, consecutively, lead to new experiences [5, 6].

A serious game, in order to be a useful tool in an educational environment, must be appropriately introduced to participants, with rules and directives clearly stated [7, 8]. Also organizational and running aspects must be carefully defined because it would have

© Springer International Publishing Switzerland 2016
A. De Gloria and R. Veltkamp (Eds.): GALA 2015, LNCS 9599, pp. 368–374, 2016.
DOI: 10.1007/978-3-319-40216-1_41

an important role on participants' learning processes [9]. Following, to turn experience into learning, an abstract conceptualization must be carried out to integrate observations and to create various insights for future applications. Finally, as a key activity of an application of serious games for learning, a debriefing must be realized to summarize the essential aspects of experiences conducted.

1.2 Applying Game Theory to Design Simulation Games

Game theory, used as a tool to evaluate situations in which the decisions of multiple agents affect each agent's payoff, could be applied to design serious games for learning in production engineering. Hence, some basic concepts emerge from the game theory [10], like non-cooperative versus cooperative games, existence of multiple equilibria or a unique equilibrium, games with perfect versus imperfect information, games based on static or dynamic characteristics, and games involving auctions and bidding [11].

According to Cachon and Netessine [12], non-cooperative static games are particularly relevant to experience industrial engineering aspects, mainly for supply chain management [13]. Under this circumstance, players need to choose strategies at the same time and are, thereafter, committed to their chosen strategies in a market involving synchronized movements. Also non-cooperative dynamic games are appropriate to simulate production management problems, particularly in situations involving sequential or simultaneous moves over multiple periods of time, which conducts to a design of games with stochastic characteristics.

Another class of serious games, the cooperative ones, have recently emerged in the market, almost certainly due to the predominance of bargaining and negotiations in supply chain relationships [12]. This kind of games, in your own way, tend to use a different approach to be designed, focusing on human aspects, including topics which take into account psychological and emotional behaviours of game participants [4].

2 Using Operations Research Models to Design Serious Games

In a business environment, managers are responsible for the planning and control of production systems to reach the objectives of the company. In that situation, operations research is a useful tool to solve such problems [14, 15], requiring some assumptions to be efficiently used: focus on decision-making aspects; process evaluation based on economical effectiveness criteria; use of a formal mathematical model; and dependence of computerized systems.

To solve management problems using operations research techniques, it is often essential to engage computerized systems, since the logistics and the production planning and control in the industry increased their complexity [16].

For this reason, the representation of a transportation system in a computational model, as a simulation game [17], could be useful to allow the understanding of the managerial environment.

3   Transportation Services Game

The design and development of the Transportation Services Game was based on supply chain management principles [18], cost management concepts [19] and operations research models. This game presents the simulation of cost management in a transportation system [20], where rival companies attempt to maximize profits through optimization of available resources.

The Transportation Services Game was designed as a multi-player game where various companies compete to provide freight services from two origins – Rio Grande and Itajaí – to three destinations – Porto Alegre, Curitiba and Caxias do Sul – as shown on Fig. 1.

Origin	Rio Grande			Itajaí		Market Share	Capacity
Destination	Porto Alegre	Curitiba	Caxias do Sul	Porto Alegre	Curitiba	40%	25
Distance	300	1.000	400	600	200	(km)	(ton per vehicle)
Median Freight Price	29,20	101,00	40,00	56,20	19,00	($ per ton)	Utilization
Minimum Freight Price	28,00	97,00	38,00	57,00	18,00	($ per ton)	40
Mark Up	25%	10%	20%	15%	30%		(days per vehicle per quarter)
Freight Price to Market	36,50	111,10	48,00	95,93	24,70	($ per ton)	Distance
Freight Rate to Market	0,1217	0,1111	0,1200	0,1116	0,1236	($ per ton.km)	500
Demand Variation vs Price Variation	20	6	15	10	30	(ton per quarter per $)	(km per day)
Total Market Demand at Price Zero	10.000	3.000	7.500	5.000	15.000	(ton per quarter)	Fixed Cost per Vehicle
Seasonal Factor	1,10	1,00	1,20	0,90	1,20		10.000,00
Total Market Demand	10.197	2.333	8.136	3.898	17.111	(ton per quarter)	($ per quarter per vehicle)
Total Market Demand in ton.km	3.059.100	2.333.400	3.254.400	2.338.578	3.422.160	(ton.km per quarter)	14.407.638
Limit per Company	1.223.640	933.360	1.301.760	935.431	1.368.864	(ton.km per quarter)	Availability
Company A	1.223.640	933.360	543.000	0	0	(ton.km per quarter)	3.000.000
Company B	0	383.337	1.301.760	650.471	684.432	(ton.km per quarter)	3.000.000
Company C	0	103.343	0	935.431	1.368.864	(ton.km per quarter)	3.500.000
Company D	611.820	933.360	702.144	752.676	0	(ton.km per quarter)	3.000.000
Company E	1.223.640	0	407.496	0	1.368.864	(ton.km per quarter)	3.000.000
Contractor	3.059.100	2.333.400	3.254.400	2.338.578	3.422.160	(ton.km per quarter)	Fleet Size
	Oversupply	0%		Limit of Oversupply	50%		
Freight Price - Company A	29,00	101,00	40,20	61,00	25,00	($ per ton)	6
Freight Price - Company B	29,20	97,00	38,00	57,00	18,20	($ per ton)	6
Freight Price - Company C	33,00	105,00	44,00	58,20	19,00	($ per ton)	7
Freight Price - Company D	29,40	98,00	39,00	58,00	20,00	($ per ton)	6
Freight Price - Company E	28,00	110,00	40,00	65,00	18,00	($ per ton)	6
							(vehicles)
Freight Rate - Company A	0,0967	0,1010	0,1005	0,1017	0,1250	($ per ton.km)	Unit Variable Cost
Freight Rate - Company B	0,0973	0,0970	0,0950	0,0960	0,0910	($ per ton.km)	0,0500
Freight Rate - Company C	0,1100	0,1050	0,1100	0,0970	0,0950	($ per ton.km)	($ per ton.km)
Freight Rate - Company D	0,0980	0,0980	0,0975	0,0957	0,1000	($ per ton.km)	Extra Freight Rate
Freight Rate - Company E	0,0933	0,1100	0,1000	0,1083	0,0900	($ per ton.km)	0,0925
Minimum Freight Rate	0,0933	0,0970	0,0950	0,0950	0,0900	($ per ton.km)	($ per ton.km)
	Direct Sales	Extra Sales	Total Revenue	Total Fixed Costs	Total Variable Costs		Total Profit
Company A	3.000.000	0	297.276,06	60.000,00	150.000,00		87.276,06
Company B	3.000.000	0	262.966,95	60.000,00	150.000,00		72.966,95
Company C	2.407.638	1.092.362	332.673,39	70.000,00	175.000,00		87.673,39
Company D	3.000.000	0	292.645,36	60.000,00	150.000,00		82.645,36
Company E	3.000.000	0	278.153,76	60.000,00	150.000,00		68.153,76
	(ton per quarter)	(ton.km per quarter)	($ per quarter)	($ per quarter)	($ per quarter)		($ per quarter)
Contractor			1.705.464,38	240.000,00	1.382.694,03		92.770,35

Fig. 1. Spreadsheet model of the transportation services game

The only parameters that the companies can control is the price of freight services and the size of their fleet, which, in turn, could periodically fluctuate only in a smooth basis – see Fig. 2.

Origin	Rio Grande			Itajaí			Capacity
Destination	Porto Alegre	Curitiba	Caxias do Sul	Porto Alegre	Curitiba		25
Freight Price - Company A	29,00	101,00	40,20	61,00	25,00	($ per ton)	6
Freight Price - Company B	29,20	97,00	38,00	57,00	18,20	($ per ton)	6
Freight Price - Company C	33,00	105,00	44,00	58,20	19,00	($ per ton)	7
Freight Price - Company D	29,40	98,00	39,00	58,00	20,00	($ per ton)	6
Freight Price - Company E	28,00	110,00	40,00	65,00	18,00	($ per ton)	6
							(vehicles)

Fig. 2. Spreadsheet model: price of freight services and size of fleet

3.1   Mathematical Model of the Transportation Services Game

The Transportation Services Game was developed as an operations research model, comprising an objective function – maximisation of the contractor profit – and a set of constraints, which includes availability of vehicles and the total demand for freight services.

The mathematical model was designed by using, as decision variables, the quantity of freight services to be provided by the companies and to be sold by the contractor – see Fig. 3.

Origin	Porto Alegre	Rio Grande Curitiba	Caxias do Sul	Itajaí Porto Alegre	Curitiba	
Destination						
Company A	1.223.640	933.360	843.000	0	0	(ton.km per quarter)
Company B	0	363.337	1.301.760	650.471	684.432	(ton.km per quarter)
Company C	0	103.343	0	935.431	1.368.864	(ton.km per quarter)
Company D	611.820	933.360	702.144	752.676	0	(ton.km per quarter)
Company E	1.223.640	0	407.496	0	1.368.864	(ton.km per quarter)
Contractor	3.059.100	2.333.400	3.254.400	2.338.578	3.422.160	(ton.km per quarter)

Fig. 3. Spreadsheet model: decision variables – quantity of freight services

As a demand constraint – Fig. 4 – it must be considered the total market demand for each freight service, which is dependent on the freight price to the market calculated with a mark-up over the median price of freight services, and the individual limit per company, defined by the maximum market share.

Origin	Porto Alegre	Rio Grande Curitiba	Caxias do Sul	Itajaí Porto Alegre	Curitiba	Market Share 40%
Destination						
Distance	300	1.000	400	600	200	(km)
Median Freight Price	29,20	101,00	40,00	58,20	19,00	($ per ton)
Minimum Freight Price	28,00	97,00	38,00	57,00	18,00	($ per ton)
Mark Up	25%	10%	20%	15%	30%	
Freight Price to Market	36,50	111,10	48,00	66,93	24,70	($ per ton)
Freight Rate to Market	0,1217	0,1111	0,1200	0,1116	0,1235	($ per ton.km)
Demand Variation vs Price Variation	20	6	15	10	30	(ton per quarter per $)
Total Market Demand at Price Zero	10.000	3.000	7.500	5.000	15.000	(ton per quarter)
Seasonal Factor	1,10	1,00	1,20	0,90	1,20	
Total Market Demand	10.197	2.333	8.136	3.898	17.111	(ton per quarter)
Total Market Demand in ton.km	3.059.100	2.333.400	3.254.400	2.338.578	3.422.160	(ton.km per quarter)
Limit per Company	1.223.640	933.360	1.301.760	935.431	1.368.864	(ton.km per quarter)

Fig. 4. Spreadsheet model: freight service price and demand constraints

As capacity constraints, it must be taken into account the resources available in each company – in terms of fleet size – and the operational characteristics of the vehicles, as shown on Fig. 5.

Fig. 5. Spreadsheet model: operational characteristics and capacity constraints

3.2   Dynamics of the Transportation Services Game

The dynamics of the game [8], for each player, consists on presenting bids in a quarterly auction, trying to achieve maximum accumulated profit in a long-term basis, usually on two or three years. Then, after a round of bids from each company, the contractor take a purchase decision based on maximization of its own benefits.

As a main decision principle, on each round, the strategy for each player consists on offering a particular price to provide freight services and to set the right capacity of the fleet, in order to maximize its own profit [21]. The final decision – how many freight services will be purchased from each company at a certain quarter – is taken based on maximization of the contractor' total profit – see Fig. 6.

Origin	Rio Grande			Itajaí				
Destination	Porto Alegre	Curitiba	Caxias do Sul	Porto Alegre	Curitiba			Unit Variable Cost
Freight Rate - Company A	0,0967	0,1010	0,1005	0,1017	0,1280	($ per ton.km)		
Freight Rate - Company B	0,0973	0,0970	0,0950	0,0950	0,0910	($ per ton.km)		0,0500
Freight Rate - Company C	0,1100	0,1050	0,1100	0,0970	0,0950	($ per ton.km)		($ per ton.km)
Freight Rate - Company D	0,0960	0,0980	0,0975	0,0967	0,1000	($ per ton.km)		Extra Freight Rate
Freight Rate - Company E	0,0933	0,1100	0,1000	0,1083	0,0990	($ per ton.km)		0,0025
Minimum Freight Rate	0,0933	0,0970	0,0950	0,0950	0,0900	($ per ton.km)		($ per ton.km)
	Direct Sales	Extra Sales	Total Revenue	Total Fixed Costs	Total Variable Costs			Total Profit
Company A	3.000.000	0	297.276,06	60.000,00	150.000,00			87.276,06
Company B	3.000.000	0	282.988,95	60.000,00	150.000,00			72.988,95
Company C	2.407.638	1.092.362	332.673,39	70.000,00	175.000,00			87.673,39
Company D	3.000.000	0	292.645,36	60.000,00	150.000,00			82.645,36
Company E	3.000.000	0	278.163,76	60.000,00	150.000,00			68.163,76
	(ton.km per quarter)	(ton.km per quarter)	($ per quarter)	($ per quarter)	($ per quarter)			($ per quarter)
Contractor			1.705.464,38	240.000,00	1.382.694,03			82.770,35

Fig. 6. Spreadsheet model: financial results and total profit

So, it depends, ultimately and simultaneously, on the price of the freight services offered by the companies and on the size of fleet available at each company.

As stated by Wisner et al. [18], "suppliers must be able to accurately forecast demand so they can produce and deliver the right quantities demanded by their customers in a timely and cost-effective fashion". Also Vollmann et al. [22] state that a key element of the demand management is a systematic search for equilibrium between supply of services and its demand, through monitoring of actual conditions of the marketplace, providing an information basis for the decision-making process.

4   Educational Experiences and Concluding Remarks

The Transportation Services Game was extensively used in undergraduate classes and its ongoing design and development was benefited from contributions presented by participants. Some experiences have shown that the accomplishment of the goals for each company depends on an accurate demand forecasting and on a tactical plan to define the short time actions in terms of the freight services prices and the availability of resources.

As the result of the companies is directly affected by the decision of the contractor, players need to choose between cooperation and competition with other players, in order to maximise their own benefits.

On using the taxonomy and metrics for serious games proposed by Popescu and Bellotti [23], and loosely based on the framework provided by the Serious Games Society [24], the Transportation Services Game could be tentatively and analytically described as shown on Fig. 7.

Features	Explanation
Primary Target Ages	18 years and up
Genres	Simulation game
Markets	Primarily for high education students
Learning Curve	About 60 to 90 minutes
Effective Learning Time	12 rounds of approximately 30 minutes each
Game Platform	Uses Microsoft Excel spreadsheet
Deployment Style	Bidding and auctions in a regular basis
Number of Players	It is a multiplayer game
Sociality	Each company is formed by small groups
Feedback and Results	Depends on the supervisor management
Motivation	To achieve the biggest profit among the competitors
Assessment	The higher the profits the higher the grades
Difficulty Levels	Varies during the game
Violation of Rules	It is impossible to violate the rules
Game Transfer	The game is based on fixed costs and price management and could be adapted for various environments

Fig. 7. Serious game characteristics of the transportation services game

This simulation game was used in an undergraduate course on logistics and supply chain management, giving to the students an interactive tool to provide a better understanding of the managerial aspects involved in a decision making process.

Preliminary results emerging from game application have shown that students with high grades in conventional evaluation methods have demonstrated additional enthusiasm to participate and, therefore, have also achieved superior results in the Transportation Services Game.

New experiments have been continuously performed – including the use of a Data Envelopment Analysis approach to evaluate efficiency and productivity of transportation systems [25] – and improvements emerging from these applications will be also included in future versions of the Transportation Services Game.

References

1. Carvalho, M.B., Bellotti, F., Berta, R., Curatelli, F., De Gloria, A., Gazzarata, G., Hu, J., Kickmeier-Rust, M., Martinengo, C.: The journey: a service-based adaptive serious game on probability. In: De Gloria, A. (ed.) GALA 2014. LNCS, vol. 9221, pp. 97–106. Springer, Heidelberg (2015)
2. Farber, M.: Gamify Your Classroom: A Field Guide to Game-Based Learning. Peter Lang Publishing, New York (2015)
3. Werbach, K., Hunter, D.: For the Win: How Game Thinking Can Revolutionize Your Business. Wharton Digital Press, Philadelphia (2012)
4. Bellotti, F., Berta, R., De Gloria, A.: Designing Effective serious games: opportunities and challenges for research. Int. J. Emerg. Technol. Learn. 5 (2010). Special Issue 3: Creative Learning with Serious Games

5. Elias, G.F., Garfield, R., Gutschera, K.R.: Characteristics of Games. The MIT Press, Cambridge (2012)
6. Kapp, K.M.: The Gamification of Learning and Instruction: Game-Based Methods and Strategies for Training and Education. Wiley, San Francisco (2012)
7. Kapp, K.M., Blair, L., Mesch, R.: The Gamification of Learning and Instruction Fieldbook: Ideas into Practice. Wiley, San Francisco (2014)
8. Chou, Y.: Actionable Gamification: Beyond Points, Badges, and Leaderboards. Octalysis Media (2015)
9. Werbach, K., Hunter, D.: The Gamification Toolkit: Dynamics, Mechanics, and Components for the Win. Wharton Digital Press, Philadelphia (2015)
10. Kogan, K., Tapiero, C.S.: Supply Chain Games: Operations Management and Risk Valuation. Springer, New York (2007)
11. Kalagnanam, J., Parkes, D.C.: Auctions, bidding and exchange design. In: Simchi-Levi, D., Wu, S.D., Shen, Z.J. (eds.) Handbook of Quantitative Supply Chain Analysis: Modeling in the E-Business Era, pp. 143–212. Springer, New York (2004)
12. Cachon, G.P., Netessine, S.: Game theory in supply chain analysis. In: Simchi-Levi, D., Wu, S.D., Shen, Z.J. (eds.) Handbook of Quantitative Supply Chain Analysis: Modeling in the E-Business Era, pp. 13–165. Springer, New York (2004)
13. Voss, S., Schneidereit, G.: Interdependencies between supply contracts and transaction costs. In: Seuring, S., Goldbach, M. (eds.) Cost Management in Supply Chains, pp. 253–272. Physica-Verlag, Heidelberg (2002)
14. Coelli, T.J., Rao, D.S.P., O'Donnell, C.J., Battese, G.E.: An Introduction to Efficiency and Productivity Analysis. Springer, New York (2005)
15. Zhu, J.: Quantitative Models for Performance Evaluation and Benchmarking – Data Envelopment Analysis with Spreadsheets and DEA Excel Solver. Springer, New York (2003)
16. Shapiro, J.F.: Modeling the Supply Chain. Duxbury, Pacific Grove (2001)
17. Kaczmarek, M., Stüllenberg, F.: Decision support by model based analysis of supply chains. In: Seuring, S., Goldbach, M. (eds.) Cost Management in Supply Chains, pp. 273–288. Physica-Verlag, Heidelberg (2002)
18. Wisner, J.D., Leong, G.K., Tan, K.C.: Principles of Supply Chain Management – A Balanced Approach. South-Western, Mason (2005)
19. Mehafdi, M.: Transfer pricing in supply chains – an exercise in internal marketing and cost management. In: Seuring, S., Goldbach, M. (eds.) Cost Management in Supply Chains, pp. 147–163. Physica-Verlag, Heidelberg (2002)
20. Slagmulder, R.: Managing costs across the supply chain. In: Seuring, S., Goldbach, M. (eds.) Cost Management in Supply Chains, pp. 75–88. Physica-Verlag, Heidelberg (2002)
21. Dolgui, A., Proth, J.M.: Supply Chain Engineering: Useful Methods and Techniques. Springer, London (2010)
22. Vollmann, T.E., Berry, W.L., Whybark, D.C., Jacobs, F.R.: Manufacturing Planning and Control Systems for Supply Chain Management. McGraw-Hill, New York (2005)
23. Popescu, M.M., Bellotti, F.: Approaches in metrics and taxonomy in serious games. In: Proceedings of 8th International Scientific Conference eLearning and Software for Education, Bucharest, April 2012
24. Serious Games Society homepage, October 2015. http://studies.seriousgamessociety.org/
25. Cooper, W.W., Seiford, L.M., Tone, K.: Introduction to Data Envelopment Analysis and Its Uses. Springer, New York (2006)

The Absolute and Social Comparative Analysis of Driver Performance on a Simulated Road Network

Gautam R. Dange[1], Pratheep K. Paranthaman[1], Marco Samaritani[1],
Oussama Smiai[1], Francesco Bellotti[1(✉)], Riccardo Berta[1],
Alessandro De Gloria[1], Mario Marchesoni[1], Stefano Massucco[1],
and Jens Pontow[2]

[1] DITEN, University of Genoa, Via Opera Pia 11A, 16145 Genoa, Italy
{gautam.dange,pratheep.paranthaman,
Marco.Samaritani,Oussama.Smiai,franz,
riccardo.berta,adg}@elios.unige.it
[2] Automotive Services and Communication Technologies,
Fraunhofer Institute for Open Communication Systems FOKUS,
Kaiserin-Augusta-Allee 31, 10589 Berlin, Germany
jens.pontow@fokus.fraunhofer.de

Abstract. The process of modeling a qualitative evaluation schema to gauge the driver performance is a prominent aspect in enhancing the driving standards. We have implemented a comparative analysis module to estimate the driver performance based on absolute and social comparisons. In this approach we simulated a road network of 40 vehicle users and analyzed the performance of the users by our interlinked system architecture dedicated for simulation, data sharing and representation of the entire information on Map-based user interface. Another key aspect that was performed in this approach was the usage of Map-Matching module to discard the inaccuracies in Geo-references while representing the coordinates on Google Maps. We believe, this evaluation approach will broaden the overview of performance analysis and provide more insight to the user on all grounds in improvising the driving standards.

1 Introduction

The application of Serious games in various domains such as military [14], corporate [15], healthcare [1] and driving [2] have created huge impact in educating and training people though a gamified environment. Indulging in serious games environment can significantly improvise the skills of players such as decision-making, teamwork, leadership and collaboration in a controlled manner. The deployment of serious games in automotive industry is a major leap in technological grounds, as it's a best way to inculcate safe driving patterns to reduce the fatalities and enhance resource utilities. Some models involving the games for supporting safe driving such as: the experiment conducted by [3] using a motivational method of displaying avatar on screen, which cheers the driver during good performance. Fiat Eco drive [4] an application promoted eco driving and iCO2 game [5] gathered driver behavior data from many users for

© Springer International Publishing Switzerland 2016
A. De Gloria and R. Veltkamp (Eds.): GALA 2015, LNCS 9599, pp. 375–384, 2016.
DOI: 10.1007/978-3-319-40216-1_42

enhancing Eco driving. There were certain research projects centric on human-machine interface (HMI) for enhancement of driving modalities such as: Project COMUNICAR [10] comprised of human-machine interface (HMI) for managing the driver information system ranging from entertainment to environment safety and the Adaptive integrated driver-vehicle interface (AIDE) [9] project which addresses the behavioral and technical issues oriented to adaptive human-machine interface. The I-GEAR [6] project (incentives and gaming environments for automobile routing) used serious games to understand the driver behavior by creating certain scenarios that driver would comply. Whereas, the serious games IC-DEEP was developed to assess driver performance using in-vehicle Information System (IVIS) for tracking the distraction in driving process [7] and IC-DEEP was also used to test an Advanced Driver Assistance Systems (ADAS) to attain cost effectiveness in testing process [8].

Most of the existing models in serious gaming context for automotive industry aims at improvising driver behavior by various methods. But, there is another viewpoint for this approach (i.e.) out of many methods that could enhance driver behavior, the chief methodology would be the qualitative driver performance analysis. We believe that, the first step in attaining better driver behavior would be devising a qualitative evaluation pattern that would analyses and provide a detailed statistical report of driver performance. These analysis can be of great assistance in comparing the individual driver performance with the performance of peers, also the comparative analysis can be used for conducting serious games to inculcate the efficient driving behavior. Having all these considerations as foundation, we have developed a comparative performance assessment schema that would analyze the driver behavior on absolute and social comparison basis.

2 Implementation Overview

The system core manages the driver performance evaluation by unifying four architectures together (see Fig. 1), here the evaluation is done based on the relative plot of the scores with the average performances of the peers.

The system core comprises of four architectures:

- Vehicle Simulation Unit
- Driver Performance Evaluator
- Aggregation server
- Live User performance enabler

2.1 Vehicle Simulation Unit

The simulation unit acts as the input part, where the vehicle signals of 40 vehicles are generated over here for this entire test scenario. The source of replication is from the real log file which comprises of vehicle signals recorded by CRF Trento, Italy [11]. Figure 2 comprises of the control flow involved in vehicle simulation unit, the first block (Vehicle signals) holds the test log file from which the signals are generated for the simulation.

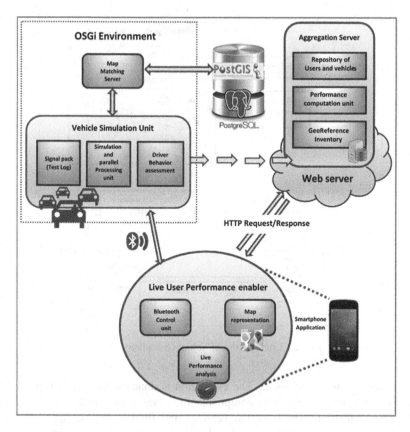

Fig. 1. Implemented system design and control flow mechanism

The signal generator unit forms the data structure for the signals that flow in and simulation inventory is comprised of certain configuration files associated for the parallel simulation. Simulation inventory handles the logical signal generation from the real signal and maintains the course of the replicated signals to match with the source signal. The 40 vehicles are associated to 40 users and the details of 40 users and the signal mapping to concerned users are done in parallel simulation unit (SP-1 corresponds to signal pack 1 and it goes on till SP-40, as displayed on Fig. 2).

2.2 Driver Performance Evaluator

Parallel simulation unit sends signals to Driver performance evaluator. To evaluate the signals, we developed certain algorithms (Linear distances, K-Nearest neighbors, Kohonen Neural Networks and Dynamic sliding Window) based on various criterion. For this simulation environment, we used Linear distances to estimate the vehicle signals, in linear distances approach the signals are segregated into harsh and smooth patterns using the slope-intercept form, in which the harsh signals are penalized and smooth ones are rewarded. The signals such as acceleration, brake, RPM and speed are

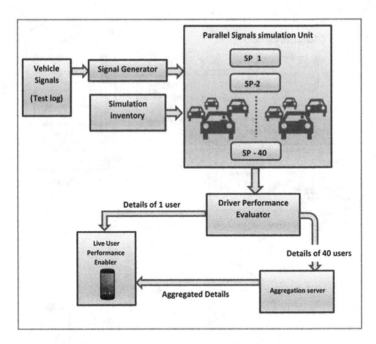

Fig. 2. Components of vehicle Simulation unit

evaluated using Linear Distances. The evaluation is done on the basis of green drive and fluid traffic, where green drive comprises of the evaluation pattern based on Brake, RPM and acceleration signals of the vehicles and fluid traffic estimates the speed signals based on the specified criterion in Linear Distances.

Post signal evaluation, the scores and vehicle details of 40 users are forwarded to the Aggregation server for the computation and only one user score is forwarded to the Live User Performance enabler unit. Later the score of this individual user is compared with the scores of 40 users for deriving the overall performance.

2.3 Aggregation Server

The Aggregation server receives the signals of 40 vehicles from the Vehicle simulation unit and stores the entire details of the vehicle signals, Geo-references and users associated with it. The key element of Aggregation server is the computation of average performances of 40 users, where the latest and historic user performances are tabulated based on the geographic links. Aggregation server responds to the live user performance enabler module for the comparison of individual performance of the user with the average performance of all the users that were recorded on the links.

Apart from computation of user performance, the visualization of the results on Google maps is another feature associated with this system. We had worked in localizing the user's Geo-references on Google maps with accuracy. In real-world recordings of Geo-references there can be a deviation from the actual position and this might result in a drastic change when the coordinates are displayed on Google Maps. To resolve the errors associated with variations in Geo-references, we used Map-Matching algorithm [12] (The map-matching API "Geotoolbox" [12]) to integrate the position data with Spatial Road Network data to identify the correct link and coordinates on which the vehicle is travelling [13]. The vehicle coordinates are sent from the Vehicle simulation unit to the Map-matching module for the correction, the Map-matching module is housed in OSGi framework. The Map-matching module relies on a Geographic database generated from the OpenStreetMaps files.

The vector file of OpenStreetMaps representing a geographic location is converted into tables and stored in PostgreSQL, where each table represents a road network as directed graph. Every road is represented by set of links (Unique identifier), therefore by querying vehicle coordinates, we can retrieve the corresponding road link from the database. Vehicle simulation unit exploits Map-matching module to fetch the entire details of Geo-references and forwards it to the Aggregation server and later these details are used by Live User Performance Enabler unit to plot the road links on Google Maps.

2.4 Live User Performance Enabler

The UI based architecture enables the visual representation of the user performance on the android phone in lively basis, where the final outcome of evaluations are plotted and displayed. The three main functionalities of this block are as follows:

- Communication control
- Performance analyzer
- Map based interactive UI

The major activity of performance enabler unit is to communicate with the other two architectures (vehicle Simulation unit and Aggregation server) seamlessly to gather and analyze the data. The entire architecture is housed into an android framework as an application, therefore the application connects to Vehicle simulation unit using Bluetooth module. From vehicle simulation unit, the absolute scores of user performances corresponding to Green Drive and Fluid Traffic behavior are gathered and analyzed. Post analysis these values are represented on UI with a grading scale of colors (green, red and yellow), where each color corresponds to the driver performance such as good, medium and bad (see Fig. 3).

The evaluation happens in two stages where the first phase involves the representation of absolute scores and second phase involves the representation of the relative scores of the users (Social comparison). In the second phase the Performance analyzer application requests the Aggregation server for the latest and historic averages of users on the link. The response of the Aggregation server is then assessed with the absolute values secured from the Vehicle simulation unit and are displayed on the gauges with the grading scale of good, average and bad (refer Fig. 3). This comparative methodology enables the comparison of user performance with the peers on all aspects of the Green driving and Fluid traffic, apart from the estimation on gauges, the performance

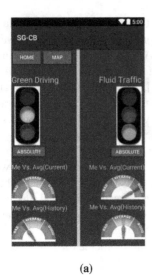

(a)   (b)

Fig. 3. (a) Live user performance screen with absolute and social comparisons, (b) Performance results on Geo-referenced links on Google maps. (Color figure online)

measured (respective to various links) are then plotted on Google Maps for further visualization.

3 Results

We hypothesize, the methodology of comparing user performance analysis with the performance of peers for deriving the detailed analysis of user caliber. As our analysis involved two different aspects (Green drive and Fluid Traffic), we have segregated the results in the graphs below (refer Figs. 4 and 5).

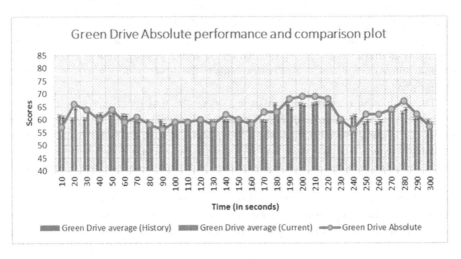

Fig. 4. Green drive absolute performance and comparison plot (Color figure online)

The first part of the evaluation involves the absolute comparison, where the user scores are received from the vehicle simulation Unit and are tabulated on the grading scale for the performance metrics (Good, Average and Bad). The test scenario consisted of samples collected for 5 min with the update frequency on the timestamp of 10 s. These values of the scores were absolute and ranged based on the evaluated user performance in Vehicle simulation unit. On other hand, the Fluid traffic has the evaluation pattern based on speed signals, where the comparison of absolute performance is displayed on Fig. 5.

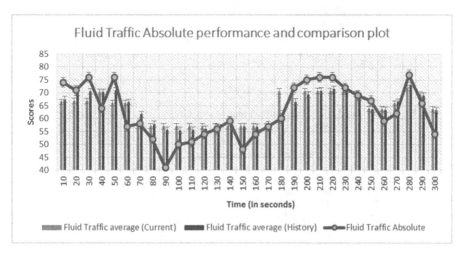

Fig. 5. Fluid traffic absolute performance and comparison plot (Color figure online)

Another significant aspect of our approach is the social comparison, where the individual user performance is analyzed with the average of all the users on the link.

The average values of all the users in a various links (Geo referenced zones) are tabulated in the Aggregation server and the user performance on a particular link is compared with the average values derived from the Aggregation Server to estimate the final outcome. Figure 6 represents the social comparison results of Green Drive on the average scale and the percentage of the performance overview.

The average scale denotes the difference of the values calculated from the Aggregation server and vehicle simulation unit for extraction of the social comparison results. From the tabulated data of green drive, it can be noted that the social comparison of user seems nominal with certain amount of coarse pattern (Fig. 7).

Whereas, the fluid traffic holds maximum amount of inadequate performance on the grading scale. As the results of the analysis are represented spontaneously on Google Maps, which would also provide the user an insight about the locations where the driving pattern can be enhanced. The social comparison also stands as a hidden factor that could motivate the driver to maintain smooth driving behavior. Therefore, this method provides an in-depth analysis of user performance on two scales (absolute and social comparison) and this can be deployed in real-time for creating a qualitative grading analysis of user performance.

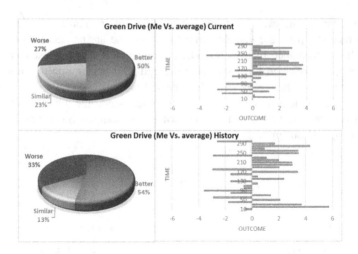

Fig. 6. Consolidated social comparison analysis of Green Drive (Color figure online)

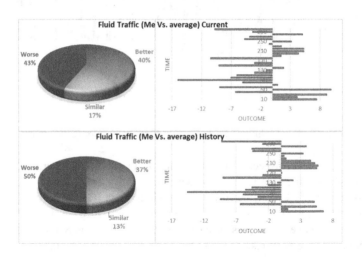

Fig. 7. Consolidated Social comparison analysis of Fluid Traffic (Color figure online)

4   Conclusion

The live user performance evaluation using a comparative approach with peers to estimate the user caliber was performed in this research work. This approach provides the wider spectrum of the user performance details for Green drive and Fluid traffic corresponding to latest and historic observations. The methods used in the simulation environment could be transformed to the real world platform by discarding the vehicle simulation unit from the architecture and direct transmission of the vehicle signal evaluation to the Aggregation server. The individual user can utilize the live user performance enabler application and fetch the performance analysis report directly on the smartphone application with the reference values from the Aggregation server. Henceforth, the methodology which we implemented emphasizes more on qualitative assessment of user performance on absolute and social comparative aspects. This way of gauging user performance would uplift the entire cluster of users coupled to it, as the betterment of driving behavior with one user would impact on all the users associated with it, thus ensuring the collaborative enhancement of driving standards.

References

1. Stapleton, A.J.: Serious games: serious opportunities. In: Health Care (Don. Mills), vol. 1, pp. 1–6, September 2004
2. Diewald, S., Möller, A., Roalter, L., Stockinger, T., Kranz, M.: Gameful design in the automotive domain: review, outlook and challenges. In: Proceedings of 5th International Conference on Automotive User Interfaces Interactive Vehicular Applications, pp. 262–265 (2013)
3. Shi, C., Lee, H.J., Kurczak, J., Lee, A.: Routine driving infotainment app: gamification of performance driving. In: Proceedings of 4th International Conference on Automotive User Interfaces Interactive Vehicular Applications, pp. 181–183 (2012)
4. Fiat eco: Drive. http://ecodrive.driveuconnect.eu/
5. Prendinger, H., Oliveira, J., Catarino, J., Madruga, M., Prada, R.: ICO2: a networked game for collecting large-scale eco-driving behavior data. IEEE Internet Comput. **18**(3), 28–35 (2014)
6. McCall, R., Koenig, V.: Gaming concepts and incentives to change driver behaviour. In: 2010 11th Annual Mediterranean Ad Hoc Networking Workshop Med-Hoc-Net 2012, pp. 146–151 (2012)
7. Goncalves, J., Rossetti, R.J.F., Olaverri-Monreal, C.: IC-DEEP: a serious games based application to assess the ergonomics of in-vehicle information systems. In: 2012 15th International IEEE Conference on Intelligent Transportation Systems, pp. 1809–1814 (2012)
8. Goncalves, J.S.V., Rossetti, R.J.F, Jacob, J., Goncalves, J., Olaverri-Monreal, C., Coelho, A., Rodrigues, R.: Testing advanced driver assistance systems with a serious-game-based human factors analysis suite. In: IEEE Intelligent Vehicles Symposium Proceedings, no. Iv, pp. 13–18 (2014)
9. Amditis, A., Andreone, L., Pagle, K., Markkula, G., Deregibus, E., Rue, M.R., Bellotti, F., Engelsberg, A., Brouwer, R., Peters, B., De Gloria, A.: Towards the automotive HMI of the future; overview of the aide integrated project results. IEEE Trans. Intell. Transp. Syst. **11** (3), 567–578 (2010)
10. Bellotti, F., De Gloria, A., Montanari, R., Dosio, N., Morreale, D.: COMUNICAR: designing a multimedia, context-aware human-machine interface for cars. Cogn. Technol. Work **7**(1), 36–45 (2005)
11. CRF. http://www.crf.it/en-US/Company/Pages/CompanyProfilo.aspx. Accessed 8 May 2015
12. FraunhoferFokus. https://www.fokus.fraunhofer.de/en. Accessed 27 Oct 2015
13. Quddus, M.A., Ochieng, W.Y., Noland, R.B.: Current map-matching algorithms for transport applications: state-of-the art and future research directions. Transp. Res. Part C Emerg. Technol. **15**(5), 312–328 (2007)

14. Lai, J., Tang, W., He, Y.: Team tactics in military serious game. In: Proceedings - 2011 4th International Symposium Computational Intelligence and Design (ISCID 2011), vol. 1, pp. 75–78 (2011)
15. De Carvalho, C.V., Lopes, M., Gomes, D.: Serious games for lean manufacturing: the 5S game. IEEE Rev. Iberoam. Tecnol. Del Aprendiz. 8(4), 191–196 (2013)

A Smart Mobility Serious Game Concept and Business Development Study

Francesco Bellotti[1(✉)], Riccardo Berta[1], Alessandro De Gloria[1], Gautam Dange[1], Pratheep Kumar Paranthaman[1], Francesco Curatelli[1], Chiara Martinengo[2], Giulio Barabino[1], Giuseppe Sciutto[1], Elias Demirtzis[3], and Florian Hausler[4]

[1] DITEN - University of Genova, Via Opera Pia 11/A, 16145 Genoa, Italy
{franz,berta}@elios.unige.it, alessandro.degloria@unige.it
[2] DIMA - University of Genova, Via Dodecaneso, 35, 16146 Genoa, Italy
[3] EICT GmbH, EUREF-Campus Haus 13, Torgauer Straße 12-15, 10829 Berlin, Germany
[4] Fraunhofer Fokus, Kaiserin-Augusta-Allee 31, 10589 Berlin, Germany

Abstract. The paper presents the concept of a serious game aimed at creating an ecosystem for connected, collaborative and green mobility. The ecosystem is based on rewarding proper user behavior through virtual and/or real-world incentives. The basis is provided by a seamlessly extensible set of apps allowing assessment of user behavior according to criteria related to green and collaborative mobility. The ecosystem looks particularly suited to the promotion of new mobility services. Users could be rewarded through incentives such as discounts from public authorities, mobility service providers, insurances. This is particularly interesting for companies willing to stay in constant contact with their customers and get data to improve their products and services. While the system has been developed for mobility-based games, the infrastructure is general and may be used in a variety of domains.

1 Introduction

Serious games (SGs) – games designed with a primary goal different than pure entertainment [1–3] – are gaining attention also in the infomobility and transportation area. Practicing in the context (situated cognition) [4] is particularly promising for a domain like green/safe driving, where the user (driver/passenger) is in the field and could exploit his experience to improve driving habits and performance.

The TEAM EU FP7 project[1] is developing new, cloud-based collaborative transport solutions based on Information and Communication Technologies (ICTs).

Road users will benefit from the new TEAM technologies through real time traffic recommendations, where the self interest is balanced with global mobility and environmental aspects. TEAM intends to turn static into elastic mobility by joining drivers, travelers and infrastructure operators into one collaborative network. Collaboration extends the cooperative concept of vehicle-2-x systems [5, 6] to include a certain degree of driver interaction and participation towards shared goals.

---

[1] www.collaborative-team.eu/.

© Springer International Publishing Switzerland 2016
A. De Gloria and R. Veltkamp (Eds.): GALA 2015, LNCS 9599, pp. 385–392, 2016.
DOI: 10.1007/978-3-319-40216-1_43

The TEAM consortium is designing and developing a system of apps for smart and collaborative mobility, ranging from Collaborative Navigation to Collaborative Parking, from support for public transport intermodality to collaborative Adaptive Cruise Control, etc. One of these new elastic mobility applications is a SG for collaborative green mobility. The complete name is SG_CB (Serious game and community building, as also the social aspect is considered important for car manufacturers for customer retention). The SG is intended as a tool for personal improvement through competition (self and social). The SG combines different user performance evaluators – typically based on the other TEAM apps – so that a user is incentivized to improve his performance. The SG app also intends to support a community of users, who share events, results and related info [7].

In this paper, we briefly describe the SG_CB app and then focus on the discussion of possible business aspects related to the proposed SG. This paper presents findings of a business modeling workshop that was held at the Fokus Fraunhofer premises in Berlin (Germany) during the TEAM project general assembly on October 23rd 2015.

2   The Concept

The main idea of the serious game is to motivate and spur improvement of the user in green and collaborative mobility behaviors.

This is achieved by creating a cloud-based infrastructure (Fig. 1 is a high level sketch) able to aggregate and manage different types of contributors. Contributors are evaluator modules that may process different types of events, contexts and signals, but send their evaluation to the cloud servers that are responsible for performance and competition management. Evaluators may run on smartphones and/or on embedded systems, for instance in a vehicle. The reference architecture is a Service-Oriented architecture [8]. The user interface is implemented on a smartphone.

2.1   Evaluators

Evaluators are components that are used as the virtual sensors of the game and provide the fundamental user evaluations according to the green and collaborative driving criteria. As the main goal of the game is to improve the user behavior, evaluators aim at assess the mobile user behaviors in various kinds of activities.

At the present stage, most of the evaluators are within apps that are being developed by the TEAM project (Table 1). Extensions are simply aimed at assessing how well the user is behaving with respect to the activities covered by that particular app. Beside the TEAM app, we are implementing also other evaluators, concerned on green driving. Third parties evaluators may be added in the feature seamlessly. As sketched in Fig. 1, data coming from the evaluators, are sent to the gaming services.

2.2   The Game Services

The TEAM app offers two kinds of game services: a virtual bank and a competition.

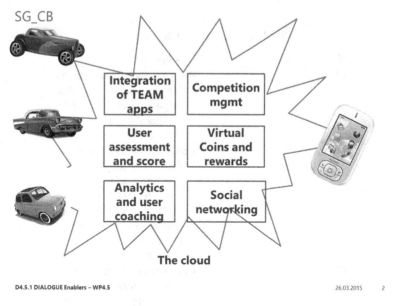

SG_CB

Integration of TEAM apps

Competition mgmt

User assessment and score

Virtual Coins and rewards

Analytics and user coaching

Social networking

The cloud

D4.5.1 DIALOGUE Enablers – WP4.5   26.03.2015   2

Fig. 1. Sketch of the TEAM serious game

The virtual bank manages virtual coins, that are gained by behaving well according to the evaluators. Virtual coins are accumulated by individuals, without sharing nor knowledge among different people (as it happens for real bank accounts). Virtual coins may be spent by the owner either on real-world items (e.g., bus tickets, parking slots, etc.) and on virtual items, such as accessing premium levels in the TEAM apps. For instance, the gaming user interface requires a premium level to display comparative results among friends.

The virtual bank service implements some gamification effects, such as saturation (in order to avoid over-scoring by a single evaluator), happy hours and happy areas.

The competition service allows creation of competitions based on area and/or time periods. Users need to subscribe to competitions, so that they can participate to the (periodic or manually set) instances of the competition. The users can see the ranking of a competition instance in real-time already when running. This allows a comparison with self and friends. At the end of a competition instance, the best scorers are also rewarded with some virtual coins and notified through a basic social networking service.

While the virtual coins system is typically suited to manage events from a single user, competitions look more suited to processing constant rates of evaluations from several different users.

2.3 Basic Social Networking

A major goal of the serious game is to support the construction and nurturing of a community of users engaged in activities related to green and collaborative driving. This is achieved through the whole system design, and also relies on a specific module

Table 1. Current SG_CB evaluators

Name	Description
EFP	Eco Friendly Parking is an in-vehicle Team app aimed at helping drivers in finding parking slots, also thanks to collaboration among them
CONAV	Collaborative Navigation is a TEAM app (implemented both on vehicle and on a smartphone) that provides navigation according to criteria suitable for large groups of people, not a single person
CPTO	Collaborative Public Transport Optimization is a TEAM app that considers preferences and real-time information from various users in order to adapt the public transport bus service accordingly
CCA	Co-modal coaching support from virtual avatar users is a co-modal transportation support app with post trip cost/benefit analysis functionalities, made through a comparison of the behaviours of the real user and the "virtual" avatar user
GD V	Green Drive Vehicular is an in-vehicle module that processes vehicular signals (e.g., RPM, pedal activity) in order to assess effectiveness of the driver for green driving
GD E	Green Drive External is a module that processes various kinds of signals (not from the car) in order to assess the driver green behavior. Typical signals are GPS and accelerometers in a smartphone

providing basic social networking functionalities, such as: friendship management; group management; notification; posting on walls and on maps.

2.4 Human-Machine Interaction (HMI)

HMI has been designed to have a very little impact on the driver, while allowing third parties (e.g., a passenger) to assess to information in real-time. There is no need, given the game logic, for the driver to know about his performance during a competition instance. This is achieved through a smartphone app (Fig. 2).

Fig. 2. Competition menu; hall of fame for a competition; user virtual bank balance

2.5 Data Availability and Privacy Issues

User assessment performed by the TEAM evaluators provides a lot of valuable information, especially related to green and collaborative driving. Other info concern user preferences and habits, such as use of the apps, competitions, expenditure of VCs. This basis of data may be of interest to several companies and organizations.

Of course, tracking of users creates significant issues in terms of privacy. A clear policy, together with anonymization are key elements for user trust.

3   Potential Business Analysis

3.1 Value Proposition

We believe that the proposed app has a value to end users, as it promotes green and collaborative driving. In particular, it provides a social gaming infrastructure (virtual bank, competition and basic social networking services), through which users can be challenged by several different apps aimed at supporting good driving behavior. The serious game aims at closing a virtuous cycle as it engages and motivates users towards improving the use of such apps. At present, only few apps have been implemented. But the system is open and other evaluators may be seamlessly added.

Beside personal improvement, there are also other items that should appeal end-users, such as personal satisfaction and fun.

This is a clear value also for stakeholders. We can think of cities, which benefit from virtuous user behaviors in terms of traffic, navigation, parking and, in general, an optimized use of resources. Manufacturers can take advantage of being in contact with a community of users. The game represents also a platform providing new ways to advertise products (e.g., public transportation, apps, parking slots), also through the real-world rewards. For a company/organization, being involved in the system – especially if certified - may become a sign of eco-friendliness. The concept may also be extended to traffic safety, by adding the proper apps.

3.2 Potential Customers

The potential customers of the gaming app are end-users, who may improve their driving experience and, overall, green and collaborative drive style, especially in the long run.

This feature could be of interest to several stakeholders, from local authorities to original equipment manufacturers.

A natural joint-venture is foreseen with third parties app and evaluator developers. Partnership with social networks may also be considered.

Beside this, availability of a mass of new, geo-referenced data about green and collaborative driving could be of interest to a variety of actors, such as local authorities, car manufacturers, navigation service providers, infrastructure operators.

3.3 Financing

How to make money from the serious game? The game supports and incentives a good use of the other apps and evaluators. Thus, a joint venture with them seems reasonable. Another source of revenues could be given by selling a quantity of data, as discussed above.

At least at the beginning, subscription should be free, as quick growth of the community is key to the success. Freemium access could be considered, especially for a massive use of apps.

Advertising, possibly based on location and other user profile data, could be a significant source of income. Investors may include "smart cities", most interested in eco-friendly behavior and in providing new services.

3.4 Value Chain

The following table summarizes the envisaged value chain (Table 2).

Table 2. Value chain

Component	Added value	Notes
Apps and evaluators	Apps supporting proper user (i.e., driver, traveler) behavior	Seamless addition to the system. Certification may be needed.
Platform	Gaming services. Secure cloud infrastructure. Motivate users to virtuous behavior	
Data	Individual, combined	
Providers	Social network, navigation suppliers	
End-user	Discount, pay-back, subscription, competition	
Stakeholders	Transport service suppliers, corporate community, cities, insurances, general companies	Advertising, promotion, new mobility services, customer relationship

4   Conclusions and Future Work

The main idea behind the presented concept is the creation of an ecosystem for connected, collaborative and green mobility. While the main focus up to now is on driving, different means of transport are considered as well. The ecosystem is based on rewarding proper user behavior through virtual and/or real-world incentives. Attention must be paid in the management of the system, that the included services are coherent with the goal of the system. The ecosystem looks particularly suited to the promotion of new mobility services.

Examples of incentives could be discounts from public authorities, transport companies and insurances, that could attract more users and build communities. Corporate communities are useful for companies to stay in constant contact with their customers and get data to improve their products and services. In general, the game system can be intended as a communication support tool.

While the system has been developed for mobility-based games, the infrastructure is general and may be used in a variety of domains.

References

1. Prensky, M.: Digital game-based learning. ACM Comput. Entertainment **1**(1), 21 (2003)
2. Zyda, M.: From visual simulation to virtual reality to games. IEEE Comput. **38**(9), 25–32 (2005)
3. Bellotti, F., Berta, R., De Gloria, A.: Designing effective serious games opportunities and challenges for research. Int. J. Emerg. Technol. Learn (IJET) **5**, 22–35 (2010). Special Issue: Creative Learning with Serious Games
4. Van Eck, R.: Digital game-based learning: it's not just the digital natives who are restless. EDUCAUSE Rev. **41**(2), 16 (2006)
5. Martelli, F.; Renda, M.E.; Santi, P.: Measuring IEEE 802.11p performance for active safety applications in cooperative vehicular systems. In: 2011 IEEE 73rd Vehicular Technology Conference (VTC Spring), pp. 1–5, 15–18 May, 2011
6. Ibanez, A.G., Flores, C., Reyes, P.D., Barba, A., Reyes, A.: A performance study of the 802.11p standard for vehicular applications. In: 2011 7th International Conference on Intelligent Environments (IE), pp. 165–170, 25–28 July, 2011
7. Bellotti, F., Berta, R., De Gloria, A.: A social serious game concept for green, fluid and collaborative driving. In: De Gloria, A. (ed.) Applications in Electronics Pervading Industry, Environment and Society. LNEE, vol. 289, pp. 163–170. Springer, Heidelberg (2014). doi:10.1007/978-3-319-04370-8_15. ISBN 978-3-319-04370-8
8. Carvalho, M.B., Bellotti, F., Berta, R., De Gloria, A., Gazzarata, G., Hu, J., Kickmeier-Rust, M.: A case study on service-oriented architecture for serious games. Entertainment comput. **6**, 1–10 (2015). doi:10.1016/j.entcom.2014.11.001

ProtoWorld –A Simulation Based Gaming Environment to Model and Plan Urban Mobility

Jannicke Baalsrud Hauge[1,2(✉)], Miguel Ramos Carretero[1],
Jerome Kodjabachian[3], Sebastiaan Meijer[1], Jayanth Raghothama[1],
and Bertrand Duqueroie[3]

[1] Royal Institute of Technology, Alfreds Nobels Alle 10, Stockholm, Sweden
{Jannicke.baalsrud.hauge,miguel.ramos,
sebastiaan.meijer}@sth.kth.se, baa@biba.uni-bremen.de
[2] BIBA – Bremer Institut für Produktion und Logistik
an der Universität Bremen, Bremen, Germany
[3] Thales Group, Palaiseau, France
{jerome.kodjabachian,
bertrand.duqueroie}@thalesgroup.com

Abstract. This workshop will offer the participants the opportunity to explore and test a gaming environment integrating simulation data from different sources. The participants will model and play different mobility options for five European cities. The ProtoWorld solution integrates different simulations and street maps in Unity and allows a playful experience in urban mobility planning. The software will be available for the participants also after the workshop for further experimentation.

Keywords: Simulation models · Game engine · Urban mobility planning

1 Introduction

The citizens' demand for optimal mobility solutions with single window entrance, always accessible, with high usability requires an integrated approach among all mobility service providers. Furthermore, the increased focus on sustainability and quality of life requires a substantial effort in overcoming both congestion and traffic jams leading to the need of improving the mobility solutions across all modes, however often within strict boundaries in old and well-established cities.

Thus, during the past decades, government and local authorities have paid more and more attention to developing new mobility concepts. However, this requires improved simulation of different transport modes like busses, trams, trains, cars, bicycles, as well as pedestrian and their interaction. This means that simulation models need to satisfy different requirements in order to serve as good visualization and decision support tools useful for investigating causes of effects. Such effects can be congestion, accidents, to study the effects of policies and designs to manage and regulate traffic, and to provide insights on urban development and planning [1, 2]. In addition, holistic mobility

© Springer International Publishing Switzerland 2016
A. De Gloria and R. Veltkamp (Eds.): GALA 2015, LNCS 9599, pp. 393–400, 2016.
DOI: 10.1007/978-3-319-40216-1_44

concepts for urban regions require that different stakeholders get together, interact and collaboratively develop suitable mobility concepts, taking the need and the requirements of each stakeholder group into account. This results in growing needs of simulating large-scale complex traffic patterns, individual behaviour etc. at the scale of large cities, possible informed by real time sensor data and visualized in real time for decision support [3, 4]. However, many traffic simulations provide highly complex, accurate models with high granularity for one mode, but do often not mirror the complexity and the high interaction and mutual dependencies of the real world needed for an holistic planning. The workshop offers a possibility to try out a gaming environment enabling the holistic exploration of complex transport systems by integrating different simulations into a gaming engine. The aim of the tool is to provide an environment in which the participants can playfully discuss and test different strategies for monitoring and control and for training personnel.

2   Description of Gaming Environment

Modern cities demand interwoven mobility solutions, while existing toolkits focus only on isolated parts and, when combined, provide sub-optimal services. ProtoWorld is a platform for federating simulations and combining data sources for exploring multimodal mobility options. Due to its interactive and playful nature, ProtoWorld provides a bridge between otherwise separated stakeholders. ProtoWorld is a platform developed in the EITICT project "MD4CR". It allows combining multi-model simulations using a game engine to develop a game scenario. The main objective behind the game scenario is to increase the awareness among different stakeholders.

Figure 1 shows the architecture diagram of our platform, which includes several components all connected by a communication bus. Among these components, there is a federation of simulations for urban mobility. For the main showcase of this project we included SUMO, an open source simulation suite for modelling realistic traffic systems, and SE-*, a simulation software developed by Thales Group with a high level of realism mimicking human behaviour. As alternatives to the latter, we also developed two own propietary pedestrian simulations: SiPS, focused on simulating pedestrian students in academic environments [2], and Flash, a large-scale pedestrian simulation for public transport commuting. Other simulations could also be integrated following the same architecture. Beside these simulations, a database is also used for the storage of information about the geography of the scenario imported from OpenStreetMap (OSM). In order to control and synchronize the federation of simulations, a gaming interface (Unity3D) is connected through the communication bus, assuming control over all the simulations and being responsible of all the visualization (geography and agents from the simulations) using the database in an automated fashion. With this, the end-user interacts with the gaming interface, which allows for controlling different parameters in the federation of simulations as well as the triggering of several events, affecting the behavior of the simulations in real-time. The next section deals with the scenario development [5].

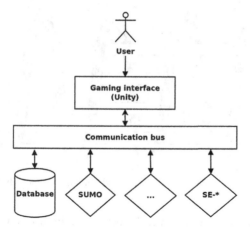

Fig. 1. Architecture diagram

3 Scenario Development

Approach. As indicated in the introduction, it is still a challenge within the requirement elicitation to define clear, correct and complete requirements for such complex systems as game environments for multi-modal mobility systems. One reason for this is that those delivering the requirements and those developing the tools and scenarios based on the requirements have different perceptions of terminology and understanding of wording. In addition, in most cases, the requirements are for future products and services for which the customer might not have a clear idea on how the product or service will look like [6]. This leads to uncertainties and inconsistencies in the requirements, as well as to misunderstanding of what is actually meant with a specific requirement. Thus, in order to reduce the risk of capturing false requirements for the scenarios, capturing end user requirements can use the story telling method. This method is not new, actually it has been used for some decades for this purpose [7]. "Storytelling is a flexible design research method with a broad range of applications, associated processes and variations" [8]. It is based on communication between the stakeholders. It allows the participants to develop the story commonly (group story-telling) and thus discuss the different perspective as it is carried out. A narrative story telling helps to put the requirement in a specific context clarifying to the reader how they are to be understood. In addition, a different advantage for the users are that it is a natural way of communicate among human beings, and thus reduces the barriers to articulate what they think they need using their natural language and by generating a common understanding.

Consequently, for the scenarios used in the workshop, a participatory, agile approach was used, as seen in Fig. 2. Based upon the identified needs, the requirements were derived in a participatory approach including the development teams and the different user groups.

The following steps where carried out (according to the development process described in Fig. 2)

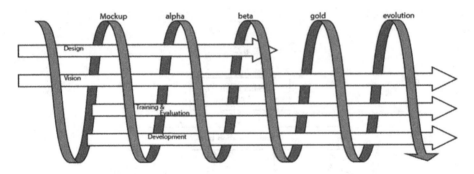

Fig. 2. Scenario development and validation approach [9]

1. Requirement analysis (process in real world scenario, needs, target of simulation, stakeholders, decision making options for each stakeholder groups, possibility for delivering real world data (traffic data, travel times etc.)
2. Mapping of the real world scenario into the simulation scenarios (including mapping different variables, definition of game mechanics)
3. Prototyping- transferring into the gamified simulation environment (either using paper prototypes (or directly a digital prototyping
4. Definition of game scenario
5. Implementing in the Petra gaming simulation environment

Regarding the requirement elicitation- there are two sets depending on the usage: One set is related to the functionalities the user (i.e. editors of scenarios) need in order to set up new and for adapting existing scenarios, the second set is related to the game play itself (i.e. the requirements a player have on the tool).

The workshop was focusing on the validation of the first type of requirements. The next sections describe briefly the object the workshop participants worked on- i.e. the scenarios.

Scenario Description. This section describes one of the five existing scenarios (Stockholm, Paris, Delft, Berlin and Rome) realized in Unity, using the ProtoWorld platform as described in Sect. 2. The idea is just to provide a feeling of the tool. The selected scenario is prepared for Berlin uses SiPS and SUMO as simulators. The area of interest is the surroundings of Brandenburger Tor.

This scenario has the functionalities:

- Increase/decrease the speed of the underlying simulation
- Delay and stop metros
- Add and move bike stations
- Bikes
- Weather conditions influencing the personal choice
- Distance to bike station influencing the personal choice
- Distribution of people selecting bikes

Figure 3 is a graphical user interface the player starts with. The red line marks a radius from a given point. This can either be from a station, an attraction etc. and helps the user to think of where to put a new parking slot etc. On the left, different options for changes like mode management or weather conditions can be selected. These changes will have an impact on the behavior of the pedestrians.

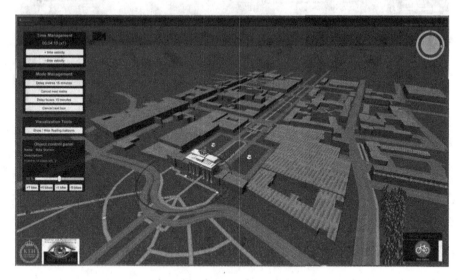

Fig. 3. Berlin Scenario overview of GUI

Figure 4 is a screen shot from a running scenario. We here see that some pedestrians have not selected the transport means yet, whereas others will take the bus or a metro (urban). The green labeled bike is a bike parking. In the right bottom corner is the function Bike parking house. This is a drag and drop functionality and the player can implement several of those where he wants. He can also move and delete already existing. After a few minutes he can observe the changes this has on the overall performance.

Figure 5 illustrates how it looks like when 3D graphics are imported from a library. This helps the user recognize the place and to feel familiar. The demonstration scenario can be easily transferred to other areas of Berlin or for other cities. The scenario can also be adapted to any other city like Rome (see below) or other cases (Fig. 6).

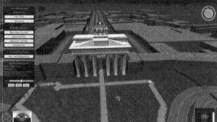

Fig. 4. Berlin Scenario screen shot   **Fig. 5.** Integration of 3D components

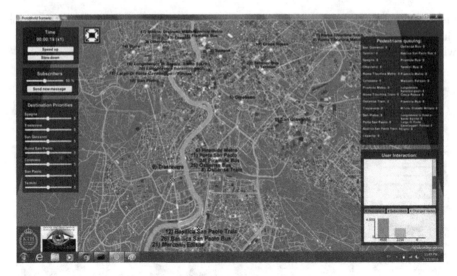

Fig. 6. Updated Rome scenario

4 Experimental Set Up

The workshop was designed for 1/2day. It started with a short introduction on the main objectives of urban planning as well as of the different gaming scenarios (different European cities) as well as with and introduction to the ProtoWorld platform. This was followed by a hands-on in which the participant could get familiar with the software using a short testing scenario. The main part of the workshop was dedicated to playing and experiencing with the game play and to do changes in the scenarios. Based upon their experience during game play with different mobility options visualizing how these affect the urban mobility in the given scenario, the participants can modify the scenario. The aims are: (1) to analyze (and provide suggestions to improve) existing gaming scenario; (2) to design new scenarios. The workshop was closed by a discussion on the usability of the gaming environment and how easy it would be to transfer the tool to the cities of the participants.

5 Validation Results

Validation is always done for a specific purpose. In order to improve the usability of the ProtoWorld tool for different user groups, we used the workshop also to validate the gaming environment. For this we used a questionnaire as well as oral feedback. Both the gaming environment as well as the scenarios were validated. The first part of the questionnaire dealt with the experience of the workshop participants related to 3D environment and simulations. Here, it has to be stated that we had an expert group, all feeling familiar with this type of tool. The second part was related to the interface and how intuitive it is- whereas the responses shows that the user interfaces are easy to understand, the interfaces an editor needs to deal with, scores much lower. Here, most of the participants says it would be required to have programming skills or a very extensive introduction in order to cope with that. The scenarios and the level of details meet the level of expectation and are sufficient. The simulation is seen to be valid. The last part of the questionnaire deals more with how to use the tool, how to make it more usable as well as how this can benefit urban mobility planning. The participants all agree upon that the tool can be very helpful, but as a valuable addition there are some differences. One participants suggest a multi-user approach, whereas two mention that the adaptability needs to be improved so that the tool (the editorial part) can be used by the expected target group- consultants without programming skills. Also a guide on how to develop scenarios step by step as well as the possibility to import transport data are suggested.

6 Conclusion and Next Steps

The experience of the participants shows that even much of the work related to the generation of scenario map can be quite easily done, the import in Unity of the Open Street Maps requires quite much manual work. This is difficult without the relevant skills. Also the handling of changes required in the database is identified as a challenge. Furthermore, even though the scenario generation as such is quite simple, it is still required that someone has done the requirement elicitation and designed the gaming scenario. This requires knowledge in both areas. If additional functionalities are required, it is necessary to engage a programmer. Thus, in order to improve the usability of the tool, we will redesign the way the scenarios are generated, automating the process in more intuitive steps to ease the labour of the user. Along with that, we will divide each of the functionalities provided by ProtoWorld in self-contained modules, allowing with this a complete customization of the tool and giving the user the freedom to select the elements that are relevant for each particular scenario.

Acknowledgment. The work presented herein is partially funded under the European Community Seventh Framework Program, PETRA project and EIT ICT Labs MD4CR project

References

1. Raghothama, J., Meijer, S.: What do policy makers talk about when talking about simulations? In: ISAGA (2015, to appear)
2. Raghothama, J., Azhari, M., Carretero, M.R., Meijer, S: Architectures for distributed, interactive and integrated traffic simulations. In: Models and Technologies for Intelligent Transportation Systems (MT-ITS) (2015)
3. Nagel, K., Esser, J., Rickert, M.: Large-Scale Traffic Simulations for Transportation Planning (2002)
4. Sewall, J., Wilkie, D., Merrell, P., Lin, M.C.: Continuum traffic simulation. Comput. Graph. Forum **29**(2), 439–448 (2010). http://onlinelbrary.wiley.com/doi/10.1111/j.1467-8659.2009. 01613.x/abstract
5. Baalsrud Hauge, J., et al: D6.3 Validation of gaming simulation project, Petra project (2016)

6. Gausepohl, K.A.: Investigation of storytelling as a requirements elicitation method for medical devices (2008)
7. Ribeiro, C., Pereira, J., Farinha, C., da Silva, M.M.: Gamifying requirement elicitation: practical implications and outcomes in improving stakeholders' collaboration. Entertainment Comput. **5**, 335–345 (2014)
8. Vink Storytelling: Conceptualize, Define, Design, Discover, Implement (2015). http://designresearchtechniques.com/casestudies/storytelling/. Accessed 11 Dec 2015
9. Hauge, J.B.: Mediating skills on risk management for improving the resilience of Supply Networks by developing and using a serious game (2014). http://nbn-resolving.de/urn:nbn:de:gbv:46-00104706-14

The Role of Surprise in Game-Based Learning for Mathematics

Pieter Wouters[1], Herre van Oostendorp[1(✉)], Judith ter Vrugte[2],
Sylke vanderCruysse[3], Ton de Jong[2], and Jan Elen[3]

[1] Institute of Information and Computing Sciences, Utrecht University,
Princetonplein 5, 3584 CC Utrecht, The Netherlands
{P.J.M.wouters,h.vanOostendorp}@uu.nl
[2] Department of Instructional Technology, University of Twente,
Enschede, The Netherlands
{j.tervrugte,a.j.m.dejong}@utwente.nl
[3] Center for Instructional Psychology and Technology,
KU Leuven, Louvain, Belgium
sylke.vandercruysse@kuleuven-kulak.be,
jan.elen@ppw.kuleuven.be

Abstract. In this paper we investigate the potential of surprise on learning with prevocational students in the domain of proportional reasoning. Surprise involves an emotional reaction, but it also serves a cognitive goal as it directs attention to explain why the surprising event occurred and to learn for the future. Experiment 1 - comparing a surprise condition with a control condition - found no differences, but the results suggested that surprise may be beneficial for higher level students. In Experiment 2 we combined Expectancy strength (Strong vs. Weak) with Surprise (Present vs. Absent) using higher level students. We found a marginal effect of surprise on learning indicating that students who experienced surprises learned more than students who were not exposed to these surprises but we found a stronger positive effect of surprise when we included existing proportional reasoning skill as factor. These results provide evidence that narrative techniques such as surprise can be used for the purpose of learning.

1 Introduction

Despite the increasing popularity of serious games or game-based learning (GBL), recent meta-analytic reviews have shown that GBL is only moderately more effective and not more motivating than traditional instruction [11]. A potential problem with GBL is that the outcomes of players' actions in the game are directly reflected in the game world. This may lead to a kind of intuitive learning: players know how to apply knowledge, but they cannot explicate it [3]. The articulation of knowledge and underlying rules is important, because it triggers students to *organize* new information and *integrate* it with their prior knowledge [5] and thus construct a mental model that is more broadly applicable. This implies that genuine learning in GBL requires additional features in the game that will provoke the player to engage in the process of knowledge

A. De Gloria and R. Veltkamp (Eds.): GALA 2015, LNCS 9599, pp. 401–410, 2016.
DOI: 10.1007/978-3-319-40216-1_45

articulation. Typically in learning environments such knowledge articulation is often prompted by explicitly asking students to reflect on their actions and thoughts. In complex GBL environments this may compromise the motivating quality of the game or can be so cognitively demanding that learning will not take place [6].

The question raised in this paper is how we can stimulate players to engage in relevant cognitive processes that foster learning without jeopardizing the motivational appeal of the game [12]. A promising technique is the generation of manageable cognitive conflicts by introducing surprises [4]. Surprise involves an emotional reaction, but it also serves a cognitive goal as it directs attention to explain why the surprise occurred and to learn for the future [1]. In the context of learning a medical procedure with a serious game [9] demonstrated that surprise yielded superior knowledge structures, indicating that such events foster deep learning. They assume that in games players construct a mental model based on the story line, the events and the underlying rules of the game. The assumption of this study is that the effect of surprise also pertains to problem solving in serious games. Ideally, the mental model will enable the student to recognize specific characteristics of a problem and how to solve that problem. Because our aim is to integrate the instructional technique (i.e. the introduction of the surprise) with the learning content [2], the surprises have to be focused on what has to be learned, i.e. the mental model of proportional reasoning problems and methods to solve them. For this reason, the surprising events change some of the problem characteristics, and the solution method previously applied, is no longer applicable and the player has to re-evaluate the situation and decide which problem characteristics are relevant and which solution method is now most appropriate. We expect that surprise has a positive effect on learning because it stimulates relevant cognitive processes such as organizing and integrating information [5] without compromising the motivational appeal of computer games.

In this study we investigate the impact of surprise on learning and how this impact is moderated by the expectancy of the student (in the second study).

2   Experiment 1

In Experiment 1 a group of students playing the game with surprises occurring during the game was compared with a group without these surprises (control group). We expected that the group with surprises would learn more from the GBL than the control group.

2.1   Method

Participants and Design. The participants were 71 students from second year prevocational education. We adopted a pretest-posttest design with a control condition ($N = 36$) and a surprises condition ($N = 35$). Participants were randomly assigned to the conditions.

Materials.

Domain. The domain of proportional reasoning comprises three problem types: comparison problems, missing value problems, and transformation problems. In comparison problems students have to find out whether one proportion is "more than", "lesser-than" or "equal to" another proportion. In missing value problems one value in one of two proportions is missing. Students have to find this "missing value" in order to ensure that both proportions are equal. Transformation problems involve two proportions as well and all values are known, but the proportions are not equal. Students have to find out how much has to be added to one or more of the proportions in order to make both proportions equal (for a more extensive description see [7]).

Game Environment. In the 2D game (Flash/ActionScript 3) called *Zeldenrust* players have a summer job in a hotel (http://www.projects.science.uu.nl/mathgame/zeldenrust/index.html). By doing different tasks the players can earn money that can be used to select a holiday destination during the game: the more money they earn, the further they can travel. During the game the player is accompanied by the manager, a non-playing character, who provides information about the task and gives feedback regarding the performance on the task. The game comprises a base game and several subgames. The base game provides the structure from which the subgames can be started. After selecting an avatar, the players receive an introduction animation in which the context of the game is presented and finally enter the "Student room" from which the player can control the game (e.g., for example by choosing a specific subgame). Each task is implemented as a subgame and covers a specific problem type in the domain of proportional reasoning. The tasks are directly related to proportional reasoning (e.g., mixing two drinks to make a cocktail according to a particular ratio directly involves proportional reasoning skills). The actual assignments are described on a *whiteboard*. With drag-and-drop or clicking, the player can accomplish the assignment, but the specific action depends on the subgame. To further motivate the player, a *"geldmeter" (money meter)* is implemented which visualizes the amount of money that the player will receive after an assignment. Correct and incorrect actions during an assignment are directly reflected in the money meter. For example, if the player breaks a bottle, the money meter will decrease (and the color becomes redder); if the player places bottles in the refrigerator the money meter will increase (and becomes greener). The money meter also shows the (accumulated) amount of money that the player has earned. The player can use a built-in *calculator*, but using it will cost some money. Depending on the subgame the player has to perform a typical action (e.g., closing the door of the refrigerator) to receive *verbal feedback* from the manager of the hotel who tells whether the answer is correct or not (e.g., 'Excellent' or 'You have too much Cola in relation to Fanta'). If the answer is correct the money meter will be increased.

The *surprise* condition comprised a non-playing niece character in the introduction animation telling that she sometimes will make it difficult to carry out the task. When a surprise occurred the niece character had popped up and told that she had changed something. This change involved specific characteristics of the task whereby the solution method of the player doesn't apply anymore and the player has to reconsider the original solution method. Figure 1 gives an example of the occurrence of a surprise.

Figure 1a depicts the starting situation. The player can solve the problem by looking at the ratio within: the number of Fanta in the refrigerator is twice as much as the number of Fanta in the desired proportion (12 Fanta) since 12 * 2 = 24, so the number of Cola also has to be doubled (9 * 2 = 18 Cola). When the player is implementing the solution, the surprise occurs (Fig. 1b). When the niece character has disappeared the characteristics of the task are modified (Fig. 1c); that is, the desired proportion is now 5 Cola per 10 Fanta. The ratio "within" is not applicable anymore and the player can better use a method based on the ratio "between" (the desired proportion is 5 Cola/10 Fanta, so the number of Cola in the refrigerator should also be half the number of Fanta, 12/24). In total the players received 8 surprises (four in both the missing value and the transformation subgames).

Tests/Measures. The arithmetic tempo test, the *TTR (Tempo Test Rekenen),* measures fluency in basic arithmetic operations i.e., addition, subtraction, multiplication, and division. The TTR score is calculated as the sum of correct answers. The range of possible scores is 0–200. Proportional reasoning skill was measured with a test consisting of 12 open questions: four questions for each problem type. There were two versions of the test. The comparability of both versions was tested in pilot study. Each answer of the pre- and posttest was coded as 0 (wrong answer or no answer) or 1 (correct answer). As game performance indicators the number of correct game tasks and the time spent on game tasks were used.

Procedure. The experiment run on school computers and comprised three sessions of 50 min. In session 1 the experiment was introduced and the pretest was administered. In the second session, a week later, the participants played the game (40 min). All actions of the players during playing the game were logged. The posttest was administered in the third session (a week after playing the game).

2.2 Results and Conclusion

In order to test the effect of surprise on learning we used the combined score of the items of the two problem types in which surprise was applied (missing value – Refrigerator subgame; transformation – Blender subgame). Table 1 shows the results for each condition on proportional reasoning skill. A paired samples T-test reveals that playing the game ($t(70) = 2.73$, $p = .008$, $d = 0.29$) improves learning. We also conducted a hierarchical regression analysis to investigate whether game performance indeed is predictive for learning. The first block comprised pretest score and TTR; the second block consisted of correct game tasks and time spent on game tasks. The number of correct game tasks explains an additional 6 % extra of the variance in posttest performance ($B = .11$, $SE\ B = .04$, $\beta = .39$, $p = .007$). An independent T-test with overall learning gain (posttest score – pretest score) as dependent variable shows no difference between control and surprise group ($t(69) = .07$, $p > .05$, $d = .00$).

The surprise group did not perform better than the control group. There are two plausible explanations for the failure to find a beneficial effect of surprise. To start with, the processing of surprise requires a certain level of cognitive flexibility and metacognitive skills. Students must perceive and understand that the changes in the

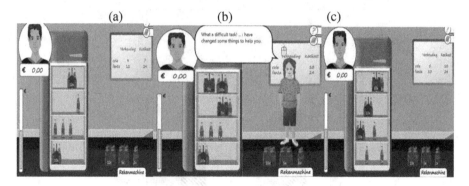

Fig. 1. (a) Starting situation in a task with a surprise, (b) surprise (c) modification of task characteristics in the game *Zeldenrust*.

Table 1. Mean scores and standard deviations on the dependent variables of Experiment 1

TTR	Control		Surprise	
	76 (12)		75 (20)	
	Pre	Post	Pre	Post
	M (SD)	M (SD)	M (SD)	M (SD)
All items	4.32 (2.33)	5.07 (2.65)	4.38 (2.01)	5.02 (2.56)
Surprise items	2.30 (2.87)	2.88 (2.34)	2.06 (1.71)	2.66 (2.31)
Comparison	2.02 (.99)	2.20 (.91)	2.32 (1.83)	2.36 (1.18)

Note: Range of All items is 0 to 12. All items means all proportional reasoning skill items. Surprise items (are missing value and transformation items) range is 0−8. Range comparison items is 0−4.

problem situation of the game are not superficial but that some deeper characteristics of the problem have been altered, see that the changes may have consequences for the chosen solution method and consider whether another method is more appropriate. For students who do not possess these skills sufficiently, the surprise can be confusing or even frustrating because their solution method is thwarted. The students in this experiment can be classified in one of three educational levels that may give an indication regarding cognitive flexibility and metacognitive skills: (1) basic with a practical orientation, (2) moderate with a larger theoretical component and (3) high with a large theoretical (cognitive) component. Probably students in the third level have higher metacognitive skills than those in the first and second level. Figure 2 shows the posttest scores on the surprise items for the three groups in each condition. Although ANCOVAs (posttest score surprise items as dependent variable; condition and educational level as independent variables and TTR and pretest score surprise items as covariate) showed no significant effects (main effect condition and level $F < 1$; interaction of condition and level $F(1, 67) = 1.36$, $p > .05$), theoretical level students seem to benefit more from surprises.

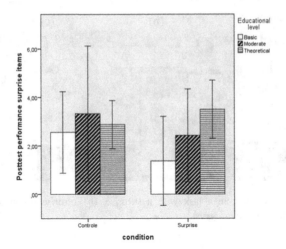

Fig. 2. Posttest performance score surprise items (missing value and transformation items) for basic, moderate and theoretical level students in Experiment 1.

The second explanation concerns the order in which problems with different characteristics were presented to the player. Often the characteristics of a new problem were different from the preceding one which may have thwarted the emergence of a strong expectation. If this is true, the potential beneficial effect of surprise may not have been fully realized. In that case surprise triggering the necessity to retrieve and update the mental model will be weak.

3   Experiment 2

In Experiment 2 we investigated the two possible explanations discussed in Experiment 1. First, participants were recruited from the theoretical educational levels instead of all three educational levels. Second, we introduced a second independent variable in which expectancy was manipulated.

3.1   Method

Participants and Design. The participants were 94 students from second year pre-vocational education. We adopted a pretest-posttest design with two independent variables *Surprises* (Yes or No) and *Expectancy strength* (Strong or Weak) that were factorial combined resulting in 4 conditions: Surprises and Strong expectancy ($N = 22$), Surprises and Weak expectancy ($N = 23$), No surprises and Strong expectancy ($N = 26$) and No surprises and Weak Expectancy ($N = 23$). Participants were randomly assigned to conditions. We tested three hypotheses: (1) Playing the game will improve learning; (2) We expect a main effect of surprise indicating that surprise will increase learning more because it triggers students to interpret the changes in the problem characteristics caused by the surprise and the consequences for the solution process; (3) In addition, we hypothesize an interaction between surprise and expectancy strength indicating that a surprise after multiple problems with the same characteristics (Strong expectancy) will have the largest learning effect because the strong unexpectedness of the surprise will incite students more (or deeper) to think about the changes in the characteristics of the problem characteristics caused by the surprise and the consequences for the solution process.

Materials.

Domain. The same domain was used as in Experiment 1.

Game Environment. The game environment was the same as in Experiment 1 with a modification in the surprise conditions. In Experiment 2 the screen first became brighter (to make the surprise more salient) and then dimmed again before the niece character appeared. The implementation of the factor *Expectancy strength* implied that the characteristics of the problems changed. Strong expectancy was defined as a series of problems with the same characteristics. Weak expectancy was defined as a series of problems in which the characteristics varied. The tests, procedure and scoring were the same as in Experiment 1.

3.2   Results and Conclusion

As in Experiment 1 we used the combined score of the surprise. Table 2 shows the results for each condition on proportional reasoning skill. To test hypothesis 1 we conducted a paired-samples T-test. The results show that playing the game improves learning ($t(93) = 2.54$, $p = .013$, $d = .25$). This is partly corroborated by the results of the hierarchical regression analysis: the number of correct tasks explains 10 % extra of the variance in posttest performance ($B = .10$, $SE\ B = .03$, $\beta = .34$, $p = .002$). Hypotheses 2 and 3 were tested with 2*2 ANCOVA with Surprise and Expectancy strength as independent variables, posttest score as dependent variable and TTR and pretest scores as covariate.

For the surprise items we found a marginally significant main effect for Surprise ($F(1, 90) = 3.16$, $p = .079$). The main effect for Expectancy strength and the Surprise*Expectancy strength interaction were not significant (both $F(1, 90) < 1$). For the comparison items we did not find main or interaction effects (all $F < 1$). The participants in this study represent a heterogeneous population which is reflected in the large SD. We assumed that better performing students would possess the (meta) cognitive skills to deal with the surprises and benefit from the cognitive processes that they trigger. We divided the sample in low and high level students based on the median score of 6 on the pretest. Figure 3 shows the results.

We ran an ANCOVA with the posttest score on the surprise items as dependent variable; surprise, expectancy strength and level as fixed factors and TTR as covariate. We expected to see an interaction between surprise and expectancy and between surprise and level, indicating that high level students would benefit more from surprises than low level students. The results, however, only show significant main effects for

Table 2. Mean scores and standard deviations on the dependent variables of Experiment 2

TTR	Surprise			
	Strong expectancy		Weak expectancy	
	Pre	Post	Pre	Post
	M (SD)	M (SD)	M (SD)	M (SD)
All items	5.71 (2.34)	6.90 (3.18)	6.00 (3.05)	6.95 (3.29)
Surprise items	3.04 (1.88)	4.28 (2.23)	4.00 (2.41)	4.79 (2.53)
Comparison	2.66 (1.06)	2.61 (.97)	2.00 (1.06)	2.17 (1.20)
TTR	No surprise			
	Strong expectancy		Weak expectancy	
	Pre	Post	Pre	Post
	M (SD)	M (SD)	M (SD)	M (SD)
All items	5.07 (2.41)	5.53 (3.46)	5.56 (1.61)	5.86 (3.16)
Surprise items	3.11 (2.41)	3.57 (2.14)	3.21 (1.44)	3.47 (2.44)
Comparison	1.96 (.95)	1.96 (1.18)	2.35 (1.07)	2.39 (1.40)

Note: Range of All items is 0 to 12. All items means all proportional reasoning skill items. Surprise items (are missing value and transformation items) range is 0–8. Range comparison items is 0–4.

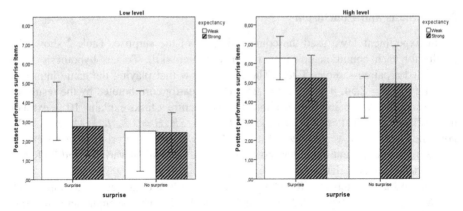

Fig. 3. Posttest performance on surprise items (missing value and transformation items) for low (left) and high (right) level students.

Surprise ($F(1, 85) = 4.12$, $p = .046$) and Level ($F(1, 85) = 18.98$, $p = .000$), but all other main or interaction effects were not significant (Expectancy*Surprise: $F(1, 90) = 1.06$, $p > .05$; all other effects $F < 1$).

4 General Discussion

In two experiments we found that learning improves by playing the game. This corroborates earlier findings regarding serious games in general (cf. [11, 12] and other studies with the game *Zeldenrust* [6]). In both experiments we also found that effective game play (the number of correct game tasks) is predictive for posttest performance. In Experiment 1 we failed to find a beneficial effect of surprise, though high educational level students did benefit. We provided two arguments for this finding. The participants did not possess sufficient (meta)cognitive skills and the expectancy factor which is important for surprise was not optimal utilized. In Experiment 2 we operationalized these new demands by focusing on higher cognitive level students and by manipulating the strength of expectancy. We found a marginal effect of surprise on learning indicating that students who experienced surprises learned more than students who were not exposed to these surprises but we found a stronger effect of surprise when we included existing proportional reasoning skill as factor. These results connect with other studies that find cognitive effects of narrative techniques like surprise in games [9, 13]. These results also imply that instructional techniques such as surprises should be applied with care. An important precondition for effective surprise is that players have sufficient cognitive flexibility and metacognitive skills to orientate on the task, to re-evaluate the results at the moment when the surprise occurs and to reflect on the performed actions. Students who lack these competencies can be overwhelmed by the additional cognitive demands that are introduced by these surprises. Possibly, the effect of surprise can be increased by offering students additional instructional support during the problems before the surprise intervention occurs which may help them to select an appropriate method for a problem. One could think of exercises that help them to automatize part-tasks such as multiplication tables so that they can more easily identify intern or extern ratios and/or worked examples in which strategies for specific types of problems are modelled.

Two other lines of research can also be interesting. First, there is some evidence that metacognitive skills in math improve with small differences in age [8]. The students in this study had a mean age of 13.9 years (second year class) and the metacognitive skills of some may have been insufficiently developed. Another point is that the students come from the least advanced of three Dutch educational tracks. It would be interesting to replicate this study with older students in the same educational level or students from a higher educational track. A second research avenue pertains to the characteristics of the game. The game *Zeldenrust* has a repetitive character, students engage in the same type of tasks which require similar actions. It is not unlikely that students finally will expect that the niece character will reappear and modify the nature of the task. In that case they may anticipate these events and thus undermine the potential effect of surprise. If that is the case more variation in surprise can perhaps further increase its effectiveness.

It may seem that the introduction of surprise adds more difficulty to the problems presented. Two comments to this suggestion can be made. Firstly, making a problem in first instance somewhat harder, e.g. by omitting particular information, can improve learning, particularly of the underlying rules of the problem [10]. Secondly, we want to point out that surprise did have a positive effect on learning, particularly of students with sufficient (meta)cognitive capabilities.

Acknowledgments. This research is funded by the Netherlands Organization for Scientific Research (project Number No. 411-00-003).

References

1. Foster, M.I., Keane, M.T.: Predicting surprise judgments from explanation graphs. In: International Conference on Cognitive Modeling (ICCM). Groningen University, Groningen, The Netherlands (2015)
2. Habgood, M.P.J., Ainsworth, S.E.: Motivating children to learn effectively: exploring the value of intrinsic integration in educational games. J. Learn. Sci. **20**, 169–206 (2011)
3. Leemkuil, H., de Jong, T.: Instructional support in games. In: Tobias, S., Fletcher, D. (eds.) Computer games and instruction, pp. 353–369. IAP, Charlotte, NC (2011)
4. Loewenstein, G.: The psychology of curiosity: a review and reinterpretation. Psychol. Bull. **116**, 75–98 (1994)
5. Mayer, R.E.: Multimedia learning and games. In: Tobias, S., Fletcher, J.D. (eds.) Computer Games and Instruction, pp. 281–305. Information Age Publishing, Greenwich, CT (2011)
6. ter Vrugte, J., de Jong, T., Wouters, P., Vandercruysse, S., Elen, J., van Oostendorp, H.: When a game supports prevocational math education but integrated reflection does not. J. Comput. Assist. Learn. (2015). doi:10.1111/jcal.12104
7. Vandercruysse, S., ter Vrugte, J., de Jong, T., Wouters, P., van Oostendorp, H., Elen, J.: 'Zeldenrust': a mathematical game-based learning environment for vocational students. In: Proceedings of Research on Domain-Specific Serious Games: State-of-the-Art and Prospects Conference. University of Leuven, Belgium (2014)
8. van der Stel, M., Veenman, M.V., Deelen, K., Haenen, J.: The increasing role of metacognitive skills in math: a cross-sectional study from a developmental perspective. ZDM Int. J. Math. Educ. **42**(2), 219–229 (2010)
9. van der Spek, E.D., van Oostendorp, H., Meyer, J-JCh.: Introducing surprising events can stimulate deep learning in a serious game. Br. J. Educ. Technol. **44**, 156–169 (2013)
10. van Nimwegen, C., van Oostendorp, H., Tabachneck-Schijf, H.J.M.: The role of interface style in planning during problem solving. In: Bara, B., Barsalou, L., Bucciarelli, M. (eds.) Proceedings of the 27th Annual Cognitive Science Conference, pp. 2271–2276. Lawrence Erlbaum, Mahwah, NJ (2005)
11. Wouters, P., van Nimwegen, C., van Oostendorp, H., van der Spek, E.D.: A meta-analysis of the cognitive and motivational effects of serious games. J. Educ. Psychol. **105**, 249–265 (2013)
12. Wouters, P., van Oostendorp, H.: A meta-analytic review of the role of instructional support in game-based learning. Comput. Educ. **60**, 412–425 (2013)
13. Wouters, P., van Oostendorp, H., van der Spek, E.D., Boonekamp, R.: The role of game discourse analysis and curiosity in creating engaging and effective serious games by implementing a back story and foreshadowing. Interact. Comput. **23**, 329–336 (2011)

iPlayAStory: A Language Learning Platform for Interactive Story-Telling

Abdelrahman Sakr$^{(\boxtimes)}$, Injy Hamed, and Slim Abdennadher

Computer Science Department, The German University in Cairo,
The 5th District, Cairo 11432, Egypt
abdelrahman.ahmed@student.guc.edu.eg,
{injy.hamed,slim.abdennadher}@guc.edu.eg
http://www.guc.edu.eg

Abstract. Edutainment is a neologism that combines education and entertainment. It has been found to promote learning in a fun and interesting environment. Edutainment applications covered several fields including language learning. However, applications that focused on reading in language learning suffered from some limitations. These limitations include low interactivity and the lack of users' reading assessment. In this paper, we will introduce iPlayAStory; an interactive online educational platform for language learning. iPlayAStory provides children with an entertaining application where they can read sentences aloud. The system then assesses the correctness of the children's reading. Children are provided with feedback and can listen to the correct pronunciation. Moreover, iPlayAStory provides parents and teachers with a clear profile for their children's performance on the application. Parents and teachers could also record stories with their voice to be played back for their children. iPlayAStory also serves as a platform for speech acquisition. The collected speech data could later be used to build an Automatic Speech Recognition system for detailed assessment of children's pronunciation.

Keywords: Edutainment · Games with a purpose · Serious games · Language learning platform

1 Introduction

Today's environment provides various technology equipment such as laptops, mobile phones and game consoles which made it easier for computer and video games to become widespread among children and adults. Moreover, the quick development of multimedia and online information has remarkably highlighted the concept of digital learning models. These models may include edutainment, game based learning, edumarket games and serious games. [22,23]

The term edutainment is a combination of education and entertainment. This can be achieved through various media such as games, television programs and movies. The main idea behind edutainment is that people can enjoy their time

© Springer International Publishing Switzerland 2016
A. De Gloria and R. Veltkamp (Eds.): GALA 2015, LNCS 9599, pp. 411–420, 2016.
DOI: 10.1007/978-3-319-40216-1_46

while learning new topics and enhancing their knowledge. According to [18], Edutainment is defined as:

"The methodology of combining the methods of teaching and the form of game to attract the students and make the most of the active effect of games to help with our education."

Edutainment proved to be a successful way to help with learning. According to previously done studies, it was shown that edutainment games have a great positive impact on children learning progress and that the concept of having a game with images, or animations was surely enjoyed much more than traditional text books [21].

Different topics have been covered in Edutainment applications such as: science, mathematics, languages, geography and history. Trivia Crack [11] is an example of a popular game that covers 6 fields: Geography, Science, Art, Entertainment, History, and Sports. This game achieved high popularity in 2014, and it occupied the eighth rank in top free mobile applications [12]. Interest in using these kinds of games to educate has grown impressively in the last period [16]. It is predicted that edutainment will develop and could be of great potential in the future, as it helps in improving the learning interests for children [18].

One of the fields covered by Edutainment applications is language learning. In this paper, the focus will be on applications that target reading through stories. Stories have a great impact on children, where they can learn new languages, experiences, values, morals, etc. One of the most important aspects that could be earned by children from reading stories is to learn a new language, or improve theirs. Efforts have been done in this area, which will be discussed in details later in Sect. 2. However, there were some limitations that existed in some of those applications such as low interactivity and unappealing designs. Moreover, all applications do not assess the children while reading the stories. If this feature was available, children can get feedback on their reading. Moreover, parents and teachers could track the performance of their children easily.

In this paper, iPlayAStory, an online educational platform for language learning, will be presented. iPlayAStory is a learning platform tailored for children as well as their parents or teachers. Children can learn and enhance their English language skills by presenting them with an interactive and fun environment where they read sentences. Children then get feedback on the words that were mispronounced with clear visual effects. Children can also listen to the correct pronunciation of the sentence. Furthermore, parents and teachers can view the history of their children and monitor their performance offline.

The rest of the paper is organized as follows: a review of the relevant literature is given in Sect. 2. In Sect. 3, iPlayAStory is presented in details. In Sect. 4, a primary evaluation for iPlayAStory is shown. Finally, Sect. 5 concludes and gives suggestions for future work.

2   Related Work

In this Section, several learning platforms that teach children through stories will be discussed. In these platforms, children can create their own stories, read them aloud, listen to them, or decide an ending for them. Each of these categories is described in the following subsections.

Story maker [9] and My StoryMaker [5] are examples of platforms for creating stories. These application provide children with an interesting and engaging environment for reading. The child gets to create his/her own stories by first choosing the main theme for the story, then choosing the main characters appearing in the story, and finally after following some steps, the story is generated.

Many applications focused on providing stories in the form of text and images for children to read. Magickeys [3] is a website that offers a variety of stories designed for children. There exists a list of stories that the user can choose from depending on what he/she wants to read. Similar to MagicKeys, there exist many other websites that offer the same functionality, such as: Kidsgen [1], Pitara [7], and Vtaide [15].

In Goodnightstories [14], children get to decide the story flow. The child chooses a story from the list, then he/she proceeds with reading it. At the end of every page, the child is left with a decision that he/she has to take in order to continue with reading the story. Depending on the child's decision, the story flow changes, and accordingly it has different endings.

Other applications allow children to listen to the system's voice narrating the story. In Kizclub [2], the user chooses a story from a full list of available stories, and then the story starts to play page after another. In each page the child can see the full text and an image, and for each word that is being narrated by the system, it is highlighted in different color. Similar applications do exist under this category such as Curiousgeorge [13], Speakaboos [8], Storynory [10], and Freechildrenstories [4]. Moreover, there exists Pinky Dinky Doo [6], which combines the feature of creating stories along with listening to stories. The advantage of these types of applications over the previously presented ones is that they allow children to listen to the correct pronunciation. This may help children improve their pronunciation skills.

All the presented applications suffer from the same limitation; there is no assessment done for the child to test his/her performance and progress in reading, or whether he/she can actually read the text correctly or not. In this paper, we will present iPlayAStory as a learning platform that overcomes this limitation. iPlayAStory provides the children with an interesting and fun environment for reading. It allows children to read aloud and assess their reading. Children get feedback as well as score on their correctness of reading. iPlayAStory also presents the children's parents and teachers with an interface where they can monitor their children's history of readings along with their performance.

3   iPlayAStory

iPlayAStory is successfully launched online on iPlayAStory.cf. In iPlayAStory, there exist two types of users that can be categorized into either children or parents.

Children have the ability to play any of the following games:

1. Quiz: which is explained in Sect. 3.1.
2. Story: which is discussed in Sect. 3.1.

Parents have two main roles in iPlayAStory:

1. View children's progress: which is illustrated in Sect. 3.2.
2. Record audio for their children: which is elaborated in Sect. 3.2.

3.1 Games

In this application, there are two types of games, which are: Quiz, and Story. In this section, a detailed description will be given for each.

Quiz. A quiz consists of a set of questions. Each question consists of an image, and three text choices. Two of those choices are not related to the shown image, and only one of the three is related. The child is required to choose the text related to the image by reading it aloud. After the child reads the text aloud, in order for the system to give feedback on whether the chosen text was correct or not, the following process is performed:

– Child's speech is recorded: this is accomplished using Web-RTC library.
– Child's speech is recognized: this is done using Google Speech api.
– The system approximates what the user has said to the nearest matching choice: this is done by comparing the speech transcription produced by Google Speech api to the three choices, and selecting the text with the highest string similarity.

If the user chooses the correct answer, it will be colored in green. Otherwise, the user's choice will appear in red color, and the correct answer will appear in green color, as shown in Fig. 1. Finally, the user can proceed to the following questions.

Fig. 1. A question in a quiz (Color figure online)

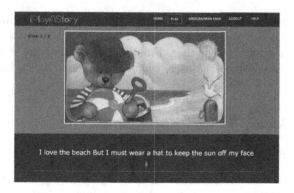

Fig. 2. Stories - new game

In [19, 20], research was done to identify the factors that make game enjoyable and fun. Among several other factors, score-keeping and different difficulty levels were found as key aspects to make games more challenging. Both factors were incorporated in the application as follows:

- Score-keeping: The child gains points for each correct answer. The score is updated after each question.
- Difficulty level: The child can choose a difficulty level for the quiz. The difficulty levels vary between easy, medium, and hard.

Story. The story is one of the most important features found in iPlayAStory. The application offers several stories that the user can choose from. A Story consists of several slides, where each slide has an image and text, as shown in Fig. 2.

After the user chooses a story, he/she starts reading each slide. After reading the text in a slide, the user is shown the transcript for what he/she said according to how it was correctly pronounced. The words that match with the original text will be colored in green, while those that do not match, or even do not exist in the original text are shown in red color.

This assessment is done through the following steps:

- Speech recording: this is accomplished using Web-RTC library.
- Speech recognition: this is done using Google Speech api.
- String matching: this is done using the Brute Force String Matching algorithm.

After the assessment is done, the child will hear the correct pronunciation for this text. It might have been recorded earlier by his/her parent/teacher and saved to the database for iPlayAStory, as described in Sect. 3.2. In case no recording is available for the parent/teacher, the default system voice is played back. The application takes into consideration the child's dialect (US/UK), which is provided by the parent/teacher at registration.

The score for each slide is updated according to the matching percentage between the transcript produced by Google Speech api, and the original text. The score is then shown to the user. Finally, if the end of the story is reached, an overall score is shown to the user, which is calculated as the average of each slide score.

3.2   Parents Mode

The role of the parents could be categorized into two main points:

- Recording their voice over stories, to be heard by their children.
- Viewing their children's profile in order to track their performance.

Recording Stories. Research has shown that it is beneficial for children to hear familiar voices with words that they already know. Moreover, their processing ability is improved when hearing those familiar voices [17]. Therefore, the application allows parents to record their voice over the stories. Children can then hear their parent's voice instead of the system's voice.

Viewing Children's Performance. iPlayAStory allows parents and teachers to view their children's history. This allows them to keep track of the children's performance anytime. In this section, the feature of viewing the children's performance will be described. The child's parent/teacher could view his/her child's profile, in which he/she will presented with the following data:

1. Quizzes: parents/teachers can view all of the quizzes taken by the child along with the overall score earned in the quiz. For each question in a quiz, they can view the child's as well as the correct answer.

2. Stories: parents/teachers can view all of the stories that were read by the child. They can view the date the story was read on, and the score the child has earned in this story. For each slide in a story, the parent/teacher can view: (1) its original text, (2) the transcript obtained from Google Speech api for the child's reading and (4) the accuracy, which is how much does the original text match to the obtained transcription. The parent/teacher can also listen to the recording of the child's reading for each slide.

4   Evaluation

A preliminary evaluation has been done in order to assess iPlayAStory. Respondents were divided into three different groups; children, parents, and teachers. Questionnaires were distributed on respondents after trying the application. In this section, the gathered data will be presented for each group.

4.1 Children

In order to evaluate the impact of the application on children, a sample of 18 respondent was randomly selected, age ranging from 6 to 8 years old. The questionnaires show the following:

1. On a scale from 1 (lowest) to 5 (highest), iPlayAStory was found to be interesting with an average of 4.3.
2. 67 % of the children stated that they prefer to hear their parent's voice over the system's voice.
3. 67 % of the children preferred the story mode over the quiz mode.
4. All children stated that they would play it again.

The following is quoted from some of the children who tried the application:
"I adore it!"
"The application is very interesting, but I want more stories."
"I had so much fun!"

4.2 Parents

A sample of 5 parents participated in the evaluation process. Parents recorded stories for their children and explored the feature that enables them to track their children's progress. The results of the parents questionnaires are as follows:

1. On a scale from 1 (lowest) to 5 (highest), iPlayAStory was found to be user-friendly with an average of 4.6.
2. On a scale from 1 (lowest) to 5 (highest), parents find iPlayAStory to be beneficial with an average of 4.8.
3. On a scale from 1 (lowest) to 5 (highest), parents find the feature of viewing their children's profile (showing his/her history) to be beneficial with an average of 5.
4. All parents agreed that the child's profile is clear enough to see his/her progress.
5. All parents agreed that online educational applications can assist in the learning process.
6. 60 % of the parents prefer their children to hear the system's voice over the parent's voice.
7. 80 % of the parents preferred the story mode over the quiz mode.

The following is quoted from one of the parents who tried iPlayAStory:
"It is amazing! I think this could really help my child to learn. We really do miss those creative and interesting ideas in today's schools. I hope that you can expand this platform to include more stories and handle different age groups, in order to publish it for schools."

4.3 Teachers

Teachers played a crucial part in the evaluation process since the game is based on reading and language learning. After showing teachers a demo for the application, questionnaires were distributed on a sample of 7 English teachers with a part of open ended questions, for giving them more space to freely express their opinions including any future enhancements. The results of the questionnaires are as follows:

1. On a scale from 1 (lowest) to 5 (highest), iPlayAStory was found to be user-friendly with an average of 4.4.
2. On a scale from 1 (lowest) to 5 (highest), teachers find iPlayAStory to be beneficial with an average of 4.86.
3. On a scale from 1 (lowest) to 5 (highest), teachers find the feature of viewing their children's profile (showing his/her history) to be beneficial with an average of 4.86.
4. All teachers agreed that the child's profile is clear enough to see his/her progress.
5. All teachers agreed that online educational applications can assist in the learning process.
6. 86 % of the teachers preferred the story mode over the quiz mode.

All of the teachers found this application very beneficial and important for kids. Moreover, they stated that children nowadays are obsessed with technology and computers, and by having an online platform like iPlayAStory, children would love to read more and learn. Considering the design of the application, they found it extremely appealing and eye-catching. Some of the teachers focused on the same point that was the need to handle and assess children's intonation, which is how correctly the child changes his voice pitch to differentiate between statements and questions or to express certain emotions.

The following is quoted from one of the teachers who were shown a demo for the application:

"This application should be patented or copyrighted and distributed over schools. The service provided in this application is unique and cannot be compared to any other existing application. Both children and schools will benefit a lot from having such an application."

5 Conclusion and Future Work

Edutainment is found to be an effective technique to help children in the learning process. Language learning is one of the fields targeted by Edutainment applications. Work done in this field focused mainly on stories for children, where the child can create a story, read a story, listen to a story, or decide an ending for a story. The main shared limitation between these applications was that no assessment for child's performance was available. To solve these problems, iPlayAStory was introduced. iPlayAStory is an online educational platform for language learning. The application provides children with a fun and interesting environment, in order to be motivated to learn reading. Additionally, it helps parents to track their children's performance through an easy interface.

iPlayAStory is successfully launched online on iPlayAStory.cf. Children and parents were presented with this application. Children enjoyed their time, and found the application very interesting. Parents as well as teachers found the application very beneficial. Parents also liked the design of the application with its easy interface. They found the feature that enables them to view their children's performance very useful and beneficial.

Moreover, the application serves as a means for speech acquisition. Throughout the duration of the evaluation, data collected has an average of 35 min of recordings with an average recognition accuracy over 80 %. Such collected data could be later used to build an ASR system tailored for the stories in the application. This will make it possible to have a more detailed assessment of the children's pronunciation to include phonemes rather than words.

In order for iPlayAStory to attract more users and to motivate children to use the application more, several improvements could be done. The following list states some of the enhancements for future work:

– Further evaluation: iPlayAStory was launched during school recess, therefore the evaluation was done on a small scale. Further evaluation is needed in order to assess the effectiveness and usefulness of iPlayAStory.
– Minimize uploading time: the application collects speech data by recording users' speech into audio files, these files are then uploaded to the server. Further research should be done in this area in order to minimize the time that the user waits for this file to be uploaded.
– Intonation: it would be extremely beneficial if the application was capable of assessing children's intonation, which is how correctly the child changes his voice pitch to differentiate between statements and questions, or to express feelings and emotions.
– More stories: more stories should be added to the application. Stories should be obtained from a publisher to have a correct level of stories for different age groups.

References

1. Kidsgen. http://www.kidsgen.com/stories/
2. Kizclub. http://www.kizclub.com/reading1.htm
3. Magic Keys. http://www.magickeys.com/books/
4. Free Children Stories. http://www.freechildrenstories.com/
5. My StoryMaker. http://www.carnegielibrary.org/kids/storymaker/embed.cfm
6. Pinky Dinky Doo. http://www.pinkydinkydoo.com/storybox.html
7. Pitara. http://www.pitara.com/category/fiction-for-kids/stories-for-kids/
8. Speakaboos. http://www.speakaboos.com/
9. Story Maker. http://learnenglishkids.britishcouncil.org/en/make-your-own/story-maker

10. Storynory. http://www.storynory.com/
11. Trivia Crack. http://www.triviacrack.com/
12. Trivia Crack Rank. http://thenextweb.com/insider/2014/11/27/latin-american-mobile-game-trivia-crack-conquered-us-market/
13. Curious George. http://www.curiousgeorge.com/kids-stories-books
14. Goodnightstories. http://goodnightstories.com/decide.htm
15. Vtaide. http://www.vtaide.com/png/stories.htm
16. Ritterfeld, U., Cody, M., Vorderer, P.: Serious Games: Mechanisms and Effects. Routledge, Abingdon (2009)
17. Levi, S.V.: Talker familiarity and spoken word recognition in school-age children. J. Child Lang. **40**(4), 1–30 (2014)
18. Wang, Q., Tan, W., Song, B.: Research and design of edutainment. In: First IEEE International Symposium on Information Technologies and Applications in Education, ISITAE 2007, pp. 502–505 (November 2007)
19. Malone, T.M.: Heuristics for designing enjoyable user interfaces: lessons from computer games. In: Proceedings of the Conference on Human Factors in Computing Systems (Gaithersburg, MD, Mar. 1517), pp. 63–68 (1982)
20. Malone, T.M.: What makes things fun to learn? heuristics for designing instructional computer games. In: Proceedings of the Third ACM SIGSMALL Symposium and the First SIGPC Symposium on Small Systems (Palo Alto, CA, Sept. 1819), pp. 162–169 (1980)
21. Wong, W.L., Shen, C., Nocera, L., Carriazo, E., Tang, F., Bugga, S., Narayanan, H., Wang, H., Ritterfeld, U.: Seriousvideo game effectiveness (2007). 62
22. Bian, W., Wang, A.I.: A guideline for game development-based learning : a literature review. Int. J. Comput. Games Technol. **2012**, 8 (2012)
23. Hsu, T-Y., Liu, H.-C., Wang, S.-L.: The effectiveness of different types of digital game-based learning contents on children e-learning - empirical study on the digital museum of children website

Co-design of a Game to Support Increased Manufacturing Insight and Interest Among Teenagers and Young Adults

Poul Kyvsgaard Hansen[1]([✉]), Manuel Oliveira[2], and Joao Costa[3]

[1] Department of Mechanical and Manufacturing Design,
Aalborg University, Fibigerstraede 16, 9220 Aalborg, Denmark
kyvs@production.aau.dk
[2] SINTEF, Strindvegen 4, 7034 Trondheim, Norway
manuel.oliviera@sintef.no
[3] HighSkillz, Lisbon, Portugal
joao.costa@highskillz.com

Abstract. This paper is focusing on the specific development of a serious game to support manufacturing insight and interest among teenagers and young adults. To achieve the necessary motivation and engagement, a co-design approach has been chosen, involving students, teachers, and industrial companies. This dynamic design process involved the different stakeholders from inception of the idea to actual use and evaluation. The first versions of the game were developed as a board game to allow for the most flexible adoption of new ideas or even re-orientation of the original ideas. However, the goal is to develop an online digital version that can be played simultaneously but flexible among a number of educational institutions.

1 Introduction

In recent years, despite the global economic crisis, manufacturing is facing serious difficulties in the recruitment of the brightest high-skilled human resources. National and international institutions have provided important guidelines to combat these skills mismatch and several innovations have been made both in STEM and manufacturing education. However, there is still a lack of concrete strategies harmonizing delivery mechanisms and pedagogical frameworks throughout the whole student lifecycle, from primary to tertiary education. Today's students are raised in an online environment where games and videos are essential parts of their communication culture. The traditional textbook approach of organizing and communicating knowledge is highly challenged by these distinctive cultural changes.

An ongoing EU Project – ManuSkills [1] – is addressing these challenges with the aim of studying the use of enhanced ICT-based technologies and training methodologies to facilitate an increase of young talent interest in manufacturing and to support their training of new manufacturing skills. The project is experimenting with a wide range of innovative delivery mechanisms such as serious games, simulation, mixed reality and teaching factories, supported by the use of social media augmented by gamification. ManuSkills is addressing all three stages of the young talent pipeline (i.e. children, teenagers, young adults), where in the early stages the focus is on raising the awareness

© Springer International Publishing Switzerland 2016
A. De Gloria and R. Veltkamp (Eds.): GALA 2015, LNCS 9599, pp. 421–430, 2016.
DOI: 10.1007/978-3-319-40216-1_47

of manufacturing education thus making it more attractive to young talent. In the later stages of the young talent pipeline, the focus is on facilitating transformative deep learning of individuals, with reduced time-to-competence.

The ManuSkills project has incorporated six specific experiments. One of these experiments, Lego Exploratorium, has been focusing on co-designing approaches that involve the three most important stakeholders in the process of designing and launching new ICT-based educational resources to support awareness, interest and application of manufacturing knowledge in teaching institutions. The most important stakeholders are: the students, the teachers, and the industrial companies. All of these stakeholders have to be involved and motivated, and to sustain motivated to continue their engagement.

The cognitive domain of manufacturing can be seen as a number of resources (machines, processes, people, materials, information, and finances) that are brought together in order to produce some kind of physical product. If combined right the collection of resources can produce in the right quality, the right amount, and at the right price. The combination of the resources is a combined technical and organizational task. Essentially, the output is determined by the decisions taken by the people involved in the specific manufacturing setup. These decisions should take into consideration both what is the immediate task and what might be the task of the future. Also the general technical development will impact the decisions. New machines or changes in the portfolio of resources might change the competitive setup. The customers might also behave different than anticipated. This can be due to new and better product from competitors or a general change in the preferences of the customers.

The traditional pedagogical approach of manufacturing education has been to teach the various disciplines individually. However, the individual disciplines have specialized deeper and deeper, and this has led to challenges in teaching the integration of the disciplines. Integration of disciplines is essentially what happens in the real life of industrial companies. In order to bring these experiences more explicitly into teaching, a co-design approach involving industrial companies was chosen. The ManuSkills approach taken is based on living labs where the co-design is embedded in a process that lasts from idea inception to deployment.

The current version of the specific game supported educational framework was initiated September 2013 and the focus of this paper has been on the first 18 months of development and application.

2 Methodology

The adopted methodology has been inspired by the "Living Lab" approach, which according to the European Network of Living Labs (Enroll) "is a real-life test and experimentation environment where users and producers co-create innovations" [2].

The four main activities that characterize the Living Lab approach are:

1. Co-Creation: co-design by users and producers
2. Exploration: discovering emerging usages, behaviors and market opportunities
3. Experimentation: implementing live scenarios within communities of users

4. Evaluation: assessment of concepts, products and services according to socio-ergo-nomic, socio-cognitive and socio-economic criteria

Initially, the adopted co-design approach involved the two stakeholder groups of teachers and industrial companies. The purpose was to define the learning scope to be addressed by the Lego Exploratorium, thus identification of specific manufacturing cases was carried out along with clear links to the relevant theoretical disciplines of manu-facturing engineering.

After the overall scope being defined, the subsequent workshops, involving mainly teachers and students, focused modernizing education through the adoption of game-based learning in the form of a serious game (Lego Exploratorium). At the start, the co-design activities were more exploratory in nature, resulting in open-ended themes, topics and measures. However, as the themes and content of the serious game became more focused the workshop topics got more focused.

Each round of workshops has led to an updated version of a serious game supple-mented by various ICT based materials. The workshop activities were documented as written summaries, which were complemented by interviews with some of the partici-pants (both teachers and students).

Interleaved with the co-design workshops has been formative assessment of the use of the serious game within different educational settings. The students exposed to the Lego Exploratorium have been high school students, vocational students, and university students. These assessment activities have been documented by observations, inter-views, and followed up by questionnaires to the students. In particular, the question-naires were designed to capture interest, awareness, usability, enjoyment and knowl-edge. All the questionnaires that we used were pre-manufactured and their validity and reliability was tested in previous projects by their designers [3].

3   Co-design in an Educational Context

The traditional conception of value creation assumes that value is created inside the firm and that consumers are separated from the value creating process [3]. The critical inter-action with the consumer is the moment of exchange. In today's markets the consumers are informed, connected, empowered, and they are increasingly learning that they can extract value beyond the traditional point of exchange [5]. Consumers are now subjecting the industry's value creation process to scrutiny, analysis, and evaluation [6]. In comparison, the value creation process in an educational setting has been seen as the teacher being the instrument by which knowledge is communicated. Students played a passive role as recipients and the traditional approach also insisted that students were taught the same materials at the same time.

The traditional approach to teaching has been surprisingly persistent though it has for a long time been questioned and considered an extremely inefficient use of students' and teachers' time [7]. An important aspect is that most of the existing teaching materials are still in the form of textbooks.

Teachers within the manufacturing field have traditionally had a mechanical engi-neering background. Many of the teachers have had some practical experiences from working in industry. Today the teachers need to qualify to tenure positions largely based on their research qualifications. Consequently, the teachers develop a higher degree of specialization, and fewer teachers have practical industrial experience.

The relevant topics in manufacturing have changed and expanded. Besides the traditional mechanical engineering topics the new areas are automation, digitalization, logistics, ecology, supply chain management, and many others. The higher degree of specialization among teachers has led to challenges in regards to the integration of the disciplines. This is further reinforced by the general lack of practical industrial experiences among the teachers.

The rapid technological development makes it difficult to keep the textbooks updated with the most recent technologies.

4   Co-designing the LEGO Exploratorium

Initially three types of workshops were defined: (1) Workshops with teachers of different manufacturing disciplines, (2) Workshops with teachers and industrial companies, and, (3) Workshops with students from various studies.

The first workshops were guided by the two open-ended questions:

- What characterizes good teaching within the broad discipline of manufacturing?
- What are the barriers and enablers in providing good teaching within the broad discipline of manufacturing?

The first round of workshops led to the following main findings:

- Both students and teachers are highly motivated by real life, realistic, and updated cases (that they can relate to). Current textbooks rarely support this.
- Both teachers and students experience a lack of cross-disciplinary and integrative understanding of manufacturing.
- Currently there are substantial investments in e-learning platforms at educational institutions. The platforms are improving rapidly in terms of performance.
- There is a rich potential in video material and informative web pages publicly available. Both students and teachers valuate good video material. However, it is difficult and time consuming to get an overview and to verify good quality.
- There is only limited experience sharing between various manufacturing disciplines and between different educational institutions. Therefore, each individual teacher often has to develop his or her own real-life cases.
- Companies are willing to deliver updated content but find the requests from the educational institutions unfocused and uncoordinated.
- Students are highly motivated by elements of gamification in teaching.

4.1   Initial Game Preparation

Initially, the workshops with teachers from various disciplines (mechanical process technology, logistics, automation, IT, supply chain management and production economics) led to little progress. Participants found the workshops interesting but felt difficulties in collaborating in the integration areas. Teachers brought cases that would highlight the focus of their particular discipline. These cases were illustrative when applied within one particular discipline, but were generally not suitable to illustrate examples of integration.

A breakthrough came when it was proposed to reframe the discussion and focus on very simple products. This led to the idea of focusing on a simple LEGO minifigure (see Fig. 1). The various disciplines provided proposals for how they could contribute to enlighten the many challenges that are associated with planning and developing a production of such a simple product.

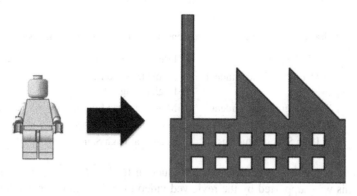

Fig. 1. Illustration of the simple problem that led to the basic idea behind the game "LEGO Exploratorium".

The formative assessment with students proved that the simple initiating problems developed into complex problems after a few rounds of increasingly more advanced challenges, and, furthermore, that teachers from the various disciplines felt it easy to scale from the simple challenges (for example simple moulding technology) to more advanced challenges associated with their particular disciplines (for example advanced simulation of moulding processes). The shared simple starting point became the integrating element.

The fast scaling from simple to complex challenges is often defined as "flow". This is the case when improved skills among participants are carefully synchronized with increasingly challenging tasks [8]. Pine and Gilmore refer to the task of engaging the participants as "staging" a user involvement. They emphasize that staging experiences is not a question about entertaining users; it is primarily about engaging them [9].

The co-design activities with industrial companies had generated commitment from the companies to deliver updated technical information about materials, machines, and supporting equipment. In parallel, a group of teachers with different background had identified and reviewed publicly available web-based video materials. The information from the industrial companies and the video materials were integrated in an application that was made available to the students via the specific e-learning platform of the particular educational institution.

The pre-test was done with only four students. In order to develop and test the initial game ideas four additional tests were planned. A total of 206 students with different educational background was schedule to test various versions of game setups derived from the pre-test activities.

4.2 Initial Game Assessment

The initial game assessment targeted different types of students and the duration of the game test varied according to their availability and the specific context where the game was introduced. Table 1 highlights the characteristics of both the students and the duration of the gaming period. The tests were conducted during September and October 2014.

Table 1. The four groups of students participating in the game test.

Group No.	Level of Students	Educational Focus	Duration
1	130 Undergraduate Students	Innovation and Logistics Engineering	5×2 h
2	30 Undergraduate Students	Manufacturing Engineering	3×2 h
3	30 Vocational School Students	Technical Integration	4 h
4	16 High School Students	Technical High School	4 h

Each test group was given a short introduction to the plastic injection moulding process. This was supported by the reviewed video material and made available on e-learning platforms at the different institutions. In each case the person in charge was the teacher of the course where the game was to be integrated. The teacher had in each case introduced the idea behind the experiment to their classes and assigned preparation tasks to the groups. This would typically involve studying the video materials in order to understand the manufacturing processes associated with producing the LEGO minifigures. The clarification of the role of the teacher was essential since this led to new co-designed options, further development, and most importantly, a foundation for a strong local ownership.

In order to apply the newly gained plastic injection moulding knowledge the groups were given the same challenges. The following describes the test with group 3 and group 4. These tests were limited to 4 h.

The larger groups were divided in smaller teams of 2–3 persons and asked to establish a production of 250,000 white LEGO minifigures (the minifigures were not supposed to be assembled). Their first assignment to the teams was to report when they would be able to deliver the order. In the assignment they were limited by having only one plastic injection-moulding machine, one mold per part of the minifigure (head, upper body, arm, hand, hip, leg), and a 64 m^2 production facility (8 by 8 m).

After half an hour the students reported that they could deliver at a given date. During the assignment they had clarified practical problems related to change of molds, change of colors, safety rules of the production, working hours per week, etc.

With the newly gained knowledge they were presented with the next challenge: Scale the production to a yearly capacity of 10,000,000 minifigures. In this task they were supported by LEGO bricks in order to prototype their factory layout (see Fig. 2). The production task was also expanded to include decoration of both heads and upper bodies of the minifigures. During this task the students faced a number of critical choices in regards to deciding on the number of machines and the number of molds. This led some of the teams to formulate an initial manufacturing strategy for their production.

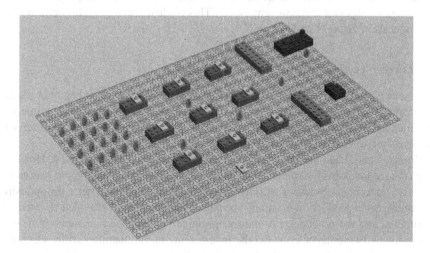

Fig. 2. A LEGO model of a production layout with a capacity of 10,000,000 minifigures per year.

The last 90 min of the 4 h were devoted to simple game sessions based on the factory layout developed by each of the small teams of 2–3 persons. Their production plans were challenged by "customer" requests for different orders. In response to each "customer" request they needed to re-schedule their production in order to comply with the delivery dates requested by the "customer". The planning and scheduling process were supported by a simple Excel Spreadsheet program that had been developed by one of the teachers as a part of the co-design activities. Most of the teams came up with proposals of how to improve the program and some of the teams did implement some of the improvements as a part of the continuing class activities after the game test.

The feedback from the groups 3 and 4 (cf. Table 1) was focusing on three aspects. First, the impact on the students' insight and potential interest in manufacturing. Second, the students' experience of utilizing video and gamification more intensively. Third, ideas from the students in regard to potential improvements of current the game setup.

The feedback was generally very positive. Group 4 (High School Students) had only limited insight and interest in manufacturing before the test. They experienced the integration of the videos and the game setup to be the most important benefit. Regarding the game setup they had a large number of potential improvements and provided examples from existing commercial games that could inspire for the further development.

Group 3 (Vocational Students) were positive in line with group 4. They specifically pointed out that they got a new insight into how technical improvements (process specifications, technical setup, technological developments, etc.) influenced the flexibility and efficiency of the manufacturing setups.

Both groups emphasized that a financial dimension of the game setup would improve both the game aspect and the insight aspect. This feedback was brought forward to the ongoing tests in Group 1 and Group 2.

4.3   Further Testing with Group 1 and Group 2

The test of Group 1 and Group 2 (both Undergraduate Students) had begun in parallel with Group 3 and Group 4. However, the two first groups had assigned more time with the game, and, more importantly, they were schedule to have two-hour sessions with the game on a weekly basis respectively for five and three weeks.

Groups 1 and 2 had the same introductory challenges as Groups 3 and 4. However, due to the feedback from Groups 3 and 4 a financial dimension of the game was added. This was done in a co-design activity between the involved teachers, the industrial companies, and a production economy specialist. The companies provided updated cost information and the production economy specialist co-designed a financial dimension with focus on two perspectives: (1) the investments in the manufacturing setup, and, (2) the estimated cost price of the produced minifigures.

The fact that Groups 1 and 2 had a full week between the game rounds meant that the challenges given to them could be rather extensive. The larger groups were divided in smaller teams of 5–6 persons and the competition between the smaller teams were made much more explicit. A LEGO enthusiast among the students proposed that the production orders should be based on LEGO's collectable series of minifigures [10]. This proposal was incorporated between round 2 and round 3 and it led to a huge variety of the potential production orders. In total the LEGO collectable series comprises 256 very different variants of the minifigure.

The feedback from Groups 1 and 2 was very positive. One of the teams made this comment: "It has been nothing less than fantastic. Teaching is varied with the switch between teaching and gaming. But especially the videos help to gain an insight into what it really is about. Then the game side comes in and do things exiting, because you can only understand things by trying them".

5   Reflections

The evidence in literature demonstrate that game-based learning will gain widespread use within the near future [11]. However, the development of the games to support the game-based learning approach is not yet delivering according to the needs and expectations of the educational institutions [12]. One important explanation is the fact that the development of commercial games for leisure purposes and serious games for educational purposes need different development processes and different business models [12].

As a response to the need for new and different development processes this paper has been focusing on applying a co-design approach that actively involve students, teachers, and industrial companies in a dynamic development of a serious game.

The co-design activity is defined as a continuous involvement from users (students) and producers (teachers and industrial companies). The involvement results in an intermediate setup that is tested with students and subsequently the reaction and active proposals is fed back to the producers. The process is then repeated [2].

The experiences have shown that the co-design approach has facilitated the creation of strong local ownerships. Initially, 206 students in various institutions tested the game setup. In the late fall 2014 and the spring 2015 additionally 5 groups of students (in total 154 students) have tested and co-design the game setup. The local ownership has led to very different game setups that have supported the specific local learning objectives. The evaluations of the game tests have been followed by questionnaires that are focusing on interest, awareness, usability, enjoyment and knowledge [3]. In every case there have been made a pre-test and a post-test.

The initial results show that the weaker students (based on the knowledge component in the questionnaire) raise the level of interest and awareness. The stronger students (based on the knowledge component in the questionnaire) lower their interest and awareness. The following interviews have documented that the stronger students feel that the game is moving too slow to retain interest. However, due to the co-design approach they also have specific suggestions on how to improve the pace and the challenges of the game. These suggestions are continuously implemented in the game.

The focus in the first period of the game development has been solely on the game content and the challenges in relation hereto. Less focus has been devoted to the learning analytics. However, in the fall 2015 a digital version of the game will be launched. The digital version will improve dramatically the gamification element since the backend server can keep track of timing and performance of the participating student teams. Through the co-design effort by the students the crucial gamification element has been identified as the financial element of the game. Every follow up interview of the students has emphasized the importance of the financial aspect. In short, the students report that without the financial aspect there is no game. The critical feedback is though that the financial aspect has to be tied closely to the technical aspects (cost of machines, degree of automation, dynamics of the market) and that the financial and technical aspects have to mirror real life conditions. This is seen as the most important benefit of the synchronized co-design involvement of industrial companies, teachers and students. The game is seen as the mediator of this complicated dialogue.

The digital version will also support the integration of the needed learning analytics and thereby provide a better research setup.

The online version will be developed in a new co-design process that will involved 400+ students and 10+ teachers from various educational institutions. The first online version will launched September 2015 but it is expected that this version will still be co-design to include new options and new supporting tools.

6   Conclusion

The paper describes a co-design approach to game development. The co-design has proven to be suitable because it invites for participation and local ownership. Though the initial results have been positive there are still a number of challenges in order realize a full-scale serious game. Among the most important challenges are the inclusion of learning analytics and the final decisions on the business model that can support a continuing development of the game.

Acknowledgments.   The research leading to these results has received funding from the European Community's Seventh Framework Programme (FP7/2007-2013) under grant agreement no. 609147.

References

1. ManuSkills EU Project: Envisioning an advanced ICT-supported build-up of manufacturing skills for the Factories of the Future, FoF-ICT-2013.7.2, Grant agreement no. 609147 (2014)
2. Eskelinen, J., et al.: Citizen Driven Innovation. European Network of Living Labs (2015)
3. Christensen, R., Knezek, G., Tyler-Wood, T.: Student perceptions of Science, Technology, Engineering and Mathematics (STEM) content and careers. Comput. Hum. Behav. **34**, 173–186 (2014)
4. Kotler, P.: Marketing Management. Prentice Hall, Englewood Cliffs (2002)
5. Prahalad, C.K., Ramaswamy, V.: Co-creation experiences: the next practice in value creation. J. Interact. Mark. **18**(3), 5–14 (2004)
6. Chesbrough, H.W.: Open Innovation: The New Imperative for Creating and Profiting From Technology. Harvard Business School Press, Boston (2004)
7. Dewey, J.: Experience and Education, pp. 1–5. Kappa Delta Pi, New York (1938)
8. Csíkszentmihályi, M.: Flow: The Psychology of Optimal Experience. Harper & Row, New York (1990)
9. Pine, B.J., Gilmore, J.H.: The Experience Economy. Harvard Business Review Press, Boston (2011)
10. LEGO (2015). http://www.lego.com/en-us/minifigures
11. Johnson, L., Smith, R., Willis, H., Levine, A., Haywood, K.: The 2011 Horizon Report. The New Media Consortium, Austin (2011)
12. Hauge, J.B., et al.: Business models for serious games developers - transition from a product centric to a service centric approach. Int. J. Serious Games 1 (2014)

Stop the Mob! Pre-service Teachers Designing a Serious Game to Challenge Bullying

Christopher S. Walsh[1] and Alexander Schmoelz[2(✉)]

[1] James Cook University, James Cook Dr, Townsville, QLD 4811, Australia
`Chris.walsh@jcu.edu.au`
[2] Universität Wien, Universitätsring 1, 1010 Vienna, Austria
`alexander.Schmoelz@univie.ac.at`

Abstract. Mobbing or bullying is a widely recognized problem in European schools, but it is most serious in Austria. We report on the game *Stop The Mob!*, which was designed during a teacher education course at the University of Vienna where students were required to play serious games to experience how deep learning occurs with the goal of designing a serious game for the course's final assessment. The focus of this paper is twofold. First we describe the course 'Digital games, simulation and virtual worlds for teaching and learning'. Then we evaluate the design of *Stop the Mob!* and illustrate how it provides viable possibilities to situate learning, minimize cognitive load, engage the learner constructively and facilitate the learning task of preventing bullying when pedagogically embedded into classroom practice. In conclusion, we argue that educators can integrate the game into their pedagogical practice to fully actualize its potential to prevent bullying.

1 Introduction

The widespread popularity of digital games like *Sim City*, *Civilization*, *Minecraft*, *World of Warcraft* and the *Walking Dead* is no longer questionable. These games now permeate and greatly influence popular culture. They are also extremely successful at teaching gameplayers (students and teachers) complex and higher order thinking skills. Because children and young people are already using these digital games, simulations and virtual worlds, it is timely to rethink initial teacher education so that pre-service teachers understand what and how individuals (gameplayers) learn through gameplay and what implications this has for teaching and learning across subject areas.

There is a multiplicity of game design courses on offer, yet few are exist or are required in initial teacher education programs outside maths and science. Katrin Becker designed and taught a graduate-level course on digital game-based learning in 2005 that was an introduction to digital games and gaming for instruction and learning. Her course required students to either design a game to be used in a learning situation or design a "learning situation or instructional intervention that makes use of a COTS or other existing game, including lead up activities, game play with goals, and debriefing" (Becker 2007, p. 5). The Massachusetts Institute of Technology's (MIT) Scheller Teacher Education Program (STEP) program licenses students to teach mathematics or science in grades 5–12. At MIT, future maths and science teachers are required to take

© Springer International Publishing Switzerland 2016
A. De Gloria and R. Veltkamp (Eds.): GALA 2015, LNCS 9599, pp. 431–440, 2016.
DOI: 10.1007/978-3-319-40216-1_48

an innovative course entitled 'Computer Games and Simulations for Education and Exploration' taught by Eric Klopfer and Jason Haas. In the 2010 course syllabus available online, students are required to complete a 'Literature Review on Games and learning' and 'Documentation and Presentation of an Educational Board Game.' Their course was, in part, an inspiration for our course.

Our course, entitled 'Digital games, simulation and virtual worlds for teaching and learning', is different because it is not a graduate-level course on digital game-based learning primarily for future maths and science teachers. Rather, our course was offered across disciplines and required pre-service teachers to play, critically evaluate and design serious games for a variety of academic subjects. We wanted our students to design playable serious games using a game engine of their choice that was aligned with topics in the Austrian National Curriculum (Österreichischer Lehrplan für allgemeinbildende höhere Schulen), where their gameful learning design (Walsh et al. 2014) was explicitly tied to identified learning outcomes.

'Digital games, simulation and virtual worlds for teaching and learning' was held at the Institute for Teacher Education at the University of Vienna (Institut für Lehrer/-innenbildung, Universität Wien) and was embedded in the module 'Theory and Practice of Teaching and Learning' (Theorie und Praxis des Lehrens und Lernens). As teacher educators (not game designers) we are aware of the potentials and frictions of digital games for learning, but troubled that most initial teacher education courses rarely require pre-service teachers to design serious games. Our course required pre-service teacher education students to engage in gameplay, critical academic game reviews, a literature review, game design and development and the playtesting of their serious game prototypes with their peers at university and then in a year 8 classrooms. The course followed a blended learning design aimed to intensified dialogue and sharing of ideas in the online environment. Introducing blended learning as a vehicle for dialogue and sharing of ideas, stands contrary to most of the blended learning courses on offer at the University of Vienna (Schmoelz and Payrhuber 2009). Moreover we were aiming to apply the peer-approach of mentoring, which was developed by Schmoelz and Peterson (2014) for the context of higher education.

As part of the course's final assessment task, pre-service teachers designed and developed a prototype of their serious game. Then they playtested their games in an lower secondary classroom. We also encouraged them to submit the final versions of their serious games to Austria's Samsung mLearning Contest. In this paper we analyze one game in particular—*Stop the Mob!* (Luftensteiner et al. 2015)—the winner of the contest. We provide a brief overview of *Stop the Mob!* Then we exemplify how teachers can incorporate the serious games into their pedagogical practice to situate learning, minimize cognitive load, engage the learner constructively and facilitate the learning task of preventing bullying. Finally, we conclude by arguing subject area teachers and educators can pedagogically embed *Stop the Mob*! into their teaching and learning practices to prevent bullying.

The course was supported by Samsung Electronics Austria GmbH who provided our pre-service teachers with professional accounts for Game Maker, Game Salad and Construct 2 that supported our students' co-creative gameful learning design. We required students to make their serious games playable on Samsung tablets, because

Samsung also provided us with a portable case of 20 tablets and a strong Wi-Fi connection through a portable wireless modem. This allowed students to present and playtest their serious games first in class at the university and then in the classroom at the school. Partnering with an innovative teacher, who was open to the idea of integrating digital games into the curriculum, was also critical to the success of our course. Our pre-service teachers were very fortunate to have the opportunity to playtest their serious games in her new middle school, NMS Schopenhauerstraße and gain intensive practical experience in the classroom and from the feedback sessions with the pupils.

2 Pre-service Teachers Designing Serious Games

The course explored research around the kinds of thinking, learning and teaching that go into the design of video games, simulations and virtual worlds. Pre-service teachers explored how gameplay might assist children and young people, to understand complex systems within virtual worlds (Walsh 2010). They also examined the use of digital games, simulations, and virtual worlds as places where 'deep learning' occurs (Aldrich 2009; Thomson and Brown 2009). Through playing digital games, students explored how simulations and virtual worlds operationalize playful structures to allow game-players to think about their choices, take action, and experience the impact of their actions. These pre-service teachers also experienced, first-hand through gameplay, games research and critique, what 'good' serious games do (Gee 2007). 'Good' serious games draw players in, teach them how to succeed, and keep them engaged with just the right level of challenge. More importantly, by being reflective of what and how they were learning, when playing serious games, pre-service teachers were better placed to answer the question, "*Why* aren't we using serious games in schools?"

Another important question that we wanted the pre-service teachers to be well equipped to answer is: "How can I pedagogically embed serious games into my future classroom's teaching and learning practices." Therefore, we lustrated how serious games can be embedded within a wider discourse of what were referred to as playful pedagogies. We presented the idea of playful pedagogies as an umbrella term that explores different aspects of play and pedagogy. In the context of pedagogies, it does not mean that learners are just playing games. Rather they explored the idea of gamification and the introduction of game elements such as storytelling, goals and progress indicators, visualisation of characters and problem-solving into educational non-game experiences. Pre-service teachers also viewed gamification as a viable way to improve student in-class participation and engagement (Cronk 2012) as well as increase motivation and self-efficacy (Banfield and Wilkerson 2014).

By introducing the pre-service teachers to the notion of playful pedagogies they were able to rethink professional judgments on the ends to which a specific serious game could be designed and embedded into subject matter curriculum. We realised introducing gamification to teaching and learning with pre-service teachers might have no relevance in regards to learning outcomes, because "not all students will be equally inclined to take all learning activities seriously enough for their own good in meeting the learning outcome objectives" (Øhrstrøm et al. 2013, p. 422). We also introduced the students to game-based learning, to help them understand that when students are playing games, they can simultaneously be learning curricular content though gameplay. This was a catalyst to helping them understand that playing serious games in school could potentially help their future students achieve specified learning outcomes within the Austrian National Curriculum.

Furthermore, we required pre-service teachers to engage in learning activities and game design projects directly related to contemporary research in the field of digital games and playful pedagogies, giving them the opportunity to explore the dynamics and principles underlying successful game design. These were grounded in three distinct areas: empowering learners, designing problem-based learning experiences and fostering deep understanding (Gee 2007). Participants used this knowledge later in the course to collaborate to design their 'playable' serious games (from beginning to end).

Because students playtested their serious games with diverse pupils in an urban lower secondary school classroom, they not only took on the role of game designers who acquired new systems-based literacy practices (Walsh 2010), but also experienced observing students actually sitting down and playing their game. This experience assisted them in better understanding whether their "game is accessible, usable, and if its mechanics are actually appealing" (St. John 2015, p. 1) to gameplayers and if it achieves the desired learning outcomes. Then for a final assignment, they reflected on the process of playtesting and outlined plans to further develop their games.

Each group of pre-service teachers designed, prototyped, developed and playtested a serious game. The topics covered by our students included bullying (mobbing), teaching English as a second language (TESOL), packaging (environmental sustainability) and politics (history). Students used different game engines for which Samsung Electronics Austria GmbH had generously provided pro-licences. The students were encouraged to use the online manuals of the game engines to learn how to build games. Students drew heavily on the course readings, assessment tasks, seminar discussions and playtesting in their game design. We outline one of the serious games designed for the course, *Stop the Mob!*, which aims to raise awareness and address mobbing or bullying. We believe *Stop the Mob!* is a salient example of a 'good' serious game that teachers can pedagogically embed into their classrooms with the aim of prevent bullying.

3   Stop the Mob!

Stop the Mob! is a serious game that provides viable possibilities to situate learning, minimize cognitive load, engage the learner experientially and facilitate the learning task of preventing bullying. In what follows we outline the game's design and evaluate its features. To evaluate *Stop the Mob!*, we drew on Catalano et al.'s (2014) guidelines for an effective design and evaluation of serious games that emerged from their wok on the Games and Learning Alliance (GALA) project funded under the Europe Commission's 7th Framework Programme for European Research and Technological Development. First we provide a brief overview of *Stop the Mob!* and then exemplify how the game's design has the potential to situate learning, minimize cognitive load, engages the learner experientially and facilitate the learning task of preventing bullying. Then we conclude by arguing subject area teachers and educators can integrate serious games into their pedagogical practice to engage learners.

3.1 Pedagogically Driven Serious Game Design

Stop the Mob! is a digital point-and-click game designed for computer and tablet use that introduces players to the topic of bullying in schools. It presents gameplayers with scenarios in which the consequences of their actions can make a positive or negative difference for a bullying victim named Bob. *Stop the Mob!* is a role play serious game, from the perspective a nameless and faceless girl, designed for students in lower secondary schools. The serious game presents students with examples of how to react when presented with five 2-part scenarios, first at school and then at home. The presentation is static using both images and text. The daily scenarios focus on assisting student gameplayers in understanding bullying. It does so by providing them with opportunities to react differently to the scenarios through a targeted question after viewing a situation where Bob is bullied by classmates in different school contexts (e.g. the classroom, gym and locker room). The scenarios focus on understanding what possible actions to take within the different contexts from joining the bullying or walking away, to taking action and help Bob. Individual gameplayers are given a direct role in the decisions made. As a result, student gameplayers experience an incident involving bullying, assess the situation and determine the best (or not so best) response strategy, then implement it and observe the consequences of their decisions. Pedagogically, this works to raise students' awareness of bullying in schools, like their own, and understand how their actions can make a difference. This is in stark contrast to being provided with a set of school rules that outline how they must behave or face punishment. The pedagogical goal is simple in that it helps them understand the consequences of bullying for the victim and know what actions they can take to minimize bullying.

3.2 Situating Learning

Stop the Mob! can be used to situate learning because it deploys an environment with appropriate interactions that are designed to fit the context of use in ways that are immediately familiar and recognizable to students. From this perspective, this serious game's raises awareness of Bob's bullying without overdoing it, meaning the gameplayers are not flooded with information about bullying, why bulling is bad or how to address the issue of bullying. This is achieved at the onset of the game when the player's character has not yet taken a stand in regards to the scenario, meaning the player needs decide how to react to Bob's bullying (Fig. 1).

3.3 Minimizing Cognitive Load

The way *Stop the Mob!* was designed, potentially minimizes cognitive load because the learning conditions, presented by the scenarios, do not represent a steep learning curve. This coupled with the serious game's user-friendly navigation makes the game potentially more engaging and playable (Fig. 2). From this perspective, we argue *Stop the*

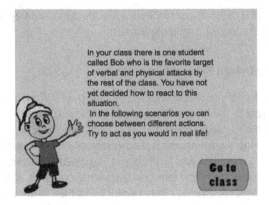

Fig. 1. Situating the learning at the beginning of *Stop the Mob!*

Mob! employs good game design, particularly for novice game designers. Players are also introduced to increasingly difficult learning tasks in terms of the game's questioning at the end of each scenario, meaning the correct answer is not obvious. Additionally, the game's interface is user friendly and does not require time to learn to navigate. The game also captures students' attention because the scenarios are immediately familiar to their lifeworlds in schools. Importantly, the learning objectives embedded into the game are not that overly simple and require the students to critically think about their actions. Every decision and action the players take awards them with a certain number of points if they take action to improve Bob's situation. Points are subtracted if they make Bob feel worse. The players also receive immediate feedback on their actions in the form of Bob's facial expression (Fig. 3).

Fig. 2. Minimizing cognitive load through user-friendly navigation.

Fig. 3. Engaging the learner constructively through immediate feedback

3.4 Engaging the Learner Constructively

Stop the Mob! can also be used to engage the learner constructively because it provides five individual scenarios that are general and stereotypical, but real enough to trigger active engagement. This is because choosing a non-obvious path leads to a different appreciation of the problem of bullying. The pre-service teachers, after playtesting the game in a real classroom, came to understand how the serious game can be used to focus on the students' own experiences of bullying in such a way that they are drawing on their own experience as they engage in exploring possible actions they can take to not bully Bob. Through gameplay, they can do this alone or collaboratively and then use the game as a catalyst for classroom discussion aimed at addressing and eventually preventing bullying. For the most part the game is not redundant with the exception that the classroom scene (image) is used twice and the at home scene is the same in each 2-part scenario. But this does not block engaged gameplay. Also the gameplayers, in this short serious game, are provided with constant and immediate feedback where Bob is either smiling or crying (Fig. 3). This highlights that the pre-service teachers were able to integrate a 'fun component' into their game's design (Catalano et al. 2014). Having this fun component helps make *Stop the Mob!* a successful serious game where winning is not the goal. Rather student gameplayers have a new opportunity to learn effectively from a relevant and realistic experience in the safe environment of the serious game and possibly in their classroom. Much of the learning will depend on how a given teacher pedagogically integrates the game into his/her classroom in gameplay debriefing and further discussions and debates.

3.5 Facilitating the Learning Task

Integrating *Stop the Mob!* into a classroom setting can potentially facilitating the learning task into an experiential and constructivist learning experience. This is especially true if the game is not treated as a stand-alone game that teachers do not pedagogically integrate into their classroom teaching and learning activities. The learning task is facilitated in the following three ways:

1. students are first provided with a brief that aims to make them aware of the issue on hand, bullying as well as the instructions/objectives of gameplay (Fig. 1). This can be augmented by the teacher when introducing the game in the classroom;
2. the gaming session ensures the five scenarios build upon each other in such a way that students are able to explore, through gameplay, the intended learning objectives (e.g. awareness of bullying, strategies for ending bullying, etc.); and
3. upon completion of each scenario there is a debriefing within the game (Fig. 4) and by transferring gameplay experiences into the classroom, teachers are well placed to further facilitate understanding and acquisition of new knowledge through exploration, debate and discussion.

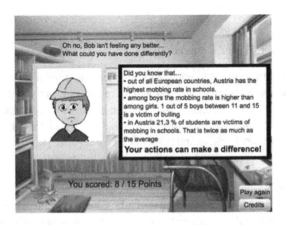

Fig. 4. Stop the Mob! Facilitating the learning task into a constructivist learning task

We cannot stress enough that a serious game, such as the one designed by the pre-service teachers—who are novice game designers—must not be used as a stand-alone learning object. This is because the game itself cannot trigger critical reflection on the actions taken within the game. This is where the active role of the teacher and learner becomes critical. The topic of bullying in school, particularly with children in lower secondary classrooms, is a serious one. Thus, while *Stop the Mob!* does help to facilitate the learning task, it is paramount to remember it was designed with an understanding that a teacher would be involved before, during and after gameplay.

4   Conclusion

We have highlighted how *Stop The Mob!* can be used by educators to situate learning, minimize cognitive load, engage the learner constructively and facilitate the learning task of preventing bullying. Furthermore, we understand the game on its own cannot address the complex issue of bullying in schools, rather it can be used by teachers and educators to present students with viable possibilities to discuss and reflect on issues of bullying that may exist in their teaching and learning contexts. As a learning object, the serious game *Stop The Mob!* has the potential to bridge the gap between student interest and how 'serious' issues are addressed in educational contexts. *Stop the Mob!* can be used by educators as a non confronting way to introduce the issue of bullying to students as partners in learning, because teachers can use it to teach empathy.

Many studies in educational research and research on technology-enhanced learning suggest the viable possibilities presented by digital devices and resources (e.g. serious games) are primarily dependent on how educators pedagogically integrate them into their teaching and learning practices (Conole and Oliver 1998; Beetham and Sharpe 2007; Livingstone 2012). Against this background our analysis of the design of *Stop the Mob!* has illustrated the possible outcomes of using the game in classrooms to address bullying. If educators are keen to include and/or design serious games for their classrooms, they must think about serious games' content and reflect on their teaching and their learners as key dimensions of pedagogy (Hopmann 2007). These dimensions involve questions about the educational substance of content (Klafki 2000), the partnership of teachers and learners (Rogers 1969) and the pedagogic tact (Herbart 1982; Muth 1962; van Manen 1991). For example they may ask themselves, when integrating serious games into their practice:

- What is the educational substance of the game's content?
- What role does the partnership with students play in their teaching? and
- How do I respond tactfully to students' actions and inquiries?

Theses key dimensions of pedagogy and their related questions highlight the need for further research that illustrates how serious games can be pedagogically embedded into teaching practices to engage learners. Furthermore, the pre-service teachers' success at designing and playtesting serious games, as well as the students' increased engagement in learning, warrants their inclusion as a required topic of study in initial teacher education programs.

Acknowledgments. We acknowledge the work of our pre-service teachers Katharina Luftensteiner, Katharina Pölzl, Markus Resch and Katrin Waldhart in successfully designing *Stop The Mob!* and their work towards building *Serious Gamers* , a new serious game collective in Vienna. We also want to thank Gerda Reissner, who works with the New Middle School NMS Schopenhauerstraße for allowing our students to playtest their serious game prototypes in her classroom.

References

Aldrich, C.: Learning Online with Games, Simulations, and Virtual Worlds: Strategies for Online Instruction. Jossey-Bass Guides to Online Teaching and Learning, Kindle Edition. Jossey-Bass, San Francisco (2009)

Banfield, J., Wilkerson, B.: Increasing student intrinsic motivation and self-efficacy through gamification pedagogy. Contemp. Issues Educ. Res. 7(4), 291–298 (2014)

Becker, K.: Digital game-based learning once removed: teaching teachers. Br. J. Educ. Technol. 38(3), 478–488 (2007)

Beetham, H., Sharpe, R.: An introduction to rethinking pedagogy for a digital age. In: Beetham, H., Sharpe, H.R. (eds.) Rethinking Pedagogy for a Digital Age: Designing and Delivering e-Learning. Routledge, London (2007)

Catalano, C.E., Luccini, A.M., Mortara, M.: Guidelines for an effective design of serious games. Int. J. Serious Games 1(1), 3 February 2014

Conole, G., Oliver, M.: A pedagogical framework for embedding C&IT into the curriculum. ALT-J Res. Learn. Technol. 6(1), 4–16 (1998)

Cronk, M.: Using gamification to increase student engagement and participation in class discussion. In: Amiel, T., Wilson, B. (Eds.) Proceedings of EdMedia: World Conference on Educational Media and Technology 2012 Association for the Advancement of Computing in Education (AACE), pp. 311–315 (2012)

Herbart, J.F.: Die ersten Vorlesungen über die Pädagogik In: Asmus, W. (ed.) Pädagogische Schriften, pp. 121–131. Klett-Cotta, Stuttgart (1982[1802])

Hopmann, S.: Restrained teaching: the common core of Didaktik. Eur. Educ. Res. J. 6(2), 109–124 (2007)

Klafki, W.: Didaktik analysis as core of preparation of instruction. In: Westbury, I., Hopmann, S., Riquarts, K. (eds.) Teaching as Reflective Practice: The German Didaktik Tradition, pp. 139–160. Lawrence Erlbaum Associates, Mahwah (2000[1958])

Luftensteiner, K., Poelzl, K., Resch, M., Waldhart, K.: Stop the Mob! (2015)

Øhrstrøm, P., Sandborg-Petersen, U., Thorvaldsen, S., Ploug, T.: Teaching logic through web-based and gamified quizzing of formal arguments. In: Hernández-Leo, D., Ley, T., Klamma, R., Harrer, A. (eds.) EC-TEL 2013. LNCS, vol. 8095, pp. 410–423. Springer, Heidelberg (2013)

Gee, J.P.: Good video games, the human mind, and good learning. In: Gee, J.P. (ed.) Good Video Games Plus Good Learning, vol. 27. Peter Lang, Chicago (2007)

Livingstone, S.: Critical reflections on the benefits of ICT in education. Oxf. Rev. Educ. 38(1), 9–24 (2012)

Muth, J.: Pädagogischer Takt: Eine Monographie einer aktuellen Form erzieherischen und didaktischen Handelns. Quelle & Meyer, Heidelberg (1962)

Rogers, C.: Freedom to Learn. Merrill, Colubos (1969)

Schmoelz, A., Payrhuber, A.: Quality assurance and mass courses – blended learning in practise. In: Chova, G., Belenguer, M., Torres, C. (eds.) Proceedings of EDULEARN 2009, pp. 4090–4099 (2009)

Schmoelz, A., Peterson, B.: Mentoring in circumstance. Zeitschrift für Hochschulentwicklung (J. Higher Educ. Dev.) 9(1), 118–132 (2014)

St. John, V.: Best Practices: Five Tips for Better Playtesting. Gamasutra (2015)

Thomas, D., Brown, J.S.: Why virtual worlds can matter. Int. J. Learn. Med. 1, 37–49 (2009)

van Manen, M.: The Tact of Teaching: The Meaning of Pedagogical Thoughtfulness. The Althouse Press, London (1991)

Walsh, C.S.: Systems-based literacy practices: digital games research, gameplay and design. Aust. J. Lang. Lit. Educ. 33(1), 24–40 (2010)

Walsh, C.S., Craft, A., Chappell, K., Koulouris, P.: Gameful learning design to foster co-creativity? In: International Conference of the Australian Association for Research in Education (AARE) and the New Zealand Association for Research in Education (NZARE), "Speaking back through Research", Brisbane, Australia (2014)

Design and Implementation of the Jomini Engine: Towards a Historical Massively Multiplayer Online Role-Playing Game

David Bond[1], Hans-Wolfgang Loidl[1(✉)], and Sandy Louchart[2]

[1] Heriot-Watt University, Riccarton Campus, Edinburgh, EH14 4AS, UK
{D.A.Bond,H.W.Loidl}@hw.ac.uk
[2] Digital Design Studio, The Glasgow School of Art, The Hub, Pacific Quay, G51 1EA, UK
s.louchart@gsa.ac.uk

Abstract. This technical paper describes the design and implementation of a game engine for historical massive multiplayer online role-playing games (MMORPGs). We explore the game and system design space with a focus on historical accuracy and provide a detailed discussion of key design goals for the support of a large-scale, distributed and scalable MMORPG. The *JominiEngine* is a modular and extensible system architecture built on C# and integrates Riak, a non-SQL database, at the core of the persistent data store in order to facilitate scalability. *"Overlord"*, the first instance of the engine is set in the medieval time period and uses rigorous UML design methodology for both game and system design. In order to enhance the immersive gaming experience, a separate Unity-based client can be used to interact with the game engine.

1 Introduction

The benefits of exploiting game technologies for learning and education are well documented and substantiated by current and predicted growths in both the serious games and gamification industries [1]. Researchers have highlighted the benefits of learning through digital games and simulations. According to Gee, digital games provide context for learning and through hard fun [2], a desired experiential state in entertainment gaming leading to the experience of flow [3], which can facilitate effective learning. Gee also highlighted similarities between models of learning in education and game mastery [4], the capacity for games to support deep learning [5] and offering a safe environment where the consequences of failure are lower than in traditional education approaches [2]. Lee et al. [6] extended on Gikas and Van Eck [7] and mapped gaming genre and activities across Gagne's intellectual skills [8] and Bloom's taxonomy of the cognitive domain [9]. In this context, MMORPGs provide the added benefit of engaging large groups of remotely located users [10] and, through their design, facilitate collaborative learning approaches [11]. They also offer the opportunity to collaboratively engage students with a wide range of learning domains and convey experiential learning [12] through an immersive simulation environment. For instance, Second-Life has been widely used in

© Springer International Publishing Switzerland 2016
A. De Gloria and R. Veltkamp (Eds.): GALA 2015, LNCS 9599, pp. 441–451, 2016.
DOI: 10.1007/978-3-319-40216-1_49

various educational disciplines [13] and Lee et al. [6] investigated a Massively Multi-Player Online approach (MMO) towards supporting English [14] and History education in the Rochester Castle MMORPG [15].

In this technical paper, we describe the *JominiEngine*, a game engine framework exploring the design principles of modularity and scalability towards developing a fully-fledged educational MMORPG. We discuss the core game engine with regards to the implementation of a concrete game model. The causal and dynamic nature of the history and heritage domain maps well on existing MMOPRG mechanics and "*Overlord: Age of Magna Carta*" ("*Overlord*" for short), our RPG, has a medieval setting (1194–1215). It illustrates the instantiation of the *JominiEngine* in relation to a concrete, playable experience and system design principles, which we believe to be essential for a successful educational MMORPG deployment. We thus establish the current context for historical MMORPG development through an educational and technical review of current implementations before we explore the primary technical issues related to the provision of scalability for a large playable universe. Finally, we discuss the game model and system design with regards to latency considerations, support for redundancy, distributed architectures and inter-operability with modern commercially available game engines such as Unity [16]. We conclude with a discussion of our current implementation of the *JominiEngine*, its planned future developments and its potential as a teaching and learning support tool.

2   Related Work

Historic Wargames (HW) represent a significant part of well-established game traditions that includes both wargames and war simulations. The wargame genre pre-dates digital gaming and has traditionally been rooted in analogue game-play, such as historical and fantasy/sci-fi simulations. The recent digitization of the genre has opened up new avenues, possibilities and a renewed appeal to current generations of gamers. Beside its entertainment values, Kirschenbaum [17] points to wargames as relevant tools for teaching and reinforcing creative decision-making; a core aspect of wargaming, recognised since Georg von Reisswitz first introduced his wargaming rules in the early 19th Century [18]. HWs represent a popular genre and an increasing number of commercial history-based games have become available, many based on historical conflicts. These games often contain a high degree of historical accuracy and vary both in, firstly, their level of abstraction (from 'traditional' wargames in which units are abstractly represented as counters on a hexagon map, to those that use cutting edge animation technology to allow the player to participate in battles) and, secondly, scale (from the modeling of a single battle, to the simulation of entire civilisations and time periods). HW's also often include role-playing elements; for example, the Crusader Kings series (which uses Paradox's ClausewitzEngine) [19]. Although, not historically accurate, Clash of Clans [20], a 'freemiuim' mobile strategy MMO, was ranked 3rd (in 2013) in the global list of iOS/Android apps revenues [21].

Kirschenbaum described wargames as "a vehicle for its participants, either through role-playing or the arbitrary rule-based constraints of the game world, to critically examine their own assumptions and decision-making processes" [17]. This is supported by a broadening range of simulations in domains such as management or cultural heritage. Anderson et al. [22] investigated the use of serious games in the field of cultural heritage and drew attention to the increasing provision of modding tools as an intrinsic part of many commercial games, allowing for them to be adapted for educational purposes. From a design perspective, accuracy is a key feature for any wargame or historical simulation. Dunnigan argued for realism in HWs [23] but also made a case for balancing historical accuracy with fun gameplay and advanced the notion of "dynamic potential" (i.e. mechanisms through which the player might interact with the game world in order to alter history) in order to better integrate both aspects of the design. Whilst this places an extra burden on the game designer who needs to ensure accuracy, both in game data and mechanisms, it allows for a contextual positioning of relevant aspects such as geography, society, and military technology and doctrine. With regards to HWs specifically, two essential sources for wargaming, emerged from the aftermath of the Napoleonic wars: von Clausewitz [24] wrote on the principles and conduct of warfare, covering topics such as the foundations of strategy, the importance of information and planning, and the best uses of offense and defense and von Reiswitz [18] produced what is regarded as the first modern set of wargaming rules, aimed specifically at the military profession. It defines a rigid set of rules and charts that can be used to simulate the events and effects of battle. In the specific context of developing *Overlord*, we further referred to relevant authorities, including Sumption [25], and Nofi and Dunnigan [26] in representing the Hundred Years War, Oman [27] in examining medieval military practices, Ross [28] in designing game-world data structures for MMORPGs, and Adams [29] for the development of in-games formulas for the development of game mechanics.

Most existing MMORPG engines use a relational database management system (RDBMS) as the underlying data storage mechanism. This design choice profits from guarantees in terms of atomicity, consistency, isolation, and durability (ACID) but incurs extra runtime costs to deliver these guarantees. This can lead to delays, hampering the user experiences: for the EVE engine, Emilsson [30] states that *"the main bottleneck that we have had to overcome is I/O performance of database storage"* and reports typically 2500 transactions per second. To address this problem, the game-world in EVE is partitioned into regions, each served by its own SQL server, but all of them comprising a single universe (or "shard") and utilizing a single back-end RDBMS. This internal separation avoids a bottleneck, but requires regular data exchange on the fringes of regions. Other techniques have been devised to allow "caching" of frequently used data, avoiding RDBMS access in these cases. Again, this leads to added complexity in the implementation, and the efficiency depends on the choice of which data to cache. One notable survey of storage methods in MMOs compares MySQL, with the CouchDB and Riak, both NoSQL (non-relational) databases [31]. The results show that both NoSQL databases outperformed the SQL database: with 200 concurrent players by 7.6 % for CouchDB and 23 % for Riak. Another study [32] compared a range of NoSQL databases with the Microsoft SQL Server RDBMS, looking at the performance of basic operations (create, read, write, delete, fetch keys). The study summarises that, whilst some NoSQL databases (e.g. MongoDB) consistently outperformed MS SQL for almost all operation types (for some write operations by a factor of 10), overall the results varied greatly across products, and across different operations, indicating a need for more research in this area.

3   The *JominiEngine*

Providing scalability for an MMORPG means catering for thousands of players and a large, playable universe. We address these issues primarily through the following choices in our system design: (i) we use a non-relational (NoSQL) database-manage-ment system (Riak) in order to reduce latencies in accessing the underlying (global) database; (ii) we build on Riak's support for redundancy, through transparent data-replication on distributed architectures; and (iii) we use a main-stream, general-purpose programming language, C#, with good inter-operability to the data-base and to other widely available game engines, such as Unity. The design of a new game engine, rather than extending an existing one, gives the opportunity to address scalability and modu-larity into the design from the start, exploring design choices for the system and the use of the engine itself. Throughout the system and game design we use UML diagrams for modelling (complete diagrams are included in Bond [33]). We primarily focus on tech-nical issues first in order to build a generic engine that can instantiate rules flexibly and be deployed across a range of domains. Figure 1 (below) provides an overview of the game model and the central components; actors (NPC, PCS), relationships and manage-ment of resources (in-game currency, tradable/non-tradable) and conflict resolution, which in the historical context means combat, with armies as a tradable resource.

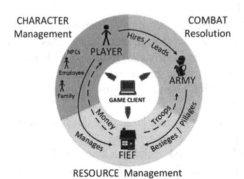

Fig. 1. Basic game model

The *JominiEngine* combines real-time interaction and turn-based mechanics, where specific actions such as conflict resolution trigger immediate events, and state changes which affect fundamental game resources are processed during an 'update', which calculates the impact of resource management policies over one game turn (typically one season), and updates available resources (e.g. money, tax income). Additionally, communications are out-sourced to external mechanisms such as using bulletin boards or social networking infrastructure (player-to-player) or expressed internally for aspects specific to the game engine (game-to-player). Thus, game events are communicated to players either immediately when events happen (synchronously) or at a later point when an update is performed (asynchronously). Similarly, administrative functions such as user management are out-sourced to an external engine. A tailored administrative interface to the component is still necessary, and currently implemented via an admin client.

3.1 Technical Considerations

Investigating a Distributed NoSQL Database for Scalability: One design principle is to avoid bottlenecks in accessing the persistent data storage. We therefore opted for a low-latency, NoSQL solution over a more main-stream SQL database, as the strong consistency guarantees offered by the latter is often not fully required in a digital game context. In contrast, low database latency (i.e. the response time to a request for updating the game data), is very important for an enjoyable gaming experience and for the scalability to thousands of players. These requirements are similar to those in big data applications, where consistency is sometimes weakened for performance. Thus, NoSQL databases have been developed that often provide a simpler view of a distributed, key-value store, without a full-blown SQL query language. Riak [34] is one such database and additionally provides built-in redundancy and the possibility to distribute the database over a network of nodes, both highly desirable aspects for MMORPG game systems.

Ensuring Modularity in the *JominiEngine*: The *JominiEngine* is composed of several key components (Fig. 1), namely; combat resolution, character management, and resource management. The representation of the relationships between these components and game interfaces are critical in determining the modularity of the overall design. As such, we followed an object-oriented design throughout in order to isolate data that is internal to main game objects (i.e. PCs, fiefs) and define a set of operations that can be performed on these objects, thus ensuring modularity through the systematic definition of an engine-internal API for the main operations of the sub-components in the engine. This approach is advantageous in that it is relevant to large-scale system design and offer opportunities for future deployment such as the embedding of a simple scripting language such as Lua [35] into the engine, which would simplify content authoring and increase mod-ability of the engine.

3.2 Game Model

Overlord serves to illustrate the *JominiEngine* game model and its three main areas of functionality (i.e. fief management, combat & army management, and household management - Fig. 1). These are represented, in the game model through the modeling of time, goals and resources management.

Time model: As previously discussed, the *JominiEngine* time model is a hybrid of real-time and turn-based and allows for a combination of real-time cooperation between players, whilst also providing a flexible management of time ('days' in the game). Where it is used as a resource that can be 'spent' on various actions.

Goals: A game should have concrete goals, leading to an achievable victory [36], but it should also provide a degree of freedom for its players [37]. Additionally, many players of historical games are looking to compare their own performance with that of historical figures [23]. The *JominiEngine* was designed to provide a variety of victory conditions, encouraging teamplay, and allowing victory to be decided based on total victory, the achievement of historical victory conditions, or team scores.

Resources: Game resources management is fundamental to enjoyment, game dynamics and the way in which players interact. In a historically-based game, resources must also be depicted authentically. Crawford [38] suggests two main techniques for allocating resources: (i) asymmetric, in which each player is assigned a unique combination of resources; (ii) symmetric, in which resources are allocated equally, and victory depends purely upon execution. The former is often more interesting but tends to be more difficult to program, as goals need to be more finely balanced. Table 1 (below) shows the resources identified for *Overlord*. Given its historical setting, the asymmetric model was chosen so that players must 'strategise' in order to ensure the most effective use of resources (this is also a historically accurate modeling of resources allocation).

Table 1. Game resources and their characteristics

Resource	Increased by	Reduced by	Used for
Money[a]	Fief income; pillage/siege; borrowing	Pillage/siege; lending	Recruitment; NPCs; fief expenses; family expenses
Population	Population growth	Pillage/siege	Recruitment; fief productivity
Game days	Passage of time (seasonal update)	Negative skills	Performance of game actions
NPCs	Birth (family); re-spawning (non-family)	Death, hiring by another player	Assuming roles of responsibility
Troops[a]	Recruitment, transfer between players	Combat, transfer between players	Combat
Titles[a]	Gaining territories, transfer between players	Losing territories, transfer between players	In-game status

[a]*denotes resource is tradable between players*

Mechanics: Using Crawford's approach [37], an initial list of verbs was compiled in order to define core game mechanics for the *JominiEngine* which could then be translated more readily into object-oriented programming structures and functions. As suggested by Sicart [36], the core mechanics were subdivided into primary (those whose employment have a direct influence on the achievement of victory) and secondary (those that do not directly result in the achievement of victory but nevertheless are useful to the player). In addition, some mechanics are defined as compound; - i.e. several tertiary mechanics which comprise a core mechanic.

Character model: A strong character model is important, both for increased player immersion, and because it allows more realistic behavior modelling, particularly of NPCs, and assist the later implementation of AI. For the *JominiEngine*, the following attributes (simplified for the initial version) were assigned: Stature, Combat, Management, Virility, Maximum health. Additionally, in order to provide increased flexibility, a number of 'traits' were defined, each of which positively or negatively influence particular game mechanics and character attributes. In the interests of simplicity, the pool of available traits was limited, and only 2–3 were allocated per character. It is hoped that future enhancements to the *JominiEngine*'s character model can be simplified via the introduction of new traits.

Rules: Game rules were also created so that they could be readily mapped to predicates and conditional checks in the game program. For this reason, it is important that even inherently obvious rules should be recorded (e.g. in the *JominiEngine,* the value of the fief tax rate must lie between 0–100). In an attempt to maintain historical accuracy, some rules were impacted by the need to ensure that the game ultimately remained fun to play; e.g. maintaining an army in the field is a straightforward matter of allocating the appropriate funds, rather than arranging for the purchase and delivery of different types of supplies.

Historical accuracy: The additional dimension of historical accuracy was reflected in the design of the *JominiEngine* game model in that: (1) goals (victory conditions) allow for the achievement of historical conditions; (2) game rules reflect the social practices of the times; e.g. the use of marriage as a tool to acquire stature; (3) game mechanics are restricted to those that would have been available in the target time period, albeit simplified. Where possible, the formulas underpinning the mechanics are based on historical research; e.g. the formula used to derive battlefield casualties [29]; (4) data for *Overlord* was taken from reliable sources [26] and includes personalities, titles and ranks, fief data, and troop types.

4 Performance Aspects

In order to assess the current implementation of the *JominiEngine*, in terms of basic performance and scalability, we assessed the performance of the underlying Riak database and ran a series of measurements, for insert, fetch and delete operations, into a simple but sizable database, performing a sequence of operations from within a varying number of threads up to 150 in total. The goal was to simulate high load on the database, and to compare the access times for each set of operations, with the access times on a standard MySQL server, as one representative of a main-stream SQL-based engine. The results in Fig. 2 (below) show that insert latencies are considerable lower with Riak (4.8 ms vs. 27.8 ms for a single thread, up to 140 ms vs. 300 ms on 150 threads) compared to MySQL. This reflects differences in design, where an SQL-based engine is conservative, always providing exclusive write access to the database, which is expensive, Riak has looser guarantees, avoiding the necessity of locks at the expense of potential roll-backs. We observe a similar picture for the performance of delete operations: 4.4 ms vs. 26.9 ms with a single thread, up to 310 ms vs. 220 ms on 150 threads. In this case the cost for roll-back operations may kick in for the Riak implementation, making it more expensive on this scale. Finally, for the latencies of fetch operations we observe that MySQL is consistently faster than Riak: 0.3 ms vs. 1.5 ms with a single thread, up to 30 ms vs. 68 ms with 150 threads. This reflects that no locks are needed for read access, and the SQL engine can profit from a highly optimised handling of read requests. We note, however, that in terms of scalability, Riak catches up with MySQL for higher thread numbers (Fig. 2 below).

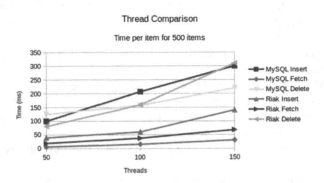

Fig. 2. Database performance comparison with increasing thread numbers (50 to 150)

These preliminary performance results show a mostly positive picture in terms of the benefits of a NoSQL database. While we have gains for write access and modifications, the cross-over in performance for deletes for high thread numbers needs further investigation, and we do observe a performance penalty for read operations. In the bigger picture, however, Riak brings benefits in terms of distribution, which is wired into the database engine, and it has been designed with data redundancy and for massive concurrency, building on the Erlang system, which is known for its efficient handling of concurrency. We thus believe that these preliminary results strengthen our case for using Riak as the database in the *JominiEngine*.

5   Conclusion

We have presented the design and initial implementation of a game engine for historical massive-multiplayer on-line role-playing games. The *JominiEngine* has been designed for the educational application domain and to support this usage it allows for the accurate modeling of historical game data as an incentive metric to encourage team play and reflection on historical context. *"Overlord"* presents such data as one instance of the game engine. We envision to use such instances as educational tools to provide insights into dependencies of societal and economic forces in a specific time period and geographic area. Thus, our immediate application domain will be (interactive) history in education. This technical paper is concerned with the performance aspects of the game engine and its requirements for *scalability, modularity, fault tolerance* through data redundancy and the authoring of both primary and secondary game mechanisms. The *JominiEngine* is a generic game engine, which can be used, in different educational contexts. This technical article discusses key decisions made during the development of the engine in terms of scalability (the use of Riak as a NoSQL database to reduce lookup latency), and modularity (C# as a flexible implementation language, an API for key functionality in the game engine, usage of established data formats for data exchange). Reflecting on *Overlord*, the initial instance of the game, we observe that accurate content authoring is challenging, requiring a high investment of research time and the assembling of a multi-disciplinary team of experts for future developments.

The *JominiEngine* has been developed in order to design a scalable and extensible MMOPRG solution for serious game interventions. The scalability aspect discussed in this article is essential for large-scale deployment and a critical condition to be met in order to distribute educational MMORPGs simultaneously in a large number of institutions. Additionally, the *JominiEngine* has been designed as a generic and modular solution so as to extend its applicability to domains other than history and battle re-enactments. The *Overlord* game has been developed using the *JominiEngine* in order to illustrate the concrete implementation of these concepts discussed in this article and to provide a basis for future deployments A Unity-based client has recently been added, without requiring major restructuring of the core engine. The complete source code is available at https://github.com/libdab/hist_mmorpg/tree/nonMVC, (under the OSI approved MIT license) and a detailed discussion of the JominiEngine is given in Bond [33].

References

1. Adkins, S.: Keynotes Serious Play Conference 2013: The 2012–2017 Worldwide Game-Based Learning and Simulation-Based Markets (2013). http://bit.ly/1s42fDL. Accessed 7 July 2015
2. Gee, J.P.: What Video Games Have to Teach Us About Learning and Literacy. Palgrave/Macmillan, New York (2003)
3. Csikszentmihalyi, M.: Flow: The Psychology of Optimal Experience. Harper & Row, New York (1990)
4. Gee, J.P.: Games, learning, and 21st century survival skills. J. Virtual Worlds Res. 2(1) (2009). http://bit.ly/1NjPdZF. Accessed 18 Oct 2015
5. Gee, J.P.: Deep learning properties of good digital games. In: Vorderer, P., Ritterfeld, U., Cody, M.J. (eds.) Serious Games: Mechanisms and Effects, pp. 63–80. Routledge, New York, London (2009)
6. Lee, M.J.W., Eustace, K., Fellows, G., Bytheway, A., Irving, L.: Rochester castle MMORPG: instructional gaming and collaborative learning at a Western Australian school. Australas. J. Educ. Technol. 21(4), 446–469 (2005)

7. Gikas, J., Van Eck, R.: Integrating video games in the classroom: where to begin? Paper presented at the National Learning Infrastructure Initiative 2004 Annual Meeting, San Diego, CA, 25–27 January 2004. http://www.educause.edu/ir/library/pdf/NLI0431a.pdf. Accessed 1 June 2015

8. Gagne, R., Briggs, L., Wager, W.: Principles of Instructional Design, 4th edn. HBJ College Publishers, Fort Worth (1992)

9. Bloom, B.S. (ed.): Taxonomy of Educational Objectives: Handbook I: Cognitive Domain. David McKay, New York (1956)

10. De Freitas, S., Griffiths, M.: Online gaming as an educational tool in learning and training. Br. J. Educ. Technol. **38**(3), 535–537 (2007)

11. Yu, T.W.: Learning in the virtual world: the pedagogical potentials of massively multiplayer online role playing games. Int. Educ. Stud. **2**(1), 32–38 (2009)

12. Kolb, D.A.: Experiential Learning. Prentice Hall, Englewood Cliffs (1984)

13. Childress, M.D., Braswell, R.: Using massively multiplayer online role-playing games for online learning. Dist. Educ. **27**(2), 187–196 (2006)

14. Kongmee, I., Strachan, R., Montgomery, C., Pickard, A.: Using massively multiplayer online role playing games (MMORPGs) to support second language learning: action research in the real and virtual world. In: 2nd Annual IVERG Conference: Immersive Technologies for Learning (2011). http://bit.ly/1kiPHWc. Accessed 18 Oct 2015

15. Eustace, K., Fellows, G., Bytheway, A., Lee, M., Irving, L.: The application of massively multiplayer online role playing games to collaborative learning and teaching practice in schools. In: Atkinson, R., McBeath, C., Jonas-Dwyer, D., Phillips, R. (eds.) Beyond the Comfort Zone: Proceedings of the 21st ASCILITE Conference (2004). http://bit.ly/1hMNzEm. Accessed 18 Oct 2015

16. Unity: Game Engine. https://unity3d.com/. Accessed 18 Oct 2015

17. Kirschenbaum, M.: War: what is it good for? Learning from wargaming (2011). http://www.playthepast.org/?p=1819. Accessed 18 Oct 2015

18. Von Reiswitz, G.H.R.: Instructions for the representation of tactical maneuvers under the guise of a wargame, s.l.: s.n. (1824)

19. Crusader Kings 2. http://www.crusaderkings.com/. Accessed 18 Oct 2015

20. Clash of Clans. http://supercell.com/en/games/clashofclans/. Accessed 18 Oct 2015

21. Mirani, L.: Why free games are increasingly the most profitable apps (2014). http://qz.com/172349. Accessed 18 Oct 2015

22. Anderson, E.F., McLoughlin, L., Liarokapis, F., Peters, C., Petridis, P., de Freitas, S.: Developing serious games for cultural heritage: a state-of-the-art review. Virtual Real. **14**(4), 255–275 (2010)

23. Dunnigan, J.F.: Wargames Handbook: How to Play and Design Commercial and Professional Wargames, 3rd edn. Writers Club Press, Lincoln (2000)

24. Von Clausewitz, C.: On War. Wordsworth Editions Limited, Ware (1997)

25. Sumption, J.: The Hundred Years War, 3 vols. Faber and Faber, London (1990–2009)

26. Nofi, A.A., Dunnigan, J.F.: Medieval life & the Hundred Years War (1997). http://bit.ly/1M4hoNH. Accessed 18 Oct 2015

27. Oman, C.W.C.: The Art of War in the Middle Ages: A.D. 378–1515. B.H. Blackwell, Oxford (1885)

28. Ross, S.J.: Medieval demographics made easy (2013). http://www222.pair.com/sjohn/blueroom/demog.htm. Accessed 5 July 2015

29. Adams, E.: The Designer's Notebook: Kicking Butt by the Numbers: Lanchester's Laws (2004). http://ubm.io/1eD8N6v. Accessed 5 July 2015

30. Emilsson, K.: Infinite space: an argument for for single-sharded architectures in MMOs (2014). http://ubm.io/1LWxaFh. Accessed 18 Oct 2015

31. Muhammad, Y.: Evaluation and implementation of distributed NoSQL databases for MMO gaming environments. M.Sc. dissertation, Uppsala University (2011, unpublished)

32. Li, Y., Manoharan, S.: A performance comparison of SQL and NoSQL databases. In: 2013 IEEE Pacific Rim Conference on Communications, Computers and Signal Processing (PACRIM), pp. 15–19. IEEE (2013)

33. Bond, D.A.: Design and implementation of a massively multi-player online historical role-playing game. M.Sc. dissertation, Heriot-Watt University (2015, unpublished). http://bit.ly/1LXhj9k. Accessed 18 Oct 2015

34. Riak KV.http://basho.com/products/riak-kv/. Accessed 22 May 2016

35. Lua. http://www.lua.org/. Accessed 18 Oct 2015

36. Sicart, M.: Defining game mechanics. Game Stud. Int. J. Comput. Game Res. **8**(2) (2008). http://bit.ly/1Hv4UJH. Accessed 18 Oct 2015

37. Crawford, C.: The art of computer game design (1984). http://bit.ly/1Tjgv4X. Accessed 18 Oct 2015

38. Crawford, C.: The Art of Interactive Design: A Euphonious and Illuminating Guide to Building Successful Software. No Starch Press, San Francisco (2002)

Towards the Blending of Digital and Physical Learning Contexts with a Gamified and Pervasive Approach

Sylvester Arnab[1(✉)], Gemma Tombs[1], Michael Duncan[2], Mike Smith[2], and Kam Star[3]

[1] Disruptive Media Learning Lab, Coventry University, Coventry, UK
{s.arnab,g.tombs}@coventry.ac.uk
[2] Health and Life Sciences, Coventry University, Coventry, UK
{m.duncan,m.smith}@coventry.ac.uk
[3] Playgen Ltd., London, UK
kam@playgen.com

Abstract. This paper discusses our perspectives on pervasive learning based on live projects at the Disruptive Media Learning Lab, UK (DMLL.org.uk), aligning with the need to respond to the blurring of boundaries between physical and digital learning spaces and contexts. The paper describes a holistic and modular approach in thinking about pervasive learning design and with special interest on games and gamification. Findings are presented on a study carried out on physical learning spaces and students' engagement with these spaces (digital and physical). The paper also describes a pilot on the use of game mechanics in a blended learning environment. The findings will inform other projects that are investigating the crossings between gamification and pervasive gaming, including the potential of indoor mobile communication to support context-aware resources and future 'learning spaces'. The holistic model may inform future initiatives in integrating knowledge, tools and services towards facilitating a pervasive and technology-enabled learning exploiting both physical and digital contents and contexts.

1 Introduction

Key to reducing the barriers of time and physical space in teaching and learning is to open up education in such a way that formal/informal learning contexts, and digital/physical experiences are blended. Exploiting current advances in digital technologies allow for learning processes to be better situated in a learner's context, needs and surroundings, where many different forms of learning experience can be combined in working toward the desired learning outcomes.

To understand how digital and physical learning contexts could be exploited to enhance the learning experience of learners, there is a need to study students' engagement with learning spaces, pedagogical (such as game-based learning) techniques as well as technologies to understand learning dynamics in physical and digital environments, and the extension of learning beyond the limitation of a physical classroom by looking at relevant enabling technologies. It is thus important for educational institutions to evaluate and possibly re-design how formal spaces are used in teaching and learning

© Springer International Publishing Switzerland 2016
A. De Gloria and R. Veltkamp (Eds.): GALA 2015, LNCS 9599, pp. 452–460, 2016.
DOI: 10.1007/978-3-319-40216-1_50

and how digital platforms can help facilitate delivery, application and assessment of learning in informal context.

Through the years, digital platforms ranging from e-learning and simulation platforms to game-based learning and mobile applications have provided alternative means for the way learning contents are being delivered. As the discipline of seamless learning merges the technological and human challenges faced by the emerging new technologies of the last decade, it is becoming clear that the ultimate learning environment will have to provide a smooth learner experience, with options to both consume and create content [1] in both formal and informal setting as well as digital and physical spaces.

Advances in ubiquitous computing, mobile and location-based technologies open up opportunities for digitally-enabled learning to be facilitated in everyday spaces, increasing flexibility for learning experience to be made more engaging, contextualized and seamless. With game-based learning in mind, potentials include games taking place in the physical world, concurrently with the normal activities of learners' everyday lives, where virtual actions may be the trigger for physical actions in the real world and vice versa [2]. Example games with serious purposes that adopt such a pervasive approach include Zombies Run -an adventure location-based mobile game that advocates running, and Ingress- transforming local landmarks into game objects in a viral and global gaming, provides an avenue for teaching and learning to be made more playful and pervasive.

Sensors built into mobile devices, such as smartphones and tablets also make it possible for context-aware educational resources to be triggered. Pervasive gaming for learning is both exciting and commercially promising and can be realised through computer games built with a combination of hybrid interfaces, multi tenacity, and context-sensing technologies. Ubiquity is expanded by context awareness, a term that "describes the ability of the computer to sense and act upon information about its environment, such as location, time, temperature or user identity" [3]. This information can be used to enable selective responses such as triggering events or retrieving and prompting information relevant to the task at hand. This affords virtualisation, which provides a more seamless means to link formal and informal learning approaches, and blend digital and physical learning mechanics.

The use of game techniques in a non-game context, known as Gamification, has also demonstrated potential impact in a wide range of subjects [4]. Gamification often exploits competition to motivate, personified by points, badges and leader boards. Success, however seems to go beyond these basic features and relies on a concrete acknowledgement of the motivational model of the user, taking into view concepts such as situational relevance, and situated motivational affordance, which strategy can either be framed under competition and/or collaboration [5].

By further investigating how learners use the different spaces for learning, how to exploit learners' preferences for enhancing the use of digital platforms and the potential of gamification, pervasive gaming and context-aware technologies in enhancing a blended learning process, the expected benefits of blended spaces and contexts can be optimised. With these perspectives, this paper attempts to explore the various facets and insights that could inform the development of a more pervasive approach in learning in a holistic and modular way. The paper will touch on two projects at the Disruptive Media

Learning Lab (DMLL), UK, which can be used to explore key factors in the use of physical and digital spaces. The modular approach is described in Sect. 2. Section 3 reports relevant insights from the projects. The first two projects provide insights on the engagement with physical and digital spaces, and the implication of using a gamified platform to scaffold team working. The paper is concluded in Sect. 4 with indications of further work within the area of pervasive learning.

2   Holistic and Modular Design

To help understand the needs and potential in a more holistic way, we adopt a modular approach that allows considerations under each layer to be investigated in an agile manner and collectively inform the gamified and pervasive learning development. Figure 1 illustrates the key layers, which can help structure study and design considerations.

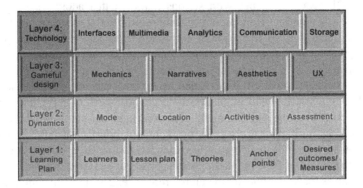

Fig. 1. A modular approach from layer 1 to layer 4

Layer 1 Learning Plan: This emphasizes the need to ensure pedagogical design informs the context, mechanics and dynamics of the intended learning process and activities. Challenges and opportunities in terms of teaching/learning practices, (co-curriculum, informal learning, learners' and teachers' needs and learning spaces help determine 'anchor points'; milestones set for learning activities and assessment measures. These points can potentially spread across the formal–informal spectrum fostering a digital-physical blend.

Layer 2 Learning Dynamics: This maps out activities with associated learning objectives (what skills to apply, what knowledge to assess), informing the content and context of learning. It will consider learners' motivational model, learners-instructors dynamics and spatial contexts of learning. The monitoring dynamics (formal–informal) can be defined to ensure that progress is continuously assessed.

Layer 3 Gameful design: This maps learning mechanics/dynamics with game mechanics/dynamics (e.g. [6]), informing the design of user experience (UX), gamified practice and pervasive context. The approach can exploit digital game technologies/gamification techniques in enhancing engagement. Narratives, for instance can be designed to wrap around the lesson plans, creating context that glues targeted learning milestones together.

Layer 4 Enabling technologies: This allows us to evaluate the feasibility and relevance of existing technologies in supporting pervasive and gameful learning processes and addresses specific teaching and learning challenges and opportunities identified in previous layers. The gamified lesson plan will inform the standard-driven integration and implementation of enabling technologies for interfaces, multimedia, analytics, communications and storage. Existing platforms, tools and applications will inform the building blocks of the desired solutions or outcomes. It also investigates and evaluates how technologies disrupt existing practices.

3   The Perspectives of Live Projects at the Disruptive Media Learning Lab (DMLL)

In DMLL, we are piloting interventions in operational environments responding to the various challenges and opportunities identified in teaching and learning practices, and the investigations lie under the layers in Sect. 2. This section describes two projects with implications for pervasive learning approaches.

3.1   Physical Space, Digital Needs and Students' Dynamic

Background and methodology: As part of activities within *layers 1 and 2*, this study looks at students' engagement with physical resources and infrastructures in order to evaluate learning behavior and dynamics within the university library. It was undertaken to identify popular usage and potential issues to address in the subsequent redesign of the library space. Of the five floors, three (Learning Lounge, Ground Floor, and the Disruptive Media Learning Lab) were categorized as 'collaborative' working floors, whilst the first floor was categorized as a silent 'individual' working floor and the second floor was categorized as a quiet floor with both 'individual' and quiet 'collaborative' working. These floors hosted the library's book stock. The Ground Floor hosted the service desk and study skills collection.

Data were gathered using two methods (photographic observations and surveys), with ethical approval provided by the host institution. Photographs were taken at 50 locations across the floors, every 3 h from 10am–10pm on alternate days for two non-consecutive weeks. Students then responded to a survey that asked for information on: regularity of resources used in the library (both student-owned and library-provided), choice of location for individual/group work, requested resources, and favourite areas.

Discussions: Data in this study were analysed with particular regard to students' usage of the different library spaces. Table 1 identifies students' locational choices for individual and group work totaled from 239 total respondents; multiple students identified several areas in which they worked both individually and in groups.

Table 1. Students' locational choices for individual and group working

Floor	Working area	Individual	Group
Learning Lounge	PCs	20	45
	Tables with sofas	16	88
Ground Floor	PCs	35	48
	Group tables with sofas	18	89
	Maths Support Office	8	11
1st Floor [silent]	PCs and Macs	114	9
	Individual tables	83	10
2nd Floor [quiet with separate silent room]	PCs and Macs [quiet]	93	17
	Individual tables [quiet]	64	20
	PCs [silent room]	79	6
	Individual tables [silent]	70	4
Disruptive Media Learning Lab	Macs	40	40
	Project areas [6–8 people, with computer screens and/or whiteboards]	19	82
	Hill [central presentation/ seating area]	7	28
	Grass [informal presentation space]	10	42
	Movable tables [10 + people]	12	48

Previous studies have shown that in order to promote self-directed and pervasive learning, it is essential for students to have access to both independent and collaborative spaces [7]. Whilst these spaces were provided for students, this study revealed that students themselves rarely categorised spaces as independent or collaborative, with a small percentage of students undertaking groupwork in silent areas and a larger percentage of students working independently in areas designated as collaborative working areas. Additionally, [8] found that students adapted library spaces for their own needs, regardless of the designated purpose of the space. Thus whilst barriers might be seen to exist between formal and informal spaces in institutions, these barriers may not be perceived by students themselves. This raises interesting challenges for the provision of resources across the institution. Whilst students in this study could and often did move books around, desktop computers could not be moved with the same ease. Figure 2 indicates the resources most often used in the library, grouped by year of study.

These findings suggest that, despite the move towards mobile learning in this institution and others, desktop computers remain by far the most regularly used resource in the library across all years. There are two possible reasons for this finding. Firstly, many students in this study requested that further plug sockets be made available for charging of laptops or tablets, suggesting a wish to use personal resources but a lack of structural capacity to support this. However, observational analyses also indicated that oftentimes university desktop computers and personal laptops or tablets were used concurrently, allowing students to research online whilst writing papers, for example, or enabling

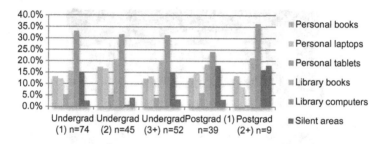

Fig. 2. Student use of resources in the library (by year) (Color figure online)

students to have both 'social' and 'work' feeds. Overall, these findings would seem to suggest that dichotomies between individual and collaborative study, or desk-based versus mobile learning, no longer exist, if indeed they ever did.

3.2 Scaffolding Learning Using Gamification on a Digital Platform Linking to Physical Assessment

Background and methodology: Framed within collaborative and social learning operating under the mechanics of team working (*layers 1 and 2*), this study explores the learning dynamics enabled by a gamified approach (*layer 3*) on a digital (web-based) platform (*layer 4*). Achievement mechanics and competition have been key to existing gamification design approaches. Motivated by the fact that collaborative and social learning has demonstrated the nurturing of soft skills, which are an important component of 21st century skills, we piloted a gamified learning platform- the StarQuest Platform (Fig. 3) that serves as a tool to help investigate the competition and collaboration mechanics and their impact in learning. The pilot study was carried out in collaboration with Playgen Ltd. Participants were 2nd year undergraduate students (n = 94) on a module titled, "A Fundamental Approach to Motor Learning and Control." It ran for 11 weeks and used a problem-based learning (PBL) approach. Students were allocated to one of 20 tutorial groups, consisting of approximately 5 students per group. Five members of staff acted as PBL facilitators and the curriculum is divided into 4×2 h lectures, 8×2 h tutorials and 3×2 h lab sessions. Problems were set from current issues in the world of sport and exercise and students had to prepare group and individual information related to providing a solution to the problem before the first tutorial. As the problems are often complex and due to the time constraints of providing a solution within approximately two weeks, students were provided with a paper-based scaffolding tool, which has been developed based on Edward de Bono's six thinking hats [9].

The mechanics of StarQuest were introduced to the students in the first lecture and students were encouraged to asynchronously upload content relevant to answering the problem, which could then be used as content in their individual solution sheet, forming part of coursework 1 (CW1). This process was repeated for 4 problems, which make up the content of the module. The groups were randomly allocated under the Collaborative, Competitive and Control modes. Interaction data and feedback from the groups were collected via the platform over the pilot duration and the modes were matched against

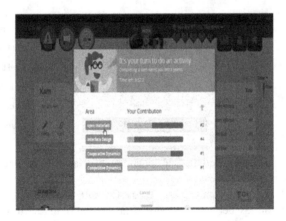

Fig. 3. StarQuest.eu interface showing progress bars based on contributions

the performance based on two course works (CW1, CW2). The initial analysis looked at how the modes correlate with the actual marks.

Discussions: A series of one-way ANOVAs were conducted to examine any differences in marks for CW1, CW2 and final module mark with group type (competitive, collaborative and control) as between subjects' factors. Results indicated that there were no significant differences in CW2 (P = .480) mark and final module (P = .148) mark as a consequence of type of engagement in StarQuest. There was however a significant difference in CW1 module mark as a consequence of type of engagement in StarQuest (P = .003). Bonferroni post-hoc analysis indicated that there was significantly lower CW1 mark in the collaborative group compared to the competitive group (P = .003, mean diff = 8.9 %) and the control group (P = .027, mean diff = 7.3 %). There was no significant difference in CW1 mark between the competitive and control groups (P = 1.00).

The study demonstrated that the context of learning and the specific module influenced the learning and learner dynamics, where competition within the team and across teams worked better with this group of students. One of the assumptions to why groups in the collaborative mode performed worse that the competitive group is due the type of cohort; Sport Science students are by their very nature competitive and consequently would like to outperform their 'team mates'. The collaborative group may have also been guilty of social loafing [10] and leaving engagement with StarQuest to the rest of the group. Furthermore, autonomy might have been better fostered in the competitive mode and the control mode. Beersma et al. [5] concluded in their study that teams with extroverted and willing members performed better under the collaborative structure, whereas teams low on these orientations performed better under the competitive structure, which highlights additional study to be conducted on the students' personality and motivation model. Findings from CW2 show insignificant outcomes that may be due to lack of support provided compared to CW1. A small-scale study carried out on gamification and its effects on brainstorming [11] also showed insignificant difference between results generated from cooperation and those from competitive gamification.

The pilot highlighted both the strengths and weaknesses of introducing something new to the students informing considerations important to *layers 1 and 2* of the holistic model, which will inform future design, development and deployments of new learning platforms. Introducing a new approach to students in their first year may be more effective; also recommended by PBL model [12]. The level 2 students had already been introduced to a systematic way of looking at the PBL pathway in the level 1 module. They had also already established their own collaborative method in the first year, for e.g. using Facebook and Whatsapp groups. This emphasizes the importance of understanding learners' needs and the learning dynamics as suggested in *layer 2*. Further work will include an in-depth analysis of group and individual activities under both collaborative and competitive modes, and to further understand students' current engagement with their module.

4 Conclusions

This paper has highlighted a modular approach in investigating considerations and enablers of pervasive learning based on the two example projects with findings that map to the different aspects of the layers (1–4). The spatial study concludes that contrasts between individual and collaborative study, or desk-based versus mobile learning are blurring, and that students adapted spaces for their own needs, raising interesting challenges for the provision of resources (digital, physical and blended) across the institution. These findings influences the key learning goals and learners characteristics explored in layer 1 and the dynamics and relevant learning activities to be considered in layer 2. Provision of new learning design, approaches and platforms in layer 3 and layer 4 should consider factors associated to the previous layers, and findings from the StarQuest pilot emphasizes that the provision may also prove to be more effective with first level students compared to other advanced levels, linking to the motivational conditions of learners (individually and collectively) that influence the learning dynamics and culture as they level up. Understanding the dynamics (layer 3) is key to designing gamified activities.

Further work will include mapping findings from other projects to the different layers of the modular model to collectively form insights and guidelines for designing pervasive learning enabled by technological approaches, including games and digital gamification. The modular model will be expanded to include findings from our research and development at the DMLL based on other existing projects such as the crossings between pervasive games and gamification to support active learning and the pilot of beacon technologies and context aware approaches to inform the design of future "learning spaces".

Acknowledgments. The work has been funded by the DMLL. The authors would also like to acknowledge Playgen Ltd.

References

1. E-Learning Guild: Seamless Learning: Forget MOOCs, Mobile Learning, and Ubiquitous Access. Learning Solutions Magazine (2014)
2. Jantke, K.P., Spundflasch, S.: Understanding pervasive games for purposes of learning. In: 5th International Conference on Computer Supported Education, CSEDU 2013, pp. 696–701 (2013)
3. Schmidt, A.: Context-aware computing: context-awareness, context-aware user interfaces, and implicit interaction. In: Soegaard, M., Dam, R.F. (eds.) The Encyclopedia of Human-Computer Interaction, 2nd edn. The Interaction Design Foundation, Aarhus (2014)
4. Hamari, J., Koivisto, J., Sarsa, H.: Does gamification work? – A literature review of empirical studies on gamification. In: Proceedings of the 47th Hawaii International Conference on System Sciences, Hawaii, USA (2014)
5. Beersma, B., Hollenbeck, J.R., Humphrey, S.E., Moon, H., Conlon, D.E., Ilgen, D.R.: Cooperation, competition, and team performance: toward a contingency approach. Acad. Manag. J. 46(5), 572–590 (2003)
6. Arnab, S., Lim, T., Carvalho, M.B., Bellotti, F., de Freitas, S., Louchart, S., Suttie, N., Berta, R., De Gloria, A.: Mapping learning and game mechanics for serious games analysis. Br. J. Educ. Technol. 46, 391–411 (2015)
7. Keating, S., Gabb, R.: Putting learning into the learning commons: a literature review. Postcompulsory Education Centre Victoria University (2005)
8. Montgomery, S.: Library space assessment: user learning behaviors in the library. J. Acad. Librarianship 40, 70–75 (2014)
9. Smith, M., Cook, K.: Attendance and achievement in problem-based learning: the value of scaffolding. Interdisc. J. Prob. Based Learn. 127–149
10. Høigaard, R., Säfvenbom, R., Tønnessen, F.E.: The relationship between group cohesion, group norms, and perceived social loafing in soccer teams. Small Group Res. 37(3), 217–232 (2006)
11. Yuizono, T., Xing, Q., Furukawa, H.: Effects of gamification on electronic brainstorming systems. In: Yuizono, T., Zurita, G., Baloian, N., Inoue, T., Ogata, H. (eds.) CollabTech 2014. CCIS, vol. 460, pp. 54–61. Springer, Heidelberg (2014)
12. Savin-Baden, M.: Facilitating problem-based learning. OUP, Buckingham (2003)

Get It Right! Introducing a Framework for Integrating Validation in Applied Game Design

Harald Warmelink[✉], Marilla Valente, Richard van Tol,
and Robbertjan Schravenhoff

HKU Innovation Studio, HKU University of the Arts Utrecht,
Lange Viestraat 2b, 3511 BK Utrecht, The Netherlands
{harald.warmelink,marilla.valente,richard.vantol,
robbertjan.schravenhoff}@hku.nl

Abstract. Validation of applied games is generally a lengthy and costly process, usually done after the game has (almost) been completed. This article argues that validation throughout the design process is vital for creating games that achieve their desired objective. It proposes a framework to integrate validation throughout the applied game design process. Iterative design and design fidelity levels form the foundation of the framework. In the framework four types of design fidelity (specifications, concepts, prototypes, and integrations) are linked to five types of validity (content, face, construct, concurrent and predictive validity), which lead to eight applicable validation tools and techniques. The framework is a starting point for further research into applied game validation.

1 Introduction

Recently many have argued that validation should be a prime concern for current serious, simulation, educational and applied game designers and researchers [1–3]. Designers need to know if and how their games achieve their objectives in order to act responsibly. Researchers need to know the same in order to advance game design theory and practice [3, 4]. Over the past decade the research community has already proven to be invaluable in this respect by providing over 11 different frameworks for game evaluation and assessment [3, 5, 6].

While the work on game evaluation and assessment is an important step, they have their limits as validation strategies. First, the late timing of this kind of validation increases the chance of disappointment. Full-scale evaluation or assessment in accordance to e.g. Mayer et al. [3] is only possible after a costly game design and development project has all but finished. Second, evaluation or assessment connotes a problematic division between design and validation, or designer and researcher. Third, evaluation or assessment tends to downplay the multifaceted and intricate nature of game design and thus validation. Game design involves a high amount of intertwined variables (e.g. audiovisual, artistic or narrative design, the design of goals, rules and feedback systems). In some frameworks many of these variables are problematically

© Springer International Publishing Switzerland 2016
A. De Gloria and R. Veltkamp (Eds.): GALA 2015, LNCS 9599, pp. 461–470, 2016.
DOI: 10.1007/978-3-319-40216-1_51

grouped together (into e.g. 'game/simulation quality'; [6]) and are at best 'tweakable' variables by the time of an evaluation or assessment.

This article therefore extends existing work by exploring how validation can be integrated into the game design process. It offers a framework for integrating validation during game design as a starting point for further research both into the framework's foundations and into potential tools and techniques of validation. We do so not only to contribute to the continually developing field of game design research, but also to aid game design education.

Throughout this article we consistently use the term applied games as we consider it a useful umbrella term, covering games as digital, analog or hybrid interactive systems of trial and error that players engage with in order to learn or be enticed into certain behavior. In doing so we acknowledge the valuable work of the different communities of serious, simulation, educational and applied game design research.

Our understanding of validation follows Graafland et al., defining validity as whether "an instructional instrument (such as a serious game) adequately resembles the construct it aims to educate or measure" [2]. In doing so we acknowledge particularly the medical, pharmaceutical and simulation design fields as having a long-standing history concerning validation trials, in general, with simulations and with games [2, 7].

Our validation framework is based on a literature review, two years of research-through-design, and reflections on applied game design projects we were involved in. The literature review is based on evaluation and design frameworks from the applied gaming research community, as well as validation frameworks of the aforementioned related disciplines. The two years of research-through-design focused on the creation of tools (e.g. a prototype of a short card game) for applied game designers not (fully) aware of the nature and need of validation. This tool creation process helped us ascertain different timings and levels of validation during an applied game design process.

2 The Framework's Foundations

2.1 Iterative Design

Our validation framework is based on an *iterative* approach to game design. In iterative design cycles a typical 'testing' or 'check' phase is or at least should be a form of validation (Fig. 1). After all, put most simply, an iterative design cycle entails conceptualising a game experience, building it, and testing what has been built in order to ascertain whether it accomplishes what was conceptualised.

Although an iterative design approach is arguably commonplace, its nature and value is too easily overlooked. We conceptualise applied game designers as aiming for novel, creative designs that motivate certain target audiences into learning or specific behavior. This means that we consider it possible to find a design that meets self-defined criteria related not only to the main objective at hand, but to state-of-the-art game design and to what motivates the target audience as well. An iterative design approach is key to reaching these particular, multiple objectives [8–10].

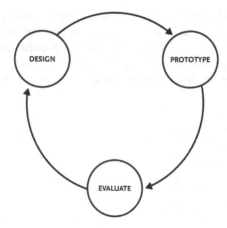

Fig. 1. Fundamental phases of the iterative design cycle, forming our framework's foundation.

Based on the iterative design cycle, our framework distinguishes three consecutive, reoccurring phases in the applied game design process: design, build and validate. The first phase, *design*, is one where specifications, concepts or prototypes are thought up, often through creativity-boosting means (e.g. the use of an ideation technique such as group brainstorming). The second phase, *build*, is one where these specifications, concepts or prototypes are developed into artefacts such as design documents and paper prototypes. The third phase, *validate*, is the phase in which these artefacts are actually validated - the focal point of this article.

2.2 Design Fidelity

Our framework also incorporates a second dimension, one depicting the gradual move towards the required *design fidelity*. With design fidelity we refer to the level of proximity a design has to the envisioned final product. For example, a paper prototype has higher design fidelity than a graphical user-interface sketch or wireframe, while such a sketch or wireframe has higher design fidelity than a design requirements list.

The inclusion of the design fidelity dimension has important consequences for our understanding of the design process, and the role of validation in it. By combining design phases with levels of design fidelity the framework accentuates the validation of multiple and different artefacts during the design process. As such the design fidelity dimension diminishes the gap between the fields of social science and design practice. It opens up new focal points for validation that have previously been overlooked in applied game validation research.

The framework depicts four levels of design fidelity: *Specifications* level, *Concepts* level, *Prototypes* level and *Integrations* level (Fig. 2). *Specifications* denotes the basic specifications or requirements the final design should meet. *Concepts* denotes the grand, basic ideas for the applied game experience, often using common, current game heuristics, e.g., well-known game genre typologies ('real-time strategy', 'simulation', 'role-playing' games). The *Prototypes* level encompasses several design fidelity levels.

For example, when designing a computer game, a paper prototype is of lower design fidelity than a digital prototype. The fourth and final level of *Integrations* depicted in Fig. 2 is the highest level of design fidelity. Once an applied game or any product is fully integrated into a context of use (e.g., an educational setting, or an organisational process), it can be considered a finished product. Hence the center of Fig. 2 is also marked with '*Finish*'.

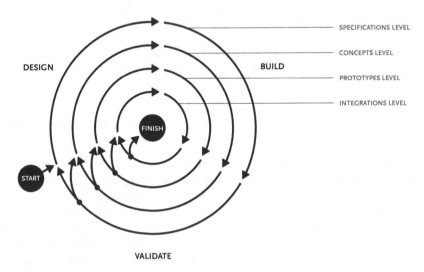

Fig. 2. Integrating validation in applied game design based on four design fidelity levels.

3   The Framework Completed

3.1   Validity Types

Because of the existence of different levels of design fidelity, we propose that applied game design validity has many faces and can take place throughout the entire applied game design process. Graafland et al. [2] provided the inspiration for what validation specifically can entail. Based on the guidelines set forth by The American Psychological Association [11], and mirroring simulation validity types [7], they state that validity research in medical education usually involves several phases and includes *content, face, construct, concurrent,* and *predictive* validity:

> "First, experts should scrutinize the game's content to determine its legitimacy (*content* validity). Second, experts and novices judge the instrument's apparent similarity to the construct it attempts to represent (*face* validity). *Construct* validity reflects the ability of the instrument to actually measure what it intends to measure (i.e., the difference in performance between groups of users with different levels of experience in reality). *Concurrent* validity reflects the correlation between performance on the serious game and their performance on an instrument believed to measure the same construct (e.g., a simulator or course). The ultimate goal is to prove a game's *predictive* validity: does performance in the game lead to better outcomes in reality?" [2].

3.2   Validation Tools and Techniques

Table 1 integrates design fidelity and the five validity types to propose a set of tools and techniques applied game designers can use during the validation phase of a particular fidelity level in the design process. In the remainder of this section we explain each of the proposed tools and techniques.

Table 1. Validation tools and techniques for each design fidelity level

Design fidelity level (low to high)	Validity type	Validation tool or technique
Specifications	Content validity: Is the game's content legitimate? How is the content validated to be complete, correct, and nothing but for the intended designated construct?	1. Design requirement framework or heuristic check 2. Subject matter check 3. SMART goal definition check
Concepts	Face validity: Is there a similarity to the construct it attempts to measure? Do educators and trainees view it as a valid way of instruction?	4. Specifications check 5. Applied game design framework or heuristics check
Prototypes	Construct validity: The ability of the instrument to actually measure what it intends to measure. Is the game able to measure different skills it intends to measure?	Same as listed under Concepts, plus: 6. Playtest, with at least an appropriate outcome variable measurement
Integrations	Concurrent validity: The correlation between performance on the designed game and performance on an instrument. How does learning outcome compare to other methods assessing the same medical construct?	Same as listed under Prototypes, plus either/both: 7. A (quasi-)experiment or randomised controlled trial
	Predictive validity: Does performance in the game lead to better outcomes in reality? Does playing the game predict skills improvement in real life?	8. Stealth assessment: behavioral data gathering and analysis

Design Requirement Framework or Heuristic Check. To ensure that the design team has defined the right design requirements, we propose that the team juxtaposes their proposed requirements onto the following simple requirement framework/ heuristic. Thus the team asks, critically, 'have we covered all possible requirements in our design requirements list?'

Technological, Institutional and Legal/Policy Constraints. The preferred or required context of use will impose technological, institutional and legal constraints. For example, within the domain of education, a formal educational institute will always have certain computer hardware (e.g. PCs, smartboards) and facilities (e.g. computer labs) at its disposal that the team will at least need to be familiar with. They might also have a support staff for equipment lending, troubleshooting or security, complete with undefiable protocols and procedures. There might also be relevant regional or national legislation or policies in place.

Target Audience Specifics. An applied game design team designs for one or more specific target audiences who should be engaged by the game, intrinsically and/or extrinsically. This obligates the design team to know all about their target audiences. Without enough insights, the design team runs the risk of designing a product that falls short of the expectations. One common technique for defining for whom the designer actually designs is the development of one or more personas. Here personas are defined as 'a documented set of archetypal people who are involved with a product or service' [12].

Subject Matter Check. All applied games have subject matter, regardless of the domain in question (e.g. health, education). The subject matter behind an applied game for education might be medieval history of a certain country, or decision-making processes in national government, for example. Behind an applied game for health might be a tried-and-true physical or mental therapy model. In any case, the subject matter of the applied game design project will be easily identified, yet hard to define concretely. It nevertheless needs to be checked, probably through literature studies with or without the help of a subject matter expert.

SMART Goal Definition Check. Despite different interpretations of the acronym, SMART is essentially a validation technique for goal definitions, allowing for the design team to focus and collaborate. Our interpretation of the often-used SMART acronym is as follows:

- Specific, i.e., the goal is so specific that there is (seemingly) no room for mis- or reinterpretation.
- Measurable or Meaningful, i.e., the goal includes a quantified or qualified level of achievement, either in absolute or relative terms (e.g. playing the applied game should be more effective than some alternative).
- Achievable, i.e., based on their individual expertise, all design team members agree that the goal is actually attainable for the design team in question, given the allotted or preferred time frame.
- Relevant, i.e., the goal entails fulfilling a need or solving a problem through the acquisition of or a change in knowledge, skills, attitude or behavior, and does not encompass the exact nature of the design (e.g. not 'an online multiplayer computer game').
- Time-bound, i.e., a (rough) deadline for reaching the goal has been set and can be achieved within the allotted time.

The Achievable and Relevant criteria of the SMART goal validation technique require not only practical design experience, they also require the design team to do further research into disciplines relevant to the goal at hand and/or to collaborate with subject matter experts. For example, if the design team wishes to achieve a long-term behavioral change, the team would need to consult (recent) psychological studies and theories into the complexities of such an endeavor in order to ascertain whether and how it might actually be achievable within the desired time frame.

Specifications Check. Once the design requirements, subject matter and design goal have been validated, a concept or prototype can in turn be juxtaposed onto them as a next validation step. The design team thus simply asks, critically, 'does the concept or prototype fit the design requirements, subject matter and design goal that have been set?'

Applied Game Design Framework or Heuristics Check. Several frameworks, heuristics or design principles have been developed and published that applied game designers can use to validate their own concepts or prototypes. Such a validation entails juxtaposing the concept or prototype onto a chosen framework. The domain of the concept or prototype at hand (e.g. health or education) dictates which framework the design team could choose. Possible frameworks include:

- The Four Dimensional Framework [13] or Marne et al.'s framework [14] that forces an applied game designer to make several (e.g. pedagogical) foundations or facets explicit;
- The Triadic Game Design or similar frameworks [15–17], focusing on finding a balance between different requirements emanating from the 'worlds' of play, meaning and reality;
- More specific design principles by Dondlinger [18], Charsky [19] or Annetta [20], focusing on e.g. challenges, increased complexity or the use of avatars.

Playtest, with at Least an Appropriate Outcome Variable Measurement. Once a paper or digital prototype has been made, it can be tested. Such a test is essentially a strategy for validating the prototype. Usually this is done by structured observation of the play test (preferably by two observers using the same protocol). Primary concern during a play test is to ascertain to what extent the desired goal of the applied game is reached. The design team needs an indication if this first paper prototype reaches the desired goal for at least the majority of players. If not, it is back to the drawing board.

Yet structured observations of the knowledge, skills, attitude or behavior that the prototype should aim for might not be enough. Most times results of particularly first play tests will be ambivalent. Some players might do what is expected, many might not.

The question that then remains is simply, why? In order to even come close to an answer to this basic yet grand question, more data is required that provided by a structured observation as described above. It need to be complemented by more qualitative or quantitative data obtained from open or semi-structured interviews or questionnaire. In-game data capturing might also be used. Existing evaluation and assessment frameworks offer ample insights into what data should be obtained [3, 5, 6].

A (Quasi-)Experiment or Randomised controlled trial. If part of the design goal is to integrate a game in a certain context that serves its purpose better than its predecessor, a (quasi-)experiment or randomised controlled trial is the best final validation technique to apply. Think of an educational game that is meant to replace a lecture (series), since it is assumed that playing the game will have the students reach the learning objective more often than the lecture (series).

Often a quasi-experiment is the most practical to set up and also rigorous enough and most relevant for the purpose at hand. The design team forms two groups of comparable size and composition, and has the first group play the game, while the second group serves as the control group, doing the original activity that the game is meant to replace. A third comparable group might also be formed as another control group, doing something else entirely or even nothing at all, if the design team wants to ascertain whether the game not only performs better than the original activity, but that it has any added value to begin with. In any case, the same measurements must be applied to all groups, which includes a baseline measurement prior to the intervention (game or otherwise).

For an applied game where the stakes are extremely high, e.g. in the domain of health [21], a randomised controlled trial is probably essential, although it may require the help of a research specialist. This full-experiment setup has additional rigor thanks to its larger scale (i.e., it should involve many more participants with more diverse backgrounds), more longitudinal focus (multiple post-game/-intervention measurements are carried out over a period of days/weeks/months) and its stricter protocols concerning the assignment of participants (i.e., study personnel is unaware of the actual assignment).

Stealth Assessment: Behavioral Data Gathering and Analysis. To validate a full integration or implementation of an applied game, one can gather and analyze behavioral data obtained 'stealthily', i.e., unobtrusively by the software that is the applied game, or by e.g. having the game's facilitator keep the paraphernalia involved in gameplay. Several applied gaming case studies offer insights into the nature and usefulness of such behavioral data gathering and analysis [22, 23].

4 Discussion and Conclusion

This article has proposed a framework integrating validation in applied game design with an aim to extend the existing work on applied game validation. It further aims to contribute to the field of applied game design research and aid game design education. For many applied game designers, validation has been considered an afterthought. Playtesting and fine-tuning one's design are seen as essential to the process. Different types of validity were introduced to broaden the scope of validation, making it encompass more than just standard evaluation trials. Our framework for applied game design validation was introduced as based on iterative design and design fidelity dimensions. The proposed framework links four types of design fidelity (specifications, concepts, prototypes, and integrations) to five types of validity (content, face, construct, concurrent and predictive validity), leading to eight tools and techniques that designers can choose to use in order to perform a validation study throughout their applied game design process. An overview of applicable validation tools and techniques was included with an aim to make validation more accessible to designers.

Limitations of this approach are as follows. Some of the proposed validation tools and techniques arguably come very close to verification ('are we designing the game right?') rather than validation ('are we designing the right game?'). Those that come too close to verification, e.g. a prototype stress test, were expressly omitted from the framework. It is also important to be aware that not all applied game design frameworks, heuristics or principles have been extensively validated, even though we refer to them in our validation framework. Further research should focus on this.

Additionally, this is not a quantitative validation benchmark which can be used in simulation or large-scale AAA companies. It is also not a large-scale validation process that validates the totality of any game. Although our framework is thus meant to be applicable to different types of game design, it favors an iterative, user-centered, co-design approach as well as the domains of education and health because of our experience with them.

Future research should test and validate the proposed framework. This is a first step towards creating a tool both accessible and useful for designers. Then again, some of the validation tools and techniques we have proposed are hardly 'new', but tried-and-true or even self-evident. The novelty of the framework lies in how it connects the design process to validity types, not necessarily in all the individual validation tools and techniques themselves.

Additionally, future research should focus on further testing the model amongst designers, as the question remains, are designers going to use this framework and is it feasible to ask this of designers whose main aim might not be to validate their applied game? As of yet, we do not know the answer. We are aware that the different paradigms behind our framework (particularly game design and social science) can be conflicting and confusing. The challenge is to integrate them in a feasible manner which does not hinder the designer in attaining both validity and a game. This article is an attempt at that integration, and a first step towards creating tools that lower the barrier to applied game validity.

References

1. Bellotti, F., Kapralos, B., Lee, K., Moreno-Ger, P., Berta, R.: Assessment in and of serious games: an overview. Adv. Hum. Comput. Int. (2013). Article no. 136864
2. Graafland, M., Dankbaar, M., Mert, A., Lagro, J., De Wit-Zuurendonk, L., Schuit, S., Schaafstal, A., Schijven, M.: How to systematically assess serious games applied to health care. JMIR Serious Games 2, e11 (2014)
3. Mayer, I., Bekebrede, G., Harteveld, C., Warmelink, H., Zhou, Q., van Ruijven, T., Lo, J., Kortmann, R., Wenzler, I.: The research and evaluation of serious games: toward a comprehensive methodology. Br. J. Educ. Technol. 45, 502–527 (2014)
4. Sanchez, A., Cannon-Bowers, J., Bowers, C.: Establishing a science of game based learning. In: Cannon-Bowers, J., Bowers, C. (eds.) Serious Game Design and Development: Technologies for Training and Learning, pp. 290–304. IGI Global (2010)
5. Connolly, T., Stansfield, M., Hainey, T.: Towards the development of a games-based learning evaluation framework. In: Connolly, T., Stansfield, M., Boyle, L. (eds.) Games-Based Learning Advancements for Multi-sensory Human Computer Interfaces: Techniques and Effective Practices, pp. 251–273. IGI Global, Hershey (2009)
6. Kriz, W.C., Hense, J.U.: Theory-oriented evaluation for the design of and research in gaming and simulation. Simul. Gaming 37, 268–283 (2006)

7. Feinstein, A.H., Cannon, H.M.: Constructs of simulation evaluation. Simul. Gaming **33**, 425–440 (2002)
8. Mueller, R., Thoring, K.: Design thinking vs. lean startup: a comparison of two user-driven innovation strategies. Presented at the 2012 International Design Management Research Conference, Boston, MA, 8 August (2012)
9. Kelley, T., Littman, J.: The Art of Innovation: Lessons in Creativity from IDEO. America's Leading Design Firm. Random House, New York (2001)
10. Kelley, T., Littman, J.: The Ten Faces of Innovation: IDEO's Strategies for Defeating the Devil's Advocate and Driving Creativity Throughout Your Organization. Random House, New York (2005)
11. American Educational Research Association, American Psychological Association, National Council on Measurement in Education: Standards for Educational and Psychological Testing. American Educational Research Association, Washington, D.C. (1999)
12. Saffer, D.: Designing for Interaction: Creating Innovative Applications and Devices. New Riders, Berkeley (2010)
13. De Freitas, S., Oliver, M.: How can exploratory learning with games and simulations within the curriculum be most effectively evaluated? Comput. Educ. **46**, 249–264 (2006)
14. Marne, B., Wisdom, J., Huynh-Kim-Bang, B., Labat, J.-M.: The six facets of serious game design: a methodology enhanced by our design pattern library. In: Ravenscroft, A., Lindstaedt, S., Kloos, C.D., Hernández-Leo, D. (eds.) EC-TEL 2012. LNCS, vol. 7563, pp. 208–221. Springer, Heidelberg (2012)
15. Harteveld, C., Guimaraes, R., Mayer, I.S., Bidarra, R.: Balancing play, meaning and reality: the design philosophy of LEVEE PATROLLER. Simul. Gaming **41**, 316–340 (2010)
16. Harteveld, C.: Triadic Game Design: Balancing Reality, Meaning and Play. Springer-Verlag, London (2011)
17. Rooney, P.: A theoretical framework for serious game design: exploring pedagogy, play and fidelity and their implications for the design process. Int. J. Game-Based Learn. **2**, 41–60 (2012)
18. Dondlinger, M.J.: Educational video game design: a review of the literature. J. Appl. Educ. Technol. **4**, 21–31 (2007)
19. Charsky, D.: From edutainment to serious games: a change in the use of game characteristics. Games Cult. **5**, 177–198 (2010)
20. Annetta, L.A.: The "I's" have it: a framework for serious educational game design. Rev. Gen. Psychol. **14**, 105–112 (2010)
21. Kato, P.M., Cole, S.W., Bradlyn, A.S., Pollock, B.H.: A video game improves behavioral outcomes in adolescents and young adults with cancer: a randomized trial. Pediatrics **122**, e305–e317 (2008)
22. Shute, V.J., Ventura, M., Bauer, M., Zapata-Rivera, D.: Melding the power of serious games and embedded assessment to monitor and foster learning. In: Ritterfeld, U., Cody, M., Vorderer, P. (eds.) Serious Games: Mechanisms and Effects, pp. 295–321. Routledge, New York (2009)
23. Shute, V.J., Ventura, M.: Stealth Assessment: Measuring and Supporting Learning in Video Games. The MIT Press, Cambridge (2013)

Design of "TRASH TREASURE", a Characters-Based Serious Game for Environmental Education

Young-suk Lee[1(✉)] and Sang-nam Kim[2]

[1] Institute of Image and Cultural Contents, Dongguk University,
26 3-Ga Phil-Dong, Jung-Gu, Seoul 100-715, Korea
tonacoco@dongguk.edu
[2] Graduate School of Digital and Image, Dongguk University,
26 3-Ga Phil-Dong, Jung-Gu, Seoul 100-715, Korea
naminamiya@naver.com

Abstract. This study analyzed household wastes from the standpoint of resources, and designed TRASH TREASURE, a serious game for environmental education. A character is a critical factor to lead a serious game. The resource recycling process of household wastes is learned through characters appearing in the game. In addition, in terms of utilization of waste resource, resource circulation processes, including collection process, waste separation process, and the process of converting wastes to energy, were implemented in the game.

Keywords: TRASH TREASURE · Serious game · Environmental education · Game character

1 Introduction

The globe is at war against wastes. According to a report released in 2010, the wastes discharged only in New York City amounted to 33 million tons. With the growing urban scale, the issues of resources and wastes have emerged as critical ones to be addressed for sustainable development [2]. In June 2014, the 1st United Nations Environment Assembly (UNEA) held in Nairobi, Kenya, accepted 16 resolutions including internationally recommended actions for air pollution, illegal trading of wild animals, and waste treatment plans for ocean plastic wastes, chemicals, and waste disposal. In addition, the UN Post-2015 Development Agenda was aimed at sustainable consumption and production and sustainable development to raise awareness of wastes and waste resources. As such, environmental issues have become the most critical to human beings, but diverse methods to raise environmental perception have yet to be developed much. The waste issue is closely related to habits of everyday life, and thus what is the most critical is people's change of awareness and their will of action. A serious game means a game that includes entertainment elements and has special purposes [11, 12]. It is effective in conveying a subject clearly. Therefore, now is time to apply a serious game including educational functions and interesting elements to the

© Springer International Publishing Switzerland 2016
A. De Gloria and R. Veltkamp (Eds.): GALA 2015, LNCS 9599, pp. 471–479, 2016.
DOI: 10.1007/978-3-319-40216-1_52

environmental education of waste separation for young children and elementary students. Recently, the scale of the serious game market has been expanded. Serious games have greatly been developed in the US and Europe. They have been applied to various fields, such as medical science, public education, intellectual education, therapies, and national defense [8]. In Korea, the serious game market has also grown. The sales of serious games in Korea were estimated to account for around KRW 166.6 billion in 2013 [6]. However, unlike in the US and Europe, serious games in Korea have focused on education. With more importance of public education, serious games for public education have grown, and especially, such games related to the environment have tended to be developed [8, 12].

Previous studies of serious games tended to define the concept of a serious game or analyze its system structure. That is because a serious game that has the features of game is recognized to be a training tool simply to implement a purpose. Therefore, this researcher tried to approach a serious game as a awareness tool for environmental issues, rather than as a training tool. In addition, unlike other researchers, this researcher paid attention to characters and storytelling of a serious game in order to design a method of delivering a purpose effectively.

Therefore, this study tried to develop a serious game for the purpose of environmental education for children to recycle waste resource for children. The study objectives to develop the program are set forth as follows:

- Based on previous studies, the elements of a serious game are analyzed, and the factors required to change environment awareness are established.
- Based on the elements and factors, user-friendly characters and stories for more effective information conveyance and awareness change are developed.
- For the purposes of users' awareness change and of information conveyance, a serious game for the environment is designed.

2 Serious Game

2.1 Serious Game

A serious game is effective in delivering a special purpose, and is helpful to offer knowledge and improve cognitive ability. In addition, it is effective in the areas requiring repeated training and for the change in awareness [12]. The game is developed for the purposes of awareness change and repeated training so that it is designed for particular users and features immediate feedback. Therefore, a serious game can be applicable to a wide range of areas. In particular, such a game has been developed for diverse purposes including military training, education, occupational training, and health care.

Unlike general games developed for fun, a serious game featuring accomplishment of purposes is mostly considered to be a sort of tool. A serious game uses a game as an effective tool for a purpose, and thus it has fewer entertainment factors than conventional games [11] (Table 1).

Table 1. Differences between entertainment games and serious games [11].

	Serious games	Entertainment games
Task vs. Rich experience	*Problem solving in focus*	*Rich experiences preferred*
Focus	*Important elements of learning*	*To have fun*
Simulations	*Assumptions necessary for workable simulations*	*Simplification processes*
Communication	*Should reflect natural*	*Communication is often perfect*

Many researchers defined a serious game as the computer-based game developed to achieve a critical purpose, rather than to focus on entertainment that conventional games concentrate on [9]. Basically, regarding design and other factors, a serious game is different from the games for industrial purposes. Unlike conventional games, a serious game lay stress on educational element rather than on fun element, the main purpose of general games. A game direction changes depending on its main goal. In a serious game, the course of solving a problem is more important than the final outcome that a user obtains. For this reason, a serious game needs to take into account more factors than general games.

A serious game is also a sort of game so that it doesn't exclude the factors of conventional games. Such a point is proved by the cases where some serious games emphasizing only functions without entertainment disappeared immediately after development. When the features of general games, such as concrete purposes, active motivation for users, and immediate feedback, are provided to serious games, users can get immersed in the games. Although an extent of immersion does not affect purpose accomplishment directly [1], it can enhance the hours users spend in games. Immersion has something to do with continuance of games and effective purpose accomplishment. In particular, in the education area, it is very important for users to recognize knowledge naturally through their immersion. In other words, a serious game needs to maintain user entertainment sufficiently and accomplish its main purpose. For this reason, it is necessary to develop a serious game that meets its purposes in the whole process ranging from game development to the outcome drawn user experience. Given that, a serious game should be different from general games in the aspects of planning and design. In the case of public issues including environmental issue, such a game is developed for the purpose of awareness change. The most important objective in the environmental education is to bring about the change in awareness of educatees. Such serious games as health care or e-learning are aimed at conveyance of knowledge and training of action, whereas serious games related to the environment are effective to raise and change awareness of environmental issues, rather than to knowledge conveyance [4]. That shows the most significant elements handled in public education.

The change in awareness is made by users' action taken in games. Users make their decisions to solve game tasks designed for their purposes. They behave depending on their judgment and take feedback immediately according to their action. Such users' actions create a game cycle [3]. Through repetition of the game cycle, users take information, have training of actions, or make changes.

According to the analysis on recent trends of serious games [12], the game features affecting users are awareness tool and game task. In particular, awareness tool is associated with information imaging [10].

Visualization of a concept is also a critical factor of a serious game [5]. As shown in previous studies, image based information is more effective to users than text based information. That is because visual information makes awareness easier to users than text information. Therefore, it is important to convert a difficult concept into visual element. Through awareness of familiar images, users are able to take information immediately and show reaction quickly.

Based on previous studies, the elements taken into account in serious games are presented as follows:

- Clarity of game purpose
- Motivation for users through concrete goals
- Inducement of users' action and creation of game cycle through immediate feedback
- Security of immersion through the control of a proper level and the task associated with a final purpose
- Information imaging and awareness tool based information conveyance

2.2   Game Characters

A character as a main factor of digital contents includes a particular disposition. It can serve as diverse roles depending on contents types. In particular, a character can become not only a human being, but can be impersonated as an animal or a plant. A character is the most important factor in a plot, and a core entity to lead OSMU (One Sours Multi Use). In the contents business, a character is associated with diverse culture contents business groups and generates economic added-value as a core item. Therefore, a character represents a product in itself. As a tool to spread communication, a character produces a great deal of economic value in association with derivatives of other contents. Previous studies extracted the elements required for serious games, but failed to focus on characters and storytelling which are directly related to game features and immersion. Although they mentioned the importance of image based information effect and the importance of immersion, they never mentioned characters and stories for them. Immersion helps to enhance continuance time of games. The elements for immersion are challenge, curiosity, and fantasy [7]. To meet them, it is important to assign proper roles to each character.

A character is a core factor in the point that it is used for a user to reflect itself and increase its immersion in games. In addition, a character helps a user approach an uninteresting theme emotionally, and thus can be used as an awareness tool of users. In particular, unlike adults who can get educated through simulation, young children are able to visualize a character as their 2nd self and experience actual action training and knowledge conveyance. In this aspect, now is time to develop a serious game based on characters and storytelling which is aimed at environmental education for young children and elementary students.

Therefore, this study tried to set up characters for young children and design a serious game based on the characters for environmental education, which can trigger awareness change and action.

3 Serious Game of Environment Education

3.1 Game Design

In this chapter, the serious game was designed based on the characters as the plan for effective realization of the problem of recognizing environment. First, serious game content for education was planned based on the practical resolution of household waste-related problem through the education in our real daily life.

The seriousness of increased amount of food waste has become the social issue in Korea together with meter-rate system of food waste recently. The trends of researches on food waste and environment become dynamic targeting the elementary school students. Especially, it is the time to require the custom-tailored environment education at the level of infants and elementary school students due to full operation of food service at elementary schools and explosive increase of food waste. It is also the time that we are facing exhaustion of food and energy resources, global warming, destruction of ecosystem, disposal of increased waste and filled ground seriously. And it is willing to teach the children the various life habits for environment through the games since they are young. It forwards the message that classification of waste and recycling process with the game characters in the easy and fun way and it enables them to recognize that the waste that he or she throw away is the article that he or she purchase by themselves.

So, this study planned the contents focusing on the characters for the emersion of serious game for environment education. It realized the process that classifies recyclable waste and resourcing in our daily life in the point of view of infants and elementary school students. And the data of environmental waster in life was analyzed and it was processed to be suitable for the contents. After that, the characters were designed based on the analyzed data and entire game was designed. And the plan for visualizing the serious game contents was sought by suggesting the prototype.

3.2 Character Design

Main characters and family characters were composed by taking the waste as the motive in this chapter. And the visualization plan was sought. The characters to perform the game consist of 2 kinds of main characters and 6 kinds of supporting characters. The characters appeared in digital contents are personified by taking human, animal and plant as the motive. The personification expresses the emotion or personality with the shape of animal or plant. Especially, in case of animation, the cast is created along the role from the first. That is, the personality of the characters are given along the intention of planning the characters and the characters are produced properly along the personality.

That is, the personality of character is given along the intention of planning and the story in digital contents and the characters are produced along the personality. Design factors to be considered when designing the characteristics of the characters by expressing them all are personality, proportion, shape and color.

First, the personality of characters are the most basic element that defines the characters. The personality is expressed first in the appearance of the characters and they are expressed by the look or form of behavior second time. So, the external setting that shows the personality is the important factor first. The exact personality setting from planning is the important factor that decides whole design of the characters.

The personality of the characters was set first in the planning process. This character was produced with life-size SD character to be suitable for serious game contents for mobile. And external shape of the character originated from basic figure such as square and triangle.

Looking into shape of the characters and characteristics of color, 2 kinds of main characters are <TRASH> that symbolizes tray bin and <Dr. Bin> that symbolizes the natural life. This is the personification of waste basket and bean that is the plant (Fig. 1). The first purpose of this game is to the collect classification of waste and change of recognition against waste. So, the waste basket was visualized as the main character by giving the symbolic meaning that collects the waste. The change of recognition was induced by setting the waste basket as the main character and giving the positive meaning. Dr. Bin that represents the nature means bean that is the plant. Bean has the strong vitality as the plant that grows up well anywhere worldwide. It plays the role of carrying out the game (Fig. 2).

Fig. 1. Main character "TRASH" and "Dr. Bin".

Fig. 2. Sub character "Mr. Owl" and "Captain Acorn", "Ping", "Windy", "Hittie".

There is <Mr. Owl> as the supporting character taking owl as the motive. The Mr. Owl is the character that takes in charge of the education for protecting environment as the role of guardian and supervisor. <Ping> was named from <Pink> that is the color of earthworm taking it as the motive. Earthworm takes in charge of representative purification and plays the role that provides the hint that is helpful for learning of the users. And there is <captain acorn> that personifies the squirrel. The squirrel is the animal at the endangered step that requires the attention that plays the role of leading the exploring team. And there are <Windy> and <Hittie>. These two are the visualization of filth as the interrupter of proceeding the game.

3.3   Suggestion of Prototype

TRASH TREASURE is the serious game of environment education for smart device (Android ver.). It is designed and produced in various mini game types. Each character offered in the previous clause is the mean to provide the educational information for the learners by being input to this course and takes in charge of supporting the process of the game.

Total 4 types of structure were set as below (Fig. 3)

Fig. 3. Process of collecting the waste.

First, the kinds of waste is learned through the process of collecting the waste as the process that collects and withdraws the waste.

Second, it shows the correct classification process of recyclable waste as the process of classifying the waste.

Third, it is the process of energization. The kinds of combustible waste and incombustible one are learned and environmental problem that can happen in case of burning incombustible waste is recognized. And the burnt combustible waste can be utilized as the energy resource that develops the city by energizing themselves.

Fourth, it is the process of making the recyclable waste be resources as the treating process. It is learned that the resource is secured by reusing the waste resources and various wastes can be used as the resources (Fig. 4).

Fig. 4. Correct classification process of recyclable waste.

4 Conclusion

This study suggested the serious game of environment education for smart device (Android ver.), "TRASH TREASURE". The process of collecting, classifying, energyzing and processing was shown in various mini games from the process that plans and designs the game characters. Each character plays the role that supports or helps the game for the learners as the core element of the game by being input to this process. Especially, the character should be used as one of tools to attract the emersion in serious game. And it is expected that the serious game grows up rapidly as the core field that can lead the technology and contents of next generation. At this time, the environmental problem should be recognized and waste should be researched in respect of resource. And the development of serious game that can implement the recycle of resource in daily life is the important issue to be discussed definitely. The production of various serious games should be discussed and developed in dynamic way regarding environment education.

Acknowledgments. This research was supported by Basic Science Research Program through the National Research Foundation of Korea (NRF) funded by the Ministry of Education, Science and Technology (2014R1A1A1005863).

References

1. Galimberti, C., Ignazi, S., Vercesi, P., Riva, G.: Communication and cooperation in networked environments: an experimental analysis. CyberPsychol. Behav. **4**, 131–146 (2001)
2. Kennedy, C., Ibrahim, N., Stewart, I., Facchini, A., Mele, R.: Research ProjectMegacities: Comparative analysis of urban macrosystems. An urban metabolism survey design for megacities, University of Toronto and Enel Foundation (2014)
3. Garris, R., Ahlers, R., Driskell, J.E.: Games, motivation, and learning: a research and practice model. Simul. Gaming **33**(4), 441–467 (2002)

4. Kim, H.-M., Lim, S.: How playing a serious game affects the player's perception of the environmental issues. Korean Soc. Comput. Game **27**(3), 69–76 (2014)
5. Belanich, J., Orvis, K.L., Mullin, L.N.: Instructional characteristics and motivational features of a PC-based game. Mil. Psychol. **25**(3), 206–217 (2013)
6. KOCCA: 2014 Korea Serious Games Business Report, KOCCA (2014)
7. Malone, T.W.: Toward a theory of instrinsically motivating instruction. Cogn. Sci. **5**, 333–369 (1981)
8. Marketsandmarkets: Serious Game Market by Vertical (Education, Corporate, Healthcare, Retail, Media and Advertising), Application (Training, Sales, Human Resource, Marketing), Platform, End-User (Enterprise, Consumer), and Region - Forecast to 2020 (2015). marketsandmarkets.com
9. Michael, T., Prince, C., Salas, E.: Can PC-based systems enhance teamwork in the cockpit? Int. J. Aviat. Psychol. **15**(2), 173–187 (2005)
10. Nova, N., Dillenbourg, P., Wehrle, T., Goslin, J., Bourquin, Y.: The impacts of awareness tools on mutual modelling in a collaborative video-game. In: Favela, J., Decouchant, D. (eds.) CRIWG 2003. LNCS, vol. 2806, pp. 99–108. Springer, Heidelberg (2003)
11. Susi, T., Johannesson, M., Backlund, P.: Serious Games – An Overview, Technical report, School of Humanities and Informatics. University of Skövde, Sweden (2007)
12. Wouters, P., van der Spek, E.D., van Oostendorp, H.: Current practices in serious game research: a review from a learning outcomes perspective. In: Connolly, T.M., Stansfield, M., Boyle, L. (eds.) Games-Based Learning Advancements for Multisensory Human Computer Interfaces: Techniques and Effective Practices (2009)

A Gamified News Application for Mobile Devices: An Approach that Turns Digital News Readers into Players of a Social Network

Catherine Sotirakou[✉] and Constantinos Mourlas

Faculty of Communication and Media Studies, University of Athens, Athens, Greece
{katerinasot,mourlas}@media.uoa.gr

Abstract. Gamification is a well known approach nowadays for achieving the ultimate goal of motivating loyalty with a brand and engaging users with given tasks in a variety of fields. However, attempts made to use gamification techniques in news industry have given poor results, pointing to the conclusion that journalism may not an open field for gamification to thrive. At the same time changes in news consumption across the globe show a rapid rise of news audiences accessing stories through their mobile devices, while social media play a huge role in distribution of online news. This paper examines the combination of these three trends, gamification, smartphones and social media in a promising and possibly successful way.

Keywords: Gamification · Game design · Digital media · Journalism · Mobile news reader · Social interaction

1 Introduction

Gamification according to recent academic publications can be a powerful human motivator and has already being utilized in domains that collect user-generated content such as mobile social reporting and citizen sensing [4, 9, 31] with remarkable outcome. Gamification is a promising mechanism to motivate people to use an application more often [28] and derive fun from their activity [3, 10, 12, 31, 32].

Digitalization, which results from rising penetration of smartphones and tablets on news consumption, along with the social media networks providing readers access to digital news throughout the day, offers space for a platform that combines news and social media. A vast majority of the readers instead of going directly to stories via a brand's homepage, uses a side door like Facebook or Twitter. As news industry becomes more dependent on different distribution platforms to find audiences over time, business strategies are forced to change. A promising approach is that of Gamification. We propose an alternative approach on gamifying digital news, by adjusting the effective principles of game design to a news ecosystem, consisted of social media friends.

© Springer International Publishing Switzerland 2016
A. De Gloria and R. Veltkamp (Eds.): GALA 2015, LNCS 9599, pp. 480–493, 2016.
DOI: 10.1007/978-3-319-40216-1_53

2 Journalism in Digital Age

Current Trends in Digital News. A key focus for the news industry over the past years has been trying to reach a wider audience, especially in younger demographics, subscribing to content, but there has been limited success.

According to recent reports [19, 20, 33] smartphones are the main devices for accessing digital news, causing a significant impact on consumption formats, while Facebook plays a dominant role in finding, discussing and sharing the news. The same report underlines the fact that even though 70 % of smartphone users have a news application installed on their phone, only a third uses it to read articles in a given week [20].

For that reason news companies have started to focus on their articles creation (changed format, added pictures, short-form video formats) and distribution through multiple channels to capture new audiences [29], while at the same time experiment with new ways to improve content by making it more relevant and valuable to each user.

Merging digital news and digital play could be an interesting combination to promote news readers and to increase user's motivation, however previous attempts had not given successful results as we can see in the following paragraphs.

Previous Attempts. Following the rise of gamification, popular news companies have adopted this idea into practice with the intent to gain greater user involvement and loyalty. Although famous news organizations like "Google News" for instance, had been extremely popular to younger people, the moment they started to gamify, the experience changed and users did not respond as planned, so months later the companies ended those services.

Research on users [8, 17] have shown that introducing a gamification layer to existing systems can obscure the main purpose of the application and therefore be perceived as disruptive to the main activity. A recent example is "Google News badges".

At 2011 Google News invested in game mechanics and introduced to its audience "Google News badges", users could earn 500 different emblems, for reading news stories for particular topics. As the user became more well-read the service added a star to the badge for that topic. Totally the user could receive five different levels of stars, bronze, silver, gold, platinum and the ultimate star. However, game rules were not clear, whereas guidance, instant feedback or sense of progress were apparent for the user to understand how to play and the experience quickly became confusing and frustrating. Thus, the given approach reduced the navigational freedom of the users, disrupted the main activity of reading the news and decreased the total usability and user's satisfaction levels.

These failures imply that if news were to use game rewards, it would have to rely on the real benefits games provide for players, such as a sense of achievement and a progression to mastery [9, 31]. People should feel like they have accomplished something unique or difficult, or that they outplayed their friends. Extrinsic motivations are not enough to engage users when they harm intrinsic motivation [6].

3   Gamification

Gamification has been proven to increase engagement, motivation and loyalty, when adjusted to mobile applications and marketing strategies, while other reports show that users who enjoy a playful activity are willing to spend more time on a task that they find interesting. [12, 14, 15, 30, 31].

Gamification attempts to harness the motivational power of games in order to promote participation, persistence and achievements [23]. The application of game design principles to non game environments renders technology more inviting, by engaging users in desired behaviors by showing the path to mastery, providing constant feedback and utilizing people's innate enjoyment of play. Studies have indicated [18, 27] that applying gamification elements in enterprise software and workplaces results in better user engagement.

The work described in this paper confronts the shortcomings of gamification adjustment to digital news by sorting out the reasons of previously tested successful implementations and best practices in other areas of applications. We initially started by the study of gamification issues related to motivational theories of psychology.

Games are able to trigger player's own intrinsic motivations by engaging them to overcome self-imposed challenges and put their skills to the test. After that there is the need to get feedback and see how well they are doing. Game elements such as points, badges and leaderboards used within a news reader application can clarify task goals and provide clear feedback. Customized suggestions that result to rewards, allow a sense of autonomy in personal goal setting [7, 16, 23].

Motivation and Gamification.   Many studies have been conducted to identify which internal motives lead people to action [1, 2, 11, 24, 25, 27, 30]. Current approaches concern two dominant clusters that play a role in determining player's motivation: extrinsic and intrinsic motivation [6, 25]. The idea of using game mechanics and dynamics to drive participation and engagement, mostly by using extrinsic rewards can undermine free choice, self reported interest in the given task and reduce pre-existing intrinsic motivation [6, 17]. To prevent this from happening, Nicholson's proposal of "meaningful gamification" is followed in this application. According to this proposal, users are able to find "meaningful connections with the underlying non-game activities" [21].

Meaningful gamification has a user-centred approach and focuses on Self-Determination Theory that sets three main human needs, autonomy, competency, and relatedness [25]. Gameful activities can satisfy the need to control the outcome of a situation and when playful activities occur in groups, social interactions arise which further contribute to satisfy the need to compete, interact, connect and belong [5]. Therefore different users find meaning in alternative features, so by allowing users to learn through the system what is meaningful to them, they can recognize and set their own goals.

Meanwhile, for some users, a point system attached to public status is important, although for others is meaningless, whereas their ranking on the leaderboard appears to be more engaging. Providing multiple ways to achieve within the gamification system allows users to select the most meaningful methods to them [22]. Empirical evidence also suggests that forced serious game play is less enjoyable and effective and autonomy appears to be a key factor to successful use of gamification [9].

4   Designing a Gamified News Reader for Mobile Devices

Our Design Methodology. Based on the motivational theories [6, 10, 30, 26] and the game principles explained above, we tried to design an approach that links mobile news, games and social media networks, via a mobile application.

The application takes into account also the recommendations of Zichermann and Cunningham [32], who underline the fact that the first minute of use can determine whether that user will continue to use the application in the long-term or whether they will delete it in seconds. Also suggests a quick tutorial that walks the user through the gamified interface, plus a welcome bonus and a social engagement loop through social media networks.

According to an approach described by Deterding [8], designers have to find "skill atoms", a feedback loop between player and game that is organized around challenges or skills that the player is trying to master so they fulfill their goal pursuits. A skill atom consists of goals, actions, tokens, feedback, a rule system, challenge, and the user's skill. The fripside of skill atom, is that after it is fully mastered, the intrinsic interest is gone, therefore for the system to continue to be engaging it must be more complex, challenging and user-centered designed. A game design has to incorporate user's goals and needs, as Kumar [18] noted "The first step in the player design approach is to understand the player and their context". The success of gamification efforts depends on this clear understanding.

Here we are developing a gameful system to facilitate the social interactions between users through a gamified news reader that provides personalized stories to its users through social feeds. The use of social networks like Facebook and Twitter contributes to building personalization algorithms and forming a sense of community.

Our application is primarily a community-based, third-party platform that features personalized news stories in the feeds of its users, using gamification elements to gain their engagement and commitment. The incentive strategy we used is based on badges, reward points, levels and leaderboards.

The Design Process. The application was designed following a user-centered approach [13], including identification, documentation of user's needs and generating interactive prototypes that can be evaluated, a fuller description of the methodology we used follows.

We started by contacting an initial data gathering and analysis of the spaces of exploration and defining target audience. Our top news consumers according to our research are young people 18–35, who own mobile devices, are comfortable using electronic equipment and have at least an average experience in gaming. Thus older demographics appeared to be quite interested in using our platform, so we assured ease of access for all users by developing an efficient and simple user interface that captures all individual needs.

Afterwards, we designed comprehensive online questionnaires to capture all aspects of news consumption and preferences in game elements. The collected data suggest that news accessed from social media has jumped significantly, as audiences consume the majority of their online news, following stories shown on their social feeds. Our findings also suggest that distribution of journalism happen through social networks as people sometimes leave their daily news updates to friends and family along with some news brands they follow in social media networks.

We made an inventory of what our responders think is important to them and conduct a set of user requirements to be used during ideation. After identifying, documenting and agreeing on specific usability and user experience goals, we conducted focus groups, card sorting techniques, and task analysis methods, until we had determined some promising concepts, in order to make interactive prototypes. Therefore we set those objectives and integrated these dynamics into the mobile application. We decided to gamify the parts that allow for user acquisition, engagement and behavior modification.

Game Design. Award based systems can define goals and send immediate feedback to encourage users to engage to the main activity of reading articles, as well as being on the leaderboard and sharing the experience in social media can strengthen social bonds and promote competition.

The player's journey has progression steps, illustrated by an award collecting system which can be monitored any time through user's profile screen (Fig. 5). On a first level, users earn points for every step they complete within the application (registering, reading, commenting) and also get a variety of colorful badges as a status signifier for their exceptional choices in news stories. On a second level, the system keeps the reader's score (Fig. 5) and based on the total points (Table 1) the reader has collected, he/she is able to unlock new levels.

In the mobile platform we propose, when a user finishes reading an article about politics, the system rewards her with points and suggests articles from different categories or articles her friends liked. By providing personalized suggestions and simultaneously give constant feedback, users feel a sense of control, freedom and a feeling that the system rewards them for their own choices.

When gamifying an experience, having rules along with a scoring system that allocates specific point values to actions, it can push gamers to engage with the main activity, which in our case is reading more news articles.

Applying game elements in a serious platform like news, remains a form of play, so we set our goal to make a well-designed game to allow the player to use playful interactions such as curiosity, creativity, and improvisation to find new ways that lead to pleasure and fun while reading the news.

We provide a non-confusing and aesthetically pleasing gamified environment, dominated by news stories imported via RSS feeds from sites and blogs, where readers can choose their favorite topics, read stories, rate the content, share their experience and get rewards for all their activities.

Table 1. The provided point system

Point value	Point awards for player activities	
	Activity	Purpose
100 points	Create an account	Early welcome bonus
200 points	Import friends	Have users imported their social media connections
5 points	Read an article	Have users read articles
30 points	Share a story or reward	Have users shared their experience
15 points	Read a suggested article from a different category	Have users read more articles & explore
10 points	Comment	Have users commented the content
5 points	Favorite	Have users rate the content
50 points	Create profile	Have users input their characteristics
100 points	Suggest to a friend	Have users invited their friends
50 points	Visit once per day	Have users rewarded for coming back frequently

Design Guidelines. In order to promote the basic functionalities of the news reader and keep the users engaged without overshadowing the real purpose of the application we incorporated the following techniques:

- Meaningful rewards, which lead to real life advantages, so extrinsic motivation does not harm previously existing intrinsic urges in staying ahead of the news and gaining knowledge and at the same time develop more intrinsic motivation concerning the news consumption.
- Simplification, step by step user's onboarding to the game, to avoid her being overwhelmed and perceive the system as difficult and abstruse.
- Discretion, game elements are incorporated in harmony into the system, almost invisible, to avoid users to focus on the gamification layer and supplant the mission of the application.
- Instant Gratification, helps the user understand her next actions, sets the rules and defines gamer's goals. Unexpected rewards will follow, after the user has a clear view of the game.
- Autonomy, users are not forced to take any kind of actions. Users are free to choose if they are willing to interact with the gamified features and engage further; otherwise they can always hide game elements from their profile settings, even not register, because sing up is optional, thus playing in order to work, needs to be voluntary [31].

- Privacy, the user can explore the application, share information with his friends and get positive feedback for her choices. There is no automated sharing system, so the user does not feel violated and his friends are not spammed in social networks.
- Social Interaction, players establish a "play community", that according to De Koven, is what direct players toward a game, thus it matters less what game they are playing and more that they are playing together [5].

Visual Design and Evaluation Process. Nevertheless, no gamification implementation is perfect, at least at first, so in order to avoid unintentional flaws in the system that can result to unwanted user behaviors, we tested the model using interactive prototypes.

We had some useful expert reviews in order to spot usability errors and we conducted simple testing from users, to get feedback and determine which features work and which don't. After that we changed our design and we developed new prototypes in order to come closer to a more successful gamified experience and higher levels of users' satisfaction. Below a simple but typical user scenario is given, describing the sequence of steps that a user will follow in order to read news articles and interact with the application.

A Typical User Scenario. After downloading the application user gets the description of the news reader and a quick tutorial of how the system works (Fig. 1). Then, user decides if she wants to sing up with Facebook or another preexisting account (when system automatically imports theirs friends), register or continue without creating a profile. After registration she is asked to choose her favorite news topics, so the system could customize the user's experience (Fig. 2). Instant feedback is very significant at this point, so some points and a welcome badge are an excellent way to reward her desired behavior, (the user just provided her favorite news categories to the platform) and keep the player from starting playing with no points (Fig. 3). The newsfeed is ready with personalized suggestions (Fig. 4) and the user can start reading. While she reads various articles, points are awarded to her along with new badges, statistics, stars that represent levels and a leaderboard. The accumulated information stored on user's profile (Fig. 5) and accessed through the main menu screen (Fig. 7), indicate the player's ranking, status and achievements, promoting greater engagement. Social interactions are important for increasing user's motivation, so share buttons are available to all the content and rewards, along with a friends' activities screen (Fig. 6), similar to Facebook's sidebar activity feed.

Fig. 1. The first screen of the application with a brief introduction and no clear hints to the gamification layer. Gamification designed to be discrete making user's journey and the first experience simple adding more value later on.

Fig. 2. Optimizing the experience. User picks at least 3 categories of news stories, so the system can begin to optimize his experience, offering personalized suggestions.

Fig. 3. First Badge. An early welcome bonus is the base upon we build a gamified design according to Zickerman [32]. In this point we want to define the main activities we want the player to participate. Users have to know what is going on and be prepared for the game journey that is ahead of them.

Fig. 4. News Feed. A list of stories is displayed along with "SAVE" feature. The user can save the article he finds interesting and read it later.

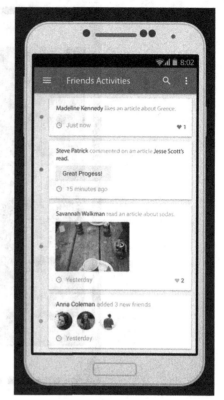

Fig. 5. Profile. By maintaining some user score, he can gradually unlock features (new badges, levels) based on the score resulted from his actions (sharing, commenting).

Fig. 6. Friends & Sharing

The Visual Prototypes. From the moment user is on board, the system starts rewarding her gradually with small expected and unexpected rewards.

Users can also visit the profile screen and get to flaunt their achievements. Users like statistics when it makes them look good. For example a user would want the world to see her in a certain way – and might do not want to have 100 % score on gossip category. Making personal consumption data public can distort behavior, so in this screen only the best score is visible to the public and overall statistics are available only to the user.

The leaderboard makes comparisons amongst friends and provides a sense of accomplishment and achievement. Its purpose is to make the user look good, so we chose the "no-disincentive leaderboard", that puts the player always in the middle, her actual ranking order is of no matter [32], except she is in the top of the list.

People want to complete the need of relatedness. Our research results suggest that users enjoy being connected to, like commenting on articles shared on their friends' wall on Facebook and would like not only to compete with each other, but have the opportunity to make personalized suggestions to their friends.

Fig. 7. Main menu

In our implementation there are buttons that enable users to share their achievements on their social-media networks. This gives to users a sense of achievement, making them more likely to stay engaged (see Fig. 6).

Card sorting results suggested that the users want to have easy access through the menu screen to their profile, newsfeed, search, friends, news folders, settings and logout (see Fig. 7).

User's actions are more formally represented in the following activity diagram (Fig. 8):

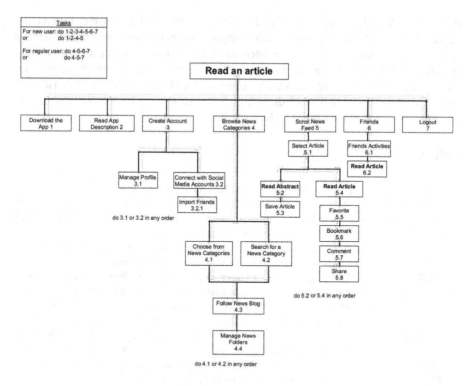

Fig. 8. Activity diagram

5   Conclusion

One of the most compelling challenges of adding game design elements to a serious environment, such as news, is how to support and promote the main activity of reading news stories via a news reader, while avoiding readers from focusing only on the attractive game features provided.

In this paper, we tried to design an innovative mobile reader towards this direction, implementing game elements into mobile news so that we improve user's experience, usability and user's satisfaction. As we have seen by using the above approach we have created a gamified environment where the user can read news stories as he would normally do, but in this case the system delivers personalized suggestions while at the same time rewards the users for their reading habits. The approach detailed above harnesses play in certain ways in order to promote greater user's involvement. The user reads an article from the personalized news feed, earns some points and a badge, that later shares to the social media network creating a new topic for discussion. Rewards do not only make users flaunt their achievements in the profile screen, but challenge them by triggering an intrinsic motivation to be better and become experts on their favorite topics. This desired behavior increases user's engagement and results in greater digital news consumption as compared to a news reader without the gamification layer.

We have proposed an approach that the user does not read and leave, instead she discreetly enters a world of game, which through constant feedback, real life challenges and social networking, aims to greater user engagement. In our opinion, it is a promising approach for implementing a gamified application on the challenging media ecosystem, giving a set of design practices that we believe can result to the development of a playful environment that does not distract users from the main activity, but encourages them to develop motivation related to the activity itself.

References

1. Bartle, R.A.: Designing Virtual Worlds. New Riders, Berkeley (2004)
2. Bartle, R.: Hearts, clubs, diamonds, spades: players who suit MUDs. J. MUD Res. **1**(1),19 (1996). Richard Bartle's webpage, http://mud.co.uk/richard/hcds.htm. Accessed 15 Jan 2015
3. Caillois, R.: Man, Play and Games. The Free Press, New York (1961)
4. Crowley, D., Breslin, J., Corcoran, P., Young, K.: Gamification of citizen sensing through mobile social reporting. In: Proceedings of Games Innovation Conference 2012. IEEE (2012)
5. De Koven, B.: The Well-Played Game: A Player's Philosophy. MIT Press, Cambridge (2013)
6. Deci, E.L., Koestner, R., Ryan, R.M.: A meta-analytic review of experiments examining the effects of extrinsic rewards on intrinsic motivation. Psychol. Bull. **125**(6), 627 (1999)
7. Deterding, S., Dixon, D., Khaled, R., Nacke, L.: From game design elements to gamefulness: defining "gamification". In: Proceedings of the 15th International Academic MindTrek Conference: Envisioning Future Media Environments, New York, NY, USA, pp. 9–15 (2011)
8. Deterding, S.: Skill atoms as design lenses for user-centered gameful design. In: From the CHI 2013 Workshop on Designing Gamification, Paris, France (2013)
9. Deterding, S.: Eudaimonic design, or: six invitations to rethink gamification. In: Fuchs, M., Fizek, S., Ruffino, P., Schrape, N. (eds.) Rethinking Gamification, pp. 305–331. Meson Press, Lüneburg (2014)
10. Deterding, S., Sicart, M., Nacke, L., O'Hara, K., Dixon, D.: Gamification: using game design elements in non-gaming contexts. In: Proceedings of CHI 2011, pp. 2425–2428. ACM Press, New York (2011)
11. Ferro, L.S., Walz, S.P., Greuter, S.: Towards personalised, gamified systems: an investigation into game design, personality and player typologies. In: Proceedings of the 9th Australasian Conference on Interactive Entertainment: Matters of Life and Death, New York, NY, USA, pp. 7:1–7:6 (2013)
12. Fontijn, W., Hoonhout, J.: Functional fun with tangible user interfaces. In: Proceedings from DIGITEL 2007 in 1st IEEE International Workshop on Digital Game and Intelligent Toy Enhanced Learning, Jhongli, Taiwan, pp. 119–123 (2007)
13. Garrett, J.J.: The Elements of User Experience: User-Centered Design for the Web and Beyond. Pearson Education, New York (2010)
14. Hamari, J., Koivisto, J.: Measuring flow in gamification: dispositional flow scale-2. Comput. Hum. Behav. **40**, 133–143 (2014)
15. Huotari, K., Hamari, J.: Defining gamification - a service marketing perspective. In: Proceedings of the 16th International Academic MindTrek Conference, Tampere, Finland, 3–5 October 2012 (2012)
16. Jung, J., Schneider, C., Valacich, J.: Enhancing the motivational affordance of information systems: the effects of real-time performance feedback and goal setting in group collaboration environments. Manag. Sci. **56**(4), 724–742 (2010)

17. Knaving, K., Björk, S.: Designing for fun and play: exploring possibilities in design for gamification. In: Gamification 2013 (2013)
18. Kumar, J.: Design, User Experience, and Usability: Health, Learning, Playing, Cultural, and Cross-Cultural User Experience. LNCS, vol. 8013, pp. 528–537. Springer, Heidelberg (2013)
19. Mitchell, A., et al.: The Explosion in Mobile Audiences and a Close Look at What It Means for News, Future of Mobile News. Journalism.org (2012). http://www.journalism.org/2012/10/01/future-mobile-news/. Accessed 1 Oct 2012
20. Newman, N., Levy., D.A.L., Nielsen, R.K.: Reuters Institute Digital News Report 2015 (2015). http://dx.doi.org/10.2139/ssrn.2619576. Accessed June 2015
21. Nicholson, S.: Two paths to motivation through game design elements: reward-based gamification and meaningful gamification. In: Proceedings of iConference 2013, pp. 671–672 (2013)
22. Nicholson, S.: A user-centred theoretical framework for meaningful gamification. In: Proceedings of GLS 8.0, pp. 223–230. ETC Press (2012)
23. Richter, G., Raban, D.R., Rafaeli, S.: Studying gamification: the effect of rewards and incentives on motivation. In: Reiners, T., Wood, L.C. (eds.) Gamification in Education and Business, pp. 21–46. Springer, Heidelberg (2015)
24. Ryan, R.M., Deci, E.L.: Intrinsic and extrinsic motivations: classic definitions and new directions. Contemp. Educ. Psychol. **25**(1), 54–67 (2000)
25. Ryan, R.M., Deci, E.L.: Self-determination theory and the facilitation of intrinsic motivation, social development, and well-being. Am. Psychol. **55**(1), 68–78 (2000)
26. Ryan, R.M., Rigby, C.S., Przybylski, A.: The motivational pull of video games: a self determination theory approach. Motiv. Emot. **30**(4), 347–363 (2006)
27. O'Brien, H., Toms, E.: What is user engagement? A conceptual framework for defining user engagement with technology. J. Am. Soc. Inform. Sci. Technol. **59**(6), 938–955 (2008)
28. Thom, J., Millen, D., DiMicco, J.: Removing gamification from an enterprise SNS. In: Proceedings of CSCW 2012. ACM Press, New York (2012)
29. Veglis, A.: From Cross Media to Transmedia Reporting in Newspaper Articles (2012)
30. Venkatesh, V.: Determinants of perceived ease of use: integrating control, intrinsic motivation, and emotion into the technology acceptance model. Inf. Syst. Res. **11**(4), 342–365 (2000)
31. Werbach, K.: (Re)Defining gamification: a process approach. Persuasive **2014**, 266–272 (2014)
32. Zichermann, G., Cunningham, C.: Gamification by Design: Implementing Game Mechanics in Web and Mobile Apps. O'Reilly Media, Sebastopol (2011)
33. In Changing News Landscape, Even Television is Vulnerable, Trends in News Consumption: 1991–2012, Pew Research Center for the People & the Press. http://www.pewresearch.org/fact-tank/2013/10/04/pew-surveys-of-audience-habits-suggest-perilous-future-for-news/. Accessed 17 July 2015

A Comparison of Film and Computer Generated Imagery Medium for the Learning of Chimpanzee Behaviours

Simon Campion[✉], Paul Rees, and David Roberts

THINKlab, The University of Salford, 7th Floor Maxwell Building, Salford M5 4WT, UK
{s.p.campion,p.a.rees,d.j.roberts}@salford.ac.uk

Abstract. Knowledge of social interactions between animals has traditionally been passed on through observation and standard teaching materials such as lectures, books and documentaries. Serious games may be well suited to teaching animal behavior as they allow for easy control of what is being presented as well as interaction, in terms of moving around the environment and effecting behaviour of the virtual animals.

We compare how the visual qualities of computer generated imagery (CGI) and film impact on learning and enjoyment. The reason for this comparison was partly as other work has shown how some human behaviour can be more easily communicated using CGI and to allow the impact of visual qualities to be better understood before studying the interactive CGI environments.

Our findings suggest that when viewpoint is fixed people can identify animal behaviour equally well in both mediums. This validates further experimentation into the advantages of free viewpoint.

Keywords: Serious games · Virtual environments · Virtual learning · Virtual animals

1 Introduction

The identification of social behaviour of humans and animals from visual mediums has a number of potential uses, such as training through to psychology. Past studies have compared film with interactive virtual environments [1], however, the impact of visual differences in the media on behaviour identification has been studied less. It is known that more detail is often represented in film, whereas unnecessary detail can be left out in CGI. Behaviour, such as the eye gaze of a child with Attention Deficit Hyperactivity Disorder (ADHD), has been shown with great clarity using simplified virtual representations [2]. Further more scenes can be tailored to fit an application rather than exactly mimic reality. Rizzo and Kim state that in some instances we may not want VR to exactly copy reality, due to constraints such as time and safety [3].

The study reported uses Virtual Chimpanzees to depict various social behaviours. This allows the user to view a simplified representation of events without being distracted by secondary actions or unnecessary detail within the scene. The aim of this experiment was to measure the relative performance and experience of identifying animal behaviours from CGI and film. Allowing the comparison of each media's

© Springer International Publishing Switzerland 2016
A. De Gloria and R. Veltkamp (Eds.): GALA 2015, LNCS 9599, pp. 494–505, 2016.
DOI: 10.1007/978-3-319-40216-1_54

qualities before potential future studies add in variables such as free viewpoint. Without exploring this, our future studies cannot accurately determine whether differences in user performance are the result of free viewpoint or visual differences.

Zoo keepers study animal behaviour to acquire knowledge needed to identify animal wellbeing from behaviour and help them avoid or diffuse dangerous situations before they occur. Confrontations in primates are extremely dangerous and can result in serious injury or even death [4]. In an effort to avoid confrontations, some Zoos design enclosures to encapsulate escape routes and visual barriers that allow for faster keeper intervention [5]. However, the ability to recognise aggressive behaviour and when to intervene is built up over time. Mimicking Chimpanzee behaviour when caring for them has been shown to increase playful behaviour [6]. Jenvoid suggests that keepers should adopt this approach when caring for Chimpanzees. Enclosures are often built to mimic the wild (Melfi 2009) in an effort to stimulate wild behaviour, so why not take this same approach when interacting with the animals VEs could teach this. Virtual training could be practiced and tested in any location in addition to onsite learning.

Conservation education is one of the main aims of Zoos globally [7]. It is known that people visit Zoos as a form of entertainment [8]. This presents the challenge of how to educate and inform visitors in an entertaining way. Currently, visitors learn from viewing animal exhibits and signage. In some instances they receive talks or interpretive presentations about the animals. Studies have been conducted to compare knowledge gained between interpretive and fact only presentations [9]. Results showed that people retained more information from interpretive presentations. Using serious games it is possible to go one step further and engage the viewer in a Virtual Environment (VE) where they could view the world through a camera, perhaps representing the animal's visual perspective. VEs could be used to teach visitors about animal behaviour and the motivations behind it.

Virtual Reality (VR) is a computer generated three-dimensional interactive environment that simulates real places and situations, allowing the user to navigate and interact with the environment in real time. When people talk about VR they often talk about the terms Presence and Immersion. The term Immersion in virtual reality is the level to which stimuli from reality are exchanged for the virtual. This can create a feeling of being there, which is referred to as Presence. VR simulations are interactive and afford high levels of presence. Of course, as suggested by Steuer [10], a sense of presence can be gained from a variety of media from books and film through to VR. Steuer uses Interaction and Vividness as variables to measure presence. This use of variables would suggest that while a film, would score highly in terms of visuals, it would score badly on the interactive scale. It should therefore offer a lower sense of presence than that of an interactive VE.

Serious games have been researched for a number of decades. The earliest example being flight simulators in 1929. Visual feedback however, was not possible until the 1950s [11]. They allow individual or collaborative learning. Multimedia content can be embedded within them. Making the environment an interactive hub of knowledge that engages multiple senses. Learning outcomes are contained within the game rather than users searching the web and getting lost in a mass of information [12]. Serious games such as these could revolutionise the way in which subjects are taught with students learning new skills through exploration and play [13]. Research suggests they will enable us to update teaching materials and add to traditional teaching methods [14] or in some cases be an alternative to text books [15].

Using serious games opens up many new opportunities for training, a lot of which would not be possible or are too expensive to act out in real life [16–18]. With the use of database back ends to store scenario events and interactions, information from training scenarios can be stored and integrated for performance. Rizzo and Kim [3] state that in some instances we may not want VR to exactly copy reality, due to constraints such as time and safety. With VR we can temporarily put these constraints aside, therefore allowing for play and the repeat of scenarios as and when required until users are ready to attempt a task in reality.

Several past studies explore virtual animals. In Gorillas in Bits [19] the user becomes an adolescent Gorilla in a Gorilla family. Consisting of a male and female at rest. Users could approach the adults, however there were rules. The male has a large personal space and intrusion into this in an aggressive way by the user resulted in behaviours such as chest beating, charges, vocalisations or even physical attack. The female Gorilla was easier to approach and allowed the user to approach her in a slow, submissive way. No response meant the user could groom her. Again incorrect approaches to the female resulted in aggressive behaviour. One attractive feature of this simulation is the "Time Out" function. The authors knew some children may deliberately evoke an aggressive response. If they did this, the screen would turn black and display "Time Out" [20]. The aim was to help children learn about biomechanics of Gorilla behaviour/movements, such as grooming and knuckle walking. The simulator was also used at Zoo Atlanta. After using the simulator they then made models of Gorillas in poses using pipe cleaners. Other studies have concentrated on simulating social interactions between animals using artificial intelligence techniques, with groups studying the behaviour of Wolves, Chimpanzees and Macaques [21–23].

The majority of the above literature survey outlines the capabilities of VEs and how they could be used to help teach animal behaviour. It was important to describe the full range of features offered by VEs in order to illustrate how they can be utilised in future studies. However, in this study we were interested in focusing on just one of these qualities. We have explored the visual qualities of VEs and how they affect user learning, enjoyment. Many studies of VEs tend to focus on the more glamorous interactive elements. We believe that it is important to isolate impacting factors therefore exploring their components. More consideration should be given to the learning capabilities of different levels of realism [24] and the comparison of different medium [25].

To summarise, the literature informs us that Zoos have an obligation to teach visitors about their exhibits and need new and innovative ways of doing this. It identifies that certain animals respond positively when keepers care for them by mimicking the animal's behaviours. It illustrates that Serious Games are a way of teaching material that may otherwise be too expensive or dangerous to teach, and that some research has been carried out in these areas on teaching primate behaviour. However, before we could move onto more advanced studies, we first needed to examine whether CGI used in VEs contain sufficient detail for the learning of animal behaviour. By isolating the visual variable and scripting the user experience, we ensure that they see the appropriate learning material. We can then compare this experience to that when viewing film, before moving onto unscripted user controlled interactions and the added benefits or distractions that they bring in later studies. In this, and subsequent studies, we aim to build on these foundations and show evidence in support of using serious games as a new and exciting way to educate people on animal behaviour, whilst ensuring that we do not use 3D technologies simply for the sake of it.

2 Methodology

A Chimpanzee keeper was motion captured mimicking Chimpanzee behaviour and the animations applied to virtual Chimpanzees. Film was then captured of captive Chimpanzees (real film). Behavioural Animations were matched to it for the virtual Chimpanzees and footage captured of this (CGI film). Both films were then condensed to less than three minutes in duration. These films were shown to n = 20 participants who were asked to identify Chimpanzee behaviour. Participants were split into two groups of ten. One tested on a standard laptop, the other on a large projected display. In each groups half of the participants watched the CGI film first and the other watched the real film first. The experiment used a repeated measure within subject design for the primary overarching task of behaviour identification and the influence of display used between subject design. The duration of the experiment was approximately twenty minutes.

2.1 Thesis and Hypothesis

The thesis of our experiment is that CGI and virtual animals can be created to represent animal behaviours mimicking those seen in real life and captured on film. We put aside the interactive aspects of virtual environments and examined how the visual qualities of CGI and film alone impact on user learning and enjoyment. Specifically we tested the following hypothesis:

H1 There will be no significant difference in identification of simple behaviour across the two visual mediums.
H2 Participant will perceive visual fidelity of the CGI film to be high enough for basic behaviour identification.
H3 Participants will perceive the real film to be more enjoyable than CGI Film.

2.2 Scope

We examine how participant experience is affected by the use of different visual medium, the first being a film that is a faithful representation, the second a film captured from a virtual environment (CGI Film). That is, an abstract representation. During the experiment we measured behavioural identification and participant's impression of visual fidelity and enjoyment. Participants could comment on each medium, allowing us to measure the visual suitability of a virtual environment for the learning of animal behaviour.

2.3 Variables

We now describe the dependent and independent variables.

2.4 Independent Variables

The conditions were visual medium and display technology. The visual medium variables were CGI film and real film. The variables for display were laptop (low immersion) and large projected display (high immersion) (Table 1).

Table 1. Independent variables

	Standard laptop	OCTAVE (single screen)
Real video	RVI	RVo
CGI video	CGII	CGIo

2.5 Dependent Variables

Three dependent variables were collected. Firstly, behaviour identification, where a simple scoring system was used. Correct identification scored 1 and incorrect 0. A maximum score of 8 could be achieved if all were accurately identified. In each medium, seven of the eight behaviours were present and one was not. Visual fidelity and enjoyment data was collected on a bespoke questionnaire using a seven point likert scale with a balanced number of questions and counter questions for each.

2.6 Procedure

Each participant read about several Chimpanzee behaviours using written descriptions taken from an ethogram (catalogue) of Chimpanzee behaviour. These behaviours were validated as being suitable by a group of primate experts from The University of Salford's School of Environment and Life Sciences. Each participant was shown two short films. One was footage of real captive Chimpanzees, the other virtual Chimpanzees. Both films were approximately two and a half minutes long, and illustrated various Chimpanzee behaviours. Participants then had a second chance to review the written behavioural descriptions before again watching the two films. They were permitted to make notes as they watched the films. On completion they were given a questionnaire that allowed for the collection of objective measures of task performance and subjective measures of experience. Behaviour recognition was only recorded if it had been viewed once or more.

2.7 Subjects and Confederated

N = 20 participants were recruited to take part in the study from University staff and students, 14 were Male and 6 female. It should be noted, that it would have been better to recruit, an equal number of male and female participants. The mode age range was 21–30 (45 %). The majority of participants either never or occasionally play games (80 %). Participants were free to leave the study at any point with no explanation needed. It was explained that the results of the experiment were anonymous and participants were not in competition with each other. Only the researcher and his research partners would see the results. Participants were not rushed at any point and were free to ask the researcher any questions.

2.8 Ethics

Ethical approval was gained for the study from the University ethics board. The approval number was CST 12/51. This included an information sheet and consent form. The information sheet explained to the participants the general theme of the study and what they might expect to see. The consent form included understanding of anonymity of data, the right to leave at any time, and to have their data completely removed.

2.9 Apparatus

We describe techniques used for CGI film and film creation and also briefly explained the display technologies used.

2.9.1 CGI Film Production

The environment and virtual Chimpanzees were produced using low polygon modelling techniques (4694 Polygons per Chimpanzee) in an effort to keep up performance while maintaining adequate visual realism. The Software used to create assets was Autodesk 3DS Max and Adobe Photoshop (Fig. 1).

Fig. 1. Virtual Chimpanzee creation process from the left motion capture then untextured and textured geometry

The virtual Chimpanzees were rigged (skeleton added) and skinned (skeleton assigned to Chimpanzee geometry). Motion capture data of a Zoo keeper acting out Chimpanzee behaviour was used to animate them. All of the models were imported into Quest3d where logic was created to allow the environment to come to life. The CGI

Film was created by screen capturing footage from our experimental virtual environment. This was edited into a short sequence with no audio (Fig. 2).

Fig. 2. An image showing the virtual Chimpanzee enclosure

2.9.2   Real Film

Film footage was captured showing Chimpanzee behaviour. This was edited into a short sequence with no audio. It should be noted that it is a time consuming process waiting for the Chimpanzees to display particular behaviours and there is no guarantee that this will happen, which in itself could add weight to the argument for some kind of virtual training application (Fig. 3).

Fig. 3. Chimpanzee feeding behaviour on the left real film and right CGI film

2.9.3 Hardware/Display Technology

Display Variable 1 used a Gaming Laptop. Display Variable 2 used a large projected screen of the OCTAVE [26] allowing for a life sized, first person experience.

2.9.4 Questionnaire Design

A questionnaire was designed split into two sections; the first a brief personality questionnaire and the second related to the experiment. The personality questionnaire determined a participant's suitability for the experiment. The experiment section contained a behavioural identification section. Participants could tick off the behaviours that they had identified in each of the films. In addition, an experience section consisting of twenty questions (including counter questions) measured enjoyment, presense and visual fidelity. A seven point Likert scale measured participant's opinion.

3 Results and Analysis

3.1 Behavioural Identification Performance

A McNemars test was used to compare performance across medium. There was a strong trend towards better performance in CGIl (83.8 % correct) when measured against CGIo (75 % correct). This was significant (P = 0.039). Participants performed better in RVl (83.8 % correct) than in RVo (82.5 % correct). This was not significant (P = 0.9999). Therefore only the CGI medium performed better in low immersion. Participants performed equally in RVl (83.8 % correct) than in CGIl (83.8 % correct). This was not significant (P = 0.9999). There was a trend towards better performance in RVo (82.5 % correct) when measured against CGIo (75 % correct). This was not significant (P = 0.143). Overall real video (83.1 % correct) performed better than CGI (79.4 % correct) but not significantly (p = 0.377).

There were differences in the qualitative data collected suggesting that the real film was busy and unpredictable, with comments such as "The film required attention to be focused everywhere to witness behaviours, however the VE (CGI Film) could focus on a particular behaviour." The qualitative data also suggested that the film contained more subtle movements and intent "Key issue is granularity. Gross actions were identifiable in both, but nuance and purpose only really came through in the film. Eg. For approach you could see contact between two individuals in film but VR (CGI Film) did not establish this and the animals could have just wandered closer."

3.2 Visual Fidelity

A paired sample test was conducted to compare participant's impression of the visual fidelity of the mediums. There was a significant difference between CGIl results (M = 5.68, SD = 1.696) and CGIo results (M = 5.18, SD = 1.289), with a trend towards better performance in CGIl (t(49) = 5.466, p = 0.001). Suggesting that low immersion offered participants a better impression of visual fidelity. Overall 80 % of participants viewing the films on the laptop or on the Octave believed that the visual fidelity was high enough to identify behaviour.

However, the qualitative data suggested room for improvement with participant comments such as "Movement of animals in VR (CGI Film) was strange at some points." Another participant stated: "Also the VE (CGI Film) has the ape's movements not so smooth and this was a bit distracting." This suggests that the movement was detracting from the user experience.

3.3 Enjoyment

A paired sample test was conducted for the conditions 'the film was more enjoyable on the laptop' and 'the film was more enjoyable on the Octave'. There was a significant difference between the RVl (M = 3.83, SD = 1.534) and RVo results (M = 4.68, SD = 1.347), with RVo performing better than the RVl (t(39) = −10.077, p = 0.001). Interestingly, the real film condition was preferred on the larger Octave screen, while the CGI film conditions performance improved and was equal to the film on the smaller laptop one.

4 Discussion

The research question set out at the start of the paper was 'How do the visual qualities of computer generated imagery (CGI) and film impact on learning and enjoyment?'. Results suggest no significant difference between CGI and film for the learning of simple animal behaviour, which is in line with a similar study examining identification of children's classroom behaviour [27] which was published as we concluded our study. This suggests that the CGI film contained enough relevant realism for gross behaviour identification, which implies additional detailing may be a waste of resource and potentially a distraction. Looking more closely at the results, a significant difference between behaviour identification was present between low and high immersion in the CGI medium. This could be due to rendering artifacts becoming more prominent however this was also true for the video as pixilation became more obvious. Further work would be needed in this area to examine this more closely. A possible way to improve our study would be to conduct further experimentation using various levels of detail to try and establish minimum requirements for gross behaviour recognition. Allowing a baseline or standard to be established. One participant noted that the CGI film did not contain sufficient detail to illustrate subtle movements and intent. This could be added with extra effort and resource however it may also be worth considering other mediums for this purpose such as 3D reconstructed video.

Identifying levels of relevant realism for specific tasks has been done in other fields. Biology books utilise media such as line drawings of anatomy or simplified images showing areas demarked by colour in addition to photography. Each type of image is used to help the learning process as the way they are presented makes it easier to identify certain features [28]. We do not have this with CGI. We may render in wireframe when we want to show off the fact that we have not used many triangles in a mesh, or to show the topology flow, but we do not have a guide that tells us which rendering style may be best for a particular style of learning. Nor do we know how much detail is needed for optimum learning. In virtual environments we are presented with a unique opportunity to tailor scenes for learning. We can remove detail and make scenes uncluttered, or design camera paths that focus the user's attention on certain attributes whether through model layout or camera depth of field. In effect, we can play with variables and try to find what we like to call the 'level of relevant realism'.

The use of CGI allows the user experience to be controlled. In serious games, behaviors and events can be triggered when required, allowing for behavior to be seen on demand. In the real world, as the authors discovered, animals choose when to do something and quite often take their time doing so. It is possible to spend hours making observations and never see the desired behavior. Therefore, serious games could supplement observation training. Past studies suggest that serious games could be used to update and add to teaching material [14]. However, they need to be fit for purpose and not created for the sake of using the technology.

People visit Zoos as a form of entertainment [8], so it is important that they enjoy the learning process. Participant's impression of enjoyment was split according to which platform the media was viewed on, with the film preferred on the higher immersion projected screen and the CGI Film performing equally well on the lower immersion laptop screen. This could potentially be due to rendering artifacts in the CGI film becoming more prominent when viewed at a larger scale or that the increased scale exposed missing detail in the CGI film. A truer test may have been to scale the resolution, as the display scaled, but due to hardware constraints at the time this was not possible. There were also positive comments. "I think the virtual environment would be a great teaching aid and as children/young people are so exposed to technology it would be easy to include with minimal disruption whilst allowing for information to be passed on in a fun and engaging manner.". This would suggest that with improvement to visual quality for larger displays, the CGI film would be fit for purpose. Overall the results do suggest that CGI could potentially be used as an alternative to film as a teaching aid for animal behaviours and also within Zoos for conservation education, which is one of the main aims of Zoos globally [7].

5   Conclusions

Currently human and animal behaviour is learnt through observation and standard teaching material. We suggest that serious games could be a new and innovative way to teach these. However prior to exploring free viewpoint serious games we wanted to investigate the impact of visual differences in the media from a fixed viewpoint. Thus allowing us to ensure that any advantage or disadvantage identified during free viewpoint studies would not be due to visual differences in media. Our findings suggest that when viewpoint is fixed people can identify gross animal behaviour equally well in both mediums and previous studies have shown this for human behaviour [27]. In addition our findings suggest a trend towards better performance in low immersion. However imagery being scaled with no increase in resolution could potentially impact up on this.

This work validates the study of free viewpoint interaction and whether it is a benefit or distraction when learning about animal behaviour. In conjunction with this It would be interesting to study how gradual increases in levels of immersion impact on learning and enjoyment and whether there is an optimal immersion level for this. To conclude below is a summary of the main advantages and disadvantages identified in the study -

Advantages of CGI visuals for portraying animal behaviour:

1. CGI allows for level of detail to be managed to stop users being distracted.
2. CGI allows behaviours to be split into levels. Basic movements could be taught first and then subtle behaviours added in.
3. CGI allows for the tailoring or scenarios. Scenarios can be designed to last for a set duration and contain all of the necessary information.
4. There was no significant difference between the CGI film and Real film for the learning of basic animal behaviours. (This suggests adequate relevant realism)

Disadvantages of CGI visuals for portraying animal behaviour:

1. CGI lacks subtlety of movement and intent. Although this could be added to an extent with extra resource. However some users found additional detail distracting.
2. CGI environment lacks visual richness. Again this could be added in with extra time and resource.

Acknowledgements.   Simon Hutchinson and Sean O'Hara for guidance on Chimpanzee behaviours. Becky Dassan for acting out the Chimpanzee behaviours for motion capture. Hannah Jarvis for guidance with Motion Capture equipment.

References

1. Morgan, P., Cleave-Hogg, D., McIlroy, J., Devitt, J.: Simulation technology a comparison of experiential and visual learning for undergraduate medical students. Anesthesiology **96**, 10–16 (2002)
2. Adams, R., Finn, P., Moes, E., Flannery, K., Rizzo, A.: Distractibility in Attention/Deficit/Hyperactivity Disorder (ADHD): the virtual reality classroom. Child Neuropsychol. **15**, 120–135 (2009)
3. Rizzo, A., Kim, G.J.: A SWOT analysis of the field of virtual reality rehabilitation and therapy. Presence **14**, 119–146 (2005)
4. Goossens, B., Setchel, J., Tchidango, E., Dilamaka, E., Vidal, C., Ancrenaz, M., Jamart, A.: Survival, interaction with conspecifics and reproduction in 37 chimpanzees released into the wild. Biol. Conserv. **123**, 461–475 (2005)
5. Coe, J., Scott, D., Lukas, K.: Technical report – facility design for bachelor gorilla groups. Zoo Biol. **28**, 144–162 (2009)
6. Jenvoid, M.: Chimpanzee (pan troglodytes) response to caregivers use of Chimpanzee behaviour. Zoo Biol. **27**, 345–359 (2008)
7. WAZA: Building a Future for Wildlife - The World Zoo and Aquarium Conservation Strategy (2005)
8. Ross, S., Gillespie, K.: Research article – influences on visitor behaviour at a modern immersive zoo exhibit. Zoo Biol. **28**, 462–472 (2009)

9. Visscher, N., Snider, R., Vander Stoep, G.: Comparative analysis of knowledge gain between interpretive and fact-only presentations at an animal training session: an exploratory study. Zoo Biol. **28**, 488–495 (2009)
10. Steuer, J.: Defining virtual reality: dimensions determining telepresence. J. Commun. **42**, 73–93 (1992)
11. Primenta, K., Teixeira, K.: Virtual Reality – Through the new looking glass (1993)
12. Njenga, J., Fourie, L.: The myths about e-learning in higher education. Br. J. Educ. Technol. **41**, 199–212 (2010)
13. de Freitas, S., Rebolledo-Mendez, G., Liarokapis, F., Magoulas, G., Poulovassilis, A.: Learning as immersive experiences: using the four-dimensional framework for designing and evaluating immersive learning experiences in a virtual world. Br. J. Educ. Technol. **41**, 69–85 (2010)
14. Pan, Z., Cheok, A., Yang, H., Zhu, J., Shi, J.: Virtual reality and mixed reality for virtual learning environments. Comput. Graph. **30**, 20–28 (2006)
15. Hew, K., Cheung, W.: Use of three-dimensional (3-D) immersive virtual worlds in K-12 and higher education settings: a review of the research. Br. J. Educ. Technol. **41**, 33–35 (2010)
16. Ieronutti, L., Chittaro, L.: Employing virtual humans for education and training in X3D/VRML worlds. Comput. Educ. **49**, 93–109 (2007)
17. Falloon, G.: Using avatars and virtual environments in learning: what do they have to offer? Br. J. Educ. Technol. **41**, 108–122 (2010)
18. Dalgarno, B., Lee, M.: What are the learning affordances of 3-D virtual environments? Br. J. Educ. Technol. **41**, 10–32 (2010)
19. Crowell, A.: Gorillas in Bits (1997)
20. Hay, K., Crozier, J., Barnett, M., Allison, D., Bashaw, M., Hoos, B., Perkins, L.: Virtual gorilla modelling project: middle school students constructing virtual models for learning. In: Fourth International Conference of Learning Sciences, pp. 212–213 (2000)
21. Tomlinson, B., Blumberg, B.: Social behaviour, emotion and learning in a pack of virtual wolves (2001)
22. Irenaeus, J.A., Boekhorst, T., Hogeweg, P.: Self-structuring in artificle "chimps" offers new hypothesis for male grouping in chimpanzees. Behaviour **130**, 3–4 (1994)
23. Puga-Gonzalez, I., Hildenbrandt, H., Hernelrijk, C.: Emergent patterns of social affiliation in primates. Model. PLos Comput. Biol. **5**(14), e1000630 (2009)
24. Karitiko, I., Kavakli, M., Cheng, K.: Learning science in a virtual reality application: the impacts of animated-virtual actors' visual complexity. Comput. Educ. **55**, 881–891 (2010)
25. Kaya, E., Peja, T., Rychlowska, M.: How good is an avatar's smile?: effects of facial expression in video- and avatar-based computer mediated communication. In: CHI 2012 (2012)
26. Roberts, D., Rae, J., Duckworth, T., Moore, C., Aspin, R.: Estimating the gaze of a virtuality human. IEEE Trans. Vis. Comput. Graph. **19**, 681–690 (2013)
27. Smith, D., McLaughlin, T., Brown, I.: 3-D computer animation vs live-action video: differences in viewers response to instructional vignettes. Contemp. Issues Technol. Teacher Educ. **12**, 41–54 (2012)
28. Dwyer, J.R.F.: Effect of varying amount of realistic detail in visual illustrations designed to complement programmed instruction. Percept. Mot. Skills **27**, 351–354 (1968)

The Effect of Simulations and Games
on Learning Objectives in Tertiary Education:
A Systematic Review

Stephanie de Smale[✉], Tom Overmans, Johan Jeuring,
and Liesbeth van de Grint

Utrecht University, Utrecht, The Netherlands
{S. deSmale, J. F. A. Overmans, J. T. Jeuring,
E. J. M. vandeGrint}@uu. nl

Abstract. The growing popularity of simulations and games invites the production of insights that help academic teachers to use simulations and games in
their courses. This article clarifies positive conditions to use simulations and
games in tertiary education. Based on a systematic review of literature we
tentatively find a positive or neutral relationship between using simulations and
games and achieving learning objectives. Also, we find three recurring conditions for successful use of simulations and games: the specificity of the game,
the integration in the course, and the role of a guiding instructor. Finally, we
express the strong need for a scientific framework to measure effectiveness of
simulations and games.

1 Introduction

Simulations and games are widely used in a diverse range of academic courses. Their
use largely depends on teachers' personal initiatives and experiences in courses rather
than on grounded information about which simulations work in which courses and for
which learning objectives. Because game-based learning is increasingly popular in
academic education, there is a need to validate the use of digital simulations and games.
This study evaluates the value of simulations and games for tertiary education.

We analyse the relationship between simulations and games in academic programs
and the achievement of learning objectives. Furthermore, we highlight what academic
teachers can learn from previous studies. In a systematic literature review, we analyzed
64 articles focusing on tertiary education, games, and learning objectives. We find a
tentative positive or neutral relationship between using simulations and games and
achieving learning objectives, and three recurring preconditions for successful use of
simulations and games: the specificity of the game, the integration in the course, and
the role of a guiding instructor. Lastly, we think there is a need for a framework to
measure effectiveness of simulations and games.

A. De Gloria and R. Veltkamp (Eds.): GALA 2015, LNCS 9599, pp. 506–516, 2016.
DOI: 10.1007/978-3-319-40216-1_55

2 Learning Objectives, Simulations, and Games

2.1 Learning Objectives

An important part of studying the value of simulations and games in tertiary education is concerned with its relationship with learning objectives. Learning objectives or learning outcomes describe what knowledge and skills students need to acquire. Learning objectives are fundamental in the design and validation of education. There are several frameworks for classifying learning objectives. Most widely known is Bloom's taxonomy, revised in 2001 by Anderson & Krathwohl [1]. The applicability of Bloom's model for studying simulations and games is disputed. A shortcoming of Bloom's taxonomy in the context of this study is that it does not account for interactions among learners. Academic discourse on games and learning frame games as technologies that engage students in deep learning [2–4]. Skills like collaboration, but also critical thinking and problem solving are crucial in achieving deep learning goals [5, 6]. While games appear to be particularly useful to engage students in skills for deep learning, traditional theories such as Bloom's taxonomy do not take these higher order skills sufficiently into account.

Simulations and games are often about acquiring skills. As a result, we adopt the taxonomy of Romiszowski [7], which focuses on these learning objectives, and explicitly differentiates between knowledge and skills. The term 'knowledge' refers to "information stored in the learner's mind" which can be differentiated into four different levels: facts, procedures, concepts, and principles. Skills refer to 'actions (intellectual and physical) and reactions (to ideas, things, or people), which a person performs in a competent way' [7]. Interactive skills, dealing with others, are one of the four skills categories of Romiszowsky's taxonomy. The other three are cognitive, psychomotor, and reactive. Additionally, Romiszowski distinguishes between reproductive skills (applying procedures) and productive skills (applying principles and strategies). Examples of these skills will be given later on in this article. We focus on the ability of simulations and games to transfer different type of skills. Which games enhance which types of learning skills?

2.2 Simulations and Games

The lack of a clear definition of simulations and games may result in what some scholars refer to as 'terminological ambiguity' [8]. In recent years many managers, educators, and other practitioners have turned to the study of simulations and games in education [9–11]. Also in academia simulations and games in education are a hot topic [12–16]. Contemporary studies on games and education use a variety of definitions: education games, serious games [17, 18], digital game-based learning [9], or applied games [19]. Despite the lack of shared definitions and terminology, authors generally focus on games in non-leisure contexts. Defining simulations and games contributes to terminological coherency and reduces ambiguity [8]. Although any classification of simulations and games is debatable, definitions of different forms are important when discussing effectiveness in academic education. In this study, we combine theory from

Narayanasamy et al. [20], Lean et al. [21] and Apperley [22] to classify different types of simulations and games.

Simulations historically refer to both management/business simulations, and computer simulations [8]. In general, simulations are models that express complex real-world systems. A simulation is used to analyze specific systems, develop mental models in learners, or research artificial environments [20]. A difference between games and simulations is intent: 'the intent of games and simulation games is to engage players in a fun and entertaining experience, while the intent of simulators is to train and develop the skills of its operators' [20]. Relevant for this study are two different types of simulations: training and modeling simulations. Firstly, a training simulation also simulates real-world processes by re-enacting a specific type of system or process in order to improve performance, and maximize efficiency of the user [20]. One example is *FlightGear Flight Simulator* (1997). Secondly, modeling simulations are simulations that model specific systems in order create and/or test model - such as weather simulations or car modeling. Because the categorization of simulations and games are often ambiguous and their framing is also discipline-specific, we stress that the proposed categorization should be considered as a continuum rather than as completely separate categories. In this specific review the focus is on tertiary education and simulations and games that are often used in academic programs (Fig. 1).

	Genre	Description	Well-known example	Example from present study
Games	Role-playing game	Assuming a character	The Sims	SCRUMIA
	Strategy game	Strategic-decision making	Company of Heroes (real-time), Civilization (turn-based)	Pax Warrior
	Action game	Physical challenges, coordination	Space Invaders	Space Goats
Hybrid	Simulation Game	Goal-oriented re-enactment of real-world processes	Gazillionaire	Venture Strategy
Simulations	Training simulation	Train to maximize performance in achieving task (e.g. psychomotor)	Flight Simulator	Skills-O-Mat
	Modeling simulation	Model processes or objects	Weather simulation, Car modeling	Virtual Construction Simulator

Fig. 1. Classification of games, simulation games, and simulations used in this review based on a combination of Narayanasamy et al. [20], Lean et al. [21], and Apperley [22].

Games, according to the traditional definition, are rule-bound systems, set in a defined space [23, 24]. Games are goal-oriented activities with clear in-game endings, as opposed to simulations, which may not have clear goal-oriented activities or end-states [20]. Simulation games have in-game goals, but successful completion of the game is not (necessarily) based on victory conditions. Firstly, role-playing games are games in which characters assume the role of a character or take control of an avatar in a fictional setting [22]. These games can be single, or multi-player, depending on the game's structure [21]. One well-known example is *The Sims* (Electronic Arts 2000). Secondly, strategy games are games in which player's decisions have a high significance in determining the outcome. These games are usually divided into real-time strategy games - such as Company of Heroes (Relic Entertainment 2006) - or turn-based strategy games - such as the *Civilization* series [22].

The third type of game is an action game, which focuses on physical challenges, such as reaction time or eye-hand coordination. A well-known game in this category is the classic *Space Invaders* (1978), but it should be noted that this type of game has many subgenres such as shooter- or fighting games. Besides simulations and games, there are simulation games, which is a hybrid form. While a simulation game is a subgenre of games, a simulation game does not have to be end-goal oriented and can be entertaining [20]. Simulation games are games that re-enact sports, flying, driving, but also real-world dynamics such as communities or governments [22]. Examples are games from the Lavamind series, such as *Gazillionaire* (2005). In this review, we found that these games appear both in a digital, physical, or a combination of digital and physical form. Therefore, in this classification all games, simulation games and simulations can be computer based, non-computer based or a hybrid of computer- and non-computer based.

3   Research Method

3.1   Protocol and Selection

A systematic review consists of five steps: (1) identification of research, (2) selection of primary studies, (3) study quality assessment, (4) data extraction & monitoring, and (5) data synthesis [25]. Our main research objective is to uncover the value of simulations and games for tertiary education by exploring the relationships between their use in academic programs and the achievement of learning objectives.

In answering the research question, we produced a review protocol with several sub questions[1], such as what type of simulations and games are used in higher education, and for what type of learning objectives games are useful?

For the selection of the primary research data, we conducted a comprehensive database search in SCOPUS. In SCOPUS, our query was: "serious gam*" or "simulation gam*". Within this query, we searched for articles related to education type, focusing on tertiary education; our query consisted of the search terms "university", "academic", or "tertiary" education. Second, since our research focused specifically on the relationship between games and learning objectives, the last part of the query consisted of a combination of the words "learning goals" or "learning objectives", or "learning outcomes".

---

[1] The research protocol can be obtained here: http://www.stephaniedesmale.nl/2015/10/22/research-protocol/.

3.2 Assessment and Extraction

The final literature review compared 64 articles. The initial dataset consisted of 728 articles. This dataset concerns journal articles with simulations, games or learning mentioned in its title and abstract. Starting with 728 articles a four stage-review process was carried out by a team of four researchers. In the first stage, articles were included or excluded from the review, using two criteria. Firstly, simulations *or* games *and* tertiary education had to be mentioned in the abstract, since the study focuses on the value simulations and games in tertiary education. Secondly, the articles had to focus on learning, i.e. on the achievement of learning objectives. If we were unsure if the article focused on higher education, the article was included in the shortlist for further examination. To provide a valid selection of articles for the shortlist, at least two researchers evaluated each title and abstract. The conflicting results were discussed by two researchers. After systematically reviewing 728 abstracts, a final shortlist of 93 articles remained; 14 % of the initial dataset. In the second stage, four reviewers all read three different articles and one identical article. This was done to check the quality of the short list and to extract relevant topics for qualitative analysis. Eleven topics were extracted, and provided a solid base for a systematic analysis of the remaining articles. These topics concern, for instance, type of learning objectives, effect of simulations and games on learning objectives, type of research conducted, or academic discipline. In the third stage, all articles 93 articles were scrutinized and all topics were ranked in a database. In this stage, the set of 93 articles was reduced to 64, because 29 articles were excluded additionally. This was done for various reasons such as: the study did not focus on higher education, or the article was written in an inaccessible language. In the fourth and final stage several group meetings were organized to discuss the research findings, which formed the backbone of this article.

4 Dataset Characteristics

When analyzing our dataset, we found some interesting facts and figures. Most articles originated from the United States, The Netherlands, and the United Kingdom. Furthermore, we found that most simulations and games were used in the areas of computer science (20,31 %), engineering (10,94 %), or interdisciplinary courses (10,94 %). Most articles describe single case studies, in which a single game is analyzed and tested in a single educational setting. These studies usually examined the effect of a game by testing it for a specific amount of time (for instance, the duration of a course) and measuring before and after effects via questionnaires or interviews.

Most of the games studied are hybrid simulation games (52,38 %), role-playing games (21,38 %), or training/modeling simulations (14,29 %). The majority of these games is computer-based (60,94 %). One example of a studied simulation game is *REALGAME*, a business simulation played by students in the Business University of Turku, Finland [26]. In this study, 133 non-business majors participated in a business simulation course (2008 until 2012). Students' knowledge was evaluated in a pre- and post-game test in the form of a mental model. *REALGAME* is a continuously processed/clock-driven simulation game. In this example the simulation contributed to acquiring factual and conceptual knowledge of business. The objective for the simulation was to introduce novice students to business logic [26]. An example of a role-playing game is the *Mastership Game*, a collaborative role-playing game to teach pedagogy students didactic dilemmas in classroom situations [27]. There are players and observers, and players have to react to specific situations such as 'dealing with negative colleagues' [27]. An example of a training simulation is SCRUMIA, a paper-based role-playing game that teaches students SCRUM, a project management methodology. The learning objective of this study was a productive understanding of the SCRUM process. Focusing on practical knowledge transfer, students had to remember, understand, and apply procession knowledge [28].

5 Value of Simulations and Games for Achieving Learning Objectives in Tertiary Education

5.1 Tentative Positive Effect on Learning Objectives

We observe a tentative positive effect between simulations and games, and the achievement of learning objectives. Although all of the studies in our dataset somehow focus on learning objectives and simulations or games, only 29 reviewed articles explicitly refer to learning theories as conceptualized, for instance, by Bloom [1] or Romiszowski [7]. However, in labeling the declared learning goals in the articles, we found that simulations and games are deployed to develop a diverse range of cognitive and communicative skills: 37 % related the simulation or game to productive cognitive skills (for example [27, 29–31], 16 % procedural knowledge (for instance, [28, 32–34]), and 12 % productive interactive skills (such as [27, 30, 34]). Important to note is that most studies mentioned several learning objectives relevant to their research.

After studying the articles we remain reluctant about the validity of previous claims made about the clear and definite positive relationship between learning objectives and games. Out of 64 articles, only 29 studies explicitly studied the effects of simulations and games on learning objectives (for instance [27, 30, 35]). Despite the large diversity in studies, illustrated effects between the use of simulations and games and the achievement of learning objectives were always positive, or neutral. In the specific articles, results between simulations and games, and learning objectives were always positive (26 articles), or neutral (3 articles). One might consider this as a publication bias, where positive results are more likely to be published than negative results. Not a single study in our dataset suggested a negative relationship between the use of simulations and games and the achievement of learning objectives.

5.2 Enabling and Constraining Factors

Studying enabling factors in the effectiveness of simulations and games in academic education leads to the question: which conditions are of importance when using a simulation or game? First, the effectiveness of learning is strongly related *to the role of the teacher/instructor/facilitator*. Thirteen studies claimed the role of the instructor is vital for achieving learning objectives through simulations and games [26, 28–33, 35–40]. Baalsrud Hauge et al. [33] show that the role of the teachers becomes more important when the emphasis on abstraction increases. In their meta-analysis, Wouters & Van Oostendorp [41] identify that the role of instructional support enhances learning, especially when learning objectives involve (higher order) skills, and in discussing and selecting new information. There are different types of instructional support during a simulation or game: reflection, modeling, advice, collaboration, control, narrative elements, modality, feedback, and personalization [41]. These studies show that without instructional support, learning effect is constrained since players may use their capacity for ineffective activities such as focusing on irrelevant information.

For the effectiveness use of a game or simulation in an educational context, the *specificity of the game* and the desired learning objectives needs to be taken into account. To a certain extent, the game can be tailored to meet the desired learning goals. Eight studies found clearly defined learning objectives in using a specific simulation or game to be an important enabling factor [32, 35, 37, 42–46]. For example, Castronovo et al. [46] integrated the modeling simulation *Virtual Construction Simulator 4* in a third year course 'Introduction to the Building Industry' and a fourth year course 'Building Construction Engineering' at Penn State University. In this case, the modeling simulation was specifically used in order to facilitate higher order thinking skills such as: evaluation, self-reflection, planning, determine appropriate construction methods. To accomplish this, the authors collaborated with course instructors to revise the existing set of learning objectives. This enhanced both the courses' and the simulation's objectives [46].

Lastly, the effect of simulations and games depends on *course integration*. Six studies found course integration an enabling factor in the effectiveness of a simulation or game [29, 30, 32, 33, 35, 47]. For instance, in Loughborough University the business game *Venture Strategy* was played by 70 senior-year students during the module 'Business Model'. It is a web-based team simulation where students start a company in the microcomputer industry [35]. This simulation deals with issues such as marketing, product development, accounting and finance. Using quantitative and qualitative analysis, subjects were asked to fill in a pre- and post-questionnaire and provide feedback during and after the courses. To improve the effectiveness of the module, some of the important enabling factors the authors suggest are: clear guidelines on coursework, realistic complexity, incentives for interaction, and face-to-face contact with course leader [35].

5.3   The Need for a Univocal Framework

Although we suggest a tentative positive relation between the use of simulations and games, and the achievement of learning objectives in tertiary education, we think it is too early to draw definite conclusions. Despite the growing attention for measuring effects of simulations and games on learning objectives, nearly all studies use self-developed evaluation instruments. These instruments vary from wide-ranging methods to very simple evaluations. This is issue is raised previously by several scholars [38, 41, 46, 48]. In addition to the large diversity of measurement tools, we find range of methods to classify learning objectives. As said, some studies explicitly use Bloom's taxonomy, whereas other studies mention obvious learning objectives. Using the studies in our dataset, we cannot draw definite conclusions concerning the effect of simulations and games on the achievement of learning objectives. Instead, we urge the need for an unambiguous framework to evaluate the effects. We suggest that this framework consists of (a) a clear classification of learning objectives which is recognizable for academic teachers, (b) a clear typology of simulations and games (in order to demonstrate which simulations and games might be helpful for achieving specific learning objectives) and (c) a sound scientific evaluation model using both quantitative and qualitative gathering techniques.

6 Conclusion and Discussion

We have studied the relationships between simulations and games and learning objectives in tertiary education. Our aim was to see if there are significant patterns between the use of simulations and games, and the achievement of learning objectives. Although the diversity of studies and experimental designs prohibit any hard results, three conclusions can be drawn from this study: we find a tentative positive effect between simulations and games and learning objectives, we suggest three recurring conditions for successful use of simulations and games, and we urge the need for a framework to measure the effectiveness of simulations and games.

This review has four theoretical and methodological limitations. Although we have tried to limit the chance, there might be a publication bias in our dataset. In performing a trans-disciplinary literature review, the articles differed in approach, methodology and situated knowledge.

The second limitation is the selection of data conducted in this study. In our own systematic review we used SCOPUS as our main database for extracting articles related to simulations and games in tertiary education. A limitation in this search strategy is the publication bias of relying on one database for our data.

A third possible limitation is the interpretation of learning objectives in the model of Romiszowski. We found Bloom's taxonomy inadequate for the study of higher order learning skills, which is why we used Romiszowski's learning theory. We interpreted the objectives mentioned in the articles and classified them using Romiszowski model. The classification depends on the reviewers' interpretation of the article. We have tried to improve the intercoder reliability by formulating a coding scheme, by reading and coding multiple articles team wise, and by discussing ambiguous learning objectives.

The fourth and last issue is concerned with the definition of simulations and games. We found that often a poor distinction was made between simulations and games. Generally it was not clear whether or not the articles were referring to games, which are goal-oriented, or simulations, which can also be open-ended. We elaborated on the differences in order to offer a frame of reference in an attempt to increase terminological coherence. However, in categorizing these simulations and games, we depended on information given in the article, which might have excluded valuable information to determine the type of game. In order to improve the intercoder reliability comparable steps were made (coding scheme, reading and coding team wise, discussing ambiguous types).

We recommend two issues for further research. The first is concerned with a grounded understanding of types of learning objectives in studying the effects of games and learning. Few studies relate learning goals with theory on learning objectives, which is fundamental when studying the effects of games in academic education. This is closely related with knowledge on the specificity of, and between simulations and games, and their key characteristics. A second issue is concerned with developing and studying a univocal framework. Many studies were heterogeneous experiments, with varying evaluation and framework. A general framework for evaluating learning effects in using simulations and games is needed.

References

1. Krathwohl, D.: A revision of bloom's taxonomy: an overview. Theor. Pract. **41**, 4 (2002)
2. Gee, J.P.: Learning and games. In: Salen, K. (ed.) The Ecology of Games: Connecting Youth, Games, and Learning, pp. 21–40. The MIT Press, Cambridge (2008). The John D. and Catherine T. MacArthur Foundation Series on Digital Media and Learning
3. Prensky, M.: Digital natives, digital immigrants part 1. Horizon **9**(5), 1–6 (2001)
4. Egenfeldt-Nielsen, S., Smith, J.H., Tosca, S.P.: Understanding Video Games: The Essential Introduction. Routledge, London (2013)
5. Fullan, M., Langworthy, M.: Towards a New End: New Pedagogies for Deep Learning. Collaborative Impact, Seattle (2013)
6. Fullan, M., Langworthy, M.: A Rich Seam: How New Pedagogies Find Deep Learning. Pearson, London (2014)
7. Romiszowski, A.J.: Designing Instructional Systems. Kogan Page, London (1981)
8. Klabbers, J.H.G.: Terminological ambiguity game and simulation. Simul. Gaming **40**(4), 446–463 (2009)
9. Prensky, M.: Digital game-based learning. Comput. Entertain. **1**(1), 12–21 (2003)
10. Gibson, D., Aldrich, C., Prensky, M. (eds.): Games and Simulations in Online Learning: Research and Development Frameworks. IGI Global, Hershey (2006)
11. Aldrich, C.: The Complete Guide to Simulations and Serious Games: How the Most Valuable Content Will Be Created in the Age Beyond Gutenberg to Google, 1st edn. Pfeiffer, San Francisco (2009)
12. Squire, K.: Video games in education. Int. J. Intell. Simul. Gaming **2**, 49–62 (2003)
13. Ritterfeld, U., Cody, M., Vorderer, P. (eds.): Serious Games. Mechanisms and Effects, 1st edn. Routledge, New York (2009)
14. Squire, K.: Video Games and Learning: Teaching and Participatory Culture in the Digital Age. Teachers College Press, New York (2011)
15. Khine, M.S. (ed.): Playful Teaching, Learning Games. New Tool for Digital Classrooms. Sense Publishers, Rotterdam, Boston (2011)
16. Shaffer, D.W., Gee, J.: The right kind of GATE, computer games and the future of assessment. In: Mayrath, M., Robinson, D., Clarke-Midura, J. (eds.) Technology-Based Assessments for 21st Century Skills, Theoretical and Practical Implications from Modern Research. Information Age Publishers, Charlotte (2012)
17. Sawyer, B., Rejeski, D.: Serious Games: Improving Public Policy Through Game-based Learning and Simulation. Woodrow Wilson International Center for Scholars, Washington (2002)

18. Michael, D., Sande, C.: Serious Games: Games That Educate, Train, and Inform. Cengage Learning PTR, Boston (2005)
19. van Roessel, L., van Mastrigt-Ide, J.: Collaboration and team composition in applied game creation processes. In: DiGRA 2011, Proceedings of the 2011 DiGRA International Conference, Think Design Play, pp. 1–14 (2011)
20. Narayanasamy, W., Wong, K.K., Fung, C.C., Rai, S.: Distinguishing games and simulation games from simulators. Comput. Entertain. **4**, 2 (2006)
21. Lean, J., Moizer, J., Towler, M., Abbey, C.: Simulations and games. use and barriers in higher education. Act. Learn. High Educ. **7**(3), 227–242 (2006)
22. Apperley, T.H.: Genre and game studies: toward a critical approach to video game genres. Simul. Gaming **37**(1), 6–23 (2009)
23. Huizinga, J.: Homo Ludens: Proeve Eener Bepaling Van Het Spel-Element Der Cultuur. University Press, Amsterdam (2008)
24. Caillois, R., Barash, M.: Man, Play, and Games. University of Illinois Press, Urbana (1961)
25. Kitchenham, B.: Procedures for performing systematic reviews. TR/SE-0401, Department of Computer Science, Keele University (2004)
26. Palmunen, L.-M., Pelto, E., Paalumäki, A., Lainema, T.: Formation of novice business students' mental models through simulation gaming. Simul. Gaming **44**(6), 846–868 (2013)
27. Hummel, G.K., Geerts, W., Slootmaker, A., Kuipers, D., Westera, W.: Collaboration scripts for mastership skills. Online Game about Classroom Dilemmas in Teacher Education. Interactive Learning Environments 0.0, pp. 1–13. Taylor and Francis + NEJM, Web (2013)
28. von Wangenheim, C.G., Savi, R., Borgatto, A.F.: SCRUMIA. an educational game for teaching SCRUM in computing courses. J. Syst. Softw. **86**(10), 2675–2687 (2013)
29. Günther, M., Kiesling, E., Stummer, C.: Game-based learning in technology management education. IEEE Educ. Eng. EDUCON **2010**, 191–196 (2010)
30. Vos, L., Brennan, R.: Marketing simulation games: student and lecturer perspectives. Mark. Intell. Plann. **28**(7), 882–897 (2010)
31. LeFlore, J.L., Anderson, M., Zielke, M.A., Thomas, P.E., Hardee, G., John, L.D.: Can a virtual patient trainer teach student nurses how to save lives, teaching nursing students about pediatric respiratory diseases, simulation in healthcare. J. Soc. Simul. Healthc. **7**(1), 10–17 (2012)
32. Julien, F., Doutriaux, J., Couillard, J.: Teaching the production/operations management core course. integrating logistics planning activities. Prod. Oper. Manage. **7**(2), 160–170 (1998)
33. Hauge, J.B., Bellotti, F., Nadolski, R., Berta, R., Carvalho, M.B.: Deploying serious games for management in higher education: lessons learned and good practices. EAI Endorsed Trans. Serious Games **1**(3), 1–12 (2014)
34. Bayart, C., Bertezene, S., Vallat, D., Martin, J.: Serious games. leverage for knowledge management. TQM J. **26**(3), 235–252 (2014)
35. Begum, M., Newman, R.: Evaluation of students' experiences of developing transferable skills and business skills using a business simulation game. In: FIE 2009, pp. 1–6 (2009)
36. Peters, V.A.M., Vissers, G.A.N.: A simple classification model for debriefing simulation games. Simul. Gaming **35**(1), 70–84 (2004)
37. Bellotti, F., Berta, R., De Gloria, A., Lavagnino, E., Dagnino, F. M., Antonaci, A., Ott, M.: A gamified short course for promoting entrepreneurship among ICT engineering students. In: ICALT, pp. 31–32 (2013)
38. Mayer, I., Warmelink, H., Bekebrede, G.: Learning in a game-based virtual environment. a comparative evaluation in higher education. Eur. J. Eng. Educ. **38**(1), 85–106 (2013). Taylor and Francis + NEJM
39. Adrian, A.: Borrowing experience: ASX share market game. Int. J. Innov. Learn. **16**(1), 81–96 (2014)

40. Hämäläinen, R., Oksanen, K.: Collaborative 3D learning games for future learning: teachers' instructional practices to enhance shared knowledge construction among students. Technol. Pedagogy Educ. **23**(1), 81–101 (2014)

41. Wouters, P., van Oostendorp, H.: A meta-analytic review of the role of instructional support in game-based learning. Comput. Educ. **60**(1), 412–425 (2013)

42. Hannig, A., Lemos, M., Spreckelsen, C., Ohnesorge-Radtke, U., Rafai, N.: Skills-O-Mat. computer supported interactive motion- and game-based training in mixing alginate in dental education. J. Educ. Comput. Res. **48**(3), 315–343 (2013)

43. Söbke, T.B.H.: Using the master copy-adding educational content to commercial video games, pp. 521–530 (2013)

44. Bellotti, F., Berta, R., De Gloria, A., Lavagnino, E., Antonaci, A., Dagnino, F., Ott, M., Romero, M., Usart, M., Mayer, I.S.: Serious games and the development of an entrepreneurial mindset in higher education engineering students. Entertainment Comput. **5**(4), 357–366 (2014)

45. Boyle, E.A., MacArthur, E.W., Connolly, T.M., Hainey, T., Manea, M., Kärki, A., van Rosmalen, P.: A narrative literature review of games, animations and simulations to teach research methods and statistics. Comput. Educ. **74**, 1–14 (2014)

46. Castronovo, F., Nikolic, D., Zappe, S.E., Leicht, R.M., Messner, J.I.: Enhancement of learning objectives in construction engineering education: a step toward simulation assessment. In: Construction Research Congress American Society of Civil Engineers, pp. 339–348 (2014)

47. Hauge, J.M.B., Pourabdollahian, B., Riedel, J.C.: The use of serious games in the education of engineers. In: Emmanouilidis, C., Taisch, M., Kiritsis, D. (eds.) Advances in Production Management Systems. IFIP AICT, vol. 397, pp. 622–629. Springer, Heidelberg (2013)

48. Freno, A., Trentin, E.: Applications. In: Freno, A., Trentin, E. (eds.) Hybrid Random Fields. ISRL, vol. 15, pp. 121–150. Springer, Heidelberg (2011)

EEG Assessment of Surprise Effects in Serious Games

Konstantinos Georgiadis[1,2(✉)], Herre van Oostendorp[1], and Jelke van der Pal[2]

[1] Department of Information and Computing Sciences, Utrecht University,
Princetonplein 5, 3584 CC Utrecht, The Netherlands
constantinosgeorgiadis@yahoo.gr, H.vanOostendorp@uu.nl
[2] National Aerospace Laboratory, Anthony Fokkerweg 2, 1059 CM Amsterdam, The Netherlands
Jelke.van.der.pal@nlr.nl

Abstract. This study examines an innovative approach for evaluating surprise effects in a serious game. In this game, players were exposed to surprising situations that challenged their level of performance which eventually should help them to acquire crucial mental readiness when real crisis situations emerge. During exposure to surprises, measurements were taken online from players' left prefrontal cortex, using an electroencephalogram (EEG) device. Two groups of participants were compared at three common surprising events (SEs) during the game, with only one group being exposed to seven preceding SEs. First, mean amplitude power (MAP) values in Delta band were indeed significantly lower during exposure to SEs compared to their baseline pre-game status which points to a more wakeful state. Secondly, comparing MAP values in the Alpha band showed a significant difference as was expected, with the group with preceding surprises having higher MAPs, indicating less cortical activation which is interpreted as being more relaxed and conscious.

1 Introduction

Many training contexts in simulation games demand for making decisions under time pressure, such as, for instance, handling emergency situations for helicopter pilots or evacuations for safety personnel. Surprising events are in these circumstances almost always present. Being able to handle them is an important condition for adequate operating and handling the situation. This study intents to strengthen the role of surprises in simulation games, as for example could be used in aviation training. We will first examine whether we can assess surprise effects in brain activity by measuring EEG patterns. Second, we examine whether dealing with prior surprises enhances the performance of players and the handling of new, subsequent surprises.

1.1 EEG Measurements

It was only in 1924 when neurologist Hans Berger managed to amplify the brain's electrical activity in order to depict it on a strip of paper. From then on, rapid progress in biofeedback technologies has been achieved, which nowadays allows neuroscientists examine and analyse various physiological responses concurrently and then correlate them in a unified analysis frame in order to reach robust conclusions such as surprise

© Springer International Publishing Switzerland 2016
A. De Gloria and R. Veltkamp (Eds.): GALA 2015, LNCS 9599, pp. 517–529, 2016.
DOI: 10.1007/978-3-319-40216-1_56

effects [1]. Electroencephalogram (EEG) has been applied for decades to measure differences in mental states. That is what we explore in this study: measuring surprise effects by EEG. Firstly, we will examine whether we can measure reliably surprise effects by EEG when surprising events (SEs) are embedded in a serious game. Secondly, we will test the hypothesis that prior exposure to SEs will lead to more efficient task behaviour in the game (and hopefully in real life) when finally a new SE occurs. Before dealing with the role of surprises in games and the research questions, we will elaborate on the topics of EEG measurements and the nature of surprises.

The human brain generates electricity that can be measured on the scalp surface in microvolts by applying electrodes. Electric output can be found in wavelengths from 0.1 to 100 Hz. This brainwave spectrum is categorized into meaningful bandwidths or brainwave types. Each type has been found to indicate certain psychological states. What is more, each brainwave type is characterized by its amplitude. The more neurons that work in synchrony, the larger the amplitude of the electrical oscillations measured in microvolts. In other words, amplitude indicates the intensity (i.e. power) of the electrical signal at each brainwave type. In a certain interval of time, the mean amplitude power (i.e. MAP) at each brainwave band can be calculated in order to define the mental condition within this time period in general.

Table 1. Brainwave types with their respective mental interpretation

Brainwave types		
Brainware type	Freq. range	Mental state
Delta	0.1 to 3 Hz	Deep, dreamless and non-REM sleep, unconscious
Theta	4 to 7 Hz	Intuitive, creative, recall, fantasy, imaginary, dream
Alpha	8 to 12 Hz	Relaxed yet focused, sensorimotor response
Low Beta	12 to 15 Hz	Relaxed yet focused, sensorimotor response
Mid Beta	16 to 20 Hz	Thinking, aware of self and surroundings
High Beta	21 to 30 Hz	Alertness, agitation
Gamma	30 to 100 Hz	Higher mental activity, motor function

Berger was also the first to classify the brainwave spectrum in certain brainwave types in 1929. In general, the most common brainwave bands discussed in EEG literature are Delta, Theta, Alpha, Beta and Gamma [2], each indicating certain mental states (see Table 1). However, there is no standard classification of brainwave types. Several frequency ranges for the brainwave bands are used and more detailed classification of the brainwave types have been suggested as well [4], including brainwave types such as Mu (ranging from 7.5 to 12.5 Hz) or SMR (ranging for 13 to 15 Hz), each defining very specific mental states not described by the aforementioned brainwave bands [5, 6]. A variety of EEG devices (e.g. intrusive or non-intrusive with one or more electrodes) are available in the retail market and manufacturers also define different frequency ranges for these brainwave bands/types for their products and applications. For example, Emotiv defines Delta band for wavelengths ranging from 0.5 to 4 Hz [3], while NeuroSky defines its range from 0.1 to 3 Hz.

NeuroSky's Mindwave Mobile. This study explores the use of non-intrusive EEG. Practical application in training situations using simulation or gaming should be feasible. For that reason a simple one-channel, mobile EEG device measuring frontal brain activity is used, namely Mindwave Mobile (manufactured by NeuroSky Inc.). This device provides a more explicit classification of the Beta band by splitting it into three different brainwave types: Low, Mid and High Beta. Each of these brainwave types is interpreted into a very specific mental state. Table 1 illustrates all bandwidths, as provided by NeuroSky, along with their respective mental state interpretation [7]. The important point now is that Delta activity (0.1 to 3 Hz) corresponds to sleepiness and drowsiness. Specifically, low Delta band means low in sleepiness and thus to be more wakeful [8]. Next to that, Alpha brainwaves (8 to 12 Hz) are generally associated with a state of relaxation [8]. Benca et al. [9] showed that increased Alpha band corresponds to a mental state of more relaxation and to be more conscious.

Prefrontal Cortex. The prefrontal cortex (i.e. PFC) is the cerebral cortex which covers the front part of the frontal lobe and it contains Brodmann areas 9, 10, 11, 12, 46, and 47 [10]. Among others, these areas are involved in significant brain functions such as in working memory, decision making, emotion processing, behaviour control, strategy change response, planning and selective attention. In general, the PFC is responsible for executive and higher cognitive functions. Therefore, this part of the brain is the most promising for measuring (short-term and/or long-term) effects that surprises (as well as other emotions) trigger in the brain. Moreover, the frontal activation models [1, 11–14] argue that the greater the frontal activation, the more intense is the emotional experience.

Frontal EEG Asymmetry. Due to frontal EEG asymmetry [15], the left and right parts of the PFC have a different response to emotions with different valence [16–18]. The right PFC is usually linked to negative emotions such as disgust, fear, sadness which are associated behaviourally to withdrawal [19, 20]. Moreover, right frontal asymmetry measures are predictors of empathic concern (compassion and concern), a relationship that is mediated by feelings such as sadness [21]. In addition, right PFC is also associated specifically with the adjustment of inferential learning on the basis of unpredictability (i.e. surprising events) [22]. In contrast, left PFC is usually linked to positive emotions such as joy and happiness which are associated behaviourally to approach [19, 23, 24]. It is vital to underline here that surprises can have any valence (positive, negative or neutral), and thus they can accordingly be partially linked to the left or right PFC. Hence, surprises can behaviourally associated to withdrawal or approach. This remark coincides with the fact that surprises may induce a fight-or-flight response [25]. What is also important to note is that, individual differences in frontal asymmetry are present in humans from early age and predict their reactivity to emotional challenges [26].

1.2 Nature of Surprises

Surprise is a complex phenomenon with physiological and psychological elements and depends considerably on situational meaning and therefore the personal background of the surprised person. Surprising events can trigger a variety of responses such as startle, surprise, confusion, stress, panic, shock, and even trauma.

What counts as a surprise, often defined as inconsistency between predicted and observed outcome [27], differs between individuals in experienced intensity (ranging from insignificant to life threatening). Furthermore a surprise can have valences such as positive, neutral, or negative, and can be pleasant or unpleasant [28].

1.3 The Role of Surprises in Gaming

Designing surprising events can be done in a variety of ways. We distinguish two main types of surprises: bottom-up surprises, using sensory elements and top-down surprises, using cognitive, narrative elements. A bottom-up surprise is generated by providing unexpected sensory input, while a top down surprise is generated by providing cognitive inconsistencies to Long Term Memory or narrative surprises. Of course a combination of both is also possible.

Visual and auditory cues in the virtual environment can be used in order to create a bottom-up surprise. In the case of visual cues, the surprise of visual stimuli can be more or less salient, determined by features like the local luminance contrast, the color contrast, the orientation and direction of motion. Moreover, the flickering of a color (especially red) in some parts of an image can also be surprising and trigger the player's attention [29]. Beside the visual cues that can be used in order to generate bottom-up surprises from the virtual environment, a scenario or game developer can also use auditory cues. Any sudden and unexpected change of tonality, loudness, pitch etc. of voices, music, sounds and noises can cause surprise to the player.

Top-down surprises can be created by building surprises from a narrative or by addressing the personal knowledge base of the trainee(s). For example, assume reading a book in which the main character starts dating a person. The information related to this event becomes surprising when it is coupled to the reader's knowledge in the long-term memory, for example that the person dated is the sister of the person's wife. As result, the surprise may trigger a physiological reaction such as facial expressions or to give a cry.

Beside the distinction of surprises on basis of how they are elicited (bottom-up, top-down or mixed), surprising events can also be related to a task or a procedure that is being executed by a player at the moment *or* not. In other words, a surprise event can also be either task-dependent or task-independent; one can expect that these surprise types can produce different impact on players. As a result, different types of surprises can be created in a game.

1.4 Research Questions and Hypotheses

The first research question is whether surprise effects in a game environment can be measured using a simple EEG device. For example, surprises are known for their capability to stir up players, which means that vigilance increases and players transit into an (even) more wakeful state. In EEG, this means lower amplitude power in the Delta band. We therefore expect that inserting Surprise Events (SEs) in the game will lead to lower

MAP values in the Delta band compared to a baseline measurement where players were in wakeful rest and no SE's were present. Furthermore we will compare the online EEG measurements of the SEs with a post-game measurement by means of a questionnaire.

The second research question involves the effect of prior experience with SEs on subsequent handling of new SEs. We expect that the more players are exposed to surprise events the more they will mentally adapt in perceiving and handling SEs, and thus the more efficient they will become during task performance when finally new surprising events occur. The learning process behind this relates to a desensitization process and the formation of a coping strategy [30]. This means less emotional response and so less cortical activation which during wake state connects to higher Alpha band activity [9]. Therefore, people that have been exposed to SEs before will reveal higher Alpha MAPs when facing with new SEs than people that have not previously been exposed to SEs because previously exposed players will be more relaxed and conscious at that moment. Furthermore we expect that people that have been exposed to SEs before, will perform better during new SEs, that is, carry out their mission faster and reach higher in-game scores.

For this purpose a simulation game including the surprise events mentioned above was designed using Virtual Battle Space (VSB2). A training scenario was developed in which the player acted as an undercover agent who had to perform a series of action in order to save an island's commercial supplies from terrorists. Two versions were constructed: the Experimental Condition (EC) and Control Condition (CC) version. The scenario was divided in three phases in order to meet the requirements of the study. The first phase (i.e. Phase A) has an introductory purpose to the game and is common for both versions. The goal here is to learn the basic movement keys and the required action-set to the players. The regular gameplay starts at Phase B. At this point, the scenario differentiates the two versions, since seven SEs are introduced for the EC, while no surprises exist for the CC. This is because, we want to examine whether being exposed to prior surprises can lead to an improved handling of surprises at a later stage. This later stage is phase C, which is common again for both versions and it introduces the same three SEs. The surprises were inserted within the missions in a random order considering their type. An overview of the two versions of the game is provided in Table 2.

Table 2. Overview of the two versions (Experimental Condition EC; Control Condition CC).

	Phase A	Phase B	Phase C
EC	Learning basic movement keys, available action-set	Surprising gameplay with **seven** SEs	Surprising gameplay with **three** SEs
CC	Learning basic movement keys, available action-set	Regular gameplay with **no** SEs	Surprising gameplay with **three** SEs

2 Method

2.1 Participants, Conditions of Experiment and Procedure

Twenty people aging from 19 to 33 participated in this experiment (10 in EC and 10 in CC). Assignment to conditions was randomised and balanced to sex and game experience. The experiment took place at the "Serious Game Lab" at the NLR facilities in order to reassure that the setting would be sufficiently quiet.

After fitting NeuroSky's Mindwave Mobile to the participants head, they were asked to remain calm and inactive in order to perform a 5 min baseline recording. When done, few verbal instructions related to the gameplay were given to the participants. Afterwards, the participants started playing the mission (either EC or CC) while concurrent EEG recordings were performed. After completing the mission, the participants were handed with a questionnaire that they had to fill in order to complete the experimental process. The total session approximately lasted for about 45 min.

2.2 Materials

Game Design. A 3D game scenario was created to provide all types of surprises (described at 1.3) by using the Virtual Battlespace 2 editor from Bohemia Interactive. In this scenario, the player acted as an undercover agent whom had to perform a series of actions in order to save an island's commercial supplies from terrorists. The gameplay was set as single player, action-based in a non-military setting using a linear, simple scenario that was playable even for participants unexperienced to first person shooter games.

Two different versions of the same mission were implemented. The first, the Experimental Condition (EC) contains 10 surprising events (SEs). Example snapshots from some of the implemented SEs can be seen at Fig. 1, i.e. upper-left a sudden fire, at the upper-right an unexpected bomb explosion in a car, lower-left an additional undercover mission is revealed and lower-right the electric provision on the island limits due to a sabotage at the electric generators. The second, Control Condition (CC), follows the same narrative, except this time only three surprising events are included during Phase C. The narrative of these two versions is divided in 3 phases (see Table 2):

Phase A: This is the introduction phase where the player learns how to navigate into the virtual world by using the standard gaming control keys for moving around in the virtual environment. Moreover, it is the learning phase where the player becomes aware about his mission and how and which types of actions can be performed. The participant is given guidance (prompts, cues) on the actions to perform. By performing some actions without surprises, we assume the participant will learn to perform the actions setting a baseline of expectations on the task and the environment.

Phase B: For the EC condition this is the surprising events phase, where the player has to perform actions which are introduced by different types of surprising events. The surprising events are introduced as cinematics of certain time duration. On the other hand, in the case of the CC mission, similar cinematics with a neutral character of the same duration are introduced, only this time the surprising stimulus is completely removed because no time differences should exist between the two missions.

Fig. 1. Example snapshots from the implemented surprise events.

Phase C: This is the last "undercover mission" phase, where the player has to perform a series of actions in order to complete the mission successfully. This phase is identical for both EC and CC, since both contain the same (three) SEs.

Analysis Tools and Process. In order to examine the participants' brain function, EEG data was collected at a sampling rate of 128 Hz by using NeuroSkyLab. By using NeuroSky's Mindwave Mobile, a dry single-electrode can be applied on the left prefrontal cortex (position Fp1 according to the International 10–20 system [8]), while embedded algorithms on its ThinkGear chipset can perform artefact correction (electricity generated by muscle movements, e.g. eye movements). During gameplay various predefined key-strokes were used in order to time-stamp critical moments (such as the SEs and the game phases) within the EEG recorded data. The recorded data was stored in a Thinkgear file that was converted to a suitable form expressed in microvolts, ranging from −825 to 825 µV. Afterwards, EEGLAB was used to further analyse them. Thus, the proper electrode location was defined and the data was filtered with respect to the Nyquist frequency restrictions that removes artefacts. When done, specific time-frames of major interest were selected by using the logged time-stamps. A MATLAB script was developed to calculate the Mean Amplitude Power (MAP) values at each brainwave band for the selected time-frame.

Before performing statistical analysis using SPSS over the collected data, all the outliers were removed by finding the according upper and lower limits for the amplitude range of each brain frequency band [31].

Additionally, in-game assessment was performed in order to register the players' correctness. For this reason, a simple point system was used that measured their total score (+100 points for every correct action). During gameplay the players could get feedback and keep track of their progress from the in-game score indicator at the upper-left part of the screen. Moreover, the players' completion times for finishing a mission were logged (in milliseconds) separately for each phase as well as their overall time for completing the whole mission.

Questionnaire. Besides the EEG and in-game assessment, a post-game questionnaire was used for rating the disturbance in task performance due to the SEs. A 7-point Likert-type scale was used ranging from "not at all" to "very much" disturbed. A screenshot was presented beside each SE, illustrating a scene moment with the SE along with a short description of the respective surprising event.

2.3 Apparatus

The simulation game was made by using the VBS2 Editor (version 1.6) created by Bohemia Interactive Studios. The game was played on a Dell Alienware AURORA_4 desktop computer using an Intel(R) Core(TM) i7-4930 K CPU @ 3.40 GHz, with a 27" widescreen monitor, a NVIDIA GeForce GTX 680 graphics card, and a large Alienware headset. The game ran smoothly on a maximum detail (of 2560 × 1600) and lighting settings. All the VBS2 audio settings (SFX, Music etc.) where set at maximum in order to get advantage of the auditorial cues used in the game. Lastly, a 64-bit version of Windows 7 Professional was used as operating system. In addition, Neurosky's Mind-wave Mobile was used for collecting the EEG data. This device consists of the Think-Gear EEG sensor module, a dry-electrode and an ear-clip. Embedded within it, is the TGAT chip, which is a fully integrated single chip EEG sensor. The chip is programmed with NeuroSky eSense, A/D, amplification off head detection, and noise filtering for EMG and 50/60 Hz AC powerline interference.

3 Results

3.1 EEG Results

Delta Band Effects. A comparison was made between the mean Delta MAP values during the baseline and during the phases with surprises (Phase B and C) in the EC group. This difference between the baseline and each of the Delta's at the moment of the surprises was significant (using One-way ANOVA with Games-Howell for post-hoc analysis showed $F(1,9) = 14.971$, $p = .004$). We used here a time-window of 3 s from presenting the SE's. Figure 2 shows that during the exposure to the SEs the Delta values were lower compared to their baseline pre-game values which point to a more wakeful state.

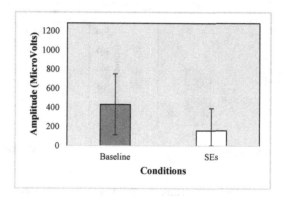

Fig. 2. Mean MAP Delta values during baseline and SEs.

Alpha Band Effects. Results from the EEG data show a significant difference $(t(50.1230) = 2.079, p < .05)$ between the EC group and the CC group in mean Alpha MAP values. Figure 3 shows that the EC group was more relaxed when encountering surprises in Phase C than the CC group.

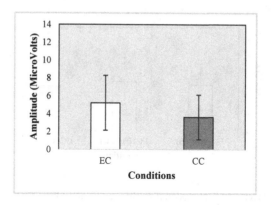

Fig. 3. Mean Alpha MAPs of last three common SEs in the EC and CC groups (Phase C).

3.2 Completion Time and In-Game Scores

Next we compared whether participants in the EC group carry out their mission faster than the participants in the CC group, and also we compared their in-game score during phase C. There was a significant difference regarding completion time $(t(18) = 2.637, p < .005)$ and regarding in-game performance $(t(18) = 1.861, p < .05)$. Figure 4 shows that the EC group was faster during Phase C and also their in-game performance score was higher.

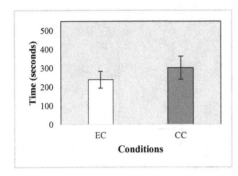 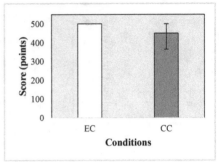

Fig. 4. Means (and sd's) of completion time (left) and in-game score (right) during Phase C for both groups

3.3 Questionnaire Outcomes

Considering the results of the players' self-ratings of disturbance due to task-performance at the post-game questionnaire, no statistically significant differences ($p > .05$) occurred, during Phase B compared to Phase C. Similarly, no significant differences ($p > .05$) were found among the two groups during Phase C. In Fig. 5 results are presented.

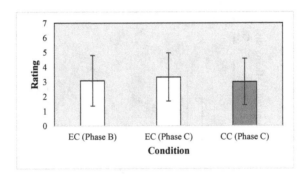

Fig. 5. Means of players' self-ratings on disturbance during task-performance due to the SEs.

4   Conclusion and Discussion

Our first research question examined whether the EEG measurement is sensitive and reliable enough to detect EEG effects of surprises. We hypothesized that surprises are considered to stir up players, i.e. to awake them. This hypothesis was confirmed for all surprising events. It appeared that the Delta MAP values were indeed significantly lower during exposure to surprising events compared to their baseline pre-game status, which points to a more wakeful state.

Considering our second research question of whether exposure to more surprises leads to an improved handling of surprises, measurements were performed in three ways: EEG measurements, in-game measurements and post-game questionnaire ratings. The results showed that even though the EC participants stated not to feel less disturbed during their task-performance based on the questionnaire compared to the CC group, they still performed better regarding their in-game performance and completion time during Phase C. When looking at the EEG results of the two groups during the surprising events within a 3 s time-window from the moment the last three common SEs were presented, the EC and CC groups differed in Alpha band, indicating that the EC group felt more relaxed than the CC group during Phase C. This fact probably helped the EC group to maintain a higher level of instant or reflex reactions towards the surprising gameplay, which consequently facilitated to achieve higher in-game scores and faster completion time.

The study mainly focused on testing the usefulness of one technique that has powerful potential in online measuring mental states: EEG measurement. With the device as used, surprises could be detected and distinguished in a virtual simulation environment. This outcome can also be used in revising/redesigning processes of a surprising scenario's, that is, it enables designers to reject or alter non-effective surprising events. Based on the results of this study we conclude that even a simple, commercial of the shelf tool that is easy to use in standard training situations, is sensitive and reliable to measure effects to surprising events. However, using the data recording and analysis software is at present not a simple task and considerable time and effort must be spent.

No matter the complexity that EEG measurement introduced in this experiment, it helped in answering the posed research questions. An important finding is the effect of surprises in the Delta band, more specifically its MAP value decreased when SEs were triggered. The most significant finding, however, was the increased Alpha band activity after being exposed to many surprises, implying that the players responded emotionally less intensive to later surprising stimuli leading to a relaxed and more conscious mental state. This is probably also the reason why they managed to be more effective during task performance. However, the post-game questionnaire results didn't align with these in-game and EEG findings. Therefore, doubts can be raised for the usefulness of a post-game questionnaire, at least as it was currently constructed.

This experiment was also an excellent chance for us to test our simulation game for assessment and training purposes. As for the simulation game used for assessment and training it is important to mention that the use of EEG provided a new scope in the analysis of players' mental states. However, what also could be (additionally) useful here is an eye-tracking device and a camera for recording facial expressions. An eye-tracking device would allow observation of the participants' reaction to surprises. Additionally, more biofeedback devices such as Galvanic Skin Response could also be used, with the trade-back however of possibly decreasing the players' immersion and natural response. While a one-channel device is easy to wear, more channels do provide more information. For example, it could be useful to examine the right prefrontal cortex since in the current scenario setting only surprises of neutral and negative valence were implemented and these are mainly represented at the left prefrontal cortex.

Acknowledgements. This study is part of the Serious Gaming project supported by the Royal Netherlands Air Force under contract 080.14.3903.10.

References

1. Murugappan, M., Ramachandran, N., Sazali, Y.: Classification of human emotion from EEG using discrete wavelet transform. J. Biomed. Sci. Eng. **3**, 390–396 (2010)
2. Hondrou, C., Caridakis, G.: Affective, natural interaction using EEG: sensors, application and future directions. In: Maglogiannis, I., Plagianakos, V., Vlahavas, I. (eds.) SETN 2012. LNCS, vol. 7297, pp. 331–338. Springer, Heidelberg (2012)
3. Emotiv EPOC 3D Brain Activity Map Premium Version. User Manual V1.0. Emotiv Inc. (2011)
4. Dressler, O.: Awareness and the EEG power spectrum: analysis of frequency. Br. J. Anesth. **93**(6), 806–809 (2004)
5. Amzica, F., Da Silva, F.L.: Celluluar substrates of brain rhythms. In: Schomer, D.L., da Silva, F.L. (eds.) Niedermeyer's Electroencephalography: Basic Principles, Clinical Applications, and Related Fields, vol. 6, pp. 33–63. Lippincott Williams & Wilkins, Philadelphia (2010)
6. Arroyo, S., Lesser, R.P., Gordon, B., Uematsu, S., Jackson, D., Webber, R.: Functional significance of the mu rhythm of human cortex: an electrophysiologic study with subdural electrodes. Electroencephalogr. Clin. Neurophysiol. **87**(3), 76–87 (1993)
7. NeuroSky: Brain Wave Signal (EEG). NeuroSky, Inc. (2009)
8. Hammond, D.C.: What is neurofeedback? J. Neurother. **10**(4), 25 (2006)
9. Benca, R.M., Obermeyer, W.H., Larson, C.L., Yun, B., Dolski, I., Kleist, K.D., Weber, S.M., Davidson, R.J.: EEG alpha power and alpha power asymmetry in sleep and wakefulness. Psychophysiology **36**, 430–436 (1999)
10. Brodmann, K.: Vergleichende Lokalisationslehre der Grosshirnrinde (in German). Johann Ambrosius Barth, Leipzig (1909)
11. Davidson, R.J., Schwartz, G.E., Saron, C., Bennett, J., Goleman, D.J.: Frontal versus parietal EEG asymmetry during positive and negative affect. Psychophysiology **16**, 202–203 (1979)
12. Dawson, G.: Frontal electroencephalographic correlates of individual differences in emotional expression in infants. In: Fox, N.A., (ed.) The Development of Emotion Regulation: Behavioral and Biological Considerations. Monographs of the Society for Research in Child Development, vol. 59(2–3), Serial No. 240, pp. 135–151 (1994)
13. Schmidt, L.A.: Frontal brain electrical activity in shyness and sociability. Psychol. Sci. **10**, 316–320 (1999)
14. Schmidt, L.A., Fox, N.A.: Conceptual, biological, and behavioral distinctions among different types of shy children. In: Schmidt, L.A., Schulkin, J. (eds.) Extreme Fear, Shyness and Social Phobia: Origins, Biological Mechanisms, and Clinical Outcomes, pp. 47–66. Oxford University Press, New York (1999)
15. LeMay, M.: Asymmetries of the skull and handedness. Phrenology revisited. J. Neurol. Sci. **32**(2), 243–253 (1977)
16. Davidson, R.J.: The neuropsychology of emotion and affective style. In: Lewis, M., Haviland, J.M. (eds.) Handbook of Emotion, pp. 143–154. Guilford Press, New York (1993)
17. Fox, N.A.: If it's not left, it's right: electroencephalograph asymmetry and the development of emotion. Am. Psychol. **46**, 863–872 (1991)
18. Heller, W.: Neuropsychological mechanisms of individual differences in emotion, personality, and arousal. Neuropsychology **7**, 476–489 (1993)

19. Coan, J.A., Allen, J.J.B., Harmon-Jones, E.: Voluntary facial expressions and hemispheric asymmetry over the frontal cortex. Psychophysiology **38**, 912–925 (2001)
20. Dawson, G., Panagiotides, H., Klinger, L.G., Hill, D.: The role of frontal lobe functioning in the development of infant self-regulatory behavior. Brain Cogn. **20**, 152–175 (1992)
21. Tullett, A.H., Harmon-Jones, E., Inzlight, M.: Right frontal cortical asymmetry predicts empathic reactions: support for a link between withdrawal motivation and empathy. Psychophysiology **49**, 1145–1153 (2012)
22. Fletcher, P.C., Anderson, J.M., Shanks, D.R., Honey, R., Carpenter, T.A., Donovan, T., Papadakis, N., Bullmore, E.T.: Responses of human frontal cortex to surprising events are predicted by formal associative learning theory. Nat. Neurosci. **4**(10), 1043–1048 (2001). Nature Publishing Group
23. Davidson, R.J., Schaffer, C.E., Saron, C.: Effects of lateralized presentations of faces on self-reports of emotion and EEG asymmetry in depressed and non-depressed subjects. Psychophysiology **22**, 353–364 (1985)
24. Harmon-Jones, E., Allen, J.J.B.: Anger and frontal brain activity: EEG asymmetry consistent with approach motivation despite negative affective valence. J. Pers. Soc. Psychol. **74**, 1310–1316 (1998)
25. Cannon, W.: Wisdom of the Body. W.W. Norton & Company, New York (1932)
26. Davidson, R.J., Fox, N.A.: Frontal brain asymmetry predicts infants' response to maternal separation. J. Abnorm. Psychol. **98**, 127–131 (1989)
27. Ranasinghe, N., Shen, W.M.: Surprise-based learning for developmental robotics. In: Proceedings of ECSIS Symposium on Learning and Adaptive Behaviours for Robotic Systems, Edinburgh, Scotland (2008)
28. Frijda, N.H.: The Emotions. Cambridge University Press, Cambridge (1986)
29. Itti, L., Baldi, P.: A principled approach to detecting surprising events in video. In: Proceedings IEEE Conference on Computer Vision and Pattern Recognition (CVPR), pp. 631–637 (2005)
30. McGlynn, F., Smitherman, T., Gothard, K.: Comment on the status of systematic desensitization. Behav. Modif. **28**(2), 194–205 (2004)
31. Iglewicz, B., Banerjee, S.: A simple univariate outlier identification procedure. In: Proceedings of the Annual of the American Statistical Association (2001)

FRAGGLE: A FRamework for AGile Gamification of Learning Experiences

Alberto Mora[1]([⊠]), Panagiotis Zaharias[2], Carina González[3],
and Joan Arnedo-Moreno[1]

[1] Estudis d'Informàtica, Multimedia i Telecomunicació,
Universitat Oberta de Catalunya, Barcelona, Spain
{amoraca,jarnedo}@uoc.edu
[2] Information and Telecommunication Systems,
Open University of Cyprus, Latsia, Cyprus
panagiotis.zacharias@ouc.ac.cy
[3] Ing. de Sist. y Aut. y Arq. y Tec. de Computadores,
Universidad de La Laguna, San Cristóbal de La Laguna, Spain
cjgonza@ull.edu.es

Abstract. Student's motivation difficulties are present in learning scenarios, even university grades. Between the techniques being applied by instructors to counteract this fact, we can find gamification techniques. Unfortunately, sometimes the result is the appearance of unwanted effects, which is a very common symptom of poor designs caused by the lack of proven methodologies for its purpose. This paper presents our first approach of a conceptual framework for designing the gamification of learning experiences. It is focused in higher education and based on the use of the Agile methodologies in order to obtain a fast Minimum Viable Product (MVP) ready for testing. Its aims are to apply different techniques all the way down to the lowest levels of abstraction through its step-by-step process.

Keywords: Gamification · Design · Framework · Learning · Higher education

1 Introduction

Nowadays, motivation is a very common problem in learners, especially when they do not find the purpose of a learning activity [10]. Therefore, instructors face the daily challenge of motivating them and, at the same time, designing student-centered activities in order to develop their skills. Learning strategies related to the use of game components look like an appropriate contribution to the development of these skills. Thus, "gamification", understood as the use of game design and game elements in non-game contexts [6], becomes a relevant technique for increasing student motivation and engagement [7,26]. By applying gamification into the classroom, students could be motivated to learn in new

© Springer International Publishing Switzerland 2016
A. De Gloria and R. Veltkamp (Eds.): GALA 2015, LNCS 9599, pp. 530–539, 2016.
DOI: 10.1007/978-3-319-40216-1_57

ways or become engaged in otherwise tedious tasks [13]. According to these principles, different experiences are being carried out [11].

Gamification of learning seems to be a promising approach to overcome these difficulties, although the achievement of that effect is not trivial. A big effort is required from the very design to the implementation and deployment of the experience [7]. Special care must be taken into account, since unwanted effects during the application of gamification have been reported in the literature [3]. On that regard, different learning experiences in higher educational contexts are reporting failures due to use of *ad hoc* gamification designs [1,2,9]. Additionally, back-end reports from instructors show designing issues as cost, time, and difficulties on implementation [14,21,28]. As a common factor, most of them do not follow a proven design process for the engagement purpose.

Hence, the need for a conceptual specific learning framework for designing the process becomes clear. A wide array of gamification frameworks exist in the literature, but it is noteworthy that most of them were developed with a business scope in mind, as shown in bibliographic reviews [19]. Above all, learning references are highly focused on specific experiences [20] and, to a lesser extent, as simple sets of guidelines [16,17]. This is the main motivation to propose our first approach to a conceptual framework for designing gamification in educative contexts, built upon Agile methodologies [8]: a FRamework for AGile Gamification of Learning Experiences. The proposed methodologies, commonly used in terms of software development, make the building process easy and efficient thanks to iterative and incremental tasks, including permanent testing and corrections. The attention to the human motivation and engagement issues gives Agile projects a particular relevance.

In summary, a formal proposal for designing and introducing gamification techniques into the learning process is presented here. The paper is structured as follows: first of all, the principles of the framework are explained in Sect. 2. Section 3 is devoted to a step-by-step guide of the process. Finally, Sect. 4 sums up the conclusions and further work.

2   Principles

Based on the previous background, the development of a formal design process for educative contexts seems essential. The development of a framework, understood as "a standardized set of concepts, practices and criteria to focus on a particular type of problem that serves as a reference, to confront and solve new problems of a similar nature set" appears to be an appropriate structure for this purpose, since it intends to solve the design gaps and difficulties found in the gamification experiences.

On the other hand, Agile methodologies aim to improve the efficiency and quality of the final developments, having the ability to respond to changes and new definitions, by providing the greatest possible satisfaction to the final user and continuous feedback. Therefore, in contrast to traditional methodologies, Agile relies on incremental developments with very short iterations, giving greater value to the individual issues with high effectiveness in unclear and changeable environments. Agile development encompasses a broad set of principles and methodologies, but the main inspiration for FRAGGLE are Lean UX [12] and Behaviour-Driven Development (BDD) [4].

On the one hand, Lean UX, (inspired by Lean Startup [22], design thinking, and the Agile development theories), is an approach for an extremely fast User-Centered Design (UCD) which aims to ensure achievements for specific targets under a model based on experimentation. By its application, it is intended to avoid the traditional slow design and production cycles commonly defined for other gamification proposals. The main approach is taking a leaf out of the Lean Startup movement and launch a valued MVP, getting early validation from users about the design and improving by iterating on a real world experience. Human-Centered interaction literature proves the useful use of User-Centered techniques in the design process, in particular by using iterative prototypes. Thus, the process is more than just a thoughtful design and will not end when the user's interactions start. Although users are not aware about their participation in the design process, they themselves are indirect designers of the experience. This way, Agile principles are a perfect fit for developments that require quick reaction time and speed, and reducing associate costs and efforts.

On the other hand, BDD is proposed as a synthesis of practices derived from Test-Driven Development (TDD), coming from Extreme Programming methodology (XP). It is based on the specification of user behaviours and how the features should perform. The most important ones for users are developed first. Thus, through the collaboration and continuous feedback, this practice becomes more clear and efficient. The main reasons for BDD application are the proposal of User Stories as outcomes. The implementation process is then limited to only those parts which actually contribute to such outcomes, measured via the Acceptance Tests. Thus, BDD practices let us turn the objectives into readable executable specifications.

Following these principles, the use of Agile methodologies beyond software development may be appropriate for an affordable design of the gamified experiences since its effectiveness has been proven over the years.

3   Design Process

The proposed approach is structured in four phases: declaration, creation, execution and learning as shown in Fig. 1. In the declaration phase, the definition and the necessary previous conceptualization for the design process are explained. The creation phase covers user interaction issues. In the execution phase, tracking is carried out using the provided user feedback. Finally, the learning phase includes the analysis and measurement tasks, including management and prediction works necessary for improvement. Due to size constraints of this publication, we will develop the declaration and creation phases, which are the most relevant ones to get a gamified solution started.

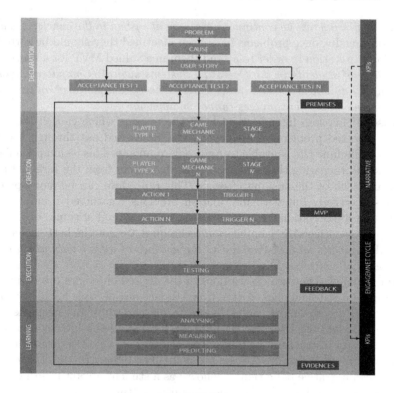

Fig. 1. FRAGGLE's overview

3.1 Declaration

The first phase of the proposed framework aims to cover the acquisition of the necessary information and the description of assumptions. During this phase, four key concepts must be sequentially declared: the problem (as the target to be solved through gamification techniques), the root cause, the necessary actions for reaching the expected outcomes, and finally, the tests for determining if the chosen behaviours lead to problem solving.

1. **Problems.** The first task consists of the identification of the difficulties to be solved by applying gamification techniques. A problem must be previously detected *a priori*, before starting a gamification process design. Some information, quantitative or qualitative, is acquired from the learning scope and it is determined that some improvement is required. Then, gamification can be considered as one of the possible solution but never the other way around (by deciding to use it and then looking for a problem that needs solving).

   Parallel to the problem description, metrics must be identified. They will help us at a later stage to figure out if the desired objectives have been achieved. Therefore, an objective must be specific, measurable, achievable, relevant and time-bound.

e.g. The passing rate by continuous assessment system in the quarterly subject.

Additionally, once problems have been identified they should be sorted for a priority iteration in order to attend them in a valued MVP for a short time. *e.g. 75 % of students in the Operating Systems subject (Computer Engineering grade) do not deliver the tasks through the virtual platform on time, so a continuous assessment process cannot be applied.*

2. **Causes.** This step intends to identify the reasons which caused the previously detected problems. This process can be carried out through the Five Whys Technique [25], suitable to Agile environments. This technique relies on recursively repeating the question "Why" five times from the targeted problem and each of the ensuing answers. This procedure can be developed not only subjectively but with information previously gathered from students. Note that a motivational root cause must be recognized at some stage during this process, otherwise, gamification techniques are not the best choice. *e.g. A motivational lack that causes the absence of work habits which enable a process of continuous assessment.*

3. **User Stories.** They are descriptions of the desired outcomes (objectives) by setting informal sentences written from student perspective. Each User Story provides a description of valued issues to learners through engagement. Be aware that feasible User Stories must be located at the intersection of the learners' and instructors' interests. The creation of such descriptions may be aided by the Role-Feature-Reason template. The basic structure consists in a quantified narrative definition as follows: as a student, i want to feel engaged in... (action), so that... (achievement), during... (time). *e.g. As a student, i want to feel more engaged to make the regular deliveries, so that I will make all of them on time during this semester.*

Therefore, the quality of User Stories should be assessed avoiding ambiguity, being achievable, timely and challenging. The appropriate metrics for achievements related with problem are related. Ethical and legal implications must also be highly considered. Finally, if the feasibility of an User Story is not assured after being described, it must be discarded.

4. **Acceptance Tests.** This step produces a list of expected concrete behaviours which measure the achievement level of each appropriate User Story, through engagement. Each User Story may have a set of Acceptance Tests, which are generated with the aid of the following template: given... (context), when... (action), then... (consequence). *e.g. Given the first deliverable of the course, then at least 90 % of students have sent a file containing the proposed work (unknown content yet) on time.*

Thus, the expected "behaviours" must be aligned with the User Story it belongs to. Although a User Story may have associated different Acceptance Tests, it is not strictly necessary a full coverage success, but recommended. The quality of the Acceptance Tests should be assessed avoiding ambiguity and they should be measurable, achievable, timely and challenging through the definition of the appropriate metrics and Key Performance Indicators (KPIs). The actions and the achievements will let us know if the tests have successful passed when running, as well as quantitative and qualitative evidences. Commonly metrics are related to recency, frequency, duration, virality and rating. An Acceptance Test is considered successful when the values taken from KPIs in data analysis (last phase) exceeded the defined threshold.

3.2 Creation

The Acceptance Tests are the starting point for any of the iterations which are carried out within the Lean process. In order to pass them, a suitable customization is a relevant issue for its achievement. According to Seaborn's view, [24], gamification in action is defined by applying a limited number of game elements. Therefore, it becomes essential the knowledge of the most suitable game elements for particular types of end-users and motivators through a personalized experience.

At the Creation stage, for each of the Acceptance Tests, the appropriate design components are incorporated under a comprehensive narrative layer (any account of connected events as a sequence into the engagement cycle). In this phase, the description of the different player's profile, game mechanics, stages, actions and triggers is developed. The result of the Creation stage will be at least a valued MVP.

1. **Players.** In learning context, they are the different students who will join voluntarily into a gamified experience. According to their attributes, in order to cluster them, several player motivation taxonomies have been developed in the literature [27]. Nevertheless, people in the real world are likely to display a mix of features of more than a concrete cluster. Therefore, considering motivational incentives are more suitable for the design process. According to RAMP [18] there are four main elements of human intrinsic motivation: relatedness, autonomy, mastery and purpose. Of course, extrinsic motivation is an available option, but not highly recommendable for a long-time engagement.

   Before first interaction with real users, different profiles must be predefined. For this reason, it is necessary to describe several *players prototypes*, as the models which would interact within the gamified learning experience. It is an hypothetical segmentation for personalized experiences and provides some of the more useful insights to better understand the different types of learners are going to interact with the environment. Such prototypes are defined according to the following template: *profile, demography and habits, motivational incentives, and potential behaviours.* Even, gender differences may also be relevant [23]. Afterwards, through the iterations and the knowledge of the real learners, an accurate design will be possible for achieving a personalized and engaged learner experience.

   It is noteworthy that the interests and motivational issues of players may change along the gamified experience, influenced by the interaction with other players within the learning experience. In this manner, its detection is considered in the last phase through the design of the appropriate analytic procedure.

e.g. Student profile 1: Peter, 38, male, Caucasian. He works as a graphic designer, high autonomy, with a limited time for the studies and medium records. It is expected a high autonomy work with low interaction in the learning platform and non-regular study habits. Mastery and Autonomy can be the appropriate motivational incentive for this profile.

2. **Game mechanics.** They are the elements around which the experience revolves. According to the game designer Jesse Schell, "Game mechanics are the core of what a game truly is. They are the interactions and relationships that remain when all of the aesthetics, technology, and story are stripped away" [23]. Thus, the appropriate selection of game mechanics for each kind of profile (learners) is a relevant issue for the engagement purpose.

3. **Stages.** Not every game mechanic is suitable for every situation. Depending on the evolved phase into the engagement process, different players will not show the same interest and sensitivity from the prescribed motivators. In this cycle, some mechanics are *better* deployed at concrete stages, throughout the experience. Therefore, Chou [5] identifies the player's journey in a gamification involvement. In order to decompose the experience, it has been broken into four stages: discovery, on-boarding, mid-game and end-game.

   e.g. For the student with profile X, according to the autonomy motivator, Avatar is an appropriate game mechanic to be applied on-boarding stage.

   Regarding the above, it can be used different brief reviews as [29] supporting the suitable use of game mechanics in order to handle the motivators of concrete stages. It must be considered as a complement to the acquired design experience by the instructors.

4. **Actions.** At this point, the desired performances, leaded by the previous design performances, should be well taken into account. Actions are the "verbs" of the gamification, these are the performances that move forward (dynamics). Therefore, different Use Cases [15] must be developed for each proposal including a player, through a game mechanic into a stage, as described before. A Use Case is a list of actions, typically defining interactions between a role, known in Unified Modelling Language (UML) as an "actor", and a system, to achieve a goal. The main purposes for its use are: giving a clear and consistent description of the user performance (desired actions), determining what the system will run (trigger). The definition of the expected conducts through the design proposal, it aims to prevent the situations that players can experience and lead to the disengagement (although it should be considered and dealt with the appropriate trigger).

   e.g. For the student with profile 1, by using Avatars in the on-boarding stage, the valuable actions are: (a) downloading the necessary material to complete the activity, (b) checking the statement of the task and (c) uploading the work on time. The unwanted action is: (d) no accessing to the relevant topic.

5. **Triggers.** Motivational factors are quite sensitive to interaction issues like feedback. Thus, any action should mean an associated response in order to keep an engagement state during the engagement cycle. Triggers give the necessary feedback to learners when some event happens (actions) in the associated stage. Therefore, triggers aims to produce emotional responses into the

player (aesthetics). Thus, they should be developed as a personalized feedback according to the specific actions described above.

e.g. For the action (a) a generic avatar is available (the same for every student). Through action (b) the student may choose between a set of additional avatars and (c), enables customization. (d) Avatar is not available but positive reinforcement is run to captivate.

3.3   Execution

At this time, at least a valued MVP has been developed, during the Execution phase, user interaction within the learning engagement cycle takes place. It will consist of a correlation of experiences which involve the learners in order to the achieve the proposed objectives. It is conceived by the logical relationship of the elements previously identified and described:

"Players" through motivational incentives do "actions" by adopting the appropriate "game mechanics" at a concrete "stage" activating a "trigger" which produce a feedback under a "narrative" layer leading to new motivations.

Additionally, it will be necessary to track and "log" all user interactions in order to allow the quantification of the efficiency and effectiveness of actions. User's feedback becomes essential, although subsequent analytic tasks can determine much finer information about the process. It must be assumed that an optimal design will not be achieved in early iterations. Therefore, adaptability issues are more important than planed design tasks. As a result, a personalized *journey* is developed to attend to learners profile and motivators.

3.4   Learning

The main purpose of the Learning phase is the analysis and measurement of activities, in order to know the achievement of Acceptance Tests, according to the predefined metrics and corresponding KPIs. A long-term experience requires regular checkpoints to ensure the experience has being effective. Therefore, the structure of an existing design can be modified by new iterations for altering the learner behaviour in order to correct possible deviations. Additionally, the detection of the commonly performances during the courses through the use of patterns must be exploited. Behavioural patterns aims to know the anomalies in individual human behaviour. By its process, the appropriate "solutions" that respond to the specific needs of learners (corrective actions) can be provided, even the execution of preventive actions (in order to avoid certain unwanted behaviours). The lack of a personalized design is one of the primary factors that contribute to the failure of gamification initiatives.

4   Conclusion

In this work has been presented a first approach to a conceptual framework for designing gamification of learning experiences, called FRAGGLE. It is focused in higher education through the use of the Agile methodologies in order to obtain a fast MVP in a short time. The approach is based on an incremental development with minimal iterations, giving greater value to individual issues. These, reach high effectiveness in unclear and dynamic environments. Concretely, it is based on low levels of abstraction for a step-by-step understandable application, inspired on the Lean UX principles and the Behaviour-Driven Development methodology, by describing four steps: declaration, creation, execution, and learning. As further work, we consider the expansion of the execution and learning phases, as well the development of a wizard/tool box in order to aid the fast design process. Moreover, the wide validation of the proposal in technical courses in diverse university scenarios in the short time.

Acknowledgments. This work was partly funded by Agència de Gestió d'Ajuts Universitaris i de Recerca (Generalitat de Catalunya) through the Industrial Doctorate programme 2014-DI-006 and the Spanish Government by means of the project TIN2013-45303-P "ICT-FLAG" (Enhancing ICT education through Formative assessment, Learning Analytics and Gamification). It also has been carried out in collaboration with Grupo ICA Barcelona.

References

1. Barata, G., Gama, S., Jorge, J., Gonçalves, D.: So fun it hurts – gamifying an engineering course. In: Schmorrow, D.D., Fidopiastis, C.M. (eds.) AC 2013. LNCS, vol. 8027, pp. 639–648. Springer, Heidelberg (2013)
2. Berkling, K., Thomas, C.: Gamification of a software engineering course and a detailed analysis of the factors that lead to it's failure. In: 2013 International Conference on Interactive Collaborative Learning (ICL), pp. 525–530. IEEE (2013)
3. Broer, J.: Gamification and the trough of disillusionment. In: Mensch & Computer 2014 - Workshopband, pp. 389–395 (2014)
4. Chelimsky, D., Astels, D., Helmkamp, B., North, D.: The RSpec Book: Behaviour Driven Development with Rspec, Cucumber, and Friends. The Pragmatic Bookshelf, New York (2010)
5. Chou, Y.: Gamification design: 4 phases of a player's journey (2013)
6. Deterding, S., Dixon, D., Khaled, R., Nacke, L.: From game design elements to gamefulness: defining gamification. In: Proceedings of the 15th International Academic MindTrek Conference: Envisioning Future Media Environments, pp. 9–15. ACM (2011)
7. Domínguez, A., Saenz-de Navarrete, J., De-Marcos, L., Fernández-Sanz, L., Pagés, C., Martínez-Herráiz, J.J.: Gamifying learning experiences: practical implications and outcomes. Comput. Educ. **63**, 380–392 (2013)
8. Fowler, M., Highsmith, J.: The agile manifesto. Softw. Dev. **9**(8), 28–35 (2001)
9. Gåsland, M.: Game mechanic based e-learning: a case study. Ph.D. thesis (2011)
10. Glover, I.: Play as you learn: gamification as a technique for motivating learners. In: Proceedings of World Conference on Educational Multimedia, Hypermedia and Telecommunications, Chesapeake (2013)
11. Gonzalez, C., Mora, A.: Methodological proposal for gamification in the computer engineering teaching. In: 2014 International Symposium on Computers in Education (SIIE), pp. 29–34. IEEE (2014)

12. Gothelf, J., Seiden, J.: Lean UX: Applying Lean Principles to Improve User Experience. O'Reilly, Sebastopol (2013)
13. Hanus, M.D., Fox, J.: Assessing the effects of gamification in the classroom: a longitudinal study on intrinsic motivation, social comparison, satisfaction, effort, and academic performance. Comput. Educ. **80**, 152–161 (2015)
14. Iosup, A., Epema, D.: An experience report on using gamification in technical higher education. In: Proceedings of the 45th ACM Technical Symposium on Computer Science Education, pp. 27–32. ACM (2014)
15. Jacobson, I.: Object Oriented Software Engineering: A Use Case Driven Approach, 1st edn. Addison Wesley, Reading (1992)
16. Kapp, K.: The Gamification of Learning and Instruction Fieldbook: Ideas into Practice. Wiley, San Francisco (2013)
17. Kotini, I., Tzelepi, S.: A gamification-based framework for developing learning activities of computational thinking. In: Reiners, T., Wood, L.C. (eds.) Gamification in Education and Business, pp. 219–252. Springer, Cham (2015)
18. Marczewski, A.: Gamification: a simple introduction (2012)
19. Mora, A., Riera, D., González, C., Arnedo-Moreno, J.: A literature review of gamification design frameworks. In: Proceedings of 7th International Conference on Games and Virtual Worlds for Serious Applications (VS-Games), pp. 1–8. IEEE (2015)
20. Nah, F.F.-H., Zeng, Q., Telaprolu, V.R., Ayyappa, A.P., Eschenbrenner, B.: Gamification of education: a review of literature. In: Nah, F.F.-H. (ed.) HCIB 2014. LNCS, vol. 8527, pp. 401–409. Springer, Heidelberg (2014)
21. O'Donovan, S., Gain, J., Marais, P.: A case study in the gamification of a university-level games development course. In: Proceedings of the South African Institute for Computer Scientists and Information Technologists Conference, pp. 242–251. ACM (2013)
22. Ries, E.: The Lean Startup: How Today's Entrepreneurs Use Continuous Innovation to Create Radically Successful Businesses. Crown Business, New York (2011)
23. Schell, J.: The Art of Game Design: A Book of Lenses. CRC Press, Boston (2008)
24. Seaborn, K., Fels, D.: Gamification in theory and action: a survey. Int. J. Hum. Comput. Stud. **74**, 14–31 (2015)
25. Serrat, O.: The five whys technique. ADB, Open Access Repository 3 (2009)
26. Simoes, J., Díaz Redondo, R., Fernández Vilas, A.: A social gamification framework for a K-6 learning platform. Comput. Hum. Behav. **29**(2), 345–353 (2012)
27. Tuunanen, J., Hamari, J.: Meta-synthesis of player typologies. In: Proceedings of Nordic Digra 2012 Conference: Games in Culture and Society (2012)
28. Villagrasa, S., Fonseca, D., Duran, J.: Teaching case: applying gamification techniques and virtual reality for learning building engineering 3D arts. In: Proceedings of the Second International Conference on Technological Ecosystems for Enhancing Multiculturality, pp. 171–177. ACM (2014)
29. Xu, Y.: Literature review on web application gamification and analytics. Technical report (2011)

Realizing an Applied Gaming Ecosystem: Towards Supporting Service-Based Innovation Knowledge Management and Transfer

Jana Becker[1]([✉]), Giel van Lankveld[2], Christina Steiner[3],
and Matthias Hemmje[1]

[1] Research Institute for Telecommunication and Cooperation,
Martin-Schmeisser-Weg 4, 44227 Dortmund, Germany
{jbecker,mhemmje}@ftk.de
[2] Open University of the Netherlands,
Valkenburgerweg 177, 6419 AT Heerlen, The Netherlands
Giel.vanLankveld@ou.nl
[3] Graz University of Technology, Inffeldgasse 13, 8010 Graz, Austria
christina.steiner@tugraz.at

Abstract. The EU-based industry for non-leisure games is an emerging business. As such it is still fragmented and needs to achieve critical mass to compete globally. Nevertheless its growth potential is widely recognized. To become competitive the relevant applied gaming communities and SMEs require support by fostering the generation of innovation potential. The European project *Realizing an Applied Gaming Ecosystem (RAGE)* is aiming at supporting this challenge. RAGE will help by making available an interoperable set of advanced technology assets, tuned to applied gaming, as well as proven practices of using asset-based applied games in various real-world contexts, and finally a centralized access to a wide range of applied gaming software modules, services and related document, media, and educational resources within an online community portal called the RAGE Ecosystem. It is based on an integrational, user-centered approach of Knowledge Management and Innovation Processes in the shape of a service-based implementation.

1 Introduction and Motivation

The European landscape for non-leisure games (applied games or formally called serious games) industries is an emerging market. Contrary to the established video game industry it is still fragmented over a large number of small and independent companies and needs to achieve defined product and service qualities to compete globally. The EU project *Realizing an Applied Gaming Ecosystem (RAGE)* [1] will support this challenge by building up an applied gaming community portal to promote collaborations and knowledge exchange between and among different stakeholders. The so called *RAGE Ecosystem* will provide an interoperable set of advanced applied gaming technology assets as well as a bundle of proven practices of using asset-based applied games in various real-world contexts. This will be achieved by enabling a centralized access to a wide range of applied gaming software modules, services and

© Springer International Publishing Switzerland 2016
A. De Gloria and R. Veltkamp (Eds.): GALA 2015, LNCS 9599, pp. 540–549, 2016.
DOI: 10.1007/978-3-319-40216-1_58

related documents, media, and educational resources. The community portal as an online social space will facilitate collaboration, especially under the condition of progress and innovation, between game developers, researchers from multiple disciplines, online publishers, educational intermediaries and end-users and will provide workshops and online training opportunities for developers and educators [2].

This paper will start to review the objectives of the RAGE Ecosystem, will show the basic considerations influencing the Ecosystem concept and development as well as the economic potential of Ecosystems and the importance of *Knowledge Management* in the execution of innovation and *value added processes*.

Therefore, the Knowledge Management fundamental SEKI model will be described supplemented by the extension into an *Innovation Knowledge Lifecycle*. The realization into the specific technological environment will be shown from a knowledge and a service oriented perspective extended by a short description of the development approach and the evaluation approach. To describe the potentials of the Ecosystem examples of similar, successful Ecosystems from different domains will be introduced and the economic value potential of the asset approach will be taken into account. Finally a conclusion will review the potential outcomes and benefits of the RAGE Ecosystem.

2   The Objectives of the RAGE Ecosystem

The main objectives of the RAGE Ecosystem are to allow its participants to get hold of advanced, usable gaming assets (technology push), to get access to the associated business cases (*commercial opportunity*), to create bonds with peers, suppliers and customers (*alliance formation*), to advocate their expertise and demands (*publicity*), to develop and publish their own assets (*trade*), and to contribute to creating a joint agenda and road-map (*harmonization and focus*). Therefore, the RAGE project is a technology and know-how driven research and innovation project. Its main driver is to be able to equip industry players (e.g. game developers) with a set of technology resources (so-called *assets*) and strategies (i.e. know-how) to strengthen their capacities to penetrate an almost new market (non-leisure) and to consolidate a competitive position. In consequence, the RAGE Ecosystem and its integration with social networks of game-developing-, gaming-, and applied-gaming communities will on the one hand become an enabler to harvest community knowledge and on the other hand it will support the access to the RAGE Ecosystem as a knowledge resource for such communities.

The applied gaming sector as an upcoming business market is at present characterized by weak interconnectedness, limited knowledge exchange, absence of harmonising standards, limited specialisations, limited division of labour, and insufficient evidence of the products' efficacies [3, 4]. The industry is scattered over a large number of small, diverse, independent players, niche products and of course specialists. Because of limited collaborations of industries and limited interconnections between industry and research, applied gaming companies display insufficient innovation power and size to open up new markets (e.g. schools, business, governments) [2, 3]. To support the development and growth of this branch the RAGE Ecosystem will foster the merging of the heterogeneous applied gaming communities by providing an effective knowledge and innovation management service tool. The Ecosystem will serve as an interactive knowledge and content management platform and provide a diverse set of services across the knowledge value chain [5].

As a single entry point for applied gaming it will realize centralized access to a wide range of applied gaming software modules, services and resources (or their metadata) by the arrangement of a well-managed and structured asset repository, digital library, and media archive system. The resulting material in the Ecosystem, particularly the textual resources, will be semantically annotated to support searching and access. Besides this, the Ecosystem will arrange workshops and offer training courses on an online training portal, covering training for developers and educators in order to amplify applied gaming uptake. The aim will be to support the self-sustainable production of assets and documentation, training material, workshops and collaboration activities. In addition the social dimension of the RAGE Ecosystem will be supported by community tools for collaboration, annotation, creativity, matchmaking [2].

3 Knowledge Management and Innovation Processes

The increase of global competition combined with limited budgets affects the frequency and quality of realizing innovations today. Under the conditions described above, the launch of innovative products for SMEs of the applied gaming industry constitutes an enormous challenge. They need strategies to have the crucial competitive advantage of being faster than others [6]. Accelerating the discovery of new (scientific) findings, the technical realization and the market launch [7, 8] is increasingly dependent on the use of advanced information and knowledge technology for building environments that support the innovation process systematically and efficiently [9]. Such environments depend on a number of advanced Knowledge Management technologies and processes and have to adapt to a wide variety of innovative practices, cultures, organizational context and application areas, where innovation takes place. Independent of the domain, innovation is a knowledge-intensive process [6].

To support innovation processes successfully, an established Innovation Knowledge Lifecycle has proven to be valuable and essential [6, 10].

3.1 The SEKI Model

One of the most important bases for these Knowledge Management considerations is the *SEKI model* from Nonaka and Takeuchi (cf. Figure 1). SEKI describes four knowledge creation and -transformation processes [11] between tacit and explicit knowledge. The learning effect and the development of the knowledge base results in the so called knowledge spiral, which occurs in several passes of the SEKI process and is described as (organizational) learning [12]. The knowledge spiral differentiate between explicit knowledge, which is stored in media and can be recorded, transmitted and stored by means of information and communication technology and tacit knowledge, which is based on ideals, values and feelings of individuals. It is difficult to

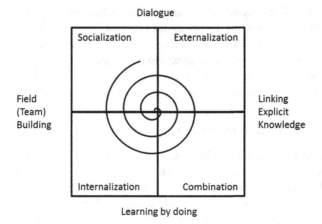

Fig. 1. SEKI knowledge spiral [13]

formulate and to pass on [13]. The core of this model is the interaction between explicit and implicit as well as individual and collective knowledge for the generation of new knowledge and innovation [14].

The four steps of the process are described as *Socialization, Externalization, Combination and Internalization* (SEKI). The cycling of these steps results in the spiral and symbolizes the continuous, dynamic change process of the resource knowledge [13].

3.2   The Innovation Knowledge Lifecycle (IKLC) Meta Model

The *IKLC model* is integrating the SEKI cycling process in an innovation process environment. The innovation process is thereby influenced by a problem cycle and a knowledge cycle. The problems were composed through market needs, innovation strategies and available resources. In the considerations of this paper problems will be simplified as needs or demand. The concept of the knowledge cycle has special significance. It distinguishes three basic knowledge types: community, organizational knowledge, shared by a specific community or within an organization, and working knowledge, the knowledge at hand in a concrete working or task context. It differs between personal knowledge of an individual or team knowledge as the relevant joint knowledge of the team members [6].

The innovation process influenced by the demand on the one hand and the working knowledge on the other hand will lead into a demand specific solution. This solution will not necessarily be a tangible product. In the case of RAGE it will be an intangible gain of evaluated and validated knowledge and experiences.

4   Realizing the Digital Ecosystem

The concept of a supporting tool for innovation processes by creating an adequate environment considering incoming needs and demand, working knowledge processes and the satisfied demand based on innovative outcome has been extended to the concept of the RAGE Ecosystem. The environment is located in the domain of applied gaming and the corresponding communities (applied game developers, game based learning initiatives, etc.). That's important because each community or domain is assumed to have its own shared context. Even in the field of applied gaming the different perspectives or "languages" across communities have an impact on the performance of the whole innovation knowledge lifecycle process [15].

4.1 Knowledge-Driven Innovation Approach

Mapping the SEKI and IKLC ideas onto the Knowledge Management within the RAGE Ecosystem can be described as follows. Driven by the need for competitive products and services, responsive to the customers fast changing requirements the applied gaming industry indicates a high demand of innovation. To establish an appropriate environment and kind of a knowledge-baseline the Ecosystem will collect media resources as well as documentation, training material, and best practices from the heterogeneous and dispersed applied gaming landscape to provide relevant communities the opportunity to participate, to share, and to benefit from these resources and to create new, innovative outcomes. In a first step available explicit as well as tacit knowledge must be made available in machine-readable shape to handle it within a technology-based infrastructure. Therefore, applied gaming users or user groups from a corresponding serious gaming or game based learning community (e.g., software developer, researcher or end-user) have to externalize their tacit needs, requirements, assets, knowledge, information, and experiences into explicit digital content and knowledge objects (text, image, video, recorded speech, taxonomies ...) and provide them to the related applied gaming communities. The RAGE Ecosystem will serve as a platform for this kind of externalization and social sharing. The service can be described as Externalization and Socialization. In the next step a Combination process of merging existing, explicit knowledge from different domains (e.g., Research, Development, Education) generates new information in the context of applied gaming. As one of the features of this system, the digital content objects will be annotated with semantic representations of knowledge objects, as e.g., taxonomies. This means an enrichment of objects with a common framework of semantic annotation supporting understanding of externalized knowledge implicitly contained in digital content, to solve problems of different perspectives or understanding as described above. As a result a systematic search and analysis of content objects and knowledge resources will be possible. Thus, the Ecosystem supports its users to find content arose from tacit knowledge with explicitly annotated semantic representations and to adapt, extend and link it to internalize this knowledge (Internalization). This step is called cognitive value creation or the generation of knowledge [10].

Connecting to this process the attached Educational Portal offers internalization resp. knowledge transfer in the sense of a learning management process. It serves as a huge knowledge library or database. The learning objectives of a user could be annotated, based on his profile, so that this annotations will be available as knowledge in the system additionally. A test/exam can then decide what content needs to be learned in order to achieve the learning objectives and which competences already exist and may be assigned to the users profile.

By working on the solutions experiences will be influencing the results and will appear as results out of the process. This kind of knowledge will complete the working knowledge and the knowledge cycle.

4.2 Service-Driven Innovation Approach

Taken this features of the RAGE Ecosystem into account the Content- and Knowledge Management Portal is integrating streams of the demand and supply side. Users will be able to inquire community specific knowledge, to search and access knowledge, to consume knowledge and information (e.g., online training courses) and they will be able to produce new media objects and knowledge in various ways.

Thus, the Ecosystem including the offered features receives a *Service Character*. In this case knowledge represents an intangible commodity and the result of the service process has intangible character. The process could be highly integrative, if the customer, frequently the user itself, will be integrated into the preparation constantly [16]. An advantage of the system lies in the automated execution of the described service processes, the Ecosystem can act efficiently and independently, it arises an automated service.

Considering the *Service Production Phase Model* [17, 18] knowledge management within the Ecosystem environment will be affected through internal and external factors. The internal factors may be tacit knowledge and experiences of the users of the applied gaming communities or other internal knowledge carriers, the explicit knowledge of already existing recourses and assets organized in the Ecosystems content management infrastructure, the ambition and motivation to create something new and the users capacity. In addition expert knowledge, information and expertise from outside the direct user community have to be taken into account as well as community collaboration support.

The users or user groups will produce a pre-combination of knowledge by combination and integration of content and their experiences from different domains and will supplement this by consultation of external experts or social communities.

The final combination will be resulting by including the customer to the service production process. The customer in this demonstrated knowledge production process will mainly be the user itself. Because of his special demand of knowledge he will enter the Ecosystem and will trigger the knowledge creation process in different ways. Maybe he will inquire more competencies in the field of applied gaming by entering to an online trainings course. Or he will inquire a new serious game based asset and will collaborate with other software developers or he will just learn from the best practice knowhow to create a new idea and bring it efficiently into the market afterwards.

4.3 Development Approach

Based on the previous considerations and to avoid the risk of not working instruments and environment the development will be an agile process involving different stakeholder resp. user communities. In the first step the researcher requests and requirements out of the RAGE consortium will be integrated. Thereafter the game development companies will be involved and in the third step the application partners will be integrated to improve the system. Using these different so called user stereotypes with different interests, experiences and skills, the Ecosystem will be evaluated during the development process. The result is a *phase-oriented user-centered agile development approach*. The accompanying evaluation process is described in Sect. 6 "Evaluating the Ecosystem".

5   Potentials Based on the RAGE Ecosystem

To strengthen the approach of the RAGE project similar Ecosystems can be referenced and the value of knowledge could be made much more transparent.

5.1   Similar Ecosystems

In order to find empirical support for success chances of the RAGE project as an applied gaming Ecosystem similar Ecosystems can be inspected that are not specifically focused on the domain of applied gaming. An example of such an Ecosystem is GitHub[1].

GitHub is a software development Ecosystem which currently has over 10 million users. Users can upload or start a software project on GitHub and collaborate on its development with other users in the community [19]. Currently active and past projects are retained and can be used as examples and sources of knowledge. GitHub demonstrates that an Ecosystem with a partial overlap of features to the RAGE Ecosystem but with a different domain can be successfully adopted as collaboration environments.

Another example for empirically supporting the potential of the RAGE Ecosystem is the *GALA project*. The GALA project involves 31 European institutions and facilitates the cultivation and dissemination of academic applied games knowledge [20]. The GALA project resulted in a successful conference; a scholar.google search reveals 37 publications for 2014 as well as a host of GALA related research. One of the relevant differences between RAGE and GALA is that RAGE aims to facilitate the business market rather than the academic community. However, both RAGE and GALA have overlap in residing in the domain of applied gaming.

5.2   Economic Value Potential

To foster the willingness of the addressed communities to participate with RAGE and to strengthen the common understanding of the necessity and usefulness of such an Ecosystem it is important to understand the project ideas behind the expected developments within the Ecosystem. RAGE focus on the creation and exchange of assets

---

[1] http://www.github.com.

that could be incorporated in different games targeting different populations and application fields. Most of the available approaches and methodologies used by game development companies typically focus on design and development of domain-specific games. The *RAGE assets* are self-contained solutions showing economic value potential based on advanced technologies related to computer games, and intended to be reused in different game platforms. To increase the added value potential value adding services and attributes, like instructions, tutorials, examples and best practices, instructional design guidelines and methodologies, connectors to major game development platforms, data capacity, and content authoring tools for game content creation will be supplemented. RAGE assets will be shared, exchanged, enriched and reused in the field of serious gaming. Looking from a knowledge management perspective the RAGE assets will be developed as a product of a digital knowledge creation- and – transformation process and then flow itself into the production of new applied games or game based learning applications.

Hence, the developed knowledge will be economized and could be monetarily evaluated at the market. Therefore knowledge becomes an economic asset itself and the process of knowledge creation becomes a value added service. Depending on the initial requirements and needs new knowledge arises in the transformation process that can be brought to the market within the meaning of value added. It may be a further qualification of a user or a new asset in the form of an accumulation or enrichment of one or more existing software assets. The user then has an increased competence and thus an increased market value on the applied gaming market. It is planned to underpin this by a certification form of training by the educational portal. The newly gained technology asset could also be monetized in the market, as it flows into the development of new and innovative games.

6   Evaluating the Ecosystem

To empirically demonstrate the quality and benefit of the RAGE Ecosystem, it will be systematically investigated in user-oriented evaluation studies. This is part of the holistic RAGE evaluation approach aiming at a comprehensive understanding of the added value of applied gaming technologies for their stakeholders. For a full coverage of the usage and stakeholder dimension of the RAGE technologies – from searching and contributing resources, to developing an applied game, to actually playing it – a multi-perspective evaluation framework is elaborated as a common reference point guiding all evaluation work [19]. For investigating the effectiveness of the RAGE Ecosystem, evaluation approaches from the field of digital libraries and virtual research environments are taken up and adapted [20, 21]. These kinds of information systems and the Ecosystem have the same core feature – i.e. providing information and resources through networked systems – and thus, they also share similar factors of system success, like usability, user acceptance, usefulness of resources, and performance. Multi-method evaluations triangulating different data sources (retrospective reports, interaction logs, and online feedback) will be carried out on the Ecosystem. The evaluation studies will iteratively involve the different stakeholder groups and communities, aligned with the phase-centred agile development approach.

7 Conclusion

The RAGE Ecosystem will provide a wide range of supporting services in the field of knowledge transfer and -creation to overcome low market access and small market share of small and medium sized companies in the applied games market, to create new effective technology based assets in order to build new ingenious learning games.

The innovation potential of the new platform based knowledge added value process underlies the following factors: a huge, mostly entire collection of community specific knowledge (e.g., content like media objects, software components and best practices), a structured approach of knowledge access, search and browse, collaboration tools as well as social network analysis tools to foster efficient knowledge creation and trans-formation processes into marketable technology assets.

The RAGE Ecosystem supports therefore the interconnectedness, the knowledge exchange and the harmonization of standards of the applied gaming branch.

Using this support and newly acquired strength, the industry should have the opportunity to assert themselves and their products to big games companies [22].

Acknowledgements and Disclaimer. This publication has been produced in the context of the

RAGE project. The project has received funding from the European Union's Horizon 2020 research and innovation programme under grant agreement No. 644187. However, this paper reflects only the author's view and the European Commission is not responsible for any use that may be made of the information it contains.

References

1. RAGE, 22 July 2015. http://www.rageproject.eu
2. RAGE Description of Action (2015)
3. Stewart, J., Bleumers, L., Van Looy, J., Mariën, I., All, A., Schurmans, D., Willaert, K., De Grove, F., Jacobs, A., Misuraca, G.: The potential of digital games for empowerment and social inclusion of groups at risk of social and economic exclusion: evidence and opportunity for policy. In: Centeno, C. (ed.) Joint Research Centre. European Commission (2013)
4. García Sánchez, R., Baalsrud Hauge, J., Oliveira, M., Fiucci, G., Rudnianski, M., Kyvsgaard Hansen, P., Riedel, J., Padrón-Nápoles, C.L., Brown, D.: Business Modelling and Implementation Report 2, GALA Network of Excellence (2013). www.galanoe.eu
5. Salman, M., Heutelbeck, D., Hemmje, M.: Towards social network support for an applied gaming ecosystem. In: The 9th European Conference on Games Based Learning, ECGBL 2015, Norway (2015)
6. Paukert, M., Niederée, C., Hemmje, M.: Knowledge in innovation processes. In: Encyclopedia of Knowledge Management (2011)
7. Haß, H.-J.: Die Messung des technischen Fortschritts, Munich (1983)
8. Grupp, H.: Messung und Erklärung des technischen Wandels – Grundzüge einer empirischen Innovationsökonomik. Springer, Heidelberg (1997)
9. Specht, G., Beckmann, C., Amelingmeyer, J.: F&E-Management. Schäffer-Poeschel-Verlag, Stuttgart (2002)

10. Vogel, T.: Wissensbasiertes und Prozessorientiertes Innovationsmanagement WPIM - Innovationsszenarien, Anforderungen, Modell und Methode, Implementierung und Evaluierung anhand der Innovationsfähigkeit fertigender Unternehmen. Fakultät für Mathematik und Informatik der FernUniversität in Hagen, Munich (2012)
11. North, K.: Wissensorientierte Unternehmensführung. Wertschöpfung durch Wissen, 3 Auflage, Wiesbaden (2002)
12. Weggeman, M.: Wissensmanagement – der richtige Umgang mit der wichtigsten Ressource des Unternehmens, 1 Auflage. MITP-Verlag, Bonn (1999)
13. Nonaka, I., Takeuchi, H.: The Knowledge-Creating Company: How Japanese Companies Create the Dynamics of Innovation. Oxford University Press, Oxford (1995)
14. Trillitzsch, U.: Die Einführung von Wissensmanagement, Flein b. Verlag Werner Schweikert, Heilbronn (2004)
15. Paukert, M., Niederée, C., Muscogiuri, C., Bouquet, P., Hemmje, M.: Knowledge in the innovation process: an empirical study for validating the innovation knowledge life cycle. In: Proceedings of the 4th European Conference on Knowledge Management, Oxford, England (2003)
16. Fließ, S.: Dienstleistungsmanagement: Kundenintegration gestalten und steuern. Gabler Verlag, Wiesbaden (2008)
17. Corsten H., Gössinger, R.: Dienstleistungsmanagement, 5 Auflage. Oldenbourg Wissenschaftsverlag, Munich (2007)
18. Engelhardt, W.H., Kleinaltenkamp, M., Reckenfelderbäumer, M.: Leistungsbündel als Absatzobjekte. Zeitschrift für betriebswirtschaftliche Forschung, Bde. %1 von %245. Jg., Heft 5, pp. 395–426 (1993)
19. Steiner, C., Hollins, P., Kluijfhout, E., Dascalu, M., Nussbaumer, A., Albert, D., Westera, W.: Evaluation of serious games: a holistic approach. Paper accepted at International Conference of Education, Research and Innovation (ICERI 2015), Sevilla, Spain, 2015
20. Fuhr, N., Tsakonas, G., Aalberg, T., Agosti, M., Hansen, P., Kapidakis, S.: Evaluation of digital libraries. Int. J. Digit. Libr. 8, 21–38 (2007)
21. Steiner, C., Agosti, M., Sweetnam, M., Hillemann, E.-C., Orio, N., Ponchia, C., Hampson, C., Munnelly, G., Nussbaumer, A., Albert, D., Conlan, O.: Evaluating a digital humanities research environment: the CULTURA approach. Int. J. Digit. Libr. 15, 53–70 (2014)
22. Bullinger, H.-J.: Einführung in das Technologiemanagement – Modelle, Methoden, Praxisbeispiele. B.G. Teubner, Stuttgart (1994)
23. Bullinger, H.-J., Wörner, K., Prieto, J.: Wissensmanagement heute. Fraunhofer Institut für Arbeitswirtschaft und Organisation, Stuttgart (1997)
24. de Gloria, A., Roceanu, I.: Serious games in the life long learning environment. games and learning alliance network of excellence. In: The 5th International Conference on Virtual Learning, ICVL 2010 (2010)
25. Dabbish, L., Stuart, C., Tsay J., Herbsleb, J.: Social coding in GitHub: transparency and collaboration in an open software repository. In: Proceedings of the ACM 2012 Conference on Computer Supported Cooperative Work. ACM (2012)

Towards Modding and Reengineering Digital Games for Education

Ioana Andreea Stanescu[1], Jannicke Baalsrud Hauge[2,3(✉)],
Antoniu Stefan[1], and Theodore Lim[4]

[1] Advanced Technology Systems,
Str. Tineretului Nr 1, 130029 Targoviste, Romania
{ioana.stanescu,antoniu.stefan}@ats.com.ro
[2] BIBA – Bremer Institut für Produktion und Logistik GmbH,
Hochschulring 20, 28359 Bremen, Germany
baa@biba.uni-bremen.de,
jannicke.baalsrud.hauge@sth.kth.se
[3] Royal Institute of Technology, Alfreds Nobels Alle 10, Stockholm, Sweden
[4] Institute of Mechanical, Process and Energy Engineering,
Heriot-Watt University, Riccarton, Edinburgh EH14 4AS, Scotland, UK
t.lim@hw.ac.uk

Abstract. Research has highlighted the positive qualities of Digital Games for Education (DGE), such as their persuasiveness and motivational appeal, which can support immersive, situated and learner-centered learning experiences. Designing, Developing and Developing (DDD) games for education remain a challenge, especially in terms of costs and of the advanced, multi-disciplinary expertise required to DDD a game. This paper highlights the challenges associated with the implementation of pedagogical requisites and analyzes opportunities for enabling modular, scalable and more elastic DDD processes. To support the approach, the authors present the Reusability Serious Games Reusability Point of Reference (SGREF), a tool that aims to facilitate game modding and reengineering by capturing and structuring information on DDD processes. Two case studies are presented to reflect the particularities teachers are confronted with when attempting to alter or extend a DEG and how SGREF is used to collect information to support DEG modding and reengineering.

Keywords: Game based learning · LM-GM · SGREF · Seconds · Bamzooki

1 Introduction

Even though there is an increased tendency to implement Digital Games for Education (DEG) in learning [1] and corporate training [2] either as an integral part or as an add-on, the overall deployment rate remains low. The use of DEGs in classes is much higher in primary and secondary schools than within higher education [3] and typically we find games like math games that can be applied without any form of modding or reengineering, since the competencies to train and the learning goals are similar in many curricula. However, research has revealed the transition between the instructional design and the actual game design implementation relevant for pedagogy is lacking [4].

© Springer International Publishing Switzerland 2016
A. De Gloria and R. Veltkamp (Eds.): GALA 2015, LNCS 9599, pp. 550–559, 2016.
DOI: 10.1007/978-3-319-40216-1_59

In most instances, it requires a leap of faith from a prospective customer (teacher) to the ability of a DEG developer to deliver a game that will achieve the desired learning outcomes for a particular target group [5]. Apart from complexity, the costs of DEGs make their deployment in meaningful curricula to remain low [6].

In addition, even if the number of game engines, authoring tools and open source games has increased significantly in the last decade, digital game Design, Development and Deployment (DDD) remain a challenge for non-IT professionals. Furthermore, for existing games using engines and authoring tools, there is only limited documentation describing in detail the game design and development and the pit falls for educational benefits, and few guidelines and best practices that would support modding and reengineering. All these produce barriers for teachers that are open to integrate DEGs into their classrooms [7].

The purpose of this paper is to identify and analyze how DEG modding and reengineering can be facilitated to support a higher uptake of DEGs in classes. Key challenges and requirements are discussed and the Serious Games Reusability Point of Reference (SGREF) is presented as a tool that manages information on DEGs in order to support modding and reengineering processes. Two examples of how SGREF can be used to capture information on DEGs are presented.

2 Challenges and Requirements of the Game Adaptation Process

Key barriers for deploying DEGs in an educational environment can be summarized as a two-fold approach [6, 8]:

(1) Even if a flexible curricular design would exist to allow teachers to mod a DEG to their unique goals and practices, at the moment DEGs do not have the required elasticity to be altered and/or extended on-demand to meet new requirements in terms of specific learning objectives listed in a certain curriculum.
(2) The teacher is not a game developer or programmer, and his/her experience in game based learning may vary. The time consumed on the technical aspects of the game can be a significant obstacle. The successful integration of DEGs in classrooms imply overcoming various challenges across an extensive process that reunite the learning objectives, teacher's gaming experience, the students' gaming experience, choosing the right game to meet the learning objectives, technical issues, managing complex DEGs etc.

To be able to mod or reengineer DEGs, teachers must have access to additional information on how the DEG was designed, developed and deployed. Such additional information is not collected and managed in specialized databases, usually are owned by developers or reside in scientific articles. Teachers need to carry out time consuming game analysis, [6, 9–11] in order to first understand the interconnection in the original game, identify the elements that can be changed, and then perform the changes.

To cover all relevant aspects for a detailed analysis, a structured analysis using a taxonomy such as described in [12] may be used. Examples of game analysis using this taxonomy can be found in [13]. A main concern is often how to change the learning mechanics–game mechanics interaction. Here, two methodologies described in [14, 15] can provide guidance. Currently, this process is carried out manually and thus it is very time consuming, as well as with instable quality, since it solely depends on the competences of the person who analyses and alters the game.

Digital games are complex artefacts. Their design and development require extensive, multi-disciplinary expertise [16]. However, in deciding on the suitability of a game and to assess if it can be changed enough to be used in a different context, often the teacher is left alone with this challenges process. Even the use of the mentioned taxonomy and methodology [6, 13, 14] requires basic knowledge of game design; there are several attempts of smart and fast adaption that resulted in badly redesigned games. Consequently, this leads to low reuse and repurposing of existing games in an educational context. A tool supporting the teacher in this process will increase the reusability and quality of the game modding and reengineering processes.

To circumvent debate over domain specific terminology 'modding' as defined herein refers to the act of modifying or customizing digital game hardware/software not originally conceived for bespoke purposes, whereas reengineering refers to low-level, systematic changes in game structure and underlying simulation model. The main aim of both is to reduce the ground-up development costs while ensuring the customization retains genre familiarity for the users.

Past research has studied the implications of modding as an alternative to compensate certain drawbacks, such as the fact that some game elements can potentially disadvantage certain social groups (e.g. avatars) [17]. However, modding alone does not necessarily provide teachers the freedom to model a digital game to better answer specific needs. Factors such as knowledge and experience in instructional design, game design, and software/hardware prowess play an important role [9]. Moreover, assessment mechanisms remain inflexible. Replaying the same game can turn into a boring experience. Access to information that enable DEG modding and reengineering empower teachers to design and deploy more successfully DEGs within classes [18], answering to specific learning objectives and distinct needs of a certain target group.

Digital game development integrates technical and pedagogical constructs, as well as communication with external applications (e.g. Learning Management Systems) into a user-friendly one-stop solution that covers all the key requirements necessary to easily create learning-oriented games remains a challenge [6, 10]. As mentioned above, in order to mod or reengineer a game, it is currently necessary to manually identify to which degree different components can be changed, as well as explain how they can be changed (e.g. using an authoring tool, changing the source code, adding plug & play components, etc.). This identification is challenging and time consuming. Thus, it has become critical to create a tool that collects and manages information on the changeability of

- Game assets: multimedia (sounds, images, videos, text), multi-language, scenarios, chats, game status, AI, narratives.
- Gameplay (goal, roles, learning objectives and scenarios, rewards, physical constants). Game rules without access to source code: customization AI algorithm; game plugin architecture for adding dynamic components.

- Type of access: full access to source code modding; access to assets like library and guidelines on how to use the library to alter the game.

In a second step, this tool can be further extended to:

- Combine information from different sources and analyze inter dependencies. In time the tool can be developed so that it will be capable of learning.
- Support profiling and characterization of games, preferably automatically, using a taxonomy for classification (e.g. an extension of the one described in [12], since current game databases does not contain specific information on game modding or reengineering.
- Include features like a semantic search engine that is able to go through literature and analyze the content.

3 Case Studies

In this section, the authors explore the modding potential of digital games and present two case studies on how to deconstruct DEGs using SGREF. SGREF is a collection of references to games, game assets and game-related resources. The scope of the tool is to support the reuse of game resources across game communities by capturing information on DDD and thus enabling modding and re-engineering of DEGs. SGREF targets mainly non-IT professionals. For the case studies we have selected a COTS game and an in-house development. The selection of the games was based on the following criteria: (1) Should already be used for educational purpose, (2) Need adaption for different type of courses and learning goals (3) Authors needs the access to do changes (4) The in-house game should also be applied at different universities.

These criterias let us experiment with the SGREF tool to see if the algorithms and search functions are satisfactorily working.

3.1 Case Study "Seconds"

"Seconds" is used for teaching different aspects of logistics, supply chain management (SCM) and production in distributed environment. The game is operated in different universities for different courses. The game engine is separated from the simulation model. To reduce the time needed to customize game scenarios, as well as to reduce the need to involve programmers in this process, an authoring tool is provided allowing an experienced teacher with knowledge both in logistics/production/SCM and SG conceptualization to develop new scenarios. A more detailed description of the game engine and of the current scenarios is presented in [9, 10, 19–21], and a taxonomy-based general game description is described in [13].

Since the "Seconds" data model is based on an SQL database, modifying its database can alter the game scenario. While this makes it technically easy to attune to the business case, it remains quite difficult for a teacher to do the changes, since there is a large degree of freedom in which data to change. This requires that the teacher has experience in game design of educational games. Past experiences have shown that a good field expert can make good simulations, since they know the processes exactly, whereas the experience with teachers with profound theoretical knowledge are less good. Thus, a tool supporting the process of changes would support current and future users to mod and reengineer existing scenarios using the authoring tool.

SGREF has been used to collect information that support the modding and reengineering of the game. Due to its design, "Seconds" can, to a large extent, be reengineered at different levels. Since it uses objects stored in a DB, there are mainly three levels of customization, for example narration. The simulation model contains objects of many types related to productions, and thus it is easy to set up a new gaming scenario. This allows the teacher to change the functions (but the role descriptions can also be changed), the product, the processes - but keep the narratives. Thus, a complete new scenario is made available to the teacher, just by changing the content, but the learning goals would be the same. It is possible to change to a different production process, a different supply chain or a different product (like changing from car production to farming), while keeping the narrative. However, the feeling of the player is changed, s/he experiences a completely new scenario, yet identifies with the same elements, which leads to improved interaction with the GUI (Fig. 1).

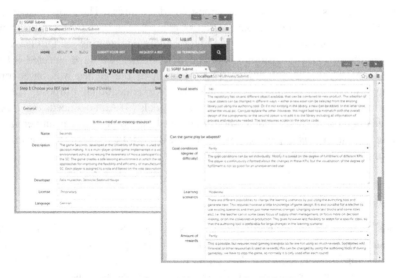

Fig. 1. "Seconds" referenced in SGREF.

The second level of change requires more knowledge, since at this level the narratives would change more. The teacher would model a new process, alter different roles and role descriptions, changing the interaction level. This would for instance be required if the learning goals change considerably – e.g. if we go from strategic decision making to operation or if the game scenario is used for sustainable supply chains. This would require that not only the narrative is changed, but also the game mechanics in place.

Finally, the most radical change that can be implemented regarding the narratives is if the teacher wants to include elements that are not in the DB or if s/he wants to change the level of granularity in the simulation model so that it is more detailed than it currently is. This would require reprogramming. Examples of such would be if "Seconds" is used to exactly mirror all processes in a multi-modal transport chain or details in warehousing handling. This would be quite expensive and time consuming, so in this case it should first be investigated if there are other available games already providing this level of granularity.

4 Case Study Bamzooki

As an alternative to classical teaching, a game-based approach to learning engineering design was investigated [22, 23]. The CBBC BAMZOOKi™ application was identified as providing a self-contained "design-build-test" environment. BAMZOOKi was developed for the CBBC, BBC TV's children's channel to enable children design creatures called zooks, which are put to the test against each other. Users construct virtual organic robots or zooks from building block elements and modify their physical, dynamic and kinematic properties. Zook physics can then be performance tested and measured against a set of standard tasks. A multiplayer capability allows for Zook Olympics. Figure 2 illustrates the atypical design cycle when engineering a product.

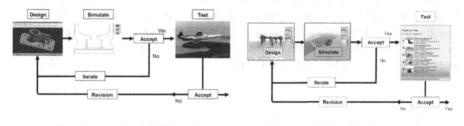

(a) Conventional CAD tools   (b) BAMZOOKi design interface

Fig. 2. Design cycle similarities.

There is an extensive body of observational research conducted on the engineering design process, resulting in various models to characterize and structure design activities. A typical model similar to that depicted in Fig. 2 was proposed by Wächtler [24], which explicitly models the learning process that develops a design. However, many academic models are defined in terms of high-level concepts remote from the details of the design process. Consequently, in teaching students about the dependencies and implications of engineering change, a means to conduct knowledge capture and information push was necessary to be implemented within BAMZOOKi.

The following design environment properties were considered:

- all stages of the design process must be supported from conceptualization to functional detailing;

- an intuitive graphical interface will allow a large number of participants (non-expert to expert) in the experiment;
- a short design cycle that incorporates integrated in-line testing of mechanical performance;
- a feasible, competitive and engaging design goal;
- a measurable design success;
- an innate design criterion; and
- accessible data logging.

The version of the BAMZOOKi software distributed by the BBC does not support any continuous user logging; however, a detailed specification was created and the software's developers, Gameware Development Ltd, enabled a mod and produced a bespoke version, BAMZOOKi Academic. Through this, researchers could define specific knowledge capture and information push to be implemented and evaluated.

The key mod was to ensure the design process data flow was captured accurately. For this each event within BAMZOOKi was tagged against various event possibilities. XML log files were automatically generated by BAMZOOKi and their data structures (Fig. 3) lend themselves naturally to user behavior predictions based upon these stochastic observations. That is, the data can be interpreted as a probabilistic model of user behavior to be developed into a structured design rationale process based upon these observations. These finite state machine views allow user behavior patterns to be observed and event filtering (such as cosmetic and name changes) can be used to identify a structured design rationale process. For example, if the user's goal is to improve the sprint performance, a high level process will be observed which involves changing the leg length (ZookPhysicalEvent), and adjusting the leg gait (ZookDynamicEvent). These types of observations are key to achieving a representative result from a large experimental data set (Fig. 4).

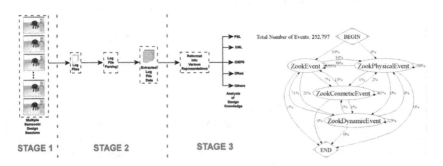

Fig. 3. Data flow and XML finite state machine

After extracting the design knowledge required to say, achieve a successful sprint, this information pattern can then be stored within a PSL (product specification language) format and 'pushed' to users working on similar design tasks in real time. This way inexperienced designers can learn and share design knowledge.

Fig. 4. BAMZOOKi™ referenced in SGREF

To conclude the strategy to modding BAMZOOKi as an application for learners to understand fundamentals of a design process and the rationale to design changes relied on pervasive logging. This required implementing a data structure within BAMZOOKi and changing the data flow process at the low level. Because of commercial rights, the mod had to be initiated by the developers based on the researchers' specifications and requirements. However, once implemented it provides a spectrum of opportunities to provide visual and formal representation to learners of the processes that occurs in an engineering design process.

5 Discussion and Future Work

Current DEGs do not incorporate information on their capabilities to be altered or extended. SGREF has been develop to facilitate the analysis of such capabilities in existing DEGs, in order to enable teachers to adapt existing DEGs to specific learning objectives. This paper reports work in progress on supporting DEG modding and reengineering and present an analysis of the modding capabilities of two educational games: "Seconds" and "BAMZOOKi". The results of the analysis are used to populate references to these games that are stored in SGREF. The current version of the tool captures and manages information that enable teachers to better understand the game design, empowering them to mod these games to answer specific learning objectives. However, the tool captures only key information and requires extensions that are able to reflect better the complexity of modding and reengineering of DEGs. Future versions of the tool will suggest compatible assets and modules from the SGREF repository that can be used in the game adaptation process.

Considering the significant effort required to achieve this goal, future work will focus on the provision of guidelines so that the identification, separation and encapsulation of game parts that can be subject to change – modding or reengineering - occur in the game design stage. Such approaches will enable games to be flexible and scalable. The aspects in a DEG that vary need to be separated from those that stay the same and should be encapsulated so that changeable parts can be altered or extended without affecting those that do not change. Also, parts that can vary need to be categorized and their behavior need to be described, so that the adaptor fully understand the consequences of change on the gameplay. Principles and patterns need to be defined for all stages of the development lifecycle, in order to support game adaptation.

Acknowledgement. The work presented herein is partially funded under the European Community Seventh Framework Programme (FP7/20072013), Grant Agreement nr. FP7-ICT-2009-5-258169 (GALA) 284860 (MSEE) and by Unitatea Executiva pentru Finantarea Invatamantului Superior, a Cercetarii, Dezvoltarii si Inovarii (UEFISCDI) in Romania, Contract no. 19/2014 (DESiG).

References

1. Seng, W.Y., Yatim, M.H.M.: Computer game as learning and teaching tool for object oriented programming in higher education institution. Procedia Soc. Behav. Sci. **123**, 215–224 (2014)
2. Vos, L.: Simulation games in business and marketing education: how educators assess student learning from simulations. Int. J. Manag. Educ. **13**(1), 57–74 (2015)
3. Ariffin, M.M., Oxley, A., Sulaiman, S.: Evaluating game-based learning effectiveness in higher education. Procedia Soc. Behav. Sci. **123**, 20–27 (2014)
4. Suttie, N., Louchart, S., Lim, T., Macvean, A., Westera, W., Brown, D., Djaouti, D.: Introducing the "serious games mechanics" a theoretical framework to analyse relationships between "game" and "pedagogical aspects" of serious games. Procedia Comput. Sci. **15**, 314–315 (2012)
5. Arnab, S., Lim, T., Carvalho, M.B., Bellotti, F., Freitas, S., Louchart, S., De Gloria, A.: Mapping learning and game mechanics for serious games analysis. Br. J. Educ. Technol. **46**(2), 391–411 (2015)
6. Baalsrud Hauge, J., Bellotti, F., Nadolski, R., Berta, R., Carvalho, M.B.: Deploying serious games for management in higher education: lessons learned and good practices. In: EAI Endorsed Transactions on Serious Games, vol. 2 (2014)
7. Tan, K., Tse, Y.K., Chung, P.L.: A plug and play pathway approach for operations management games development. Comput. Educ. **55**(1), 109–117 (2010)
8. Eastwood, J.L., Sadler, T.D.: Teachers' implementation of a game-based biotechnology curriculum. Comput. Educ. **66**, 11–24 (2013)
9. Baalsrud Hauge, J., Duin, H., Thoben, K.-D.: Reducing network risks in supply networks by implementing games for mediating skills on risk management. In: Cunningham, P., Cunningham, M. (eds.) Collaboration and the Knowledge Economy: Issues, Applications, Case Studies, pp. 707–714. IOS Press, Amsterdam, Berlin, Oxford, Tokyo, Washington, D.C. (2008)
10. Bellotti, F., Berta, R., De Gloria, A.: Designing effective serious games: opportunities and challenges for research, special issue: creative learning with serious games. Int. J. Emerg. Technol. Learn. (IJET) **5**, 22–35 (2010)

11. Greitzer, F.L., Kuchar, O.A., Huston, K.: Cognitive science implications for enhancing training effectiveness in a serious gaming context. ACM J. Educ. Resour. Comput. 7(3), 1–16 (2007)
12. Popescu M., Bellotti F.: Approaches on metrics and taxonomy in serious games. In: Proceedings of the 8th International Scientific Conference on eLearning and software for Education, Bucharest, Romania, 26–27 April 2012 (2012). ISSN 2066-026X
13. Gala consortium. studies.seriousgamessociety.org
14. Carvalho, M.B., Bellotti, F., Berta, R., De Gloria, A., Islas Sedano, C., Baalsrud Hauge, J., Hu, J., Rauterberg, M.: An activity theory-based model for serious games analysis and conceptual design. Comput. Educ. 87, 166–181 (2015). doi:10.1016/j.compedu.2015.03.023. ISSN 0360-1315
15. Arnab, S., Lim, T., Carvalho, M.B., Bellotti, F., Freitas, S., Louchart, S., De Gloria, A.: Mapping learning and game mechanics for serious games analysis. Br. J. Educ. Technol. 46(2), 391–411 (2015)
16. Fernández-Manjón, B., Moreno-Ger, P., Torrente, J., del Blanco, A.: Creación de juegos educativos con <e-Adventure>. Revista del Observatorio Tecnológico. Instituto Superior de Formación y Recursos en Red para el Profesorado (ISFTIC) del Ministerio de Educación, Política Social y Deporte (MEPSYD) de España (2009). ISSN 1989-2713. http://observatorio.cnice.mec.es/
17. Ratan, R., Sah, Y.J.: Leveling up on stereotype threat: the role of avatar customization and avatar embodiment. Comput. Hum. Behav. 50, 367–374 (2015). doi:10.1016/j.chb.2015.04.010. ISSN 0747-5632
18. Stanescu, I.A., Warmelink, H.J.G., Lo, J., Arnab, S., Dagnino, F., Mooney, J.: Accessibility, reusability and interoperability in the European serious game community. In: Proceedings of the 9th International Scientific Conference on eLearning and software for Education, Bucharest (2013)
19. Baalsrud Hauge, J., Stanescu, I.A., Carvalho, M.B., Lim, T. Louhart, S.: Serious game mechanics and opportunities for reuse. In: Proceedings of the 11th International Scientific Conference on eLearning and software for Education, Bucharest (2015)
20. Hüther, G.: Die neurobiologische Verankerung von Erfahrungen. In: Elsner, n, Lüer, G. (eds.) Das Gehirn und sein Geist. Wallstein Verlag, Göttingen (1996)
21. Hunecker, F.: A generic process simulation-model for Serious Games in manufacturing. In: 38th Annual Conference, SAGSET 2008, Nottingham, UK (2008)
22. Sung, R.C.W., Ritchie, J.M., Lim, T., Rea, H.J., Corney, J.R.: Automated capture of design knowledge using a virtual creature design environment. In: Proceedings of the 40th ISAGA Conference, vol. 110007 (2009)
23. Sung, R., Ritchie, J.M., Rea, H.J., Corney, J.: Automated design knowledge capture and representation in single-user CAD environments. J. Eng. Des. 22(7), 487–503 (2011)
24. Pahl, G., Beitz, W.: Engineering Design, a Systematic Approach. The Design Council, London (1988)

Approaches to Gaming the Future: Planning a Foresight Game on Circular Economy

Mikko Dufva[⊠], Outi Kettunen, Anna Aminoff, Maria Antikainen,
Henna Sundqvist-Andberg, and Timo Tuomisto

VTT Technical Research Centre of Finland Ltd.,
Tekniikankatu 1, PL 1300, 33101 Tampere, Finland
mikko.dufva@vtt.fi

Abstract. Foresight is used to anticipate future developments and trigger responses to them. Serious games can enhance foresight by creating engaging experiences and increasing interaction between participants. In this paper we study how serious games can be used to generate new insights about alternative futures. We structure existing approaches based on their type and purpose and describe a case study of developing a web-based foresight game on circular economy. Based on the review and case study we suggest that foresight games that are balanced between the dimensions of idea generation, informing and experience are well suited to provide insights into the practices and strategy of the players' organisation.

1 Introduction

Major disruptions and systemic changes such as a transition to the circular economy require a long-term perspective and challenging of existing mind-sets. Companies and other organisations as well as whole industrial sectors need to anticipate future developments in order to be prepared for them [1]. While it is relatively easy to prepare for short term linear changes, longer term shifts in the socio-technical system and the impacts of technological disruptions are harder to cope with and are regarded as the "black hole of strategy" [2]. Foresight is an approach to support the longer term anticipation of alternative futures and for triggering responses to them [1, 3].

However, if not integrated well into the everyday activities of the organisations, foresight processes can become separate and laborious interventions with little impact [4–7]. The process may have too much focus on collecting information about the futures and less on creating future-orientation and a futures mindset. Too much focus on knowledge synthesis does not facilitate the challenging of existing mindsets. It omits the learning opportunities in a foresight process, which are crucial especially in the context of socio-technical transitions or major disruptions. Thus, the results of foresight are not internalised or utilised to their full benefit.

Serious games offer one solution to enhance learning in foresight. They can be used to support internalising knowledge, communicating and sharing ideas, increasing and broadening participation and creating new futures knowledge [7, 8]. Games can create fun and engaging experiences that increase the interaction between participants to the foresight process as well as with the data gathered.

© Springer International Publishing Switzerland 2016
A. De Gloria and R. Veltkamp (Eds.): GALA 2015, LNCS 9599, pp. 560–571, 2016.
DOI: 10.1007/978-3-319-40216-1_60

In this paper we study how serious games can be used to generate new insights about alternative futures. As a case study we analyse the development of a game aimed at creating new business models in the emerging circular economy. In the last few years Circular Economy (CE) has been receiving increasing attention worldwide as a way to overcome the current production and consumption model based on continuous growth and increasing resource throughput. Circular economy is an industrial system that is restorative or regenerative by intention and design [9].

Within the circular economy, new business models are developed that reduce the need for virgin raw materials. The basic notion of circular economy is to eliminate waste by designing out waste. Products are designed and optimized for a cycle of disassembly, reuse, and refurbishment, or recycling, with the understanding that the foundation of economic growth is the reuse of material reclaimed from end-of-life products rather than extraction of resources. CE implies the adoption of cleaner production patterns at company level, an increase of producers and consumers' responsibility and awareness, the use of renewable technologies and materials as well as the adoption of suitable, clear and stable policies and tools [10]. In circular economy the concept of user replaces that of consumer. Unlike today, where a consumer buys, owns and disposes a product, in circular economy durable products are leased, rented or shared whenever possible. Also, when the goods are sold, new models and incentives are planned to motivate users to return or reuse product or its components and materials at the end of its period of primary use.

New innovative business models, when changing from ownership to performance based models, are instrumental in translating products designed for reuse into attractive value proposals. Accenture has identified five underlying business models in its case studies [11]. These are circular supplies, resource recovery, product life extension, sharing platform and product as a service. These business models have their own distinct characteristics and can be used singly or in combination to help companies achieve massive resource productivity gains and, in the process, enhance differentiation and customer value, reduce cost to serve and own, generate new revenue, and reduce risk. As an example of product as a service, Michelin, one of the world's leading tire manufacturers, has made significant strides toward adopting the model to create an innovative program in which fleet customers can lease instead of purchase tires outright. Under this program, Michelin effectively sells "tires as a service." Customers pay per miles driven. They don't own the tires, and don't have to deal with the hassles of punctures or maintenance of any kind. By adopting a Product as a Service model, Michelin is incentivized to develop longer lasting tires. And, by getting worn out tires back, the company is motivated to make sure through design and material selection that they can be reprocessed into a valuable input for new tires or something completely different [11].

Understanding the changes in the way business is done in CE requires future-orientation and challenging of existing mind-sets. Innovating business models in this challenging and dynamic environment sets a big challenge while currently many actors and processes supporting these business models are still lacking. The game in the case study is aimed at supporting learning about the shift to circular economy and generating new applicable business models for the players. Thus, it is an example of how to use games to both anticipate and understand the consequences of a paradigm shift as well as support action in the present.

The article is structured as follows. After this introductory section we give a short review of what type of games have been used in foresight. Based on this we describe a categorisation of three purposes of foresight games: idea generation, informing and experience. Then we describe the process and challenges encountered in the foresight game development in the case study, focusing especially on problems arising from future-oriented nature of the game. We conclude with general discussion on using foresight games for generating insights about alternative futures.

2 Types of Games in Foresight

The IT-based tools to support foresight have been categorised into databases, prediction markets, social rating systems and collaborative scenarios [12]. Of these four categories, the tools in collaborative scenario development have most game-related characteristics in them. The most prominent example, and one that is most relevant for the scope of this paper, are MMORPGs (massive multiplayer online role playing games), such as the foresight engine by IFTF (Institute for the Future) [13]. These foresight-oriented games can bring together up to thousands of players to create, share and rate ideas about future development. However, the end result is often a relatively unstructured massive dataset, which then needs to be analysed and interpreted after the game [12].

Game-related characteristics, such as points and reputation levels, have also been applied in databases, prediction markets and social rating systems to motivate the collection and assessment of futures knowledge [12]. For example, the TrendHunter website[1], which crowdsources ideas and trends, has top lists for the best contributors. Likewise the iKnow Innovation, Foresight & Horizon Scanning Community[2] tracks member contributions. However, apart from collecting points or trying to "level up", these systems lack game dynamics and a specific goal. They also face the same problem as the games in collaborative scenarios: how to shape the gathered and assessed data into something that is of use in the present?

In addition to the four categories of IT-based tools mentioned by Schatzmann et al. [12], also computer simulation has been used to support foresight [14]. While simulation is more closely connected to forecasting, it can be used to support more qualitative futures work. Simulation enables games that mimic a real world situation, possibly taking place in the future. It has been used in so called business games [8]. The downside of simulation related to futures work is that it often requires fixing a lot of assumptions in place, effectively closing down the range of possible futures. In other words, it is useful for exploring and learning about defined futures, but often not flexible enough for defining futures.

---

[1] http://www.trendhunter.com/.

[2] http://community.iknowfutures.eu/.

IT-based games are of course not the only type of games played in foresight. Since participation is a key characteristic of foresight [3, 15], many methods have been created to facilitate the joint futures exploration of foresight exercise participants. These include card based games introducing different future developments, as well as board games for exploring futures. For example, both Foresight Cards[3] and the Drivers of Change cards by Arup Foresight[4] present different trends and future events to the participants, who then try to make sense of what it would mean for the topic at hand. Other card games such as Mobility VIP[5] and The Thing From The Future[6] are aimed at facilitating the imagination of alternative futures based on the frame provided randomly by the cards. Likewise, Board games such as the Foresight eXplorer[7] and JRC Scenario Explorer[8] support the creation and exploration of alternative future scenarios.

In addition to card and board games, improvisation, role-play and drama skits have been used in foresight [16, 17]. A notable example is the Sarkar game [17], which puts emphasis on learning and surfacing the assumptions about the current and future situations and systems. In the Sarkar game, the players adopt one of four roles – worker, warrior, intellectual and capitalist – and play through an everyday situation related to the topic of the foresight exercise. Through role-play new insights about the problems, assumptions and preferences emerge, and they are discussed after the game.

There have also been performances using role-playing to simulate a future scenario, such as the case of Byologyc[9], which described the rise and fall of a biotech company. The Byologic story unfolded through social media, websites, different types of events and live-action theatre, demonstrating the possible implications and threats of biotechnology. In these types of performances the audience does not necessarily realise they are players in an elaborate game about a specific futures scenario.

3 Purposes of Games in Foresight

As the previous short review illustrates, games of various forms have been developed and used in foresight. In addition, they have been used for different purposes. We categorise the approaches to games in foresight roughly based on their emphasis on three purposes: idea generation, informing and experience (Fig. 1). By idea generation we mean the creation and aggregation of signals, trends and future developments without processing them further. Idea generation is emphasised especially in web-based games such as the Foresight engine by IFTF, although they also aim at enhancing learning through experiencing the future. On the workshop method side, the card games mentioned above are usually aimed at facilitating ideation.

---

[3] http://foresightcards.com/.

[4] http://www.driversofchange.com/tools/doc/.

[5] http://www.mobilityvip.com/.

[6] http://situationlab.org/projects/the-thing-from-the-future/.

[7] https://www.unteamworks.org/node/454008.

[8] In development in the Joint Research Centre.

[9] https://www.singularityweblog.com/april-fools-the-truth-about-byologyc%E2%80%8F/.

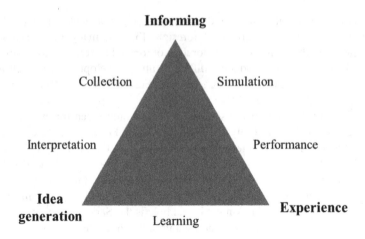

Fig. 1. Three main purposes of games in foresight.

By informing we mean the communication of existing ideas, scenarios, trends etc. In idea generation the future is open, while in informing it is closed [18]. The motivation behind informing is often educating the player about a certain topic, as is the case in C2C BIZZ[10], a game on circular economy. Close to informing, but more towards ideation is the collection of different signals, which is the main aim of databases such as TrendHunter, as well as services such as FutureScraper and SenseMaker [7]. Further towards ideation is interpretation, which exploits existing futures knowledge to create new insights and explore alternative futures, as is the case with the JRC Scenario explorer board game.

By experience we mean moving towards other "ways of knowing" [19], that is feeling, sensing and going through alternative future developments. Role-playing, especially the Sarkar game, is a good example of experiencing the future. Performances, such as the Byologyc example, are also ways of creating experiences about futures. Coming back to the IT-based tools, business games aim to produce experiences by simulating different real world scenarios [8]. In performances, business games and simulation the future is more closed and the emphasis is also more on informing than it is in role-playing.

The purpose of the game depends of course on its use. If the game is used only at the starting phases of an foresight exercise for gathering ideas, then emphasis on idea generation is suitable. On the other hand, if the idea is to present readymade scenario, then the emphasis should be on informing. However, in both of these cases putting more emphasis on experience could be useful. In idea generation it enables learning and in informing it supports internalising the presented futures knowledge. In the next section we describe an attempt to develop a game with a balance between all of these three purposes.

---

[10] http://www.c2cbizz.com/cradle-to-cradle-game/.

4   Case Study: Developing "Circulate.Now"

This section describes the process and problems we have faced when trying to develop a foresight game on circular economy called Circulate.Now. The process is still on-going. In our game development we set out to emphasise experience and learning. The aim was to design a game where players develop new ways of creating value for their company by tapping into the potential in circular economy. In the game players create new business ideas that are economically, socially and environmentally sustainable and aligned with future trends. Idea generation is an important part of the game, but the business ideas are also assessed and "implemented" in the game, and have an influence in how the game moves forward.

The players act as both CEOs and investors in the game, creating ideas and investing in others' ideas. For each idea a self-assessment of key indicators is made, which is then validated by the other players. If many players disagree with an assessment, it is changed and the idea proposer gets a penalty for trying to mislead investors. The score is based on the indicators and divided into three parts: economic, environmental and social. The return on investment for a business idea is based on all three of these. There are also changing trends in the game, which impact how much emphasis is put into a specific indicator. For example, if the regulations concerning landfill are tightening, increasing the amount of recycling is emphasised.

Below is a short narrative of the game play, set in the context of future of office furniture business:

> The player adopts the identity of Frank Circular, a CEO of a company that currently makes office furniture. He joins his colleagues in the game, who have also created alter egos for themselves. Frank starts his round with a glimpse of the current situation. He checks the current trends: urbanization is continuing, people value access increasingly over ownership and regulations regarding landfill are tightening. He decides to create a new business idea for his company based on the trends.
>
> He writes the headline and description of the idea and some other details, so other players can have a clear picture of what the idea is all about. He then assesses the impact using the indicator list. Impact to recycling? Sales? CO2 footprint? Finally he sets the amount of money to be invested in the idea and submits it so other players can see it too.
>
> After submitting his own idea he decides to browse through the ideas that other players have submitted. Brenda Business has submitted an idea that sounds promising. Frank reviews the idea and decides to invest in that too. Also Rick Recycler has submitted an idea, but upon closer inspection Frank disagrees with some of the assessments made by Rick. He pushes the "disagree" button next to the indicator, submits a value he thinks is right and briefly argues why.
>
> Frank gets feedback on his actions through scores that are updated after each new idea or investment. He notices that while the financial and social scores are good, he needs to pay more attention to the environmental factors. After a while he starts to receive money from his investments, allowing him to invest in other ideas. He submits another idea, which unlocks an "Social Entrepreneur" achievement due to its high social impact.
>
> A news flash informs Frank that there is now a new trend: digital nomads. This trend immediately starts affecting the score and return on investments. Frank reads the short description about it and continues investing and creating ideas...

4.1 Game Design Process and Structure

The game design process was highly iterative and consisted of a series of workshops with the project team. The project team consisted of 3 experts on circular economy, 3 experts on foresight and 1 expert on software development. None of the experts had prior experience in designing a game and thus the focus in the first stages was on learning about the best practices, and benchmarking and participating in other game design processes. The goal of the project on the organizational level was, in addition to developing the game, on opening up new avenues of research for the organization and building new capability.

To give a more structure description of the game design, we apply the Activity Theory-based Model of Serious Games (ATMSG) [20], which considers both the learning and gaming actions, tools and goals used in the game (see Table 1). On the game side, the goal is to maximize score by creating good business ideas and investing in others' ideas. Randomness and surprise is brought into the game via changing trends and hiding the direct influence of indicators that the player assesses when creating an idea.

Table 1. Game design structure in the ATMSG.

	Actions	Tools	Goals
Gaming activity	Player creates and invests in business ideas	Other players' ideas, constantly updating score, randomly changing trends	To maximize financial, social and environmental score
Learning activity	Creating new business ideas, evaluating their success, understanding the role of trends	Assessing indicators, receiving feedback, reading others' ideas and arguments	To understand the effect of trends and the important factors in CE business models
Intrinsic instruction activity	Constant feedback on the ideas through scores, ROI and achievements	Indicator checklist, performance assessment	To create an implicit understanding of CE business potential and the effect of trends
Extrinsic instruction activity	Info on CE, game possibly played as part of a facilitated workshop	Reflection after the game, summarising the ideas and lessons learned	To help develop next steps towards adoption of CE business models

The player gets constant feedback in the form of scores (divided into environmental, social and financial), achievements and return on investments (ROI). This feedback supports the learning goal: to understand both the impact of trends and the new thinking required in circular economy. While the game supports the creation of this implicit understanding in itself, it is perhaps more useful as part of a facilitated workshop process. This way the experiences made during the game can be reflected upon and explicit next steps planned.

4.2 Challenges in Capturing the Future Development to a Web-Based Game

There are many challenges in developing a serious game such as ensuring that the game is fun, educational and visually appealing [8]. In our case there were additional problems related to the future-orientation of the game (see Table 2). First, there was a need to simulate a future world without modelling it. Modelling would have required too much resources as well as data on an emerging shift, the implications of which are still largely unknown. We did not want to "get stuck with" a small number of alternative futures that the modelling would have resulted in, but rather wanted to have multiple, surprising and open futures in the game. We resolved this by basing the future world on relevant trends and their implications. We gathered a trend pool from which to draw randomly a set of five trends for a game. The trends also change during the game, simulating a changing operational environment. The trends provide the weights to the indicators, therefore influencing the how different ideas are scored.

Table 2. Problems faced during the development of the Circulate.Now game.

Problem	Key question	Our solution in the game
Avoiding world simulation	How to have enough information about the future world, without simulating it in detail, and how to keep the future open?	Describe only the relationship between trends and key indicators, draw randomly from a pool of trends
Solving assessment	How to assess the business idea without detailed information about the future world?	Player self-assessment validated by other players.
Ensuring actionable outcomes	How to facilitate the creation of new ideas, which are relevant for the present?	Assessment and ranking of ideas through gameplay, iteration of ideas
From preaching to insight	How to teach the mindset of circular economy without being preachy?	Designing the scoring and gameplay based on the principles of circular economy to enable implicit learning
Balancing accuracy and simplicity	How to have a scientifically solid depiction of circular economy while ensuring the game is simple?	Choosing what is essential for gameplay and leaving other aspects for later iterations of the game

Related to avoiding simulation was the question of assessment. Since the game revolves around creating and assessing ideas for new business models for circular economy, it was important to create an easy and educational way of assessing these ideas. Again we did not want to create an elaborate computer model. Instead we decided to rely on player self-assessment with peer-control. Players assess their ideas themselves according to a set of indicators. Other players can disagree with the assessment, which creates a dynamic of self-control. Furthermore, the formula to calculate the score for each idea is hidden from the players and dependent on which trends are chosen for the game. Since the goal is not so much to win the game, but rather to collectively explore new business opportunities, we decided to try if self-assessment would work. As the game testing is still in progress, this remains to be seen.

The third problem we faced was to ensure that the ideation in the game results in actionable results, or at least something that is relevant for the players and does not require too much further analysis. This tension between exploration and exploitation is common in foresight and strategy development [21, 22] and also apparent in the examples of foresight games mentioned above. We tried to find the right balance by building assessment and ranking of ideas generated to the gameplay itself. This also enables the iteration of ideas during the game.

During the game players get an implicit idea of what works and what does not. We wanted to avoid explicitly telling the players what would be the best action in order to enhance the learning experience. In other words, we did not want to preach, but to enable the generation of own insights. This is especially relevant in foresight, since while the principles of future-orientation or foresight can be articulated [3, 18], they are more likely embodied through practice [23]. The aim of our game is that the players learn about circular economy and the implications of various trends, and can apply the insights gained also outside the game.

Emphasising the implicit learning experience led to the fifth problem: ensuring that the game represents circular economy and the implications of trends accurately enough while still keeping it simple enough for playing. At first we had a rather complex version of the game from a player viewpoint that included different categories of business models [11] and assessment of value to various stakeholder groups [24]. In the end we decided to focus on the indicators of circular economy [25]. The business model categories and stakeholder value was approached through these indicators, but not explicitly mentioned, as they were not essential to the gameplay. We also decided to start from a simple version and build more aspects of circular economy into it based on feedback from players.

In summary, the future-orientation of the game brought along problems related to the uncertainty and openness of futures. Our solutions are one attempt to respond to these challenges, but we do not claim that they would be the most appropriate in other contexts. Rather, the point is that during the development of a foresight game choices have to be made about how to approach the future. The key question is how open or closed are the futures i.e. how much is given and how much is left for the players to create? In the next section we discuss this question from the viewpoint of using games to generate new insights about alternative futures.

5 Discussion and Conclusion

Depending on their purpose, foresight games have different assumptions about the openness of futures, and thus different approaches to the pluralism of futures. Games that emphasise only idea generation assume – implicitly or explicitly – that there are infinite possible futures and imagination is the only restriction. At the other end, games that are aimed just to inform have narrowed the possible futures to a finite set of scenarios to be explored. In practice, most games fall somewhere in between these two extreme ends of the openness – closedness continuum.

Games emphasising experience take a slightly different approach regarding the openness of futures. They assume a finite number of possibilities, but try to simulate the surprising and dynamic nature of future. Thus the focus is not on how open or closed the futures are, but rather what can be learned from them, not just through thinking them through explicitly, but also through living and experiencing them. Feelings, emotions, intuition, associations etc. play a key role in this experience. The learning process is not about learning to predict the future, but about orienting towards the future. This means being open to alternative futures, sensing weak signals of change and proactively working towards a preferred future.

Games, especially more formal ones such as IT-based games, require much more effort than working with post-its and pen, which are the common tools of a foresight practitioner. Therefore the benefit from them needs to be significantly greater. In addition to the possibility of introducing complex dynamics and easily gathering and analysing information, one of the key benefits of well-designed games is enhanced learning. A game that is balanced between the dimensions of idea generation, informing and experience provides insights into the practices and strategy of the players' organisation. This requires the game to be relevant for the players' context. A common approach to ensure this, used in the IFT foresight engine as well as in the Circulate.Now game, is to make the game easy to modify to different contexts.

Foresight games can be used in a multitude of situations to support the generation of insights about alternative futures. For example, the Circulate.Now game can be used to support a larger foresight exercise, as a stand-alone process to enable thinking differently about business opportunities or as a continuous part of the foresight culture of an organisation. The key thing is that it provides opportunity to experience and learn from alternative futures.

Finding the balance between idea generation, informing and experience in foresight games is challenging and dependent on the context. But once the balance is found the end result is a game that opens up new opportunities but is connected to the everyday work of the player – a game that can be used to generate new insights about alternative futures.

Acknowledgments. Funding from the iBET project Gamified Foresight and VTT Graduate School is acknowledged.

References

1. Rohrbeck, R.: Corporate Foresight. Springer, Heidelberg (2011)
2. Uotila, T., Melkas, H., Harmaakorpi, V.: Incorporating futures research into regional knowledge creation and management. Futures **37**, 849–866 (2005)
3. Miles, I., Harper, J.C., Georghiou, L., Keenan, M., Popper, R.: The many faces of foresight. In: Georghiou, L., Harper, J.C., Keenan, M., Miles, I., Popper, R. (eds.) The Handbook of Technology Foresight, pp. 3–43. Edward Elgar Publishing Limited, Northampton (2008)
4. Miles, I.: Dynamic foresight evaluation. Foresight **14**, 69–81 (2012)
5. Hines, A., Gold, J.: An organizational futurist role for integrating foresight into corporations. Technol. Forecast. Soc. Change **101**, 99–111 (2014)
6. Hines, A.: An audit for organizational futurists: ten questions every organizational futurist should be able to answer. Foresight **5**, 20–33 (2003)
7. Raford, N.: Online foresight platforms: evidence for their impact on scenario planning & strategic foresight. Technol. Forecast. Soc. Change **97**, 65–76 (2015)
8. Petridis, P., Hadjicosta, K., Guang, V.S., Dunwell, I., Bigdeli, A., Bustinza, O.F., Uren, V.: State-of-the-art in business games. Int. J. Serious Games **2**, 55–68 (2015)
9. Ellen MacArthur Foundation: Towards Circular Economy: Accelerating the Scale-Up Across Global Supply Chains, vol. 3 (2014). https://www.ellenmacarthurfoundation.org/assets/downloads/publications/Towards-the-circular-economy-volume-3.pdf
10. Ghisellini, P., Cialani, C., Ulgiati, S.: A review on circular economy: the expected transition to a balanced interplay of environmental and economic systems. J. Cleaner Prod. **114**, 11–32 (2016)
11. Lacy, P., Keeble, J., McNamara, R.: Circular Advantage - Innovative Business Models and Technologies to Create Value in a World without Limits to Growth. Accenture, Chicago, IL, USA (2014)
12. Schatzmann, J., Schäfer, R., Eichelbaum, F.: Foresight 2.0 - definition, overview & evaluation. Eur. J. Futures Res. **1**, 1–15 (2013)
13. Vian, K., Chwierutt, M., Finlev, T., Harris, D.E., Kirchner, M.: Catalysts for change: vizualizing the horizon of poverty. Foresight **14**, 450–467 (2012)
14. Rausch, E., Catanzaro, F.: Simulation and games in futuring and other uses. In: Glenn, J.C., Gordon, T.J. (eds.) Futures Research Methodology - Version 2.0, pp. 1–51. Millennium Project, Washington, D.C. (2004)
15. Van der Helm, R.: Ten insolvable dilemmas of participation and why foresight has to deal with them. Foresight **9**, 3–17 (2007)
16. Myllyoja, J., Koivisto, T.: Improvisation in supporting organizational development and change. In: Melkas, H., Buur, J. (eds.) Proceedings of the Participatory Innovation Conference, pp. 249–252 (2013)
17. Inayatullah, S.: Using gaming to understand the patterns of the future - the sarkar game in action. J. Futures Stud. **18**, 1–12 (2013)
18. Bussey, M.: Concepts and effects: ordering and practice in foresight. Foresight **16**, 1–16 (2014)
19. Wildman, P., Inayatullah, S.: Ways of knowing, culture, communication and the pedagogies of the future. Futures **28**, 723–740 (1996)
20. Carvalho, M.B., Bellotti, F., Berta, R., De Gloria, A., Sedano, C.I., Hauge, J.B., Hu, J., Rauterberg, M.: An activity theory-based model for serious games analysis and conceptual design. Comput. Educ. **87**, 166–181 (2015)
21. March, J.J.G.: Exploration and exploitation in organizational learning. Organ. Sci. **2**, 71–87 (1991)

22. Heger, T., Rohrbeck, R.: Strategic foresight for collaborative exploration of new business fields. Technol. Forecast. Soc. Change **79**, 819–831 (2012)
23. Rhisiart, M., Miller, R., Brooks, S.: Learning to use the future: developing foresight capabilities through scenario processes. Technol. Forecast. Soc. Change **101**, 124–133 (2014)
24. Bocken, N., Short, S., Rana, P., Evans, S.: A value mapping tool for sustainable business modelling. Corp. Gov. **13**, 482–497 (2013)
25. Ellen MacArthur Foundation: Circularity Indicators - An Approach to Measuring Circularity - Project Overview (2015). https://www.ellenmacarthurfoundation.org/assets/downloads/insight/Circularity-Indicators_Project-Overview_May2015.pdf

Author Index

Printed in the United States
By Bookmasters